techniques
in
transactional
analysis

FOR PSYCHOTHERAPISTS
AND COUNSELORS

techniques
in
transactional
analysis

FOR PSYCHOTHERAPISTS
AND COUNSELORS

by
Muriel James
and
Contributors

Addison-Wesley Publishing Company

Reading, Massachusetts
Menlo Park, California • London • Amsterdam • Don Mills, Ontario • Sydney

In Chapter 1, the paraphrase of material from *The Power at the Bottom of the Well* (1974), by Muriel James and Louis Savary, is used by permission of Harper & Row, Publishers, Inc.

In Chapters 1, 4, and 5, the quotations from *Sex in Human Loving* (Copyright © 1970 by the City National Bank of Beverly Hills, Calif.), by Eric Berne, are used by permission of Simon & Schuster, Inc.

In Chapters 1 through 5, the quotations from *Transactional Analysis in Psychotherapy* (1961), *Games People Play* (1964), *Structure and Dynamics of Organizations and Groups* (1966), and *What Do You Say After You Say Hello?* (1972), all by Eric Berne, are used by permission of Grove Press, Inc. British distribution of material from *Transactional Analysis in Psychotherapy* is by permission of Souvenir Press, Ltd., and that from *Games People Play* and *What Do You Say After You Say Hello?* is by permission of Andre Deutsch, Ltd. World distribution of quotations from *Principles of Group Treatment* is by permission of Oxford University Press.

Acknowledgment is made to the International Transactional Analysis Association for permission to reprint the articles which appear in this book as Chapters 7, 24, 25, 26, 27, 28, 31, 32, 33, 34, 37, 38, 41.

ISBN 0-201-03256-2
CDEFGHIJ-MA-7887

In memory of Eric Berne, M.D.
teacher, supervisor, friend

And when he fell in whirlwind, he went down
As when a lordly cedar, green with boughs,
Goes down with a great shout upon the hill,
And leaves a lonesome place against the sky.

Edwin Markham

preface

I like Transactional Analysis (TA) because it's effective, nonpretentious, and can be used for everyday problem-solving for mentally healthy people, as well as to correct the serious distortions of reality experienced by people who are mentally less than healthy. My first encounter with TA was in 1958, when I read Eric Berne's first paper on the subject and, as a result, started meeting with him regularly. He became my teacher, clinical supervisor, and friend, and I felt his death in 1970 as a great personal loss. But since that first contact with TA, I have continued to be intensely involved in its theory and methods.

This book is the ninth book on TA that I have authored or co-authored, and though I am not the only author writing about TA, I suspect that the subject will never be fully covered. Whenever I begin to think it is, I suddenly perceive a different facet, dimension, or application of TA. Once more I am excited and motivated to develop additional TA theory and methods that can be used to help people who feel like losers to become the winners they were born to be. I am also delighted and excited that people who are already winners, including many psychotherapists and counselors, can use TA to become even more so.

This book is written for these people, for persons who are already in one of the helping professions and for students with similar professional goals in mind. I am assuming the readers, like myself, are interested in many theories of personality and human communication, in how the theories developed, how they are used, how philosophical beliefs support them, and how the methods can be applied to various problems, goals, and situations. The focus of this book is on one particular theory, Transactional Analysis, yet it includes chapters that compare it with other major psychological systems as well as chapters on application. Although much of the writing is mine, much is from other Transactional Analysts. A few of the chapters have been previously published as articles in professional journals; most, however, are original.

Part I focuses on the underlying philosophy, theory, and treatment techniques of TA, how TA developed, and how it is currently being used. It is written with a special emphasis on how psychotherapists and counselors can apply TA concepts to themselves as well as to their patients and clients. One of the chapters in this section will be of special interest to persons who are seriously interested in becoming Transactional Analysts. It includes historical background and new information on Eric Berne, M.D., the founder of TA, as well as information about training standards and accrediting procedures for professionals.

Part II, a brief and important section, shows the relationship of mind and body to psychosomatic disorders and how these can be understood from a TA perspective.

Part III is related to training and supervision of Transactional Analysts. Innovative techniques for staff-patient training are presented and TA procedures for supervising trainees are spelled out in detail.

Part IV contains a verbatim of Eric Berne as group therapist and chapters which compare TA to other therapeutic modalities including: Psychoanalysis, Gestalt, Psychodrama, Bioenergetics, as well as Jungian, Adlerian, and Client-Centered theories and techniques. Each of these chapters gives brief details about a particular form of psychology and the originator of the theory before comparing it with Transactional Analysis.

Part V discusses how to use TA in different situations. These chapters are not intended to cover all the problems (such as chronic schizophrenia) that psychotherapists and counselors continually confront. Instead, they are included to illustrate TA's wide usefulness, flexibility, and adaptability.

Part VI, the last section in the book, is a compilation of a few selected papers I have written. These are included as a response to many requests and because they further illustrate the versatility of TA.

I am very appreciative of those authors whose original works are included in this book. I also appreciate those authors and journals who have given permission for reprinting other articles. I salute the International Transactional Analysis Association and the many colleagues who belong to it and whose friendships I treasure. I also respect and love the many clients who have shared their despair, fears, dreams, hopes, and plans with me. They taught me a lot. In particular they taught me that the search for autonomy and health is a lifelong journey, and that thoughtful caring and enjoying speak louder, much louder, than words.

Lafayette, Calif.
November 1976   M.J.

contents

philosophy
and
techniques
of TA

Muriel James, Ed.D.

PRINCIPLES OF TA
ERIC BERNE, THE DEVELOPMENT OF TA, AND THE ITAA
TA THERAPISTS: AS PERSONS AND PROFESSIONALS
SELF-THERAPY TECHNIQUES FOR THERAPISTS
TREATMENT PROCEDURES

principles of TA

Psychotherapy should never be used as
an end in itself; it should be used
solely and forthrightly as an instrument
toward better living.
Eric Berne

TA AND AUTONOMY

Autonomy is a rare possession. According to Eric Berne, most people have the illusion that they are autonomously making their own decisions when actually they are more like persons sitting down to a player piano, playing notes that have been previously programmed. They are not autonomous; they are "scripted" to feel, think, and act in certain ways. Transactional Analysis (generally called simply TA) can be used to clarify these scripts and change what needs to be changed.

Eric Berne, psychiatrist and originator of Transactional Analysis, defined TA as "a theory of personality and social action, and a clinical method of psychotherapy, based on the analysis of all possible transactions between two or more people, on the basis of specifically defined ego states."[1]

Transactional Analysis is both a psychological theory and a psychological method. It is also educational. It turns losers into winners. Like the kiss in the fairytale of The Frog Prince, it frees people from their froggy feelings and behavior so they can be the princes and princesses they were meant to be. Transactional Analysis is universally useful for anyone who wants to be a real person instead of a frog, or who wants to cure others so that they can be real. A real person is one "who acts spontaneously in a rational and trustworthy way with decent consideration for others."[2] Those who do this well are autonomous.

A major TA concept is that *people can be autonomous.* They do not have to be enslaved by their past. They can decide who to be and who not to be, what to do and what not to do, how to feel, and how not to feel. With the use of TA they can "work through" and transcend past influences, plan creatively for the future, and learn to respond in freedom to the here and now of daily existence.

To become autonomous, most people need to rethink the decisions they made in early childhood about themselves and about other people. Many of these decisions were a result of parental programming. "Parental programming is not the 'fault' of parents—since they are only passing on the programming they got from their parents—any more than the physical appearance of their offspring is their 'fault,' since they are only passing on the genes they got from their ancestors."[3] Parental programming is a fact of life and is both negative and positive.

Many children pick up *positive* messages from their parents. These messages are given verbally and nonverbally—messages to think, to feel, to be healthy, to succeed, to rejoice. These children, when grown, are likely to be more autonomous than others. They are not likely to need therapy. They have winner's scripts.

Other children pick up *negative* messages, given verbally or nonverbally, from their parents. These messages are often prohibitive injunctions. According to Mary and Robert Goulding, common ones are: "Don't be," "Don't be you," "Don't be a child," "Don't be grownup," "Don't be close," "Don't," "Don't make it," "Don't be sane," "Don't be important," "Don't belong."[4]

In response to these kinds of parental injunctions, children make decisions such as "I won't grow up," "I won't be close," "I can't make it." These decisions tend to be acted out in later life. With TA, they can be changed through a process of redecision. Effecting the change, at both cognitive and emotional levels, is an important focus of TA. As Berne notes:

> Psychotherapists know more about "bad" scripts than about "good" ones because they are more dramatic and people spend more time talking about them. . . . Only a few winners bother to find out how they got that way, while losers are often very anxious to know so that they can do something about it.[5]

People who, since childhood, have felt and acted like losers need to redecide in favor of becoming winners. People who decided in childhood that others were not-OK need to redecide in favor of the many people who are indeed OK. People who, when young, were taught or somehow learned to be unreal, even phony, need to recover their realness, their humanness. Transactional Analysis provides an opportunity for change and redecision. A client's statement shows a loser acquiring a new point of view:

> The main thing TA has taught me is that I can change anything I want to change, but I have to want it first. If I don't want to change something I will just keep playing games with myself to make me believe that there is no other way. Being exposed to TA has taught me to ask myself if I really like something the way it is and if not what do I have to do to change it and am I really willing to do what I have to in order to change it? Now it is easier for me to define the areas in which I want to make changes and the areas I really don't want to change.

Change is a continuing process for those who want to be real people. Real people are autonomous, and autonomous people, according to Berne, are able to demonstrate "the release or recovery of three capacities: awareness, spontaneity, and intimacy."[6] These capacities are spelled out in *Born to Win:*

Awareness is knowing what is happening now. Autonomous people are aware. They peel away the layers of contamination and hear, see, smell, touch, taste, study, and evaluate for themselves. They shed old opinions that distort their present perception. They perceive the world through their own personal encounters rather than the way they were "taught" to see it. . . .

Aware people listen to the messages of their own bodies knowing when they are tensing themselves, relaxing themselves, opening themselves, closing themselves. They know their inner world of feelings and fantasies and are not afraid or ashamed of them.

Aware people also hear other people. . . . They don't use their psychic energy to form questions, create diversions, or plan counterattacks in their heads. Instead they attempt to make genuine contact with the other people. . . .

Aware people are all there and fully aware. Their minds and bodies respond in unison to the here and now; their bodies are not doing one thing while their minds focus on something else. Aware people know where they are, what they're doing, and how they feel about it.[7] They can spontaneously choose from the full spectrum of Parent behavior and feelings, Adult behavior and feelings, and Child behavior and feelings.

Autonomous people are not only aware, they are also spontaneous—flexible, not foolishly impulsive. They see the many options that are open and use what behavior they judge to be appropriate to their situations and goals. These spontaneous people are liberated. They make and accept responsibility for their own choices. They rid themselves of the compulsions to live predetermined life styles. Instead they learn to face new situations and to explore new ways of thinking, feeling, and responding. They constantly increase and reevaluate their repertoire of possible behavior.

Spontaneous people use or recapture their ability to decide for themselves. They accept their personal history but make their own decisions rather than remaining at the mercy of their "fate."

In addition to having the qualities of awareness and spontaneity, autonomous people are also capable of intimacy. They learn to "let go," revealing more of themselves by dropping their masks. They refrain from transacting with others in ways that prevent closeness. They attempt to be open and authentic, existing with others in the here and now. They also attempt to see others in their own uniqueness, not through the distortions of past experiences.

People who do not experience awareness, spontaneity, and intimacy are not in touch with their potential. Transactional Analysis enables these people to change.

A basic TA concept is the belief that people are of value and that their personalities and lives are enriched and enhanced by the release or recovery of autonomy, which includes awareness, spontaneity, and intimacy.

The TA techniques that are designed for this purpose, and to resolve the confusion that many clients who enter therapy seem to have, are a series of well-planned operations—decontamination, recathexis, clarification, and reorientation. Berne writes:

> Decontamination means that where the patient's reactions, feelings, or viewpoints are adulterated or distorted, the situation will be rectified by a process analogous to that of anatomical dissection. Recathexis means that the effective emphasis the patient puts on various aspects of his experience will be changed. Clarification means that the patient himself will have some understanding of what is going on so that he can maintain the new condition in a stable form and, hopefully, extrapolate the previous processes without the help of the therapist into new situations that he will encounter after the treatment is terminated. Reorientation means that as a result of all this, the patient's behavior, responses, and aspirations will be changed to be what some reasonable consensus would regard as more constructive.[8]

ADVANTAGES OF TA

Currently, TA is being used in hospitals, convalescent homes, schools, families, prisons, government agencies, business, and industries—in both private and public sectors—by people of all ages and educational backgrounds, wherever people want to understand themselves and what goes on between people. A very creative use of TA is being made by a fourth-grader who knows how to apply TA principles and conducts "groups" on her back porch. It is such a practical, useful tool that its use is skyrocketing throughout the world; numerous materials in transactional analysis are being published in many languages.*

Almost all book stores carry one or more of the many TA books. Some are written for professional therapists, some are written for the general public. However, even those books written for professionals, as Eric Berne's were, have been purchased, read, and comprehended by lay persons. It is a sign of our times that people want to understand who they are, why they are, where they are going with their lives. They also want to understand other people and how to transact with them in mutually satisfying ways.

Karpman, in his foreword to *Born to Win,* wrote that it presented "psychological insights in an immediately recognizable way. It is in line with the '70's trend of making all information more readily available to people, and the "Aquarian Age" of bringing together information from both worlds. Humanistic Man, interested in personal growth and high levels of awareness, can now handle information intelligently that before he could handle only intellectually."

The popularity of TA books such as *Born to Win, I'm OK–You're OK,* and *Games People Play* means that the time spent in therapy can be greatly shortened. Clients are usually willing to read something that they think will accelerate the therapeutic process and TA therapists are usually willing to recommend such reading.

Common advantages of TA are:

1. *TA is a self-help psychology.* While most traditional psychologies are not readily understandable by lay persons and can be used only by highly trained professionals, TA theory can have a startling effect on people simply by their reading about it. They discover they can really help themselves. Although they may decide that it is also valuable to have professional guidance, somehow they feel more intelligent and competent because the basic concepts are not sacred nor secret. It is shared, readily available information.

2. *TA is a nonthreatening psychology.* It deals with readily observable behavior, words, tone of voice, gestures, facial expression, body posture, etc. Other theories —which focus on the unconscious cellars of the psyche and preoccupy themselves with sexuality, primal traumas, death drives, and so forth—often seem so threatening that many people avoid getting help.

---

* For example, *Born to Win* is now in Spanish, Dutch, German, Portugese, Danish, Japanese, Swedish, French, Arabic and Finnish. *Games People Play,* by Eric Berne, and *I'm OK–You're OK,* by Thomas Harris, have also been widely translated.

3. *TA is a psychology of change.* Some psychologies are seen only as ways of helping people to conform to society, to be as other people expect them to be. TA focuses on changes and how people can change what they want to change.

4. *TA is immediately effective.* The use of most therapeutic systems involves long periods of time for the client before problems are uncovered and solutions found. Not so with TA. Within the first hours of treatment, people gain insight about themselves, their needs, and the ways they can change.

5. *TA is for mentally healthy as well as for disturbed people.* People don't have to be sick to get better. Even healthy people can learn to feel more OK about themselves and can learn to communicate more authentically with others.[9]

6. *TA is also for people with severe emotional problems* and for people who are sometimes thought of as retarded or delinquent. It is widely used in hospitals and other situations where people require continuous care.

7. *TA can be used by families.* Even very young children can understand and profit by the concepts. So can their parents.

8. *TA is also an on-the-job communication tool* for government, business, and industry. It improves staff relations, decreases staff turnover, and increases staff morale as well as productivity.

DIAGNOSTIC LABELS AND TA VOCABULARY

Labels both help and hinder. In general, medically trained psychotherapists are the term "patients," therapists not medically trained use the words "clients" or "counselees," pastoral counselors are likely to use the word "parishioners," and teachers use the term "students."

Unless there is a specific reason for doing otherwise, I will use the word "clients" in this book. I think it dignifies the people involved and implies that they have the freedom to choose whether or not to seek help, although obviously they do not have this freedom in some situations. The reader is naturally free to translate the word "client" into whatever vocabulary fits his or her orientation. The word "therapist" is used in a broad sense to include both psychotherapists from various disciplines and counselors with various orientations.

People who are institutionalized are most often called "prisoners," "inmates," or "patients." TA is used for people in each of these situations. Unfortunately, the label that is used often determines how such people are treated physically, as well as how they are treated psychologically and the therapeutic goals that are established for them. Would they be treated differently if they were called "clients," or even "students"?

The way therapists speak of the people they work with not only affects the treatment process, it affects the way other people, such as their families, respond to them. Most TA therapists are trained to use words that an eight-year-old can understand, to use words that describe behavior rather than words that label a person. I personally am opposed to phrases such as, "Oh, he is a schizophrenic." I prefer something like "he has schizophrenic symptoms." This phrase implies the person *has* a problem without *being* the problem itself. Not all TA therapists agree with me. Some believe that clients should be labeled clinically and told what the label is.

For example, one TA psychiatrist tells some patients that they don't need to be afraid of going crazy—that they already are crazy and that craziness means simply acting irresponsibly. He adds that their job is to learn how to act responsible while finding more efficient ways to handle problems, since the only people who go crazy are those who have not yet figured out how to handle their problems.

My dislike for labels may come from having read a powerful article written by Karl Menninger some years ago. In this he strongly claimed that "a label applied to an illness becomes almost as damaging as the illness itself."[10] Menninger gave several examples, one being that of a young doctor who for a time, suffering from anxiety and indecision, consulted a psychiatrist and recovered. His professional career, however, was damaged by a rumor which labeled him "tentatively" schizophrenic.

A label can blight a person's life even after recovery. It can panic the patient and his or her friends and family, and can discourage a therapist. Labels mean widely different things to different people; therefore, mental illness is not a thing for which a label must be found. It is a state of functioning, a way of behaving. Menninger believes that if someone is diagnosed psychotic, manic depressive, borderline, etc., the person's treatment and prognosis is much less favorable than a description of the behavior, or the subjective lay figure of speech such as "I'm falling apart" used by the person seeking treatment.

This concept—that mental health is easier to achieve if people are not given clinical labels of mental illness—fits into basic TA theory and methodology. Although in some instances the American Psychiatric Association official classifications may be needed and used—for example, when meeting the demand of an insurance company or when referring someone to a hospital—most TA therapists tend to avoid them. Rather than labeling people's behavior they describe it in terms of ego states, transactions, games, scripts, and time structuring. According to Berne:

> *A good policy is not to use any label in clinical work.* A surgeon need not tell the patient he needs "an operation" (which is only a label); he can simply tell him what he proposes to do: "You'll have to have your appendix out," or "You should have it removed." A group therapist can similarly use verbs instead

of nouns: "I think you should go into a group," instead of "I think you should have group therapy (or group treatment)."[11]

All professions (and often the subgroups within them) have their own vocabularies. TA vocabulary is precise; it can be readily understood by both clients and therapists who are interested and willing to learn simple basic definitions. The use of simple words and colloquial terms lowers the clients' anxiety. It dilutes much of the magic spell that people seem to fall under when the mumbo-jumbo of clinical terms is used. TA practitioners do not accept a concept of irreparable personality damage or unsolvable interpersonal problems. Instead, they believe TA motivates people toward mentally healthy attitudes and behavior toward themselves and others.

Almost anyone can look around and compare noninstitutionalized people with those who are "locked up" for one reason or another. Although an impartial comparison would be hard to make, it appears as though many of those on the outside of institutions could easily be (and need to be) on the inside, and that many of those on the inside could easily be on the outside, making their own way. Which raises an interesting question: When is the therapist healthier than the patient or client? Berne advised, "If you want the patient to be your therapist, be sure first that you can afford to pay him your usual fee."[12]

INTRODUCTION TO TA THEORY

For those who are unfamiliar with TA theory and method, a brief summary will be useful. In its basic form, TA is concerned with the four different types of analysis listed here and discussed at greater length in the next few pages. Those types are:

1. Structural analysis
2. Transactional analysis proper (The term "Transactional Analysis" is also used to identify the system as a whole.)
3. Game analysis
4. Script analysis

Structural Analysis

Structural analysis is the segregation and analysis of the Parent, Adult, and Child ego states which comprise individual personality. The goal of this procedure is "to establish the predominance of reality-testing ego states and freeing them from contamination by archaic and foreign elements."[13]

In structural analysis, the Parent ego states (exteropsyche) are the incorporation of the specific parent figures people have when they are young. As each person has unique parent figures, so each has a unique Parent ego state. This ego state

is outwardly expressed toward others in prejudicial, critical, and nurturing behavior—behavior which is identical or very similar to that of the original parent
figures.

In any person the Parent ego state also conducts an inner dialogue with the
Child ego state, continually telling it what to do or what not to do as an inwardly influencing factor.

The Child ego state (archaeopsyche) contains all the *natural* feelings, needs,
impulses, and potentialities of an infant. It also contains creative, manipulative,
intuitive capacities as well as the *adapted* feelings and behavior learned during
childhood, such as compliance, rebellion, and procrastination.

The Adult ego state, (neopsyche) is not related to a person's age. It is concerned
with the autonomous collecting and processing of data and the estimating of
probabilities as a basis for action. It organizes information, is adaptable, and
functions by testing reality and computing dispassionately.[14]

The structure of personality is as shown in the accompanying diagram.

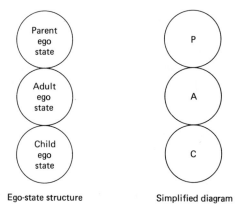

Ego-state structure   Simplified diagram

When people act, think, or feel as their parent figures once did, they are in the
Parent ego state. When they are living in the here and now, gathering facts,
computing them, and acting on the basis of facts, rather than on the basis of
parental tradition or childhood feelings, they are in the Adult ego state. When
people feel, act, and respond to others as they learned to do when they were
little, they are in their Child ego state—using, however, the increased facilities
they have gained while growing up.[15]

Shifts in ego states can be observed in all people. According to Berne the shifts
may be accounted for "by using the concept of psychic energy or cathexis, on

the principle that at a given moment that ego state which is cathected in a certain way will have the executive power."[16] The ego state cathected will feel like the real self.

Berne postulates three states of cathexis: bound, unbound, and free. He uses an analogy of a monkey in a tree: If the monkey is inactive, his physical energy is only potential, or bound; if he falls off the tree, it is unbound; if he jumps off by choice, the energy is free. The executive power is in the ego state in which the "net sum of unbound, plus free cathexis (active cathexis) is greatest at the given moment than that which is bound."[17]

I believe changes in ego state which people self-induce may be accounted for by their Inner Core. Psychologically, the Inner Core may be described as a permanent universal self, independent of the three ego states, that can influence the flow of cathexis within an individual.*

Transactional Analysis Proper

The term "Transactional Analysis Proper" is used to distinguish this phase from the theory of Transactional Analysis *as a whole*. Berne says that the goal of this phase is "social control: that is, the control of the individual's own tendency to manipulate other people in destructive or wasteful ways, and of his tendency to respond without insight or option to the manipulations of others."[20] Transactional Analysis Proper consists of determining which ego state in one person is transacting with which ego state in another and in what ways—what is the transactional stimulus and what is the transactional response.

A transaction consists of two or more strokes. The word "stroke" is a TA colloquialism meaning any form of recognition. Without sufficient strokes children die or become physically and/or emotionally ill.†

Strokes can be positive, like a smile or friendly greeting, or negative, like a frown or sarcastic greeting. They can be unconditional, like "I love you 'cause you're you," or conditional, like "I love you if you. . . ." "Hello" is a single stroke. A "Hello" in return is another stroke. The two strokes make up a transaction. There has been a stimulus and a response.

---

* The concept of the Inner Core was developed in two of my previous publications[18] and is amplified in *A New Self*, coauthored by myself and Louis Savary.[19] I am not including details of the Inner Core here as the basic concept is so new to the mainstream of TA that it needs a book in itself to explain the theory and use in therapy.

† My previous book, *TA For Moms and Dads* uses strokes as the theme. Many TA practitioners use this book when teaching or ask their clients who are parents to read it as bibliotherapy which will accelerate the therapeutic process.

Patterns of stimulus and response are categorized into three basic kinds of transactions: complementary, crossed, and ulterior.

Complementary transactions. These include Adult-Adult stimulus and response, an example of which is shown here.

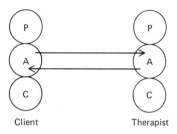

C.: Dr., what is your fee?

T.: It's $30 an individual session.

But they are not only Adult to Adult; in healthy relationships, people transact openly and directly from any ego state and receive responses that are expected and appropriate. In these cases, the vectors of sending and receiving are usually parallel and communication is open. For example, if one person uses a nurturing Parent transaction to an unhappy Child in someone else, that unhappy Child often responds by feeling better. The response *complements* the stimulus. Complementary transactions can go on indefinitely unless one of the participants gets tired or bored.

Crossed transactions. These, too, may occur between any ego states. When a message sent from one person gets an unexpected response, the vectors cross. Communication is usually broken off or someone feels misunderstood or hurt or angry. Gestures, facial expressions, body posture, tone of voice, words, all contribute to the meaning of any transaction, crossed or otherwise. Berne claims that 72 types of crossed transactions are possible, yet only four of them occur frequently in daily life.[21] The diagram shows a crossed transaction.

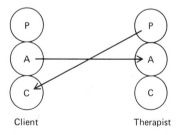

C.: Dr., what is your fee?

T.: Now don't you worry about that.

or

T.: Can't you see the prices posted on the wall!

Ulterior transactions. These transactions have a hidden agenda. Along with the spoken words is sent a nonverbal message. Very often the verbal stimulus and the nonverbal stimulus are quite different. The accompanying diagram shows an example in which the whine and the frown (broken lines) convey the ulterior message.

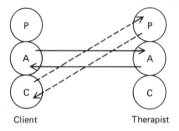

Client   Therapist

C.: (whining) Dr., what is your fee?

T.: (frowning) It's $30 per session.

There are two types of ulterior transactions—*angular* and *duplex*. In each of these there is a *covert* meaning or message under the surface of the ostensible social transaction. Communication may or may not continue after an ulterior transaction.

An *angular transaction* involves one ego state in one person and two ego states in another. I frequently choose to use angular transactions, especially with new clients. When doing this, I give and receive information, Adult to Adult. At the same time I indicate, usually with my eyes or facial expression, Adult to Child, that the client is actually OK and capable of making new decisions that will be life-enhancing. I don't believe it is necessary for professionals to be "poker faced" when using TA. I suspect I sometimes use an Adult-to-Adult social transaction with a Parent-to-Child nonverbal message. Such would be the case if I convey the message to clients that they "should" read books and put the knowledge to work. This was a message I got from my own parents. I sometimes pass it on to others, justifying it, of course, with my sometimes inaccurate Adult!

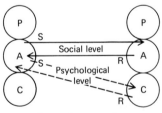

An angular transaction

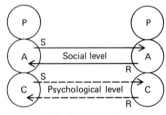

A duplex transaction

The *duplex transaction* involves two ego states in each person and is often more obvious than the angular one. It most frequently involves a Child-to-Child covert message. *Berne's* classic example is:

Cowboy: "Come and see the barn."

Visitor: "I've loved barns ever since I was a little girl."[22]

Game Analysis

Game analysis is the analysis of a series of overt social transactions that are accompanied by covert ulterior transactions which lead to a well-defined payoff. The goal of this phase is for clients to gain awareness of the psychological games they play, how they initiate those games, and how they get hooked into them by others. The goal also includes awareness of how games can be broken up in favor of more satisfying ways of structuring time.

For a detailed consideration of games, see Eric Berne's book *Games People Play*. A later section in this book describes games therapists often play, techniques for identifying them and techniques for giving them up.

A game is an on-going series of transactions, seemingly complementary, covertly ulterior, which lead to a well-defined *payoff*. Payoffs are usually negative feeling such as fear, anger, sadness, inadequacy, etc., for one or both of the "players" involved. Sometimes however, payoffs are feelings of self-righteousness. In either case, the feelings are unknowingly exploited by the players to justify their behavior.

Psychological games are similar to card games. It takes two or more to play (unless it's solitaire, and some people *do* play internal games—between their Parent and Child ego states—in their heads).[23] All games have a beginning which is the initial stimulus, a set of rules and expected "plays," and a conclusion. People tend to have favorite games that they play over and over again. Thus they "collect" the old familiar feelings from childhood at the end of the game.

Kick Me is a common game played in the counselor's or therapist's office. When it occurs, two players are required, one who is willing to play the role of a punitive kicker and one who is willing to play the helpless or rebellious kick-me role, provoking others in order to get putdowns. This game can be initiated by a client who neglects to pay the therapist's fee, or by one who sounds desperate while making an appointment by phone but then forgets to come or arrives late.

People play games with different degrees of intensity from the socially accepted, relaxed level to the criminal homicide/suicide level. Berne writes:

a) A First-Degree Game is one which is socially acceptable in the agent's circle.

b) A Second-Degree Game is one from which no permanent, irremediable damage arises, but which the players would rather conceal from the public.

c) A Third-Degree Game is one which is played for keeps, and which ends in the surgery, the courtroom or the morgue.[24]

The payoff at the end of a first-degree game is like a small "prize," such as a temper tantrum or crying jag. At the end of a second-degree game the prize is bigger and often involves a quit of some kind—quit school, quit a job, quit a marriage, etc. The third-degree game player, like a big game hunter, usually is going for broke—homicide or suicide.

Games tend to be repetitive. People find themselves saying the same words in the same way, only the time and place may change. Perhaps the replay contributes to what is often described as "I feel as if I've done this before."[25]

Everyone, including therapists, plays games. Games are most often played from the Child or Parent ego states and usually are outside of awareness; therefore they are not always easy to identify in others. Furthermore, although therapists often accuse others of playing games, they seldom see themselves as playing the complementary roles.

Script Analysis

Script analysis is the analysis of life dramas that people, usually without awareness, act out compulsively. The goal of this phase is the discovery of scripty behavior which is based on early childhood decisions. Because the decisions made in these scripts often interfere with autonomy, the focus is on redecisions that will put a better show on the road.

Although people are not usually aware of it, their psychological scripts, like those of stage plays, contain not only the themes, but also the roles they expect to play, the roles they expect others to play, the dramatic action, climax and denouement.

Generally speaking, it is people with destructive, nonproductive, or banal scripts who enter treatment, since those with constructive scripts seldom feel the need for psychotherapy. Berne writes:

In general a script is based on a childhood theory that somewhere there is a kind of Santa Claus who will bring the individual a magic gift to crown his life. People wait varying lengths of time before they fall into despair about the appearance of this Santa Claus, and it is this despair which, other things being equal, determines when they seek treatment—some at 20, some at 40, and some at 60. Failing "Santa Claus," there are four alternatives from which the individual can choose. The most decisive is suicide in one form or another.

The second choice is sequestration from society, along with other people in despair, in a state hospital or a prison (or sometimes in isolated areas or in certain types of roominghouses found in big cities). The third alternative is to get rid of the people who are held to be responsible for the failure—by divorce, homicide, sending the children to boarding school, etc. The fourth alternative is getting better, which means to give up the hope of Santa Claus, to abandon previous destructive games, and to start anew living in the world as it is. It will be apparent that script analysis by its very nature has an existential quality.[26]

Techniques used in TA are designed to break up the Santa Claus fantasies so that scripts can be rewritten. They are designed to identify games and unsatisfactory transactions that need to be given up in favor of authentic intimacy. They are designed for the diagnosis and treatment of personality problems. With the use of TA techniques, therapists, as well as clients, have the opportunity to become free—free to be "real" because they have attained some measure of autonomy.

REFERENCES

1. Berne, Eric, *What Do You Say After You Say Hello?* (New York: Grove, 1972) p. 20.

2. Ibid., p. 32.

3. Berne, Eric, *Sex in Human Loving* (New York: Simon & Schuster, 1972) p. 198.

4. Goulding, Robert, "New Directions in Transactional Analysis: Creating an Environment for Redecision and Change." In *Progress in Group and Family Therapy,* edited by Clifford J. Sager and Helen Singer Kaplan (New York: Brunner/Mazer, 1972), p. 107.

5. Berne, *Hello,* p. 107.

6. ———, *Games People Play* (New York: Grove, 1964) p. 178.

7. James, Muriel, and Dorothy Jongeward, *Born to Win: Transactional Analysis with Gestalt Experiments* (Reading, Mass.: Addison-Wesley, 1971) pp. 264–265.

8. Berne, Eric, *Principles of Group Treatment* (New York: Grove, 1968) p. 213.

9. James, Muriel, and Louis Savary, *The Power at the Bottom of the Well* (New York: Harper & Row, 1974) pp. 3–5.

10. Menninger, Karl, "Psychiatrists Use Dangerous Words." *Saturday Evening Post,* 25 April 1964.

11. Berne, *Principles,* p. 86.

12. Ibid., p. 358.

13. Berne, Eric, *Transactional Analysis in Psychotherapy* (New York: Grove, 1961), p. 22.

14. James and Jongeward, *Born to Win,* pp. 16–24.

15. Berne, *Principles,* p. 220.

16. ———, *TA in Psychotherapy*, p. 38.

17. ———, *Hello*, pp. 40–41.

18. James, Muriel, *Born to Love: Transactional Analysis in the Church* (Reading, Mass.: Addison-Wesley, 1973). Muriel James and Louis Savary, *Bottom of the Well.*

19. James, Muriel, and Louis Savary, *A New Self: Self-Therapy with Transactional Analysis* (Reading, Mass.: Addison-Wesley, in press).

20. Berne, *TA in Psychotherapy*, p. 23.

21. ———, *Games*, p. 30; cf. *Hello*, p. 17.

22. ———, *Games*, p. 34.

23. For the diagram of an internal game, see James, Muriel, and Dorothy Jongeward, *The People Book: Transactional Analysis for Students* (Menlo Park, Calif.: Addison-Wesley, 1975) p. 133.

24. Berne, *Games*, p. 64.

25. James and Jongeward, *Born to Win*, p. 34.

26. Berne, *Principles*, p. 229.

CHAPTER 2

Eric Berne, the development of TA, and the ITAA

Information is of no value for its own
sake, but only because of its personal
significance.
Eric Berne

The basic concept of Transactional Analysis began with Eric Berne when he noticed that his patients were not getting well as fast as he hoped they would. As an analyst, practicing in Carmel, California, he often treated people on an individual basis, one hour a day, five days a week, for three years. Obviously, many people were unable, or unwilling, to invest that amount of time and money on treatment. This awareness led to a search for a new theory and method that would be more effective than traditional psychoanalysis.

THE CASE OF MR. SEGUNDO

It was the case of Mr. Segundo that first stimulated Eric Berne to develop the concept of structural analysis upon which the entire system of Transactional Analysis is based. Berne tells the following story:

An eight year old boy, vacationing at a ranch in his cowboy suit, helped the hired man unsaddle a horse. When they were finished, the hired man said: "Thanks, cowpoke!", to which his assistant answered: "I'm not really a cowpoke, I'm just a little boy."

The patient then remarked: "That's just the way I feel. I'm not really a lawyer, I'm just a little boy." Mr. Segundo was a successful courtroom lawyer of high repute, who raised his family decently, did useful community work, and was popular socially. But in treatment he often did have the attitude of a little boy. Sometimes during the hour he would ask: "Are you talking to the lawyer or to the little boy?" When he was away from his office or the courtroom, the little boy was very apt to take over. He would retire to a cabin in the mountains away from his family, where he kept a supply of whiskey, morphine, lewd pictures, and guns. There he would indulge in childlike fantasies, fantasies he had as a little boy, and the kinds of sexual activity which are commonly labeled "infantile."

At a later date, after he had clarified to some extent what in him was Adult and what was Child (for he really was a lawyer sometimes and not always a little boy), Mr. Segundo introduced his Parent into the situation. That is, after his activities and feelings had been sorted out into the first two categories, there were certain residual states which fitted neither. These had a special quality which was reminiscent of the way his parents had seemed to him. This necessitated the institution of a third category which on further testing, was found to have sound clinical validity. These ego states lacked the autonomous quality of both Adult and Child. They seemed to have been introduced from without, and to have an imitative flavor.

Specifically, there were three different aspects apparent in his handling of money. The Child was penurious to the penny and had miserly ways of ensuring pennywise prosperity; in spite of the risk for a man in his position, in this state he would gleefully steal chewing gum and other small items out of drugstores, just as he had done as a child. The Adult handled large sums with a banker's shrewdness, foresight, and success, and was willing to spend money to make money. But another side of him had fantasies of giving it all away for the good of the community. He came of pious, philanthropic people, and he actually did donate large sums to charity with the same sentimental benevolence as his father. As the philanthropic glow wore off, the Child would take over with vindictive resentfulness toward his beneficiaries, followed by the Adult who would wonder why on earth he wanted to risk his solvency for such sentimental reasons.[1]

These three parts of Mr. Segundo's personality were subsequently labeled the Parent, Adult, and Child ego states. Everybody has these three states in their own personality; however, in each person the ego states are unique. All people have different parent figures in their Parent ego states, different inherited characteristics and childhood environmental influences in their Child ego states, and different information, education, and experience in later life in their Adult ego states.

Ego states are defined as consistent patterns of feelings and experience which are directly related to corresponding consistent patterns of behavior.[2] Phenomenologically, an ego state is described as "a coherent system of feelings related to a given subject." Operationally, it is described as "a set of coherent behavior patterns; or pragmatically, as a system of feelings which motivates a related set of behavior patterns."[3]

The findings of Dr. Wilder Penfield, neurosurgeon, support these definitions. He found that an electrode applied to different parts of a person's brain evoked memories and feelings long forgotten by that person.[4] Berne writes:

> ... in this respect the brain functions like a tape recorder to preserve complete experiences in serial sequence, in a form recognizable as "ego states" —indicating that ego states comprise the natural way of experiencing and of recording experiences in their totality. Simultaneously, of course, experiences are recorded in fragmented forms ...[5]

The implications are that what happens to people is recorded in their brain and nervous tissue. This includes everything that they experience in their childhood, and all that they incorporate from their parent figures, perceptions of events, feelings associated with these events, and distortions they bring to their memories. These "tapes" can be replayed, the events can be recalled and even reexperienced. This concept was built into all Eric Berne's TA writings.

ERIC BERNE AND HIS WRITING

Eric Lennard Bernstein, born in Montreal in 1910, was the son of David Hillel Bernstein and Sarah Gordon Bernstein. Eric's father was a general practitioner who often took Eric on his rounds, and his mother was a professional writer and editor. After Eric's father died, when Eric was nine years old, Eric's mother supported Eric and his sister by her writing. When Eric was eleven, he too began writing, and he continued to write until his death. His witty, brilliant writing was sometimes complicated and difficult to decipher, especially when he was inconsistent. I think his nine-year-old inner boy was traumatized at his father's death. It sometimes shows through his writing, contaminating his Adult as though to say, "How am I doing, Dad?" Another image that comes to mind is of a little boy climbing a tree, waving toward the house, shouting with glee, "Look Ma, no hands!"

After receiving his M.D. in 1935 from McGill University, Eric changed his name. He dropped the Lennard, shortened Bernstein to Berne, and came to the United States, where he took American citizenship. He became Psychiatric Resident at Yale University of Medicine, next was Clinical Assistant at Mt. Zion Hospital in New York City, and entered the Army Medical Corps as a psychiatrist in 1941.

It was in the army that Berne first began to do group therapy; the focus of his groups was to get men into shape for return to active duty. Doing group therapy with people who were in the position to make more autonomous decisions than those in the Army began in 1946. He took seriously his own words: "Psychiatrists know many therapeutic procedures but less about what in a particular procedure is therapeutic."[6] With groups and individuals, Berne worked concontinually to find out which procedures *cured* clients. He was not in favor of "making progress," only in favor of cures—with the phantom ideal goal being a one-session cure. In TA terms he was a "cowboy" therapist, meaning "a relaxed therapist who walks into any room where any group of patients is collected, without regard to selection, and proceeds to cure as many as he possibly can in the shortest possible time."[7]

Throughout his career Berne wrote for both professionals and nonprofessionals. Both his books and his journal and magazine articles reflect his feeling that psychology is for everyone. In fact, his first book, *The Mind in Action* (1947), was later republished as *A Laymen's Guide to Psychiatry and Psychoanalysis.*

The development of his early ideas in Transactional Analysis can be observed in his six articles on intuition written between 1949 and 1962.[8] In a biographical sketch of Berne, Warren Cheney refers to three specific articles Berne wrote in 1957 and 1958: "Intuition: The Ego Image," "Ego States in Psychotherapy," and "Transitional Analysis: A New and Effective Method of Group Therapy." Cheney writes:

> Using references to Paul Federn, Eugen Khan and H. Silberer, Eric in the first article indicated how he arrived at the concept of ego states and where he got the idea of separating "adult" from "child." In the next article he developed the tripartite schema used today, namely *Parent, Adult,* and *Child,* introduced the three-circle method of diagramming them, showed how to sketch contamination, C-A, and P-A, labelled the theory *"structural analysis"* and termed it "a new psychotherapeutic approach." The third article, written a few months later, was first presented at the Western Regional Meeting of the American Group Psychotherapy Association, in Los Angeles, November 1957, by invitation, carrying the title, "Transactional Analysis: A New and Effective Method of Group Therapy." With the publication of this paper in the *American Journal of Psychotherapy,* October 1958, the name of Berne's new method of diagnosis and treatment, *transactional analysis,* became a permanent part of the psychotherapeutic literature.[9]

Eric Berne's first TA book, *Transactional Analysis in Psychotherapy*[10] was published in 1961 and is still his most important in that subsequent writings are based on the principles delineated in this first text. The application of TA to group dynamics was detailed in 1963 by Berne in *The Structure and Dynamics of Organizations and Groups;*[11] the use of TA in analyzing psychological games can be found in his best seller, *Games People Play,*[12] published in 1964. The principles of TA for psychotherapists are spelled out in his *Princi-*

ples of Group Treatment,[13] and the theory of scripts are to be found in *What Do You Say After You Say Hello?*[14]

Each of these books was primarily written for a professional audience. However, Berne also wrote *The Happy Valley*[15] for children and *Sex in Human Loving*[16] for the general public as well as for professionals.

The *Transactional Analysis Bulletin,* with Berne as editor, came into existence in 1962, as interest in TA grew and members were eager to share information. After Berne's death, the *Bulletin* developed into a professional journal, first published by the ITAA in January, 1971. Since then the ITAA has published the *TA Journal* quarterly, presenting theory, methods, and research materials.

The ITAA also serves as a clearing house for TA publications through an operation called Trans Pubs. Trans Pubs screens all TA publications that authors wish to have sold through the association.

In his writings Berne often referred to himself as "Dr. Q." and in his *Organizations* book described part of his own script.

> A therapist whose protocol had to do with "curing lots of people" (siblings) had a palimpsest by the age of 5 where he would invite his neighborhood contemporaries en masse to his house to play doctor. The protocol was based on a beloved family physician and much illness in his family. . . . The adaptation occurred years later when he was able to become a group therapist, which was a socially acceptable way of trying to "cure a lot of people at my house." During the period of the adaptation, his efforts were tentative and not very successful. . . . Finally, his script underwent a secondary adjustment, in which his therapeutic efforts were better controlled, involved fewer games, and were still more successful. . . . This "meeting at my house" was the first act of a long script which led to a satisfactory professional career when it was properly adjusted.[17]

A Personal Reminiscence

Probably each person who knew Eric had a unique perspective of him. For example, Claude Steiner's[18] is different in many ways from those recorded by Thomas Harris[19] or by Jules Levaggi, Viola Callaghan, and Charles Berger.[20] Someday the many perspectives may be gathered together; meanwhile, here is a small part of mine.

I saw Eric as responsible, brilliant, shy, fun to be with, and very clever, both personally and professionally. When he first became my clinical supervisor, I shared the supervision time and cost with psychiatrist Martin Groder. This was a valuable experience. When more time became available on Eric's calendar, I asked for individual supervision and received it. Naturally, this increased the cost, which at that time was difficult for me to meet. One day, when I was no doubt playing *Poor Me,* I told him I was going to terminate, complaining that my two-hour drive to see him and the money it cost when so little was available seemed too much. His response was, "Muriel, if you continue your supervision, I guarantee you'll double your income shortly." He was right. I did. In fact, I tripled it. When I happily reported this to Eric, his retort was, "Good. Now you can pay me the $50 I'm worth each session instead of the $15 you have been pay-ing." An avid poker player, Eric won that hand. I agreed to continue learning, and at the higher rate.

It has been recorded that Eric was against touching in the therapeutic relation-ship. At one time that was true. However, this began to change toward the end of his life. One time he was co-leading a marathon with me; my clients were the participants and were used to some touching. Spontaneously, they reached out to hug him as the marathon was coming to a close. He looked surprised, then interested, and later said, "I'm going to think some more about touching."

My feeling of respect and closeness for Eric may have started one noisy night at the Spaghetti Factory when he was working on his early experiments with intimacy. There, in a crowded noisy situation, Eric asked me to do this experi-ment with him. The process involved two people sitting opposite each other with their faces no less than 20 to 30 inches apart. The purpose was to stimulate eiditic perception such as an infant has with its mother, so that the two involved would really "see" each other and thus experience intimacy. The rules were: no psychological withdrawals, no rituals, pastimes, games, or activities during the 15 or 20 minutes it lasted. The effect was powerful for us both, and, as a result, I enjoyed some lovely fantasies and dreams about him for a period of six weeks.[21]

This concept of six weeks as an important period of time emerged again when Eric claimed that a therapist could drop ideas to their clients, say nothing about them, and the clients would bring up the ideas six weeks later as though they had just discovered them for themselves. I didn't believe it, so I tested it and carefully recorded the process. The six-weeks phenomenon was often true.

Another memory I have is of our long conversations after the evening seminars. Eric would sometimes say, "Muriel, go have a cup of coffee, then come back after everyone has gone. I want to talk to you." I was willing to do this. He would come out to my car and sit there talking in the darkness. I responded, not as a therapist but as a concerned friend. Our last conversation concerned his need for therapy. He explained what he thought was his problem and asked for two professional appointments. I asked, "Why me?" "Why not?" he said. "You have a fairy godmother in your Child, and I particularly need a fairy godmother." I strongly believe and often say, "It takes one to know one," so in Eric's Child there must have been the male counterpart of what he saw in mine.

Eric loved children, including the Child in his clients and colleagues. Although his Adult was clearly the executive, his own Child was often active, especially when he danced or banged away on his son's drums. Furthermore, when leading the TA seminars he often used some of his hard-working Parent.

Eric encouraged many of his followers to write, saying, "Write for an eight-year-old," though he himself did not quite accomplish this goal. He then added the words, "Send me the tenth draft to read." No doubt this was to diminish the belief in a writer's Child that Santa Claus would come if something was just put down on paper, for nothing could be further from the truth. Now an increasing number of TA writers are using the advice he didn't quite follow himself. "After hello," he wrote, "the next thing is to get to work."

In my own experience, writing that is easy to read is difficult to write. I had always felt inadequate in this field, never having taken any courses in writing or English. In fact, the struggle of writing my doctoral dissertation was so difficult that I vowed never to write again. Yet Eric directly influenced my writing; he gave me permission to write in 1967 when he asked me to contribute a brief chapter to his reissued third edition of *A Laymen's Guide to Psychiatry and Psychoanalysis.* Naturally, I was delighted.

Shortly after this Dorothy Jongeward and I met while we were speaking on a panel. We had many interests in common, including our ways of treating clients, some of whom had difficulty understanding Berne's *Games People Play.* Our meeting led to a decision to write *Born To Win.* Eric never saw it. He died of a heart attack the day we signed the publishing contract. I wish he had seen it, I think he would have liked it.

Another permission came in reference to a paper I wrote titled, "Curing Impotency With Transactional Analysis."* I was to present it at the Golden Gate Group Psychotherapy Association in San Francisco in June, 1970. When they saw it listed on the program, several male therapists ridiculed me for writing on the subject. I became very anxious just before the presentation, so I asked Eric, who was attending the conference, to come in and hear it and give me feedback.

A few moments after I started reading the paper, Eric took out the tiny black book that he usually carried in his shirt pocket and started making notes. I knew then that I had said something that interested him, since he only used

---

* Included in this volume.

this little book when he was jotting down ideas to use later in his own writing. When the paper was finished, he defended it strongly in an argument with a couple of antagonistic, non-TA therapists and said to me, "Muriel, get that published immediately and keep on writing." This was an important directive to me, one that I treasure.

THE ORIGINAL TA SEMINARS

Even as I was influenced by Eric Berne, so were many others. The study of TA began in the small town of Carmel, California, where Eric Berne lived and had a private practice. According to Joe Concannon, social worker and "grandfather" of TA, Berne already had a reputation around Carmel for being able to treat more veterans with psychiatric disabilities than other therapists in the area, and with fewer dropouts.[22] The TA study group started in the early 1950's when he invited a small group of professionals to meet regularly and discuss clinical material. There, at what was called "The Seminar," he began to present his ideas about the structure of personality.[23] At about the same time, Berne began dividing his time between Carmel and San Francisco (a practice which he continued until his death in 1970), seeing patients in both places and writing. In San Francisco, in addition to his private practice, Berne also served as psychiatrist at Mt. Zion Hospital and the Veterans' Administration Mental Hygiene Clinic, as well as Consultant to the Surgeon General of the U.S. Army. A seminar group similar to that in Carmel was organized in 1958 in San Francisco. I joined it and began studying TA.

This new professional organization met every Tuesday night at Berne's apartment on Washington St. and was known as the San Francisco Social Psychiatry Seminar, Inc.[24] Later the meetings were held at a house Berne purchased on Collins St. Berne was a strict Parent in some ways. "No eating or drinking coffee during the seminar," he would say. "These things are for the Child, and the seminars are for the Adult." As for his continual pipe-cleaning and smoking, I do not remember anyone ever confronting him with "that too is for the Child!" Inconsistency seems to be a universal characteristic.

A few of those who were part of this original seminar, and others who have since joined, still meet Tuesday evenings. The name of the group has been changed in honor of its founder and is now known as the Eric Berne Seminars.

It was at the Washington St. address that two course numbers were adopted which have become common in all TA circles and readily identify two types of learning experiences. The first is 101 (one-oh-one, not one hundred one), an *introduction* to TA which takes from 12 to 20 hours. It includes didactic instruction with clinical examples, discussion, and demonstration. The other number is 202 (two-oh-two), and it refers to the Tuesday evening meetings. In the early 202's, clinical material would be presented by Berne or one of the seminar members. The presentation would be followed by discussion and often by a trip to the well-known Spaghetti Factory, where the seminar would continue—but now freely punctuated with jokes and laughter. (Occasionally, a broad-jumping contest or a "jumping-up-and-down" dance in Berne's living room was preferred to the Factory.) During the seminar, all participants were expected to "work"—to present their ideas clearly, with good documentation, and without "sloppy thinking."

The presenter, before presenting the clinical material for the evening, asked the other members of the group a question to think about during the evening. It was not a rhetorical nor trick question, but something he or she had not quite figured out about the case. This question served, during the later discussion, as a point of reference. It specified the focus for the listener. It also decreased the likelihood of Child or Parent ego state "performances" by the presenter (as occur in many professional seminars) in favor of problem-solving by the Adult.

From the meeting of only three people early in 1950 to a membership of over 7000 people in the International Transactional Analysis Association by 1976 is considerable growth. That growth was due in large part to the genius of Eric Berne himself and his continuing concern for professionalism and scholarship.

ITAA ESTABLISHED

As interest in TA developed, some of the people who were originally supervised by Eric Berne moved to other locations and formed seminars and institutes of their own. Because of this dispersal, the growing number of institutes, and the increasing interest in TA, the International Transactional Analysis Association was established in 1964. Since then the members have come together each August for a large international congress in which workshops, papers, demonstrations, and panels are presented to the membership as a whole and to other interested persons. Each January a smaller conference is held. It is open only to advanced members in the association who wish to deepen their friendships and knowledge in direct meeting with each other.

Leadership of the ITAA has been provided through a number of Standing Committees, an Executive Committee, an Editorial Board, a Board of Trustees, and the officers.

ACCREDITATION OF TA PRACTITIONERS

Historically, Eric Berne often welcomed the uninformed and nonprofessional to his seminars. By word and action he illustrated his belief that TA could be used by anyone.

Because of this the ITAA is open to all people who wish to enroll and pay the modest fees. There are, however, various classifications of membership. In brief, any interested person may become a member and be eligible to receive the Journal if they have taken the ITAA Introductory Course (101), which is from 12 to 20 hours of didactic material and discussion.

Advanced membership, which requires additional training and supervision, includes Special Fields Members, Clinical Members, and Teaching Members. Special Fields Membership is for those who are educators, trainers in business and industry, and in other special fields which are nonclinically oriented. Clinical Membership is for those who are practicing psychotherapists who are, or can be, legally licensed in the geographical location in which they practice, and who have extensive TA training in addition to basic training in psychology, group dynamics, and so forth. Either one of these two membership categories usually takes two years of study and supervision followed by oral and written examinations. Teaching Membership, which is the most advanced category, requires additional training and experience. At this writing there are approximately 80 persons throughout the world who are Teaching Members and, consequently, have the rights, privileges, and responsibilities related to this classification.

TRAINING

Currently, people are being trained in the use of TA in many locations throughout the world and in many different ways. To date, training is not yet standardized.

In the United States there are various ways to get training. For example, TA is taught in over 1,000 colleges and universities in various departments including: public health, medicine, business administration, psychology, education, social welfare, and law. Master's degrees and Ph.D.'s in TA are available in some universities.

TA is taught at undergraduate, graduate, and postgraduate levels, as a psychological theory and method, or as a communication theory and method, or as an education theory and method, as a business management theory and method, and so forth. It is taught as a specific subject and as part of a larger subject.

TA is also taught in the many institutes that are authorized by the International Transactional Analysis Association. Different institutes organize their programs in different ways. Some have residential week-long or month-long programs; others have academic courses that meet weekly and/or weekend intensive marathons for personal growth and therapy; most of them provide a wide range of educational opportunities, consultation, and supervision. Currently, these institutes are in the process of organizing themselves into a more cohesive group with interchangeable courses.

It is customary for potential TA therapists, counselors, and educators to study in several institutes. Each institute has unique emphasis, therefore each has unique strengths. As the details of TA training have not yet been standardized, the experience of working with several supervisors is a growth process. In this process, supervisees begin to make specific decisions about how they personally will use TA. They seldom come out as carbon copies of a particular institute or a particular supervisor.

One of the reasons TA therapists tend to be unique is because of the strong emphasis on *continuing* training and treatment.

For the person who wishes to become a good TA therapist, personal treatment as well as training is always essential. Psychoanalysts *must* have a "training" psychoanalysis; psychiatrists, as part of their training, may or may not. Other therapists sometimes do, sometimes don't. In TA circles this aspect is becoming more and more important, and personal treatment is recommended for those seeking advanced membership and accreditation in the ITAA.

In 1973 a group of psychoanalysts in Caracas, Venezuela, invited me to train them in Transactional Analysis. When asked what they specifically wanted in their training, they said their preferred form of training was group *treatment*. They did not want information "about" TA given didactically nor through discussion, but wanted to *experience* TA personally six hours a day for one week.

Some of my colleagues cautioned that these highly trained psychoanalysts would "play games" with me. Such was not the case. They were developed therapists who knew that the best training is often experiential and that learning through group treatment provides internal, gut knowledge and insight, a necessary adjunct to intellectual, academic book knowledge. Currently, under the leadership of Humberto Blanco, A.M.D., there is a strong TA movement in Venezuela.

Although TA treatment and experiential learning is useful for people who want to be good TA therapists, occasionally it is possible to accomplish this if basic psychological knowledge has been acquired and if the TA literature is carefully studied. Such was the case at the University of Buenos Aires, where, at Berne's request, I went for a conference in 1969 and met a panel of psychiatrists presenting TA. Their only experience with TA had been through two of Berne's books, *Transactional Analysis in Psychotherapy* and *Games People Play*. Yet this group had analyzed these two books carefully, formed a professional TA study group, were using TA as a mode of treatment, and confronting each other personally as a method for internalizing both theory and method.

In India, the TA movement is growing rapidly, largely because people such as Mary and Robert Goulding, and Katherine and John Dusay have gone there to lecture, but also because people have come from India to the U.S. to study and then returned to teach and treat others. An example is Father George Kanda-thil, who came to the TA Institute in Lafayette, California, and studied TA intensively for nine months. When he returned to India, to the state of Kerala, Father George gathered together a group of interested professionals. He trained some of them, encouraged others to train in the United States, and started publishing a journal in the native language. Since then, several well-accepted TA centers and activities have been established in India. One of them in Bangalore is led by Saroj and Carlos Welch, who also received their training in the United States. Another, in Bombay, is led by Jaswant Singh and Meena Kamani.

From many other countries in the world, people have come to various TA In-stitutes and returned to their homeland to use TA in creative and effective ways. At the same time a number of leaders in the ITAA have traveled through-out the world, lecturing and leading TA workshops and introducing thousands to the theories and methods developed by Eric Berne and his associates.[25]

In 1975 the first European TA congress was held, and in 1976 the first Pan-American congress occurred. Numerous training institutes and treatment clinics are springing up throughout the world. The trend seems to be toward increas-ing expansion and national autonomy.

Currently, there is an increasing number of therapists who are not trained in TA but use some TA concepts with other modalities. There are also an increas-ing number who are committed to extensive training. One such therapist wrote: "I've been avoiding serious study of TA. My clients were doing pretty well because I was warm and supportive and would occasionally throw in some TA language. But really I was using any method I enjoyed that I thought might work. Then one of my clients who had done some reading kind of confronted me on my poor use of TA. Now I want to be accredited. I want to learn TA well—at the head as well as the gut level. Then, when I use other modalities, it will not be just because 'I *feel* like it' but for very specific, rational reasons."

One of the best ways to begin becoming an effective TA therapist is to write to the ITAA for information, to enroll in one of the TA institutes for an in-tensive or an extensive program, and to sign a "contract" with a teaching mem-ber for sponsorship and supervision. Specific contracts are available for each category of memberships and include details of cost, the kind of training that is required, and other pertinent details.

It is wise to get data when selecting someone to be a training supervisor or therapist or an instructor. See how that person leads a group or a workshop. Talk to other supervisees, students or clients. Find out if people who were sponsored and supervised passed their exams, if students who were taught learned the material, if the clients who were treated learned to solve their problems and get well. Observe the use of Occam's Razor.

Occam was a Fourteenth-Century philosopher. He believed that when there are several possible solutions, the right one was probably the most obvious. Using questions in order to dissect the problem, he encouraged people to think. Famous for his hard-headed approach to problem solving, his axiom was *Entia nun sunt multiplicanda praeter necessitatem,* or, "Entities ought not to be multiplied except from necessity."[26]

The axiom was called Occam's Razor because of Occam's style of shaving away all extraneous details and all unnecessary facts. The well-trained TA therapist learns to do the same.

REFERENCES

1. Berne, Eric, *Transactional Analysis in Psychotherapy* (New York: Grove, 1961), pp. 33, 34.

2. ———, *Principles of Group Treatment* (New York: Grove, 1968), p. 364.

3. ———, *TA in Psychotherapy,* p. 17.

4. Penfield, W., "Memory Mechanisms," A.M.A. *Archives of Neurology and Psychiatry* **67** (1952), pp. 178–198.

5. Berne, *Principles,* p. 281.

6. ———, "The Natural History of a Spontaneous Therapy Group," *International Journal of Group Psychotherapy* 4 (1954), pp. 75–85.

7. ———, "Review: Four Books on Group Therapy," *American Journal of Orthopsychiatry* **34** (1964), pp. 584–589.

8. Berne's studies on intuition are summarized in Dusay, John M., "Eric Berne's Studies of Intuition 1949–1962," *TA Journal,* Jan. 1974, pp. 34–44.

9. Cheney, Warren D., "Eric Berne: Biographical Sketch," *TA Journal,* Jan. 1971, p. 19.

10. Berne, *TA in Psychotherapy.*

11. ———, *The Structure and Dynamics of Organizations and Groups* (New York: Grove, 1966).

12. ———, *Games People Play* (New York: Grove, 1964).

13. ———, *Principles.*

14. ———, *What Do You Say After You Say Hello?* (New York: Grove, 1972).

15. ———, *The Happy Valley* (New York: Grove, 1968).

16. ———, *Sex in Human Loving* (New York: Simon & Schuster, 1970).

17. ———, *Structure and Dynamics,* pp. 167–168.

18. Steiner, Claude, *Scripts People Live* (New York: Grove, 1975).

19. Harris, Thomas, "A Tribute to Eric Berne," *TA Journal,* Jan. 1971, pp. 59–60.

20. Levaggi, Jules, Viola Litt Callaghan, and Charles Berger, "A Living Ephemerus Never Dies," *TA Journal,* Jan. 1971, pp. 64–70.

21. Berne, Eric, "The Intimacy Experiment," *TA Bulletin,* Jan. 1964, p. 113: "More About Intimacy," *TA Bulletin,* Apr. 1964, p. 125.

22. Concannon, Joseph, "My Introduction to Eric Berne," *TA Journal,* Jan. 1971.

23. Kupfer, David, "In the Beginning," *TA Journal,* Jan. 1971.

24. Cheney, "Eric Berne."

25. James, Muriel, "Survey of International Growth," *TA Journal,* Jan. 1973, pp. 8, 9.

26. Brewer, E. Cobham, *Brewer's Dictionary of Phrase and Fable,* Centenary ed., edited by Ivor H. Evans (New York: Harper & Row, 1972), p. 773.

CHAPTER 3

TA therapists: as persons and professionals

For the group therapist to be the master of his own destiny requires a commitment which misses no opportunity to learn, uses every legitimate method to win, and permits no rest until every loss has been thoroughly analysed so that no mistake will ever be repeated.
Eric Berne

EFFECTIVE AND INEFFECTIVE THERAPISTS

Adler wrote, "The technique of treatment must be in yourself." Berne added, "Preparation of the therapist must precede preparation of the patient."[1] Therapists are made, not born. A therapist who has received good training, who stays involved in continuing education, and who has integrity as a person, is likely to be effective. The personal characteristics of effective therapists vary widely. For example, some are physically attractive, some are not; some have high energy levels, others do not; some have the ability to be at ease with other people, others have not. Yet these are but a few of the qualities that can usually be acquired. An equally important aspect of effective therapists is that they have worked through their major personal problems satisfactorily. This is true for therapists who use TA exclusively or who use it in conjunction with other modalities.

Tragically, a few therapists (both TA and otherwise) have considerable intellectual information but practice treatment without sufficient awareness of their own problems. Consequently, these problems may be worked out on their clients. Specifically, people who are not effective therapists until they work out their own hangups include those who:

1. are not liked by others,
2. in their subconscious do not want to be liked because of the demands other people's affections might make on them,
3. would rather be alone than with other people,
4. are unwilling to discipline themselves to the requirements of training and treatment, or
5. do not plan for continuing personal and professional growth after being certified to practice.

Even therapists who have themselves well put together emotionally should not attempt to use TA without sufficient TA training. On the surface, TA appears simple, but it is a long way from being so simple that a therapist can master it by just taking the ITAA accredited 101 introductory course, reading a few TA books, and attending a few TA workshops. The information gained this way can and should be of great value to the individual—but it is far from enough to qualify a therapist as a practitioner. This is not meant to reflect on any accredited psychotherapist's proficiency with other therapeutic modalities; it is merely to point out that the proper use of such a highly specialized technical tool, like any other, requires considerable training and expertise. It need not be the *only* tool the psychotherapist uses—and he or she should have complete command of it.

Berne speaks of various styles of therapists who can be labeled. There are:

1. Phallus in Wonderland, who is fascinated by the clients and what happens to them.
2. The Delegate, who seemingly knows everything and has the "whole weight of psychoanalytic tradition behind him."
3. The Smiling Rebel, who tends to keep secret what's on his or her mind, experimenting with clients and seldom telling people what's really going on.
4. The Patient Clinician, who gets along slowly, rescues somewhat, and never gets upset.
5. The Jargon Junk Juggler, who enjoys using large words that nobody understands.
6. The Conservative, who is so bland and passive that nothing much happens.
7. The Hypochondriac, who is afraid to try anything new because of the concern over his or her own comfort.[2]

Competent TA therapists are aware of the possibility of fitting into one of these phony roles and reject them in favor of being real.

TA THERAPISTS AND "REAL" DOCTORS

Transactional Analysis therapists, who are accredited by the ITTA, hold clinical or teaching membership in the organization. They are people who consider themselves to be in the curing, treating, and teaching professions. Some of them are state licensed to do therapy, some are not. Institutions of various kinds are able to hire unlicensed people as therapists (though usually under another title) because of the licensing responsibility held by the institutions themselves or by their medical directors. Many of these people do admirable work. States have varying requirements for licensing and different laws under which the licensee may practice. The reader who is thinking about becoming a therapist is encouraged to seek out information on such laws and requirements in his or her state.

In California, for example, licenses to practice psychotherapy may be issued to psychoanalysts, psychiatrists, clinical psychologists, licensed clinical social workers, and marriage, family, and child counselors. Each of these, before licensing, has earned a master's degree or higher in the behavioral sciences, has had extensive supervision, and has passed both oral and written examinations.

Not everyone may be aware of such requirements, however, or value them highly. A psychiatrist at a staff meeting was heard to ask a new staff member about his professional training and title. The new staff member specified his degrees, his years of training and supervision, and added that he was licensed as a Marriage, Family, and Child Counselor. The psychiatrist retorted, "Oh, a counselor. That means you give advice; *I* give treatment!" Both of these people had been trained in TA but, according to TA, the psychiatrist's clear-thinking Adult was for the moment contaminated by Parental opinions of "what's best," and Childlike feelings of grandiosity. This is not surprising. Many therapists, irrespective of background, are so busy getting their own education that they may not know that others are likewise busy studying and that learning from a different perspective can also be useful.

It is probably true that counselors do give advice. So do psychiatrists. It is also true that psychiatrists give treatment. So do counselors. The advice or treatment may be good, bad, or indifferent. Neither group can be labeled with the best or worst qualities found in therapists.

Historically there has been considerable medical/nonmedical controversy (often between psychologists and psychiatrists) over who can do psychotherapy. It is not yet resolved. To some people the points seem petty; to others they appear vitally important. Wolberg raises a pertinent question with, "When a nonmedical person works with an individual is he 'helping' a 'client,' but when a medical person utilizes the same process is he 'treating' the same 'patient'?" He notes that there is no uniformity of sentiment and quotes from "California Dialogue: Defining Psychotherapy Insight" (Roche Report, 1965)

> Dr. F. James Gay (Neuropsychiatric Institute, Westwood, L.A.): Regarding the definition of psychotherapy, should its connotation be so broad that it includes nonmedical people—such as social workers and psychologists? If so, aren't we jeopardizing the responsibility of our role in the medical profession? There are many instances where those outside of our specific medical field do not exercise the same clinical care for people they are working with as we do. I think the term, psychotherapy, perhaps ought to be restricted to working with feelings, fantasies, resistances, defenses as it is done by psychiatrists.

> Dr. Alexander S. Rogawski (Past-President of the Southern California Psychoanalytic Society): I cannot agree. What is important is that a psychotherapist be a professional person educated for this task and that he belong to a self-policing and/or legally licensed group subscribing to a code of operational standards.[3]

Some of the greatest contributors to psychotherapy have been nonmedical people: Anna Freud, Erik Erikson, Erick Fromm, Theodor Reik, Otto Rank, S. R. Slavson, Robert Linder, and Carl Rogers. It is not likely that any of these people would consider themselves nontherapists just because they do not have medical degrees. Although the debate over who is entitled to do therapy will probably continue, there is no question about the increasing demand for therapy and the inability of any one group to provide enough of it. The ITAA recently initiated pioneer action among psychotherapy organizations when its boards of trustees, many of whom are medical doctors, voted unanimously, and publicly stated that *all* qualified ITAA therapists—medical and nonmedical— hold equal status in the ITAA.

Berne weighed titles and functions judiciously and seldom expressed degree snobbishness. Although he used the word "patient" in the traditional way because of his medical orientation, he used the word "doctor" in a nontraditional way. In fact, one of his hospital stories is of psychiatric staff—a group of psychiatrists, psychologists, and social workers—who had lunch together regularly and joked about themselves as being unreal doctors in contrast to the surgeons and internists who occasionally joined them and who were considered "real." In Berne's view, "real" doctors could be described as follows:

1. A "real doctor" is specifically oriented throughout his training toward curing his patients and that is his overriding consideration throughout his practice.
2. A "real" doctor can plan his treatment so that at each phase he knows what he is doing and why he is doing it.

3. A "real doctor" clearly distinguishes research and experimentation from good medical or surgical care, and the former is always subsidiary to the latter.
4. A "real doctor" takes sole and complete responsibility for the welfare of his patients.[4]

This book is intended for those who wish to be "real doctors" irrespective of the academic degrees and licensing they may or may not have earned.

WHY PEOPLE BECOME TA THERAPISTS

People enter the mental health fields and become TA psychotherapists and counselors through widely divergent routes. Some may in their childhood decide "to be a real doctor" (as Eric Berne did); some may transfer from very different disciplines such as mathematics, architecture, or chemistry; others transfer from allied fields such as education or nursing. When asked why he was making the transfer, a chemist replied, "I've just decided that understanding people by using TA is more interesting than test tubes." An economist added, "After having had treatment myself, I realized relationships with people were the most important thing in my life." The academic background of people such as the chemist or economist is so entirely different from those in mental health fields that they usually need to start their psychological training as beginning students. However, the ability to discipline themselves in their original studies usually carries over into their TA training.

When people transfer to psychology from allied fields, such as education, it is often because they find the task of being a therapist more compatible to their interests and skills. One teacher who decided to become a therapist did so because "the questions being asked me in the sociology and family life courses that I taught were obviously related to personality idiosyncrasies and psychological problems." A nurse who made the vocational switch said she did so because, "I'm tired of always being a nurturing parent to people. I want more eyeball-to-eyeball ways of curing ·people. Using psychotherapy, especially TA, I can do that."

Currently, many clergy seek TA training as therapists because of their frequent personal involvement with people and their need for tools other than those given to them during their years of theological training. Some clergy use TA in their churches when counseling; some go into private practice outside the institutional church, or become chaplains, or work in centers specifically designed for pastoral counseling.

A clinical psychologist working at a state hospital entered training angrily, "Damn it," he said, "I've got to find some effective tools that I can use quickly and that the patients can understand and use after they get out of the hospital."

Kenneth Everts, psychiatrist and past president of the ITAA went into TA because he was bored with conventional psychiatry. Reflecting on years in office and how it affected his practice, he wrote:

> My personal interest in TA has been and will remain the dissemination of the knowledge as accurately and as widely as possible, and the preservation of the integrity and high ethical standards of ITAA. During the past four years I have maintained a modest group practice, and my income has been comparable to the pre-Berne days. I did not pursue TA for fame, money, or personal gain. What I've gotten from it is great satisfaction and gratification in my practice. Before TA, I found conventional psychiatry boring and its results dubious.[5]

I became a therapist in a roundabout way, sort of after the fact. I had completed an Ed.D. in Adult Education at the University of California with a focus on the psychology of adult learning, and was teaching at the University and in various adult education programs. Gradually, it occurred to me that many people were coming for some kind of guidance, for clarification of life goals, for help with severe personal problems, for tools to use in times of crisis, and so forth, and that further training in psychotherapy was clearly indicated. I then took appropriate post-doctoral studies, interned in both state and private mental hospitals, received 2500 hours of direct competent supervision, was licensed, and established a private practice. I have not regretted this choice.

My introduction to Eric Berne and TA was in 1958 through Kenneth Everts, past president of the ITAA. He showed me one of Eric's first papers and invited me to the Tuesday night 202 seminar in San Francisco. I attended this fairly regularly until Eric's death, at which time I organized the TA Institute in Lafayette, California.

Because it was an hour's drive from my home to the 202 seminar, I often went with some reluctance. I also fantasized from time to time, "There's nothing new to learn. I've learned it all." Then Eric or some other member of the seminar would present theory using slightly different words, or present an especially challenging case, and it would be a new "ah-ha" insight; my interest would rise once more. Even now, after all these years with TA, there's always something new in it for me.

I have enjoyed teaching, observing, and supervising many persons interested in TA. I have come to believe that people's decisions to become competent therapists are directly related to their personal goals, including those they may not be fully aware of, and their interest and concern for other people. All kinds of people can and do become therapists. Regardless of their backgrounds, they will be good ones if, objectively and with a minimum of games, they enjoy other people, believe that everyone has potentiality for growth, have feelings of good-will and interest toward others, are ethical and self-disciplined, are neither exploitative nor "fly-at-night," and if they get competent training. Such people will always be sought out by those who need therapy.

It seems to me that most people who make conscious decisions to become TA therapists are willing to do what is necessary to achieve their goal—to give time and energy, make personal changes, and handle the financial cost. It may mean considerable sacrifice; the time spent in training will leave less time for something else. Nevertheless, good training and treatment are essential to the development of effective therapists.

People with authenticity, integrity, creativity, and training are effective. They are able to be *potent* when faced with treatment challenges. They give people *permission* to get well, and they *protect* them psychologically during the process.

POTENCY, PERMISSION, AND PROTECTION

Potency, permission, and protection are interrelated words that refer to particular qualities and skills a TA therapist needs to have.

Genuinely *potent* TA therapists are so because of a personal sense of authenticity, credibility, trustworthiness, and responsiveness. These people do not use time or energy in putting on a performance, nor do they play at being therapists. Instead, they respond appropriately to therapeutic challenges and work to protect the worth and well-being of their clients.

Potent therapists do not need to know all the answers in TA, but they do need to have a clear understanding of some of the answers, especially the basic definitions of ego states, strokes, transactions, games, and scripts, how they are interrelated, and how problems related to each can be solved.

Potent therapists are in a continuing learning process. They have an increasing awareness of their own ego states—their Child feelings, their Parent opinions, and their Adult data. They know when and why their ego states are in conflict or in agreement and how each may affect their clients. They are aware of how their own health is affected by their life styles and their eating, sleeping, and exercising patterns. They know that an informed, experienced Adult will be more potent than an uninformed, inexperienced one. They are able to analyze their own transactions and change them when appropriate, decrease the frequency and intensity of their games, and rewrite their own script through reeducation of their inner Child.

One technique for a therapist who wishes to measure the potency of his or her Parent ego state is to use a fantasy—that is, a fantasy of the client's Parent figure confronting the therapist's Adult and fighting, in one way or another, for the health, happiness, and well-being of the client. If the fantasy shows that the therapist could win in such an encounter, then he or she has a distinct advantage over the client whose inner Parent often does not want the Child to change and is weaker than the therapist who does. If the client's Parent is stronger than the therapist's Adult, then referral to another therapist is in order.

Another interesting technique can be used to measure Child ego state potency. It is for the therapist to: (1) visualize each client as an animal, (2) visualize himself or herself as an animal, and (3) fantasize what would happen if they met. Who would win if a battle ensued? Fantasy techniques often bring unresolved archaic feelings into awareness so that they can be worked through. For example, one therapist, whose script was Little Black Sambo, came to realize that the tigers (people) he feared were really only paper and that sometimes he too was a paper tiger to the clients he worked with.

Other ways potency can be measured is by Adult evaluation of the length of time in treatment in relation to the kinds of contracts made and completed. For example, an unemployed client might contract to get a job, and get one, in a month's time. However a client living alone and seriously withdrawn, who leaves home only once a week to see the therapist, would take longer to fulfill a contract, for example, to acquire two friends.

Berne sometimes asked his supervisees to analyze what they were doing that week to prevent their clients from healing themselves. Potent therapists are willing to think about that. They are not afraid to say, "I don't know the answer. I'll look it up." They are not embarrassed when searching out a well-qualified supervisor or when confronted by peers. They learn from their mistakes as well as their successes.

Potent TA therapists also learn how to give *permission* to their clients. The permission is given either verbally or nonverbally so that people can experience positive feelings, thoughts, and behavior about themselves and others instead of living by negative childhood scripting.

Permission may be given *indirectly* and verbally with remarks such as, "Winners learn to think for themselves. It's OK for you to do so," or "You don't need to be afraid to ask for positive feedback. It's OK to ask for it and to act in ways that will get it." Permission may also be given *directly* with words such as, "I give you permission. . . ." (The latter technique needs to be used discreetly, as many clients will interpret it as paternalistic and thereby be "hooked" into their Rebellious Child.) Permission is also given *nonverbally* with a smile, nod, and clap on the back, a handshake or some other sign of caring or good-will.[6] It is given with any positive act that reinforces a client's achievements and changes, thus giving permission for more achievements and more changes. Permission can be given *from any ego state*. A therapist who jokes or laughs play-fully from the Child often gives as potent a permission to have fun out of life as one who gives a Nurturing Parent remark or gives some rational Adult in-formation.

Although TA was originally designed as a nontouching form of treatment, an increasing number of therapists are using well-timed physical touching—even holding—when redecisions are made and old negative injunctions are worked through. This reenforces permission. Permission transactions encourage change and, like positive reenforcement, accelerate growth. The therapist often serves as a model.

Potent TA therapists who are able to give permission often need to provide *protection* simultaneously because the client's Child may be very vulnerable at this point. As a rule of thumb, if a person is genuinely hurting—physically or emotionally—therapists need to be both tender and strong and thus protective. In a crisis, therapists need to be available themselves or have a dependable referral source. To establish what is a crisis and what is not, a therapist could say something like, "Phone me immediately if you think you might hurt your-self or anyone else. Otherwise, only phone me for appointments." This kind of statement not only provides the client with needed protection, it also provides some for the therapist who needs private, uninterrupted time. Further protec-tion is provided by not putting anything in the files that might be construed negatively, or held against a client if the files were stolen.

During a group session, a potent leader may provide protection by interrupting and changing the subject if a group member is revealing information that might cause great embarrassment or punitive action at a later time. Because group confidentiality is sometimes precarious, some TA therapists suggest that his-tories of homosexuality, forced hospitalization, or crime be discussed in private rather than in group sessions. For example, a homosexual teacher might be fired if his or her sexual orientation were discovered by others in the commun-ity who have not worked through their own sexuality. As the dignity of every individual needs some protecting, most effective TA therapists do not try to elicit any kind of information prematurely that the client may wish to keep secret. In fact, some may tell a client, "You do not have to tell me anything unless you want to," or words to that effect.

Crossing a transaction is an intervention technique which provides both per-mission and protection.[7] It can, for example, be used with clients who, without full awareness, strongly antagonize others and set themselves up for a psychological "kick." Although some clients can take a kick, others need a stronger Adult ego state before they can handle heavy rejection. For example, if a client continually whines, and collects put-downs from others as a result of whining, a therapist might intervene and say, "What kind of a response do you expect when you look and talk as you're now doing?" This question is designed to hook the client's Adult and give it permission to think. Or, "What is the worse thing that could happen if you did or didn't. . . ?" This question is meant to elicit the catastrophic expectations in the Adapted Child and give it permission to get in touch with archaic feelings. Or, "It would be OK if you got into the Adult-Leveling position for the balance of this session." This statement is used to give the person permission to put the Adult in executive control over the somewhat acting-out Child. Berne used to say, "If the Child is in control, give the Adult something to do."

I well remember a period during my training when I found it necessary to give my Adult an assigned task that would control my Child. It was at the 202 seminars when I was often feeling excited by an idea and wanted to talk about it. At the same time, the atmosphere was often male chauvinistic and I was shy, listening to an inner tape of "Children should be seen and not heard," or to another tape of, "If you can't say anything nice, don't say anything at all," and so forth. Both my Adapted Child and my Parent interfered with my Adult.

I handled this by giving myself something to do: It was to diagram the complementary, crossed, and ulterior transactions between the seminar members during the discussion and to diagram the games that were frequently played. This paper-and-pencil assignment required my Adult to be the executive, and I learned well the favorite games played by others in the seminar. I also discovered some of mine! The notebooks I have of those sessions are still of interest as I observe that some of the old-timers no longer play those same old games and a few old-timers play them harder than ever.

The Adult-leveling position is leveling the body, a method developed by Franklin Ernst.[8] It can be used by a person who acts inappropriately or is "out of control," whose feelings are overly painful or who wishes to have the Adult as executive of the personality for problem-solving purposes. To level physically, the person sits or stands with feet flat on the floor, hands, legs, and arms uncrossed and parallel to the body, back straight, head untipped, and chin parallel to the floor. This technique inevitably protects the Child and gives the Adult permission to be in the driver's seat.

Potency, permission, and protection—everyone wants them, everyone needs them, and everyone can have them—therapists as well as clients. Effective TA therapists use these three "Ps" of treatment.

PSYCHOLOGICAL POSITIONS OF THERAPISTS

All children, including those who grew up to be therapists, take OK or not-OK psychological positions about themselves and others.[9] The positions taken are seemingly logical though usually outside of awareness. They result from specific childhood experiences and the specific decisions that children make because of them. For example, children who are brutalized by one parent and not protected from such brutality by another, will logically decide to be fearful of the brutalizing parent and indifferent or angry toward the nonprotective one. In cases such as these, the specific decisions are later expanded to the general psychological position that people as a group are not-OK. About themselves, such children may decide: I'm OK in spite of the way they treat me (they're crazy), or I'm not-OK (otherwise they would love me and treat me differently).

Psychological positions are generalized opinions based on specific decisions and strongly adhered to throughout life. These positions are as follows:

1. "I'm OK, you're OK."* This is the mentally healthy position, and the person who holds it is willing to *get on with* people.
2. "I'm OK, you're not OK." This is the projective position, essentially paranoid, in which the person would prefer to *get rid of* other people.
3. "I'm not OK, you are OK." In this introjective position, basically depressive, the person would rather *get away from* other people.
4. "I'm not OK, you're not OK." In this position of futility, the person feels hopeless and schizoid, and expects *to get nowhere with* other people.[10]

Franklin Ernst uses this concept in a grid diagram colloquially called "The OK Corral."[11]

---

* The OK positions may be read "we" and "they" instead of "I" and "you" if that is appropriate. That is, "We're OK, they're OK," and so on.

Therapists in the I'm OK, you're OK position are *confident*. They are master craftsmen or women. They are artists at their work. They believe life is worth living and convey that message to others.

Therapists in the I'm OK, you're not-OK position feel and communicate a *superiority* position of, "I'm OK because I'm the therapist, you're not OK as you're the client." They may show this by being indifferent, or over-critical, or over-nurturing and paternalistic. The message they give out is, "Your life is not worth as much as mine."

Therapists in the *anxious* or depressed position of I'm not-OK, You are OK allow themselves to be used and abused by clients. They may "forget" to set time limits for the session, or "forget" to tell clients not to phone them unless it's a crisis, or "forget" to collect their fees. The message they give out is, "My life is not worth as much as yours."

Therapists in the *hopeless* position of I'm not-OK, you're not-OK experience chronic failure or unhappiness in their own lives and manage to select clients equally destructive. If they are in private practice, they often have a high rate of hospitalizing clients or referring clients to others more competent. Their message is, "Life isn't worth anything anyway."

One of the reasons it is important for therapists to discover their life positions is so that they may become aware of episcripts and how they can be passed on without awareness through not-OK transactions. The episcript, according to Fanita English, is a secret plot based on the magic assumption that tragedy to the self can be avoided by passing it on to a sacrificial object, a victim, or scapegoat. It is a condensed version of a script, including the tragic ending, which a person tries to "pass on" to someone else.[12]

An episcript, like a hot potato, may be passed on, generation after generation, by a culture or in a family. Therapists may also pass on their own destructive episcripts which are "too hot to handle," or they can encourage the process between clients.

RIGHTS OF CLIENTS AND THERAPISTS

Clients who are seeking TA treatment and/or training have certain inalienable "rights." These are similar to a hospital patient's rights which, according to the American Hospital Association, are:

1. The right to considerate and respectful care.
2. Complete and current information concerning diagnosis, treatment, and prognosis in language the patient can reasonably be expected to under-

stand. In such cases that it is not medically advisable to give such information to the patient the information may be made available to an appropriate person in his behalf.

3. The right to know by name and specialty, if any, the physician responsible for coordination of his or her care.
4. The right to every consideration of his privacy and individuality as it relates to social, religious, and psychological well-being.
5. The right to respectfulness and privacy as it relates to the medical care program.
6. The right to expect the facility to make a reasonable response to the requests of the patient.
7. The right to obtain information as to any relationship of the facility to other health care and related institutions insofar as his or her care is concerned.
8. The right to expect reasonable continuity of care.

These rights, translated into the private practice of psychotherapy, mean that clients are entitled to be selective when choosing their therapist. As such, it is appropriate for them to query their potential therapist or supervisor as to background, training, accreditation, fees, and so forth. "Real" doctors are willing to supply that information without resentment or impatience. I believe it is also a client's right to switch therapists or supervisors. Whereas there are many advantages to staying with one, there are few advantages to staying out of a sense of loyalty or fear of changing.

Confidentiality, continuity of care, consideration for the person's life style (if that style is not actually destructive), respect for their religious orientation, a reasonable amount of attention that is generally free of interruptions, and information on diagnosis and treatment in words that are readily understood are standard rights of all clients. Last but not least, is the right *not* to be involved in research or experimental methods without full consent.

I believe therapists also have "rights," and that many of these are similar to those of their clients. For example, therapists have the right to privacy, the right to time off, to vacations. To get this, they may need to instruct their clients that they are not available between therapy sessions either on a face-to-face basis or by phone, except for emergencies or to make appointments.

Therapists are also entitled to a coffee-break, or time between sessions to bring files up to date, or time to take a deep breath. Some therapists need training on how to do this—how to terminate sessions with clients who, at the last minute, have several more things to say. They also need to learn how to structure their own time to take care of their own needs. Neophyte therapists, especially if they see themselves as helpers and rescuers, may have difficulty with each of these issues. I did.

When I first opened my private practice, I wanted to spend most evenings with my family, so I scheduled my four TA groups on two nights a week, in such a way that I could take a one-hour break between two sessions. However, I invariably allowed last minute "shy" speakers or people with "fascinating" problems to continue past the hour set for closure. After all, one of my games was, "I'm only trying to help them." My break between groups became shorter and shorter. In the attempt to discipline myself, I rescheduled the groups closer together, knowing that one batch of cars and clients would have to leave before there would be enough space for the next. The result was still not satisfactory; my break was even shorter. Obviously, I was not setting or maintaining consistent limits. With a jolt I looked hard at the problem, made new contracts with myself, and changed my behavior. One way I did this was to say, "I notice that the group often runs overtime. Hereafter, we will stop on time." Another technique I used was to interrupt, even if someone was speaking, 10 or 15 minutes before the group was to terminate, and make a comment such as, "There's 10 minutes left of the group session." These limits were quickly accepted by the group members. They learned to speak sooner and finish on time.

The therapist also has the right to honest pay for honest work, and usually to be paid when the fee is due. Many therapists bill their clients monthly, and psychological games are often played around money, its payment, and its collection. To avoid some of this, a therapist can have fees posted in the waiting room. I prefer to discuss fees with the client at the end of the first session, rather than have the receptionist (if there is one) do so. I tell clients that, although I keep financial records, I do not send bills; that the Adult ego state within can be responsible and figure out what is owed. I then ask them how they wish to pay—weekly, monthly, or what, and I accept their answer. The one exception is that if the first interview indicates that the client plays the game of Debtor, I say the fee will need to be paid weekly to break up that pattern. In the many years I have been in practice, I have had only one person who "mixed up" an account, so I feel pretty relaxed about fees.

Eric Berne was in favor of the relaxed therapist who had permission to be happy and "transmitted this license to his patients."[13] He did not, however, equate being relaxed with being casual. Promptness, thoughtfulness, creativeness, kindness (when needed), and ethical behavior in every way were qualities that he expected of all his supervisees. "Psychotherapists are parapeople," he wrote, "but they are entitled to laugh occasionally just like real people—only for a few seconds, however, and then they must get back to work."[14]

REFERENCES

1. Berne, Eric, *Principles of Group Treatment* (New York: Grove, 1968), p. 357.

2. Ibid., pp. 337–340.

3. Wolberg, Lewis R., *The Technique of Psychotherapy*, 2d ed. (New York: Grune & Stratton, 1967), p. 332.

4. Berne, *Principles*, p. xvii.

5. Everts, Kenneth, "The President's Page," *TA Journal*, Jan. 1974, p. 4.

6. Crossman, Patricia, "Permission and Protection," *TA Bulletin* **5**, 19 (1963), pp. 152–153.

7. Karpman, Stephen, "Option," *TA Journal* **1**, 1 (1971), pp. 79–87.

8. Ernst, Franklin, *Activity of Listening*, 1st ed. (Vallejo, Calif.: Golden Gate Foundation for Group Treatment, 1968), pp. 13–14.

9. Berne, Eric, "Classifications of Position," *TA Bulletin* **1**, 23 (1962): Harris, Thomas, *I'm OK—You're OK* (New York: Harper & Row, 1969).

10. James, Muriel, and Dorothy Jongeward, *Born to Win: Transactional Analysis with Gestalt Experiments* (Reading, Mass.: Addison-Wesley, 1971), pp. 35–37.

11. Ernst, Franklin H., Jr., "Psychological Rackets in the OK Corral," *TA Journal* **3**, 2 (1973), p. 19: See also James, Muriel, *The OK Boss* (Reading, Mass.: Addison-Wesley, 1975), for application of the OK positions to management styles.

12. English, Fanita, "Episcript and the 'Hot Potato Game'," *TA Bulletin* **8**, 32 (1969), pp. 77–82.

13. Berne, *Principles*, p. x.

14. Ibid., p. 338.

CHAPTER 4

self-therapy
techniques
for therapists

Self-Analysis is like giving oneself a haircut:
with sufficient care and practice it can be done.
Eric Berne

Therapists are in powerful positions. Not only can they run their own lives, they can run the lives of others. Whereas personal therapy and clinical supervision are requirements for TA therapists, continuing self-therapy, in spite of its limitations, is also a prerequisite for being an effective, "real" doctor. If self-therapy is a continuing process, the lives that therapists run, or try to run, are likely to move in the direction of autonomy.

Although this chapter focuses upon the therapist, it also provides vital diagnostic rationale and techniques which can be used with clients. Subsequent chapters which focus on the client and treatment procedures in more detail will also be useful for therapists who are willing to do self-therapy.

EGO-STATE DIAGNOSIS

Self-therapy first requires clear knowledge of ego states and how different people use them differently. There are four ways to diagnose ego states: behaviorally, socially, historically, and phenomenologically. Each diagnostic process has value.[1]

In brief, *behavioral diagnosis* includes analyzing posture, voice, facial expressions, gestures, words. Behavior that often reflects the use of the Parent ego state is sometimes expressed with authoritarian words, voice, gestures: scowling, shaking a finger at someone, commanding "you must," "you should," "you have to," etc. Parent ego-state behavior may also be expressed in nurturing, tender ways: patting someone on the shoulder, smiling indulgently, giving unsolicited but well-meaning advice, using encouraging words, etc.

Behavior that often reflects use of the Adult ego state is straightforward and focused on reality testing: working efficiently, asking direct questions, giving straightforward answers, computing information.

Behavior that often reflects use of the Child ego state is like the behavior of a young child: pouting, having temper tantrums, giggling, teasing, expressing oneself with "Gimme," "I don't care," "Wow."[2]

Historical diagnosis involves the identification of past events or people that contribute to an individual's unique personality development and patterns of interpersonal relations. For example, a man who comes to treatment and is resentful of his children's bids for his attention may be asked about his father and discover that he is reacting from his Parent ego state precisely as his father did by being overly busy. A woman deserted in childhood by a parent or losing one through death, may, if married, live in constant fear from her Child ego state that her spouse might also desert her. Recalling these facts and discovering the ego states involved is historical diagnosis.

Social Diagnosis does not focus on what the person does or did, but on the current *responses* that others make to him or her. For example, people who attract others who continually ask them for advice or help are likely to be using their Parent ego states more than they realize. People who feel competent themselves, who seek others who are also competent, and who exchange information on the basis of mutual respect, are likely to be in their Adult ego states most often. People who continually seek out others as voices of authority, either critical or nurturing, and who resist taking responsibility for their own lives, are likely to be in the Child ego state most often.

Subjective or phenomenological diagnosis is validated by the reexperiencing of childhood feelings in a similar situation. For example, a person who in childhood is badly frightened by thieves robbing his or her house may, when fully grown, reexperience the terror and the need for protection if verbally attacked by a group of men. A person frightened as a child by a snake or dog may reexperence a similar feeling when seeing a snake or a dog. Conversely, pleasant experiences from the past may also be relived.[3]

COMPLEXITIES OF BEHAVIORAL DIAGNOSIS

Neophytes in TA sometimes limit their ego state diagnosis to *behavioral* data. For example, they equate parental behavior with the Parent ego state, child-like behavior with the Child ego state, and data-processing behavior with the Adult. Such equation is not always valid.

Second-order structural analysis, which is analyzing the substructure within each ego state, shows why, for example, rational data processing can actually come from the Adult part of the Parent ego state. After all, most parents are some-what rational and able to process data some of the time. (Parenting behavior may also come from the Adult in those who have studied the subject of parent-ing.) Childlike behavior can also come from the Parent; parents were once children who laughed and cried and responded with conditioned behavior. The Parent ego state is an incorporation of all the ego states of the parent figures.

Parent ego states are "borrowed from parental figures and reproduce the feel-ings, behavior, and responses of these figures."[4] They are experiential, be-havioral, and civil realities; you can find the telephone number of a Parent.[5] A therapist, *playing a supportive Parent role,* may really be in the Child ego state, "very much like a little boy playing doctor."[6]

People's parent figures are not necessarily their natural parents. A person reared by grandparents, older siblings, housekeepers, etc., will have these people in his or her Parent ego state. Some may have a number of persons in their Parent ego state, some may have only one.

The Parent is expressed in two ways—outwardly toward others and inwardly, in dialogue with the Child. Two typical second-order structural diagrams of the Parent ego state are shown here.

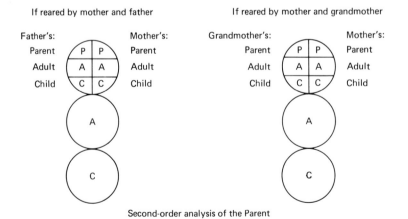

Second-order analysis of the Parent

The simplest way for therapists to determine whether parental attitudes and behaviors are coming from their own Parent ego state is to ask themselves a historical diagnostic question: "Did any of my parent figures act or speak as I am now doing?" If the answer is "yes," then the behavior is probably from the Parent ego state. If it is "no," then the behavior is either from the Child playing at being a mommy or daddy, or from the Adult who has decided on a particular kind of parenting behavior. When the Adult ego state parents others, the parenting is usually more rational rather than traditional.

I believe it is important to determine from what ego state parental behavior comes. Treatment needs to be related to accurate diagnosis. Many people— therapists as well as clients—have inadequate Parent ego states and need self-parenting.[7] Sometimes the Parent ego state is spoken of *functionally* rather than structurally. Structure refers to *parts* of the personality; function refers to *how* the person is perceived as functioning. General terms used for functional description of parenting behavior are "Critical Parent" and "Nurturing Parent." When this is the case the diagram is:

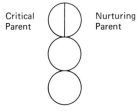

Critical Parent   Nurturing Parent

I personally believe that this way of categorizing the Parent is incomplete. Many people have *indifferent* parents, parents who stay uninvolved emotionally and "cop-out" on setting limits or showing concern in appropriate ways. Others have *inconsistent* parents, or *conflicting* parents, or parents who are *emotionally over-needy* or *over-organized.*[8] Whereas the words "nurturing" and "critical" are likely to get the point across at an introductory level, at a more precise level they may not fit a particular person. Therefore, I work with the specific words clients use when they talk about their parents.

Therapists who wish further understanding of themselves can jot down the adjectives that would have described their childhood parent figures, then speculate on how a child, parented by these people, might grow up.

The Child ego state can also be subdivided, either functionally or with second-order structural analysis, as shown on the next page.

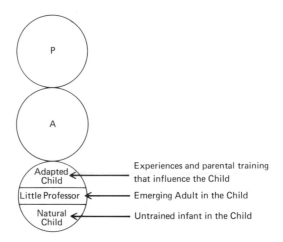

Second-order analysis of the Child

The Natural Child is that part of the Child ego state that is the very young, impulsive, uncensored, untrained, expressive infant still inside each person. It is often like a self-centered, pleasure-loving baby responding with cozy affection when its needs are met or with angry rebellion when they are not.

The Little Professor is the unschooled wisdom of a child. It is that part of the Child ego state that is intuitive, responding to nonverbal messages and playing hunches. With it a child figures things out, such as when to cry, when to be quiet, and how to manipulate mother into smiling. The Little Professor is also highly creative.

The Adapted Child is that part of the Child ego state that exhibits a modification of the Natural Child's inclinations. These adaptations of natural impulses occur in response to traumas, experiences, training, and, most importantly, to demands from significant authority figures. For example, children are, by nature, programed to eat when hungry. Shortly after birth, however, this natural urge may be adapted so that eating is on a schedule determined by the parents.

Although I prefer to use a structural diagram with my clients because of its preciseness, some TA therapists effectively use a functional diagram. When they do, it is usually with Adapted and Free Child categories. When used this way, the Free Child includes characteristics of both the Little Professor and the Natural Child.

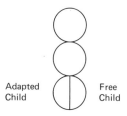

Adapted Child   Free Child

In TA treatment the first goals center around strengthening the boundaries of the Adult ego state so that it is not adulterated or distorted by the Child or Parent. This process is *decontamination.* In many cases, the next focus is on the pathology in the Adapted Child which needs curing so that the power of the Natural Child and the creativity and interests of the Little Professor can be expressed through the Adult. This is often followed by restructuring the Parent. When this is accomplished, a person is well on the way to becoming an integrated Adult.

Persons whose Adult ego states are integrated process data rationally, and they also exhibit certain childlike characteristics and ethical concerns. Seemingly these qualities are filtered from the Parent and Child through the Adult ego state.

People who have integrated Adults take responsibility for others and for themselves. They also have the natural Child capacity for pleasure.

Berne described the integrated Adult:

> . . . it appears that in many cases certain child-like qualities become integrated into the Adult ego state in a manner different from the contamination process . . . it can be observed that certain people when functioning *qua* Adult have a charm and openness of nature which is reminiscent of that exhibited by children. Along with these go certain responsible feelings toward the rest of humanity which may be subsumed under the classical term "pathos." On the other hand, there are moral qualities which are universally expected of people who undertake grownup responsibilities, such attributes as courage, sincerity, loyalty, and reliability, and which meet not mere local prejudice, but a world-wide ethos. . . . Transactionally, this means that anyone functioning as an Adult should ideally exhibit three kinds of tendencies: personal attractiveness and responsiveness, objective data-processing, and ethical responsibility. . . . This "integrated" person *is* charming, etc., and courageous, etc., in his Adult state, whatever qualities he has or does not have in his Child and Parent ego states. The "unintegrated" person may *revert* to being charming, and may feel that he *should* be courageous.[9]

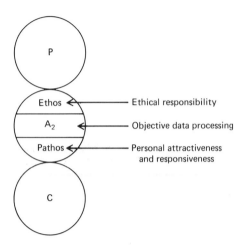

Second-order analysis of the Adult

If the Adult is not integrated it is either contaminated (see next section) or has such rigid ego state boundaries that the person is not in touch with the Parent and Child components of personality. In the case of contamination, the feelings will not be appropriate to the situation; rather they will be like rubber bands to the past. If the Parent and/or Child are blocked out because of a rigid boundary of the Adult, then the person may function more like a data-processing machine, an objective computer without feelings.

Feelings that are *copied* from significant others, usually as parental attitudes or beliefs, are likely to be in the Parent ego state. Feelings that were originally *experienced* in infancy and childhood, and rubber-banded in later life, are likely to be in the Child ego state. Feelings that are a *genuine response to an actual situation happening now* are likely to have some Adult involvement. Either the Adult informs the Child of the situation so that the response is authentic, or certain feelings have been integrated into the Adult.

For example, angry temper tantrums are rackets of the Child, indulged in with Parental permission or encouragement, but legitimate indignation or outrage that is based on observation of an actual injustice indicates Adult responsibility. Sympathy is likely to be copied from a parent; understanding involves Adult information.[10] Trust and admiration are feelings of the Child who believes people are OK. Genuine respect of others, based on objective observations of them, is Adult. Berne writes:

> *Trust comes from the Child, respect from the Adult,* with the Child's permission. Respect means that the Child looks someone over and decides that he is trustworthy. The Child then says to the Adult: 'Go ahead. You can trust him.

I'll keep an eye on the situation and review it from time to time.' The Adult then translates this into an attitude of respect and acts accordingly. Sometimes, however, the Parent interferes. The Child and the Adult may be all ready to go ahead, and then the Parent brings up a prejudiced objection: 'How can you trust a man with long hair?' or 'How can you trust a fat woman?' To the Child, of course, long hair or fatness is quite irrelevant to trustworthiness, and he would much rather be with a long-haired man and a fat woman who love him than with a short-haired man and a thin woman who don't. Nothing interferes with Child intuition more than Parental prejudices.[11]

Depression is self-indulgence of the Child. Despair implies Adult awareness of a tragic reality. The person's Adult, in a dialogue with the outer world, is overheard by the Child.[12] Guilt feelings can be a "stamp."* added to the Child's collection or can be an authentic response to an actual wrongdoing.[13] In the latter case it can be Adult response. What is important to remember is that people who are in their Adult ego states *may have feelings.* The Adult is not merely a machine; the Adult is concerned with social issues and has feelings about involvement in them. Consequently, an autonomous integrated person, client or therapist, will, according to Berne, crusade against The Four Horsemen—War, Pestilence, Famine, and Death.[14]

A person whose Adult is integrated may revert at times to behavior from his or her Parent or Child. Fritz Perls claims that there is no such thing as total integration. The reason for this is that old problems that have not been solved or new problems that need solving continue to push into the foreground of awareness until something is done about them or until solutions are reached.

The person in the *process* of integration takes responsibility for everything he or she feels, thinks, and believes. During this process the ego states go through a series of changes.[15]

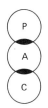

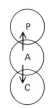

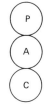

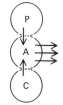

Unaware and
contaminated
Adult

Adult aware-
ness of Parent
and Child

Adult re-
alignment and
decontamination

Integrated Adult
appropriately using
Parent and Child

---

* In TA the particular feelings that a person collects and saves are called psychological trading stamps. The term "stamps" is borrowed from the practice in some places of collecting stamps when making purchases and later redeeming them for a prize.

My experience is that all people, therapists, and clients have some areas of contamination. For example, a person may be uncontaminated in the area of sexuality—free of Parental prejudices, Child fears, and with Adult information —and yet be contaminated about the use of money or leisure time. Such a person may be programed to save everything or to "work hard" or "try hard" with the injunction "Don't enjoy yourself." A therapist with this kind of contamination often has problems in close relationships, especially with a spouse who might easily complain, "You never have time for me!" In the ongoing process of decontamination and integration, people become more and more responsible for their own lives.

EGO-STATE BOUNDARY PROBLEMS

Diagnosis and treatment of ego states may be delayed or difficult for therapists who are new to TA because of defects in their own ego-state boundaries or in those of their clients.

There are four ego-state boundary problems: exclusion, contamination, lax, and lesions. These need correction. It is not enough for therapists to simply be able to identify Parent, Adult, and Child behavior in themselves and others. This is useful to a beginning client or student, but effective therapists use more sophisticated diagnostic tools when analyzing ego states—either in or out of their offices.

Exclusion

Ego states can be thought of as having boundaries which are like permeable membranes through which a person's psychic energy can flow.[16] At any moment, an ego state can be cathected and have executive power. In some people, however, the boundaries are so rigid that the energy may be locked in, unable to flow easily from one ego state to another.[17] This problem is called *exclusion* and can be diagrammed as:

The Parent,
excluding the
Adult and Child

The Adult,
excluding the
Parent and Child

The Child,
excluding the
Parent and Adult

Some people, instead of staying primarily in one ego state and excluding the two others, favor the use of two and exclude only one. For example, it is not uncommon for beginning TA therapists to exclude their Child when doing treatment by denying their own needs and feelings, and for the client to exclude the Parent and Adult by staying exclusively in a sad or mad Child. In such cases the relationship would be a symbiotic one because the two people (client and therapist) are using three ego states instead of six.

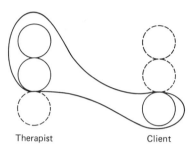

Therapist   Client

The first requirement for treating ego-state boundary dysfunctions is an awareness that there is a problem. Awareness of exclusion sometimes develops because of group response. For example, in groups where there is no laughter, the therapists have probably excluded their own Child ego states. Awareness may also emerge in response to techniques of historical diagnosis, the use of ego-state portraits, or egograms.

Ego-state portrait. This is a simple, quick way to determine which form of exclusion exists.[18] It varies according to the persons involved and the situation. The technique is to use circles of different sizes that illustrate the use of "favorite" ego states as they are cathected at specific times. Here are three of the many possibilities:

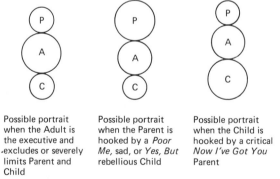

| Possible portrait when the Adult is the executive and .excludes or severely limits Parent and Child | Possible portrait when the Parent is hooked by a *Poor Me,* sad, or *Yes, But* rebellious Child | Possible portrait when the Child is hooked by a critical *Now I've Got You* Parent |

Many people have a variety of ego-state portraits which they change as the situation changes. Many others tend to stay in one ego state as much as possible. People who *maintain* the kinds of portraits shown here are frequently monotonous; they are so predictable that they're boring. The psychic energy does not flow readily from one ego state to another as the boundaries are too rigid.

Therapists who want to evaluate this phenomenon for themselves will find social diagnosis an effective way of determining how clients see them, and, consequently, how they (the therapists) have set themselves up to be seen that way. If the answer is not satisfying, then contracts to change are appropriate.

Egogram.   This is a more detailed technique for determining the relation of different ego-state parts. A typical one, described by John Dusay, is of a preorgasmic woman:[19]

The PP represents Prejudicial Parent (in this case probably prejudiced against sexual enjoyment). The AC represents a highly compliant Adapted Child; FC is the Free Child, which is a combination of Natural Child and Little Professor. A is the Adult and NP is the Nurturing Parent.

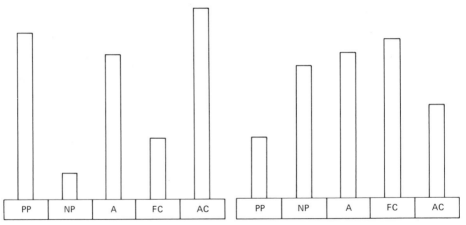

Mary's egogram before orgasm   Mary's egogram after orgasm

It is hypothesized that if one ego state increases in intensity, another must decrease, because the *total* amount of psychic energy available remains constant. When Mary, with the use of specific contracts, increased her Nurturing Parent, her Prejudiced Parent and Adapted Child decreased, and her Free Child was freer to be orgasmic.

A different form of egogram subdivides the Child into its structural components, using the three categories: Natural Child, Little Professor, and Adapted Child. This form often sheds a different light on therapists' uses of their ego states.[20] For example: Some therapists do not use their intuition on the job; other therapists do. One therapist's egogram might look like (a), while the other's might look like (b). But at home, either therapist's egogram could be more like (c).

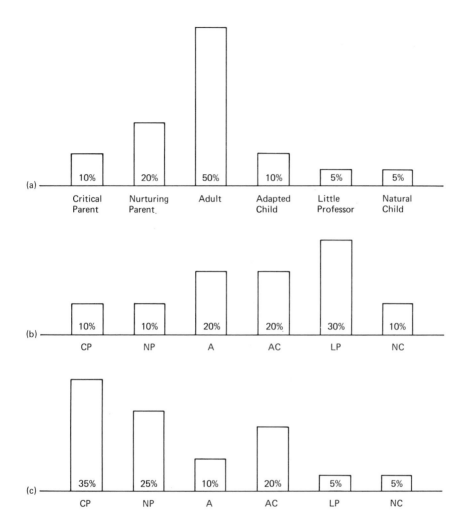

If desired, the generalized functional categories, critical and nurturing Parent, can be translated into historical structural terms. However, it's not necessary when using an egogram as information to release intuition.

Berne claims, "There is a time for scientific method and a time for intuition—the one brings with it more certainty, the other offers more possibilities. The two together are the only basis for creative thinking."[21]

I have found that releasing the Little Professor is often necessary for people like physicists, chemists, and engineers, who often have a strong Adult on the job and a turned-off Little Professor at home or in social situations. They may show this need by remarks such as "I just don't understand what's going on."

As a part of the therapeutic treatment, it may be necessary to put the Parent and Adult temporarily out of commission and open the Little Professor to the environment like a radar screen.

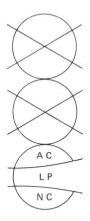

In group therapy, instructions are given: "Don't think or parent others for 10 minutes, just pick up "vibes" from others in the room. After 10 minutes reactivate your Adult. Tell others what you picked up and get feedback on your accuracy." If the intuitions are correct, the Little Professor has been activated. If not, they have been projections of the Adapted Child.

For the therapist to use his or her own Little Professor's intuition is also a valuable asset in therapy, and an intuitive clinician is one who "deliberately uses his intuitive faculties when desirable in his diagnostic and therapeutic work. Descriptively, such a clinician is curious, mentally alert, interested, and receptive of latent and manifest communications from his patients."[22] Logical Adult thinking and Parental moralistic judgments usually interfere with intuition.

Contamination

The second, and most common, problem of ego-state boundaries is called *contamination*. This occurs when the clear thinking of the Adult is interfered with by the archaic feelings of the Child and/or the prejudicial feelings of the Parent. Clients who have hallucinations—including the obscene epithet and the deadly injunction—are heavily contaminated by the Parent. Those with delusions—including grandiosity and catastrophic expectations—are heavily contaminated by the Child.[23] Contamination is diagramed as:[24]

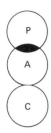

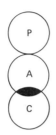

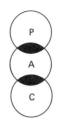

The Adult
contaminated
by the Parent

The Adult
contaminated
by the Child

The Adult
contaminated by
the Parent and
Child

One way therapists can diagnose their own contaminations is to reflect on their clients' responses. If, in response to the therapist's information, clients often look puzzled or use phrases such as "I don't understand," the therapist is likely to be transacting in an unclear manner, giving a mixed message. Unclearness is one sign of contamination. Usually, it is the Adult contaminated by the Child.

Prejudicial attitudes expressed as absolutes are another sign of contamination. Frequent use of such words as "always" and "never," "should" and "must" indicates contamination. There are two very common patterns of client response. The first is from compliant persons who nod or agree verbally with the therapist's particular biases; the second is from rebellious persons who disagree or who pretend to agree but later sabotage the therapist's statement in some way. Prejudice usually indicates that the Adult is contaminated by the Parent.

My experience is that all people—therapists as well as clients—are sometimes contaminated. Grandiosity, from the Child, may be expressed verbally or nonverbally as, "My brand of therapy is better than anyone else's"; and overnurturing or overcritical attitudes from the Parent may be expressed verbally or nonverbally as, "I can fix you up if you do what I say." Both attitudes are common signs of contamination.

Therapists need to figure out how each of their ego states are involved when doing therapy. Historical diagnosis of the Parent and Child, and Adult evaluation of the facts that are already known and the facts that are needed, bring ego states into sharp awareness. A technique that is very effective for decontamination is shown on the next page.[25]

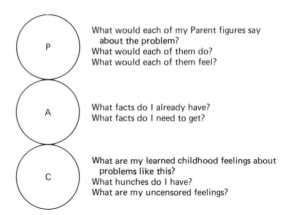

What would each of my Parent figures say about the problem?
What would each of them do?
What would each of them feel?

What facts do I already have?
What facts do I need to get?

What are my learned childhood feelings about problems like this?
What hunches do I have?
What are my uncensored feelings?

Lax Boundaries

A person with lax ego state boundaries appears to lack identity and gives the impression of being slipshod in behavior. As the boundaries do not fully exist between the ego states, the psychic energy continually moves back and forth. The problem is easily observable in back wards of state hospitals in patients who have little or no Adult control. An occasional therapist might have this problem in a less extreme form and therefore he or she would probably be very ineffective. The problem of lax ego state boundaries can be diagramed as you see here.

Lesions

Boundary lesions are another serious problem. Occasionally they are in the Parent, but they are most likely to be in the Child, and can be diagrammed like this.

In this diagram the Child has a "sore spot" which, if touched, results in un-controllable, irrational behavior. This is a person who has been seriously in-jured in childhood by a traumatic event or a series of unhappy experiences. When something rubs the sore spot, the injury breaks open. Lesions are mani-fested by a gross overreaction to the reality of the stimulus. If therapists have this problem, self-therapy is not enough; they are seriously in need of profes-sional help from someone else.

DIAGNOSIS OF STROKES

Some people, both clients and therapists, are enjoyable to be with. The feelings they express are appropriate and accepting, the messages they send out, with words and gestures, are welcoming and open. The "vibes" that emanate from them are comforting and lively. Such people encourage others to feel good. According to TA, the art of encouraging others to feel good, alive, alert, and important is called "positive stroking."

Some people, both clients and therapists, are unpleasant to be around. The messages that come through their words and gestures are unwelcoming. Their "vibes" make others uncomfortable. They may be cool and withdrawn or hos-tile and aggressive. According to TA, they practice "negative stroking."[26]

Another group of people, both clients and therapists, are pleasant, have good intentions, and often are well informed, yet need further seasoning. They send out "vibes" that reveal their sense of awkwardness, of lack of confidence, or gaps in knowledge. Their Little Professor's intuition may not be used with their Adult knowledge or vice versa. These people need more experience, or more integration of what they already know, or more self-acceptance or acceptance by others so that they can feel confident *and* competent and therefore effective.

Effective therapists are aware of their stroking patterns as they affect their clients in the therapeutic situation. Their stroking can be verbal or nonverbal. Clients are particularly susceptible to therapists' strokes, for they perceive them as having a magical quality. Therapists, especially new therapists, are often vulnerable to clients' or supervisors' strokes. Their self-esteem tends to go up or down with the positive or negative responses they receive.

Therapists who wish to discover their own stroke needs and stroking patterns can first consider their own childhood strokes—conditional and unconditional —by asking themselves some questions. A conditional stroke, implying "I ac-cept you if . . ." includes some kind of demand, so the question is, "What did I have to do to get recognition, approval, or affection?" An unconditional stroke has no demands. It is a message stated or implied "I accept you (approve of you, love you) just because you're you." The question is, "Did I receive un-conditional strokes in childhood, if so, from whom?"

Next, the therapist can evaluate current relationships—both personal and professional—in light of the kinds of strokes he or she gives and receives from others. When evaluating oneself or others, people need to consider the cultural and subcultural scripting patterns related to verbal and nonverbal transactions.

Clients usually *hope for* unconditional strokes and *expect* conditional ones similar to those they receive in childhood. The therapist's facial expressions, tone of voice, gestures, and body language will inevitably convey the "real" message.[27] Most people, therapists as well as clients, seem to long for particular kinds of strokes, the "perfect" ones they once received, or fantasized receiving, and live in fear, even catastrophic dread, of other deadly strokes they once received, or fantasized receiving. These longed-for or feared strokes are called target strokes (discussed in my book, *The OK Boss*) because they hit the target in ways that are destructive or in ways that are healing and life-enhancing. Target strokes can be sent *from* any ego state in one person *to* any ego state in another. They are the words or behavior that hurt the most or feel the best. At different times, in different situations, people may have stroke needs in one ego state and not in the others.

Strokes that involve physical comfort or pleasure are usually positive target strokes to the Natural Child. The Little Professor likes to be stroked for its intuition and creativity. Strokes of approval or disapproval may please an ego state, depending upon which one is cathected at a particular time. However, strokes of approval or disapproval most often are received by the Adapted Child. Disapproval in the form of sarcasm may hurt some clients the most. Approval in the form of listening and responding may be what someone always longed for in childhood.

Therapists are commonly seen as substitute parents. Therefore, they need to be aware of what kind of strokes their historical parents (now in their Parent ego state) once expected. For example, my parents naturally had many expectancies. Some were related to behavior such as: doing well in school, thinking for myself, being polite, and not interrupting others who might be speaking.* When my Parent ego state is cathected, I am likely to convey these same expectancies to others, which in some cases are not appropriate. Many people learn to placate their own Parent by doing some thing that decreases the discomfort that may be experienced when parental values are rejected.[28]

---

* For readers who might be interested in my own background, I am "Suzanne" in my book, *Born to Love. TA for Moms and Dads* is also highly autobiographical.

Target strokes for Adult thinking are being requested by more and more women who historically have been stroked, almost exclusively, for taking care of others from the Parent ego state or for being helpless or sexy from the Child ego state.[29] In contrast, many men are requesting more and more strokes for their Nurturing Parent capacities and for their fun-loving Child. The Adult in them may have been overstroked for rational thinking.

Integrated persons, whether clients or therapists, develop an easy flow of energy from one ego state to another. They are able to send target strokes *from* each of their ego states, and to ask for and receive target strokes *for* each of their ego states.

Giving target strokes from the Adult or to the Adult is a potent tool for therapists. It reinforces objective thinking and rational behavior and continues the process of decontamination. Therapists involved in self-therapy become aware of what they say or do to get or give Adult strokes. In my experience, the Adult needs to be used, otherwise it may become like a rusty, out-of-date piece of machinery. Thinking oils it and seems to be a self-stroking process.

TRANSACTIONS THAT HOOK

In TA, two common phrases used when referring to transactions are "throwing a hook" and "being hooked." A person throwing a hook is deliberately sending a stimulus to a particular ego state in someone else. A person being hooked receives the stimulus as sent by someone else in a particular state. As when fishing, it's not always easy to hook what is wanted. When the hooking is successful it's hard for the fish to get unhooked.

One of the goals of TA is to learn how to switch ego states, thus changing the transactional patterns with others through the process of hooking and unhooking. If transactions are always complementary and predictable, the therapeutic process is likely to become static.

Therapists who frequently hook Child ego states in their clients are those who, for example, get involved in complementary Child-Child competitive, hostile transactions, or complementary Child-Child laughter, sexy, or fun transactions. Also, therapists will often hook a Child—either compliant or rebellious—if they transact in the manner of either a Critical Parent or a Nuturing Parent.

Therapists who hook their clients' Parent ego states are those who hold the same kinds of prejudices. Thus they are likely to have complementary Parent-Parent transactions. Therapists who show something like a rebellious *Screw You* or *Screw Them* Child ego state or a compliant *Look How Hard I'm Trying* Child are also likely to hook clients' Parent ego states.

Therapists who hook their clients' Adults are those who do not threaten the Parent or Child, who give relevant information clearly and without contamination, who know their material and can time their interventions well.

It is important for therapists to know the ego state they most commonly use in treatment and to be able to use social diagnosis on themselves as well as on their clients.

A technique some therapists use is to make an egogram of themselves. Next, they make additional egograms by imagining how they appear to several clients. Some therapists even check out their perceptions with clients, peers, or a supervisor. Careful observance of a video or audio tape is another popular technique. While listening to or observing tapes, therapists who wish to diagnose and treat themselves can draw a series of circles and, as the tape progresses, fill in lines indicating complementary, crossed, and ulterior transactions (see Chapter 1). This process may require the replaying of a small section of tape several times, and often the result is a moment of truth. A later chapter in this book presents detailed techniques for taped supervision, including self-diagnosis.

"Throwing a hook" is a stimulus; "being hooked" is a response, and most therapists *do* get hooked by their clients from to time. A client's sad story, woebegone face, or body language may hook a therapist's Nurturing Parent. A resistance to change expressed in passive behavior, avoidance techniques, or open defiance may hook a therapist's Critical or even Punitive Parent.

A client's Adult, processing data adequately, and getting on with treatment contracts intelligently, may also hook a Parent in the therapist who may not really want the client to change. Or the therapist's Adult may be hooked and the therapy may proceed rapidly with a sense of mutual esteem. Sometimes a therapist's Child can be hooked by the client's Adult if, for example, a hospitalized or imprisoned client is using Adult data and the therapist is into some kind of Child game such as *"If it Weren't for Them."* (If it weren't for the establishment, you could get out of here.)

Therapists also have Child ego states which, like those of other people, are likely to be the strongest part of the personality. The Child in a therapist may get hooked by a Critical Parent in the client who frowns disdainfully, who objects to the fee structure or the availability of the therapist, or who criticizes Transactional Analysis, its founder, its organization, its practitioners, and so forth.

The therapist's Child may also be hooked by a client's Nurturing Parent, who, for example, may fix a cup of coffee for the therapist, look sympathetic if the phone rings or if the therapist sighs and says the appointment book is crowded.

Many therapists can also be hooked into Child-Child transactions with their clients. A come-hither look from a sexy woman or man may turn them on. A client's anger racket against authorities, or against particular life styles, or against certain kinds of people may hook a therapist who has similar predilections.

To get in touch with this, a common Gestalt therapy technique is to place two chairs (preferably not lounge chairs) so that they are facing each other about two feet apart.[30] In this process, a therapist who wishes to understand her or his transactions with clients sits in the first chair (or hot seat), take a few deep breaths, uses a few sentences directed toward bodily awareness (e.g., "Now I am aware of the tensions in my shoulders, of my feet resting on the floor"), then starts talking to the client, who is imagined as sitting in the opposite chair.

The second chair is called the projection chair because any object or person or dream fragment may be projected onto it.

After speaking to the client, the therapist switches chairs and *becomes the client,* responding to the therapist's verbal and nonverbal messages. The switching back and forth between the two chairs continues until some kind of resolution or insight occurs that reveals typical styles of transacting or particular ways of transacting with individual clients. This is often an "Aha, now I understand" experience.

Gallows Transactions

When doing therapy, many therapists spend most of their time in their Adult and Parent ego states. They may choose these states either deliberately or without awareness, or they may be "hooked" into them by their clients. If this is a regular pattern, they may discover their inner Child feels deprived of some of the "goodies" of life and becomes sad, angry, or bored—and then they may get hooked into gallows transactions.

A gallows transaction is one with an ulterior dimension, and it's common enough and destructive enough to deserve being mentioned specifically. The stimulus, often from a client, sometimes from a therapist, comes when someone laughs or jokes about destructive behavior.

In essence, the laugh says, "Don't take me and what I say seriously." It also invites the listener to laugh in response, thus confirming that the person making the joke is in fact not to be treated seriously. For example, a young man might laughingly say, "I smashed up my car again last night." In other words, while he is telling about self-defeating behavior, he smiles as if it is clever. He thus reinforces the Child to keep himself in trouble. The laughing response from group members or therapist reinforces his self-defeating behavior.

The real issue that needs to be talked about is thus avoided. Nobody says, "Why are you laughing? It's not funny." Such a serious response might at first feel uncomfortable, but it would effectively take off the noose by refusing to go along with this self-destructive pattern.

The most common way to diagram a gallows transaction is:[31,32]

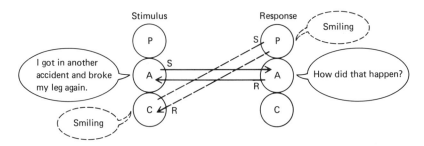

Underneath the smile of the person who initiates the gallows transaction is a rebellious Child with the position "Ha ha, you can't make me ... (get well, keep my contracts, etc.)."

THERAPISTS AND THEIR GAME ROLES

Games are played at various levels of intensity, and, from time to time, everyone plays them. Berne believed it is the therapist's duty to be aware of the games that he or she might play in treatment groups and to apply appropriate correction.[33]

The Parent and Child aspects of his motivations influence the therapist much more systematically and pervasively than he may realize. It may take him several months to perceive that he is consistently acting like a jerk, a slob, or worse of all, a sulk, in his interventions. It may take even longer to become clear that almost everything he says has the exploitative quality that is characteristic of a game leading to a masked ulterior goal. In any case, the more productive question is not "Am I playing a game?" but rather "What game am I playing?"[34]

Therapists can diagnose their own games by discovering how they get themselves into the roles of Victim, Persecutor, and Rescuer. A later chapter will discuss several important ways to diagnose and treat games, but the focus in this section is on Karpman's drama triangle, the game roles,[35] the switches between the roles (as indicated by the arrows), and the implications for self-diagnosis and treatment.

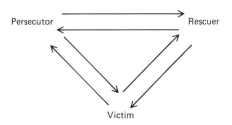

Games roles are commonly played outside of Adult awareness. These roles can be played externally with others or internally as a "skull" game. Usually, but not always, the Victim is played from the Child ego state and the Rescuer and Persecutor from the Parent. When these three words are capitalized, they will refer to the game roles. When they are not, they will refer to legitimate behavior.

Examples of legitimate roles are: the *persecutor,* someone who sets necessary limits on behavior or is charged with enforcing a rule; the *victim,* someone who qualifies for a job but is denied it because of race, sex, religion, or national origin; the *rescuer,* someone who helps nonfunctioning or poorly functioning persons to rehabilitate themselves, to stand on their own two feet and take responsibility for their feelings and behavior.

When not in their games, therapists may find themselves in each of these roles. For example, the therapist, as a legitimate rescuer, will help people who need psychological understanding and who will accept it. As a legitimate persecutor, he or she may justifiably criticize or express resentment at some behavior the client is exhibiting—may even, for example, say, "You must stop beating and mistreating your children immediately, or I will have to notify the authorities." As a legitimate victim, the therapist might be persecuted by colleagues who prefer their particular method, or even be victimized and brutalized by a psychotic client. When TA therapists are *legitimately* rescuing, persecuting, or being victimized, they are dealing with the here and now, are aware of the current situation, data-process their possibilities for getting into game roles, and know the games they are likely to play.

When these roles are game-related, they are like short scenes in a drama and are meant to manipulate. Thus: *Persecutors* are people who are overly critical, or who set unnecessarily strict limits on other people's behavior, or who are charged with enforcing the rules and do so sadistically. In games, they often switch to a Rescuer role after they have hurt someone. Game *Victims* are people who perhaps do not qualify for a job but falsely claim they are denied it because of race, sex, or religion. In games, they may switch to a Persecutor role, blaming others for "victimizing" them. *Rescuers* are people who, in the guise of being helpful, keep others dependent upon them. In games, they too may switch to a Persecutor role if others do not accept their advice.

When therapists are in the game roles, their clear-thinking Adult is contaminated by Parental prejudices, behaviors, and opinions from the past, or contaminated by Child experiences of the past, or by expectations, hopes, or fears of the future. People are seldom aware of the games they play because the games feel familiar, having been played since childhood.

Therapists, as well as clients, may have learned how to be *Persecutors* in childhood if they were given heavy parental responsibility over younger siblings when they were too young to handle it, or if they were allowed to bully others to get their own way, or if they had a parent figure as a model who persecuted others and implied that it was OK for the child to do likewise.

Therapists, as well as clients, may have learned how to be *Rescuers* in childhood, if they were often encouraged to rescue their parent figures who may have been feeling unhappy, or nurture younger siblings who were feeling likewise, or if they strongly identified with a parent figure who was a big Rescuer.

Therapists, as well as clients, may have learned how to be *Victims* in childhood, if they were victimized physically or verbally by those with more power over them. Those with more power include parents and grandparents, siblings and neighbors, teachers, baby sitters, and so forth.

These three roles are so programed into people's personalities that people often have great difficulty recognizing them as learned feelings and behavior. Consequently, people tend to intellectualize and justify being the way they are. They find it difficult to give up the roles and the particular games which are played to fulfill them.[36]

Common Persecutor games often played by therapists are *Blemish*, and *Now I've Got You, You S.O.B.* In the game of *Blemish*, the therapist acts as a nitpicker, finding small things wrong with clients and verbally stating or inferring that these small things need changing, much like parents who demand perfection from their children. Such therapists do not teach others to know the difference between trivial and important problems. In the game of *Now I've Got You, You S.O.B.*, the therapist *waits* for the client to make an error; and, when it happens, pounces strongly on the person with a sense of inner relish, much like parents who justify their abusive behavior in the guise of "Now I'll teach you a lesson."

Common Rescuer games often played by therapists are *I'm Only Trying To Help You* and *Why Don't You?* Both games look the same from the therapist's "helping" position, but the end of each game is quite different because of different responses. In *I'm Only Trying To Help You,* the therapist gives some "well-meaning" advice and the client seemingly takes the suggestions. Later he or she messes up in some way, then returns to blame the therapist for things not going right, playing a complementary game of *Look What You Made Me Do* or *Look How Hard I'm Trying.* In *Why Don't You?,* a client pretends to be taking the advice but does nothing about it, or says it won't work. He or she plays a complementary game of *Yes, But,* which is to reject all offers of help with "Yes, but . . ." and then tell why that particular form of help won't work.

Common Victim games often played by therapists are *Look How Hard I'm Trying* and *Why Does This Always Happen To Me?* In *Look How Hard I'm Trying,* therapists may work overtime, be always available to their clients, do the client's thinking for them, frequently make unwanted suggestions and feel inadequate when the "trying hard" doesn't work. In *Why Does This Always Happen To Me?,* therapists find themselves in similar dilemmas. For example, they may often have clients who do not pay, or who are slow in paying their bills. Or they may often have those who exhibit either extreme passivity or aggressive "try and make me" or "prove it to me" attitudes. In any case, therapists, feeling victimized by their clients, may be caught up in Victim games, wondering why it always happens just when they're trying so hard.

Solon Samuels, TA psychiatrist, makes a strong appeal for therapists to discover their own games so that the usual success rate of two out of three cases, regardless of what method is used, can be increased. *Kosher,* he says is "the basic game of all psychotherapy—'I believe, therefore, what I do is right!' " This is played out of the need to feel honest and justified by inner approval. Samuels writes:

> In psychotherapy today, *Kosher* is being played in three major faiths. First, there are the true believers in the organic biologic theory of mental illness. They are bolstered in their belief by the good, short-term recoveries obtained in the treatment of endogenous depressions by electroshock, and also by the rapid reduction of psychotic agitated states of chemotherapy. These therapy successes encourage the organicists to proclaim with great conviction that "by and by in the scientific sky we will find our full salvation in the discoveries of neurophysiology and neurochemistry. Some day soon we will be able to help more than the eternal two out of three."

Those who cleave to the psychological theories of personality development are bolstered by Freud's insightful success with intuition as a way of science, and are therefore able to make contracts for prolonged shaman-like sessions, convinced that imparting emotional reliving and insight will deliver their patients to a personal salvation. They, too, are very happy to report that two out of three of their patients offer no resistance to their theories. Many of these patients recover a stability that is sometimes better than the one that the therapist has achieved, because they have *someone to believe in.* (Sustained positive parent transference.)

Finally, there are the sociological therapists who see society as a socio-illogical cauldron of good and bad *environments* which boils up and periodically spews out individual casualties. By this theory, the casualties need a humanistic *reconditioning* to toughen their outer social coverings and so develop an indestructible nosecone with which to make re-entry into the hot pot-luck of life.[37]

Samuels says he used to play *Kosher* from each of these faith positions with the usual success rate of two out of three cases. Now with TA he achieves better results, getting in touch with his own games and roles that interfered with the social gains of his clients.

The simplest way therapists can get in touch with whether or not they are caught in drama and game roles is to ask themselves, "How do I usually feel when things go wrong? And how do I act? Like a Victim? A Persecutor? A Rescuer?" If the answer is "I don't have feelings like those of a Victim, Persecutor, or Rescuer, nor do I act like one when things go wrong," then the therapist is not playing the drama roles. If the answer is "Yes, I do feel victimized or feel like persecuting or feel like rescuing when things go wrong," then there is the strong possibility that the therapist is involved in a game.

The most common role therapists play is that of Rescuer. While supportive techniques may be useful in the preliminary steps of treatment, especially if clients are severely depressed or psychotic, they will interfere with the client's movement toward autonomy if they are continued.

Therapists who play rescue roles may encourage clients to continually wait for Santa Claus.[38] In "waiting for Santa Claus" groups, members become passive, make progress, then fall back to their previous position or attend group irregularly only to see if Santa Claus has yet arrived. They are looking for some form of supportive group therapy where the therapist plays a parental role.[39]

One simple way to break up one's own games is to become aware of the Persecutor, Rescuer, and Victim feelings when they occur. The Adult ego state can data-process them as coming from the Parent or Child, can stop intellectualizing and justifying, and can relinquish them, though sometimes reluctantly.

Another way therapists can identify their own games is through the use of the Game Plan as developed by John James.[40] The Game Plan is based on the understanding that each psychological game has a plan of action, much like the kind of plans that are designed for football plays.

The Game Plan focuses on predictable patterns and payoffs. The basic technique is a series of questions:

- What keeps happening over and over again that leaves someone feeling bad?
- How does it start?
- What happens next?
- And then what happens?
- How does it end?
- How do you feel after it ends?
- How might the other person feel?

After each question the answers are written down in brief form. This immediately reveals the process of "what keeps happening" over and over that usually leaves one person feeling sad, mad, scared, confused, and so forth, and the other person often feeling self-righteous.

The technique for breaking up a game is to reflect on each answer and ask "What could have been done differently at this point?" Usually, there are many options around which decisions can be made to "do something differently." James gives an example of the Game Plan regularly played by a father and daughter:

Sis: (Asks a favor)

Pa: No

Sis: Why not?

Pa: Because, last time . . . (put-down) . . .

Sis: Well, that's not true . . .

Pa and Sis: (Argue loudly)

Sis: (Leaves the room, yelling)

Pa: (Reads the paper)

Pa: (Feels mad)

Sis: (Feels mad)[41]

When they first became aware of this Game Plan, both Pa and Sis thought the other person ought to stop doing this or that. Eventually, they made a mutually acceptable contract regarding the granting of favors. They also contracted that neither person would put the other down and that neither would yell. Thus, they contracted to respond differently at several steps in the game.

Therapists who recognize games have, according to John Dusay, four possible ways to respond:

1. Expose the game
2. Ignore the game
3. Offer an alternative
4. Play the game[42]

In my opinion, the best alternative to playing games is learning how to get and give positive payoffs which, according to John James, are the real reason for playing.[43] The positive payoff is the healthy or striving-for-health element that underlies games. It is what comes after the game is finished. For example, after a game of *Uproar* a positive payoff for some people would be to have time to be alone. Time to be alone is what they really wanted and didn't know how to get directly. As another example, some people might play a game of *Kick Me* when what they really want is sympathy—and maybe that's what they need.

One way to discover the positive payoff is to ask, "After you feel bad, what happens *then,* so that you get what you really want without asking for it directly?"

Therapists, like clients, have needs. Like clients they often play games to get these needs met, unaware of what they are doing. And like clients, they can learn to be more direct in healthy ways. Then can seek positive payoffs without ulterior transactions and the negative feelings that go with games.

In summary, all people play games and play them at different levels of intensity. They can decide whether to play, when to play, and who to play with.[44] To accuse others of playing games is not an effective way to stop them. Accusation is always some form of a blaming game played from the Persecutor's position to make others feel guilty. Discovering one's own games and replacing them with authentic, open, and honest transactions is self-therapy of the highest order.

SCRIPTS THERAPISTS LIVE BY

Scripts show up in repetitive, compulsive behavior and the games people play are like brief scenes or acts in a drama. Often they are replays of previous "acts," though sometimes with new scenery and characters. The accompanying figure illustrates the script cycle.[45]

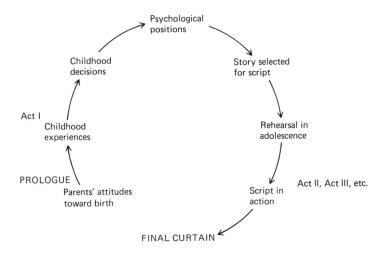

Therapists, as well as clients, have individual scripts that are chosen in childhood and designed to last a lifetime. Seldom are people aware that they are living in a preprogramed way as though reading from a theatrical script.

A *script* can be briefly described as a *life plan,* very much like that of a dramatic stage production which an individual feels compelled to play out. Life plans are based on the early decisions children make about themselves and others. Berne says they are "reinforced by the parents, justified by subsequent events, and culminating in a chosen alternative."[46]

The script is an adaptation. It is in the Child ego state, "written" from transactions between children and parents, and is usually developed before the age of six. Roles of Victim, Persecutor, and Rescuer advance the script and although people are not aware of it, each person compulsively plays out the parts.

Like theatrical plays, psychological dramas have themes. The most common themes are love, hate, revenge, or jealousy.[47] These themes are somewhat like threads that run through a person's life; they can be identified and classified.

Scripts are constructive, destructive (to self and/or others), or going nowhere. People with *constructive scripts* are winners. They care about the world and its people and value others as well as themselves. They achieve a measure of "greatness," though it may never be written out in book or newspaper. Fame is not the criterion. Whether known or unknown, people with constructive scripts leave the world a bit better for their having been a part of it. They not only care about their own success, health, and happiness, they also care about the success, health, and happiness of others. People with constructive scripts work actively to change situations that contribute to poverty, disease, discrimination, and to alleviate problems leading to unhealthiness and unhappiness.

People with *destructive scripts* are losers. Sooner or later they injure themselves and/or others. They may do so gradually, over an extended period of time, or suddenly, in dramatic fashion. Self-destructive people may, for example, drink, eat, or work themselves to death, may drive recklessly, or commit suicide in some more obvious manner. People who are destructive of others will destroy or hurt them, either physically or psychologically. Their attitude toward the suffering of the world may be one of indifference. Such people will allow, sometimes encourage, the maiming, killing, and starving of helpless victims of political or social machines and do so without a sense of guilt.

People with *going-nowhere,* banal scripts are nonwinners. They restrict their own growth, limit their own opportunities, and avoid the full realization of their potentialities. These persons often follow the stereotype expectations of the larger culture. On the surface they may appear successful, as though they had constructive scripts. However, they inevitably undermine themselves in some way, often explaining their misfortunes as bad luck. In other words, when the curtain is up, the person may be oriented toward useful activities; yet when the final curtain comes down, nothing really important has been accomplished. This is the script of many people who complain, "I tried." They do not set realistic goals or realistic plans of action. Consequently, they don't succeed. These people are on the proverbial treadmill—not going anywhere because they are too busy trying instead of doing and being.[48]

Individual scripts are affected and to a large degree determined by the cultural, subcultural, and family cultural patterns transmitted generation after generation as cultural scripting. A cultural script functions like a collective Parent, passing on cultural scripting messages from Parent ego state to Parent ego state. Children then decide whether to comply with or rebel against the cultural expectations. According to *Born To Win*:

> Cultural scripts are the accepted and expected dramatic patterns that occur within a society. They are determined by the spoken and unspoken assumptions believed by the majority of the people within that group. Like theatrical scripts, cultural scripts have themes, characters, expected roles, stage directions, costumes, settings, scenes, and final curtains. Cultural scripts reflect what is thought of as the "national character." The same drama may be repeated generation after generation.[49]

A common script theme in the United States is the "work-hard" script, often called the Protestant Ethic. Inherited from those who first came to this country to exploit it or escape persecution, the work-hard script was acted out by people who were pioneers and/or settlers.[50] It is still a strong cultural script, although many people are currently rebelling against it. Perhaps laissez-faire or "more play and less work" is a cultural script that emerges with an affluent society where there *seem* to be fewer pioneering challenges.

Subcultures are often defined by geography, language, religion, age, sex, race, ethnic grouping, or in some other general way. The family may be considered a small subculture. Political parties, religious, socio-economic, and racial groups —even professional associations—may influence others much as parents do. In fact, Freud and the psychoanalytic tradition form a subcultural Parent to many psychotherapists. Cultural or Subcultural parents may be paternalistic and punitive or paternalistic and controlling like "an iron hand in a velvet glove." Others may be nurturing, permissive, or indifferent.

Originally, all people experience their culture in the family. Some families are angry and punitive. Some are cold and indifferent. Others are warm and loving. Each family culture lives by myths it believes to be true; often these myths are related to sexual roles, academic achievement, how to rear children, etc. Each family also perpetuates traditions and prejudices. Myths, traditions, and prejudices that are strongly adhered to—whether or not they are valid—become part of the family script.[51]

Other subcultures are often more influential than the family. For example, many children are so desirous of peer approval that their *peer subculture functions as a strong parent,* making demands, withdrawing favors, etc. Cultural and subcultural scripts share the Parent ego state with the historical parent figures. This can be diagramed as:

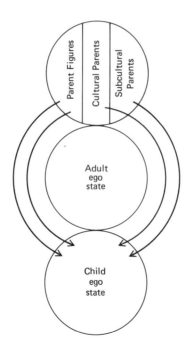

When people comply with the cultural or subcultural scripting, such scripting is continued generation after generation. An example of this is demonstrated by the Protestants and Roman Catholics of northern Ireland who continue to fight to prove superiority, to get even, or to survive.

When people rebel, either openly or covertly, cultural patterns and scripting often change. This is happening with many minority groups who see themselves as an important part of the culture and are demanding fair treatment. Cultural scripts also change when people, using the educated Adult, *decide* that certain traditional behavior and values learned in childhood and reinforced by the Parent ego state are no longer appropriate. Whether the change comes by rational thinking or rebellion, new customs, new laws, new institutions may be instigated. Thus a Cultural Parent is revised—for better or worse—and the new values become part of the cultural script.

Therapists who wish to consider how their cultural scripting may aid or hinder them as persons and as professionals can start by reviewing the cultures and subcultures to which they have belonged. What did these groups have to say about psychology, being helpful, and being a therapist? Awareness of cultural scripting is essential in the exploration of an individual script.

CULTURAL SCRIPT CHECK LIST

Describe each of the following cultures, *as you have experienced them,* in three to five words. The subcultures may be social, ethnic, geographical, socioeconomic, religious, etc. (Choose subcultures which had the most influence in your life or currently do.)

My Family Culture	Subculture 1	Subculture 2	Subculture 3	Dominant National Culture
_____	_____	_____	_____	_____
_____	_____	_____	_____	_____
_____	_____	_____	_____	_____

List strengths of each:

_____	_____	_____	_____	_____
_____	_____	_____	_____	_____

List weaknesses of each:

_____	_____	_____	_____	_____
_____	_____	_____	_____	_____

List common mottoes, sayings, phrases, or jargon of each:

_____	_____	_____	_____	_____
_____	_____	_____	_____	_____

My Family Culture	*Subculture 1*	*Subculture 2*	*Subculture 3*	*Dominant National Culture*

List heroes, character types, myths, legends of each:

_____	_____	_____	_____	_____
_____	_____	_____	_____	_____

How might someone from each culture feel when things go wrong?

_____	_____	_____	_____	_____
_____	_____	_____	_____	_____

How might the majority of the people in that culture act when things go wrong?

_____	_____	_____	_____	_____

List the script theme of each culture:

_____	_____	_____	_____	_____

Categorize each as constructive, destructive, or going nowhere:

_____	_____	_____	_____	_____

How are your cultures in agreement; how are they in conflict?

_____

_____

What aspects of your cultural scripts are you most likely to use? How?

_____

_____

How are each of your ego states involved in your cultural script?

_____

_____

Discovering Individual Scripts

There are many techniques for discovering *individual scripts*. Certainly one of the easiest for self-therapy is based on three simple questions, "What happens to people like me?" and "If I go on as I now am, what will be the logical conclusions?" and "What will other people say about me when it's all over?"

An answer to the first question reveals the expected "action" and what the action is going to be as the drama progresses. The answer to the second question reveals the final scene, the conclusion of the drama. The answer to the third question reveals the audience response to the final curtain. For example, a therapist who plays *Harried* by working too hard might say that what happens to harried people is that they take on more and more responsibilities, die prematurely due to something like high blood pressure or ulcers, and receive an obituary of "Too bad. All the hard work seems to have little meaning."

Therapists, like clients, act out constructive, destructive, or going-nowhere scripts on hypothetical "stages" which call for scenery and settings, as well as for drama themes and plots, casts of characters, and action dialogue.

Some therapists, as well as clients, have several stages on which they act out their lives. The two most common stages are home and work. The scripts played on each may or may not coincide. For example, a person's scripting for work may call for competency and authenticity on the job. The same person's script when "on stage" at home may call for going-nowhere or for destructive acting-out behavior.

Going-nowhere or destructive scripts are often related to the kind of attention received in childhood. All children need positive attention—both conditional and unconditional—and few people have enough of it. Attention is like a spotlight. It stimulates growth and development. At birth, most infants, including future therapists, are in the spotlight and get the attention that comes from being at center stage. The attention may be positive—"You're just what we wanted."—or it may be negative—"Why aren't you different?" or "Why did you have to be born at all?"

If the attention is positive and unconditional, children usually develop healthy personalities and constructive scripts. If it is positive and conditional, with approval dependent on performance, children often select hard-working scripts. Later these may lead to successful on-the-job performance but not necessarily to successful home performance.

If parents' attention is seldom available or if it is continually negative, children usually adopt scripts that are destructive of themselves and often of others. Unless their scripts are rewritten, therapists with this kind of background are often unsuccessful and may, especially in private practice, have a high rate of hospitalizations and suicides.

When the attention in childhood fluctuates between positive and negative, the result is often a going-nowhere script with two steps forward and two steps backward. Attention may fluctuate or seem to, if a child is moved out of the spotlight at a very early age and another person moves in—perhaps a parent, a sibling, or a grandparent who needs or demands center stage.

Learning to take turns is a skill that develops at about age three. When children are forced to take turns or share the spotlight at an earlier age, they often feel resentful and hang on to these feelings throughout life.

Scripting first occurs nonverbally. Almost as if they had radar, infants begin to pick up messages about themselves and their worth through their first experiences of being either touched or ignored by others. Soon they see facial expressions and respond to them as well as to touch and to sounds. Children who are cuddled affectionately, smiled at, and talked to receive different messages than those who are handled with fright, hostility, or anxiety. Children who receive little touch and who experience parental indifference or hostility are discounted. They learn to feel that they are not-OK and perhaps may feel like "nothings." Children's first feelings about themselves are likely to remain the most powerful force in their life dramas. The significantly influence the psychological positions they take and the roles they play.[52]

Getting in touch with the spotlight aspects of a script. This technique for discovering one's individual script is done by drawing simple diagrams of theatrical stages at various periods of life—birth, preschool, kindergarten, etc.—indicating the people involved and their location on stage. For example, you might diagram yourself as a baby in the center-stage spotlight, with your mother as a supporting character getting little attention for herself and your father offstage but perhaps directing the action from behind the curtain. Recall

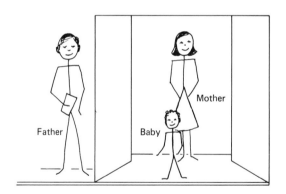

whether you were encouraged to leave this central position early in life and move to the rear of the stage, perhaps because of a family crisis. If you were, speculate on how it may have affected your script. Draw a series of stages for different periods in your life—when you were growing up (i.e., starting kindergarten, as an adolescent) and currently. Intuitively place the other characters involved where it seems appropriate and ask yourself, "What kind of a show was it?" Most children want to be stars (unless programed otherwise). If, for example, a new character such as a new sibling comes on stage, the first child may become resentful or depressed and withdraw psychologically or act out in some way so that attention will once more be focused on him or her.

Some children are able to stay in the spotlight, in one way or another—by being the first-born son, looking like mother, etc. In such cases, a sibling or other family member may be delegated to the background. This also affects the scripting process of those involved.

Among the interesting phenomena in group therapy are the ways people seek out, or try to avoid, the spotlight. One may talk continuously and persecute others with verbal diarrhea; another may be silent and anxious-looking, presenting a Victim posture to the group; a third may be "helpful" Rescuing others who may or may not need it, and so forth. In most cases people learn in childhood to seek or avoid the spotlight in ways to get approval or to avoid punishment. Therapists who compete with their clients or cotherapists for either position are likely to have "audiences" that slowly decrease in attendance. The therapist must draw a very fine line between being overactive and thereby encouraging clients to be dependent, and being underactive and thereby allowing clients who need some structure to be confused. Therapists can review their spotlight-seeking or spotlight-avoidance by replaying in their heads the past week's therapy sessions with particular focus on their own roles. Some therapists' personal lives are so sterile that they do not get the positive attention their inner Child needs to continue topnotch performances. This can be changed.

Identifying the theme and roles that are played out. This technique for script discovery is classifying the drama as tragedy, comedy, farce, melodrama, saga, adventure, and so forth. The use of fantasy reveals these categories immediately. The process is to sit in a relaxed position with legs, arms, and hands uncrossed and imagine being alone in a theatre where a video tape of your life is being played. The tape starts with your earlier years, shows the people around you, and what they are doing and saying to each other and to you that are scripting messages or modeling behavior. Take time and slowly watch the drama unfold from the early years to the present time. Then imagine that an audience has been watching the drama with you. Look at the people. What are they saying or doing? What does the audience response indicate about whether your script is constructive, destructive, or going-nowhere? What were the roles and how were they played? How would you classify the drama? What kind is it?

Let this awareness sink in slowly, then once more take a fantasy trip. This time to your death-bed. Imagine that you are very old and dying. Who is there with you? What are you saying to each other? Now let yourself go further. Imagine you have actually died. What are people saying about you and what would your epitaph be? Is there anything about yourself that you need to change?

When I first got in touch with my own epitaph, it came as a surprise. I felt that the words "She was responsible" would be on my tombstone. I decided that wasn't enough. Responsibility is ok, I didn't want to give up that characteristic, but I also wanted something more. Therefore, I made a contract with myself to be in such a way that the words "and fun" would be added to my epitaph. "Fun," I said to myself, "What's that?" For so many years I had been so busy being responsible from my Adult and Parent that I had almost shut off this part of my Child. It took time to release it, time to learn how to choose other fun-loving Childs to be on my stage and to be invited to share theirs. It also took time to experiment with and practice new behavior. However, it worked and I am convinced that if I died today the epitaph would be "She was responsible and fun," and that now pleases all three of my ego states.

The James-Jongeward Script Process. This is another technique that can be used to discover a script.[53] It can be used by therapists who are engaged in self-therapy or with clients, and is as follows:

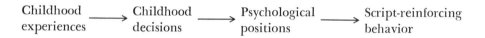

Childhood ——→ Childhood ——→ Psychological ——→ Script-reinforcing
experiences   decisions   positions   behavior

Childhood experiences include: events that occurred, training that was experienced, and injunctions that were given. *Childhood decisions* are the strong attitudes taken by children because of their experiences. The decisions include script selections and the selection of games that fit the script. *Psychological positions* are the generalized attitudes based on the decisions. They provide an emotional climate that is then acted out through the script and the *script-reinforcing behavior.*

An example of the script process would be that of a young boy who loses his mother through death, desertion, or because she is institutionalized. He is likely to make the decision (if there is no effective, nurturing mother substitute), "I will not trust or get close to a woman again; she might go away." Games such a person might play could be *If It Weren't For Her, Rapo,* or *Look How Hard I'm Trying.*

The psychological position would likely be "I'm not-OK" (or she wouldn't have left), "Women are not-OK" (they leave). The script-reinforcing behavior is to create scenes similar to those in childhood: for example, unknowingly to select women whose scripts call for them to be untrustworthy and leave, or to select women who stay on and on until driven away by the non-trusting Child.

To change this script, the person would need to change his basic decisions and redecide something like, "I *will* trust and get close to some women. They won't necessarily go away." The psychological positions would correspondingly change to "I'm OK and women are also OK." The script behavior would also change. Games played to "get rid of" or "get away from" women would be given up in favor of authenticity and intimacy.

Therapists who wish to use the script formula on themselves can jot down some important childhood experiences, then think through the balance of the format. If one is unable to recall details, it is possible to start with the script-reinforcing behavior and work backward. To do this, ask the question, "What keeps happening to me over and over again?" "What keeps happening" is the reinforcement. The next question is, "What kind of OK and not-OK psychological positions are reflected in this repetitive scene?" Then ask, "What decisions might I have made in childhood to arrive at these positions? What experiences or training preceded them and what injunctions did I receive?"

Using a script checklist.   This is common with TA therapists. The most extensive list was developed by Berne, and it includes some 220 questions.[54] Some therapists use this or other script checklists and go through them question by question with their clients. Some therapists, with considerable success, use them for themselves.

The accompanying brief checklist I've developed as a technique for motivating clients past personal awareness of their script to contracts for change that will enhance their current life as well as their future. I use this after a client has looked at his or her drama in the guided fantasy previously described.

INDIVIDUAL SCRIPT SUMMARY[55]

Try to fill in the blanks honestly, without censoring yourself.

- The kinds of things that happen to me over and over again (with money, with family, with job) indicate that my script is basically:

  Constructive_____Destructive_____Going nowhere_____

- It is similar to a:

  Comedy_____Tragedy_____Melodrama_____Adventure _____

  Pilgrimage_____Farce_____Other _____

- The script role I play most often with people close to me is:

  Persecutor_____ Rescuer_____Victim_____

- I often expect other people to play the role of_____ with me.
- What I do to attract others is: _____
- The kinds of things that happen to people like me are: _____

_____

- The theme of my script could be summarized in the words: _____

_____

- If an audience saw a movie of my life, from birth to today, the audience would: _____
- If the audience talked about me and my drama they would say: _____

_____

- If I keep going the way I am now, the final curtain will come down on a scene of: _____
- When I think of this final scene I feel: _____
- The kind of audience response I want at my final curtain is: _____
- What I want people to say about me after I die is: _____
- The kind of heritage I want to leave my family and friends is: _____

_____

- To get what I want I will need to:_____instead of_____ which I am now doing.

The script matrix. This is another useful technique in script analysis, a diagram to illustrate the messages given from parents to children. The matrix was designed by Claude Steiner[56] based on Berne's concepts.[57]

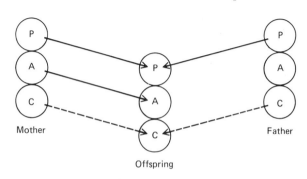

Offspring

Conventional script matrix

The line from Parent ego state in the parent to Parent ego state in the offspring represents the mottos and moralisms that are verbalized to the offspring. This line is called by some TA therapists the "counterscript," meaning against the script.

The Adult-to-Adult line is the "here's how"—the demonstration of how to carry out the scripting messages—that is also transmitted from parents to children.

The Child-to-Child dashed line is an important ulterior transaction as it is an injunction that becomes a script control. For example, a parent who often declares, "Don't cry over spilt milk," (a Parent-to-Parent counterscript message) sends the ulterior message, "Don't show your feelings" (C-C scripting message). The parent may also *show how* to do this (A-A) by acting stoic from a non-expressive Adult. People with these messages are likely to feel guilty if they cry or if they show their feelings in some other way.

An easy way to begin filling in a script matrix is to list common parental statements a client heard when little, and then to ask, "Was there another message *under* those words?" That under-message is part of the person's script. If the script is destructive or going nowhere, it is likely to be related to one of the negative "Don't" injunctions discovered by the Gouldings.[58] If the script is constructive, the script messages, from the Child of the parents to the Child of the offspring, will be in the form of positive "do's."

Therapists who believe that self-understanding and self-therapy is a life-long adventure can go another step by listing the verbal and nonverbal positive and negative "Do's" and "Don'ts" they received in childhood. For example, persons who are *told* to "work hard" may get another *nonverbal* message such as "... and *don't* enjoy it," or "... and *do* enjoy it." The working hard *and* not enjoying it is likely to be part of a destructive or banal script. The working hard *and* enjoying it is likely to be part of a constructive script.

The word "counterscript" does not always fit, as the Parent-to-Parent verbal message may *match* the Child-to-Child injunction rather than run *counter* to it. In such cases, people exhibit more consistent behavior than do those who have messages that are counter to each other.

Since the conventional matrix was designed, many variations have been discovered. Stanley Woollams shows a revised script matrix. It is of an alcoholic in which the counterscript and script are in agreement.[59]

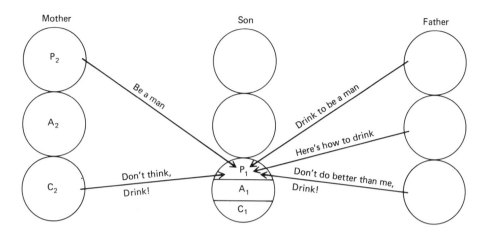

Revised script matrix

Another *matrix,* or how the messages are sent and received from three parent figures, is given in my book *Born to Love,* with a case history of positive scripting. The case is that of a clergyman named Tom Hardy who was named after the biblical "Doubting Thomas," which scripted him to have a questioning attitude and insist on proof even as a youngster.

As a boy he was unusually healthy. He so seldom caught colds that his father used to brag about it. "You really are a hardy one." This was reinforced by his physician grandfather who declared, "Doctors are for sick people. Now think about that. You don't need to be sick."

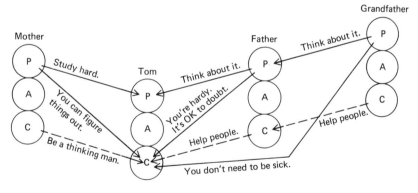

Scripting messages

When Tom was in the sixth grade, his favorite books were the Hardy Boys series, and he became deeply involved in their detective-like abilities to solve mysteries. He also spent long hours with jigsaw and crossword puzzles, encouraged by his mother.

Tom's first name had also received attention. As a bright adolescent who had to attend church regularly, Tom occasionally argued with his father over some of the points made in his father's sermons. Tom's father, from his theological corner, would respond indulgently with "You're just like your namesake, Thomas. He doubted everything. Someday you'll figure out the mysteries of faith for yourself. Just keep thinking."[60]

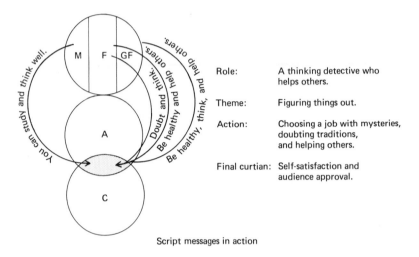

Role: A thinking detective who helps others.

Theme: Figuring things out.

Action: Choosing a job with mysteries, doubting traditions, and helping others.

Final curtian: Self-satisfaction and audience approval.

Script messages in action

The inner dialogues, learned in childhood and replayed in later life, are like stage directions to advance the script. To the extent that people are not aware of their scripts, they function from a contaminated Adult.

Analyzing a client's favorite childhood stories. This technique reveals script themes, the dramatic roles that are played, the kinds of characters selected to be on stage, and the transactions enacted.

Eric Berne claimed that children go around having various kinds of experiences and then one day they hear, read, or see a story that they identify with. "That's me!" they say. From then on they act out the story in fairytale roles like Cinderella, Peter Pan, Pinocchio, and so forth. Or they may choose to act out roles found in Greek myths, such as Prometheus, Aphrodite, Hercules, or Medusa.[61]

Some therapists, as well as clients, do not remember this part of their childhood. If this is the case, here is a technique for you. I first saw it used by Maurice and Natalie Haimowitz, and it is designed for the creative Child. This is a timed exercise to be completed in four minutes by writing a child's story as fast as possible, beginning with the words, "Once upon a time there was a . . ." (continue with the name of some kind of animal or fish). To turn on your Child, say to yourself, "Get on your mark, get set, and go," then write as fast as you can. When you've finished, but not before, turn to reference 62 at the end of this chapter.

Therapy needs to start and continue with oneself. It seems to be a lifelong journey which can be constructive, destructive, or going-nowhere. When in their Adult ego state, people may not be in a script. When they are in their Adapted Child, or perhaps in the Child in the Parent ego state, they are likely to be in their scripts. Therefore, many therapists, as well as clients, need to bring down the curtain permanently on the "same old act" and rewrite the balance of the script so that a better show can get on the road. Of course, they need to include in the rewrite new answers to the basic script questions, "Who am I?" "What am I doing here?" and "Who are all those others?"[63]

The miniscript.   Discovered by Taibi Kahler and Hedges Capers, this is another useful TA technique. It is defined as a "sequence of behavior, occurring in a matter of minutes or even seconds, that results in a reinforcement pattern for life."[64] There are not-OK miniscripts and OK ones. The not-OK miniscripts start with Parental counterscript slogans called *drivers*. These seem to be helpful when originally imposed by parents, but actually become a life-long burden. There are five drivers: "Be perfect," "Try hard," "Hurry up," "Please me," and "Be strong." When people are in their not-OK miniscript they believe they are OK *only if* complying with the drivers—being perfect, trying hard, hurrying, pleasing people, or being strong. Inevitably they fail at this and get in touch with their negative script injunctions, which are called *stoppers* in miniscript theory. To avoid the unpleasantness of stoppers, they move to a *vengeful Child* position, which is spiteful, critical behavior or passive-aggressive procrastination. Eventually they get their *final miniscript pay-off*—feeling alone, unloved, helpless and so forth.

The OK miniscript has *allowers* rather than drivers. These five are the positive opposites: "It's OK to be yourself, to take your time, to do it (rather than just try to do it), to consider and respect yourself, to be open and take care of your own needs." Instead of stoppers, the OK miniscript has *goers*. Instead of a Vengeful Child it has an Affirming Child. Instead of bad feeling, it has good feelings called *wowers*.

TA therapists need to be aware of their own miniscripts and how their drivers show in words and behavior. With awareness, they may not interlock with the miniscripts of their clients. Without awareness, they probably will. For example, the therapist with a "Be perfect" driver is likely to elicit pleasing and trying-hard behavior from clients. This, of course, would never be good enough for a "Be perfect" therapist.

The cure for people in not-OK miniscripts is to move from the not-OK drivers to the OK allowers and to practice living by the allowers until they become an integral part of the self. Thus the script can be rewritten.

Some TA therapists talk about being script-free. To me, this seems like pie in the sky, because I have never met a script-free person. I think that when a person moves into a Child ego state, he or she is likely to go into a script. I also think an OK script is *often OK.*

For Further Consideration

In therapy group one night, a man asked his wife, "Whose scripts are *you* living?" Without waiting for an answer he added, "You're not acting like yourself today, you're acting just like your mother."

That comment energized me to think about a new theoretical issue: this is, do all people live by a script that is in their Child ego state? How about those who are constantly in their Parent ego state? In the development of their Parent ego state, through the process of incorporating parental traditions, prejudices, life styles, etc., they probably also incorporated the scripts of their parents. Would they not then be acting out their Parent's scripts?

As for me, whose writing script am I living? When Eric first heard my paper on impotence (included later in this book), he said, "get it published fast and keep on writing." Now with the eight books authored or co-authored since then and with four more "in the works," I've seemingly obeyed. Is it a new Child adaptation from Eric, or is Eric incorporated into my Parent, as part of my new Parent? Thus, am I living his script of being a writer or living my own new one?

TIME STRUCTURING

Therapists, like clients, may structure their time like winners, like losers, or like people going nowhere. Whether on or off the job, there is a basic hunger for time structuring. People satisfy this need by structuring their time in any of six different ways: withdrawal, rituals, pastimes, games, activities, and intimacy. The use of each of these can be related to the ego state that is cathected at a particular time.

Psychological withdrawal from others can be a Parental copied behavior, an Adult decision, or a Child adaptation. People in their Parent ego state will withdraw, or not withdraw, in the same ways their parent figures once did. An Adult decision to withdraw could be based on the need to fantasize or plan, or from being bored with a situation, or if only a physical presence is required for a routine task. In their Child ego state, they may withdraw because of needs of their Natural Child, because their Little Professor intuits that it's a smart thing to do, or because their Adapted Child is anxious, fearful, or trained to behave thusly.

The other five forms of time structuring can be related to ego-state activity in a similar manner. For example, *rituals,* which are stereotyped transactions, such as everyday greetings, can be a Child adaptation, an Adult decision that a particular ritual is appropriate, or a Parent tradition passed on generation after generation (Parent ego state to Parent ego state) which includes specific behavior, tone of voice, words that are used, and so forth.

Pastimes are like extended rituals, though not quite as stereotyped. In the Parent ego state, people will talk about the same concerns their parents once expressed, such as how to rear children, spend money, use leisure time, and so forth. In the Adult, people may choose to pastime because it seems appropriate for the occasion—as, for example, during the few minutes before a business meeting when people are assembling. In the Child, they may feel inadequate to, fearful of, or disinterested in other people and choose pastiming to avoid other forms of time structuring which could be used if they wanted to get closer to others.

Games, which are series of transactions with ulterior purposes and negative payoffs, may be played from the Parent, as the parents once played them. They may also be played from the Adult, for example, by a therapist who goes along with a client's games temporarily while the games are being de-escalated. Games are also played from the Child who learned them in childhood as a way to get strokes in order to survive. Perhaps all games stem from contaminations.

Activities, commonly thought of as work, can be verbal or nonverbal, can include physical activity, intellectual activity, or both. In the Parent, people may, for example, play cards together as their parents did. In their Adult they may balance their budget accurately. In their Adapted Child they may clean up their desks in preparation for a visit from "the boss," a parent figure.

Intimacy, which seems to involve Child-to-Child closeness, trust, and openness, may actually emerge from a Parent ego state. After all, each parent figure also had an inner Child who had feelings (as illustrated by second-order structural analysis). Consequently, intimacy between two people in the Parent ego state may occur because of their common parental concern over an injured child. In the Adult ego state, it may occur because of a common interest in a particular job or hobby. In the child, intimacy can also occur because of a common interest, but it often has the added dimension of shared laughter, play, or sexual expression. Regardless of which ego states are involved, the intimacy usually occurs within the context of an activity, when neither person is withdrawing nor engaging in rituals, pastimes, or games.

Therapists, as well as clients, can easily evaluate their time structuring by the use of a time-o-gram. Given a certain number of minutes, hours, or days, they can ascertain how they are using their time by drawing a vertical bar representing the minutes spent in each category.

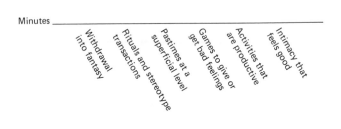

I find this technique effective in evaluating my own participation as a group therapist and for group members who may also make time-o-grams for themselves or others. If made with the Adult, the graphs will be realistic. If made by the Parent or the Child, they will be distorted.

It is not always necessary to know which ego state is structuring a person's time. However, if clients or therapists are not satisfied with the way their lives are going and the way they are acting out their scripts, then analyzing the use of time, as related to ego states, can be a useful technique for decontaminating and establishing new contracts.

It is not unusual for therapists to complain privately about their clients, to object to the time they spend with them, to label them as boring. Yet, according to Berne, "there is no such thing as a boring patient, but only bored therapists."[65] Clear goals, backed up by well-formulated plans which are implemented according to schedule, change boredom to excitement.

Good therapy is educational, good education is therapeutic. To be educated to oneself is to be alive and enjoying the continuing road to autonomy.

REFERENCES

1. Berne, Eric, *Transactional Analysis in Psychotherapy* (New York: Grove, 1971), p. 76.
2. For an extensive listing of ego-state behaviors, see: Jongeward, Dorothy, and Muriel James, *Winning With People: Group Exercises in Transactional Analysis* (Reading, Mass.: Addison-Wesley, 1972), Appendix C.

3. James, Muriel, *Born to Love: Transactional Analysis in the Church* (Reading, Mass.: Addison-Wesley, 1973), pp. 47, 48.

4. Berne, Eric, *Principles of Group Treatment* (New York: Grove, 1968), p. 220.

5. Ibid., p. 216.

6. Ibid., p. 105: Cf. Berne, *TA in Psychotherapy*, pp. 233–234.

7. James, Muriel, "Self-Reparenting: Theory and Process," *TA Journal*, Oct. 1974, pp. 32–39 (included in this volume).

8. Ibid.

9. Berne, *TA in Psychotherapy*, pp. 194–195.

10. James, Muriel, and Dorothy Jongeward, *Born to Win: Transactional Analysis with Gestalt Experiments* (Reading, Mass.: Addison-Wesley, 1971), pp. 271–272.

11. Berne, Eric, *Sex in Human Loving* (New York: Simon & Schuster, 1970), p. 118.

12. ———, *Principles*, p. 278. Also see p. 311.

13. Ibid., pp. 308–309.

14. Berne, Eric, "Editor's Page," *TA Bulletin* **8**, 29 (1969), pp. 7–8.

15. James and Jongeward, *Born to Win*, p. 270.

16. Berne, *TA in Psychotherapy*, pp. 37–43.

17. James and Jongeward, *Born to Win*, p. 228.

18. Schiff, Aaron, and Jacqui Schiff, "Passivity," *TA Journal*, Jan. 1971, pp. 71–72.

19. Dusay, John, "Egograms and the Constancy Hypothesis," *TA Journal* **2**, 3 (1972), pp. 37–41.

20. Jongeward and James, *Winning With People*, p. 89.

21. Dusay, John, "Eric Berne's Studies of Intuition 1949–1962," *TA Journal*, Jan. 1971, p. 35.

22. Berne, Eric, "Intuition VI, the Psychodynamics of Intuition," *Psychiatric Quarterly* **36** (1962), p. 295.

23. ———, *TA in Psychotherapy*, pp. 61–67.

24. James and Jongeward, *Born to Win*, p. 231.

25. James, Muriel, *Transactional Analysis for Moms and Dads* (Reading, Mass.: Addison-Wesley, 1974), p. 70.

26. For extensive details and exercises on stroking, see: James, Muriel, *The OK Boss* (Reading, Mass.: Addison-Wesley, 1975) and James, Muriel, and Louis Savary, *A New Self* (Reading, Mass.: Addison-Wesley, in press).

27. For a scientific study of body language, see: Spiegel, John P., and Paul Machotka, *Messages of the Body* (New York: The Free Press, 1974).

28. James and Jongeward, *Born to Win*, p. 249.

29. James, Muriel, "The Downscripting of Women for 115 Generations: A Historical Kaleidoscope," *TA Journal* **3**, 3 (1973), pp. 15–22 (included in this volume).

30. Cf. James and Jongeward, *Born to Win*, pp. 8–9.

31. James, Muriel, and Dorothy Jongeward, *The People Book: Transactional Analysis for Students* (Menlo Park, Calif.: Addison-Wesley, 1975), p. 84.

32. See Steiner, Claude M., *Games Alcoholics Play: The Analysis of Life Scripts* (New York, 1971): Cf. Steere, David, "Freud on the 'Gallows Transaction,'" *TA Bulletin* **9,** 1 (1970), pp. 3–5.

33. Berne, *Principles,* p. 368.

34. Ibid., p. 22.

35. Karpman, Stephen B., "Fairy Tales and Script Drama Analysis," *TA Bulletin* **7,** 26 (1968), pp. 39–43.

36. For further discussion on how games are learned in childhood, see: Zechnich, Robert, "Games in Infancy and Childhood," *TA Journal* **4,** 2 (1974), pp. 5–9.

37. Samuels, Solon D., "Games Therapists Play," *TA Journal* **1,** 1 (1971), pp. 95–99.

38. Berne, *Principles,* pp. 121–122.

39. For distinctions among supportive group therapy, group analytic therapy, psychoanalytic therapy, and Transactional Analysis, see: Ibid., pp. 101–136.

40. James, John, "The Game Plan," *TA Journal* **3,** 4 (1973), pp. 14–17.

41. Ibid.

42. Dusay, John, "Response," *TA Bulletin,* April 1966, p. 136.

43. James, John, "Positive Payoffs After Games," *TA Journal,* July 1976.

44. Berne, *Principles,* p. 308.

45. James, *Born to Love,* p. 135.

46. Berne, Eric, *What Do You Say After You Say Hello?* (New York, Grove, 1972), p. 446.

47. Ibid., p. 447.

48. James, *Born to Love,* pp. 122, 124.

49. James and Jongeward, *Born to Win,* p. 70.

50. Ibid.

51. ——, *The People Book,* pp. 68–100: White, Jerome, and Terri White, "TA Psychohistory," *TA Journal,* July, 1974, and "Cultural Scripting," *TA Journal,* Jan. 1975: James, Muriel, "Ego States and Social Issues: Two Case Histories from the 1960's," *TA Journal,* Jan. 1975 (included in this volume): Jongeward, Dorothy, "What Do You Do When Your Script Runs Out?" *TA Journal,* April 1972.

52. James and Jongeward, *Born to Win,* p. 75.

53. Ibid., p. 38.

54. Berne, *Hello,* pp. 425–439: McCormick, Paul, *Guide for Use of a Life Script Questionnaire* (San Francisco: Transactional Publications, ITAA, 1971): Holloway, William H., *Clinical Transactional Analysis with the use of the Life Script Questionnaire* (Akron, Ohio: Midwest Institute for Human Understanding, 1973).

55. James, *Born to Love,* pp. 145–146.

56. Steiner, Claude M., "Script and Counterscript," *TA Bulletin,* April 1966, pp. 133–135.

57. Berne, *Hello,* p. 283.

58. Goulding, Robert, "New Directions in Transactional Analysis: Creating an Environment for Redecision and Change," In *Progress in Group and Family Therapy,* cited by Clifford J. Sager and Helen Singer Kaplan (New York: Brunner/Mazer, 1972).

59. Woollams, Stanley J., "Formations of the Script," *TA Journal* **3,** 3 (1973), pp. 31–37.

60. James, *Born to Love,* pp. 125–126.

61. James and Jongeward, *Born to Win,* pp. 90–95: Cf. *The People Book,* pp. 166–167.

62. Now ask yourself, "How does this reflect some part of my life?" This question was put back here so it would not influence your performance of the exercise. For more information on this technique, see: Berne, *Hello,* pp. 39–50: Haimowitz, Natalie, "Fairytale Scripts in TA Therapists, the Powerful Adapted Child of the Therapist," *TA Journal,* April 1971: O'Hearne, Lillian, "Use of Fairytales in Redecision," *TA Journal,* Oct. 1974: Cheney, Warren, "Hamlet: His Script Checklist," *TA Bulletin,* July 1968: Berne, Eric, "The Mythology of Dark and Fair: Psychiatric use of Folklore," *Journal of American Folklore* **1,** 12 (1959).

63. Berne, *Sex in Human Loving,* p. 193.

64. Kahler, Taibi, and Hedges Capers, "The Miniscript," *TA Journal,* Jan. 1974, p. 28.

65. Berne, *Principles,* p. 152.

CHAPTER 5

treatment
procedures

The transactional analyst says, "Get better first,
and we can analyse later." Surprisingly enough,
in most cases the patient will oblige.
Eric Berne

THE THERAPEUTIC SETTING

A basic TA principle of "what to do first" is to plan the treatment so that a client's Adult ego state is decontaminated and gains executive control over the Child and Parent. Even the therapist's clothes and office setting affect the process of decontamination. Experienced therapists are aware that anything they say or do, including how they decorate their offices, is a stimulus to one or more of their client's ego states.

In brief, the Child needs a comfortable setting in which a relationship of trust may develop; the Parent needs a setting that is nonthreatening to his or her traditional values. The Adult needs a setting conducive to thoughtful work. Some therapists claim the physical surroundings are not important as long as they are not too uncomfortable.[1] I disagree. I believe the setting requires considerable thought.

First, the use of color should be analyzed. The inner Child in each person responds to colors—especially primary ones—and as the *Luscher Color Test* points out, different people have different color preferences. In my experience and experimentations (and I've experimented with many colors), I have found light, sunny yellow to be most therapeutic. Draperies, carpeting, and sofa in this color, leather chairs in soft golds and tans, lamp bases and a cabinet in muted wine tones, all seem to provide a setting not of swank, but of warmth and excitement. Rarely does a client enter this group room for the first time without saying something like: "Oh, how pretty," or "Oh, I like it here."

Chairs are another consideration. Since people's bodies are of different sizes and shapes, they require different sizes and shapes of chairs. What is comfortable for one person may be agony for another. Some institutions function as though they had a big, critical Parent ego state, and the administrators are unwilling to consider this basic fact of chairs and do something about it. Clients in these situations who have to put up with uncomfortable chairs may deserve a moment of sympathy. Therapists who have uncomfortable chairs could, if they so chose, go out and buy some decent chairs out of their own pockets. Even simple canvas "director chairs" are likely to be more comfortable than some other types, and they provide a feeling of safety to the Child because they have some semblance of arms and, therefore, of protection. Obviously, a king-size chair for the therapist and peasant chairs for the clients gives a "You're not-OK" message that could be avoided.[2]

Generally speaking, TA therapists do not have clients sit on pillows on the floor unless they want to cathect the Child ego state. Reasonably comfortable chairs are more effective for strengthening the Adult. An overly comfortable lounge chair may have the same effect as pillows on the floor. I had one such chair in my office and finally got rid of it because everyone who sat in it either withdrew into a cocoon position or leaned back and pontificated mightily. No one using it was able to stay in the Adult except for very brief periods.

Tables and desks, if the room has any, need to be off at the side. Nothing should be between the therapist and clients. Careful observation of body language is a must in TA and furniture may block this.

The walls of the therapy room are part of the setting. One therapist may allow clients to write on the wall as a way of "leaving their mark," which is a technique to free the Child. Another may have a wall full of diagrams and posters. Each may find their style of decorating to be effective. On my walls are pictures carefully selected to give subtle messages to those in the room. One is of orange poppies growing profusely in a sunny field. It gives permission to enjoy the earth. Another is John Pearson's photograph, which is on the cover of *Born To Win*. It is a child with arms stretched open to the universe. It gives permission to be joyful and self-revealing. On a third wall are three low-key lithographs—one by Renoir, another by June Wayne, the third by an unknown artist. Each is a subtle permission to enjoy sexuality and the sexual expression of it.

Architectural aspects of the room may also affect the therapeutic process. At one time two women who were over six feet tall were in treatment with me. It appeared that the average height ceiling did not allow them enough psychic space, so I had the ceiling raised. The effect was immediately positive. Evidently the extra space gave a subtle "permission" that they needed.

Some TA therapists permit clients to smoke during groups, some do not. I'm one of the latter. The smell may be offensive to others in the group who do not smoke or provocative to those who wish to give it up. I give clients this information and add that if they can't stand being without a cigarette they may step outside while smoking. As a rule, people discover thay can indeed go without. They may also discover some interesting data about the oral needs of their Child as related to anxiety and how and when their Child needs are activated in the group.

An electric coffee pot with hot water is in one corner of my office. Instant coffee, de-caffeinated coffee, tea, foam cups, etc. are available for people who come early and want to fix something for themselves. Many of my clients commute long distances, and it is a small service to provide that may comfort the Child, decrease the Critical Parent, and activate the Adult. To date, this service hasn't seemed to have any detrimental effects on treatment. A snack may be available during a marathon, or minithon, or some kind of extended session, but not at other times. Yet, whenever eating or drinking is going on, the therapist will have rich opportunities to observe rituals, pastimes, and games—of clients and of self.

Heat, proper ventilation, sound-proofing, bathroom facilities, and air-conditioning (when indicated) must be available. I am appalled by institutions that provide air-conditioning in the offices of administrators and therapists but ignore the needs of inmates or hospitalized patients for physical comfort. In a hot climate even as simple a thing as a small, relatively quiet fan can be used, to good advantage, so I advise therapists working in such a situation to stop playing *Ain't It Awful* (that the Administration won't provide amenities) and to "get on with it" by providing such things themselves.

The ringing of a phone, sound of a tape recorder, or intrusion of videotape equipment is distracting to many clients—but if it is deemed necessary it can aid, rather than hinder, the treatment process. When Berne was with clients who were exhibiting passive behavior and "not working," he often answered a phone if it rang. This technique acted as a stimulus to the client with a message to get going.

Tape recorders and videotape can be used therapeutically if the client is told the purpose of such equipment and believes that confidentiality will be maintained. In the diagnosis of games, for example, an audio or video playback often shows the clients more clearly than anything else just how they are playing games. They can hear their own voices from each ego state and hear the ulterior messages that "hook" others into playing with them.

THE INITIAL INTERVIEW

Currently there is no standard way to conduct the initial interview. Different people have used different methods successfully. The usual one is to greet the person with a "Hello" and observe what happens next while getting his or her name, address, referral source, etc. (if that has not been done previously). According to Berne,[3] there are two initial therapeutic rules that must be followed during this process:

1. Psychotherapy should be initiated only during periods of minimal confusion.
2. No active psychotherapeutic moves should be made until the patient has had a chance to appraise the therapist, and he or she should be given an opportunity to do this.

Some clients sit silently and wait for the therapist to take the lead; others rapidly launch into their story; still others start speaking with hesitation—sometimes with tears and despair, sometimes with agitation and anger; some act shy; some act bold. Many weigh their words and behavior as they "psych" out the psychotherapist. With the Little Professor in their Child, they may intuit whether the therapist is interested or bored. They may try to "con" the therapist with the rackets of their Adapted Child, or be so distraught that their Adult is almost totally decathected with the energy locked into their Natural Child.

On the other hand, their Adult may be functioning well, or the Parent in them may be in control. If it is the Parent in executive position, the clients will tend to transact with the therapist much as their parent figures might have done had they been there. If it is the Adult—and by chance uncontaminated—the person may be objective and impersonal, able to think well about problems and how to solve them. Using whatever tools they have, clients at the first session tentatively decide from one of their ego states what is safe to reveal (A), what is scary to feel (C), and what is "best" to conceal (P).

The effective therapist, computing with the Adult, using intuition, training, and experience, observes these initial transactions and considers: What ego state does the client seem to be in? What ego state in the therapist is this client *trying* to hook? What ego state *is* hooked and why? What are the ulterior transactions? Does a game plan or script theme seem to emerge? If the client has initiated a game, is it appropriate to go along with it at this time? Why or why not? One of the basic principles of TA is not to take away people's games until they have discovered better ways to structure their time.

Whether by soliloquy, tirade, conversation, or silence, the client will usually be communicating out of some kind of pain stance. After all, that's why people come to therapists—to get some relief from their pain. The pain may be obvious, revealing itself through despairing body language, facial expression, words and tears, or it may be partially hidden behind defensiveness, stoicism, silence, bravado, accusations, or false optimism. Whatever the mask a client chooses to wear during the initial interview, an ethical therapist will not rip it off with mild ridicule, accusations, arguments, or in other ways that would present the psychological position of I'm OK (being the therapist), you're not-OK (being the client). Therapists who do have this position badly need to seek out treatment for themselves.

Very often, before the initial treatment hour is over, a TA therapist may give a brief explanation of Transactional Analysis, using some of the information given by the client and indicating that this will be the basic method used. Of course, the therapist would not do this if the client is so emotionally disturbed as to be unable to hear the information. I have a small blackboard beside my chair on which I draw a structural diagram and put some of the words clients have used beside each circle. My experience in private practice is that most clients feel relief after being listened to for approximately 30 minutes and consequently are able to cathect their Adult ego state. Their ability to do so and their awareness that there is a tool which can at last be learned and used to solve problems are a great relief to them. For some, the feelings are like those that follow a positive first day in kindergarten after days of worry. Clients not only feel relief, they also experience interest and hope. Hope can be a strong motivating factor for getting well.

If not discussed previously, a statement of fees can be made toward the end of the initial session and the method of payment agreed upon. As mentioned earlier, if people play a game of *Debtor,* one way it can be broken up is to say that payment is expected each time they come. I do not send bills to clients, as I find it therapeutic to ask them to use their Adult and be responsible for payment—weekly, monthly, or whatever has been agreed upon. Although I keep a record of amounts owned and amounts paid, people do not mix up their accounts and no one has neglected to pay. This is valuable to me as a therapist as it saves secretarial expense. It is also of value to clients who learn in this first session that they are expected to use their Adult in a responsible manner. The Adult as executive of the personality is one of the first goals of TA. With a strong Adult, a person can decide what to use from each ego state, when to use it, and who and how to use it with. The Adult can also act as a referee between the Parent and Child. Thus, the Adult, as a substitute good parent, brings comfort to the Child, who at last feels safe.

Many times I find it useful at the end of the initial session to say something like, "Now I know a little about you, and you know a little about the theory and method of TA that we will be using, so go think about our conversation. Later, if you decide to do so, you may phone for another appointment. If I continue to see you, it might be individually but preferably in a group." If questioned about the whys and wherefores of a group, I give an explanation of the structure and values of the group process.

TA can be used in individual therapy, but much of its power comes from its use in groups; and the preparation of a client before entering a group is important. Although therapists who work in institutions may have no choice about when to admit a client to a group, and may have to take persons in without an initial interview, it is best to have at least one individual session first. Therapists tend to believe that some essential data is necessary, but they recognize that significant information may be withheld for various reasons, such as fear of the therapist, or not knowing what information is important and what is unimportant. Some therapists use a formal case-history method, others say this is not necessary. Most agree on the need for a clear statement of the presenting problem or major complaint, the history of when it began, and the efforts, if any, previously made to solve the problem. The client's personal history may then also be taken, briefly or in detail, and a short introduction to TA be given during the initial session. In this process, the therapist and client get the chance to look each other over and perhaps decide whether their relationship will be conducive to growth.[4]

With some clients, it is clear from the beginning that a therapeutic relation can be established. If clients know what they want for themselves, what they need to change, what they are willing to do to make the changes, an initial treatment contract can be established often by the end of the first session.

Successfully terminating an interview is a skill that is important and often developed only with practice. Many therapists do not do this well because they fear that they may offend the client, and indeed they may if that is what they expect. Therapists with these feelings need to examine their Overly Protective Parent or Overly Compliant Child and discover ways to state verbally or nonverbally that the time is up. They may use statements such as, "We can continue this next time," or such gestures as looking at a watch. A valid exception to maintaining a firm 50-minute hour (which allows the therapist to stretch or write notes between clients) would be in the cases of suicidal or homicidal persons or those exhibiting severe schizophrenic symptoms. In such situations, the immediate well-being of the client must take precedence over the appointment book.

TA RECORDS AND WHAT TO INCLUDE

Many institutions and individuals use standard forms, or forms they have developed, for keeping financial and psychological records. I'm not going to discuss these tried and true forms in this section, but instead to present a particular way to keep both individual and group TA records. This is not a universal TA technique but one that I have used successfully for many years.

Although many therapists do not take notes during the therapy sessions, I have found it useful to make very brief ones, usually about one-quarter of a page in an hour's time. I have heard some opinions against note-taking from those influenced by psychoanalytic schools of thought, but I have not seen any data that prove it to be detrimental either to client or therapist. I tell all clients that I will not write down anything that could be held against them by family, friends, or any authorities. I do not, for example, make notes of crime records, homosexual proclivities, or anything else that might be damaging to a client's reputation if my files were ransacked. When working with someone with paranoid tendencies, I explain even more carefully how and why I take notes.

As I do not find psychiatric labels useful, I do not use them in my notes. I prefer TA terminology for diagnosis of the problem. For example, instead of thinking of a person as schizoid, I'm likely to think of him or her as someone with lax ego-state boundaries that need to be realigned and strengthened, so my treatment is designed with this goal in mind. I do not think of a particular client as manic depressive, but rather as having a rebellious Child trying to get free from a punitive inner Parent.

One of my most useful tools is what I call my summary sheet, which consists of a piece of paper $8\frac{1}{2}$ by 11 inches that is laid out as shown in the accompanying figure. The top half and bottom half are identical because I see many couples, and having them on the same sheet makes it easier for me to review their patterns of transacting with each other, their games, scripts, and basic life positions of OKness and not OKness and how they fit together.

The top of the first column is for the person's positions, games, and scripts. The bottom of that column is for contracts, with the date that the contract is agreed upon and the date it is completed. As most people I see have a series of contracts, this is a useful checkup. Often, after termination, a client will decide to come in yearly for a "TA mental health checkup." A review of these contracts makes the checkup practical and productive.

The second column is for a list of symptoms—physical, psychological, those observed, and those reported by clients. I jot down their self-descriptive words, using quote marks so that their symptoms, as they see them, can be discussed

NAME ———————— ADDRESS ———————— PHONE ————

Initial Session (Date)   Referral Source

Positions, Stamps, Games, Scripts	Symptoms	Current Situation	Parent Figures	Childhood
	Client's Complaints			
Contracts: dates made & completed				

Positions, Stamps, Games, Scripts	Symptoms	Current Situation	Parent Figures	Childhood
	Client's Complaints			
Contracts: dates made & completed				

later and not mistranslated in my head. A psychiatric history and a brief physical history may also go here—including any medication the client may be taking. It is very important for TA therapists to know something about the physical health of the persons they are seeing. Many of the people I see need more complete physical examinations than they are accustomed to getting. I tell them that this is essential. For example, long-standing depression is occasionally related to functional hypoglycemia, which can easily be controlled. The exam may also break up a game of hypochondria—or it may reveal a serious condition that has been ignored but needs treatment. The care or lack of care that clients give their bodies is often symptomatic of psychological problems.

The next item in the second column is complaints—meaning *their* complaints, their presenting problem and subsequent ones, again in their words to avoid mistranslation.

The third column, current situation, is where I jot down items such as hobbies, job, marital status, the names and ages, of any children they may have, and so on. If a couple has a stereotypical way of transacting with each other, I sometimes add a small relationship diagram such as:

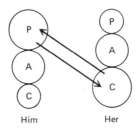

Him   Her

In the column on parent figures, I first put an initial for each significant parent figure the client had in childhood: for example, M for mother, SM for stepmother, listing all persons who had parental responsibility. This might include older siblings, housekeepers, grandparents. After each initial I list adjectives, again in the client's language. I ask, usually during the initial session: "Who were your parent figures when you were little? What words would describe them, *the way you perceived them when you were little?*" This is an important technique, as it will reveal who is in the client's Parent ego state and what might be expected when the Parent has inner dialogue with the Child or transacts outwardly with others. It may also reveal the need for reparenting (which will be discussed in a later chapter).

The last column is for childhood data including the age and sex of siblings, traumatic experiences such as death, serious illness, or desertion of a family member and the client's age when it occurred, adjectives to describe his or her home and where he or she lived (for example, children reared in a large metropolitan city are likely to have different experiences than those reared in rural areas) and a word or two of how the client was disciplined and what he or she did for fun.

In my experience, the element of fun is often overlooked by therapists. Yet many clients need to recover this capacity—or even to learn, sometimes for the first time, that it's OK to be happy, to laugh, and to enjoy life. Learning how to do this is a common TA contract.

CONTRACT THEORY AND TECHNIQUES

The establishment and completion of contracts is one of the most important TA techniques that can be used for effective therapy.

A contract is a bilateral, not a unilateral, agreement between the therapist and client.[5] It is a clear statement in operational form of the individual or interpersonal problems to be solved and the action required to solve them. It is absolutely essential that the statement be clear, concise, and direct, rather than vague or generalized; it must be realistic, with an achievable goal.

According to Cassidy and Steiner, the TA contract must have four basic requirements that are adapted from the field of law: mutual consent, valid consideration, competency, and lawful object.[6] *Mutual consent* means that a client specifies what he or she wants to be cured of and the therapist agrees to perform certain services related to the cure. *Valid consideration* is the benefit that is agreed upon, such as money, attendance, participation, etc. *Competency* refers to the client as well as the therapist; minors, incompetents, and people under drugs cannot enter a valid contract. *Lawful object* means that the contract must not violate the law or be "against public policy or morals."

Contracts can be made around the relief of (1) physical symptoms, such as ulcers, (2) psychological symptoms, such as a phobia, or (3) a change in behavior, such as getting a job. They may also be quantitative, such as increased earnings or lowered blood pressure. Berne writes:

> . . . the contract may refer to symptoms characteristic of particular disorders, such as hysterical paralyses, phobias, obsessions, somatic symptoms, fatigue, and palpitation in the neuroses; forgery, excessive drinking, drug addiction, delinquency, and other such game-like behavior in the psychopathies; pessimism, pedantry, sexual impotence, or frigidity in the character disorders; hallucinations, elation, and depression in psychoses.[7]

Contracts usually require some kind of change based on specific goals. Contracts involve an awareness that a problem exists, a decision (made by the Adult) to solve the problem, a plan of action related to the goal, and a means of evaluating the progress and the completion.

While in therapy clients may work on several contracts simultaneously, preferably starting with small ones that are easily achieved and which act as positive reinforcement. Thus they are encouraged to continue their personal growth with ever-increasing strengths and competencies. Sometimes the original contracts do not turn out to be the most effective ones or the most important. If so, amendments are made from time to time.

Initial contracts are designed to decontaminate the Adult. Later in the treatment process they are designed to deal with a client's pathology. The reason for this order is that if the client's Adult is relatively decontaminated, it will act as an aid to the therapist and a protector to the possibly psychotic- or neurotic-acting Child.

William and Martha Holloway speak of two kinds of contracts—a *social control* contract which is designed to change behavior that interferes with satisfying social relationships, and an *autonomy* contract which is designed to restructure the personality so that clients have more freedom to choose from the many options available to them and to experience intimacy.[8]

Lois Johnson has developed a contract for couples who are considering divorce. It is called Decourting for Divorce. She writes that a decourting period is necessary because it provides opportunity for legitimate transactions while recovering from the romantic fantasies of "living happily ever after." Contract elements of decourting are that each person agrees to "(1) enjoy each other's OK Child, (2) unravel the relationship gently, (3) deal realistically with childlike wishing, (4) acknowledge that *all* persons are important, and (5) become aware that, 'If I devalue you, I devalue myself.' "[9]

The technique I most often use when establishing contracts is to ask five questions, the first of which is: "Is there anything you want that would enhance your life?" The second is: "What would you need to change to get what you want?" If the client starts complaining about spouse, children, business associate, etc., I restate the question with, "Well, unless they come in, we are not likely to change them. Are there any changes *you* could make in yourself that would enhance your life?"

After this is clarified, I ask the third question: "What would you be *willing to do* to effect the change?" As many clients go to therapists with the expectation that the therapist will "do them something," this question indicates that the client is also expected to work. Some contracts require two plans of action—

one for how the client will work on the contract outside the group, another for how he or she will work on it inside the group.

The fourth question is "How would other people know when the change has been made?" This often comes as a surprise. "What difference does it make!" clients might retort. I tell them about the value of positive strokes as reinforcement. For example, parents who stop screaming at their children do better if the children note it and comment on it. Such parents may need to put a sign on the refrigerator saying, "Please notice how I've stopped screaming at you." The sign acts as a reminder and children are often amazed when they find out their parents can change. The modeling process gives them permission to do likewise.

The fifth and last question is, "How might you sabotage yourself?" The answer to this reveals the behavior and games that a client would engage in to undermine himself or herself.[10]

A concrete example of this technique is of a woman who contracted to lose five pounds (the desired change). She was willing to ignore sweets (which was easy as she didn't really like them), and curb her indulgence in French bread and butter (which she liked very much) by limiting herself to one piece once a week. She was also willing to swim and golf regularly, though not willing to jog or do sitting-up exercises, and said that others would know when she completed her contract by the way her clothes would fit. Her sabotage would be to get overly tired by playing *Harried,* at which time she would listen to her mother tape in her head that would advise her to "eat to keep up your strength."

Another example is that of an insurance man who contracted to drink no more than three ounces of hard liquor a day, who was willing to eat dinner earlier and avoid eating luncheons at restaurants with bars, who said his wife would notice it first because he would not fall asleep right after dinner and would be potent sexually. His sabotage would be to continue making sales calls through the dinner hour until he would get "too tired to eat, to start drinking so as to forget the whole day."

It is vitally important that contracts be very specific. Then they are measurable by both client and therapist. Contracts that are not achieved are those that are like New Year's Eve resolutions of the Child. Careful listening to the common words and phrases used in making contracts often reveals that a noncontract has been made:

"I'd *like* to change (this thing)," or "I think I might (do this)," are noncontract phrases. Nothing will happen. Contract phrases would be, "I'm going to change (this thing),'' or "I've thought about it and I will (do this)." "I'd like to explore . . ." is a noncontract phrase *unless it's followed by specifics,* such as, "I'd like to explore various vocations *and* I will do it by. . . ."[11]

Another technique which I often add to the third question I ask when setting a contract (What is the client willing to do?) is to detail when, where, how, and with whom. Valid contracts are not flabby, evasive, or unrealistic. They are practicable, reasonable, and measurable. For example: "cutting down on smoking" is a non-contract. A valid contract will specify the number of cigarettes to be smoked or cut out.

If both client and therapist keep a record of contracts, when they are made and when completed, the record serves as a focal point during group and individual sessions and as a tool for review. Occasionally, people are disappointed in their progress. Looking over the contracts that have already been completed restores to them a sense of potency.

When clients move away, they sometimes wish to maintain contact by phone. When this is the case, an appointment is set and the therapy session is conducted almost as though we were in the same room. The summary sheet shown earlier, which includes all contracts, is an important aid in this process.

PHASES OF TREATMENT

For convenience, it can be said that there are three phases of treatment. The first is primarily that of establishing a working relationship between therapist and client in which healing and problem-solving can take place. The middle phase might be called the working-through phase, because the causes and dynamics of the problems are identified and worked on. The client takes an increasingly active role in solving the problems. The third phase is the termination process, which, hopefully, both client and therapist agree to.[12]

Phase 1: Establishing the Relationship

The establishment of an adequate working relationship between client and therapist is of primary importance in the beginning phase of treatment. Motivating, informing, understanding, and goal-setting are parts of this phase. Some clients are motivated to accept therapy, others are not. They may have been sent by a judge, a physician, employer, or someone else with power to suggest the necessity for treatment. If they are not motivated, time must be spent developing this incentive, which is related to a feeling of trust. A sense of trust must be developed in the beginning phase of treatment so that clients are more able to deal with the anxiety often experienced in the middle phase. Some therapists hurry through this initial phase or ignore it out of a desire to get on with "the real problem." Consequently, they are likely to be unsuccessful in establishing or achieving winning contracts.

It is also important during this beginning phase for the client to receive some straight information about TA as a theory and as a therapeutic tool. Its current popularity is an aid, but it is necessary to clarify concepts and remove misconceptions about therapy in general, and about how TA in particular is used in therapy. In my office I keep a supply of the pamphlet by Leonard Campos and Paul McCormick, *Introduce Yourself to Transactional Analysis,* and often give one to a new client, suggesting that it be read for useful information. Several other effective TA therapists ask clients to use the workbook, *Winning With People,* which I coauthored with Dorothy Jongeward, and to fill in the blanks of each exercise as homework to be discussed in subsequent meetings or to work through the material in *Born to Win,* or, if appropriate, *TA for Moms and Dads.* My new book, *The New Self* (in press), which I coauthored with Louis Savary, is specifically designed for therapy. It has over 300 brief exercises and techniques that can be used by an individual or by groups.

A third crucial task for the therapist in the beginning phase is to let the client know that his or her problem is understandable and the pain can be alleviated. Clients often use their Little Professors during the initial sessions to "psyche" out the therapist's ability to understand the pain and the problem. To say "I understand" is not as effective a technique as active listening, clear information, and the sending of noncondemning verbal and nonverbal responses which serve as messages to the client that this is a new kind of relationship and help is forthcoming.

A basic policy many TA therapists use to show their ability to understand is to not interrupt if a client is talking readily and spontaneously. They obtain specific information after the spontaneous account by asking pointed questions. In some cases, however, they take a more active role and interrupt, encourage, and comfort. They may do this with clients who:

1. seem totally helpless and overcome by their problems or are too upset to talk, or act resentful, ashamed, or guilty for needing therapy;

2. verbalize and rationalize about therapy in general or about other therapists in particular rather than discuss their own problems; or

3. act tongue-tied, as though not knowing what to say, or go silent for extended periods of time.

In any of these cases, giving active feedback to clients about the feelings they may be experiencing usually helps free them from understandable resistances they have built up over many years.

Another therapeutic task during the beginning phase of treatment is the tentative setting of goals and the contracts that are needed to achieve those goals. This may be met with some resistance. After all, people who come for therapy usually have unsatisfactory patterns of behavior that are so long-standing that any suggestions of change may be threatening. However, if the previous three steps have been achieved, then the setting of goals is often eagerly sought.

At any time during the beginning phase, the therapist may decide to refer a client to some other person or to some other situation. If it is an early decision, the therapist may interrupt and give this information, supporting it with a reasonable explanation. Clients who have gone through a lengthy discussion of their problems may be resentful at not being told earlier and may feel unwilling to transfer to someone else.

Therapists who know they have no time available on their schedules should ask themselves why they agreed to conduct an initial interview. The reasons may be valid or not valid if related to a game they are playing. A valid reason could be that it is a true crisis and no one else is available, or that the client is too upset to even consider someone else. An invalid, game reason would be that the therapist's games are, "Look How Hard I'm Trying (to give appointments to everyone who wants to see me)," or "They'll Be Glad They Knew Me (I'm so available, effective, or charismatic)."

Valid reasons for referring someone include: (1) the belief that some other therapist would be more effective with the client because of the nature of the problem or because of the client's personality, (2) the therapist's and client's available hours may not coincide, (3) the fees cannot be worked out, the client may prefer a different therapeutic method or someone of a different sex, age, or race.

Game reasons for referring clients include: (1) the unresolved need to be a temporary Rescuer, trying to impress clients with skills or importance or trying to impress other therapists by giving them a referral, (2) the unresolved need to be a Persecutor by sending clients away after indicating they might get some help, or (3) the unresolved need to be a Victim by crowding the calendar, then "giving up" an interesting or profitable client and referring the person to someone else.

According to Berne, regardless of how active or inactive therapists are during the beginning phase of treatment, there are two basic concerns that must always be kept in mind:

> The first concern of all healing arts is not to injure, to cut only when and where necessary, but then to cut cleanly and with clear knowledge of what

is being cut into. The group therapist, then, must become aware of the possibilities of damaging his patients by bruising them, by misleading them (especially sinful and wicked toward the young), by opening up areas of pathology without proper preparation, or by losing them in such a way that they will be unable afterward to avail themselves of the services of other psychotherapists. Specifically, he should wield the interpretive knife gently, though firmly and steadily; he should avoid entering sequestered areas of psychosis until the patient has been fully prepared to meet face to face what he has so long sequestered; and he should be careful not to agree too quickly with derogatory statements of a patient concerning a parent or spouse. He should not poke into any traumatized areas until he is ready to finish what he begins and feels assured that the patient can survive the procedure. His first task, therefore, is to locate such areas and estimate their extent, in order to avoid them until the time has come for them to be explored.[13]

The therapist's second concern, says Berne, is to locate the healthy areas in each person's personality so as to nurture them and strengthen their potential. Some physical and mental healthy areas are always underneath the unhealthy parts. They may only have been obstructed, and these obstructions can be removed.[14]

What these concerns mean in concrete terms is that TA therapists need to know just what it is that they know and, equally important, what they don't know. For example, therapists who are not medically trained need to know the dynamics of psychosomatic problems so that they don't use non-TA methods which may be injurious to their clients, such as allowing persons with high blood pressure or ulcers to bang pillows to express anger. Therapists not theologically trained need to understand how the dynamics and values of people with strong religious beliefs may be positive factors in their lives, not necessarily negative ones to be discounted or destroyed. And therapists not trained in education need to know developmental psychology and how learning does or does not take place and what can be done about it.

All therapists, regardless of their basic orientation, need to develop techniques so that they do *not* open up problems in areas where they have no expertise. Switching the subject is one way; referring the client to someone else is another. All therapists also need postponing or delaying techniques which can be used when clients need more inner strength before dealing with their pain. Building on the healthy parts of the personality before dealing with the unhealthy parts is a potent way to do this.

Phase 2: Working-Through

The middle phase of treatment begins when a working relationship has been established between client and therapist and when the client is motivated to accept therapy, has initial information about TA, feels accepted and understood, and has established a temporary or initial contract.

Unique personality patterns and patterns of transacting with others become apparent in the middle phase. Attitudes and values, symptoms and defenses, feelings of security and esteem (and the lack of them), can be dealt with during the middle phase, all within the context of the contracts that have been adapted and the clients' willingness to work on the contracts. Contracts can be associated during this phase with several forms of TA analysis: (1) ego states and how to correct ego-state boundary problems, (2) transactions and how to use strokes and target stroking, (3) games and how to break them up, (4) scripts and how to rewrite them, and (5) time structuring and how to improve it.

For example, a person who contracts to make friends may want to discover what in each ego state hinders or aids the process, what kinds of transactions are most effective in the developing of friendships,[15] the games he or she would get involved in to avoid meaningful friends, the script themes that interfere with this goal, and the different ways time would have to be structured for the contract to be completed.

The way TA is used during the middle phases depends upon the therapeutic contract and the knowledge, skills, and style of treatment that the therapist uses. To date there have not been any statistical studies on TA therapists and the ego state they use most often in treatment groups. It appears as though some therapists favor one ego state over the other with the expected rate of successes as well as failures. Each may knowingly or unknowingly use TA as what has been traditionally known as supportive therapy, as reeducative therapy, or as reconstructive therapy. It is important that TA therapists understand the differences between these three types of therapies. Wolberg writes:

> In supportive therapy, we may merely seek to identify and to bring the patient to an awareness of discordant elements in his environment that activate his turmoil, so as to help us in their control. Here, an examination of factors that promote the situational entanglement, and study of the effects on the patient of his disturbance, may be all that is attempted. In reeducative therapy, there may be an exploration of the patient's more conscious interpersonal reactions, the ensuing difficulties that follow expression of his personality patterns, and the provocative individuals and situations that keep existing distortions alive. These therapeutic tasks are implemented by the conventional interviewing techniques.

> In reconstructive psychotherapy, the task is more ambitious, since the level of exploration is on the unconscious strata of mind. The symbolic extensions of unconscious conflicts are explored through a number of techniques. . . . The contamination of rational behavior with derivatives of the unconscious is investigated and analyzed. There is also an inquiry into the genetic origin of the individual's conflicts, the determining childhood experiences that initiated and produced character distortions and maladaptive mechanisms of defence.[16]

Translated to TA terminology, *supportive therapy* is often the chicken-soup variety that supports people in destructive or going-nowhere feelings and behavior. "From the transactional point of view, supportive therapy is regarded as intrinsically spurious. Parental supportive statements (known colloquially as "throwing marshmallows" or "gumdrops") are fundamentally patronizing, and transactionally they are brush-offs." Berne was against supportive therapy except with particular cases, such as with schizophrenics orphaned in childhood.[17] Supportive therapy in these cases focuses on the reduction of pain and symptoms. The client's not-OK feelings are lessened and the person is freer of debilitating anxiety. TA supports this growth.

Reeducative therapy, in TA terms, aims to correct unsatisfactory behavior by changing transactional patterns of response. Clients are taught to give up "hard" game playing in favor of more satisfying social relationships. Behavior modification is one type of reeducative therapy some therapists use with TA.[18]

Reconstructive therapy focuses on difficulties of personality caused by ego-state boundary problems. These problems are solved in therapy. A client is able to develop new resources because of achieving an uncontaminated Adult. Psychoanalysis is one type of reconstructive therapy.

Throughout TA therapy then, each of these three therapeutic orientations may be used. Even in the first phase, techniques that are supportive of health will be used. As simple a tool as active listening and feedback often reduce painful symptoms. This healing process continues into middle phase and it is usually during this second phase of therapy, preferably within a group structure, that reeducation occurs. Clients become aware of how they transact with others, what response they may expect because of their transactions (including transference and countertransference), the resistances they have to change, and the many options they have for different behavior.

Reconstructive therapy may start during the first phase and may continue, depending on the contract, until the client is ready for termination, hopefully having translated insight and understanding into action.

Whenever restructuring the personality is a focus of the therapeutic process, techniques such as those from Gestalt therapy may be used for the working-through. This process may be slow as basic patterns based on childhood decisions are being challenged. Therapists and clients may become discouraged because of what seems to be erratic or no improvement—or even a regression to old defenses. When this occurs, I find it useful to explain how therapy is like learning to speak a new language, or how to walk. When learning a new language, people often become frustrated and impatient and want to quit. If their motivation is high enough, they continue to study in spite of their negative feelings and eventually master their new skills. When learning to walk, children also become frustrated. They revert to crawling, to lying down and screaming, to sucking their thumbs passively. Then they get up and practice walking again. This seems to occur frequently when learning something new. Resistance to change is normal, so is the desire for change. The therapist can put weight on the latter so that the desire becomes a reality.

According to Berne, therapeutic operations that form the techniques of TA fall into eight categories. As a general rule, they are used in logical sequence. The first four are called interventions. Using these the therapist interrogates, specifies, confronts and explains to *decontaminate* the Adult. The second four are interpositions. With these, the therapist illustrates, confirms, interprets, and crystallizes. Each of these are attempts by the therapist "to interpose something between the patient's Adult and his other ego states in order to stabilize his Adult and make it more difficult for him to slide into Parent or Child activity." All eight are used in certain situations, not in others.[19] Briefly, the four interventions are:

1. *Interrogate:* To ask questions to clarify points that will be of clinical value. Interrogation is used when something needs to be documented and the client's Adult is likely to respond, not the Parent or Child, or when the therapist needs to find out which ego state would respond to a particular question.

2. *Specify:* A statement made by the therapist to "fix" information in the client's mind that might be referred to later. It is used when the therapist believes the client might later deny that he or she said or meant something, or as preparation for an explanation that will follow.

3. *Confront:* The use of previous information to disconcert and point out inconsistencies for the purpose of cathecting the uncontaminated part of the client's Adult. It is well used when the client *is* playing *Stupid* and the therapist is *not* playing Persecuting games such as *Blemish,* or *Now I've Got You,* or Rescuing games such as *Why Don't You?*

4. *Explain:* To strengthen and decontaminate the client's Adult. Explanation is used when the Adult is listening and sometimes if the client is wavering between game-playing and authenticity.

The interposition operations are:

5. *Illustrate:* Used to stabilize the Adult. It may follow a successful confrontation *if* the Expressive Child, as well as the Adult, is likely to hear. It may also soften undesirable effects of confrontation as the Adult is likely to hear.

6. *Confirm:* Is used if the Adult is strong enough so that new information won't be used by the client's Parent against his or her inner Child or used by the Child against the therapist. It continues the process of reinforcing ego-state boundaries.

7. *Interpret:* Is what the therapist may do when the client's Adult has joined forces and become cotherapist. Interpretation is related to the pathway of the Child. It is not used if it directly opposes the Parent or asks too much sacrifice from the Child or arouses too much fear of Parental retaliation or desertion.[20]

8. *Crystallize:* Is only used when each ego state is prepared for it. It is a statement from the therapist's Adult to the client's Adult that summarizes the client's positions and the available choices.

At this point, with or without interpretation, the middle phase of therapeutic task is finished in the areas that are covered by the contracts. For each new contract these techniques can be repeated.

As a supervisor of TA therapists, I have found these eight words difficult for many trainees to remember as they are so abstract. Beginning TA therapists might memorize the list yet not have the concepts integrated into their own practice. More advanced therapists might use them simply by intuition and experience.

For self-supervision the therapist can replay tapes to observe the techniques used and the sequence for using them. He or she can then question their appropriateness for particular clients. In any group, at a particular time, one client may need to be confirmed, another may need to be confronted. Each is unique and needs a plan of treatment specifically tailored to his or her blocks to growth and mental health.

Phase 3: Termination

The third phase of therapy is termination. It may be a temporary interruption or it may be permanent. It may be accidental, as in the case of a client who has to move from the area, or it may be a cooperative plan by both client and therapist. It may sometimes be an autonomous decision made by the client alone.

Termination may also be a game—as it would be, for example, if the client entered therapy not to get cured, but only to learn how to play games more comfortably. Premature termination is especially noticeable if a client de-escalates games from third degree (with a payoff of homicide or suicide) to second degree (with the payoff of a quit). The client usually feels so much better that unless the therapist is alert to the possibility of suddenly finding that client's chair empty—it is. When I sense that this is a possibility I explain it, and often suggest a contract that de-escalates games even further—from second degree to first degree—to be replaced by more activity and initimacy. If clients still choose to terminate prematurely, I suggest that they come back, at least yearly, for a mental health checkup. Thus we part on an amicable basis without any games of *Blemish* or *Now I've Got You.*

Berne says there are other reasons clients quit prematurely:

> ... he will *quit* if the therapist declines to play entirely, and also if the therapist is a pigeon and can be too easily conned. In this respect, transactional games are like chess: an enthusiastic chess player is not interested in people who do not want to play at all, nor in people who do not offer any real opposition. In a treatment group, a confirmed *Alcoholic* player will get angry if no one offers to rescue or persecute him, or play the patsy or the connection, and will soon leave. He will also leave if the rescuers are too sentimental, or the persecutors too vehement, because there is no fun if he hooks them too easily. Like other game players, he prefers a little finesse and some reticence on the part of his partners or opponents.[21]

Termination does occur, however, and it is the therapist's responsibility to see it coming, advises Berne, "and not try to pick up the pieces afterward."[22] Furthermore, if a group is truly therapeutic, other group members may need to discuss their own feelings about someone leaving.

If clients have enough control so that they will not injure themselves or others, then each time they complete a contract the question can be raised about whether or not further therapy would be useful. I think that in some instances clients need to continue even though they may choose to terminate. Such was the case with a client of mine whose contract was to decide whether or not he wanted a divorce. He was very depressed and knew it, and was not interested in changing that condition. I prefer people to experience joy and laughter in living. Usually they are willing to go along with this value of mine (which I no doubt show, though seldom mention). This man would not. The depression was a part of his script that he was not interested in rewriting. "All I want out of therapy," he said, "is to decide about my marriage." Because contracts are bilateral and allow for individual choice and decision, termination was acceptable, though perhaps premature.

When termination is therapeutic and clearly indicated, I find it useful to review contracts made and contracts completed, to ask clients to imagine what other persons who know them well would think about the changes that have been made. I ask if they want group feedback—and if so, why, and if not, why not? If they want feedback, it often indicates their new "I'm OK–You're OK" position. If they don't, it often indicates that their life position is still unhealthy.

Sometimes I ask clients if they would be willing to experiment, being put under stress to see if they can manage it from the Adult. This technique is often used in stress units in prisons and hospitals before people are released, and I find it useful in private practice. If the client agrees to this procedure, then I, and often the entire group, say the kinds of things—and often roleplay the people —that originally flipped the client into scripty behavior. When these transactions are well handled by the client, who is now relatively free of games, it is not unusual for the group to cheer or show some other form of approval. And why not!

During the second or third stages of treatment, I sometimes suggest that clients make a contract to stimulate the natural Child from is long hibernation so that the sense of pleasure and delight with life can be freely experienced. I consider the recovery of the sense of joy so important that I regularly hold weeklong marathons in situations that are conducive to this process. There, laugh therapy, body enhancement, altered states of consciousness, and sensory enjoyment are stressed. These emphases, rather than the working through childhood traumas or increasing Adult information, become the focus of contracts. For most participants the results are exciting, positive, and permanent, because replacing pain and distress with joy and laughter is conducive to health and autonomy.

THE TA GROUP PROCESS

Groups can be categorized in several ways. One way is as homogeneous or heterogeneous groups. Some organizations require therapists to have homogeneous groups, for example when dealing with alcoholics, drug addicts, juvenile delinquents, etc. However, the preferred TA group is heterogeneous.[23]

TA trainees often ask supervisors such questions as: "How do you get a group started?" and "What do you do first?"

Many therapists organize a group simply by telling their individual clients or professional peers of their intention. As some therapists are also educators, they sometimes tell their students about their plans to have groups. Advertising in a newspaper or magazine is usually considered to be unprofessional, and licensed therapists seldom resort to this kind of announcement.

Although many clients prefer evening groups, there seems to be a growing number of persons who can arrange for noontime or later afternoon sessions. In private practice, groups usually meet once a week for an hour and a half (though some therapists prefer two hours). In institutional care, groups may meet weekly, semiweekly, and even daily. Traditionally, groups have been made up of eight members, which seems to be about the most that a therapist can observe well. More than that often increases the amount of energy therapists must put out and simultaneously decreases therapeutic effectiveness, but not always.

Some groups are open-ended, meaning that they continue indefinitely; some are established for a specified number of weeks. Both have advantages and disadvantages. Advantages of the open-ended group include: the convenience to the therapist of having a regular schedule, the convenience of being able to add new members whenever space becomes available, and the feeling that there will be enough time to work things through so that no one needs to be pressured to hurry. When a group is open-ended, new members may be encouraged by the progress reports of others. Old members may be educated by the new problems and solutions. A disadvantage of open-ended groups is that clients and therapists may settle in for an indefinite period of time, be passive, and work slower than necessary.

Advantages of groups meeting for a specified number of weeks include: the ease of referral or renegotiation of contract at the end of that time, the willingness of some clients to commit themselves to brief therapy when they would not agree to an indefinite time commitment, the challenge to the therapist to be effective quickly, and the sense of pressure to achieve contracts while there is still time. Also, when the number of meetings is specified, the phases of therapy are generally more identifiable in the group as a whole than when the number of meetings is open-ended. And yet, any of these so-called advantages may also be disadvantages.

Some clients are sophisticated regarding group therapy. Others are skeptical or unreceptive, reluctant or unready, fearful of the group, or, in a few cases, ineligible.[24] Each needs to be considered individually so that the group work can be effective.

As previously noted, it is advisable to have at least one interview with clients before they enter a group. If this is not possible, then some explanation can be given by the therapist, and perhaps other group members, about TA—its use in the group, and how and why contracts are established. This information should be presented briefly, in small doses, and over a period of several group sessions, to clarify what is going on in the group. Additional information for new group members should include the time the group will begin and end, the way fees will be paid, permission for anyone to "say anything whatsoever with no exception,"[25] and the fact that no physical violence is allowed.

As the group begins to assemble, there is often a brief period of rituals and pastimes while the members get settled. Good TA therapists are in the business of curing people, not making them feel "comfortable," so they do not introduce group members to each other. Instead they carefully observe what goes on, who transacts with whom and in what way.

As the therapist sits down, hopefully with a clear mind and fresh perspective, the meeting seems about to begin. Often clients look around, using their Little Professors to psyche out others so that they can determine what might happen next. New therapists sometimes feel the need "to do something." When this is the case, and the therapist needs more experience to feel more adequate, an advance plan for what to do is useful. Often a simple restatement of the hours that the group will meet is sufficient.

Everyone who enters groups, including the therapist, does so with a personal agenda which may or may not be part of a contract, and, knowingly or unknowingly, also brings what Berne called a *provisional group imago*.[26] The group imago is the image or fantasy of what the group will be like and how the members will transact with each other. It is likely to be different in the mind of each client as well as in the mind of the therapist.

With new groups, I sometimes inquire about these fantasies. The answers frequently reveal catastrophic expectations or expectations of Santa Claus, especially the Santa Claus role expected of the therapist. Some clients tend to believe that the therapist is a magician, and that if they comply with the magician's demands they will get presents as though from Santa Claus. The giving up of this delusion is a gradual process that occurs as the Adult becomes stronger and recognizes the real world for what it is. If asked to give up the belief in magic too soon, clients may terminate therapy prematurely or experience severe depression. The alert therapist will not allow this to happen, being careful to respect people's defenses and not removing them until something better has been put in their place.

A basic technique to provide that "something better" is to focus on contracts that have been established in a previous private session or in the group itself. Although group members may become involved in each other's contracts, those contracts are not basically made with the group members; they are bilateral agreements between the therapist and the client.

During the first group session, after the usual brief rituals and pastimes, it is useful to have members state their contracts and how they are going to work on them—especially how they are going to work on them in the group. In a marathon group, these contracts and the four steps involved are written out on large sheets of paper and fastened to the walls or curtains. They thus become a referral point that serves to focus their client's energies. Groups that meet weekly often find it very helpful to use the same process of having written contracts. It is a way of hooking the Adult, and thus beginning the process of decontamination.

In open-ended groups the review of contracts is likely to occur anytime a new member joins, and the way the review goes can provide the therapist with important information. It *is not* appropriate to go around the circle asking each one in turn. That sets up a teacher-student or Parent-Child relationship. It *is* appropriate to make the request, then to observe in what order the group members speak, and then to think about the possible significance of the order.

If people are unsure about what contracts they wish to make, I suggest that they learn to identify ego-state behavior as a starter, or to think over, for a few sessions, what they want to work on.

Although some therapists effectively do one-to-one therapy in the presence of the group, TA is designed for group interaction as well as for the therapist's interventions and interpositions. The amount of group involvement often is related to how active a role the therapist takes during the early phases of the group. An overactive "being-helpful" therapist will encourage dependence and passivity in clients. An underactive therapist will encourage confusion, frustration, indifference, or anger in clients. This is an issue the therapist needs to deal with, for what is overactive in one person's eyes may be underactive to another.

A continuing important issue in the group process is how problems are recognized and solved or how they are ignored and therefore remain unsolved. In the latter case, it is usually because of some form of discount. Aaron and Jacqui Schiff write:

> There are four possible ways to discount.
> 1. *Discount the problem.* Example: The baby is crying. The mother turns up the radio or goes to sleep.
> 2. *Discount the significance of the problem.* Example: The baby is crying. The mother says, "He always cries this time of day."
> 3. *Discount the solvability of the problem.* Example: The baby is crying. The mother says, "Nothing satisfies him!"
> 4. *Discount the person.* Example: The baby is crying. The mother says, "There's nothing I can do!"[27]

Very often, even during the first group session, the discounting of the problem, or of oneself, or of others, will be obvious. However, the confrontation by the therapist when clients do this must be carefully timed, or the therapist will be seen as a Persecutor. In a few cases, after the Adult has been well stabilized, I have asked clients who sabotage their contracts by discounting them, to try an experiment for one session. The rules of the experiment are that each time they verbally or nonverbally discount a problem, themselves, or someone else, they put a dollar in a cup in the middle of the floor. One man who agreed to this discovered that in 15 minutes he discounted 10 times, and accordingly had put out $10. His new awareness of this pattern motivated his Little Professor to find ways to earn it back and his Adult to solve his problems rather than avoid them.

The use of a treatment plan is essential in TA, and therapists tend to keep their clients informed of what is happening to them, how far they have progressed, and what still needs to be done. They also teach clients the few words that make up the basic vocabulary of TA, as well as the structural and transactional diagrams. These things are best explained briefly with illustrations from the group—and always with the goal in mind of establishing "open and authentic communication between the affective and intellectual components of personality."[28]

Because TA is a "talking" therapy, questions about feelings and how they are dealt with are often asked. TA therapists distinguish between authentic feelings and spurious ones. The latter are called rackets, because they allow the client to indulge himself or herself in feelings of guilt, inadequacy, hurt, fear, and resentment.[29] These self-indulgences may be encouraged by some therapists who are of the opinion that the expression of specific feelings is "good" for people.

Many therapists seemingly think that the loud expression of anger is *the* magic key to effective therapy. I don't. I think there are other feelings that are equally important and that the experience and expression of feelings may come from any part of the personality. For example, anger is often a racket of a Child, but which Child? The Child of the Parent, in which case the client is using acting as one of their parents actually acted? Or is it coming from the Adapted Child as a rebellious, manipulative device? Or from the Natural Child fighting for survival? Sometimes it comes from the Adult who observes the real tragedies of society and is concerned over people's inhumanity toward each other.

One technique that often works for determining the ego-state source of anger is listening to the pronouns used. A phrase using the word "you," such as "You made me so angry," usually comes from the Parent. A phrase using the word "I," such as "I'm so angry I feel like kicking you," usually comes from the Child. A phrase such as, "I'm really angry at the way some teachers seem to treat children in our school," or "Some legislators ignore their constituents, and I am going to find out if anything can be done about it," usually comes from the Adult.

Laughing as an expression of feelings can also come from any ego state.

> Parental laughter is indulgent or derisive. The Child laugh in the clinical situa-
> tion is irreverent or triumphant. The Adult laugh, which is therapeutic, is the
> laugh of insight, and arises from the absurdity of circumstantial predicament
> and the even greater absurdity of self-deception.[30]

When people laugh, they take in as much oxygen as when they breath deeply.
So the use of laughter can be therapeutic, and there are no statistics to show
that crying or yelling is better than laughing. In fact, I frequently use laugh
therapy as a way of discovering Parent admonishments and Child compliances
against having fun in general and against laughing in particular.

The technique is simply to ask the group to laugh and to keep laughing
whether anything is funny or not. The therapist laughs with the group, laughing in various ways such as a simpering Child and a jolly Santa Claus. It often
becomes funny, always becomes revealing, and frequently gives new permissions. Some may laugh only briefly, often indicating an inner critical Parent
who is against fun. Others may cover their mouths with their hands or endeavor
to laugh silently, which indicates earlier injunctions to "Be quiet" or "Keep
your mouth shut" and so forth. Clients who are or have been ashamed of their
teeth may also resist expressing the Child in this way.

Autonomy implies freedom from patterns and situations that enslave. The
"road to freedom is through laughter," according to Berne, "and until he learns
that, man will be enslaved, either subservient to his masters or fighting to serve
under a new master."[31]

About 10 minutes before the end of a group session, especially if someone is
new to the group and has not spoken, a therapist may direct an open-ended
question to him or her such as, "Is there anything you'd like to say?" This is
often an effective "permission to talk," and aid to active involvement. However,
silence is not necessarily bad, nor does it need to be interpreted as a problem.

As a general rule, meetings should finish on time. Groups or therapists who
ignore the clock, or who have private conversations with some of the members
after other members have gone, are likely to be caught up in some kind of
game. Giving up games is a major step toward autonomy. It helps decontaminate the Adult and radically changes the script because the short negative scenes
that comprise games are no longer acted out.

Gaining autonomy is a lifelong process. When people solve one problem,
another comes into their awareness. As clients and therapists become more
effective with TA, problem-solving becomes a way of life, a challenge that does
not erase the experience of joy. In fact, the process of problem-solving increases
joy, and that is a potent experience.

REFERENCES

1. Wolberg, Lewis R., *The Technique of Psychotherapy*, 2d ed., Part 1 (New York: Grune & Stratton, 1967), pp. 437–439.

2. Therapists working in a clinic or an institutional setting, who may like to see how administrators, managers, and supervisors reveal their OK and not-OK positions through furniture, written communications, job descriptions, etc., see: James, Muriel, *The OK Boss* (Reading, Mass.: Addison-Wesley, 1975).

3. Berne, Eric, *Principles of Group Treatment* (New York: Grove, 1968), pp. 140ff.

4. Ibid., p. 10.

5. Ibid., pp. 88–97: Cf. James, Muriel, and Dorothy Jongeward, *Born to Win: Transactional Analysis with Gestalt Experiments* (Reading, Mass.: Addison-Wesley, 1971), pp. 231–234; 245–251.

6. Berne, *Principles*, p. 90.

7. Steiner, Claude, and William Cassidy, "Therapeutic Contracts in Group Treatment," *TA Bulletin,* April 1969, pp. 29–30.

8. Holloway, William, and Martha Holloway, *Change Now* (Akron, Ohio: Midwest Institute for Human Understanding), pp. 22–23.

9. Johnson, Lois, "Decourting for Divorce," *TA Bulletin* **9**, 35 (1970), p. 100.

10. See James, Muriel, and Louis Savary, *A New Self: Self Therapy with Transactional Analysis* (Reading, Mass.: Addison-Wesley, 1977) for additional questions and subquestions. The book also contains lengthy contract-setting forms: one for use in establishing *individual* contracts, another for use in establishing *interpersonal* contracts.

11. Cf. James, Muriel, and Dorothy Jongeward, *The People Book: Transactional Analysis for Students* (Menlo Park, Calif.: Addison-Wesley, 1975).

12. Richard Erskine isolates six stages of treatment, which reflect the client's particular attitudes and behavior: (1) being defensive, (2) being angry, (3) being hurt, (4) seeing self as a problem, (5) taking responsibility, and (6) forgiving parents. A client may enter therapy at any of these stages. "Although the stages are linear in their progression towards autonomy, a patient may recycle back through one or more stages before progressing." See: Erskine, Richard Gordon, "Six Stages of Treatment," *TA Journal* **3**, 3 (1973), pp. 17–18.

13. Berne, *Principles*, p. 62.

14. Ibid., p. 63.

15. James, Muriel, and Louis Savary, *The Heart of Friendship* (New York: Harper & Row, 1976).

16. Wolberg, *Technique,* p. 615.

17. Berne, *Principles*, pp. 314–315.

18. For details on a carefully controlled and documented comparison study of 904 delinquent young men (15 to 17 years of age), using TA and Behavior Modification, see: McCormick, Paul, "TA and Behavior Modification: A Comparison Study," *TA Journal,* Jan. 1973.

19. Berne, *Principles,* pp. 233–247. Fritz Perls wrote, "What we don't assimilate we eliminate." This is not easy to assimilate and requires careful study of Berne.

20. Berne, *Principles,* p. 244.

21. Berne, Eric, *What Do You Say After You Say Hello?* (New York: Grove, 1972), p. 350.

22. Ibid., p. 354.

23. Mullan, H., and M. Rosenbaum, *Group Psychotherapy, Theory and Practice* (New York: The Free Press, 1962).

24. Berne, *Principles,* p. 47.

25. Ibid., p. 43.

26. Berne, Eric, *The Structure and Dynamics of Organizations and Groups* (Philadelphia: Lippincott, 1963), pp. 5–9. This book is probably Berne's least known, but is essential reading for group therapists.

27. Schiff, Aaron, and Jacqui Schiff, "Passivity," *TA Journal,* Jan. 1971, pp. 71–78.

28. Berne, *Principles,* p. 216.

29. Ibid., p. 309.

30. Ibid., p. 288: Berne, *Hello,* pp. 338–339.

31. Berne, Eric, *Sex in Human Loving* (New York: Simon & Schuster, 1970).

PART 2

mind/body, medicine, and TA

Contributors

ORIENTATION TO PSYCHOSOMATIC DISORDERS
Louis Forman, M.D.

PHYSICAL EXAM AND SCRIPT DECISION: ONE HOUR
William Lowe Mundy, M.D.

CHAPTER 6

orientation to psychosomatic disorders

LOUIS FORMAN

HISTORICAL OVERVIEW

As long as people have recorded their ideas they have been aware that the "mind" is an important factor in physical illness. Socrates, 500 years before Christ, knew that in order to bring about a cure of somatic disease the "whole person" needs to be considered. In poetic literature as old as the Bible there are physical expressions descriptive of emotional attitudes; in an ancient Hebrew prayer the word which refers to obstinacy is literally translated "stiff-necked." Shakespeare's writing is abundantly sprinkled with phrases expressing emotions in somatic terms. Gregory Zilborg's "History of Medical Psychology" is an interesting and informative source of information on this subject.

In view of this long period of awareness of physical and emotional interaction it might seem strange that only within the last 50 years has there been any concerted and serious approach to the scientific exploration of this interdependence. Flanders Dunbar[1] published her first edition of a basic work on this subject in 1935; in this she brought together an already extensive bibliography of previous papers on the mutual effects of physical and emotional factors, and integrated them within some proposed theoretical concepts. This was one of the early works of its kind and it has stimulated what has become a vast literature in the field of "psychosomatic" medicine.

The reasons for the long delay before the beginnings of objective study of somato-psychic interrelationships are interesting for speculation. Probably some explanations may be found in the broadened philosophical perspectives of science generally. Anatomy, chemistry, and physiology were long regarded as the basics; psychological and sociological factors became predominant in the era that nurtured Freud. A truly integrated approach has only begun with the return of the pendulum to a more central position. (Each return of the pendulum from an extreme excursion brings additional ideas or data or both. Acceptance and application of these additions require the imaginative Child and objective Adult that are characteristic of the great scientific minds.)

Some of the most fundamental work in the field was begun by Franz Alexander[2] in the late 1930's. The concepts of "personality profiles" stimulated by Dunbar, currently in vogue in such work as Friedman and Rosenman on coronary disease "personality,"[3] and the concepts of specificity of relationships between emotions and body organs or organ systems have waxed and waned in popularity. In the three decades that have followed, the general subject of "psychosomatic" concepts has burgeoned to such an extent that it infiltrates the whole field of therapy. It is still true that vast numbers of medical practitioners have not been taught anything more of this than the basic facts that emotions (a) influence physical processes, (b) are concomitant with physical disease, and (c) often are the consequence of physical illness. However, there is now an increase in demand for, and teaching of, a clearer understanding of the details of the psycho-physiological unity of the human being.

Large numbers of people in the medical fields still tend to lump together all patients who do not have demonstrable somatic pathology into the categories of "neurotic," "functional," or even "crock," reflecting at best a lack of detailed knowledge and at worst a pejorative attitude. Only relatively few practitioners of the healing arts seem genuinely interested in the differentiation of "psychosomatic" symptoms in Alexander's sense from "hysterical" symptoms; this and others of an important nature were noted in the mid 40's by Grinker and Spiegel.[4,*] These authors carried out investigations which gave rise to a host of additional scientific inquiries into such common knowledge as the occurrence

---

* Alexander described "psychosomatic" processes as emotional stimuli causing both affective experience and chronic prolonged stimulation of smooth (visceral) muscle leading in time to anatomical changes—e.g., increased dependency needs leading to biologically appropriate stimulus of gastric motility and acidity—in time causing ulceration of the gastric mucosa. Hysterical (conversion) symptoms, however, are considered to express in somatic terms some emotion which is repressed (not conscious), and the symptom represents both the forbidden impulse and the punishment for it, e.g., paralysis of the arm when a person is repressing a hostile wish to strike.

of blushing with feelings of shame; the pallor, rapid heart rate, and diarrhea associated with fear; and the reddening of the skin during anger. They pursued the investigation into physiological and biochemical phenomena such as the rise in blood pressure with anger and changes in liver function during anxiety.

NEW DEVELOPMENTS

In the more sophisticated latter half of the 20th century it is easily forgotten that only 40 years ago there were relatively few who knew much about the mechanisms by which unexpressed anger may lead to headache and hypertension, a sense of responsibility and burden to backaches, a hunger for affection and frustrated dependency to gastric ulcers. Similarly, there was little understanding of the bases on which diarrhea and constipation could express anxiety and obstinacy respectively; how asthma and related pulmonary dysfunction resulted from unresolved emotional conflict. In all these, as in the sensation of chest constriction in coronary disease, or in anxiety without coronary disease, the observational data had long been at hand. The scientific study of the underlying processes is the outstanding characteristic of the last 40 years.

The current wide-spread knowledge of and interest in "body language" attests to the increasingly rapid dissemination of information, to the intense interest in "psychosomatic" illness, and to the tremendous advances that have been made in the understanding of the concept. Some of the most useful therapeutic and diagnostic techniques for dealing with psycho-physiological symptoms have been developed in the Gestalt theories that are prominent at the present time. Virginia Satir, primarily concerned with family therapy, offers highly illuminating illustrations of the muscular consequences of attitudinal personality traits.[5] The concepts of Transactional Analysis provide a useful framework for recognizing the wholeness of a person in the expression (by somatic symptoms or overall behavior) of emotions which are "outside awareness." Strong Parent constraints which lead to inhibitions on verbal expressions of Child feelings may result in the common phenomena of a relatively constant Adult who has an ulcer, high blood pressure, a backache, sexual difficulties, or a wide variety of less advanced, or more transient physical symptoms. This is not to mention the whole range of behavior which expresses those feelings which the Child does not verbalize and which his Adult does not recognize. (It seems unnecesary in this book to identify the growing body of literature in the fields of TA and Gestalt. For any who are not aware, however, several basic items are noted in the references at the end of the chapter.)[6,7,8]

Among the most recent developments in studying psychophysiological processes are Biofeedback techniques which also may prove to be exceedingly valuable in the field of therapy. Certainly this development has already proven highly valuable as a means of obtaining information about voluntary control over bodily processes. The methods of Biofeedback Training, in conjunction with the techniques of Operant Conditioning, seem to offer a vastly increased field of usefulness in further explorations of somato-psychic relationships.

An outstanding result of the advent of Biofeedback methods has been the startling awareness that much body process and function which has been considered "unconscious" and outside of voluntary or willful control has now been shown to be susceptible to the influence of conscious, deliberate intent. Traditional anatomical and physiological teaching has held that certain bodily functions are under the influence of the "autonomic" or "vegetative" nervous system, as opposed to those functions under the control of the "voluntary nervous system." The latter functions are, in general, those carried out by the skeletal or "voluntary" muscular system. The former are those that have to do with the cardiovascular system, the gastrointestinal system, the basic respiratory functions, and the endocrine glands. The notion that one can even control his or her own cerebro-cortical electrical discharges has been stunning to many people. An interesting observation is made by Neil Miller, in his introduction to the 1973 Aldine Annual [9] concerning a long-known phenomenon, the placebo effect.* This is in itself, he notes, perhaps an illustration of conscious influence over somatic functions and symptoms which are in the category formerly considered to be under autonomic control.

The work of Alexander and others in the 1930's through the 1950's focused scientific inquiry on the processes by which emotions were expressed physically and influenced by physical pathology, and listed certain groups of disease as "psychosomatic": these are bronchial asthma; gastrointestinal diseases of eating, digesting, and eliminating; cardiovascular disturbances, mainly hypertension, cardiac rate disturbances, and certain headaches including migraine; certain skin disorders; sexual dysfunction, rheumatoid arthritis and "accident-prone" individuals; and metabolic-endocrine dysfunctions of the thyroid, diabetes, and fatigue states.

At about the middle of the 20th century, further important contributions were made by Hans Selye[10] in his attention to the concept of "stress" diseases. In his work and that which has derived from it there has been considerable additional stimulus to understanding the biochemical and anatomical-physiological processes which lead to symptoms and the development of disease. In addition another very important facet in the concept of illness has been thrown into much sharper relief—namely the environmental, social, or "external" influences which stimulate emotions which in turn lead to the development of somatic

---

* The effect of an inert substance given without the knowledge of the patient that the substance has no physiological effect.

symptoms or pathology. Some precursors of this are to be found in the concept of the longitudinal life study of an individual as presented in the work of Adolph Meyer.[11]

Of perhaps even greater practical importance currently is the subsequent focus on an understanding of "changes" in an individual's external life as precipitants of illness. The work of Holms and Rahe[12] provides a readily applicable and often extremely illuminating device in this regard. They derived a list of 40-odd items which measure the relative emotional importance of the events in an individual's life. When, within a given period, a sufficient emotional impact is reached, as measured by this rating scale, it is probable that the individual will develop some form of illness. Conversely, in seeking for possible causes or precipitants for an individual's symptoms this rating scale technique may be applied and much useful data may be obtained regarding the patient's recent life changes.

The emphasis here, unlike the focus on *stress,* is simply on *change.* Whether an event is a happy or sad one is less significant than the amount of change required in life adjustment; whether an individual is promoted or demoted or shifted laterally in his work is less significant than the fact of the change itself. The numerous items listed on the rating scale are in effect a check list of social events —they range from the death of a spouse or a divorce, which have very high emotional impact value, to change in health of a family member, son or daughter leaving home, trouble with the boss, change in church or social activities, to relatively unimportant items such as vacations or minor law violations. This is a useful, practical and relatively simple technique; the limitations are clearly recognizable.

The highly controversial nature of these new developments and techniques is met with excitement, astonishment, rejection, or challenge in varying degrees. Therapists who are highly conservative, traditional, and rigid are, of course, likely to dismiss new developments whenever they are contrary to old beliefs (Prejudicial Parent types). The more open-minded and "young at heart" are likely to investigate, at least. From a combination of open-mindedness (Adult) with excitement, creativity, and imagination (Child), comes increased knowledge and scientific progress.

FRAME OF REFERENCE

The question of how to treat the "psychosomatic" patient, either in the specific sense of Alexander's use of the word or within the broader framework of psychophysiological interrelationships and symptomotology, is often posed eagerly and expectantly. To those with such hopefulness I am inclined to call attention at once to the basic reality in psychotherapy that neither a disease, a symptom, nor an organ is properly the subject of treatment. Rather it is the person who seeks help who is suitably the focus of the treatment. Psychiatrists have been hoping for many years to stimulate the medical profession to give something more than lip service to "functional" illness; and to inculcate a concept of learning about, understanding, and treating the *person* as a whole.

It is just as valid to point out to psychotherapists that a patient with already-defined physical illness requires a similarly total approach. Although that patient may have been referred for treatment of the emotional or psychological basis of the illness, it is the person as a whole who is properly the focus of the therapeutic work, rather than a particular and limited set of symptoms. Whether the patient has an ulcer, eczema, headaches, or other physical syndrome, the therapeutic approach will need to focus on the habits and attitudes, relationships with present and past individuals, self-concepts, goals, and other factors which, in TA language, are subsumed under the notions of Script, Games, Decisions and Injunctions, Options, and Positions.

The same basic factors which are needed in the therapist for the cure of obesity, high blood pressure, and torticollis are also important in the therapist who would treat a patient for angina, impotence, and backache—to the extent that these conditions are related to emotional causes. These requirements of a therapist are interest, skill, and knowledge of the *therapist's own personality* as well as of personality theory. These characteristics will be mediated in therapy by (again TA language) Permission, Protection, and Potency. This is true in psychosomatic disorders no less than in conditions of anxiety, depression, self-defeating behavior, and other primarily emotional dysfunctions.

There are important exceptions, of course. When the patient is undergoing a surgical procedure, under anesthesia, the main requirement of the therapist is skill. It is the Adult of the surgeon which is most important during the period at the operating table. This does not deny the tremendous value of the surgeon's reassuring Parent in the preoperative and postoperative periods. When a bone is broken the patient does not need to be particularly cooperative if he is anesthetized; the physician can do his work alone. Even in the case of an individual already in psychotherapy, when a peptic ulcer hemorrhages the time is not appropriate for a discussion of relationships with mother; the time is appropriate for surgical intervention.

I hope the foregoing has reduced the expectations of psychotherapists who hope to find gems of succinct direction that are specific for curing patients of their psychophysiological and somatic complaints.

It is valid to note that the treatment of a psychosomatic patient is in *some* respects different, at least in the initial stages, from psychotherapy with most patients who voluntarily seek help for overtly psychological or social problems. The patient whose presenting complaint is physical, and who is not yet aware that the cause and the therapy lie in the realm of emotional factors, may be resistant to the idea of psychological treatment. This problem usually arises in the office of the physician who has not found some demonstrable pathology by which to account for the patient's complaint. When the patient has accepted referral to a psychotherapist, hopefully this difficulty has been eliminated or at least reduced. Unfortunately, all too often that is not the case; the patient may have come to the psychotherapist on the persistent recommendation of the physician, but without any insight into the simple fact that somatic symptoms may be caused by emotional conflict. Sometimes the referring physician is not much more aware than the patient is, of the nature of the psychophysiological relationships, but is in effect saying to himself "This must be psychological, there's nothing physically wrong." Unfortunately, almost these identical words are occasionally used with the patient, so that referral to psychotherapy is by exclusion.

REDUCING RESISTANCE

The resistance of a patient to accepting emotional and social factors as contributing to his physical symptoms may be dealt with in various ways. One is simply to focus attention on interests and concerns of the patient other than his symptoms. Questions regarding his activity, work, family, recreation, etc., often lead the patient readily into presentation of considerable material which is informative to the therapist and useful in illuminating the situation for the patient.

Another technique useful for some patients is to give an explanation of physical-emotional interdependence in terms that the patient can hardly avoid recognizing. For example, virtually anyone will recognize that fear leads to an increase in heart rate and that feelings of embarrassment are apt to cause the skin to flush. These and other clear-cut examples of somatic expression of emotion may move the patient to an attitude in which it becomes easier for him to understand illustrations of more symbolic nature. For example, if the patient will double up his fist and hold it tightly closed for a short time he probably will be aware that there is aching and pain in the tightened muscles. By analogy he may then find it easier to accept the idea that when he has reason to be angry and resentful, his neck muscles might be tight even if he doesn't feel angry; instead he might have a sensation of tightness and constriction in the back of his neck and head, i.e., a tight headache, literally "a pain in the neck!" Similarly, the analogy sometimes is readily seen that a sense of carrying a heavy burden may lead to tightening of the muscles of the shoulder girdle or the back, with a resultant backache.

Still another technique for dealing with a patient whose initial interview or interviews are noteworthy for resistance consists in focusing on the "here and now," with little or no reference to the possibility of psychosomatic interrelationships. The patient's manner, mood, and present immediate awareness can be focused on in some instances; the feelings of the patient about coming to psychotherapy can perhaps be recognized as similar to other feelings at other times and other places, etc.

Other techniques depending upon the therapist's observation and understanding of the patient can be significant and decisive. For example, some patients will respond if the psychotherapist emphasizes his or her awareness that pain is just as real whether the origin is emotional conflict or somatic trauma. For other patients the "hooker" may be in the therapist's explicit indication of awareness that the patient does have pain and isn't pretending.

Once the therapeutic process has moved into the phase which focuses on the person who is the patient, rather than on symptoms, the symptoms themselves may soon disappear or be markedly reduced. This is a common phenomenon and is not, of course, the end point in therapy. There is frequently a tendency for the patient and for his or her family and friends to look upon the psychotherapist at this period as somewhat of a wizard. A referring physician, especially one who is aware of the patient as being "a functional case," but who is not particularly "tuned in" to the psychotherapeutic process, may also be highly enthusiastic, and somewhat extravagant in admiration and praise for the psychotherapist's "miracle cure." It is hardly necessary to note that the psychotherapist might also be tempted to believe in his or her extraordinary power, but will do better not to confuse skill with magic.

Some patients come to psychotherapy on the recommendation of a physician, clergyman, or personal friend, with the Child seeking help and the Adult open-mindedly willing to explore. Others come only in response to persistent urging, and these people may be in an Adaptive (conforming) child state. However, they often start in the Adaptive (rebellious) child and play such Games as *Yes, But* (I'll show you, you can't cure me), *If It Weren't For Him (Her),* (I don't need to be here—he (she) does), *Now I've Got You, You S.O.B.* (Who wouldn't be angry—look how much time I'm wasting!), etc., etc.

In short, some patients come to psychotherapy while extremely resistive to the notion that physical symptoms can occur without physical basis. These patients often continue to believe that there is anatomical or physiological dysfunction which the therapists simply have not yet found, and sometime, somewhere, the "real reason" for symptoms or illness can be discovered by someone (Santa Claus, I think). In this connection it is especially important that the psychotherapist be clear about the relationship between the patient, the referring individual—physician or otherwise—and the psychotherapist; the attitudes of each of these people toward the patient's illness are important, although often unexpressed.

THE THERAPEUTIC RELATIONSHIP

An essential therapeutic requirement is that the psychotherapist maintain a strictly confidential relationship with the patient, and that the patient have no doubt about this. When the psychotherapist and the referring physician are to have contact, the patient will be more comfortable knowing that the psychotherapist does not need to reveal *details* to the referring person even though an exchange of some information is desirable. It can be made clear to the patient that the psychotherapist need only confirm for the referring physician such data as "Yes, Mr. Jones does indeed have some considerable degree of anxiety (depression, tendency to suppress feelings, or other significant feature)," or "This patient has a considerable amount of emotional conflict (dysfunction, disorder, and so forth) which is appropriate to his present symptoms," or "This patient has some external stresses which could well account for the increase in his signs and symptoms recently," or "This patient does have emotional stress, of which he is aware, but about which he is unwilling to talk and which is sufficient to have precipitated the symptoms for which he recently came to you."

Not infrequently a patient will disclose to a psychotherapist data which he will not reveal to a referring physician or clergyman despite what has always seemed to be a very close relationship between the patient and these others. As a matter of fact, it is often because of the patient's feeling of closeness that he will not reveal data about which he would be embarrassed, or which he thinks would be embarrassing to the other person. It is also fairly commonplace that a patient who sees an internist, an ENT, OB-GYN, or other specialist may very well talk with each one of these people about just those aspects of his condition which the patient feels the physician wants to hear about, so each of these physicians may get a somewhat different impression of the patient. That impression may be accurate enough but very limited, somewhat in the manner of the famous story of the several blind men describing an elephant by their sensation of touch of tail, leg, belly, trunk and tusk. The best interests of this patient are, of course, going to be served, ultimately, by someone who considers this possibility, investigates it, and coordinates the data—at least for the edification of the patient. This "ultimate" person can well be the psychotherapist.

Case study. A 54-year-old woman, active in business, organizational, and social fields, despite a high colostomy of 12 years duration, developed symptoms which were diagnosed in a clinic distant from her home as cancer of the lymphoid tissue. The prognosis was not encouraging and she did not return to her own physician at home, but instead went to a hematologist recommended by the diagnostic clinic. For months thereafter she became increasingly home-bound because of diarrhea and concern over her future. Plans for work or social or recreational activity were difficult because of her anxiety and depressed mood, but the diarrhea, which had become difficult to anticipate, gave additional reason for the patient to remain at home—and thereby, of course, added to the depressive mood.

When she consented to see a psychiatrist, on the urging of her family, she was urged to become involved in some of her former activities, and only then did the psychiatrist learn that the patient never discussed the diarrhea, the anxiety, or the depressive mood with the internist. She had habitually maintained a cheerful "in charge" facade, but in addition she stated simply that she didn't think the doctor was interested in anything but the blood studies and other data relating to the malignancy. She indicated that even if she would push herself to go out—and that she often felt a strong wish to resume part-time work—she could never predict when a sudden episode of diarrhea, through the colostomy, would occur.

The psychiatrist initiated a brief consultation with the internist who promptly scheduled an appointment with the patient. He assured her that he would indeed want to know about her condition more completely; he prescribed Lomotil and the patient agreed to call him about the results. The diarrhea came under much better control, the patient began to participate in some of her various activities, the improvement in mood was notable and rewarding. Active psychotherapy remained minimal.

The patient who does accept the concept of emotional and physical interrelationships and is willing to work in a psychotherapeutic approach may retain physical symptoms or may redevelop them after periods of remission. Very often these symptoms may be dealt with as resistance to change, and handled as the psychotherapist handles any manifestations of resistance. At these times the psychotherapist will be more effective if he or she maintains a fine balance between giving Permission and providing Protection. This is emphasized again in view of the fact that there often are enthusiastic moments in psychotherapy which result from the patient's getting permission to express feelings that have long been frustrated—following which the patient behaves in a manner which is somewhat inappropriate, or develops feelings with which he or she is not yet ready to cope.

(Sometimes a patient may develop a different concurrent illness, and it is helpful to remember that a "neurotic" can also catch the flu and feel depressed, or pick up a bacterial infection and get vague prodromal symptoms, or slip a disc and have a backache, etc.)

In these connections, as in others, it is sometimes advisable to have some appropriate medication prescribed by the referring or consulting physician. For short periods, when anxiety or insomnia are so severe as to disrupt function at work, then suitable medication may be helpfully employed. Careful avoidance of reliance on the drug can be an integral part of the plan; the dangers of overdosage and habit formation are so well recognized that they need not be emphasized at this point.

PILLS, CAPSULES, POWDERS, AND SYRUPS

Tranquilizing drugs such as Valium, Librium, meprobamate, and so forth are extremely useful for limited periods and for limited purposes. Similarly, real benefits may at times be derived from the employment of such antidepressants as Tofranil, Norpramin, Elavil, and others. Thorazine, Stelazine, and other phenothiazines designed to alleviate psychotic symptoms are certainly useful; the contraindications, side effects, and dangers, are not valid reasons for avoiding their use under all conditions. Useful data relative to these and other important drugs are readily available and should be familiar to any therapist whether he or she does the prescribing or is collaborating with someone who does. Among many sources of such information are deRopp[13] and Walker.[14]

A simple and useful part of an initial psychotherapeutic interview consists of finding out if the patient: (1) has a physician, (2) is taking any medication, prescribed or otherwise, or (3) has any special dietary limitations or habits. Along with the data relating to sleeping, recreation, and other facets of life style, these questions will often elicit important information.

The specific indications, contraindications, side effects, and dangers of medications which significantly influence emotion and mood—and the physiology of their action—are ordinarily expected to be part of the understanding and knowledge of the physician who prescribes these drugs. It is nonetheless a fact that sometimes psychotropic drugs are rather inaccurately prescribed due to lack of clear distinction between psychotic and neurotic conditions or to a reluctance to use really adequate dosages of such drugs. It is also true that sometimes patients use medication on recommendation of friends and without medical advice.

For the nonmedical psychotherapist it is important to recognize the effects of various medications and to be alert to the signs and symptoms which may be due to the use or overdosage of these drugs. Among the most commonly used groups of drugs which may be encountered by the nonmedical psychotherapist are the following: sedatives, tranquilizers, antidepressants, central nervous system stimulants, narcotics, contraceptives, and antihistamines—and in some age groups and areas hallucinogens are frequently used. Medications for cardiac and cardiovascular diseases are frequently part of the regime of individuals in psychotherapy.

Familiarity with the more common drug effects which the psychotherapist is likely to encounter will be useful in evaluating the reasons for a patient's mood, manner, and general intellectual functioning at various times. The more severe and late effects of overdosage are readily recognized; the early and relatively minor or moderate symptoms need careful attention. These include the depressive mood, relative apathy, and lassitude that sometimes are seen with the use of barbiturates. The symptoms are similar to those of an individual who is moderately depressed, and the usage of barbiturates may be overlooked. With barbiturates, in addition, tolerance may develop over a period of time and addiction is not infrequent. Paradoxical reactions may occur and should be kept in mind in an individual who rather suddenly shows symptoms of confusion, excitement, or paranoid hallucinations. Barbiturates are potentiated by the use of alcohol and this needs to be clearly understood by the patient. Various other medications used for the purpose of producing sleep may have similar effects; one of the outstanding features usually claimed or emphasized in the promotion of any new "sleeping pill" is the absence of these side effects. In dealing with elderly patients it is particularly helpful to keep in mind that chloral hydrate has long been recognized as an excellent sedative; this drug, however, can lead to excited, confused, and paranoid states. Similarly, bromides are notorious for the development of bromide poisoning over a period of time; memory impairment, disorientation and confusion, delusions and hallucinations, and irritability are symptoms of bromism.

In patients who are taking some of the well-known tranquilizers, primarily and properly prescribed for the purpose of reducing anxiety, it is important to keep in mind that drowsiness, a minor degree of lethargy, and some complaints of "light-headed" feelings akin to dizziness may occur. The several groups of drugs generally classified as "tranquilizers" include Librium, Valium, Serax, and others. Elavil, Aventyl, Etrafon, and Triavil function both as tranquilizers and antidepressants and produce a paradoxical increase in anxiety for some patients, sometimes nearly to the point of hypomania. Some minor degree of confusion may occur at times; complaints of dryness of the mouth and of constipation should be inquired about if they are not spontaneously reported. The possibilities in such cases include the alteration of the dosage to suit an individual so that he or she gets the benefit of the drug without the undesirable side effects. A change from one to another of these groups is often very useful; of considerable importance, however, is the basic tenet that these in general are limited in their usefulness, are appropriately given to reduce or modify the symptoms so as to enhance the patient's capacity to carry on psychotherapy, and are not validly given as "a cure" for the symptoms. Meprobamate (Miltown or Equanil) is generally regarded as a mild but effective tranquilizer with the potential for producing excitement or even hallucinations. It is important to keep in mind that alcohol potentiates the effect of this drug.

The phenothiazines (Thorazine, Sparine, Stelazine, Mellaril, Trilafon, Compazine and others) are potent tranquilizers and often properly used as "antipsychotic" preparations. These drugs are sometimes misused for relatively minor degrees of anxiety, as the potent antibiotics are misused for a minor degree of the common cold. In general the phenothiazines have a range of usefulness that includes antihistaminic and antiemetic effects, as well as their psychological indications. The undesirable side effects which may occur include weakness, lassitude, anxiety and confusion, depressive moods, skin pigmentation or rashes, visual disturbances, insomnia, and muscle spasm, especially of facial and hand muscles. Facial grimacing as in Parkinson's disease is not uncommon, especially with continued use or in larger dosages; sexual problems particularly of an inhibitory nature may occur. The tardive dyskinesia may be reduced or managed by the use of various medications such as Cogentin or Kemadrin, and often this is desirable when an individual has urgent need for the phenothiazine. Some therapists dislike giving one drug to counter the effects of another, of course. Reduction in dosage or change to another medication often eliminates side effects while still accomplishing the desired therapeutic result.

An important consideration for the psychotherapist is a minor but persistent depressive mood that often occurs in patients who are taking medication of the Rauwolfia group (Reserpine, Serpasil, and others) which are frequently used for high blood pressure. Remarkable relief from this depressed mood often follows when the physician substitutes another antitensive medication of a different chemical class. (The Rauwolfia drugs, interestingly, were first utilized as tranquilizers.) Digitalis, one of the oldest and most classical drugs used in cardiac illness, may produce gastric intestinal disturbances, including loss of appetite, nausea and vomiting, or vague neurological symptoms such as weakness, visual disturbances, disorientation, or depressed moods.

Not infrequently a man taking one of the anti-high-blood-pressure medications will have a diminished sexual interest. This is readily confused with impotence of a psychogenic nature; considerate investigation is often rewarding.

Other commonly prescribed drugs are the diuretics. Important in reducing edema in cardiac decompensation, in high blood pressure, and in other severe or acute situations, diuretics are also frequently used for relief of premenstrual symptoms. Unless carefully managed, there is apt to be a potassium depletion resulting in weakness and tiredness similar to that of mildly depressed persons. Consultation with the prescribing physician is usually helpful. Contraceptives are recognized for the possible dangers of thrombo-embolic phenomena; and for some women they seem apt to aggravate, if not incite, depressive reactions.

In many of the drugs and drug groups there are highly individual responses from different people. Accurate assessment of an individual's response requires careful observation. Some people will be unaffected by a dosage level of a tranquilizer or sedative which will render another person drowsy or unfit to drive a car. People taking phenothiazines or other tranquilizers should be alerted to these possibilities, and should not be driving perhaps, or handling potentially dangerous machinery during the period of getting accustomed to major, potent drugs.

BODY/MIND SYNDROME

Just as it is valuable for any psychotherapist to be alert to the drug effects of an emotional or "mental" nature, so also is the psychotherapist likely to be much more effective if he is aware of the psychological symptoms that accompany various physical disorders and diseases. In some cases physical illness manifests itself by psychological symptomatology even before somatic pathology can be discovered. There are numerous such conditions which occur rather rarely and which will be only referred to in this chapter; recommended reading in this field includes Walker's book[14] referred to above, as well as Wahl[15] and Silverman.[16] Among these pyschological symptoms are the apathy and flatness that seem indicative of depression but often are among the earliest signs of organic brain disease. Though uncommon, this is important to the psychotherapist because of the possibility of avoiding futile and frustrating efforts in psychotherapy based upon misdiagnosis; and because of the possibility of useful management when the patient, his family, and the goals are more validly understood.

> *Case study.*   Bill, age 51, apparently physically very well, was seeing a psychiatrist because of symptoms of apathy, a generally depressive attitude, a tendency to withdraw from his customary degree of social contact, loss of interest in his work, and the concern of his wife which precipitated his seeking psychiatric help. He had long been in business with two older brothers and one brother was now the dominant person in the organization. That brother was aggressive, authoritarian, domineering, and the patient, always a relatively quiet individual, was now even more so. Very slight indications of resentment and hostility were occasionally elicited but the full force of these negative feelings seemed to be—and were assumed by the therapist to be—largely repressed. Various other facets of the patient's life, including a somewhat cool, reserved, unaffectionate wife, added to the seemingly valid impression of a social and psychological situation that could well lead to a reactive depression. The patient was clearly aware that his business life was not likely to increase in rewards or opportunities.
>
> One day the therapist, aware of his own sense of frustration and puzzlement at the lack of any improvement in the patient's condition, noted and asked

the patient about what seemed to be a slight indication that the patient was having some difficuly in identifying and expressing his thoughts and feelings. The patient's response was an emphatic nodding of the head and widening of the eyes which expressed quite emphatically, although nonverbally, something like, "Yes, yes, yes—*now* you understand me!"

With this sudden indication of some kind of a dysphasic condition the therapist requested psychological and neurological consultations; these revealed definite impairment in intellectual functioning, and in a relatively short time the diagnosis was made of Alzheimer's disease (a presenile dementia). Treatment thereafter continued but with a considerably different prognosis, expectation, and approach to the family.

Impairment in mental function, such as memory disorders, often gives an early clue to the presence of intracranial disease, but sometimes an individual will be in psychotherapy for considerable time with the complaint of anxiety, irritability, depressed mood, or headache before anyone considers the possibility of organic brain disease. A useful clue to underlying pathology of this nature may come in a reference or description by a relative that the patient has undergone a considerable change in personality.

Other important physical conditions which give rise to emotional symptoms include multiple sclerosis (euphoria, emotional lability, hysterical features), collagen diseases such as disseminated lupus erythematosis (irritability, confusion, and periodic depressive moods). Irritability, decrease in sexual interest or function, menstrual irregularities, fatigue, sluggishness, and depression may be early signs of various endocrine disorders.

There are important physical disorders which give rise to emotional symptomatology, either as a consequence of the patient's awareness of his illness or as primary symptoms of the disease process. Among the most important of these is the anxiety which is a classical symptom of angina pectoris. The physical concomitant here is a sense of constriction or pressure in the chest; the cause may be anxiety without any demonstrable cardiac pathology, or there may indeed be dysfunction of the heart muscle and impairment of the coronary vessels. Unless the patient is already under the care of a physician because of known or suspected heart disease, it is safer to have a medical consultation regarding the possibility of cardiac disease, rather than to overlook this just because of obvious psychological stress.

A physiological condition which is probably more common than generally recognized, although somewhat debated in medical circles, is "functional hypoglycemia." In this condition the individual has a tendency to metabolize carbohydrates in such a way that there is a rapid rise in blood-sugar level after the ingestion of carbohydrates, followed by a fall to below-normal levels which persist for a period of several hours. During the interval when the blood sugar is low the individual may feel lethargic, apathetic, somewhat depressed, readily fatigued; in addition, this individual may manifest such general symptomatology on first awakening in the morning. One of the additional significant clues to the presence of this disorder is that some "quick sugar," such as orange juice, a candy bar, or the like, will give the patient rapid relief from the symptoms; typically the relief lasts only a brief time and the patient soon returns to the fatigued or irritable or lethargic state. (Faintness and sweating may occur as well). Coffee often provides relief somewhat similar to that afforded by sugar; the reason for this lies in the caffeine-stimulation of the adrenal glands which in turn elevates blood sugar through the hormonal system. In such a patient, as in others referred to above, there also may be ample psychological basis on which to base the diagnosis of a reactive depression. An adequate laboratory analysis of the glucose metabolism will often provide the answer to the question of coexisting physiological metabolic dysfunction, which can be markedly alleviated by dietary measures. If psychological problems are indeed existing, these, too, of course, can continue to be treated but the overall situation will be markedly improved.

The apathy, lassitude, and tiredness typical of psychological depressions may also be a reflection of an anemia. This is fairly common, especially in women, and is simple to illuminate by means of a complete blood count. Relative pallor may provide a suggestive clue to more severe anemia; a psychotherapist can certainly be on the alert for this and suggest a medical consultation.

In many of the conditions considered above one of the problems lies precisely in the fact that there may be adequate psychological reason for the patient's symptoms; in such instances it is easy to overlook the possibility that there may also be somatic pathology as well. It is important to keep in mind the concept of multiple causation of symptoms; the tendency to look for "*the* cause" of any illness or problem is strong, and needs to be guarded against.

In this connection the "iatrogenic"* factor in producing anxiety or increasing already-existing anxiety is important. When a psychotherapist recognizes and considers the possibility of some basic or concomitant physical illness which has not been given attention or examination, all too often the therapist himself may become anxious. This is applicable not only to nonmedical phychotherapists; many physicians become anxiety-ridden by the nature of their own personalities because of concern for their patients, because of unfamiliarity with the condition they now suspect, or for various other reasons. (This is

---

* From Greek *iatros* (healer or physician) and *genesis* (origin), this generally refers to symptoms, especially anxiety, induced by the physician himself. (Interestingly, the word is frequently used in medical writing, but rarely in speech).

somewhat analogous to the tendency among some psychiatrists and psychotherapists to take a suddenly different attitude toward a patient when the
label "schizophrenic" is applied.)

Case study.   Elaine, married, mother of four, had always been a very apprehensive, anxiety-ridden, and compulsive individual. She was conscientious,
devoted, and a very "nurturing" Parent to her family and friends. No one
considered there would be any reason whatsoever for Elaine, of all people,
to need psychiatric help.

When a small lump was discovered in one breast by her own self-examina-
tion, at age 37, she efficiently, apparently coolly, and with her usual degree
of capability, made an appointment with her doctor. He suggested that although there did not seem to be anything very definitive about the lump
it might be well to have a biopsy done to relieve any doubts. The procedure
was expected to be simply an overnight stay in the hospital and she entered
late in the afternoon for biopsy scheduled the following morning. That evening her internist came to see her, took her blood pressure, pulse, and a
cursory "look" in the interest of giving her the ordinary kind of attention
and support that the occasion seemed to indicate. When he discovered a
pulse rate in excess of 130 his own expression of alarm was so clear to the
patient that she became virtually unnerved. His immediate ordering of an
electrocardiogram only increased her apprehension, of course. The fact that
the electrocardiogram showed nothing abnormal about her heart function,
other than a rapid rate, did little to comfort her. Her anxiety only diminished
to her normal level after the surgery had been completed and some trusted
medical friends, who were well acquainted with Dr. J., were able to convince
her that *his* own anxiety level was well recognized by all his colleagues.

From a somewhat different point of view than those considered above there is
considerable value for the psychotherapist in being aware that the process of
psychotherapy itself may very well precipitate physical symptoms. These may
be the concomitant occurrence of some externally precipitated toxic condition,
of course, or they may be an expression of the regressive phenomena that occur
when Games and Rackets are rather deliberately given up before the patient
has found and employed other means of expressing himself. It is in this connection that Protection is needed as well as Permission; careful psychotherapy
helps assure that the patient is not prematurely exposed to feelings with which
he is not ready to cope.

An interesting and thoughtful presentation is made by Silverman[17] of psychological manifestations that may be used as clues to probable development of
physical symptoms or illness. During the course of psychotherapy, if some
stresses in the life situation are recognizably increasing but the patient habitu-

ally—or at this period—tends to block off the expression of feeling, it is quite likely that some physiological dysfunction may ensue, particularly if the psychological symptoms are not increasing. In TA terms this might well be the case in dealing with an individual who is a relatively constant Adult.

Another clue to the probability of development of physical symptoms is seen when guilt feelings (expectations of the worst, sacrificial attitudes, and so forth) seem to decrease in intensity despite increasing external stress. (The Punitive Parent here may be about to punish the Child by more severe means since there is not sufficient apology, remorse, or admission of guilt in a psychological form.)

There is much from the whole vast area of "psychosomatic" illness that can be studied, understood, and valuably integrated into the knowledge and experience of a psychotherapist. The subject of preoperative and postoperative anxiety, the emotional reactions to multilating surgery, the emotional concomitants and reactions to the new surgical techniques in heart and blood vessel surgery, psychological reactions to the diagnosis of cancer and to surgery for cancer; the subject of "hypochondriasis," which is often used in a vague, loose "wastebasket" manner but which does indeed have a specific meaning as well; the emotional factors in connection with periodontal disease—these are some of the areas in which psychological and physiological interrelationships are important.

In terms of this chapter one might consider what he or she understands by the term "psychosomatic." Does this mean psychological manifestations of anatomical and physiological change such as in alcohol, drugs, cerebral-vascular accident, brain disease? Or does this refer to somatic manifestations of "repressed" emotions such as anger, fear, sexual excitement? Does this mean concomitant physical and psychological symptoms due to a basic single cause? Does this mean conscious avoidance of demands or responsibility? Malingering? Is the term "psychosomatic" more reasonably limited to those disease processes identified by Alexander? Does it include the dwarfism and psychological and mental retardation of the very young child who is emotionally severely deprived through lack of Stroking? Or is the term valid for all these? Or is it important?

Perhaps one of the most basic features in the development of a psychotherapist who is qualified and comfortable in dealing with psychosomatic disorders is exactly that same feature which applies to the development of a competent practitioner in any kind of therapeutic endeavor—namely, self-knowledge, stated centuries ago in the admonition, "Physician, heal thyself." Martin Grotjahn[18] has stated nicely and simply what is basic to the therapeutic relationship between patient and therapist: "Medical treatment is based upon the relationship between a patient and his physician which is not made in heaven but developed on earth by hard work, experience, and skill." I think this is as readily applicable, if not even more so, to the psychotherapeutic relationship.

"A medically trained patient may easily misguide his doctor, slowly, softly, and often unnoticed by anybody." It is equally true about a psychotherapist treating a patient who is also a psychotherapist, or who is a medical therapist. Treating one's peers often stimulates self-doubts, insecurities, and "not okay" feelings which the therapist's Child usually manages to avoid. The more clearly one knows oneself, the better therapist he or she can be, other requirements being reasonably met.

REFERENCES

1. Dunbar, Flanders, *Emotions and Bodily Changes* (New York: Columbia Union Press, 1935).

2. Alexander, Franz, *Psychosomatic Medicine* (New York: Norton, 1950). See also Roy R. Grinker, Sr., *Psychosomatic Concepts* (New York: Aaronson, 1963).

3. Friedman, Meyer, and Ray Rosenman, *Type A Behavior and Your Heart* (New York: Knopf, 1974).

4. Grinker, Roy, and John P. Spiegel, *Men Under Stress* (New York: McGraw-Hill, 1963).

5. Satir, Virginia, *Peoplemaking* (Palo Alto, Calif., Science and Behavior Books, 1972).

6. James, Muriel, and Dorothy Jongeward, *Born to Win* (Reading, Mass.: Addison-Wesley, 1971).

7. Berne, Eric, *Transactional Analysis in Psychotherapy* (New York: Grove, 1961).

8. Polster, Erving, and Miriam Polster, *Gestalt Therapy Integrated* (New York: Bruner/Mazel, 1973).

9. Miller, Neil et al. (ed.) *Biofeedback and Self Control,* The Aldine Annual, 1973.

10. Selye, Hans, *The Stress of Life* (New York: McGraw-Hill, 1956).

11. Meyer, Adolf, *Psychobiology; a Science of Man.* Edited by Winters and Bowers (Springfield, Ill.: Charles Thomas, 1957).

12. Holmes, T. M., and R. H. Rahe, "The social readjustment rating scale," *Journal of Psychosomatic Research* 11, 2, (1967), pp. 213–218.

13. deRopp, Robert S., *Drugs and the Mind* (New York: Grove, 1960).

14. Walker, Sidney, *Psychiatric Signs and Symptoms due to Medical Problems* (Springfield, Ill.: Charles Thomas, 1967).

15. Wahl, Charles W. (ed.), *New Dimensions in Psychosomatic Medicine* (Boston: Little, Brown, 1964).

16. Silverman, Samuel, *Psychological Aspects of Physical Symptoms* (New York: Appleton-Century-Croft, 1968).

17. ———, *Psychological Clues in Forecasting Physical Illness* (New York: Appleton-Century-Croft, 1970).

18. Grotjahn, Martin, quoted in Wahl [above, 15], p. 118.

CHAPTER 7

physical exam
and
script decision:
one hour

WILLIAM LOWE MUNDY

Prior to using TA principles in patient care, the routine use of ventilation therapy, sympathy, and reassurance was helpful, but this rarely offered me, or the patient, a definite direction to take toward a real solution of psychosomatic problems. During a one-week period in the office, two patients with physical symptoms were asked, "How old were you when you decided to...?"

CASE NO. 1

A 58-year-old woman was recently discharged from the hospital after therapy for a spinal injury and rib fractures received in an auto accident five months earlier. She had become more and more disabled with headache, pain, and weakness and aside from initial consultation with an orthopedic surgeon had not had medical care in four months. During hospitalization it was discovered by electromyogram studies that she had a polymyositis involving paraspinal muscles and all four extremities.

From *TA Journal* **2**, 3 (1972). Reprinted by permission.

When she was seen for the second time after discharge, the conversation went as follows:

Doctor: Do you feel better?

Patient: Well, I keep having these headaches.

Doctor: Do you feel better, worse, or the same as you did before going to the hospital?

Patient: I get tired so easily.

After at least five such evasive answers, I found that she could be up from three to four hours before headache and weakness forced her to lie down. This, of course, was better than the one to two hours which was her limit before therapy.

Questioned about weakness, she said it took her three days to put her suitcase on the shelf. She finally yielded the information that she couldn't raise her arms over 90 degrees with any weight in her hands.

Patient: You don't know how embarrassing it is to not be able to do anything. I wonder what the grocer and those people think when I come in every day.

Doctor: Can you tell me what they notice?

Patient: Well, I had to put the sack on a post at the parking lot. You know how you would feel if you were going to drop something.

Doctor: Did they see you drop something?

Patient: I have to go in each day instead of twice a week so I can carry small sacks. I'll bet they think I'm crazy.

Doctor: Have you thought about telling them you were hurt and asking for help?

Patient: You just don't go around telling people how you feel.

Doctor: Do the folks at work know how weak you are?

Patient: Now, doctor, they know I don't feel good. You just can't ask other people things. Nobody is interested in how you feel.

With a mixture of argumentative bitterness, and on the verge of tears, which I have seen many times when I have discussed symptoms with her, she said, "The only time I really feel bad and show it is when you ask me questions like now."

I replied that I purposely wanted to have her recognize how her feelings could make her physically sick by creating muscle spasm, fatigue, headache, and weakness. She admitted that she always argued with me and got angry but that nobody knew any more than I did or was a better doctor so she would keep seeing me. With tears in her eyes she waited on the conversation.

I then asked her, "How old were you when you decided never to need anybody and to give yourself away to other people?"

Patient: I was nine years old.
Doctor: What happened then?
Patient: My father died.
Doctor: Go on.
Patient: My aunt took us four kids into a room and said, "From here on, you
   have to take care of your mother. If you don't and she gets sick or dies,
   you'll have to go to an orphanage."

I made a very gentle attempt to discuss with her how this decision, which was
one she had to make at that time, had created feelings in her which she had
used for the rest of her life. I had personally recognized that she had not verbalized her feelings over the years, but at the same time had made it perfectly
evident to those around her that she was feeling badly.

Purposeful neglect of symptoms for long periods of time had gotten her into
trouble time and again. Although she had had some degree of warmth and
closeness with her husband, now deceased, there was still the element of "hid-
ing feelings" most of the time.

For the next few minutes, she was still in the same ego state which kept her
recollecting the care she took of her mother and she volunteered that she herself was always upset whenever mother was tired or had so much as a headache.
My memory went back to the terminal illness of her mother ten years before,
and I recalled how irritated I had become with the daughter's constant anxiety
and apprehension over each symptom, and the feelings of the professional personnel, including myself, who noticed the nonverbal distrust in the daughter's
face. She constantly played a game of *Tell Me I'm Well, Doctor.*

She spent only a few minutes recollecting her concerns with her mother, and
when I again referred to the possibility that her feelings today might resemble
those she had when she was a little girl, she quickly changed expression, became angry and said, "That's just silly; I'm a grown up person now." At this
point I ceased further discussion of past feelings and reemphasized, in a gentle
nurturing way, that I hoped she understood that my discussion of her feelings
was with the hope that she would have less fatigue, less muscle spasm, pain, and
weakness. I left her with the thought that feelings could produce physical symptoms, and that I didn't want to leave anything out in helping her feel better.

The odds are that this patient is not motivated sufficiently to pursue therapy
to effect real changes in her approach to her life. The rest of her family has
little insight into her emotions and on the few occasions when they have discussed "mother's ways" I thought they would have more concern than enthusiasm for a psychotherapeutic approach. Hopefully, the patient and I may, over
a period of time, develop enough trust so that she does a better job talking to

me about symptoms, and relinquishes to some degree, her script based on self-denial.

CASE NO. 2

The patient is a 50-year-old divorced woman. Her original symptoms in 1955 included a lack of pep and ambition, a choking sensation and fullness in the neck and throat, headache, hyperventilation, palpitation, and musculoskeletal complaints. In two years she had gained 20 lbs. to 147. Two significant episodes occurred in the next 15 years. One was a thrombophlebitis of the leg with embolization. The other was an injury to foot, knee, and ankle. In the last 10 years she utilized a gynecologist for most of her medical care, varying doses of various hormones and thyroid against her obesity and recurrent symptomatology.

She held part-time positions in speech and drama with a university which finally led to full-time work. She was not seen in our office for seven years until she came in on the advice of her aging gynecologist to be examined for her blood pressure. At this time I found her to be socially pleasant, and she talked quite freely about personal and family problems. She had gained to 180 lbs. and had a blood pressure of 160/120 with KW Grade fundi, an accentuation of A2 and a Grade I systolic aortic murmur. These were new findings which I considered quite significant.

I questioned her about sources of caloric intake and found that she had at least three drinks of alcohol daily. She admitted to tranquilizing in this way. In discussing her children, I found that one son, age 16, was living at home and doing well in sports, which was a great source of pleasure to her. One son, age 29, in another state, was recently institutionalized as an alcoholic. He had significant marital problems, but, she related, "I now have a nice minister seeing them both." A daughter, age 27, recently lost her job, having been apprehended as a drug user. I asked the patient what she had done for this daughter and she said it was hard for her to keep meeting financial obligations until her daughter got on her feet. She admitted to paying her rent and giving her money for other items. I asked her to tell me again the ages of the two children and then asked her how long she planned to be responsible for their welfare. When she told me she wasn't sure how long she should go on "taking care of them," we discussed her guilt feelings whenever she failed with the children, or when they did not come up to her expectations. I then asked her if she did not find it fatiguing to carry the responsibility for her own children as well as be concerned with the success of all her students. She became very thoughtful and her expression showed fatigue. I then asked her what happiness she had found just for herself. I waited a few moments and noted that she was close to tears and then asked, "How old were you when you decided never to need anybody?"

Without hesitation she said, "I was three." And she looked at me open-eyed with surprise. "What happened at that time," I asked. And she replied, "My father died." And with this, despite her efforts to keep from it, she began to sob into her handkerchief. Since I had been quietly going on about a physical examination during this conversation, I stopped at that time and took her hand in mine and assured her that it was perfectly all right to cry, at which she finally sobbed so she could be heard. I let her cry for a few minutes more and told her to hold on to my hand with both her hands. When she had quieted some, I asked her if she could ever remember crying out loud, and she said, "No." Then I asked her if as a child, she cried only into her pillow or when alone, and she said, "Not only that, but I used to go into my grandmother's room because she was deaf and couldn't hear me."

After she had composed herself to some degree, we finished the physical examination and she was quite able, to consider both her needs for therapy: the first, blood pressure and weight; the second, her feelings, which she thought undoubtedly produced most of her symptoms, caused her to eat and drink to excess, probably played a great part in her hypertension, and allowed her no happiness. We discussed the very significant decision she made at age three which allowed her to live at that time. It was a child's decision made under extremely stressful conditions, and perhaps was then apropos for a little girl to adapt to her environment. She saw very clearly how she had utilized this early decision to continue for the rest of her life, denying needs for herself, and giving, giving, giving all in an effort to make her mother happy. It will take, obviously, a period of time with further consultation either in our office or with one of our referring psychiatrists for her to further understand her acceptance of total responsibility for others' welfare, and to make a change in her feelings which will allow a happier way of life.

Her complete examination and interview time was a routine hour which we utilize for so-called complete office examination.

PART 3

training
and
supervision

Contributors

STAFF-PATIENT STAFF CONFERENCES
Eric Berne, M.D.

TECHNIQUES OF CONTRACTUAL SUPERVISION
Graham Barnes, M.A.

THE PATIENT AS COLLABORATOR
John J. O'Hearne, M.D.

CHAPTER 8

staff-patient
staff conferences

ERIC BERNE

The author describes a procedure whereby, following a ward meeting or group-therapy session, the staff holds its professional conference—including treatment planning—in the presence of the patients. If certain rules (which he lists) are followed and each member of the staff speaks frankly and to the point, patients of all ages and diagnostic categories are almost unanimously appreciative. A few staff members find this procedure distasteful while others find it congenial, stimulating, and therapeutically valuable.

The objects of a psychiatric staff conference may be listed, in order of explicitness, as follows: (1) to give the patient the advantage of the best available professional opinions; (2) to instruct the staff, particularly the residents; (3) to enhance the morale of the staff; (4) to teach participation and the free expression of opinions; (5) to "survey" and "get acquainted with" the residents; (6) to increase the experience of the senior members; and (7) to stimulate thinking and the organization of thoughts. In general, if the first two are well planned, the others will take care of themselves.

From *The American Journal of Psychiatry* **125,** 3 (1968), pp. 286–293. Copyright 1968, the American Psychiatric Association. Reprinted by permission.

Insofar as the psychiatric staff conferences parallel the medical and surgical staff conferences from which they are descended—that is, insofar as they deal with "hard" matters, such as somatic diagnosis, shock treatment, or medication —it may sometimes be better for the patient's peace of mind if he is not present during the arguments for various diagnoses and prescriptions. But where the conference deals with "soft" matters, as is the case in psychotherapy, social work, and psychoanalytic conferences, it is not so easy to justify what is, from a strictly objective point of view, talking behind the patient's back.

Many psychoanalysts would object to the patient being present during a staff conference on the ground that this would result in a "smudged transference."[4] But this objection is advanced a priori rather than after skillful experimentation. Even if it turned out that "the purity of the therapeutic relationship would be sullied," that might be irrelevant (or even beneficial), since the object of treatment (as distinguished from research) is not purity but therapy.

At present, the staff conference as conducted in many hospitals and clinics is one of the most highly institutionalized aspects of psychiatry. It has its own language and its own customs and culture. The language is the "therapist-therapist" dialect (as distinguished from the "therapist-patient" and the "patient-patient" dialects), which may be operationally defined as that mode and vocabulary of talking which, if indulged in by a patient, would be called "intellectualization."

A typical custom is to drink deep draughts of hot coffee while other people are talking and sometimes even while the patient is in the room. A typical cultural attitude is that nurses should be kept in their places, while other females, such as doctors and social workers, are accepted by the men as "equals." Patients are also kept in their places, but in return they have the privilege of "expressing affect," an indulgence which is denied the nurses.

THREE TYPES OF CONFERENCES

In general, such staff conferences exist in three forms, which may be called the classical, the didactic, and the romantic.

In the *classical* form, the resident or attending psychiatrist presents the "material" he has "gathered"; the patient is then brought in and interviewed; the third phase consists of diagnostic, prognostic, and therapeutic discussion after the patient has left. This phase, in turn, has two forms. In the "old-fashioned" or "European" protocol, the junior member of the staff gives his opinion first, and so on up the hierarchy until the chief gives his summary. This has the advantage that everyone has a standing invitation to speak in his proper turn and is not inhibited or intimidated by previously expressed opinions of those with more experience. In the "modern" or "democratic" protocol, each member of the staff speaks as the spirit moves him, giving an impression of "participation" and equality, but leaving many opportunities for ulterior motivation, overtalking, remaining silent, and complaining afterward.

The *didactic* staff conference is essentially a clinical teaching demonstration which is not always immediately relevant to the patient's needs but rather to the instruction of the junior staff.

The *romantic* staff conference is a "group dynamic experience" in which the staff is more interested in self-expression and mutual criticism than in the welfare of the patient—in many cases, more interested in their own psychological hypochondriases than in the patients' schizophrenias. Such conferences may be legitimate if they are not regarded as the primary or even the sole matrix for making executive decisions about patients.

SIX RULES

In my own hospital and clinic practice (principally at the McAuley Neuropsychiatric Institute* in San Francisco), which consists of ward meetings, group therapy, and only rarely an individual patient, I have established the custom of having all staff conferences in the presence of the patients. The rules which regulate these, and which have evolved over the past two years from experience, are as follows:

1. The ward or group meeting is sharply separated from the staff conference. During the meeting all the patients sit in the inner circle, and the staff members are confined to the outer circle. At the appointed time the meeting breaks up and the patients are informed that the staff conference will take place in five minutes and that they are all invited to come and listen. In five minutes—no more—the staff assembles, and *they* now sit in the inner circle of chairs or perhaps in another section of the ward. Those patients who choose to stay and listen are offered the outer circle to sit in, but if they prefer, and there is room, some of them may sit in the inner circle.

2. This procedure makes it clear to the patients that this is not merely a continuation of the meeting but is a new session. They have been invited to listen and not to talk, join in, or interrupt. The invitation to listen will implicitly

---

* Michael Khlentzos, M.D., director.

convey this restriction to them in nearly all cases. If a patient does join in or interrupt, he is reminded gently and firmly that he is there to listen only, as a courtesy to him if he wishes to avail himself of the opportunity. The patients soon learn that if they want to interrupt they must first obtain permission, which may be granted or denied according to the pertinence of what they want to say. Once this is established, even the most disturbed people will not break in. The main reason for this self-restraint is that most patients are appreciative of frank and thoughtful discussions about themselves and will suspend their psychopathology in order to pay careful attention.

3. Every staff member who observes the meeting is required to stay for the staff conference and to say something. Visitors are usually informed of this before they sit in. This makes the situation bilateral. The staff has the privilege of listening to how each patient expresses himself, and in return the patients are given the same courtesy. If a staff member or visitor (even a first-year nursing student) is reluctant to talk, it is often the patients who will inform him that this is required of him in return for sitting in, and in every case thus far the staff member or visitor has then obliged. This is made easier by following the classical "European" protocol.

4. The conference is absolutely "straight." When it ends the patients leave and so does the staff. There is no other staff conference or "post-conference" conference. If some staff members go to lunch together they may review what happened, but it is considered very bad form to withhold significant opinions until lunch time. Thus the staff is trained and expected to say everything worth saying while the patients are listening. An uneasy member who is holding back or is not talking "straight" is so informed, usually then and there.

5. The use of technical polysyllables or other words beyond the probable grasp of the majority of the patients is discouraged. It is perfectly possible to hold staff conferences of maximum usefulness in plain English using a minimum of technical terms, whose meaning can be taught to the patients. I know of one psychiatrist who has conducted several staff conferences per week for the past 10 years without using a technical polysyllable and without appreciably impairing the usefulness of the conferences. "He had sexual feelings for his mother" or "He has sexual fantasies about his mother" is a synonym for "oedipal elements," etc., which has proved acceptable to both patients and staff. "He enjoys (beating) (being beaten up)" is an adequate and informative substitute for "sadomasochistic tendencies."

Similar operational phrases are used throughout, referring to actual clinial data which emerged during the patients' meeting, rather than the poorly defined adjectives which are commonly scattered throughout staff discussions. Thus "dependent," "passive," "identification," "homosexual," "narcissistic," and similar terms behind which less well-informed people can often hide are completely dispensed with. At these staff conferences no patient has ever been accused of "acting out oedipal hostility." If it has been established that he was significantly disturbed by oedipal conflicts as a child, that these conflicts involved a significant hostility which has continued to the present day, and it is known precisely which aspect of this hostility motivates his behavior on the ward, it might be mentioned that his reaction to a known specific stimulus from one of the nurses was influenced by a sexual fantasy known to be related to similar fantasies in childhood. Thus: "Tom got angry at Miss Jones when she offered to rub his back because, as he said last week, his mother . . ." etc. Or if it is a transaction between two patients: "Mary got into bed with Tom because, as we already know, she's a sexy girl and hasn't decided to control herself yet, and yesterday she saw Tom put . . . (etc.) which, as she said, reminded her of the time her father . . ." etc.

The fact is that there are few if any clinical items which cannot be described more precisely, validly, and intelligibly by a few short common words than by a long technical term.

6. Good therapy requires planning, and it is the duty of the instructors to impress this on residents. The therapist need not hesitate to discuss his plans in the presence of the patients if he "comes on straight." But if he is ambiguous or coy, he will only complicate the situation. For example, when one discussant said: "Some day we may hope to find out why Sally feels a need to reject you whenever you approach her verbally and perhaps she will eventually tell us how she felt about her father at an early stage of development" (coy smile), Sally muttered "Garbage!" which in her dialect meant that she, like most of the others present, was bored and slightly repulsed.

The therapist later expressed the same thought by saying: "Sally is in love with me but she hollers at me when I talk to her, just like she hollers at her father, so the next step is to find out why she hollers at people she loves." To this, Sally commented loudly "Rubbish!" which in her way of talking meant that she would think about it; and she did during the ensuing meetings with good results.

Similarly straightforward is: "Ricardo is obviously afraid to talk sense, so he talks crazy except when he thinks it's safe not to. So the next step is to find out what 'safe' means to him, and how come." This was quite acceptable to Ricardo and opened the way for the therapist to make him feel safe so that he could stop "talking crazy," as will be recounted below.

THE RATIONALE

The philosophy behind this procedure is that older methods of treatment are not producing optimal therapeutic results. Instead of getting well, the majority of patients "make progress"—sometimes for 10, 15, or 20 years. A prudent therapist and a compliant patient can thus form a relationship which will keep both of them contented for an indefinite period. Neither of them will "make waves" of the sort required for the patient to get well and strike out for himself. Therefore a change is indicated: not new maneuvers based on the old premises, but a new set of premises.

The staff-patient staff conference first attacks the comfortable and well-established sociological roles of "therapist" and "patient" and substitutes a "bilateral contract" with rational exceptions. Everyone is treated as a "person" with equal rights on his own merits. Thus the patients have as much right to hear what the staff has to say as the staff has to hear what the patients have to say; and if the staff have the courtesy to remain silent while the patients are talking, the patients are expected to extend a similar courtesy to the staff.

The rational exception here is the one referred to above. When a discussion of the therapeutic prescription may be too harrowing for the patient, this may perhaps be justifiably carried on in his absence—for example, an argument about the effects of different kinds of shock treatment, or the possible side-effects of various combinations of drugs. In my own practice, however, no exceptions are made in this regard, so that each patient is aware of all the possibilities brought up by various staff members, with no detrimental effect and considerable appreciation of this frankness.

As a logical product of this "equality," categorization of patients has been abolished. The most dramatic and satisfying example of this is the abolition of "teen-agers," and of course, "delinquents," although everyone present recognizes that "guys going to high school" have to deal with teachers, parents, other guys at high school, and sometimes also probation officers and judges; while men who have a hard time on their jobs, women who don't menstruate anymore (or sometimes "women past the menopause"), and people who drink too much are each in a different situation.

As for diagnostic categories, "people who feel sad" are asked if they really do feel angry, because somewhere along the line, almost invariably, someone has told them that is really their trouble and has in effect demanded that they produce a satisfying exhibition of anger. On the other hand, Freud, who first studied this matter systematically, termed such demands "wild analysis" and advised against it. Therefore the question may be gently asked, but no such "demand" to produce is made. "People who have been called paranoid schizophrenics" (as they almost invariably know from sneaking a look at their charts somewhere in the course of their hospitalizations) are offered the alternatives of continuing to "act crazy" or of getting well. The patient himself, however, is permitted to use diagnostic categories if he so desires. For example, "Am I schizophrenic, doctor?" "At the moment, yes, and that's what you're here to be cured of." (Or, if the moment is right, the therapist might add: "And that's what you're here to be cured of, so how shall we go about it?")

The abolition of such categories makes simple the selection of patients for a therapy group: any eight patients taken at random or in some expedient order such as successive admissions constitute a therapy group, regardless of age, diagnostic category, or their relationship to each other. (In my own practice I do distinguish between people over 14 and people under 14, mainly because I do not have specialized training in child psychiatry. This, and deaf-mutism, acute mania, and degenerative brain disease are the only distinctions, I think, that have to be taken seriously, mainly so as not to hold up the other patients in the group.)

On the staff side, the abolition of professional categories during the conference is a license for everyone to think without artificial restrictions: nurses can think like doctors if they wish, doctors can think like nurses, psychologists can think like social workers, and so on. All the staff members are equal because they are all observers and have observed the same meeting; none of them has been distracted by coffee-drinking, which is not permitted; and they cannot segregate themselves by using specialized professional argots and phraseologies since the meeting is carried on in a language which is common to all the professions.

Neither can a staff member wander off into "bright ideas" or speculations, since whatever he says he must substantiate on the basis of what he has actually observed, which (except for information brought in by the ward staff or the patient's individual therapist) everyone else present has also observed, so that there is little room for distortion. (This undercuts the classical staff conference joke, where one member says: "I feel it's anal," another, "I feel it's oral," and so on with "phallic," "dependent," "oedipal," etc., until just as the clock strikes ten the last social worker says: "I feel it's sado-masochistic," whereupon a skeptical resident says as everybody gets up to go: "Thank God they got that in under the wire.") At these conferences, "I feel" is discouraged unless it is demonstrably pertinent, because the staff are not there to "feel," they are there to think.

The rational exceptions to the equality and bilaterality are based on the fact that the patients are paying to be there, while the staff is being paid, and for good reason. It is a reasonable assumption that the staff knows more about how to cure psychiatric disabilities than the patients do, and this is explicitly acknowledged. Thus there is a difference between the staff and the patients, but this difference is not elaborated into social roles; it is accepted on its own merits as part of the proceedings.

A logical extension of this is that since the leader of the group meeting, who is usually also the leader of the staff conference, is taking the responsibility for attaining the goal of both—the cure of psychiatric disabilities—he must be given the corresponding authority. He is thus entitled to make rules and decisions and to enforce them by imposing sanctions such as banishment. Only under such conditions can the proceedings go ahead in an orderly fashion so as to attain the greatest therapeutic benefit for each patient.

On the other hand, the leader must not let himself be beguiled into thinking that he is there to "run," "take," or "lead" a group. That is merely a means to an end; it matters little whether or not the group is "well run," or whether "that was a good meeting" according to some irrelevant standard; the only relevant criteria for judging *anything* that he does or does not do is whether the individual patients get well faster as a result. This is the main thing that has been impressed on the 100 or so observers and the 200 or so patients who have been present at such meetings.

LANGUAGE OF TRANSACTIONAL ANALYSIS

It has been found, in my experience, that the language most suitable for such a program is the language of transactional analysis.[1,2] Transactional Analysis, as a spoken argot, uses a simple English vocabulary of no more than 5,000 words, nearly all of them of one or two syllables; the occasional three-syllable word and the rare four-syllable one are all in common street usage. Its five technical words are also words in common usage whose specialized meaning can be easily taught to hospital and clinic patients and staff members. These are Child (roughly, archaic ego states), Adult (roughy, reality-testing ego states), and Parent (roughly, nurturing or prejudiced ego states), game (roughly, social operations with an archaic ulterior motive), and script (roughly, archaic preconscious life-plan).

In these terms, what happens at the ward or group meeting and the ensuing staff-patient conference can be described thus. During the ward or group meeting the patients "come on Child" or "come on Parent," with the occasional exhibition of an Adult ego state, but more often of a "pseudo-Adult" or "precocious Child." The announcement of the staff conference then "hooks their Adult," so that the Child and Parent ego states of the patients are decommissioned and they listen intelligently and critically during that phase.

Since the pathology resides mostly in the Child and Parent ego states, there is in effect a suspension of pathology during the staff conference. The mere fact of this suspension is in itself therapeutic, since it demonstates to the patient that he is capable of "normal mental functioning" at will for at least a short period of time—30 to 60 minutes—which means to him as well as to the staff that he is curable. This is particularly dramatic in the case of people diagnosed as paranoid schizophrenics and hysterics.

The reactions of the patients (ranging in age from 14 to 74) to this procedure are uniformly appreciative. Remarks such as the following have been heard: "I got even more from the staff conference than from the group meeting," "I can hardly wait until next week when we have this again," "You guys are tough on us, but you sure talk straight," "It's sure good to hear doctors talk in a way that I can understand." And from a particularly thoughtful patient: "It's interesting that the staff is getting better just as fast as we are."

Staff members do not have the same consensus. Some who attend a few times stop coming. There is also some grumbling from therapists who do not attend but whose patients are in the ward group or the therapy group because the patients expect them to talk the way the staff talks at the conference. Others express delight and relief at the frankness of the proceedings and the patients' reactions to them. These personal reactions of the staff, favorable and unfavorable, are actually irrelevant to the goal of the conference, which is not to please the staff, but to get the patients well. Some therapists who have this goal in mind and have observed the proceedings have adopted the staff-patient staff conference as their normal method of procedure and state that they would find it difficult and uncomfortable to return to the old system of one-way mirrors and segregated staff conferences.

FOCUS IS ON PATIENT

The staff-patient staff conference is not an entirely new concept, as it has been foreshadowed in many ways in various therapeutic communities, but its present development is, I think, more clearly formulated and more systematic than it has been previously.

Both Maxwell Jones[3] and Harry Wilmer[5] discuss in instructive detail their policy of "daily community meetings." The primary purpose of these is to reduce tensions and clear up misunderstandings among patients and among staff members and between patients and staff—a form of social psychiatry which is of therapeutic value because it smooths out the social organization of the ward or section, with all the benefits resulting from that. At such "community meetings," of course, both patients and staff must be present in order to attain that goal.

In this paper, however, we are not talking about social psychiatry in their sense, we are talking about conventional clinical psychiatry: the professional scientific staff conference. At the "community meeting," the daily life of the ward is the center of attention. At the staff-patient staff conference, the focus is on the clinical needs of each patient. Thus at the staff conference, the resident or attending psychiatrist may present pertinent information about a patient's medical or psychiatric history, and the patient may be questioned to validate or invalidate hypotheses about his psychodynamics or prognosis, in this way heading off the unsubstantiated "bright ideas" and speculations referred to above.

The ward staff may also report pertinent details about ward incidents referred to by the patients, but these are treated from a clinical point of view, leaving their community significant to be worked out elsewhere. While such critical incidents occur as a matter of course with inpatients, this area is almost eliminated in the case of outpatients who attend small treatment groups unless something untoward happens on their way from the front door of the clinic to the treatment room.

Perhaps two anecdotes, both relating "unusual occurrences," will clarify by contrast how the principle of staff-patient staff conferences usually works.

TWO EXAMPLES

In the first example, Ricardo, a hyperactive boy of 16 who habitually sat next to the therapist, spent most of his time during the group treatment session muttering, interrupting, delivering monologues about baseball, and calling jocular threats across the room to his friend Dan: e.g., "I'm gonna take Dan to a butcher shop and cut his head off, hahaha." At which Dan, of similar age, would break through his auditory hallucinations and reply, perhaps three or four minutes later and regardless of who else was talking: "Hahaha, I'm gonna give Ricardo a karate chop that will break his neck," at which they would both giggle. In transactional language, they were both "coming on confused Child." This was very disturbing to some of the observers, particularly those who thought that only one person at a time should speak in the group, without being able to explain the advantage of such a policy.

When the staff conference began, since Ricardo could not sit next to the therapist he would sit next to Dan and keep up his usual chatter. Dan would do his best to listen to the staff with his Adult, but from time to time Ricardo would "hook his Child," and Dan would answer him. The other patients, who with only an occasional lapse would listen to the staff conference with their Adults, would get angry at Ricardo and tell him to shut up because they couldn't hear what the staff was saying. Some of the staff members would reinforce this by angry looks at Ricardo or by well-controlled corroboration: "I can't hear either." The more experienced observers, however, were able to tolerate Ricardo's chattering without much discomfiture.

When he decided that the time was ripe, the therapist one day interrupted the staff meeting to tell Ricardo that he would have to keep quiet if he wanted to stay—specifically, that he would have to move to a chair at the very end of the outer circle (as far away as possible from Dan) and stop talking, or else leave. There ensued a battle of wills between Ricardo and the therapist, with Ricardo making all sorts of promises, offering to move to the second chair from the end, etc. The therapist insisted: "Either move to *that* (the end) chair, or leave."

Eventually Ricardo made his decision and moved, saving face by saying: "Then the meeting has to end at 12 o'clock." The therapist agreed to this since that was the time it was supposed to end anyway, as Ricardo knew. Away from the stimulation of Dan, Ricardo's Child subsided enough to allow his Adult to listen to some of the discussion. This became evident at the following week's group session, where to everyone's surprise and gratification, for the first time he referred to topics for which he had previously exhibited a conspicuous lack of attention and interest, such as his early childhood experiences.

The observers were much impressed because Ricardo's overt and oft-stated position was that he did not see any reason either to come to the group meetings or to stay on afterward for the conference; yet under pressure he elected to stay, even though he lost face by doing so, rather than exercising his option to leave. This was discussed quite openly in front of him immediately after the incident. The therapist said that he knew he was gambling by giving Ricardo such an ultimatum and explained the thinking that had led to his decision to do it at that time. One of the observers, who habitually confined himself to "positive thinking," favorable prognoses, and compliments to the patients, became very sentimental about Ricardo's fortunate choice; the therapist interrupted to ask if he would not say something negative for a change, and the other observers agreed that that would perhaps be "straighter" than his usual "marshmallow throwing."

This example illustrates the following points: (1) The staff conference can be interrupted on occasions when the therapeutic indications are strong enough. (2) The group need not be run according to some preconceived model, but with a "minimax" strategy which will yield the greatest good for the greatest number of patients. In the situation cited, all were agreed that everyone (except two or three who were standing still) was "getting better," whatever that meant in each individual case. This included Ricardo, Dan, the other patients, the observers, and the therapist. (3) An observer who does not "talk straight" must be corrected. (4) With a strong leader, it is possible to "hook the Adult" of even the most disturbed patient.

The second example concerns the locked ward meeting. On one occasion there was a new patient, a European girl who had been in this country only a short time; she gave a rare exhibition of grand hysteria—moaning, swaying, and swooning throughout the meeting. When the staff conference began, all the patients remained silent and listened to the discussion except the new girl, who continued moaning and swooning. The therapist did not understand why. A nurse whispered to him: "I think the reason she doesn't stop is that she doesn't realize that this is a staff conference; she thinks it's still the therapy group."

"Oh!" said the therapist. He decided that he had better intervene, so he addressed the patient: "The patients' meeting is over now, Maria, and this is a conference for the staff. You can stay and listen if you want to." At this Maria looked up from her swoon, straightened up in her chair, and began to listen attentively.

This example illustrates the following points. (1) It is important to listen to nurses. (2) A firm approach will temporarily "hook the Adult" of even the most disturbed patient. (3) The therapist's job is not to sit passively but to make decisions.

In order to have a "sane society" in psychiatric hospitals, which is what our authors[3,4,5] are striving for, the patients need even more than the conventional concessions of the therapeutic community. Experience shows that nearly all patients can call up just as much ego strength as therapists can if they are "given permission" to do so, and the staff-patient staff conference is one way of giving that permission. Experience also shows that it is in general more difficult to give the staff permission to talk freely in the presence of the patients than to give even very disturbed patients permission to listen quietly and attentively to what the staff has to say.

Further discussion is not indicated at this point because any clinician who works in a hospital or clinic can try this way of proceeding for six months or a year and see for himself how it works.

SUMMARY

The staff-patient staff conference is a procedure whereby, following a ward meeting or a group treatment session, the staff holds its professional conference in the presence of the patients. The basic rules are as follows:

1. The staff conference is sharply separated from the meeting by an announcement and a short interval, so that all the patients can readjust themselves to the new situation.
2. The patients are invited there to listen and not to interrupt.

3. Every staff member is required to express an opinion at the conference.
4. The staff members must talk "straight," with no fudging, and there must be no other staff conference or postconference conference about the aspects already discussed.
5. The use of technical terms beyond the probable grasp of the majority of patients is discouraged.
6. If these conditions are properly met, therapeutic planning can be discussed frankly and usefully in the presence of the patients.

The reaction to this procedure of patients of all ages, from 14 to 74, and of all diagnostic categories, is uniformly favorable. Among staff members, some find it distasteful; some, particularly those who are able to express themselves in simple language, adopt it as standard procedure in their own practices.

REFERENCES

1. Berne, E., *Transactional Analysis in Psychotherapy* (New York: Grove, 1961).
2. ———, *Principles of Group Treatment* (New York: Oxford University Press, 1966).
3. Jones, M., *Social Psychiatry* (Springfield, Ill.: Charles C. Thomas, 1962).
4. Talbot, E., and S. C. Miller, "The Struggle to Create a Sane Society in the Psychiatric Hospital," *Psychiatry* 29 (1966), pp. 165–171.
5. Wilmer, H., *Social Psychiatry in Action* (Springfield, Ill.: Charles C. Thomas, 1958).

CHAPTER 9

techniques of contractual supervision

GRAHAM BARNES

My goal in supervision is to create a context in which clinical trainees can become aware of and develop their potential as therapists and experienced therapists can improve their effectiveness through the use of Transactional Analysis. Following are the ways I use to supervise audio or videotape presentations of therapy sessions that help make training in TA thorough, productive, and enjoyable.

VALUE OF CONTRACTUAL SUPERVISION

Contractual supervision respects the autonomy of trainees and decreases the likelihood of games trainees may play, such as *Kick Me, Stupid, Do Me Something,* and supervisory games such as *Blemish, I'm Only Trying to Help You,* and *Now I've Got You.*[1] Tape recordings of ongoing treatment groups provide specific, objective, and systematic ways to follow a therapist's work with particular clients over a period of several months.

Some therapists perform quite well in supervised peer groups. Others do not. How trainees work with people in the real world of treatment groups is more important than how they work with peers who are generally highly verbal and motivated to change. Tape recordings of therapy sessions provide an opportunity to follow the ongoing work of trainees with people who have themselves stuck, act helpless, and demonstrate hopelessness. Conversely, supervision based on a therapist's note-taking or memory of what took place in treatment groups lends itself to missing or overlooking significant transactions and dynamics. There is a human limit to the number of things one can keep in mind during a therapy session. Productive and effective therapy is more likely to take place when the therapist functions almost entirely from the perceptive Free Child ego state with Adult processing and the Nurturing Parent looking on over his or her shoulders. Listening later to a recording of a therapy session provides an opportunity to fully engage the Adult first to listen for particular themes and then to listen to every word. This procedure encourages flexibility in listening, and the experience expands one's ability to *hear* and *see* during actual treatment sessions.[2]

By developing expertise in the critique of tape recordings of treatment sessions, trainees increase their clinical sensitivity and prepare themselves to more adeptly identify and resolve clinical issues when working with their clients. After following the procedures in this paper, a senior resident in psychiatry became aware of "how little time I allow myself to learn from myself by systematically looking back to reflect on what I do."

I have heard tape recordings of group work that trainees would not have brought to supervisory sessions if they had listened to them a few times in advance and if they had followed some guidelines for preparation, such as the ones I shall suggest. On occasions, trainees have asked me to help them identify problems in a particular treatment situation. When I have listened to their tapes with them, they have often discovered for themselves, without my assistance, what they had missed earlier.

PROCESS OF SUPERVISION

I do most of my supervision in groups. All supervisees in the group participate in the critique. This arrangement encourages role-playing of difficult clinical cases. Even experienced therapists appreciate the explicit therapeutic orientation of the training sessions. Personal therapy for supervisees is an integral part of the supervisory process. This model moves away from the traditional master/apprentice relationship as a way of teaching skills in transaction analysis. B. Gaoni and M. Neumann delineate four stages in the supervisory process from the point of view of the supervisee: (1) the teacher/pupil relationship, (2) apprenticeship, (3) focus on the intra-psychic and interpersonal problems of the supervisee to aid in the development of his or her "therapeutic personality," and (4) mutual consultation among equals. At the fourth stage "supervision becomes an exchange of openness, advice, and experience between equals, though one is more experienced than the other." Contractual supervision resembles their fourth stage although it incorporates therapy for the supervisees and takes place generally in a group setting.[3]

Ethical issues abound when therapy or treatment sessions are audio- or videotape recorded and, especially, when the tapes are used by the therapist for supervision. An explicit contract needs to be established by therapists with their clients as to how the tapes of treatment sessions will be used, by whom, and when. This rule holds even for group sessions where everyone in the group has agreed to the same rules of confidentiality as the therapist. As a compensation and consideration to clients for using tapes of their work for supervision or for one's own professional growth, I provide a place where members of the group can listen to their own work. Some patients have found this an invaluable therapeutic tool. Furthermore, I let people know what professional use I plan to make of the tapes and who, if anyone other than I, will hear them. Videotapes made with the goal of future playback require written clearance before they can be legally replayed. Each person in the group has to sign a release statement and a contract that specifies how and by whom the tapes will be used.

In addition to establishing a clear contract as to how tapes will be used, by whom, and when, it is important to have a dependable recording system with playback capabilities that permit listening without strain. Generally, a reel-to-reel system and an omnidirectional microphone provide the clearest recordings for me.

Supervisees are encouraged to listen to at least one tape recording of their group sessions weekly to get a bird's eye view of their work, and to concentrate on several three- to twelve-minute segments monthly for a close-up worm's-eye view. The overview usually provides an opportunity to hear results for which supervisees can stroke themselves positively. Here they can give particular attention to segments of their work with which they are particularly pleased. They can also concentrate on sections of work that were exciting and productive for their clients. During this process they may note sections that puzzle them and where they feel unsure about what they did. When therapists cannot explain their reasons for a particular segment of work, they need to listen to that segment until they have figured out to their satisfaction what was happening within the group, within the client or clients, and/or within themselves. By listening to tapes of their work between training sessions, supervisees usually make their work more effective. A supervisee shared the following discovery: "I'm making a review of my tapes a learning experience rather than a task to perform to get ready for supervision. I am using my tapes (1) to give myself feedback weekly on what I am doing, (2) to pick up ineffective transactions with clients before I get into patterns of nonproductive behavior, (3) to improve my listening, (4) to think of new options for my work, and (5) to give myself positive strokes. I am keeping my energy level up between training sessions rather than getting excited in the training sessions and then feeling drained as the days accumulate after supervisory sessions."[4]

When supervisees listen to segments of tapes of their treatment sessions several times before presenting them for supervision, the supervisory sessions are lively, the energy level is high, and the investment to learn is immense. Contracts for supervision are explicit. Resistance to criticism is usually low. Criticism is more often accepted as Adult-to-Adult even when it is not.

A successful group-therapy session contains both scientific and aesthetic elements. Listening to recordings of therapy sessions can be similar to the experience of listening to a symphony. When I listen to one of Beethoven's symphonies I experience joy, excitement, even ecstasy. To improve the quality of my hearing, I may follow the score and single out the different voices carrying the theme. First the strings, then the woodwinds, the percussions come in, and now the brass. Rhythmic movement continues. Beethoven's music reflects the societal pressures of revolution and oppression of his time. By listening to his works I gain appreciation for the revolution in his music that brings joy and a sense of oneness with the human race.

When I listen to a tape of a group therapy session I experience an hour or two filled with struggle, courage, love, and hopefully, triumph. Supervisees report that preparing their group tapes for supervision becomes a fascinating enterprise when they permit themselves to listen to them as spontaneous compositions. They listen to all or part of the session just to be absorbed in the process of what took place. Then they select a section to listen to for particular themes, to give careful attention to the score and to follow the voices. Transactions between people are analogous to a symphony, and the transactions can be broken down to analyze structure, transactions proper, games, and script.

Upon beginning training in TA, therapists want to know how to make their way through all the material on their tapes without getting lost or becoming overwhelmed. To learn TA is also analogous to learning another language. Early in their training, supervisees do not spontaneously think conceptually in TA. They usually work to translate into TA what is happening. I suggest to experienced therapists that they continue to use their own treatment style, and then as they listen to their tapes to use TA as another conceptual framework to answer the question, "What are the real forces operating here?" When therapists learn the language of TA, and when it becomes meaningful to them, they no longer have to translate. They can think in the language. It becomes integrated to provide an additional conceptual framework. Experienced therapists are multilingual: they have several frameworks to use in their work with their patients. Moreover, they are open to discovery and let their theory develop out of their experience.

USE OF TAPES

Early in my training in Transactional Analysis Robert Goulding reported that Eric Berne recommended to his supervisees that they listen to their tapes at least six times.[5] I found that this made the translating process more explicit. Furthermore, I discovered that when I listened to my tapes six times I did not need the supervision that I had needed previously. I also detected more quickly where I was having difficulty and then proceeded to contract with my supervisors for information or assistance in that area.

I suggest to supervisees that they prepare three- to twelve-minute segments of their tapes and follow these steps:

1. *Structural analysis of the client.* Play the selected segment of the tape to identify the clients' ego states. While listening for his or her ego states block out everything else on the tape. Listen for ego-state shifts, and possible contaminations and exclusions. Use first-order structural analysis until you are adept at identifying ego states. Keep a tally sheet. Note each shift and indications of internal dialogues. Be willing to form hypotheses. For instance, a brief silence may indicate a rapid internal shift from Child to Parent and back to Child. When you feel ready move to descriptive and second-order analyses. (Attempts to combine second-order structural analysis with functional or descriptive analysis may confuse rather than clarify the situation, since descriptive analysis is a spacial concept and second-order structural analysis is a temporal or developmental concept.)

2. *Structural analysis of yourself.* Play the segment of tape again to identify your ego states, blocking out everything else on the tape. Keep a tally of each ego-state change. After you have collected the data on the clients' and your ego-state changes prepare egograms on each.[6]

3. *Transactional analysis of the client.* Listen to the tape segment a third time to record the clients' transactions. Which of his or her transactions were Complementary? Crossed? Angular? Duplex? When do the client's transactions become crossed or ulterior? How many transactions were Adult to Adult? Child to Parent? Parent to Child? Child to Child? Parent to Parent? Ulterior? Other? Note discounts and cons.[7] What are the clients' stroking patterns?[8] How does the client structure his or her time here and now?

Pay particular attention to the first few minutes of each clients' work. In the first few sentences a client may give signals or hints of what will happen or what he or she wants to happen.[9] Note the clients' contract. At what point did the client establish a contract? Was it clear? Was it what the client wanted? Did the contract contain Adult, Free Child, and Nurturing Parent elements? (Where there is not a succinct contract, clearly and authentically articulated by the client, little if any change is likely to take place.)

4. Transactional analysis of yourself. Ask the questions about your transactions as suggested above for the client. In addition, question yourself about what was going on in the session. Einstein reportedly gave his mother credit for prodding him to develop his inquiring capacity by asking him each day when he returned home from school, "Did you ask any good questions today?" Therapists develop skill by learning to ask themselves "good questions." Here are some suggestions: Did I hear what the client said? Was I listening to the Client? To myself? What did I hear? How did I hear? From what ego state? Were my transactions crisp, clear, and direct? Was I perceptive? Permissive? Protective? Potent? Spontaneous? Creative? Did I lead or follow the client? What was I trying to do to the client? What was the client trying to do to me? Did the client remind me of someone else? Was what I said useful to the client? How was it conducive to change and growth? To elicit additional self-insight, ask and answer from each ego state: What did this work do to or for me?

Keep a record of how many seconds you talk, how many seconds the client talks, and the number of seconds of silence. This may give some clues to when the therapist is talking too much or too little or giving too little or too much cognitive feedback to the client. Of course the issue of appropriate timing of transactions cannot be determined by a stop watch.

Therapists have a responsibility to share their moral, political and social views with their clients. This is part of the protection the therapist offers his or her patients.[10]

5. Game analysis. Play the tape a fifth time. Listen for games. What game was initiated or played? Learn to detect ulterior messages, cons, and discounts. What was the payoff? Racket? Did the patient get stroked for his or her racket? Diagram the games that were initiated and/or played. Use the Goulding-Kupfer formula,[11] Berne's G-Formula,[12] and Karpman's Drama Triangle.[13] What were your options in game analysis with the patient?[14] What, if anything, would you do differently now?

6. Script analysis. Listen to the recording a sixth time for injunctions, counter-injunctions, decisions, programs, and life positions. Do a script matrix, using only the data supplied by the client on this portion of the tape. Script analysis is, of course, the most important part of your work. Often a client will state his or her entire life script in one sentence. For instance, a 27-year old female said "I will act like a happy little girl until my father says he loves me." What degree of impasse did the client experience?[15] Did the client resolve the impasse? Listen for how you confront these transactions. When supervisees consistently miss an injunction, they may need to do some personal work for themselves. I have noticed that when therapists repeatedly miss or overlook an injunction, they often have unfinished business with respect to an early decision around the injunction they miss.

The spirit of scientific inquiry that is inherent in the self-critique process re-enforces the executive function of the Adult ego state. This moves energy from the Child that may secretly fear criticism and see it as a negation of self-worth or of professional competence.

To prepare yourself for supervision and to become aware of your projections, imagine your supervisor in the room listening with you. Play the role of your supervisor and critique your tape as he or she would.

After you have listened to your work, stroke yourself positively by writing down all the things you like about what you did. Conversely, write down all the things you are concerned about. Note how you would now do the latter differently by asking yourself, "If I were working with this client now, how could I respond more effectively?" Rather than stroking yourself for doing ineffective work, stroke yourself for being clever and able to figure out more useful ways to help people change.

Ask yourself, "When I take my tape in for supervision, what will happen? What do I want from my supervisor?" Analyze which ego state your responses are from. "What will I feel or experience during and after supervision?" Your answers to these questions may help you formulate a contract for the supervision of your work. It is as important to have a contract for supervision as it is to have a treatment contract with clients. As supervisor, I want to know before I listen to a tape, "What specifically do you want me to listen for? What do you want from this session?" After establishing what the trainee wants and expects, I will say what I am willing to do. In therapy, Adult-to-Adult contracts lessen the possibilities of transference and counter-transference or, in TA terms, Parent-to-Child or Child-to-Parent transactions, especially when the social level transactions are not congruent with the psychological level transactions. I hasten to add that they have the same function in supervision. Moreover, contractual supervision provides a context for immediate confrontation of passive behavior.

Prepare for your presentation a (1) seating diagram,[16] (2) egograms, (3) script matrix diagram[17] (sometimes as complete as possible, including all you know about the client; at other times include only information derived from the segment of work you plan to present), (4) game diagrams, demonstrating facility with using the various game formulas.

THE GROUP SUPERVISION HOUR

During a supervisory session someone presents a tape on game analysis. Another participant takes off on structural analysis, and someone else attempts script analysis. The original presenter is looking at game analysis from the operational or behavioral level; others from the phenomenological perspective. All during the session, everyone talks past one another, and no one understands why there is so much confusion and/or disorganization or lack of clarity, despite the use of such clear TA concepts. Berne offers an explanation, "Transactional analysis is such a rich mesh of intertwined concepts, all consistent with each other, that it is possible to wander around in any direction and come up with something interesting and useful." He suggested a grid that I have found useful in supervisory sessions. Berne's grid is based on the four different frameworks that may be used in transactional analysis: (1) transactional with four key terms: ego states, transactions, games, scripts; (2) validating, again with four key terms: operational or behavioral, phenomenological, historical, and social; (3) modifying, either according to psycho-biological principles (structural) or functional descriptions; and (4) methodology, either logical or empirical arguments. Berne warns that there are at least 64 possible paths for discussion: "Unless everybody follows the same path, the various discussions cannot be correlated without an enormous amount of labor and definition. . . . The only way to have a well-reasoned and decisive argument is to choose one path through the grid and stick to that."[18] I do not contract in advance for which path I will follow supervisees through. I use this methodology as a road map afterwards to identify where I am coming from and what I am responding to. The discussion becomes mechanical when I literally follow this grid. I prefer to have supervisees identify the path their comments will follow so others can go there with them.

Some of the reasons supervisees give for seeking tape supervision include:

1. To become skillful in using transactional analysis to help me identify the real forces or phenomena operating here and now.
2. To fulfill part of my training contract for advanced membership in the International Transactional Analysis Association.
3. To keep my sponsor aware of what I am doing in my ongoing groups so he or she can evaluate my work.
4. To learn other options for working with people who refuse to take responsibility for feeling, thinking, or acting.
5. To learn new techniques to cultivate my ability to use myself in therapy.

6. To learn whether I want to please or displease others, especially my supervisor, and, if I want to please or displease, make a contract for change.

7. To get negative or positive strokes.

8. To check out my impressions, hunches, and observations with others, looking for possible contaminations and/or blind spots.

To learn to diagnose ego state, analyze games, and identify life scripts increases one's competence as a therapist. The emphasis in this chapter has been on discipline, attention to detail, and a commitment to rational explanation and scientific inquiry. These elements are essential to make therapy, including Transactional Analysis, more than magic and to help therapists become more than gurus. Now a warning about supervision.

Kierkegaard mentions the seamstress who makes the cloth for the altar. When people look at it if they admire only the work she has done—the beauty of the flowers and stars she has minutely and artistically reproduced—or if they find a defect, they miss the purpose of her work. She designed the cloth to call attention to "something else."

It was "an insulting misunderstanding of the poor needlewoman, when someone looked wrongly and saw only what was there. . ."[19]

Since the experience I am hearing on the tape may have been the beginning of a new venture, a piece of significant new behavior, or a clarification of an important decision, it is "an insulting misunderstanding" of the patient if I hear only what is on the tape.

My goal in supervision is to use the training milieu to devise steps that encourage trainees to look candidly, reflectively, and constructively at what they do and, through this process, to teach themselves. Contractual supervision as outlined above is designed to challenge supervisees to become clinically proficient in TA, and, at the same time, it demonstrates respect for the autonomy of supervisees and supervisors.

REFERENCES

1. Fagan, Joen, "Graduate School Games," *TA Bulletin* **6**, 24 (1967), pages 103 and 107 are relevant to supervision also.

2. Cf. Spence, Donald P., and Marta Lugo, "The Role of Verbal Clues in Clinical Listening," *Psychoanalysis and Contemporary Science*. Edited by Robert R. Holt and Emanuel Peterfreund. (New York: Macmillan, 1972), pp. 109–131.

3. Gaoni, Bracha, and Micha Neumann, "Supervision from the Point of View of the Supervisee," *American Journal of Psychotherapy* **28**, 1 (1974), pp. 108–114.

4. Seipp, Katrina, personal correspondence, February 22, 1974.

5. Goulding, Robert L. (ed.), "The Training of Psychotherapists in Transactional Analysis," *Voices* 10, 3 (1974), pp. 29–34.

6. Dusay, John M., "Egograms and the Constancy Hypothesis," *TA Journal* 2, 3 (1972), pp. 133–137: Cf. also Schiff, Eric W., "Symbiosis Illustrated by Egograms," *TA Journal* 4, 4 (1974), pp. 13–15, and Karpman, Stephen B., "Overlapping Egograms," *TA Journal* 4, 4, (1974), pp. 16–19.

7. Schiff, Aaron W., and Jacqui L. Schiff, "Passivity," *TA Journal* 1, 1 (1971), pp. 71–78.

8. McKenna, Jim, "Stroking Profile: Application to Script Analysis," *TA Journal* 4, 4 (1974), pp. 20–24.

9. Everts, Kenneth, and Eric Berne, "Interpretation of Tapes," *TA Bulletin* 3, 11 (1964), p. 139. "It is possible to predict what an individual patient X is going to do during a given group meeting, and often also what the course of his 'therapy' will be for the next few months, by listening carefully to a few initial transactions."

10. Halleck, Seymour L., *The Politics of Therapy* (New York: Science House, 1971), p. 56. "Ultimately, the only protection the patient has is his knowledge of where the therapist stands politically, of what kinds of therapeutic outcome the therapist would welcome."

11. Cited in Woollams, Stanley, Michael Brown, and Kristyn Huige, *Transactional Analysis in Brief* (Ann Arbor: Huron Valley Institute, 1974), p. 27, and in Graham Barnes, "Steps for Developing and Implementing Problem-Solving Contracts." (Chapel Hill: Southeast Institute, 1974), p. 6.

12. Berne, Eric, *What Do You Say After You Say Hello?* (New York: Grove, 1971), pp. 23–25.

13. Karpman, Stephen B., "Fairy Tales and Script Drama Analysis," *TA Bulletin* 7, 26, April 1968, pp. 39–43.

14. Dusay, J. M., "Response," *TA Bulletin* 7, 26, April 1966, pp. 136–137.

15. Goulding, Robert L., "Thinking and Feeling in Transactional Analysis: Three Impasses," *Voices* 10, 1 (1974), pp. 11–13.

16. Berne, Eric, *Principles of Group Treatment* (New York: Grove Press, 1966); p. 140.

17. Steiner, Claude, "Script and Counterscript," *TA Bulletin*, 5, 18, April 1966, pp. 133–135. Cf. Stanley J. Woollams, "Formation of the Script," *TA Journal,* 3, 3, January 1973, pp. 31–37.

18. See reference 12, pp. 409–413.

19. Kierkegaard, Sören, *Purity of Heart,* Douglas V. Steere, translator (New York: Harper and Brothers, 1938).

CHAPTER 10

the patient as collaborator

JOHN J. O'HEARNE

RATIONALE FOR INVOLVEMENT

In 25 years of teaching group psychotherapy, I have often looked for a method of keeping the students' interest, of getting them emotionally involved in an active learning process and sensitizing them to the resistances that patients experience in their group treatment. I have found one that works for me. This took a long time.

Early in my career, famous group psychotherapists told me that they did not permit students to be in the room or even to watch them through one-way vision mirrors because they felt they would be so concerned with their own temptations to "show off" for the students and slight their patients. As I gained experience, I concluded that this was not only untrue but unfair. We asked our patients to exhibit themselves before us with all their assets and liabilities; I thought it only fair that we let them see us. Thus, I began another phase in my career development. I risked coming out from behind a mask of pseudo-neutrality and of showing myself with some of my own feelings. Then I risked advanced psychotherapy students being present in the room when I was treating a group of patients. I expected my students to expose their errors when I supervised their tape-recorded group sessions; Why not let them see me as I actually worked? This seemed only fair to me, so I invited them into the treatment room and at first asked them to sit behind me so that I would not be distracted by their nonverbal communications. I found it took me approximately four sessions or less each year that I began working with a new group in order for me to become comfortable with them there—even when I could see them. During these years, however, I would teach the trainees only after the patients had finished their session and left the room.

Some years after I had begun to treat and teach in this fashion, I was invited to treat and teach in another mental health center. Here, the available rooms were so much smaller that it was not possible to have both patients and trainees in the same room. During the treatment session, the patient group plus a therapist-in-training and I met in one room and were observed by trainees through a one-way vision mirror. Again, when the treatment group was concluded, patients left and the teaching session began.

In the Spring of 1970, these trainees complained that the teaching sessions were becoming too much "teacher-tell." They wanted more action. (Almost all of them had had two prior years of training, including substantial time in T-groups.) In exploring their desires and various possibilities, we agreed to change the usual order for one session only. Patients and therapists would go into the room behind the one-way vision mirror while the trainees would occupy the group treatment room. Trainees were told they could say anything they wished. The patients found this exciting; now *they* could be the voyeurs. The comments of the students and their interaction together were very stimulating to those of us who were now the onlookers. In following weeks, patients made many references to this experience. They were most impressed with the fact that the trainees were neither entirely comfortable nor spontaneous. They could discern that some therapists "pulled their punches" by being less than frank in their comments. They also made such comments as, "that man with the beard who thought you let me get by with too much" or "that woman who thought I whined like a baby." The patients were almost uniformly delighted with this experiment; not all the trainees were delighted. Some of them had found it much easier to talk about the patients in a typical staff conference fashion—i.e., theorize about them while speaking about them in a somewhat condescending manner.

This experiment gave sufficient impetus to both the therapy and the teaching that I thought it would be profitable to use such feedback on a systematic basis. "In learning and teaching newer techniques, such as Transactional Analysis and Gestalt work, to practicing psychotherapists, I had had experience with the student therapist leading a group of his peers, then immediately following that with a critique of his methods. I had never tried this when the therapy I was teaching was more traditionally psychoanalytically oriented. I reasoned that if therapists could learn when they were 'under the gun' of their critical peers, then perhaps we could teach and learn group psychotherapy in similar ways and with greater advantages for the patients. When first proposed to the staff and trainees, the idea of having therapists conduct group therapy in the same room with the trainees, then swap places for immediate feedback, met with some resistance. The resistance was lessened not only by dealing properly with anxieties but also by the fact that the air conditioning failed in the small therapy room and adjacent room which were separated only by the one-way glass wall. This additional stimulus contributed to the ease with which the idea was fathered."[1]

Plan and Process

The staff at this mental health center agreed to divide the two hours allotted each week for treatment and teaching into three separate sections:

Group A was a group of outpatients plus myself and an assistant therapist. We met for one hour in the center of a large room and were surrounded by Group B, which was composed of clinical trainees such as residents in psychiatry, psychiatric nurses, psychology interns, social workers and others on the staff of this center. The majority of them had already had two years of training in group processes and group psychotherapy. At the conclusion of one hour of group psychotherapy for Group A, Group B (trainees) came to the center of the room while Group A (patients and the 2 therapists) went to the periphery of the room. Group B could discuss anything they wished for 25 minutes, then would make room for Group A to join them in a large circle, called Group C. This group included everybody in the room—patients, therapists, and the trainees from Group B. This group met for 35 minutes.

In summary, there was a one-hour treatment session of outpatients which was witnessed silently by a group of therapists in training who then discussed for 25 minutes the treatment they had seen. Then everyone in the room joined one large group which lasted for 35 minutes.

Let's take a look at the setting in which this occurred. The center combined hospital and outpatient facilities. All of our patients were from outside the hospital, although some had just been released from the hospital. Some were neurotics, some had severe marital problems, some were ambulatory schizophrenics. None of them were "winners" in the T.A. sense of living up to their own contracts with themselves. Their fees ranged from $0.50 to $12.50 per session. We were not allowed to collect these fees. The center was changing to computerized account keeping and their charges were often months behind.

At this center, almost all group treatment was done by teams of so-called co-therapists. I do believe that there are occasionally two therapists who can actually work as a team, but I seldom see this in operation. I definitely do not believe that a highly trained, experienced group psychotherapist and a student in the early phases of his training make a cotherapy team. I believe that such a pair constitute a therapist and an assistant therapist. With this belief, I was at variance with the accustomed spoken attitude in this center.

In this mental health center, virtually all members of Group B (primarily composed of therapists in training) had spent one semester in T group ex-perience. Since there was a feeling on the part of the trainees that they did not want teacher-tell type training, the therapists did not participate in the discussion during Group B's 25 minutes in the center of the room. This group was led by several different group therapists who also had considerable ex-perience as T-group trainers. They were chosen so that if trainees chose to ask questions about theory, they could answer them or refer them to me as consultant. They were chosen so that if trainees chose to interact as they had in T groups and express their own feelings, they could also do that.

Directions to Group B were that: (1) They must not speak during Group A's treatment session of one hour. (2) In the 25 minutes allotted for Group B to be in the center of the room, they could say anything they wished. They could ask questions, discuss theory, differ with the therapy they had seen, criticize or praise therapists and patients.

Naturally, they did not believe us when we said they could say anything they wished. Quite predictably, patients were comfortable with this approach sooner than were the trainees. At first, the latter almost uniformly saw themselves as therapists and tried to resume treatment with the patients as soon as we met in Group C, when everyone in the room was in one large circle. They learned how patients feel when they corner a therapist after a group session and start to tell things they had not wanted to discuss in the group. How did they learn this? They tried to tell the therapists things they had not felt comfortable say-ing in the group and were surprised when they also were told, "Bring it up in the group next week." Early in the year, they discussed primarily theory and technique. Later, they said in Group B that they thought, for example, that a therapist was too confronting with a certain patient. In Group C, they could ask the patient if this were so. At times, a trainee observed that certain patients talked more to one therapist than the other. In such instances, the patient usually said that he felt more comfortable talking with one than the other. And the staff member could ask if they were going to work this out in the group next week, thus confronting them and the therapists with an issue which had not been recognized in Group A. In these ways, patients and trainees became collaborators with the therapists.

Such collaboration was not trouble-free. The role of patients here is clearer, more traditional, than is that of the trainees. Trainees fear that they possess enormous power to hurt patients by saying what they feel or think. They frequently discuss Parent concepts such as whether the so-called cotherapists are being properly "co-." I told them my belief that cotherapy seldom occurs; that the model I have seen many people espouse is symbiotic; that I do believe that two therapists may work together if they complement each other.

Later in the year, patients would "level" with some of the trainees in such a way that some trainees felt discomfort. In one such sample, the trainee was told by a patient that he (the trainee) talked about wanting his patients to grow up and become independent but that the patient saw him in Groups B and C as primarily wanting to stay superior to patients, thus encouraging their dependency and hostility.

Results

At the conclusion of the first academic year of this plan, the majority of patients had successfully finished their treatment. There was almost total agreement from both the trainee and patient populations that they preferred this plan when compared with their previous modes of treatment and training. Patients liked it because they were our collaborators; they did not feel "in the dark" about their illness and its treatment; they knew the entire staff was interested in them; they no longer expected staff to be omniscient. They thought their treatment went more rapidly; they were usually relieved when not everyone present thought about them the same way; they were usually pleased to find that the therapists did not have to always agree with each other or with the staff. Those who had been previously treated were definite in preferring this approach.

Trainee interest, attendance, and participation were all maintained at an unusually high level for the year. All of them preferred this method over watching through the one-way mirror and then discussing patients in abstentia; trainees felt they learned more from discussing patients while they were there even though they had to reduce their comments to words that patients could understand.

As a teacher, I believe that the amount of emotional involvement of the staff with the patients and how to help them was much greater than any other way I had tried. I was impressed at how difficult it was, early in the year, for trainees to "talk straight." By this, I mean it was difficult for them to actually say what they meant and not to use psychological jargon to obscure their points from patients.

Enthused by the success of this method over one year's time, I searched the literature for similar ventures. There are few related references. Chief among them is Berne's 1966 article.[2] In this, he describes treating some in-patients while surrounded by trainees. At the end of the therapy session, he invited patients to listen at the teaching session, provided that they did not interrupt. Berne expected each trainee to speak. I differ from him in not insisting that each trainee speak; neither do I end the session without giving patients another chance, as in Group C, to tell us what they feel here and now. Berne greatly decreased the amount of time spent in staff conference type games, such as *If It Weren't For You (For Them)*, etc. I believe that my method reduces the psychological distance between patients and trainee staff, that it reduces regressive tendencies and magical expectations quickly, that it teaches therapists how much they can learn from patients if they will use them as collaborators and teachers. It has the further advantage that the patient does not have to wait until the next session to deal with some upset feelings he may have relative to what someone said about him in the discussion period.

One dilemma I have had in the four years of using this method is: When shall I teach Transactional Analysis to both groups? Another is: For the sake of teaching, shall I confine my therapy almost exclusively to TA? I have settled the first of these by teaching TA during any of the sessions if I believe it is appropriate to do so at the time. I do not teach it before beginning treatment. I have decided not to use TA exclusively during treatment because I do not believe it is always the best method to use at a particular time. For example, Gestalt or psychodramatic or behavior modification or encounter techniques may work better in particular instances. I often contrast TA and psychoanalytic methods during Groups B and C. I do this for two reasons:

1. Many of these therapists have psychoanalytic backgrounds and can learn easier if their previous training is not discounted.
2. I want them to realize that I know more than one treatment method (indeed, that I pity the therapist who only knows one theory, one method) and that I usually select TA as the treatment of choice.

Only four years ago, some of the therapists in training wanted to know formulations of the therapy in non-TA terms, especially psychoanalytic. Now some of them complain that they do not get enough TA in these sessions. A very rapid change in this one mental health center!

In four years of using this method, I have noted that the boundaries between the three groups become blurred as the group nears termination or even earlier. For example, when one trainee came late and the only empty chair in the room was in Group A, he smiled. I asked if he would like to join us. He smiled that he would. I told him to participate in any way that he wished. He did not speak during the remainder of Group A but almost as soon as it was completed, he said he was surprised at how much more involved he felt with what was happening in the group. (He was usually one of the most involved participants in Groups B and C.) After looking at videotape replays several weeks after they are made (tapes are of all three groups), trainees frequently move their chairs in with those of the patients. Almost midway through the year, we usually ask Group B if they will stop giving so much nonverbal direction to people in Group A.

As the external group boundaries of Groups A and B become blurred later in the year, I may occasionally ask some trainees from Group B if they will help us in using non-TA treatment modalities such as dramatizing a conflict for a patient. For example, when a patient complained of being walled in by her Parent's injunction of "Don't be you," I asked her to describe the wall. When she said it was thick and long and she didn't know any way to get through it, I asked if she wanted to see what she felt like when literally walled off from participants in the group. She agreed. I asked eight trainees to come form a wall between her and us in the therapy group. She felt very safe behind this wall; the trainees looked uncomfortable. Eventually, she tired of the wall and wanted to rejoin the group. I asked what she'd have to do to get back in the group. She replied that she would have to move. We waited. She moved. In the ensuing discussion, trainees told of how they did not like to wall her off but they saw that she did this to herself by remaining motionless behind the wall. They commented that they liked being closer to the group and being even more involved with it.

Patients almost always say to at least several trainees during the year, "I don't know whether to tell you what's on my mind or not. I don't want to hurt your feelings." Trainees have usually felt this way toward patients earlier in the year.

In further evolution of this three-group method, we first had the group therapists become leaders of all three groups. For the most part, this worked well. During this last year (1975), all of us agreed to abolish Group B (trainee group) and to prolong the therapy session for Group A another half hour. Reasons included the desire of patients and trainees that the therapy group last longer; they all felt that they could ask questions, make comments, etc. in a half hour. As of May 1975, we now spend an hour and a half in Group A, the patients and therapists; then we spend one-half hour in a large group with everyone—patients, therapists, and trainees—in a circle. Directions still include a statement that anyone there can say anything she or he wishes. With the elimination of what we had called Group B, the trainee group, there was less confusion about whether trainees were to act like a leaderless therapy group, a seminar, a T group. I believe that part of this earlier confusion was because various therapists at the center believed in cotherapy, had a lot of T-group experience, and were uneasy at not having a clear role in this new treatment-training approach. All the trainees knew that they were there as learners (at least they knew it cognitively, in their Adult ego states). I suspect that the Child ego states in the trainees may have envied the patients to some degree. However, I have not validated this to my own satisfaction yet.

OTHER APPLICATIONS

I have seen such rapid learning take place with this method that I have taken another look at the peer-group treatment so common in TA training centers. I decided that if trainees could critique each other under the supervision of a teaching therapist, and if patients could serve as our collaborators in treatment-training institutions, why not in private practice and in TA training also? Accordingly, in peer-group treatment-training, I believe that the first persons to give feedback and critique to a trainee-therapist should be the persons he or she is treating. I know that many trainers have the supervisor speak first. I believe that they use the wrong order and tend to set up a climate in which it is difficult for the less-skilled therapists to comment comfortably.

I have therefore used this method in office supervision of therapists who are in advanced TA training by asking one of my therapy groups to come at no fee for an extra session of two hours in which they would be treated by therapists in advanced TA training. At the end of 20 to 30 minutes treatment by a trainee, the action is stopped and patients are the first to give feedback and critique to the therapist. Many of them seem delighted to teach the therapists. Rivalries that some patients tend to hide from me are readily seen as they compete with some of the therapists. Cohesion in the patient group increases rapidly. Patients' perspectives of themselves and of therapists broaden and deepen. Patients are more likely to help themselves, each other, and me in our therapy session in following weeks.

SUMMARY

I have described a method for having the patient be our collaborator not only in psychotherapy but in training. Advantages of the method for patients are:

1. Regression, including magical expectations, is minimized.
2. Objectivity regarding patients' troubles increases rapidly.
3. Patients quickly learn that therapists are people too; that none of them are infallible.

Advantages of the method for therapists in training are:

1. They stay awake.
2. Their learning is facilitated by less geographic and psychological distance from patients.

3. They learn that no therapist always has all the answers for all questions.

4. They learn that patients are much tougher than they thought; that the therapists' words and theories are not magic.

Thus far I have not been able to discern any disadvantages of this method to the patients, and find that the only disadvantage to the therapists in training is that they are likely to feel some anxiety during their first few experiences in the group.

REFERENCES

1. O'Hearne, J., "Shall Patients Be Included in Supervisory Sessions?" paper read at 1970 meeting of American Group Psychotherapy Association, New York.

2. Berne, E., "Staff-Patient Staff Conferences," *American Journal of Psychiatry* 125 (1966), pp. 286–293.

PART 4

TA and other therapies

Contributors

PSYCHOANALYSIS AND TA
Robert C. Drye, M.D.

ADLERIAN PSYCHOLOGY AND TA
Jacqueline Simoneaux, M.S.W.

ANALYTICAL PSYCHOLOGY AND TA
Eugene A. Merlin, M.A.

PSYCHODRAMA AND TA
Alan Jacobs, C.S.W.

GESTALT THERAPY AND TA
Muriel James, Ed.D.

BIOENERGETICS AND TA
Joseph Cassius, Ph.D.

CLIENT-CENTERED THERAPY AND TA
Thomas J. Long, Ed.D.
Lynette A. Long, Ph.D.

OTHER TREATMENT MODALITIES AND TA
Doris Wild Helmering, M.S.W.

ERIC BERNE AS GROUP THERAPIST: A VERBATIM

CHAPTER 11

psychoanalysis and TA

ROBERT C. DRYE

Eric Berne, the founder of Transactional Analysis, was trained as a psychoanalyst at the New York and San Francisco Institutes, and frequently referred to psychoanalytic treatment in combination with TA. In both his early and late writings[1] he draws many theoretical comparisons and connections between TA and psychoanalysis, some of which will be presented later in this chapter. Psychoanalysis is a method for treating patients, a psychological theory, and an investigative method. I will (1) describe psychoanalysis, historically, theoretically, and clinically; (2) indicate some parallels and contrasts of that theory with TA theory; and (3) indicate how using these two theories in a complementary way offers a logical system from which the therapist may differentially choose his or her approaches to a particular clinical problem.

FREUD AND THE HISTORY OF PSYCHOANALYSIS

Psychoanalysis was originally developed entirely by one man, Sigmund Freud. Freud was born in 1856 in what is now Czechoslovakia but was then part of the Austrian empire. His father was a successful Jewish merchant, and Freud had a classical education at the University of Vienna. A brilliant student, he was master of several languages, and used quotations from Shakespeare as readily as from Goethe to illustrate his points. He was at first a neurologist, and published a number of monographs, including one on cerebral palsy which is still a classic. He studied with Charcot and Bernheim in France, and observed the use of hypnosis in the treatment of hysterical symptoms such as bizarre paralyses, pain, numbness, amnesias, and confusions (often called *dissociations**). Treatments accepted in those days consisted of rest, electric shocks, and baths, and, even with the addition of hypnosis, the results were unpredictable. Freud's friend and patron, Joseph Breuer, a senior internist in Vienna, told him of a woman he had cured in 1882 after a year's intensive work of daily visits. Freud persuaded him to write this as a case study which Freud included with some of his own case histories in their joint publication *Studies in Hysteria,* in 1892.[2] Psychoanalytic treatment had begun.

With his own patients, Freud had already discovered that hypnosis was not really necessary, but that patients obtained relief by simply speaking freely to describe *whatever* came into their minds that related to their symptoms. This technique of *free association* has remained in psychoanalytic practice to this day. Freud noted that these associations lead to the discovery of a conflict between a wish or memory and the person's morals or self-picture. The offending wish or memory is split off from awareness (*unconscious*). The energy of the wish or memory reappears in the symptom, hence the term "dynamic unconscious." Freud noted that these wishes or memories were usually sexual or angry. For instance, a woman with persistent leg pain obtained relief upon remembering that she had thoughts of marrying her brother-in-law at a time when her sister was seriously ill. Between 1900 and 1905 Freud wrote a series of books, *The Interpretation of Dreams,*[3] the *Psychopathology of Everyday Life*[4] and *Three Contributions to a Theory of Sexuality*[5] in which he showed how similar conflicts coud be understood through the analysis of dreams and errors. Freud himself was most excited about his discovery that dreams could be understood as disguised fulfillments of repressed childhood wishes. He developed the *psychosexual* model of early human development.

According to Freud, human sexuality covers a whole range of psychophysiological responses. It develops first through an oral phase, with energy invested in the sensations felt and expressed through the oral cavity, then an anal period with energy invested in the sensations around defecation and the struggles of toilet training, then a phallic phase with genital preoccupation and infantile masturbation, and finally a genital phase in which the other zones could be included in normal heterosexual foreplay, and the feelings of the *object* (person towards whom the urges are directed) are important. Unintegrated phe-

---

* In this paper, italicized words are technical words, usually defined by the preceding phrase or sentence.

nomena from the earlier developmental periods could appear as perversions or as unfulfilled childhood wishes likely to reappear via dreams or symptoms. Such unintegrated phenomena are known as *fixations*. These are islands of energy left behind in the course of development. Freud's metaphor was of an advancing army that needed to leave detachments behind to fall back to in case of later difficulties. This retreat to an earlier developmental phase Freud called *regression*. Fixations may occur because of too much or too little gratification in that period. Freud's emphasis on the sexuality and aggressiveness of children was very disturbing to his colleagues. Freud understood this. "I am disturbing the sleep of the world." Breuer discontinued psychoanalytic practice when his first patient showed unmistakable sexual feelings toward him. Most of Freud's opposition, however, came from physicians who had no personal experience using his approach, but were horrified that he postulated these wishes for even normal children and grownups.

Upon being scorned or threatened by his colleagues, Freud withdrew for several years to relative professional isolation. He maintained his private practice, continued to analyze his own dreams, and entered into an intense and famous correspondence with a surgeon in Berlin named Fliess.[6] As he achieved some successes with his patients, his practice gradually grew and a few men began studying with him. Some of them, like Adler and Jung, and later Rank and Reich, made major contributions to psychoanalysis before starting their own different systems.

The history of the psychoanalytic movement has been punctuated by several different schisms. The theoretical difference in each new system has been to decrease the emphasis on infantile sexuality, and to emphasize another aspect of human psychology, for instance Jung emphasized myths and symbols as an inheritance from a universal unconscious. There was often some bitterness between Freud and his previous disciples. Today the different schools seem to once again be willing to meet as fellow scientists. For instance, there were several symposia organized recently by Freudian and Jungian analysts after the Freud-Jung letters were published in 1974.[7] Freud himself continually modified his theory, writing a number of important papers from 1914 to 1923; the model of the mind developed through these works will be discussed further on. Space does not permit me to discuss the Alderian or Jungian variants, beyond noting that both Adlerian and Jungian training are available in the United States, although on a much smaller scale than classical (Freudian) analysis. By 1914, The International Psychoanalytic Association had been founded; journals were regularly published, and Freud had lectured in the United States. Psychoanalysis survived the war, and Institutes to teach it were rapidly established in Germany, Hungary, England, and the United States. Teachers from this period of rapid expansion were Karl Abraham, Hanns Sachs, Ferenczi,

and Ernest Jones, all of whom made major clinical and theoretical contributions; they, with Rank, formed a small council with Freud called "the six."

Freud continued to write prolifically, but from 1922 on struggled with a series
of painful operations for mouth cancer. He appeared at major meetings only
briefly, and spoke rarely. He was awarded the Goethe prize in Germany for
literary excellence in 1932, and finally received a Professorship at the University of Vienna which had been delayed more by anti-semitism than by his controversial views. Even then, he always felt unrecognized in his own country.
The City of Vienna honored him posthumously in 1971 with a special meeting
in his honor. His old office in Vienna is now a public museum. He continued
his clinical practice in Vienna until 1938 when the Gestapo seized his home
and library and he was saved from prison only through the intervention of
Marie Bonaparte, a wealthy French analyst. He spent a year practicing and
writing in London and died of cancer in 1939. During the Hitler era, many
European analysts were driven from their countries and provided much of the
leadership in the United States, England, and South America. Reich, Alexander, Hartmann, Kris, Fenichel, in this country, and Anna Freud and Mela-
nie Klien in England, are famous "second-generation analysts" some of whom
are still teaching at this writing.

CURRENT USE OF PSYCHOANALYSIS

Treatment: Today, psychoanalytic treatment is usually conducted in from
three to five 45–50 minute sessions a week. The patient usually lies on a couch,
but may sit up and face the analyst if he feels more comfortable. The patient
is asked to follow the basic analytic rule, which is to report whatever he is
thinking and feeling without censorship, including "here and now" thoughts
and wishes, however trivial they may appear to him. Freud observed that whenever patients were silent and he asked them what was going on, they were experiencing some feeling about him that they were not expressing. This phenomenon of "not-wanting-to-report" is called *resistance*. The analysis of resistance is a cornerstone of psychoanalytic technique, for the resistance is a
sign to the analyst of the ways in which the patient has kept his conflicts out
of his own awareness. These ways are called *defenses*. The feelings about the
analyst, the *transference*, are a specific resistance. The term "transference" is
used because the feelings and thoughts about the analyst, and the defenses
against awareness of these, are often repetitions of phenomena involving people in the patient's early life, assumed to be transferred from unconscious
mental representations of the early situations. In order to increase the likelihood that these feelings can emerge from the past, the analyst does not intrude,
but maintains a relatively inactive role, mainly listening. He comments only
when he perceives a resistance, or sees a need to focus the patient's attention

on his wishes, actions, and reactions to the analytic situation. The patient is more likely, in the absence of cues from the analyst, to use his own old techniques to avoid, to reach, and to understand people. The analyst's interventions are intended to help the patient develop a *self-observing* as well as an experiencing faculty, so that the patient can both understand and experience the process. In addition to observing behavior in the office, the analyst will also invite the patient to observe his dreams, since these give valuable clues to the current state of the analysis as well as to past conflicts.

In a successfully conducted analysis, the patient's symptoms eventually come to focus on the analyst and the *transference neurosis* becomes more important than the neurotic symptoms originally complained of; often some improvement will be noted in the patient's outside difficulties while his difficulties with the analyst become central. The resolution of the transference neurosis comes out of the *working through* of crises in which time after time the patient experiences his own feelings and wishes, observes his own ways of handling them, gradually recognizes the differences between the past and the present, and gives up his childhood wishes in exchange for the possibility of realistic success in the present. Themes emerge gradually and they often are repeated (worked through) several times, before the details become clear. Characters in the drama may be seen differently over time: last year mother was the villain, this year the heroine, with father the opposite. Each patient's style and objects are their own; for instance, I was unable to understand one woman until I realized that she was experiencing me as her older sister, with whom she used to have long periods of sharing feelings. With the termination of the analysis, the patient can finally recognize the analyst as a fair, caring, and knowledgeable guide rather than as a guilty parent who ought to make reparations to him for his childhood frustrations. Now that he can master his troubling emotions, he no longer needs to defend himself with symptoms. This entire procedure ordinarily takes a matter of several years, although successful analyses of less than a year have been reported.

Time, as well as money, limits the number of people who can be analyzed. Another limitation is that patients who have symptoms other than the classical neuroses (hysteria, phobia, and compulsions) and the related neurotic personality disorders, may have difficulty developing a transference, or may be unable to split experience and observation so that their feelings become too intense for them or the analyst. Even with these patients, a number of analysts in recent years have reported succesful work.[8,9,10] However, psychoanalysis is principally indicated for patients who have some personal stability despite a neurotic problem. The use of "psychoanalytically oriented" psychotherapies, that is, those based on psychoanalytic theory, will be discussed in the last part of this chapter.

PSYCHOLOGICAL THEORY OF PSYCHOANALYSIS

As a psychological theory, psychoanalysis has been primarily developed from psychoanalytic treatment, and to a lesser extent from child observation and from other psychological data, such as projective tests and the behavior of psychotic patients. Psychoanalytic theory holds that much adult behavior, including neurotic symptoms, is determined by childhood fantasies and experiences. The child is frightened by some of his wishes, since he believes from what he knows of his world that they will have disastrous consequences. In addition to external stimulation of wishes, Freud postulated a continuous internal stimulation by the *drives* (sometimes mistranslated as instincts). These are biologically produced and can be labeled sexual, aggressive, and (in current theory) narcissistic, which are also descriptive of their derivative wishes. As he grows through childhood, his fears may include (1) fear of unmanageable excitement from the drives, (2) fear of loss of the nurturing object, (3) fear of injury to the self, particularly castration,* (4) fear of loss of love, (5) fear of disapproval, and in relation to narcissism (6) loss of self-esteem and (7) loss of esteem for the parent. As the child grows, he stores memories and fantasies, as pictures which include wish, self, *object,* (the gratifier of the wish), affect, and outcome. These factors are called a complex and the picture of all or part of the complex is called an *internal* representation.

Freud postulated that when a child finds a situation overwhelming—that is, when he responds to the situation with intense terror, helplessness, disgust, and/or rage—he will attempt to avoid present and future distress by reorganizing himself psychologically to explain its occurrence and to prevent distress in the future. For instance, a small boy is playing with his penis. He is enjoying the sensation and is excited about his body. Mother discovers this play and suddenly and massively disapproves, showing him her own anger, fear, or disgust. If the child, who is relatively helpless, feels flooded by his own fear, shame, hurt, or anger, and is unable to readily recover his psychologic balance, this is called a *traumatic* experience. The child, in order to explain and to attempt to master this experience, uses his own fantasies about sex and about Mother's disapproval and reorganizes psychologically to avoid a similar experience in the future. This might mean not letting himself get as excited, or not to share his excitement with another. The entire scene and its associated fantasies must be kept out of his awareness, and wishes and feelings connected with it that might reactivate the memory must be psychologically avoided, ignored, or hidden. If the child does not feel seriously disturbed, no matter how upset the parent, he may simply *consciously* avoid future discovery by mother, rather than change his own potential for experience.

---

* The little girl, of course, can't lose what she hasn't got, but she may fantasize that she once had one, or has one inside her which will grow, or that mother didn't give her one in the first place because she was bad, etc.

Freud suggested that when a person is about to experience anything which might recall the original experience, he will mobilize psychological defenses to keep it out of awareness.[11] These memory traces however, including complete scenes, can be brought into awareness during analytic treatment via dreams and the analysis of resistance, or at least can be convincingly inferred from their obvious derivatives. These notions can be represented in this model of the mind, the *structural model* of analysis. The term "structure" is used because the parts of the model are seen like biological organs, each with definite psychologic functions. As with any model, the psychological functions are placed in subgroups in a way that seems to organize our present knowledge in a meaningful way. Statements such as "the Ego does" are intended as shorthand for "I am grouping the following functions together under the heading 'the Ego' because they seem regularly closely related and I think you can understand the phenomena we are observing more easily if I do such grouping."

STRUCTURAL MODEL OF PSYCHOANALYSIS

The model shown here is the structural model of psychoanalysis.[12] Biologically fed drives push toward the surface. They are not directly experienced but inferred. For instance, I can experience a continuum from smooth movement toward another person to obtain something, to anger that he isn't doing what I want, to a rage in which I attack him, to a tantrum in which I attack anything or anybody, to an epileptiform convulsion in which my body simply moves randomly—and imagine behind this sequence a drive called *aggression*. Drives may also merge, i.e., aggression and sexuality in rape. Generally, less modulated experiences come from earlier phases of development, and their representations are shown at the bottom of the diagram. However, a particular event and the feelings associated with it may be shown at more than one place on the diagram, usually with some differences in content or affect.

In addition, the most primitive area, the *Id,* is characterized by a different kind of thinking, *primary process,* where there is no sense of time, logical contradictions can exist side by side, reality is not differentiated from fantasy, and representations are linked symbolically; i.e., a flag is the same as a country, or a snake the same as a penis. Because of this ability to create and retain symbols, we can link incoming stimuli to past experience.

The part of the mind that mediates between external reality and internal drives is the *Ego.* The Ego accomplishes this through the functions of observing, remembering, thinking, and mobilizing the appropriate body functions, as well as defending against disruptive levels of feeling. The nondefensive functions of the Ego are sometimes called *autonomous,* meaning that they have no specific psychic meaning and are therefore not affected by psychic conflict. For instance, we usually walk easily and automatically whatever our state of mind. If other defenses fail, however, these functions may be reinvolved, for instance we may obsessively count our steps.

The most powerful defense is *repression,* the complete blocking from awareness of a disturbing complex. The repression barrier is shown on the right side of the diagram. If repression is not entirely effective, other defenses are mobilized to support it, such as *conversion,* the symbolic expression of the conflict in the neuro-muscular system, or *displacement,* where the feeling is shifted to another person or situation, or *identification,* where the person blocks or otherwise handles the conflict in the same way that an important person in his life did, or *disavowal,** where the person does not admit disturbing reality perceptions. These defensees can also operate to the left of the barrier to deal with less significant experiences which do not require repression and do not relate to the highly charged complexes that originally required repression. Note that the defenses all operate outside of awareness. This is shown on the model by the dashed line between the unconscious and the *preconscious* (that which is potentially available to consciousness). Note that this line passes above the Id as well as above most of the Ego and the Superego.

The structure on the far left of the model, the Superego,† functions by means of self-observation and self-criticism, and the mobilizing of approval and disapproval. The affects related to these functions are pride, shame, and guilt. This structure is shown on the diagram as dipping deep into the Id, because we clinically observe that self-criticism can be extremely primitive, even murderous, as in suicidal depressions. The Superego can also provide unrealistically high self-esteem, *grandiosity.* The Superego seems to particularly relate to one's self picture.

---

* A common way of dealing with psychologic reality is to combine disavowal with *projection:* "I'm not angry—you are." Another very early defense is splitting, in which the mind acts as if only one side of an issue at any one time really matters. For instance, on one occasion a person might say, "I know my mother must have been angry at me but all I can remember is the good times," and on another occasion, "I know my mother must have been good to me but all I can remember is our fighting." This defense is very primitive, since the person has to ignore half of reality at any one time, but it also means that the mind only has to handle one side of a problem.

† In early writings, Freud used the term *ego-ideal* ("an ideal in himself by which he measures his actual (self)"[13]) for the functions of self-observation and self-criticism. This term is currently used to refer to the narcissistic portion of the Superego, the function of self-admiration and self-depreciation, sometimes as a subagency of the superego, and sometimes as a fourth portion of the mind equal and parallel to the superego.

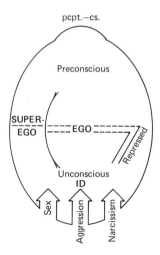

At the top of the model is "pcpt.-cs.", an abbreviation for perception-conscious. This represents an eye, or window through which external perceptions enter the mind. External here means external to the mind, so that my sore foot, for instance, is external to my mind, although I may develop a picture of it in my mind. External stimuli are ordinarily conscious, or capable of becoming so if they were magnified; disavowal may prevent certain external stimuli from becoming conscious.

In this model the Ego is also given the function of mediating and *synthesizing* the demands of the Id, the prohibitions or encouragements of the Superego, and information about reality whether experienced as demands or opportunities. This synthesizing mostly goes on automatically and outside of awareness. Freud commented that the Ego could be seen as the rider on a horse, sometimes guiding the power of the animal, and sometimes only appearing to be in control, while actually following the animal's wishes. For instance, on the one hand, I am explaining psychoanalysis as part of a project, yet I may on the other hand, out of my awareness, be responding to powerful internal pressures to show off my erudition. Incidentally, the successful expression of a drive through socially acceptable behavior, with the original aim disguised, is called *sublimation*.

Symptom formation, in this more elaborate model, proceeds as follows: (1) Incoming external stimuli reverberate with a repressed complex, or the repressing forces are momentarily weakened, or both. (2) As the impulse presses towards awareness, extra energy is required for the repression. If repression is successful, the person may only be aware of some diminished energy subjectively, some decreased flexibility in thinking, or a general dullness. The blocked impulse may now seek discharge through regressive paths, and a new struggle goes on at the repression barrier, with symptoms occurring as more defenses are mobilized. For instance, a married woman goes to a party by herself, and finds herself flirting with an attractive stranger who propositions her. If this is not a heavily conflicted issue with her, she can either continue the affair, with attention to her own values and the possible external risk, or discontinue it, and enjoy the encounter either way. If this is a conflicted area for her, she may have several experiences: (a) a loss of excitement, whether she says yes or no, (b) anxiety or guilt out of proportion to her actual behavior or even in opposition to it (even if she says no she may react to the fantasy of saying yes), (c) regressive expressions of her excitement, for instance from genital to anal with anal itching or diarrhea, (d) finally, she may have phobic avoidance of parties in the future, as an attempt to prevent a recurrence. These connections are largely out of her awareness and are recovered during therapy.

The most recent addition to this model is Kohut's formulations about narcissism.[14] The infant begins with the perfect mothering provided, and a feeling of omnipotent power at getting needs met by an omniscient parent, with the self and object almost fused. However, human defects quickly lead to frustration: mother fails. Now the infant, to repair his sense of hurt and fright (that the perfect mother has failed him and/or that he has lost control over her), recreates either a grandiose self-image that can expect unconditional mothering and/or establishes a picture of an idealized omnipotent parent, who can be expected invariably to provide the strength and confidence the helpless infant is needing. When such expectations are an important part of the patient's psychologic life, he is termed a narcissistic character, who may have a wide variety of symptoms, including depression, hypochondriasis, and supersensitivity to shame or praise. Following an episode in which the therapist fails to meet expectations, or fails to recognize the importance of the patient's unrealistic self-picture, a severe *regression* may occur with temporary psychotic disorganization, anger, or body concerns. However, if the therapist recognizes empathically the nature of the episode, these patients rapidly recover to their normal base-line. (Note the backache example near the end of this article.) These concepts are parallel to the OK-not OK feelings of TA, although at a level of primitive intensity which the OK-not OK descriptions in TA often do not seem to recognize.

THE PSYCHOANALYTIC MODEL AND TA STRUCTURAL ANALYSIS

The accompanying table lists psychological functions from the psychoanalytic model and indicates where they go on the analytic and the TA structural models.

Function	TA	Psychoanalysis
Self-observation	P, A	Superego, Ego
Approval/disapproval	P, P1, CP	Superego
Nurturing	P, P1	Ego
Reality Testing	A	Ego
Planning	A	Ego
Memories	P, C, A	Ego, Superego, Id
Synthesizing	A, A1	Ego
Intuition and Creatvity	A1, C1	Ego in regression
Impulse control	A, P, P1	Ego, Superego
Defenses	Exclusions, boundaries	Ego
Symptom formation	Contamination, exclusion Archaic C or P with A blocked out	Id impulses, in conflict with Ego and Superego restrictions, compromise formation that expresses impulse as well as defenses.
Drives	C1	Id
Narcissism	C1, P1	Id, Superego
Impulses	C1, P1, CP	Id, Ego, Superego
Sense of self	Ego state with free energy	Self-representations in Ego and Superego
Executive	Ego state with unbound energy	Ego

Comparing these two models, both of which are to explain internal, influencing dialogues, and *not* external social transactions, I see more similiarities than differences. The TA model, however is less explicit about earlier, more primitive states, which Berne included in his notion of "archeopsyche,"[15] a primitive biologic internal program which might influence the C and other ego states. He also suggested further order structural analysis of the C, each further order being more primitive and having more primitive anlage of P and A.[16] He repeatedly refers to ego states within C as well as P. This corresponds very closely to the notion of multiple representations within the psa. model, which are called complexes. These are usually not specified on the TA model, however. There is also some difference in the way symptom formation is explained. Both models use the notion of conflict, but the TA model includes the possibility of direct expression of frightened Child, with the A blocked out. Psa. talks of "weak ego" in such a situation, while TA talks of "permeable ego-state bound-

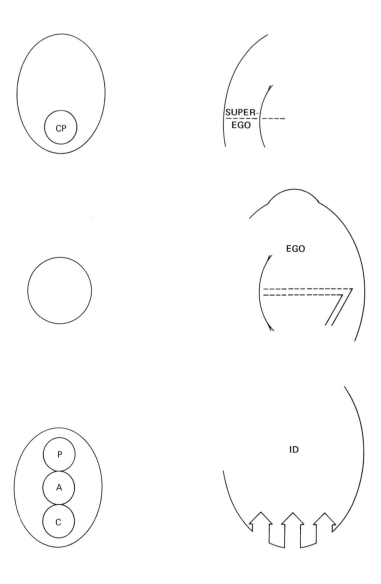

aries"[17] and objects to the notion of weak ego, saying the A is present but not used. At this point, the difference between the two models most often stated— that Id, Ego, and Superego are constructs and P, A, and C are social realities —is not convincing to me. I agree that P, A, and C are social realities in a transactional model, but in this interpersonal model the more the C ego state is described in detail structurally, the closer the subdivisions resemble the psa. model. Similarly, in the work of TA researchers looking at early C ego states as part of reparenting[18,19] there is a close correspondence with the developmental phases described by Freud and more recently developed in detail by Mahler.[20]

The largest difference between the two models is the absence in the TA model of "unconscious" as a quality. Although Berne speaks of using couch and free association to reach the "archaic Child",[21] he does not refer to the unconscious as such, but does refer to scripts, a preconscious life plan.[22] Incidentally, I think the script, which cannot be directly placed on the model, is a concept which can replace the notion in psa. of *repetition compulsion,* which can be represented on the psa. model as persistant pressure from the id, superego punishments for id/ego prohibited activity, and ego attempts to master an earlier trauma. Repetition compulsion is a way of describing someone doing the same behavior over and over against his obvious interest, e.g., repeatedly marrying alcoholic spouses.

The psa. model also can be used to represent a related notion, *acting out.* Instead of identifying and working through a conflict or expressing it by a symptom, I may express it by behavior. For instance, I may express anger I would be uncomfortable expressing directly by forgetting to do something for the person at whom I'm angry. The ego allows motor discharge of the impulse in a disguised form. This does not change the nature of the underlying conflict, merely relieves it temporarily. Since it somewhat relieves the drive pressure without evoking feared unpleasant feelings, as if the conflict were confronted directly, someone may do this repetitively, and this may become another source of the repetition compulsion. For instance, repeated homosexual transient contacts may be attempts to get the approval of a more powerful man (perhaps originally the father); in this example, narcissistic needs of which the man is intensely ashamed are replaced by still somewhat shameful behavior which briefly relieves the tension without settling it. Some of this could be represented on the TA model as C behavior and wishes, but the model still does not have a place for the unconscious aspects, or for the *notions* of displacement.

COMPLEMENTARY TREATMENT WITH TA
AND PSYCHOANALYSIS

The usefulness of psa. thinking, like TA thinking, is easy to test. Does it help us understand people better, and consequently can we make more effective therapeutic interventions? For the purposes of this chapter, does it add to the skills of a therapist who knows the TA model and other TA thinking? At times the approaches seem so similar that I expect the reader to say "That's just another way to say the same thing." For instance, the psa. therapist listens to the associations, A to B to C to D etc., and notices the sequences, such as impulse, scare, retreat, shame, impulse. He can then formulate the *dynamic line,* that is the way in which each action is partly a response to its predecessor—as the impulse pushes for discharge, arousing scare, and the patient withdraws to reduce scare, but then feels shame at his withdrawal, and again expresses the impulse. Berne[23] describes a patient cycling through flirtatious tittering, stealthy appraisal, and prim attention to auditory hallucinations. The two models are closest as we look just below the surface of behavior. The closer to the surface, the better fit the TA model has, the more I wish to understand underlying processes, the more useful the psa. model.

The psa. model represents by the Id that the archaic C is always present and that there are several different developmental areas within the C. These are manifested indirectly and are largely out of the patient's awareness. Knowing they are there, I can determine whether they are manifesting themselves in some significant way in the present and whether they need to be included in the patient's contract.

Since the Id also includes the pre-logical thinking of the C (primary process), the therapist may be less surprised at the illogical or even crazy behavior of some clients who seem otherwise well organized. These earlier organizations of the C can be understood psychoanalytically in several dimensions. Not only are the impulses more primitive, and primary process present, but the representations of the self and the object of the impulse may be fragmented, fused, partly linked, or separated. The focal body area (oral, anal, etc.) also varies as outlined in psychosexual development. See Berne: "think sphincter,"[24] and for general organization of these levels, Gedo and Goldberg.[25] For instance, the C of 3–6 years is beginning to reality-test, and gather a lot of information, specifically about sex differences. He treats the mother and father as separate people who are also separate from him. The major impulse is phallic. Because the major affect is anxious jealousy of the father (for the boy) and love for the mother, this level of the C often called oedipal, after the legend of Oedipus— a man who killed his father and married his mother. Clinically, depending on the psychopathology, earlier levels of C will be in evidence, such as the anality of the previous example (anxious lady). The psa. therapist is always watching for the regression to previous levels of development under the stress of the frustrating situation. This includes the question, what developmental level is the *best* this person already has achieved? This will influence the way the patient is approached, whether using psa. terminology or TA.[26]

The multiple representations of particular conflicts in the psa. model alert the therapist to the possible need to examine particular conflicts repeatedly as part of working through, and not to be surprised when a single decontamination or redecision does not permanently cure a symptom. One of my patients, for instance, has at least three memories, at 8, 10, and 14, where for different reasons she felt worthless and wished for death. Not only are she and her family pictured in the memories, but she has representations of important associated memories of them and herself which influenced the decision she made in each scene, and memories of later experiences which reinforced each decision. To the extent that these memories are influential in her current behavior, they will need working through, so that the patient herself becomes aware of the multiple ways she maintains her bad feelings. The psa. thinker expects that with this awareness, the patient will feel an increased mastery of herself, and less a victim of mysterious forces.

The techniques of becoming aware can be considered separately.* The psa. thinker does not necessarily assume this has to be an exhaustive process, only that it *may* be.[27] In other words, if a patient returns with a recurrent symptom, this may not be a failure, but a discovery of an important unresolved conflict at an earlier developmental level. For a discussion of this issue with the TA model see Goulding.[28] The psa. model notion of defense is also useful, I believe, in contrast to Berne's suggestion that TA can bypass these processes.[29] For instance, the person who is using intellectualization as a defense is doing more than excluding C. He is doing it in a special way which the therapist can recognize is important to him. The process of identification is useful for introducing new people into the patient's P.[30] In the same way, I believe that transference phenomena, as they occur, are more specific than the C-P or P-C crossed transactions Berne reduces them to. To work with a particular patient, this specificity may not be necessary, but I believe it often is. (Again, the technique used, such as gestalt, to obtain the specificity, is outside what I am discussing.)

The best recent paper describing how a psa. psychotherapist might think is by Offenkrantz and Tobin.[31] They specify clearly what contracts they make and what they believe can be used from psa. in once-or-twice-a-week therapy, whether or not the patient is suitable for classical analysis. This clarity has been missing in most papers about psa. psychotherapy, and one useful aspect of the TA model is that TA language seems easier to use in a clear way, particularly in describing transactions. The authors do not include or exclude TA, which I believe is certainly a psa.-oriented system because of the close correspondences noted above.

The authors give many examples of "folk wisdom," ways of treating many common conditions which I believe will be readily understandable to anyone who has read this article; they particularly emphasize throughout the usefulness for all psychotherapists of two notions, based on the psa. model. The first is to pay careful attention to transference phenomena which may interfere with the treatment process, and the second is that the patient gets well by identification with the therapist. They believe all patients, regardless of diagnosis, arrive at the therapist's office ashamed that they have not been better

---

* Berne describes using free association on the couch in combination with TA groups as a good way to rapidly reach archaic C once C/A boundaries have been clarified in the group so that the patient's A is available to study the experience rather than being overwhelmed by it.

able to control their thoughts, behavior, and feelings. The patient can immediately use from the therapist a recognition that he might be feeling this way, and can use the therapist's commitment to his work, sense of himself as someone worthwhile, honest about his own humanity, and reasonable control (through understanding) over feelings and impulses, as a model. "I understand how painful it is to be angry at me and yet to be so afraid to express it." This contacts the patient's experiencing Ego, which "feels itself caught" between the Id impulse (hostile feelings) and the Superego reaction (guilt, inferiority, helplessness, fear of retaliation). This interpretation promotes an identification with the therapist's ego that "is better able to tolerate both sides of such a conflict." The therapist does not demand anything from the patient beyond their contract. Particularly, the therapist does not depend on a particular patient's recovery, continuing therapy, discontinuing therapy, returning, or staying away to feel competent, admired, or loved.

What if someone fails to understand? Let me cite an example from my own experience, in which a man sustained an accidental injury. Initially his spouse seemed concerned, but then she suddenly shifted to her own problems, asking for his sympathy. The man experienced this shift as a complete withdrawal and suddenly had a backache unrelated to the present injury, but referring to pain from an operation months before. As soon as the therapist conveyed his understanding of this sequence, the pain disappeared. This can be described in TA as a symbiotic switch, but the specific narcissistic regression to be concerned about his own body is more clearly described by psa. This system, carefully described in the article, seems to me richer in the details of the defensive operation than currently available TA language.

Finally, if this model is useful, the TA therapist may consider obtaining consultation from a psychoanalyst, or even referring a patient to a qualified analyst for psychoanalysis. To summarize, the major indications for psychoanalysis are:

1. Persistent impasses despite reasonably conducted TA therapy (with the use of some gestalt to clarify out-of-awareness behaviors of the patient), particularly if the patient has a phobia, conversion symptom, or obsessive compulsive neurosis, or related personality disorders.

2. Some patients with brief but stormy eruptions of archaic C (borderline syndrome) which disrupt problem-solving despite an apparently available A. The level of distrust and distancing early decisions here may be so severe that they need a more continuous relationship, as in psychoanalysis.

3. Patients with major narcissistic disorders, where narcissistic transferences can also be more clearly observed in a several-times-a-week structure.

4. A strong personal preference, based on previous useful experience with psa. psychotherapy or the desire to know oneself in depth as well as obtain

relief. Menninger[32] commented that improved psychotherapies that would be faster than psychoanalysis would be found, but that analysis would remain important for therapists and educators because of the increased self-knowledge they would obtain. Naturally, a TA therapist will be free to consider that this leisurely approach might be part of a loser or non-winner script.

REFERENCES

1. Berne, Eric, *Principles of Group Treatment* (New York: Grove, 1966), pp. 101–137, and *Transactional Analysis in Psychotherapy* (New York: Grove, 1961), pp. 160–164.

2. Freud, Sigmund, and Joseph Breuer, "Studies in Hysteria," (1893–5) in *Standard Edition of the Complete Psychological Works of Sigmund Freud,* Vol. 2 (London: Hogarth Press, 1955).

3. Freud, "The Interpretation of Dreams" (1900), *Standard Edition,* Vols. 4 and 5 (London: Hogarth Press, 1955), pp. 339–630.

4. ———, "The Psychopathology of Everyday Life" (1901) *Standard Edition,* Vol. 6 (London: Hogarth Press, 1955).

5. ———, "Three Contributions to a Theory of Sexuality" (1905), *Standard Edition,* Vol. 7 (London: Hogarth Press, 1955), pp. 125–248.

6. ———, *The Origins of Psychoanalysis, Letters to Fliess* from 1897–1902. Edited by Marie Bonaparte, Anna Freud, and Ernest Kris (New York: Basic Books, 1954).

7. ———, and Karl Jung, *The Freud/Jung Letters.* Edited by William McGuire (Princeton University Press, 1974).

8. Kernberg, Otto, *Borderline Conditions and Pathological Narcissism* (New York: Jason Aronson, 1975).

9. Giovacchini, Peter, and L. Bryce Boyer, "The Psychoanalytic Impasse," *International Journal of Psychoanalytic Psychotherapy* 4 (1975), pp. 25–47.

10. Searles, Harold, *Collected Papers on Schizophrenia and Related Subjects* (New York: International Universities Press, 1965).

11. Freud, "Inhibitions, Symptoms, and Anxiety" (1926), *Standard Edition,* Vol. 20 (London: Hogarth Press, 1955), pp. 92–110.

12. ———, "New Introductory Lectures" (1932), *Standard Edition,* Vol. 22 (London: Hogarth Press, 1955), p. 78.

13. ———, "On Narcissism" (1914), *Standard Edition,* Vol. 14 (London: Hogarth Press, 1955), pp. 93 and ff.

14. Kohut, Heinz, *The Analysis of the Self,* (New York: International Universities Press, 1971.)

15. Berne, *TA in Psychotherapy,* pp. 23, 31, 36.

16. Ibid., pp. 191–194.

17. James, Muriel, and Dorothy Jongeward, *Born to Win,* (Reading, Mass.: Addison-Wesley, 1971), pp. 226–234: Cf. also Berne, *TA in Psychotherapy,* pp. 39 and 64.

18. Levin, Pam, *Becoming the Way We Are* (San Francisco, *TA Pubs.*, 1974).

19. Fawzett, Bill, and Jean Maxwell, *OK Childing and Parenting* (Pamphlet, 1974, available from TA Institute, P.O. Box 14357, West Ellis, Milwaukee, Wisconsin 53214).

20. Mahler, Margaret S., "Infantile Psychosis," *On Human Symbiosis and the Vicissitudes of Individuation*, Vol. 1 (New York: International Universities Press, 1970).

21. Berne, *TA in Psychotherapy*, pp. 224–231.

22. ———, *What Do You Say After You Say Hello?*, (New York: Grove, 1972), p. 25.

23. ———, *TA in Psychotherapy*, pp. 29–33.

24. ———, *Hello* (New York: Grove, 1972), pp. 320–321.

25. Gedo, John, and Arnold Goldberg, *Models of the Mind* (Chicago: University of Chicago Press, 1973).

26. Fawzett and Maxwell, *OK Childing*.

27. Freud, "Analysis Terminable and Interminable" (1937), *Standard Edition*, Vol. 23 (London: Hogarth Press, 1955), pp. 216–253.

28. Goulding, Robert L., "Thinking and Feeling in Transactional Analysis: Three Impasses," *Voices* 11, (1975), pp. 11–13.

29. Berne, *Principles*, p. 296.

30. James, Muriel, "Self-Reparenting: Theory and Process," *TA Journal* 4, 3 (1974), pp. 32–39.

31. Offenkrantz, William, and Arnold Tobin, "Psychoanalytic Psychotherapy," *Archives of General Psychiatry* 30 (1974).

32. Menninger, Karl, and Philip Holzman, *Theory of Psychoanalysis Technique*, 2d ed., (New York: Basic Books, 1975).

CHAPTER 12

Adlerian psychology and TA

JACQUELINE SIMONEAUX

Of all those who preceded transactional analysis, Alfred
Adler comes the closest to talking like a script analyst.
Eric Berne[1]

PUTTING THE THEORIES TOGETHER

Since 1966 I have been intrigued by the concepts of Alfred Adler's "Individual Psychology" because they have enabled me to use Berne's *principles* of Transactional Analysis effectively without requiring that clients know TA.

The term "Individual Psychology" was chosen by Adler to stress *the uniqueness of the individual as a self-consistent unity striving for the overall goal of mastery of the environment* rather than a passive element worked on by "drives," subject to a conflict between conscious and unconscious forces common to all persons. Adler believed that neither heredity nor objective reality governs the responses people make to life, but that their own unique apperception of what's going on leads them to the creation of their own "Life Style." The individual creates a goal which is his own conceptualization of success, and everything he does and thinks is a movement toward that goal. The most essential components of the goal concept are that it is creative, subjective, and unconscious.[2]

Berne also noted the difference between actions in terms of objective inner drives or mechanisms and the motivation of the individual, and he stressed the

importance of the latter. He said, "We are interested in motivations and gratifications rather than defenses, and that is why we like the word transaction,
in which you talk to someone because you get something out of it."[3] In a sense,
both systems of psychotherapy are similar in that clients are not asked to
accept any posited theory or construct from the hands of a sage authority
figure but are directed to observe the realities of interpersonal behavior which
they can see with their own eyes in friends, family, and self.

Both systems are also similar in that the jargon sometimes gets in the way of
therapy. The main resistance I have experienced in the use of TA is the need
to accept what appears to be a fragmentation of the self into three "ego states"
which are in turn divided into a seemingly endless set of parts, each with its
own catchy title. In like manner, people dismiss Adler (if they have heard of
him at all) as that fellow who invented the "inferiority complex," "the will to
power," and "overcompensation." However, there are more similarities than
differences between Berne and Adler. Their combination allows for the re-
moval of the stumbling block of jargon in each, thereby proving to be a power-
fully potent method for reeducation in living—which is, after all, the essential
goal of therapy.

Berne was using Adler's terms when explaining TA in Vienna. He said, "Obviously, the script has a lot to do with the life-style barometer based to a large
extent on the family. This has a lot to do with things that Adler and Jung and
Horney have said on the role of the parent in forming the script." In the same
talk, he again acknowledged Adler with "We also believe in positive effects
which Adler gave."[4] Encouragement in every step of the treatment was essential to Adler. He "never denied his patients' difficulties, he merely showed
them where their exaggeration of their difficulties lay, and how to tackle whatever was the real obstacle in a sensible manner. 'You cannot alter facts . . . but
you can alter your way of looking at them.' "[5]

Berne and Adler believed that a person's actions could be examined and corrected with the full knowledge and cooperation of the person himself.

ADLER THE MAN, 1870–1937

A study of Adler's life history yields a partial blueprint of his later theories.
Adler was born in Vienna in 1870, the second son of a prosperous middle-class
grain merchant. Because he grew up in a section of town where there were
few Jews and little anti-Semitism, this did not become an important factor in
his life. He was converted to Protestantism, which may reflect some of his
feelings about his Jewish mother whom he did not like.

What appears to be important, in light of the development of his later theories, is the fact that he was sickly in early years, having rickets at age two and near-fatal pneumonia at age five. One of his younger brothers died when Adler was four. He reports that from the age of five onward he was determined to become a physician to overcome death and his fear of death.[6] Had he not made this choice, he might have become a musician; he had a beautiful, strong singing voice and, until his death, enjoyed performing for his friends.

Adler's older brother was athletic, brilliant, successful, and his mother's favorite. Evidently Mrs. Adler was a cold, aloof, reserved woman and young Alfred turned from her to his father for closeness, comfort, and warmth. In his "Autobiographical Notes" he says that he did not enjoy staying at home and spent much of his time playing outside. Although he says he never surpassed his brother's skills and accomplishments, he does remark, with satisfaction, how well he succeeded socially. "Because of my friendliness and liveliness I was well received wherever I went. My elder brother was the only one with whom I did not get along well, and he never took any part in our games. At an early age I became part of a wide social milieu ... It was not so much my childhood experiences in themselves that were important; rather the manner in which I judged and assimilated them."[7]

Adler received his medical degree from the University of Vienna Medical School in 1895. At first he practiced as an opthalmologist in the Poliklinik, a Viennese benevolent institution which provided free medical care for working-class people. This reflected his deep interest in Socialism at that time. His first private practice was as a general practitioner in a lower-middle-class section of Vienna. Gradually his interest in the connection between emotional and physical processes led him to become a *Nervenarzt,* or "physician of the nerves." At that time, according to Adler, "... nervous disorders were treated simply symptomatically, through cold-water cures, etc ... All these methods ... seemed to me not to get at the root of the problem ... I searched deeper and deeper to get at the basis of the psychological connections ... Then in 1899 I attended a lecture by Dr. Freud, who, like myself, was attempting to find psychological connections of the various neuroses ..."[8]

In 1902 Freud invited Adler and three other young men to come and discuss the problem of neurosis with him at his apartment. This became the Psychological Wednesday Society which met for the next nine years as the new science struggled into being. Adler took an active lead in the society; seemingly, he used Freud as a counterfoil to stimulate his own thinking.

Adler never attended Freud's university lectures nor did he undergo psychoanalysis by him, always insisting that he had never been a pupil or disciple of Freud. Gradually Adler disagreed more and more with Freud's theory. In

1911 he published a paper on the Aggressive Instinct, which he called the "masculine protest" and was totally opposite to what Freud was saying. Freud was enraged and refused to have further association with him. He remained Adler's bitter enemy until Adler's death in Scotland in 1937. Freud, 14 years older than Adler, died in London in 1939.

THE EVOLUTION OF ADLER'S THEORIES

Because of their long working relationship, the similar subject matter, and the difference in age, Adler's Individual Psychology is usually considered a variant of Freud's psychoanalytic theory, but in truth Adler was a pioneer in Social Psychology. It was radically different from Freudian theory in that it followed a humanistic fulfillment model rather than a mechanistic conflict model of personality. Adler defined the difference in a 1931 article as follows:

> ... the decisive basic difference between psychoanalysis and Individual Psychology ... is that Freud starts with the assumption that by nature man only wants to satisfy his drives—the pleasure principle—and must, therefore from the viewpoint of culture be regarded as completely bad. The Freudian view is that man ... covers this unconscious badness through censorship merely to get along better in life. Individual Psychology on the other hand states that the development of man ... is inclined toward social interest ... We find neurotics, psychotics, suicides, etc., only when social interest is throttled.[9]

Four years before the break with Freud, Adler published a monograph titled *A Study of Organ Inferiority and its Psychical Compensations,* which furnished the foundation of his theory. He started with the accepted idea that in the human body there is an "organ of lesser resistance" which may become the area of complications during a general infection. Biological processes compensate for these inferiorities either within the organ itself, through another organ, or through the nervous centers. Adler discovered that mental processes can be involved in this compensatory process. Concentration of attention upon the inferior organ can result in a training that leads to a satisfactory or even superior level of adjustment. Adler gave as examples artists with poor vision (such as Manet), musicians with poor hearing (such as Beethoven and Franz), and the classic case of the stutterer who became a great orator, Demosthenes. In a description of Adler's ideas, Berne sums this process in one succinct sentence, " 'Inferiorities' arouse an intense desire to make up for them and gain power and prestige in some other way."[10]

After his break with Freud, Adler further developed this idea that physiological compensation sets in motion a psychological process of self-assertion, and added "... the notion that feelings of inferiority can also be brought forth by purely social factors, such as early competition between siblings and the position of the child in the sibling row. Even when there is organ inferiority the psychological reaction becomes the main element."[11] Adler saw the individual making compensatory choices in the field of human endeavor on a social basis. If one child in the family is designated the academically brilliant one, a younger sibling may feel that opportunity for development closed to him, and so choose to become proficient in sports or in the arts. If one girl in the family is domestically talented, her younger sister often will become a "tomboy." This is immediately verifiable in experience.

Adler stresses the importance of the first social group—the family. The child's felt inferiority is measured either against the parents or a sibling. Therefore, in treatment it becomes crucial to investigate the family constellation to find the "Gegenspieler" or the one whom life is "played against." TA, on the other hand, does not stress the importance of the siblings in the early decisions of the individual unless the sibling is of enough seniority in age to provide some of the information which forms the Parent ego state.

But in both systems the decisions about oneself and the way life is to be lived are made by the time the child is four or five years old, based largely on nonverbal and prespeech interpretations of the child. The life goal is not determined either by heredity or environment but is the individual's creative response to the initial social situation in which he finds himself at birth. Berne called it an early script decision; Adler called it the style of life.

The basic tenet of Adler's system is the unity of the human organism. Each individual is a unified, self-consistent whole striving toward a social goal. Every choice made by the individual in life is a movement toward that goal. No matter where one begins with the person—in stories of the past, in problems of the present, or in plans for the future, his "life style" can be deduced. This is the script-reinforcing behavior James and Jongeward discuss and is related to the O.K. positions.

These are the beginnings of Adlerian theory, which is understood quickly by every client to whom it has been presented *when it was presented without the use of either Adlerian or TA terms.* The principle of the selection of a life style and its hidden goal is easily understood if it is explained in terms of survival and in the behavioristic terms of positive and negative reinforcement. The child enters a world populated by others and begins the struggle for acceptance which guarantees survival. A client can see that an infant or young child will do literally *anything* required to find and keep his place. Positive or negative behavior makes no difference to the child. If physical needs are satisfied in response to cuteness, to ferocious crying, to temper tantrums or destructive behavior, or simply intermittently without relationship to what the child does, he will repeat and repeat and repeat those movements till the day he dies. He thinks his place and survival are ensured by those maneuvers and he remains so involved in them that he cannot become objective about them or about how they affect others.

Once a client has accepted the child's need to decide what to expect from others and how to behave to get his needs met—based on what works in the situation he is in as he perceives it—the client becomes willing to join the therapist in the detective work of discovering the goal choice and evaluating its worth. I have found it logical to proceed at this point to the study of the parents, the family constellation, and the culture without particular reference to "ego states" as such, but just as a search for data about the objective situation to which the client had to relate as a child. As Adler wrote in *What Life Should Mean To You,* "Mistakes in the meaning given to life can be corrected only by reconsidering the situation in which the faulty interpretation was made, recognizing the error, and revising the scheme of apperception."[12]

THE POWER DRIVE

Adler's original next step from organ inferiority was to the felt inferiority of the organism at birth and its drive to become superior to that inferiority, to overcome—as he put it, to move from a felt minus to a plus situation. This is the famous power drive which can only be understood in the way Adler meant it if one becomes aware of the source of the phrase, "will to power." It came from Nietzsche, who meant by it " . . . not domination over others but the dynamics toward self-mastery, self-conquest, self-perfection."[13] The drive from inferior to superior, therefore, is to be understood as the drive to overcome difficulties, to acquire the ability to cope with life's difficulties oneself. It is necessary to differentiate normal from neurotic striving. Adler uses the yardstick of "whether the striving is directed toward the useful or the useless side of life. The useful side is that of the common good, which follows the highest level of 'common sense,' where development and progress prove valuable to society."[14] The neurotic's attention is trained on himself as he tries to compensate for his felt deficiency and he lacks that social interest which is the criterion of mental health. Unfortunately for the potential neurotic, he not only misjudges the depths of his inferiority but he also misjudges the heights he must reach to overcome. He sets himself a goal of perfection. He then either tries harder than he needs to (overcompensation) or he doesn't try at all in order to protect himself from the knowledge that he cannot possibly attain his unrealistic goal of perfection.

The feeling of inferiority sometimes results in an "inferiority complex," in which an individual feels helpless without any realistic cause to do so. The same ceaseless striving on the useless side of life occurs; that is, the individual withdraws from participation in the community and expects special benefits or privileges.

MISTAKEN STYLES OF LIFE

There are three situations in childhood which generally lead a child to choose a mistaken goal, one aimed at manipulating others to take care of him: when the child is (1) physically handicapped, or (2) pampered and over-protected, or (3) neglected, hated, or abused. These three situations do not *compel* the choice of a mistaken goal, but they often lead to it as the child interprets his particular condition and treatment by others to signify that he is hopelessly incapable of independent striving. Later Adlerians have categorized the mistaken goals into four groups: (1) Attention-Getting, (2) Striving for Power and Control, (3) Revenge, and (4) Inadequacy used as an Excuse.

SOCIAL INTEREST

Whether they are mistaken or not, each goal chosen is socially oriented, involving the issue of whether or not people are hostile or are to be trusted. The insistence on the social origins and purposes of man is Adler's unique contribution. He called it "Gemeinschaftsgefuhl," a German word variously translated, but which means overall a communal feeling or social interest. It is the innate aptitude man has to live in the existing social condition. Whatever stands in the way of an individual's ability to develop this potential for social interest (interest in the interests of others) is pathology, and the therapist's task is to lead the person to greater social usefulness and cooperation.

THE PROCESS OF ADLERIAN PSYCHOTHERAPY

Adler's therapeutic methods, then, are concerned with guiding the person into goals with greater social usefulness. To do so, the therapist must explore and understand the person's style of life. The first step is the collection of data, accomplished by asking for information in the following five areas:

1. *The family constellation and the client's order in the series of siblings.* Adler believed there were characteristics so universal about the birth position of siblings that a reliable indication from it could be made to the person's life style. The first or oldest child is usually responsible. The second is usually always pushing to achieve as much as or to surpass the eldest. The middle child generally feels in danger of being squeezed out or deprived of his place. The youngest either works harder than the second to surpass all the others or becomes completely discouraged and remains pampered. The only child is similar to the youngest; he puts the adults of the family in the place of the elder siblings and feels completely unqualified to overtake them or he receives from

them an extra amount of training which enables him to succeed admirably. The constellation was always studied for instances of "dethronement," which is what the birth of a new baby in the family does to an older child, unless the latter has already achieved the thrust outward from the mother to the larger community.

2. *Earliest recollections.* Adler understood that people only remember that which is significant to them. In the case of neurotics or psychotics, memories would be those which buttressed their positions in relation to their hidden goals. A person who is convinced that others are hostile and unhelpful could not remain suspicious and doubtful if he recalled instances of assistance. He must keep telling himself "People are not to be trusted" and select only those times to remember which confirm this. The first memory usually shows the fundamental attitude toward life, the interpretation being based on such things as those included or excluded, accidents, deaths, births, solitude or group activities, etc. Mistaken goals such as that of the pampered child ("I must have someone always to take care of me.") or the fearful child ("The world and its people are so dangerous that I must withdraw.") can be deduced from the early memories. It does not matter what age the person is at the time of the memory or whether it is true or not. Because of the unity of the personality, it will be chosen to describe the goal. Collecting several memories confirms or corrects the initial interpretations.

3. *Dreams.* Adler believed that the person's dreams were used to create whatever emotion was necessary to motivate himself into another movement toward his hidden goal. As with memories, the essential unity of the personality ensures that the expression of the style of life is the same while sleeping as when awake. Dreams are roughly equivalent to the repeated messages to oneself that one must believe in order to continue movements toward a mistaken goal. There are no fixed universal interpretations because each individual is unique, but generally fear of falling means fear of loss of prestige, improper clothing signifies fear of being detected in an imperfection, etc. The most important aspect of the dream is the affective mood the person awakens with. Adler reports the story of the man unhappy with his family life who dreamed of a family with a lost child; he woke in a bad temper and behaved antagonistically to his own wife as though she were responsible for what occurred in his dream. Recurrent dreams give unmistakable indications to the goal. They show the style of life best, as do dreams which remain in the memory for many years. Adler was convinced that as a person's courage and ability to cope with reality increased his need to dream decreased. He also felt that a change in dream content during therapy revealed changes occurring in the person.

4. *The three life tasks.* Adler believed that life presents each person with three main problems to be solved: occupation, sex, and friendship. The man-

ner in which the person deals with these social tasks is an indication of his private goal of success, his life style. A healthy social feeling is the standard for mental health and every activity reveals the degree of development of that social feeling. Adler was aware that the neurotic attempts to hide the real state of affairs from the therapist as a part of his essential negativism. He just kept inquiring for details in a friendly, relaxed, companionable manner.

5. *Childhood behavior disorders.* Adler knew from his own experience that any physical or behavioral disorder in childhood would be a clue to the choice of life style. A hostile child will always find a way to attack his parents at their point of greatest weakness. If they concentrate on eating, he will refuse or become a picky eater; if they handle toilet training in a manner to force opposition, the child will suffer from enuresis or constipation, etc. Lying and stealing are ways children try to hide and make up for their felt inadequacies; daydreaming and lazy children have no faith in their own abilities; aggressive children have intense needs for self-assertion. Adler would handle these by explaining the motives to the child and discussing alternative methods of handling the situation with the parents. It is crucial to therapy to understand the person's private logic—the sum of his own creative interpretations of life around him. This must be done in such a way that the person knows he has been understood and his childhood reasoning accepted as a perfectly logical rseponse to the situation in which he found himself at the time. The TA investigation of the Child ego state is similar. The client's cooperation can be enlisted to discover what the Little Professor's creative response to the existential predicament was and what he advised the Adapted Child to do. The Adult ego state can then decide whether redecisions are appropriate.

The process requires a great deal of empathy and much intuitive guessing and a ready willingness by the therapist to change his initial diagnostic hypothesis if later data proves it untenable. When the therapist believes he fully understands, he proceeds tenderly, gently, and carefully, with the greatest kindness, to interpret and explain to the client and to assist him to discover his own mistakes. There must be an inexorable return with the evidence of the client's own life movements and a pointing out of how they invade his whole life space until the client gives up and begins to think of alternate ways of coping with life.

In his book *The Science of Living,* Adler illustrates this procedure with the story of a suspicious, isolated man who was unable to solve any of his life problems.[15] This man had been "dethroned" by a younger brother, leaving him with the expectation that another will always be preferred to him. He became unable to make friends; he remained silent in company; he broke off with each girlfriend as it got close to marriage; he was so tense about work that he overstrained himself and could not succeed. He was constantly suspicious, looking always for signs that another was preferred, and consequently making too much out of normal little disturbances. The only solution for such a suspicious person is the goal of isolation, but that is not normal. Adler describes the therapist's task as to increase this man's social interest. To do so he must understand: how he undervalues himself; his tendency to be over-tense; and how his fear that others may be preferred is standing in his way. He can understand that his early memory of his mother putting him down to pick up his younger brother started him on a long train of concentration on being slighted, so that he interpreted it where it didn't exist. Over time (though Adler was known for his "quick cures") and if handled with great tact and good will, this man would relax his vigilance, accept himself and others, and lead a more socially useful life.

CHILD GUIDANCE CLINICS:
THE UNIQUE CONTRIBUTION OF ADLER

Adler began to believe that he could reach many more children through teachers than through trying to educate each individual family. He felt that if teachers understood and used the principles of Individual Psychology they could help all pupils in the development of socially useful goals. In 1920 he organized consultations with teachers to discuss problems with individual children in their classes. He soon found it necessary to include the parents of the child concerned, so they were invited. The teacher would prepare a file on the child prior to the clinic, which was attended by other teachers, Adler's associates, and other educators as a training process for them. Adler spoke first to the mother, then with the child, and last with the teacher. The observers served as representatives of the common sense as against the child's private interpretation and gave the child the feeling of being part of a social group genuinely interested in his or her welfare. I have personally observed children at this type of consultation respond with shy enthusiasm and pleasure.

Adler became so convinced of the value of *educational therapy* and its increased effectiveness with the very young child that he even started several kindergartens. He saw that the child needed more rational information in sorting out his impressions than we adults customarily give him.

SUMMARY: TA AND INDIVIDUAL PSYCHOLOGY

There are many more instances of similarity between Berne and Adler than there are differences. The first and most obvious difference, of course, is that TA is a group therapy and Adler never used groups except for the child guidance clinics. This is strange, especially in view of the emphasis he placed on the "common sense" of the community and the need to confront the client from every angle to make him aware of his movements. A similarity is that those movements are repetitive patterns of behavior between persons which are much like Berne's games.

In Individual Psychology, the early decision about life and the people in it compares almost exactly, except for nomenclature, with Berne's script and life positions. Both systems use what Adler called "organ jargon" and body language —the body speaks for the person.

Adler, like Berne, insisted on an economy of vocabulary and resisted the invention of nomenclature to bedazzle his clients. He didn't overwhelm clients with authority or hide behind them as they lay on a couch. He sat comfortably across from them, speaking gently, observing all and missing nothing, quite like Berne.

Both TA and Individual Psychology stress the social nature of man and both emphasize studying the client's behavior in relation to others. Adler's recommendations for an increase in social interest are similar to TA's advice to give positive strokes and gold stamps. (To give is to get.)

Adler, like Berne, maintained that the therapist does not cure; the person cures himself when and if he decides to change his life style and its hidden, mistaken goals. The therapist's task is to be prepared to struggle with the client's doubt, criticism, forgetfulness, tardiness, special requests, etc., and to remain friendly but persistent in the interpretation of the objective facts, not on the basis of the client's private logic but on the basis of the common sense or the realities of life and the "iron logic of communal life."

The therapist also fulfills a belated maternal function and supplies a prototype of fellow feeling. It is originally the mother's task to teach the child to first trust her, then to transfer that trust to the father, and then out of the family to the social scene. If the mother fails in this job, the therapist is called in to do it. After this transfer of trust occurs, the client takes it from there and therapy is complete.

Individual Psychology faded for a time after Adler's death, but since the end of the second World War there has been a steady increase in Adlerians throughout the world. Transactional Analysis did not falter upon Berne's death; his followers increase yearly by leaps and bounds. TA is also branching into the schools as a form of therapeutic education.

Alfred Adler was an unpretentious man, not particularly charismatic, who was unable to write well or to lead a group of followers. He seems quietly to have done his own thing superbly well in the shadow cast by Freud and his emphasis on sex in a repressed society. The libido and the Oedipus Complex did not exist for Adler. For him, the first goal was mastery, competence, self-acceptance and self-realization. Social autonomy was the second goal. Persons are cured as soon as they can connect themselves with their fellow men on an equal and cooperative footing.

Like Berne, Adler did not ask people to believe a witch doctor's magical concept. In *The Problem Child*, published in Germany in 1930, his final statement is "You should study other theories and points of view. Compare everything carefully, and don't blindly believe any "authority"—not even me!"[16]

REFERENCES

1. Berne, Eric, *What Do You Do After You Say Hello?* (New York: Grove, 1972), p. 58.

2. Ansbacher, H., "The Fictional Final Goal: Comment," in *The Individual Psychology of Alfred Adler,* edited by H. Ansbacher and R. Ansbacher (New York: Harper & Row, 1964), pp. 87–90.

3. Berne, Eric, "Transcription of Eric Berne in Vienna, 1968," *TA Journal* **3**, 1 (1973), p. 66.

4. Ibid., pp. 67, 70.

5. Bottome, Phyllis, *Alfred Adler* (New York: Vanguard, 1957), p. 98.

6. Adler, Alfred, *The Individual Psychology of Alfred Adler,* edited by H. Ansbacher and R. Ansbacher (New York: Harper & Row, 1964), p. 199.

7. Ibid., p. 200.

8. ———, *Superiority and Social Interest,* 3rd ed., edited by H. Ansbacher and R. Ansbacher (New York: Viking, 1973), pp. 336–337 footnote.

9. Ibid., pp. 210–211.

10. Berne, Eric, *A Layman's Guide to Psychiatry and Psychoanalysis* (New York: Simon & Schuster, 1968), p. 255.

11. Ellenberger, H., *The Discovery of the Unconscious* (New York: Basic Books, 1970), p. 607.

12. Adler, Alfred, *What Life Should Mean to You,* edited by Alan Porter (New York: 1958), p. 13.

13. Ansbacher, H. L., "The Adlerian and Jungian Schools," in *American Handbook of Psychiatry,* Vol. 1, edited by Silvano Arieti (New York: Basic Books, 1974), p. 793.

14. Adler, Alfred, *The Problem Child* (New York: Capricorn, 1963), p. 2.

15. ———, *The Science of Living* (Garden City, N.Y.: Anchor Books, 1969), pp. 40–47.

16. ———, *The Problem Child,* p. 172.

CHAPTER 13

analytical psychology and TA

EUGENE A. MERLIN

INTRODUCTION

Carl Gustav Jung (1875–1961) was a Swiss psychiatrist and an early collaborator of Sigmund Freud's. He was a depth psychologist along with Freud because he went beyond the conscious mind and delved into the depths of the unconscious. However, he parted ways with Freud and developed his own approach. Jung first called his way of looking at psychic realities and doing therapy Complex Psychology, based on the concept of the "complex" which he developed. Later he called his approach Analytical Psychology, probably to differentiate it from Psychoanalytic (Freudian) and Individual (Adlerian) psychologies. He did not like the term "Jungian."

The thought that he had established a new set of beliefs, a school, was very unpleasant for him. He did not want others or even himself to be believers. He thus said, "I am not a Jungian," and "Thank God I am Jung and not a Jungian."[1] Commenting on this attitude of Jung's, Laurens van der Post, his friend for many years, writes:

> He did not like the idea of having disciples or blind followers, or even a school, and in his old age agreed most reluctantly to the establishment of

the C. G. Jung Institute in Zurich for studies relevant to his own approach to psychology.[2]

Jung disliked dogma, "isms," and systems in general. He saw his own efforts as subjective, as a point of view. They were "suggestions and attempts" and "a series of different approaches, or one might call it, a circumambulation of unknown factors."[3]

Therefore, Analytical Psychology is basically tentative. Hesitation and caution are built into the theory; uniqueness is the very goal of the therapy. This may present a problem if we ask what it is that analytical psychotherapists do. If there is no set theory, how can a practical approach have been developed?

Jung developed a practical way of doing therapy by holding that his concepts were "as if" statements. It looks, for instance, as if there is such a reality as the "shadow." Dreams, myths, projection, many personal experiences support the thesis. Thus Analytical psychotherapy developed on the basis that its overview of the psyche is a working hypothesis, based on empirical fact, is therapeutically effective, but nonetheless open even to radical change, should the facts warrant it.[4]

The real problem in discussing analytical psychotherapeutic techniques is: Whose practice do you describe? Even within the relatively small group of analytical therapists there are some major different emphases. There are three main groups. One is that of "orthodox Jungians" who follow Jung's concepts almost unchanged. A second are the "neo-Jungians" who modify Jung's ideas by the use of some psychoanalytic thought such as that of Erickson or Klein. The third may be called a center group which, while "firmly linked to Jung's teachings," accepts changes in light of further experience.[5]

I will be describing here what Jung himself did—and thus what "orthodox Jungians" and much of the center group do. This may not be the total picture, but it does illustrate the basic elements of the analytical approach.

Why might it be important to consider Jung and his work, however? It is important because Jung is important. Jung has made an impact on contemporary culture in many ways. In the history of psychology and psychotherapy he is known for his word-association tests, "the first projective test of any significance"[6] which empirically confirmed Freud's theory of repression. In psychiatry and academic psychology he is known for his work on psychological types, known to us by the terms "introvert" and "extravert." He is also famous for his theory of archetypes and complexes. Many of his terms have actually filtered down into our everyday speech, so that we find ourselves saying, "Oh, he has a complex about that" and "She's really an extravert." Interestingly enough, the use of these words is often not too far from what Jung himself meant.

Jung has also had a great influence on philosophers, writers (he met James Joyce and briefly treated his daughter), artists, contemporary college students, and much of the current youthful subculture. His emphasis on self-fulfillment, his optimism about the psyche, his interest in spiritual matters and the overall breadth of his thought appeal to many today.

There is also a growing number of people interested in being in therapy that follows Jung's approach. More therapists are being trained in analytical methods; there are training centers in New York, Chicago, Los Angeles, and San Francisco. Courses on Jungian dream interpretation and Jungian workshops are widely given. Even Jungian psychotherapy groups are appearing. Films, programs, lectures on Jung and analytical thought never fail to attract large numbers of people interested in an interior journey. It seems that a time for an expanded influence of Jung's thought and method is at hand.

JUNG THE MAN

C. G. Jung was born on July 26, 1875 in Kesswil, Switzerland. After a childhood in the country and the later completion of the Gymnasium, he studied natural science and then medicine at the University of Basel. In 1900 he finished the state examinations in medicine and became assistant to Eugen Bleuler at the Burghoezli Mental Hospital. After reading Freud's *Interpretation of Dreams* for a second time, Jung contacted Freud and met him in Vienna in March of 1907.

After a somewhat stormy intellectual and personal relationship with Freud and psychoanalysis, Jung gradually broke away from his former colleague in the period 1911–1914. As we have seen, Jung had a dislike of dogma. Adherence to any set line of thought violated his highly developed individuality and scientific integrity. It was Freud's request that Jung hold to the theory of sexuality as a dogma that struck at the heart of their relationship.

It is hard to know whether Jung ever really believed all of Freud's theories or whether Jung ever was a true psychoanalyst. In any case, after the break, Freud and Jung had no contact with each other, either personal or intellectual. Any of Jung's comments on Freud and his subsequent theories should be read in this light.

In the following years Jung continued his own interior exploration, a self-analysis, developed and refined his own approach to therapy, taught and trained other psychologists, therapists and scholars, and wrote proliferously. He died on June 9, 1961.[7]

These bare facts of Jung's life do not really tell a story about him, of course. The spirit of the man, the direction and guiding insights, require some reflection to be seen.

Jung the man and his life, as I see them, are marked by contrasts and tensions. It is the presence of these opposites that mark his genius and greatness.

He spent an important part of his youth growing up in the country. There he found his own simplicity and a deep love for the earth, wind, and water. This simpleness pervaded his life. He built his own tower at Bolingen near the lake, cutting some stones and doing the sculpting that went into it. In its simple, medieval interior Jung would spend weeks alone, cooking and caring for himself without any modern conveniences. Plain, rough, simple things were enough.

Yet Jung was a most complex and sophisticated man at the same time. He traveled extensively, wrote learned and copious works (his *Collected Works* are 19 volumes with much yet to be published),[8] lectured widely, and was internationally famous as a psychiatrist and thinker, a man who has deeply influenced his own century. His interests included experimental research in parapsychology, work as a psychiatrist with schizophrenics, involvement with Freud and psychoanalysis, original thought about the basic force of the psyche and libido, and development of his own approach to the mind. Jung developed a way of understanding people by attitude and function types, investigated world religions, mythologies, and gnosticism, studied astrology and alchemy (he had a valuable collection of alchemical texts), developed the concept of synchronicity to go beyond causality, and studied and wrote about literature and the arts. Jung was no stranger to the world of complex and sophisticated thought and life.

Peasant simplicity and tastes, and complex thought and research, were two poles Jung brought together in his own life and lived fully the tension between them.

Another example of contrasts in Jung's life regards sex. In his psychotherapeutic theory and practice, Jung did not see sex as central. When he publicly broke with Freud with the publication of *Wandlungen und Symbole der Libido* (later, *Symbols of Transformation*) in 1912, the main contention was Freud's assertion of sexuality as the basis of psychic life. Jung saw libido or psychic energy as undifferentiated; sometimes it would manifest itself in sexuality and a concern for the erotic; many other times it would show itself in the search for meaning or wholeness.

In his personal life Jung, at least at one point, claimed basic disinterest in the importance of sex:

> I cannot say I have a Freudian psychology because I never had such difficulties in relation to desires. As a boy I lived in the country and took things very naturally, and the natural and unnatural things of which Freud speaks were not interesting to me. To talk of an incest complex just bores me to tears.[9]

There was, however, another side of Jung. In his writings he treats the need to integrate the power of eros into one's life. For Jung, if one did not live and solve the questions of sex, one could not go onto questions of meaning in life, could not really achieve wholeness. If a patient had problems in the area of sexuality, Jung was quite ready to use Freudian techniques and questions to get at them. In fact for Jung, one of the four stages of analysis included the personal, the "Freudian" sexual-questioning.

Sexuality touched Jung's own life and he was certainly not indifferent to his own needs. That eros was central to him is shown by the fact that the earliest dream he could recall was one of a huge phallus enthroned in an underground chamber. It was, at the age of three or four, his initiation into "the secrets of the earth."[10]

Jung's relationships with women were deep and extensive. Most of his patients were women, some of whom became colleagues and good friends. His marriage to Emma was long and fulfilling (1903–1955), producing many children and grandchildren. So important to him was this relationship (sexual in the deepest sense) that after his wife's death, even Jung's laughter was not the same. Yet Jung's passion was not fully met by a good and comfortable marriage, for a long time he also had a mistress.[11]

The main contrast in Jung's life, however, was that of consciousness and the unconscious. As a child he was aware of these two sides of his parents' personalities. His father, consciously a minister, theologian, and true believer, was inwardly devoid of religious experience, had no personal knowledge of the God when he preached. His mother, externally a good, innocuous, kind, human mother to Jung, was interiorly, in an unconscious personality, uncanny, powerful, authoritative, somber, and imposing.

Jung, even as a child, believed that he himself had two personalities: Numbers 1 and 2, as he called them. Personality Number 1 was the Basle schoolboy who had to study mathematics, gymnastics, and drawing; Personality Number 2 was a world of mystery and intuition, of oneness with and experience of God, images, dreams, fantasy. In later life, Number 1 led Jung to study natural science, medicine, philosophy; Number 2 moved him to look at anthropology, religion, mythology, gnosticism, alchemy.

It was the need to do justice to these two personalities that moved Jung to take up psychiatry. In this way he could fulfill the needs he had for understanding and making a living (Personality Number 1) and at the same time pursue interior experience, religion, mythology, dreams, and the dark and mysterious in his own life and the lives of others.

It was not only a need to fulfill both sides of himself that moved Jung. He needed to relate each side to the other. The constant urge to relate the conscious and unconscious is the hallmark of Jung's approach. He believed that consciousness needed to ever expand, taking in elements of the unconscious. Where this was not possible (so large is the unconscious), consciousness must take up a relationhip to the unconscious that was self-aware, open, and humble.

These are but three examples of contrasts in Jung's life and thought: simplicity/sophistication, sexual interest/sexual disinterest, conscious/unconscious. In these he saw the goal as a union of opposites. This permeated his theory and practice.

JUNG'S SYSTEMATIC APPROACH TO THE PSYCHE

Jung sees the mind of man or the psyche as having two major aspects: the conscious and the unconscious. The conscious is that of which we are aware and that which we call "I." The unconscious, on the other hand, has two levels or layers.

The first level is that of the *personal unconscious.* Jung describes it:

> The personal unconscious contains lost memories, painful ideas that are repressed (i.e., forgotten on purpose), subliminal perceptions, by which are meant sense-perceptions that were not strong enough to reach consciousness, and, finally, contents that are not yet ripe for consciousness. (CW 7, p. 66)

This first layer comes from and rests on the second, that of the *collective unconscious,* or as Jung later called it, the *objective psyche.* This level "does not derive from personal experience and is not a personal acquisition but is inborn." The collective unconscious is thus different from the personal unconscious because

... it has contents and modes of behavior that are more or less the same everywhere and in all individuals. It is, in other words, identical in all men and thus constitutes a common psychic substrate of a suprapersonal nature which is present in every one of us. (*CW* 9i, pp. 3–4)

The contents of the collective unconscious are the archetypes. Archetypes *appear* as images in dreams, myth, fantasies. They are also ways of thinking and experiencing, of understanding, of behaving. They are not just age-old ideas that may or may not pop into a person's head.

Archetypes are ways of being that come with humanity. They have been formed "... during the thousands of years when the human brain and human consciousness were emerging from an animal state ..."[12] They are unconscious in themselves but are experienced in images or ways of thought, or in specific ways of behavior that are molded by a given era or culture (e.g., the returning hero in Rome wore a laurel wreath and drove a chariot; today he gets a ticker-tape parade).[13]

There are some principal archetypes that appear in almost everyone's life. The first of these is the *persona*. Jung describes this archetype:

The persona is a complicated system of relations between the individual and society, fittingly enough a kind of mask, designed on the one hand to make a definite impression upon others, and, on the other, to conceal the true nature of the individual. (*CW* 7, p. 192)

The persona is that face we put on to society. It is the experience we have, the do's, don'ts, and expectations of any group we're in. It is also the way we apportion ourselves according to the needs of the moment—e.g., a doctor will act differently when he is playing with his children and when he is performing neurosurgery.

In facing the persona the task is not to get rid of the mask, but rather to know how and when to wear it—and especially not to identify with it. Thus the doctor would know that he is not just a surgeon or a child's playmate, but these things and more.

Part of that "more" would be experienced through another archetype, the *shadow*. Jung defines it:

The shadow personifies everything that the subject refuses to acknowledge about himself and yet is always thrusting itself upon him directly or indirectly —for instance, inferior traits of character or other incompatible tendencies. (*CW* 9i, pp. 284–285)

Whereas the persona is that which we want to be, the shadow is that part of ourselves that we don't want to be, or are not supposed to be. It is the unacceptable part of us that we intensely dislike in others and that appears in our dreams often as a dark, threatening character. It is the unconscious, repressed side of the sex that we are that we have not faced. The contrasexual part of a man, the *anima,* is his unconscious feminine aspect. The contrasexual part of a woman, the *animus,* is her masculine aspect.

These archetypes are most often experienced first in projection. They are seen and experienced as parts of someone else's personality. This is most directly seen in the process of falling in love. A great deal of what happens between a man and a woman in love is based on the unconscious contrasexual aspects of each person that they see in the other. The thrill of being in love is the excitement of finding a lost part of oneself.

These archetypes, as all others, need to be faced as part of oneself, brought into relationship with consciousness, and integrated into one's life. The projections can be withdrawn. This can be done in a positive way by an expansion of the conscious life. It can also be done with a negative effect. In a marriage, for instance, the husband may withdraw an anima projection from his wife. He may incorporate those projected feminine elements into himself. Or these elements may slip away by themselves (i.e., because of an unconscious awareness that the projection really didn't fit). With the projection gone, this man may well find that there is nothing to sustain the marriage, since all he related to was the anima and not to the person whom it covered. Such a man would not really know or love his spouse but only a part of himself.

Another negative thing that may happen with the anima/animus is something like possession. A bout of moodiness or sentimentality, for instance, may overtake a man. A woman may suddenly become very cold and rational or argumentative and aggressive. Later he or she may say to themselves, "What came over me? I wasn't myself." This would be an instance of an unintegrated, unfaced anima or animus taking over, having its say with all the power of pent-up unconscious force. To prevent this and like eruptions, one must know oneself well, bringing into conscious awareness the persona, the shadow, and the anima/animus, for all of these, unknown and uncontrolled, many break forth and take over for a while.

These and other archetypes (e.g., of father and mother) are first experienced on the level of the personal unconscious in the form of complexes. Jung defines a complex as "a collection of various ideas, held together by an emotional tone common to all" (*CW* 2, p. 599). He further defines it:

It is the *image* of a certain psychic situation which is strongly accentuated emotionally and is, moreover, incompatible with the habitual attitude of consciousness. (*CW* 8, p. 96)

A complex is, then, a highly charged grouping of ideas and feelings that are unconscious. In addition, the complex acts on its own, as if it had a central, independent directing core. Thus Jung says:

... it is subject to the control of the conscious mind only to a limited extent, and therefore behaves like an animated foreign body in the sphere of consciousness. (Ibid.)

These characteristics of the complex come from its center, the archetype. The complex, the experience of the archetype on the level of the personal unconscious, is thus powerful, independent, and unconscious. In fact, our first experience of the archetype is through the complex, through the picture we have of it from the facts of our lives. Thus, if we have a father complex, we are experiencing the age-old relationship of child to father (archetype in the collective unconscious) through our experience of father in our culture and especially in our own lives (complex, and the archetypal image, in the personal unconscious).

This may seem quite complicated. However, if one pushes Jung's approach and uses it, he finds that it is helpful. For instance, we may realize that the complex/problem we have in relating to our fathers has at its center not just our own experience of our own personal fathers, but also the pains and problems that humanity has found for eons in relating to the paternal.

For Jung, archetypes and complexes are not signs of illness, but are part of being human. Even emotional symptoms, Jung feels, are not to be judged bad, for he sees them as efforts of the psyche to grow and change. Illness is the call of the unconscious that something is amiss, that something needs looking at and changing.

Jung's optimistic view is based on his positive evaluation of the psyche. He sees the personality as always striving for completion, for fullness. Thus, when something in the conscious life is incomplete, the unconscious will step in with a dream, or a symptom, or an experience of depth, to point out a need for growth and expansion. This Jung calls the self-regulating function of the psyche which compensates for any lacks. There is thus a directive, prospective aspect to this self-regulation and compensation. The unconscious will tell us what we need to do and where we need to go.

The process of coming to fullness, of becoming the person we are "meant" to be, Jung calls *individuation,* to show that the job of life is to separate oneself from unconscious identification with the collective. Yet this is done only by recognizing and experiencing one's *connection* with the collective, by keeping it in relationship to and rooted in the objective psyche. This happens through the archetype of the *Self.*

The Self is the central experience of individuation. It is often symbolized in dreams and fantasies by religious images (e.g., figure of a god or of a holy sign) and by geometrical figures, especially a *mandala.* This is a Sankrit word for magic circle and refers to concentric images arranged around a central point. Such a symbol has occurred in all religions. Jung found that such symbols occurred spontaneously in the dreams of his patients and would be accompanied by feelings of harmony and peace.

Such feelings are accounted for by the nature of the Self. This archetype is the way we experience and understand the unity of the conscious and unconscious. As the ego is the center of consciousness, so the Self is the center of conscious/unconscious relationship. To reach this experience, therefore, it is necessary to accept the inferior parts of one's nature, the personal unconscious, as well as the irrational and chaotic in life, and one's own grounding in the objective psyche. It means an awareness of our own uniqueness and of our close union with all of the cosmos, animal and plant, organic and inorganic.

How we go about this and what we will need to integrate in the process of individuation is to a great extent determined by what Jung calls our attitude and function typology.[14] This way of analyzing people some have called Jung's psychology of consciousness. It is by far the most accepted element of his approach among other schools of psychology. Jung came to this method while trying to understand how and why Freud and Adler took such different approaches to the psyche. He concluded that they were both radically different characters in their approach to things; their attitudes were basically different. Adler was *introverted.* The flow of psychic energy was inward, for he emphasized the interior attitude, the will to power. Freud was *extraverted,* for he saw the important determining factors in life as outside people and events.

Once one had established the attitude type of a person, there was still a question of the primary psychological *function* within that type. There are four functions, four ways we relate ourselves to the interior and exterior worlds. Two of the functions are the way we gather information: *intuition* and *sensation.* Sensation is perception through our senses. Intuition is perception via the unconscious, by hunches, suspicions, vague but intense feeling. The other two functions are assessing modes, ways of judging. *Thinking* judges on the basis of meaning and understanding. *Feeling* evaluates on the basis of the general feelings of a person; it is an accommodation to the likes and dislikes of the personality.

Each of the attitudes has four functions. You may be an introverted intuitive type or an extraverted intuitive type, for example. When all the possibilities are explored there are eight basic types. These are not hard categories, of course, but more a matter of emphasis. And even though these classifications are not meant to be absolute, they do help in understanding how and why people, ourselves included, act the way they do.

It is the goal of the psyche to integrate all its elements. Since each person has all four of the functions, with one the most developed, another as secondary, etc., one of the jobs of individuation is to bring into awareness and development those functions that are hidden, unused, unconscious. A person whose primary function is feeling would have thinking as the most undeveloped and unconscious function. It would be such a person's task in striving for wholeness to develop this function and bring it out of unconsciousness so that it will be a completion of the personality and not an unconscious block to growth.

Thus, depending upon our type of conscious psychology, we will have diverse talents and unconscious abilities to develop. This task centers around the part of life we are in. The first half of life has its own needs and questions. These include: developing a strong self-identity, an ego; learning to relate to society; finding a sexual identity; earning a living; finding a vocation. The second half of life has different goals: establishing a relationship to the collective unconscious; asking the question of meaning in life; facing the reality of death.

The concept of "first" and "second" halves of life refers not so much to a person's years as it does to the emotional tasks a person has accomplished and the basic questions he asks himself. One person who is 18 may be involved with second-half-of-life matters, while another person who is 45 may still be involved with elements of the first half of life. However, if one is to come to fullness, to emotional wholeness, he or she must eventually deal with questions relating to the second half of life—and that after having completed the tasks connected with the first half of life.[15]

In the process of individuation all of what we have seen here must be taken into account, become known, and be brought into harmony within the personality, under the guiding influence of that experience called the Self. In all of this, wholeness or individuation should not be thought of as a goal, as a static end or position. It is not a thing or state to be achieved and eventually to be rested in. Individuation is ongoing, a process never ending. To ever be finished in it, since it is a facing of the collective unconscious, would be like trying to empty an ocean into a tea cup. There will always be more to integrate. Consciousness can always expand.

JUNGIAN THERAPEUTIC TECHNIQUE

Change, growth, expansion of consciousness, individuation—all can happen without analysis, outside of therapy. Jung saw this as having happened throughout history through the mediation of great cultural symbols and systems (e.g., religion, astrology, alchemy) and through the individual's own dreams, fantasies, and creative expression.

Analysis can intensify the process of contacting the unconscious and developing neglected aspects. This is done through the use of the therapeutic relationship, the use of dreams, and the use of active imagination.

The analyst learns these techniques mainly from his own analysis and from doing analysis with his clients. There is very little written on Jungian techniques. This is because these ways are deeply experiential and must be lived through before one can know what they are. Also, each analyst, being the unique person he is, does analysis differently, from his own personal base. What one does in analysis depends on who one is.

The Relationship

If this is true of the analyst, it is also true of the client. Analysis is the meeting of two separate and different persons, both trying to find their own psychic way to individuation. Because the experience may be intense and intimate, the relationship in which this self-awareness happens is most important.

Jung agreed with Freud that the transference was the heart of analysis. Freud held that the patient would project onto the analyst, as though onto a blank screen, all the unfinished conflicts and problems of psychosexual development. Thus the originating problems would be recreated in the analysis through projection, a mechanism of defense.

In Freudian treatment, the transference is analyzed for its infantile and unconscious roots. Then comes reeducation to an awareness that the ego is now strong enough to face unconscious elements without fear. No longer is a frightened, unconscious projecting of needs and desires necessary.

For Jung, on the other hand, transference is the meeting of two individuals. There is indeed projection going on. But for Jung projection is the first step in incorporating unconscious elements as new possibilities for growth. For example, a man projects the anima but can retrieve her as part of himself, consciously nourish his feminine side, and grow because of this. He can bring projections back to himself only if he has a real person to dialogue with. Thus one analyzes the transference, but the heart of the analysis is the *person* of the analyst reporting to and talking with the client about what fits and what doesn't, about what he thinks and feels, about what it is like for him to be faced with the thoughts and feelings of the client.

Analysis is primarily a relationship. For the client it is a growing in individuality by meeting another individual. In the love and respect that occurs in analysis, client and analyst have a fundamental experience of the meeting of two different realities. This is the basis and the model of the patient's own joining of his own psychic differences, the union of opposites which is the method and goal of individuation.[17]

Within the relationship of analysis there are two major tools or techniques: analysis of dreams and active imagination.

Dreams For Jung, dreams are not symptoms of illness. Rather they are ways the unconscious has of contacting the conscious. They are the psyche trying to take care of itself. Through dreams the unconscious tries to tell a person what needs to be done, how one might best go about it, what to look for, what paths to explore.

Jung did not believe that there was a hidden meaning in dreams. Rather he took dreams at face value. The thing to do with dreams, therefore, is to learn their language "... like a text that is unintelligible not because it has a facade, but simply because we cannot read it."[18]

The main language of dreams is symbolism. In learning this language one first has to respectfully listen. One does not look for a book of fixed universal symbols of interpretation, but rather looks to symbols as efforts to express the not-yet-expressed. Therefore, the first thing to do when dealing with dream symbols is to take them seriously.

For Jung a dreamer listens to dream symbols and takes them seriously because he wants to learn from the unconscious. He trusts the psyche and its drive for wholeness and health. Yet the dreamer, especially in analysis, is not passive. He applies a method called *amplification* to dreams to understand their language.

Amplification may be seen to include something similar to the free association used by Freud. Thus both analyst and client try to find out the latter's personal context for a dream and its symbols. The dreamer should first look to personal factors in the dream, to the literal meaning of the images.

Second in amplification is to compare the symbols to the typical motifs of humanity which occur in myths, fairy tales, religious systems, etc. In doing this one is looking for the archetypal images that well up from the collective unconscious.

An example of an amplication of symbols in a dream is that of a man who dreams about leaving his father and feels frightened and powerless. This dream can be seen first on the personal level of amplification as arising within the context of the dreamer's own family. The dream would thus speak to his own personal history, to what he must do emotionally if he is to change, and how he is feeling about it.

Looked at in the light of the archetypal imagery, the second aspect of amplification, the dreamer faces some new facts. First, the power of the dream and the situation itself comes not just from his own life but also from a profoundly human, age-old experience of the race. Men have been separating themselves from the power of their fathers since we emerged from the trees. The problem and its weight are passed on to each man at birth with the physical and cultural inheritance he gets as a human.

In addition, the symbol of father is seen in myths and religions as referring, for example, to rationality. Seen this way the dream presents the dreamer with the additional task of separating himself from slavish adherence to his own rationality and of developing additional ways of approaching life.

There are also two levels of dream images: the objective and the subjective. Interpretation on the objective level sees dream images referring to real objects and coming from "complexes of memory that refer to external situations" (*CW* 7, para. 130). Interpretation on the subjective level "refers every part of the dream and all the actors in it back to the dreamer himself" (Ibid.).

Thus an objective-level aspect of the dream may tell the dreamer about people he has known, places he has been, talks he has heard, etc. On the subjective level the same images may be seen to mirror the dreamer's own "tendencies and components" (Ibid.). A dream about one's brother may give information about that brother and the dreamer's relationship to him. It may also speak to the dreamer's relationship to the brother within, the shadow, the unacceptable and/or unrealized part of his own personality.

In giving such information on both the objective and the subjective levels, dreams not only say what the situation has been in the past, they also point to the future. They are not just retrospective, they are also *prospective*. They may get people ready for a problem or its solution, may give suggestions about both subjective and objective materials in the dream, and may have advice for the analyst.

Having roots deep in the psyche, with an awareness far surpassing the conscious, rational ego, the dream can see dangers and possibilities. Dreams, then, are often messages from the unconscious saying, in effect, "If you go on the way you are now, then such-and-such will happen," or "You should do this."

This prospective aspect of the dream is based on an even deeper, more fundamental function of the dream: *compensation*. In observing the compensatory function of dreams we see one of the main ways the psyche regulates itself, takes care of the gaps caused by overemphasis in the conscious attitude. If the ego is too much of one thing, the unconscious steps in and demands development and integration of the opposite. For example, if thinking is too developed, dreams may call for paying attention to feeling. If a woman's self-assertiveness and her thinking are underdeveloped, her animus, her masculine side, may appear in dreams, threatening, cajoling, beckoning.

Thus both client and analyst can pay close attention to dreams to see what needs looking after in the personality. Jung says here:

> When we set out to interpret a dream, it is always helpful to ask: What conscious attitude does it compensate? . . . Every dream is an organ of information and control . . . dreams are our most effective aid in building up the personality. (*CW* 16, paras. 330–334)

One must therefore know the conscious attitude well if he is to know what the dream may be compensating for. If the dreamer finds that an interpretation is just what he was expecting, there is a good chance that the interpretation is incorrect. The purpose of dreams is to correct conscious attitudes, not to agree with them. Jung describes it:

> If the meaning we find in the dream happens to coincide with our expectations, that is a reason for suspicion; for as a rule the standpoint of the unconscious is complementary or compensatory to consciousnes and thus unexpectedly 'different.' (*CW* 14, para. 48)

Finally, it is important to see that dreams often don't occur independently of the general situation of the psyche. Thus important messages from the unconscious, especially those that are not getting heard very well, happen in series of dreams, are repeated, sometimes in varying forms. It is precisely these recurring dreams that should be paid most attention to. They are the urgent voice of the psyche calling for change, for growth. Not only do such dreams call for change in the personality, but also for a change in the analysis. Series dreams are thus ways the unconscious has of emphasizing a message and of correcting the understanding of that message. Jung's advice to the therapist who works with dreams is:

> All in all, dream interpretation is an art, like diagnosis, surgery, and therapeutics in general—difficult, but capable of being learned by those whose gift and destiny it is. (*CW* 17, para. 198)

Active imagination   The other major technique Jung uses is that of active imagination. This is an experience in which the patient is both active and passive. Jung describes the procedure:

> I therefore took up a dream-image or an association of the patient's, and, with this as a point of departure, set him the task of elaborating or developing his theme by giving free rein to his fantasy. (*CW* 5, para. 344)

This is not like consciously developing or constructing a daydream. It is more a letting the images develop themselves with the conscious ego standing back and watching. It seems somewhat similar to the experience one may have in meditation of being conscious and yet being aware of images coming and going in the mind seemingly of their own will. The only difference here is that in analysis the client reports what is happening in the fantasy.

In active imagination there is an active dimming-down of consciousness, along with "intense concentration on the background of consciousness" (*CW* 7, para. 366). This is an awareness of the movements of the unconscious in the fantasy and thus an experience of symbols developing, of archetypal images speaking. It is a method that takes a long time to develop well, demanding much practice.

Since this is an active listening to the unconscious, it demands that one start out with no expectations, giving as much freedom to the activity of the unconscious as possible. The material may emerge through many forms: "dancing, painting, drawing, or modeling" (*CW* 5, para. 344); also, as Gerhard Adler says, "in verbal form, for example, as in stories or dialogues . . . dancing and music are rarer but not unique formulations . . ."[20] Once the material has emerged through this process, one can enter into conscious dialogue with it, much as with the elements of dreams. One analyzes the content with the hope of integrating the unconscious elements into consciousness.

Active imagination is both a diagnostic tool and a therapeutic experience. It lets both the client and therapist know what the unconscious is trying to say, much as dreams do. In addition, it gives expression to material of great emotional intensity, draining off much charged material. This may prevent an unconscious eruption, or possession by an archetype, and/or eliminate the need for an unconscious projection by the psyche.

This method is one in which the unconscious and conscious come into direct dialogue and active relationship, sometimes quite intensely. It is therefore a paradigm of the goal of analysis, the joining of opposites, the *coincidentia oppositorum* Jung so often spoke of. Here, that which has not been integrated confronts that which has; conscious faces unconscious.[21]

These methods can be used throughout the different stages of analysis.[22] Jung held (*CW* 16, paras. 122ff) that there are four such stages. They are:

1. *Confession.* This is the cathartic way. It is mainly a getting-it-off-your-chest stage. The client here tells the rapist "everything concealed, repressed, guilt-laden, which isolates him from the society of his fellow men."[23] This section of analysis brings the shadow into sharp detail.

2. *Elucidation.* The first stage often leads "to a childish dependence either on the doctor or on his own unconscious."[24] Interpretation here analyzes this transference on the basis of unconscious fantasies which move the client. This is near the Freudian approach.

3. *Education.* Once these personal contents are assimilated and some adjustment to the interior man is made, the next step is an adjustment to society. Here one educates oneself as a social being, learning to relate to social demands and needs. This is something like Adler's approach.

4. *Individuation* or *Transformation.* This is the stage of Jungian analysis proper. One begins to develop his own particular pattern, differentiating himself from the collective, yet still relating to it and his roots in the collective unconscious. This is the stage of experiencing the archetype of the Self. It is a coming to be the person one was meant to be.

At the beginning of an analysis Jung would see the person several times a week, but eventually would work down to once or twice a week. Also, every ten-to-twelve weeks, he would break off the analysis for awhile.[25] The point of the interruption was to get the patient to work on his own. In such cases a patient might come to see Jung with much to talk about, use the time profitably, be responsible for his own welfare, and save himself money.[26] (Muriel James often uses this same procedure so that clients do not get "addicted" to therapy.)

Because of Jung's great respect for the psyche, he saw the analyst's position as that of listener. The analyst should have no preset goal, no plan. Rather he should heed the unconscious—both his own and that of the client. If he did not do so he might find himself going wrong in the analysis. In such circumstances he might find the psyche objecting—for example, through the client's resistances. "The resistance might very well prove that the treatment rests on false assumptions" (*CW* 16, para. 237).

This respect both for the unconscious and for the person of the client led Jung to be wary of preset theories and techniques of therapy. Thus his approach was to listen and to learn. His advice to the beginning therapist was: "Learn the best, know the best—and then forget everything when you face the patient" (*CW* 10, para. 882).

JUNG AND TA

I believe that Transactional Analysis and Jungian technique are basically two different but not antithetical ways of examining the psyche, social interaction, and emotional development. The differences between the two approaches are based on the individuality of their "founders," the different psychotherapeutic tasks each had, and the different cultural-historical milieus to which each spoke.

Their similarities are based first on the persons of Jung and Eric Berne. Jung was an introverted intuitive type. His approach reflects this and attracts such types to his way. Muriel James tells me that she believes Eric Berne was also an introverted intuitive type, a contention which is bolstered by Berne's early penetrating studies on intuition.

This similarity in personality types accounts for much in the two men's work. Both show a deep respect for the personality and a trust that it wants and is capable of health and wholeness. Both are concerned with intrapsychic function, with what goes on inside a person when he is acting, thinking, and feeling. Both developed approaches that avoided heavy psychiatric words and that would allow a person to early on do his own emotional work without dependence on an analyst and frequent therapeutic meetings.

A Jungian might first look a TA and say that it is basically a way of examining the personal unconscious. It therefore can be seen as a method for the second and third stages of analysis. Given TA's strong social orientation and group setting (Jung did not believe in group therapy), it would not seem to have much to do with the Jungian fourth stage and with the collective unconscious.

Upon reflection, however, such judgments might not hold for the Jungian. For example, ego states, because of their definition as constant in humans (everybody has them) as ways of thinking, feeling, and behaving, show that they are perhaps archetypal in nature. Our experience and understanding of them is thus a study of archetypal images and a confrontation with an aspect of the collective unconscious.

Even more important is the concept of scripts in TA. To the Jungian this concept shows TA's way of approaching the power of a myth in the life of an individual, its seeming independence and authority, and the way it has of interpreting everything through its own view. An analytical therapist would also see a great convergence between the Jungian concept of personal myth and that of script. Both of these can be positive and/or negative, can be changed, and are the ways one has of deciding how to live, what one's goals are, what life is about, and whether one has a right to happiness.

The Jungian may also find that TA can be helpful in filling in some of the gaps in his understanding of the functioning of archetypes. For instance, the concept of persona both theoretically and practically is clarified when it is seen as the interaction between Parent and Adapted Child ego states. Similar awareness of other dynamics of analysis could show the Jungian that TA has much to say to the person in all stages of analysis, including individuation. TA can be a help in understanding how one functions, deciding what to do about it, and taking up a relationship to others and to one's own interior life and its roots in the objective psyche.

The TA therapist can also learn much by looking to analytical psychology. He may see that the work of Jung is grounded in the depth psychologist's extensive studies and writings concerning myths, symbols, ritual, religion, and anthropology, as well as psychotherapeutic practice much of what TA also talks of. Ego states, transactions, games, scripts are all archetypal in character, deriving much of their power not only from the individual but also from the collective unconscious. Exposure to Jung can thus deepen the TA therapist's dedication and awareness of the profundity of what he is doing, seeing that he is dealing in a work with the psyche that has been going on for millennia.

Contact with Jung also may supply TA with added empirical, clinical, and epistemological supports that might once and for all put to rest the charge that TA is simplistic and without depth. In addition, such contact may clarify and/or emphasize some matters for TA. Again, the example of the persona is a good illustration. The Adaptive Child is often seen as a negative experience. However, when one looks into the concept and functioning of the persona, Jung's way of describing much the same thing, one sees that there is a highly positive side to adaptive responses: A person may be selective about his expression, which is often good for him and his situation. Roles, even automatically assumed, are often helpful.

Analytical psychology has an awarenes that there is hardly any aspect of the conscious personality that does not have an unconscious side. If the TA therapist can avoid the urge to equate the unconscious with the Natural Child,[27] he may see with Jung that all ego states may have unconscious aspects.[28] Such an insight may be of great value for him in clarifying resistance and confusion in therapy. For example, if a client seems incapable of developing a particular aspect of his personality, it could well be due to its being part of the shadow. This awareness might lead the therapist to understand the power of the resistance, why the client really could not understand what was happening (the shadow really is unconscious!), and to listen to the psyche in fantasy and dreams for some possible ways out.

This means, then, that TA might learn some technical aspects of therapy from Jung. A tentative use of Jungian dream and fantasy techniques, along with a respectful stance on the therapist's part in listening, might well add to TA's already many-faceted approach.

However, I am not suggesting that both the Jungian and the TA therapist jump into a wandering and unstructured mixing up of the two approaches. Rather, I believe that the most important thing that would come from an exposure of each to the other would be the jolt that comes from seeing what one has looked at through one's own eyes in turn described by the other. Such a new perspective would hopefully return both the Jungian and the transactional analyst to their own approaches for a newer and deeper look into that which they already know.

Thus I would think that dialogue between analytical psychology and TA would clarify concepts, expand techniques, and increase respect for another's way. In addition, finding your way around a new place is often lots of fun.

REFERENCES

1. Jung, quoted in: Progoff, Ira, *Jung's Psychology and Its Social Meaning* (Garden City, N.Y.: Anchor Press/Doubleday, 1973), p. xiii: Whitmont, Edward, "Jungian Analysis Today," *Psychology Today* **6**, 7 (1972), p. 68.

2. Van der Post, Laurens. *Jung and the Story of Our Time* (New York: Pantheon Books, 1975), p. 4.

3. Jung, in the Foreword to: Fordham, Frieda, *An Introduction to Jung's Psychology* (Baltimore: Penguin Books, 1966), p. 11.

4. For a description of this way of looking at Analytical Psychology, see: Whitmont, Edward C., *The Symbolic Quest* (New York: G. P. Putnam's Sons for the C. G. Jung Foundation for Analytic Psychology, 1969), pp. 15–35.

5. See: Henderson, Joseph L., "Analytical Psychology in England," *Psychological Perspectives* **6**, 2 (1975), pp. 197–198: Adler, Gerhard, "Methods of Treatment in

Analytical Psychology," in *Psychoanalytic Techniques—A Handbook for the Practicing Psychoanalyst,* edited by Benjamin Wolman (New York: Basic Books, 1967), pp. 338–378.

6. Redlich, Frederick C. and Daniel X. Freedman, *The Theory and Practice of Psychiatry* (New York: Basic Books, 1966), p. 229.

7. On Jung's life see: Jung, C. G., *Memories, Dreams, Reflections* (New York: Vintage Books, 1963): Jaffe, Aniela, *From the Life and Work of C. G. Jung* (New York: Harper Colophon Books, 1971): Wehr, Gerhard, *Portrait of Jung—An Illustrated Biography* (New York: Herder & Herder, 1971).

8. Jung, C. G., *The Collected Works of C. G. Jung* (Princeton: Princeton University Press) (Bollingen Series XX). The volumes of these works are referred to later in this essay by the shorthand "*CW*." The volumes I will use are:

    2. *Psychiatric Studies* (1957)
    4. *Freud and Psychoanalysis* (1961)
    5. *Symbols of Transformation* (1956)
    6. *Psychological Types* (1971)
    7. *Two Essays on Analytical Psychology* (1953)
    8. *The Structure and Dynamics of the Psyche* (1960)
    9i. *The Archetypes and the Collective Unconscious* (1959)
    10. *Civilization in Transition* (1964)
    13. *Alchemical Studies* (1967)
    14. *Mysterium Coniunctionis* (1965)
    16. *The Practice of Psychotherapy* (1954)
    17. *The Development of Personality* (1954)

9. Jung, C. G. *Analytical Psychology—Its Theory and Practice* (New York: Pantheon Books, 1968), p. 141.

10. Jung, *Memories, Dreams, Reflections,* p. 28.

11. Roazen, Paul, *Freud and His Followers* (New York: Alfred A. Knopf, 1975), p. 231.

12. Fordham, *Introduction,* p. 24.

13. For a fuller treatment of the archetype, see: Jacobi, Jolande, *Complex/Archetype/Symbol in the Psychology of C. G. Jung* (New York: Pantheon Books for the Bollingen Foundation, 1959) (Bollingen Series LVII).

14. See: Jung, *CW* 6: Fordham, *Introduction,* pp. 29–46: Wheelwright, Joseph, *Psychological Types* (San Francisco: C. G. Jung Institute of San Francisco, 1973).

15. See Jacobi, Jolande, *The Way of Individuation* (New York: Harcourt, Brace & World, 1967), pp. 21–48, on the two stages of individuation.

16. On technique see: Adler, *Methods of Treatment*: Hart, David, "Jungian Therapy," in *Inside Psychotherapy,* edited by Adelaide Bry (New York: Basic Books, 1972), pp. 21–39: Hochheimer, Wolfgang. *The Psychology of C. G. Jung* (New York: G. P. Putnam's Sons for the C. G. Jung Foundation for Analytical Psychology, 1969): Jung, *CW* 16.

17. On transference see: Jung, *CW* 16, pp. 129–323: Adler, *Methods of Treatment,* pp. 344 ff: Hart, "Jungian Therapy," pp. 34 ff: Hochheimer, *The Psychotherapy,* pp. 93–103.

18. Jung, C. G., *Modern Man in Search of A Soul* (New York: Harcourt, Brace & World, 1933), p. 13.

19. On dreams see: Jung, *CW* 4, pp. 25–34 and pp. 48–55: *CW* 8, pp. 237–280 and pp. 281 297: *CW* 16, pp. 139 162: Adler, *Methods of Treatment,* pp. 355 ff; Fordham, *Introduction,* pp. 97–107; Hochheimer, *The Psychotherapy,* pp. 104–123.

20. Adler, *Methods of Treatment,* p. 365.

21. On active imagination see: Jung, *CW* 8, pp. 67–91: Adler, *Methods of Treatment,* pp 365 ff: Fordham, Michael, *The Objective Psyche* (London: Routledge and Kegan Paul, 1958), pp. 67–80: Hochheimer, *The Psychotherapy,* pp. 87–89: Weaver, Rix, *The Old Wise Woman* (New York: G. P. Putnam's Sons for the C. G. Foundation for Analytical Psychology, 1973).

22. Adler, *Methods of Treatment,* p. 366.

23. Von Franz, Marie Louise, *C. G. Jung—His Myth in Our Time* (New York: G. P. Putnam's Sons for the C. G. Jung Foundation for Analytical Psychology, 1975), p. 66.

24. Ibid., p. 67.

25. Jung, *CW* 16, pp. 26–27.

26. Ibid., p. 27.

27. For an example of this approach, see: Herman, Lisa, "One Transactional Analyst's Understanding of Carl Jung," *TA Journal* 5, 2, pp. 123–126.

28. For a brief treatment of this approach, see my response to Ms. Herman, "Jung and TA: Some Clarifications," *TA Journal* 6, 2, pp. 169–172.

CHAPTER 14

psychodrama and TA

ALAN JACOBS

MORENO AND THE ORIGIN OF PSYCHODRAMA

Jacob L. Moreno broke with psychoanalysis and created Psychodrama in 1911. From the outset he was attracted to observation and explanation of spontaneity and creativity.

He'd sit in the park in Vienna and talk with children, and learned that if one allowed them to act on their problems spontaneously, it produced therapeutic results. He observed them becoming other persons in their lives and that this "role play" was often spontaneous and creative. For example, if a child was angry with a teacher, she might become that teacher and assume his posture, attitudes, expressions, and even his voice in an effort to assimilate his role, thus understanding him more and perhaps fearing him less. She might also get one of her playmates to become the teacher and then say things ordinarily disallowed in "real life." Moreno noted that these enactments often closely approximated the real situation and prepared the child to meet the future through enactment and change of the past in the now.

He also was the first to use the term, "group psychotherapy," and is responsible for the creation of role theory, sociometry, and sociodrama. His contributions to sociology make him as famous in that field as in psychotherapy.

In *Childhood and Society*, Eric Erikson talked about how psychology, sociology, and biology need not, indeed should not, be divided into separate disciplines, for to do so fragments an otherwise more complete picture of human behavior. Moreno addressed himself to two of these disciplines, sociology and psychology, and made enormous contributions to both fields. In so doing he married them with an action theory and method which has application in a wide range of areas, including psychiatric facilities, prisons, business, education, and the community.

Many years later, Eric Berne too was observing and thinking about creativity and struggling with the dismal failure of a psychoanalytic treatment method which had not produced results fulfilling the promise of its theory. Berne's subsequent observation, that the human personality could be seen as divided into three distinct behavioral and psychological realities called ego states, started with his interests in spontaneity and creativity.[1] He observed the Child in all of us and concluded that we very much need to reclaim it in order to utilize the creative forces normally available to children.

Berne, like Moreno, was a psychiatrist who began his career as a psychoanalyst and left that tradition to produce a theory and method applicable to a wide variety of human experience. He, too, realized the enormous importance of creativity in problem solving, though he failed to grasp its relationship to action during the therapy session. He did, however, create perhaps the clearest, most comprehensive view of human interaction to date. His discovery of ego states remains a genius stroke of crystallization. He had the rare ability to simplify the complex and to explain that action in understandable terms.

Modern psychotherapy has many active methods, approaches, and techniques which have been developed by Moreno.[2] Moreno was the pioneer in action methods and in the concept of catharsis being an integral part of growth and change. He believed, possibly before anyone else, that without a person's active physical participation in therapy, there could be no real change; that without action there is no catharsis and without catharsis there is little or no growth. Active means just that—action or movement during a psychotherapy session, and not simply talking.

Transactional Analysis forms the theoretical base, the view of what a person is doing, and Psychodrama provides a way for both patient and therapist to do something about it. TA explains the how, when, and why of behavior and Psychodrama is a powerful way to experience and change it. TA can be used as a theoretical base, the skeletal system, the structure. Psychodrama is the action, the muscles that move the bones.

Much of the work of modern psychotherapy has at its roots the sequence of awareness, catharsis, and retraining or relearning. Many methods focus on one, or perhaps two, of these steps and neglect the third. Transactional Analysis is very good for enabling both therapist and client to see, understand, and describe what the latter is doing; that is, it provides awareness. It also has given birth to a new kind of regressive therapy called reparenting, which is an excellent method of retraining. However, TA in my opinion, is weak in the second phase of the sequence—catharsis.

PSYCHODRAMA FOR CATHARSIS

Psychodrama has as its very base the concept of catharsis. It is similar to TA in its approach to new Parent messages and permissions. However, it is weak in the first phase, awareness. Combined, Psychodrama and TA are powerful tools which encompass all three basic requirements.

TA is not as strong as Psychodrama when it comes to experiencing feeling, because it does not employ action methods. Psychodrama does not have an elegantly simple cognitive system with which to understand now behavior and its relationship to a person's life plan or script. When both systems are used together, however, people not only become aware of what they do, but can also employ action methods to enhance experience. For example, a woman in a psychotherapy training session proclaimed to the group in a shaky, teary-eyed voice, her need to sing during the session. She was afraid to ask because nobody would listen. What we discovered with the transactional method was her decision to take care of others. She expressed wanting to sing as a need rather than as a way of entertaining. She was asked if she recalled an incident when she was responsible for others and had to put her needs second. She said she did and we invited her to a Psychodrama of the incident. She agreed.

In the process of warming up, which included setting up an imaginery dinner scene, I walked with her onto a porch attached to the kitchen. (What we do is make the Psychodrama stage into what we need in order to help people enter their past experientially rather than by recall, and we were recreating the physical scene in preparation for her reexperience of the incident.) On this recreated porch, we discovered a trunk containing many of her early adolescent belongings, and I invited her to open it. She discovered the Nancy Drew stories, which she hadn't remembered until she opened the trunk. I asked what kind of girl Nancy Drew was, and she said, "She was a good little girl who took care of other people." I froze the warmup at this point and said, "Are you aware of the kind of scripting you had in order to become attracted to these stories?" She said, "I never thought about it before, but I guess that's so. I was identifying with a girl who took care of others before she got her own needs met." The warmup is a Psychodrama method. The concept of a script decision is TA. Here is a good example of the two, using a kind of loose and free-flowing structure, the warmup, in order to get to script material. Use of the warmup is Psychodrama; stopping and telling the person you think this might be a decision is Transactional Analysis. She was aware here of her decision to take care of others. She arrived at this awareness through a Psychodramatic technique and a TA cognitive understanding.

There are three things here which need further explanation before we can continue to describe this session: first, the components of Psychodrama; second, the techniques of Psychodrama; and third, the Bernian view of script.

PSYCHODRAMA COMPONENTS

Psychodrama has five basic components: the group, the subject or protagonist, the psychodramatist or director, his or her therapeutic aides or auxiliary egos, and a system of methods and techniques adaptable to the situation. All of these form a system of necessary elements.[3]

The group is helped to enact a meaningful situation in the process of warmup. This is the first part of Psychodrama. It helps to free the spontaneity and creativity of each member so that when moving into the action portion they do so naturally, with enactment and experience as well as memory and recount.

Actually, we warm up to everything we do. We don't jump out of bed and start working. We wash, dress, eat, ride or walk, think, and prepare ourselves. A child doesn't just jump off the diving board. She stops and assesses, ponders, imagines what it's like, checks that it's safe, etc. We may have dinner, go dancing, listen to music, talk, kiss, and pet before lovemaking; we don't just begin. We need some preparation, some warmup in order to find and prepare the needed parts of ourselves for virtually all activities. Athletes, musicians, actors, and artists are all disciplined to warming up before they perform. Without this, their beginning may be flat, cold, without totality, and may influence and destroy the meaning, fullness, and sensitivity of the entire performance. It is a logical extension, then, that warming up is to be employed in the psychotherapy session, since it is happening anyway. I have seen many a session dull, flat, and superficial because permission to warm up is not given and people are expected to start right in and work. Even when the session is rewarding, the first one or two people working unknowingly warm up the group and what happens after they work is more the "real thing."

There are three kinds of warmups: the cluster, the chain of association, and the directed. Using the cluster means the group starts discussing anything, any subject. Usually there is more than one subject discussed and the group starts to cluster around different subjects. These clusters begin to interact and there is a kind of merger of interests through which a common theme may be evolved. In this way what is happening now, what people are concerned with now, is emerging from the group. Eventually a person who best exemplifies this emergence becomes the protagonist or patient and begins action.

The chain warmup is kind of a mutual free association. The group comes in and starts discussing anything. Eventually someone says something about himself in a way which demonstrates a deeper level of association. He then moves into further action.

Directed warmups are by far the most popular and most used. They may be done by the leader, the whole group, or an individual in the group.

These psychodramatic warmups form the foundation for all the group exercises we know. The encounter and sensitivity groups so popular a decade ago owe their innervation to the warmup.

In the leader-directed warmup, the leader may have specific information about the group and devise a series of exercises before the group begins. He may feel the group is stuck at a certain place, say about the issue of resolving death. He may decide to use a lifeboat exercise, where people are asked to imagine that they are in a lifeboat and that one person must be thrown overboard if the others are to survive. Naturally this evokes much feeling and helps to ready people for more personal exploration. On the other hand, the leader may be working with a group of nurses, business people, police, or parents. He might have specific information about what their problem is and institute warmups which focus the problem more specifically. The possibilities here are well-nigh unlimited, and though there is a vast glut of exercises already in existence, it is often rewarding and enlightening to create one on the spot—one that is directed toward the natural emergence of a protagonist/patient who best represents the group feeling. At this point the warmup moves to action.

"The protagonist acts for himself and for the rest of the group. This is done with the support, help, and insight of the rest of the group, who may become auxiliaries or assistants to the director and protagonist."[4] The protagonist demonstrates problems within a specific situation. It is this situational quality which does much to free the child, the spontaneous, free, flowing stream of creativity.

In *Picasso's Guernica, the Genesis of a Painting*, Rudolph Arnheim makes a point about the miracle-working spirit or psyche that runs and hides when it notices it is being watched. "The creative process must continue uninterrupted from the feeling and idea to the physiological limit of the performed act."[5] Arnheim quotes Paul Valery, who said, "One could almost derive a whole philosophy from it: Sometimes I think and sometimes I am." This is not to say that thinking isn't an important part of the therapy process. It is. However, when we are reexperiencing the past it inhibits spontaneity and what we get is historical recounting. Picasso did his thinking after he made a painting. He would sit sometimes for hours staring at the product of his spontaneous expression. And so it is with children. They make paintings that are honest. Thinking in the midst of the creative act produces works which are contrived and inane, if not tawdry and banal.

Consider a man setting up a grocery store on the psychodrama stage, complete with its colors, smells, and sounds. When he begins to deal with how his mother discounted him there, he is less likely to perform because he *is in* the store, not merely talking about it. When he is able to immerse himself in the incidentals, his problem/conflict emerges naturally and without his immediate observation. Defenses become obvious in this situation and the protagonist can then move to deeper levels.

The director or therapist must be very spontaneous. There is virtually no end to the different kinds of roles demanded of him or her, including role-playing a member of the opposite sex. He or she may be required to be a demanding father or a sympathetic aunt or whatever. It is the director's responsibility to create new situations which will enable the protagonist to change self-limiting, self-defeating behavior. This may require the use of auxiliary egos or assistants who become the different people the protagonist needs. Often the director will not enter the action, but may stand aside and allow the auxiliary egos to do the work. The director's job is to stay in touch with all that is happening; to watch the group, protagonist, auxiliaries, and central theme, and to keep all in touch.

The auxiliary egos are extensions of the director, who might tell them various things to do and say. It is helpful if the auxiliaries are trained, but not always necessary. For example, if another group member has affinity for a particular role needed by the protagonist, he may be much more effective. However, auxiliaries are usually trained people. I might add here that one of the benefits of auxiliary/director work is a sense of community during the session. Perhaps three or four trained people are active and this does much to alleviate the kind of alienation therapists who work alone often feel.

Psychodrama techniques include role reversal, the double, the soliloquy, and the mirror. There are hundreds of methods which have evolved after many years of psychodramatic procedure: dream enactment, interrupted action, self-realization, psychodramatic shock, silent auxiliary ego, therapeutic images, bi-focal psychodrama, auxiliary chair, behind your back, exit technique, future projection, video method, role therapy, rehearsal technique, etc. Some of these are discussed in the following paragraphs.

Role Reversal Role reversal is the procedure in which A becomes B and B becomes A; for example, a protagonist playing her role as wife may reverse roles with her husband, where the situation indicates, for any of the following purposes:

1. The protagonist playing the role of the relevant other often begins to feel and understand his position and reactions in the situation, thus possibly adding more effective "telic" sensitivity (two-way empathy).

2. Role reversal may be used to help the protagonist see himself as if in a mirror. The wife playing the role of her husband will see herself through his perception. This instrument has the effect of producing insights for better understanding of the protagonist as he sees himself through the eyes of another.

3. Role reversal is often effective in augmenting the spontaneity of the protagonist, through shifting him out of defenses. In general, however, role reversal helps the protagonist understand others in the situation through being them.

4. In order to aid an auxiliary ego better to understand how a role was played in particular situations, the auxiliary, not having been on the actual scene of a situation, attempts to fulfill the requirements as projected by the subject. The subject, who is usually the only person who has experienced the situation, will take the role of the other through role reversal, so that the auxiliary may more effectively fulfill the necessary role. This will enable the protagonist and auxiliary to move more effectively into the problem situation.

The Double The difference between the double experience and empathy lies in the loss of separateness of identity for the two people in the action. This results in a single production of two people. The double attempts to warm up to and become the protagonist. If the protagonist is A, the double is A. The double can give the protagonist necessary support. At other times, the double will express feelings of fear, hostility, or love which the protagonist when alone is unable to act out. The double may take a chance and express certain hypotheses which appear in the situation. The protagonist may or may not agree with the many thoughts which the double expresses. In this respect the double is useful in helping the protagonist produce new cues for lines of further understanding. The double produces an added dimension of the protagonist which he, for various reasons, cannot present himself.

The Soliloquy The soliloquy is a useful technique for expressing the hidden thoughts and action tendencies of the protagonist. The protagonist's improvisations are parallel with his overt actions and thoughts, with the hidden action tendencies and thoughts which he has in reference to a specific person or a specific situation. When the protagonist soliloquizes, he may clarify and structure insights and perceptions, and prepare himself for future situations. The double technique may be combined with the soliloquy. The double may soliloquize for the protagonist in a production or at crucial moments, stepping in and out of the situation.

The Mirror The mirror effect is produced through having auxiliary egos portray the protagonist in his presence. He sees for himself how he acts in situations of relevance. The mirror is used whenever it is indicated that seeing himself in action, as if in a psychological mirror, would be productive for him; for instance, a nurse portraying the behavior of a catatonic patient in typical situations. It helps withdrawn subjects to warm up to self-presentation. The protagonist is always encouraged to comment on, or react to, the auxiliary therapist playing the role. At times the protagonist will participate, come forward, and take over his own role from the auxiliary when he is sufficiently warmed up.

Methods and techniques are only aids for helping to produce therapeutic production and interaction in psychodrama. They are never ends in themselves. They are only available means, and may be sensitively adapted to produce therapeutic benefits for the protagonist and the group.[6]

Psychodrama often is too long for most nonactive group participants to stay involved in without becoming bored. In fact, this is the one consistent criticism of the method. With TA, the early incidents can be reached with greater speed within the session itself because of the systematic approach to early life decisions and how we make them. It affords us a structure with which to understand more clearly that early time.

PSYCHODRAMA AND TA

Many years ago, Moreno said, "Throw away your old script and write a new one." This idea, that we have a script or life plan, was further developed by Eric Berne and Claude Steiner. We make decisions early in life about who we are, who we will be, and what we will strive toward. These "choices" are the child's way of surviving within the family system. The stronger reinforcement patterns, to a large extent, force the child to what he believes are choices. For example, a group of people are standing in a circle holding hands. One person is standing in the center. Two people are instructed to stop holding hands with each other, so that there is a single opening in the circle. A is asked to leave the circle as quickly as possible. He exits at the point of least resistance, where the opening is. Now he comes in again, and the first two join hands and another pair disengage. Again A is asked to leave in the quickest possible manner. He again chooses the open space. He has made some choices, but who is really controlling them? He appears to be making them, but they are controlled by others. So too with adults. We look as though we are making our own choices, but they are most often controlled by those made many years before in childhood. Actually those forced many years before in childhood. A number of these forced choices make up a script or life plan. It is the psychotherapist's task to help a person free himself or herself from this past, so that he or she might live freely and autonomously, and make decisions now. And this is precisely what TA does—helps people to change this early programming. It helps people demystify their past, to understand it, and to make choices about changing it. Transactional and script analysis are fast ways to understand our script, how and when we got it, and how and why we are controlled by it.

It is interesting that both Moreno and Berne were aware of this kind of life plan, that both men were extremely interested in the Greeks, and in the whole idea of being controlled by a past. What we are up to as psychotherapists is challenging the power of the oracle,[7] challenging the power of the feeling that is cathected around certain behaviors, and helping a person to redecide—this time, autonomously.

Often in transactional therapy I have pointed to a script decision and asked the patient if he remembered making this decision and at what age. Often he is able to tell me, "When I was five years old I decided that I was going to have to take care of my little sister, and this was the primary way I was going to get love and care in my family." We then proceed to ask the person to make a redecision[8] and to stop taking care of other people and start taking care of himself. This seemed premature, and once I started employing psychodrama methods, I discovered the relative nature of time. It is one thing to ask a person about a decision, it is another thing to see that person, in the midst of a psychodrama, make it as if he were five years old again. Here is the difference between talking about and remembering, and experiencing and becoming. If people do not cathect, or energize, the feelings behind this kind of decision, the probability is that they will not make a change. That is, they will not make the redecision in their body and in their feelings as well as in their head.

Now we can return to the woman who takes care of others. In a TA group, we would have first identified the problem and then worked at getting a contract to change this decision. We probably would have devised some exercise for changing behavior, such as getting the patient to ask others in the room to take care of her. And this is where I think the psychodrama process belongs—in between problem identification and asking for fulfillment of unmet needs. So after we identified the problem, we went back to an early incident in the kitchen where she was required to take care of her brother by getting his food, jumping up and down, etc. She couldn't, however, discipline her brother too much, as this upset her father who said, "Don't argue. Can't you see your mother is tired?" Rather than telling us what her father, mother, and brother were feeling, she became the others in her family and spoke as if she were them. This reversal revealed much that ordinarily does not surface, because when she became them she didn't watch herself as closely. She became spontaneous. Some may say, "Well, Gestalt techniques such as the empty chair produce the same kind of spontaneity." But the Gestaltists do not regularly employ methods such as setting the scene. Also, the patient has to do all the work alone. He or she does not have the help of an auxiliary who becomes what is needed in the situation. Setting the scene carefully and employing others helps a great deal to recreate reality. It is this realness that occupies the patient's observing part and allows for the free flow of expression.

Again our example. After she experienced what "happened," she was asked if she'd like to change it. Only after the experience could she make a decision about this. And she did! She became her family again and this time gave herself what she really needed and wanted. After this portion we brought her back into the now and asked her to get what she needed. Now when she asks to get taken care of it is with all of her, because she has reexperienced and changed at an early level.

Psychodrama frees us from ordinary clock time in that it does not see it as constant and unchanging. It allows us to compress and expand time to whatever degree is needed. We can work very quickly with regressions, etc. There is a natural relationship to life and energy, and what Einstein showed us about inert matter may very well be applicable to social, psychological, and biological needs as well. If we can speed up the way in which we work with early script decisions by changing time, we can get enormous releases of creative energy. This energy is absolutely essential to problem-solving.

TA gives us a way to understand and choose rapidly what we need to return to. It offers a comprehensive explanation of how, when and why we decided to limit ourselves, but it does not employ methods which enhance experience of that time. Psychodrama does, but it often takes a while to decide which time. TA makes that process faster. So TA speeds the Psychodrama process by helping to focus quickly, and Psychodrama speeds the growth process by helping a person experience what the TA method has uncovered.

REFERENCES

1. Berne, Eric, *Transactional Analysis in Psychotherapy* (New York: Grove, 1961).

2. Yablonsky, Lewis, and James Enneis, "Psychodrama Theory and Practice," in *Progress in Psychodrama*, Vol. II. Edited by Brower and Abt (New York, Grune & Stratton, 1956).

3. Blattner, Howard, *Acting In* (New York, Springer, 1973).

4. Ibid.

5. Arnheim, Rudolph, *Picasso's "Guernica," the Genesis of a Painting* (Berkeley: University of California Press, 1962) p. 1.

6. Blattner, *Acting In*.

7. Steiner, Claude M., *Games Alcoholics Play: The Analysis of Life Scripts* (New York: Grove, 1971) p. 26.

8. Goulding, Robert, "New Directions in Transactional Analysis: Creating an Environment for Redecision and Change." In *Progress in Group and Family Therapy*, edited by Clifford J. Sager and Helen Singer Kaplan (New York: Brunner/Mazer, 1972).

CHAPTER 15

Gestalt therapy and TA

MURIEL JAMES

For a long time I inwardly debated about whether or not to write this chapter. Some of my inner dialogue was about asking someone to do it who is more directly identified with Gestalt therapy, people such as Mariam and Erving Polster, Joan Fagen, Abraham Levitsky, Jim Simken, Bob Hall, Irma Shepherd, and others. These are some of the "out-front" leaders in the use of Gestalt therapy. Although I have not studied with them nor observed their work, I respect their reputations for competency.

I also thought about asking teaching TA therapists such as Mary and Bob Goulding, who like myself have studied with, loved, and learned from Fritz Pearls, originator of Gestalt therapy, and who have chosen to use it in creative unique ways with Transactional Analysis. I then used the double-chair technique with myself to find out what was going on with me. After all, Gestalt therapists, like competent TA therapists, use their therapeutic methods on themselves. Thus I came to some closure and I decided to write this by drawing on my own experiences in training workshops with Fritz and on the Gestalt writings that are rapidly increasing in number.[1]

FRITZ PERLS AND GESTALT THERAPY

Gestalt *psychology* is not new; Gestalt *therapy* is. It is largely the work of one man, Frederick S. Perls; the S is for Solomon, the Frederick is usually shortened to Fritz. The German word *gestalt* has no exact English equivalent. In essence it means the forming of an organized whole.

When I first read Fritz' book, *Gestalt Therapy Verbatim*,[2] I hoped that the case of Muriel would be about me. Surely, fantasized my Child, I was important to Fritz. Well, maybe I was and maybe I wasn't. However, the case is not me and I was disappointed. I guess there is still some "unfinished business," years after his death, of still wanting more of his attention—just as at the age of two I wanted more attention from my grandfather, who looked quite a bit like Fritz!

That's what Gestalt therapy is directed toward—unfinished business. The task of finishing up is a lifelong process. When one issue is solved, it fades into the background and another issue moves forward.

This Gestalt principle is reflected in Perls' autobiography, published posthumously.[3] In it he claimed that finally, at the age of 75, he had reached closure on his habit of compulsory masturbation. As a youth, Perls, impressed with Freud, was convinced that he had damaged his own memory by masturbating. Perhaps his anger for not being accepted by Freud contributed to his habit. In TA terms, his rebellious Child may have been trying to prove something.

Perls had not, however, reached closure on another habit that concerned him— chain smoking. Like many children he experimented with smoking, then stopped until the end of the first world war when, as a medic in the defeated German army, he marched some 20 hours a day with little food. At this time he began chain smoking and continued to do so until his death, often throwing up a smoke screen between himself and others, especially when doing therapy.

In his free-association-style autobiography, Fritz Perls gives many examples of his far from perfect health and his struggle with self-acceptance and acceptance by others. This self-disclosure may have reflected an intuitive awareness of his impending death. I wish Eric Berne had left a similar detailed legacy.

Born in 1893, Perls grew up in Berlin. He enjoyed art, ice-skating, and swimming. He liked his elementary school teachers and was at the top of his class. He knew his multiplication tables before entering school and continued to be fascinated by mathematics. Later, school became a painful experience. He was suspended for being incorrigible and had to repeat the seventh grade. His incorrigibility and "black-sheep" status continued from this time.

Perls claimed that in spite of his Bar Mitzvah, he had only a few weeks reprieve from his black-sheep role but blames his early behavior on his father's deceitfulness and grandiosity. Once Fritz broke into his father's locked "secret" room in high anticipation of books to read. All he discovered was that the room was a mess and that it was piled high with books about Free Masonry. His father always wanted to be a Grand Master, and when he didn't succeed he founded several lodges where he could make ponderous speeches.

Perls' father was not a healthy model. When home, he continually fought loudly with Fritz' mother. As a traveling wine salesman, he was often with other women. Fritz' lifelong lechering toward women and his self-description as a "gypsy" seem to have been part of the script he copied from his father.

Throughout his life Fritz Perls was fascinated by art and acting. Both interests were related to his mother, who scripted him to draw by often taking him to visit art galleries. She also had a great interest in the theatre and carefully saved her pennies so that her son could at least have standing room there. At home she and his aunts often produced amateur plays, and Perls was part of the production. In high school he began as an extra in the "real" theatre. Later he studied with Max Reinhardt, one of the greatest stage directors of all time. This influence is reflected in one of the major techniques of Gestalt therapy, which concerns role-playing and breaking up the artificial roles people play to avoid authenticity.

Perls had two elder sisters. Grete, whom he liked, was a stubborn tomboy who was nervous, talkative, and a worrier. She used to send him cookies during his first months in America. His other sister, Else, he disliked because of her clinging manner. Else died in a concentration camp, and Perls says he hardly cared. He continued to dislike clinging people who depend on others for outer support rather than taking responsibility for their own authentic inner support. He called such people poisonous, saying that they play bear-trapper games:

> The bear-trappers suck you in and give you the come on, and when you're sucked in, down comes the hatchet and you stand there with a bloody nose, head, or whatever. And if you are fool enough to ram your head against the wall until you begin to bleed and be exasperated, then the bear-trapper enjoys himself and enjoys the control he has over you, to render you inadequate, impotent, and he enjoys his victorious self which does a lot for his feeble self-esteem.[5]

In 1914 when the war broke out, Perls was in medical school and volunteered as a Red Cross soldier "to be used outside the combat zone." He went through the war and the deterioration of Germany that followed and continued his analysis while serving as an assistant to Kurt Goldstein at the Institute For Brain-Injured Soldiers. In 1927 he took an assistantship in a hospital in Vienna and met Lori, later his wife. In his autobiography he claimed that she was competitive, opinionated, and righteous, that they were co-travelers with many common interests, and that he really didn't understand her.*

In 1933, when the Nazis took over Germany, Perls fled to Holland. Later he was able to get an appointment in Johannesburg, South Africa, as a training analyst. There he prospered financially, learned to fly and sail, and claims to have been "clobbered" by his wife, much as his father had been by his mother.

In 1946 he immigrated to the United States, but did not find a hospitable community in which to work until 1966 when Esalen welcomed him. At the time of his death, four years later, he had finally become famous and Gestalt therapy had won wide acceptance.

ORIGINS OF GESTALT THERAPY

Perls had the ability to analyze other therapists' ideas and incorporate what he approved of into his own theory. What he didn't approve of he often attacked. For example, through much of his writing he carried on a running argument with Freud. Obviously influenced by him, he spent a lot of energy to prove Freud was wrong with his focus on the unconscious and the libido theory, and that he (Fritz) was right with his focus on awareness.

Part of Perls' script was to be impressed or pleased with people in the early stages of relationships, later to become disappointed and critical of them. In spite of that, he used many of their insights. As another example, although Perls was as disappointed in Wilhelm Reich (noted for his discovery of muscular armor) as he was in Freud, the Gestalt focus on *how* clients block themselves with body rigidity was directly influenced by Perls' early training with Reich.

Another major idea Perls added to Gestalt therapy comes from S. Friedlander and his writing on "Creative Indifferences." This concept is that every event is "related to a zero-point from which a differentiation into opposites takes place. These *opposites* show *in their specific context* a great affinity to each

---

* For more fascinating details on Perls' life, see Martin Shepard's *Fritz* (New York: Bantam, 1976), which I regret that I did not read until after I had written this chapter.

other."[6] Creative indifference is not the same as an "I don't care" attitude. It is "full of interest, extending toward both sides of the differentiation,"[7] yet not staying at either one side. To do so is to be trapped into either/or thinking.

The concept of opposites, or opposing forces that need to be integrated, is a basic principle in Gestalt therapy. When the opposites are integrated, the imbalance disappears and once more the person is at the zero point.

Paul Weiss, because of his interest in Zen, was another influence on Perls. Although Perls studied Zen, expecially its focus on breathing, and saw its value for the enlargement of awareness and the release of the human potential, he wrote that neither Zen nor psychoanalysis was efficient because "they are not centered in the polarities of contact and withdrawal, the rhythm of life."[8]

Perls conceived neurotics as having holes in their personalities. "Many people have no soul, others have no genitals. Some have no heart; all their energy goes into computing, thinking. Others have no legs to stand on . . ."[9] Symptoms of holes are phobic avoidance behavior, not dealing with the obvious, not seeing the obvious. Perls goes on to say that the holes are expressed as the "patient's projection on to the therapist." This concept originated with Wilson Van Dusen, who saw people with schizophrenia as having this problem. Perls combined this idea with one of Freud's which was of the neurotic having blanks or amnesia in his or her memory. Perls writes:

> As long as the patient blocks his memories, he keeps the Gestalt incomplete. If he is willing to go through the pain of his unhappiness and despair, he will come to closure; he will come to terms with his resentments and will repair his memory . . .[10]

To aid this process, the Gestalt therapist frustrates clients so that they will develop their own potential.

The influence of Gestalt psychology on Gestalt therapy is often assumed, yet Perls brags that he never read the Gestalt psychology textbooks, only some papers by Kurt Lewin, Wertheimer, and Köhler. He says that their most important idea was that of the unfinished situation, the incomplete Gestalt, and makes this a major concept in his theory—the differentiation of the Gestalt into figure and ground.

The ground, or background, is the context, connection, or situation. The figure is that which can be experienced as distinct from the ground. It is the focus of interest. Gestalt *psychology* was concerned with auditory and visual *external* figures. Gestalt *therapy* adds a concern—a concern for how clients perceive their own feelings, emotions, and bodily sensations.

In a healthy person the figure and ground are sharply differentiated, not confused. Therefore, in the healthy person, behavior is selective: A need comes to the person's attention, it is met in an organized way, and the need disappears. For example, if a person is thirsty and gets a drink, the thirst is no longer a pressing need. According to Richard Wallen, this example is the prototype of Gestalt formation and destruction.

> The phenomenal world is organized by the needs of the individual. Needs energize behavior and organize it on the subjective-perceptual level and on the objective-motor level. The individual then carries out the necessary activities in order to satisfy the needs. After satisfaction, the mouth recedes into the background, the concern with the particular figure of water or beer disappears, and something new emerges.[11]

The Gestalt formation and destruction is a continuous process. It can be interfered with in three ways: (1) by poor perceptual contact with the external world and the body, (2) by blocking the open expression of needs, or (3) by repression or "holding back" of a muscular response to the need.[12]

PRINCIPLES OF GESTALT THERAPY

The awareness of needs and how they are blocked physically are the particular insights of Fritz Perls in the development of Gestalt Therapy.

Awareness, says Perls, is the hub of the Gestalt therapy approach. With awareness, a need is recognized and the Gestalt is formed and moves to closure. Awareness is achieved by focusing on the "how" and staying in the present, rather than focusing on the "why" from the past and the "perhaps" of the future.

Gestalt therapy is done in the present tense—in the "now." For example, if a person talks about something that happened in childhood, he or she is encouraged to replay it using the first person, present tense. However, this kind of therapy is not appropriate for everyone. According to Irma Lee Shepherd:

> Gestalt therapy is most effective with overly socialized, restrained, constricted individuals—often described as neurotic, phobic, perfectionistic, ineffective, depressed, etc.—whose functioning is limited or inconsistent, primarily due to their internal restrictions, and whose enjoyment of living is minimal.[13]

Gestalt techniques must be used with caution with individuals who are poorly organized, severely disturbed, acting out, or psychotic—and then only if the Gestalt therapist has great skill and a long-time commitment to the client. Otherwise the client may be left in worse shape because of being opened and left with unfinished business that is too heavy to handle.

The levels of neurosis have been discussed in Gestalt literature in two different ways. Fagan and Shepherd list them as

a) phony or game layer

b) phobic layer of avoidance

c) impasse layer of feeling stuck

d) implosive layer of grief, despair, self-loathing, fear, and doubt

e) explosive layer where unused energies are freed[14]

Perls lists them differently and cautions that the layers are not strictly separated but only guidelines.

a) cliché layer

b) roles and games

c) implosion

d) impasse and explosion

e) authenticity[15]

The differences in these lists may or may not be of major importance. I think that Fagan and Shepherd would agree that authenticity follows the explosion, and that cliché behavior is the same as phony behavior. Evidently Perls includes phobic avoidance under games.

The belief that people are fragmented is another basic Gestalt principle. Perls perceives many personalities as lacking wholeness, as being fragmented. He claims people are often aware of only parts of themselves rather than of the whole self. For example, a woman may not know or want to admit that sometimes she acts like her mother; a man may not know or want to admit that sometimes he wants to cry like a baby.

The aim of Gestalt therapy is to help become whole—to help the person become aware of, admit to, reclaim, and integrate his or her fragmented parts. Integration helps one make the transition from dependency to self-sufficiency.[17]

Undergirding the principles of Gestalt therapy are what Claudio Naranjo calls implicit moral injunctions. He calls these *moral* injunctions because they refer to the pursuit of the good life. They are

1. Live now. Be concerned with the present rather than with past or future.

2. Live here. Deal with what is present rather than with what is absent.

3. Stop imagining. Experience the real.

4. Stop unnecessary thinking. Rather, taste and see.

5. Express rather than manipulate, explain, justify, or judge.

6. Give in to unpleasantness and pain just as to pleasure. Do not restrict your awareness.

7. Accept no *should* or *ought* other than your own. Adore no graven image.

8. Take full responsibility for your actions, feelings, and thoughts.

9. Surrender to being as you are.[16]

TECHNIQUES IN GESTALT THERAPY

Gestalt therapists believe that the problems people have result from the lack of awareness and the blocking of awareness. Therefore, claims John Enright, Gestalt therapy "consists of the reintegration of attention and awareness."[18] Attention is focused by the therapist who suggests techniques, such as exaggeration of a hand or foot movement, to foster awareness. Thus clients discover how they frustrate themselves, how they avoid taking responsibility for their own feelings and behavior. In this process the Gestalt therapist works with clients so that they move from dependence on others to dependence on themselves.

Critical to the process is finding the impasse which originally occurred when the clients' supportive needs in childhood were not met and they were not yet self-supportive—when they therefore learned to manipulate their environment by starting to play roles.

Impasses are fantasies that are experienced as being real. Symptoms of impasses include confusion, panic, whining, and other childlike behaviors. Working with impasses includes frustrating clients until they break through the impasse. This leads them to reclaim their own power and authenticity.

There are certain guidelines to Gestalt therapy which Levitsky and Perls call rules.[19] Actually, they are not intended to be used as dogmatic "shoulds" and "should-nots," but to promote the *essence* of Gestalt therapy. Like signposts pointing to techniques, like principles that underlie all subsequent techniques, they are:

1. *The principle of the now.* This is promoted by questions such as, "What is your present awareness?" "What is happening now?" "What do you feel at this moment?"

2. *I and thou.* This is used so that the client makes direct contact with other individuals instead of, for example, talking to the ceiling or to the floor. This is facilitated by such questions as, "To whom are you speaking?" "Will you use that person's name when you speak?"

3. *"It" language and "I" language.* Changing the word "it" to "I"—for example, changing "It makes me cry" to "I am crying"—leads the client to

recognize how he or she is disowning behavior instead of taking responsibility for it.

4. *Use of the awareness continuum.* This is involved with *how* a client is experiencing body feelings, sensations, and perceptions. For example, a client who becomes aware of "uptight shoulders" may discover, by staying with them, that he or she is still living in some *past* fear rather than in the present.

5. *No gossiping.* Gossiping, in Gestalt terms, is speaking in the third person *about* someone who is physically in the room. Thus, the gossiper avoids talking directly to the person.

6. *Asking questions.* Some questions are genuine. Many more are manipulative pleas from a "helpless" Child position or rhetorical commands from a "helpful" Parent position. When the question seem manipulative, the therapist instructs the client to "Change that question into a statement."

I believe the most important "technique" for any therapist is the therapist as a person. In one way or another, the personhood always shines through. It transcends and supports techniques or undermines and destroys even the best.[20]

Another important technique for Gestalt therapists is the setting. Central to this is the "hot seat," a chair placed next to the therapist which clients take when they want to "work" on some issue. There is also a box of tissues for runny noses and tearful eyes. A second chair faces the hot seat; this is the projection chair. The client uses it to project onto it a part of a dream, another person, or a disowned part of self. These disowned parts are fragmented parts, holes in the personality, or opposing forces within. Everyone has some of these.

In *Born to Win,* the first writing to integrate TA and Gestalt therapy, the hot-seat method is described and used for a teacher who had no friends in spite of her friendly and helpful manner.

> Although she denied any angry feelings, common expressions she used were "You'll be sorry for that," and "I feel sorry for anyone like you." Others heard this as threatening and hostile.

> When this woman role-played her fragmented parts, she acted her "friendly self" from the hot-seat and imagined her "angry self" on the opposite chair. She switched chairs when she switched roles and slowly began a dialogue:

> *Hot-seat:*   I don't know why I'm here. I'm always friendly and helpful.

> *Opposite chair:* You do too know why you're here. You don't have any friends.

Hot-seat: I can't understand it. I'm always doing things for people.

Opposite chair: That's the trouble with you. Always being "helpful Hannah."
                    You have everybody obligated to you.

In a short time the teacher's voice grew shrill and loud. When she was in the hot seat, she struck out against the "helpful Hannah" comment. Amazed at her own aggressiveness, she commented in disbelief, "I never knew I could feel so angry." Although other people had seen this aspect of her personality quite often, this was the first time she admitted to her opposites of anger and helpfulness—her polarities.

Sometimes a person is aware of only *one* of his poles, as in the case of the teacher above. Sometimes a person may be aware of both and say, "I'm either as high as a kite or weighted down with depression," or "I'm either angry and aggressive, or afraid and full of doubt."

A person whose personality is fragmented by polarization operates in an either/or manner—he is either arrogant or worthless, helpless or tyrannical, wicked or righteous. When a person is stuck at the impasse of his own opposing forces, he is at war with himself. By using Perl's role-playing technique these opposing forces can have it out with each other, forgive each other, compromise, or at least come to know each other.[21]

When working with dreams, the Gestalt therapist is unique. He or she makes no interpretations at all, either during the work or after closure, and group members are instructed to also follow this procedure. It is based on the belief that the meaning of any dream is "the royal road to integration," and that every image in the dream represents an alienated part of the self.

An entire dream may be worked with or a small scene. The technique is that the client takes the hot seat, usually closes his or her eyes, gets in touch with emotional feeling and bodily sensations through using here-and-now procedures, then tells and retells the dream in the present tense. The client is instructed to tell only what is seen in the dream, not what is imagined as being there. The dream is retold, often several times, from the perspective of each image and always in the here and now.

For example, a large, strong man dreamed of walking down stairs, pushing open a door, and discovering a frightened man cowering on the other side. Asking him to play the door revealed that he was able to make a major change in his life. Asking him to play the frightened man led to an outburst of tears and revealed his opposing forces—strength and weakness. His playing of these parts allowed the process of integration to begin.

There are an unlimited number of methods for warming up a group, many similar to those designed by Jacob Moreno, who as early as 1919 was using psychodrama and encounter type techniques. Such techniques are used at the discretion of the therapist. In Gestalt circles they are sometimes called games, but their function is to promote awareness and the term is used differently than it is in transactional analysis. According to Levitsky and Perls,[22] these gestalt games are:

1. *Games of dialogue* are used for any split in the personality. The dialogues are conducted using the double chairs, two fists talking to each other, and so forth. One of the most common dialogues is between the top-dog and under-dog parts of the personality. The top dog is like a bossy parent, the underdog like a rebellious, or compliant, or procrastinating child.

2. *Making the rounds* is when the client needs to make *direct contact with each person in the group*—either verbally or physically—and does so under the direction of the therapist.

3. *Unfinished business* concerns the unresolved issues each person has. Resentments are the most common. Perls says resentments are demands that others feel guilty. Therefore "resentment sessions" in which the old ones are completed, then let go of, or where the current ones are voiced, then also let go of, is an important technique for any group.[23] Some people, instead of being afraid to voice their resentments, are afraid to voice their appreciations. They live in a "catastrophe unreality," feeling that if they give a compliment to someone it might be rejected. Like the Chicken Little of the childhood story, they expect the sky to fall in if rejection occurs.

One technique I use is to ask each person in a therapy group to voice resentments they are harboring toward others in the group. (No rebuttal is allowed, as it interferes with the process and often leads to games.) Next, each person voices his or her appreciations. Then clarifications or apologies (if in order) are given. The air is clear, the closure completed until another issue comes to the foreground.

4. *"I take responsibility."* With this technique, clients are asked to use the phrase, "I take responsibility..." after each statement or movement. In a combined TA-Gestalt group a person might say, "I like to use my Nurturing Parent with others and I take responsibility for it," or "I am withdrawing and sulking and I take responsibility for it," or "I am sabotaging my own contracts and I take responsibility for it."

5. *"I have a secret."* In this each person thinks of a secret and then either boasts about it or imagines how others would react if they knew it. John Stevens suggest that occasionally groups are asked to write down their secret

and the unsigned papers are shuffled and put in the middle of the floor. Then each person selects one and reads it aloud as though the secret was his or hers. The group then suggests techniques for dealing with the secret.[24]

6. *Playing the projection* is a technique used for clients who complain and blame and who are not aware of how they project both negative and positive traits on to others.[25] Persons who accuse others of being critical are asked to role-play these critical people and thus discover alienated parts of themselves. Persons who admire other people who are competent are asked to role-play being competent. Thus, they integrate disowned power and skill.

7. *Reversal techniques* are similar to those used for projection awareness. Clients are simply asked to play the reverse of their complaint or other kind of behavior. A silent person who seldom interrupts may be asked to be talkative and to interrupt often. A tough, rigid person may be asked to be soft and pliable. These reversals help clients become aware of their polarities. Some people know about their poles, some do not. When a person says, "I'm continuously high as a kite or lower than a snake's belly," he or she is owning up to the opposing forces within.

8. *The rhythm of contact and withdrawal* is part of life itself. People encounter each other, then withdraw either physically or psychologically. The client who is withdrawing "... is asked to close his eyes and withdraw in fantasy to any place or situation in which he feels secure. He describes the scene and his feelings there. Soon he is asked to open his eyes and 'come back to the group.' The ongoing work is then resumed, usually with new material provided by the patient who has now had some of his energies restored by his withdrawal."[26]

9. *Rehearsal* is what people do in their heads in preparation for some event or as a replay of it. Sometimes this preparation or replay is appropriate. More often it is tied in with a sense of stage fright—which is tied in with a sense of anxiety and a blocking of excitement. This can be relieved with breathing exercises[27] and sharing the "rehearsals" in the group.

10. *Exaggeration* is used when clients are unaware of what they are saying or doing in the now. They are asked, for example, to exaggerate a gesture they are using without awareness, or a tone of voice, or a sentence. They may be asked to repeat something they have said, over and over again, louder and louder. With such a technique a person may quickly break through an impasse and move to closure.

11. *"May I feed you a sentence?"* The therapist suggests a client use a particular sentence, in the group, that reflects the client's attitude. If the sentence fits, the client becomes aware of something previously unnoticed.

12. *Marriage consulting games* include resentment and appreciation statements that the partners make to each other. They take turns making "I" statements, using different verbs, for example, "I hurt you by . . . ," or "I please you by . . . ." These are designed by a creative therapist who does not get caught up in a game of Courtroom (passing judgment on who's right and who's wrong), yet has a feeling of good will toward clients. Throughout the process the client is encouraged to "stay with the feeling," rather than avoid the pain of the moment.

COMPARISONS OF GESTALT AND TA

Like Eric Berne, Fritz Perls was a fascinating man, a rebellious genius who thought for himself, confronted the psychoanalytic authorities, diverged from the traditional psychoanalytic approach, and developed his own theory and methods.

Like the two men who developed them, the TA and Gestalt therapies have many similarities. For example, both have similar positive *values*. For the individual client, these values include autonomy, sensory awareness, playfulness, effectiveness, competency, creativity, and emotional self-support. On an interpersonal level, similar positive values include abilities to make direct, straightforward contact with others, to be consciously flexible in relating to others, to be able to be close and intimate with others, to be game-free.

Both systems incorporate the *use of extra chairs for projection purposes*. This originated with Gestaltists and is now used by many TA therapists.

Gestaltists use a hot-seat chair and a projection chair with an initial emphasis on body and sensory awareness, on fantasies and dreams. They often decommission the Adult before working with the client to have better access to the Child. In fact, the Adult seldom is aware of what goes on during the working-through period even after closure has occurred, although the Adult *does* know that the Child feels a sense of relief.

TA therapists have modified the use of the double chairs and often use them in a different way. The released emotion may be less intense or deep relief and accompanying closure may occur. Typically, TA therapists use the multiple-chairs technique developed by Edgar Stuntz.[28] This technique involves three chairs, labeled Parent, Adult, and Child. The therapist teaches the client how to have a dialogue with these parts of the self. This is effective for sorting out and decontaminating, for making redecisions and developing parenting and self-reparenting contracts.

John McNeel designed a technique called, "The Parent Interview." This is a method of recognizing and working through the defense responses that come from the Scared Child of the parent figures when these figures are projected by the client in double-chair work. The purpose of it is for the client to discover that the parent "did not act with malice but from a threatened position."[29] Using this technique, the therapist, in a friendly way, talks to and questions the fantasied projected parent as though that parent was actually present. In observing the question and answer process, the client recognizes that his or her actual parent figures had a Scared Child who, feeling threatened, responded defensively to the client's childhood needs and demands. This technique is not used if the client is psychotic or potentially so or if the parent figure was, for "It is better not to invite the client into someone else's hell."[30]

Both TA and Gestalt therapists know failure as well as success. For example, when clients stay stuck in an impasse, whether in a TA or a Gestalt group, they often exploit their "rackety" feelings by acting helpless. Group members may reinforce the exploitations if they become hooked into being "helpful." In such cases, the person stays phony or phobic rather than breaking through the neurosis of avoidance to authenticity.

Gestalt focuses on *now*. Childhood experiences are not talked *about* but are brought into the now by using the present tense. For example, if a client starts talking about how it was when he or she was five years old, the therapist is likely to say, "Be five now. Speak in first person and use present tense." The client then begins with something like, "I am five years old. My name is _____. Sometimes people call me _____. Today I am _____." And so forth.

In addition to *focusing on the now,* TA therapists often focus on the past, using historical diagnosis as well as phenomenological reexperiencing. They also focus on the future by setting contracts that lead to improved living.

Therapists in both systems are *alert for body language* such as muscle tensions, facial expressions, breathing patterns, avoidance behavior, and tone of voice. They agree that psychological pathology is reflected in the body and vice versa.

Both systems *focus on psychological games.* To the Gestaltist these are neurotic manipulations learned in childhood; to the Transactional Analyst they are recurring patterns, also learned in childhood. To both, games are played just under the level of awareness. They can be brought into awareness and given up by redecision or by "working through" the original situations in which the games were played. These games are like curses. As clients begin to get in touch with them, they often play heavy blaming games about their parents. These need to be worked through. As Perls writes:

As you know, parents are never right. They are either too large or too small, too smart or too dumb. If they are stern, they should be soft, and so on. But when do you find parents who are all right? You can always blame the parents if you want to play the blaming game, and make the parents responsible for all your problems. Until you are willing to let go of your parents, you continue to conceive of yourself as a child.[31]

Berne takes the same position:

Parents, deliberately or unaware, teach their children from birth how to behave, think, feel, and perceive. Liberation from these influences is no easy matter, since they are deeply ingrained and are necessary during the first two or three decades of life for biological and social survival. Indeed, such liberation is only possible at all because the individual starts off in an autonomous state, that is, capable of awareness, spontaneity, and intimacy, and he has some discretion as to which parts of his parents' teaching he will accept. At certain specific moments early in life he decides how he is going to adapt to them. It is because his adaptation is in the nature of a series of decisions that it can be undone, since decisions are reversible under favorable circumstances.[32]

What is needed is "a friendly divorce from one's parents (and from other Parental influences) so that they may be agreeably *visited* on occasion, but are no longer dominant."[33]

Both agree with Oscar Wilde, "Children begin by loving their parents, later they judge them, sometimes they forgive them." To forgive parents for being human brings much unfinished business to closure.

The *use of questions* is also basic to both theories. In Perls' last, and at last well-edited, writing he focuses on the important ones:

I am convinced that the awareness technique alone can produce valuable therapeutic results. If the therapist were limited in his work only to asking three questions, he would eventually achieve success with all but the most seriously disturbed of his patients. These three questions, which are essentially reformulations of the statement, "Now I am aware" are: *"What are you doing?" "What do you feel?" "What do you want?"* We could increase the number by two, and include these questions: *"What do you avoid?" "What do you expect?"* These are obviously extensions of the first three. And they would be enough of an armamentarium for the therapist.

All five of these are healthily supportive questions. That is, the patient can only answer them to the degree that his own awareness makes possible. But at the same time, they help him to become more aware. They throw him on his own resources, bring him to a recognition of his own responsibility, ask him to muster his forces and his means of self-support. They give him a sense of self because they are directed to his self.[34]

Clients in Gestalt groups can ask questions when they are not an avoidance of responsibility and are answered directly. When they are manipulative, the therapist directs the client, "Turn that into a statement."

The script questionnaire is one example of the extensive use of questions by TA therapists. For clients, however, there are three continuing basic questions which may not be asked directly. Yet, they are are brought continually to the therapeutic hour as they are basic to every script. Who am I? What am I doing here? and Who are all those others?

In both types of therapy the *therapist is active,* intervening appropriately according to his or her own knowledge, experience, and use of intuition. Neither a TA nor a Gestalt therapist will get caught up in games in which a client may ramble on without awareness of how he or she is affecting others. Nor will either therapist, if effective and efficient, get hooked by a habitual *Poor Me* or *Look How Hard I'm Trying* continance. These and other similar behaviors are brought into awareness so that new choices may be made.

TA therapists tend to limit the *size of their groups* to eight members to allow *group* therapy to take place. In such cases, group members, as well as the therapist, interact therapeutically. Gestalt therapists may have groups twice as large because the focus is on *individual* therapy in a group setting rather than group therapy using group process. The therapist is like a stage director telling the client in the hot seat what to say and do to "rewrite the script."

The therapist acting as a *stage director* is clearly due to Max Reinhardt's influence on Perls, who brags that when he puts on a beautiful performance he then expects applause.[35] Berne never said so, but the glint in his eye after he would make a particularly insightful remark indicated he had the same need. In TA groups, when a contract is successfully completed, members often respond with Parental approval, Adult recognition, or Child-like pleasure.

In Gestalt groups an *audience response* is often given to a client who has worked through an impasse. This response is facilitated when the therapist instructs the person to "make the rounds." Using this technique, the client stands up, moves around the group confronting each member as an individual, making direct contact, verbally or nonverbally, trying out new insights and behaviors, and getting feedback.

Both Gestalt and TA therapists hold weekend *marathons,* week-long training sessions, or extended therapy sessions of three or more hours. These allow clients more time to become aware of their impasses and work through them. Many Gestalt and TA therapists *mix professionals with nonprofessionals* in groups where the focus is to be on personal growth and the solving of problems rather than on professional training. Some prefer to separate lay persons from professionals. I have followed both formats in my TA groups and in my Gestalt groups, and found that either way can be effective.

Another similarity between Gestalt and TA is that both *expect and encourage clients to take personal responsibility*. The clients specify what they want to work on, and this becomes the basis for a TA contract or the focus of Gestalt double-chairing. In either situation the spoken or unspoken contract may be deliberated, modified or changed if the client becomes aware of a new need that seems to be more important than the need previously experienced. Thus both systems have flexibility and fluidity. Naturally, they both require a potent therapist. Joen Fagan claims:

> To justify his hire, the therapist must be able to assist the patient to move in the direction that he wishes, that is, to accelerate and provoke change in a positive direction. We are rapidly leaving the time when the therapist, in the absence of more specific knowledge, relies on "something" in the relationship that will result in "something" happening. We are approaching the time when the therapist can specify procedures that promote rapid change in a way that the patient can experience directly and others can observe clearly.[36]

Homework is a technique often used by Gestalt and TA therapists. TA therapists give exercises or experiments to do outside of the group that are related to clients' contracts and will accelerate change.[37] For example, when a person is self-reparenting, much of the work they do is on their own in the form of homework. Morris Haimowitz gave an interesting assignment to three hundred college students in TA classes. The homework was to "Say hello to ten people you ordinarily don't say hello to. Observe your internal messages and feelings, before, during, and after each hello. Write a description of each."[38] This classroom assignment has also proven effective for clients who are willing to make a contract to stop withdrawing from people and instead make new friends.

In my own groups I seldom use the word "homework" because it often hooks either the rebellious or the compliant Child in a client. The rebellious Child is likely to refuse or procrastinate; the compliant Child may do the homework like a good girl or boy, but without the intellectual and emotional breakthrough that is possible. Therefore, I use the term "self-discovery." This is more likely to hook the Little Profesor *and* the Adult. Together they become involved in solving the puzzle that is related to the problem.

Joen Fagan, Gestalt therapist, tells of a series of assignments used with a client.[39] The homework was based on material from Perls, Hefferline and Goodman's book *Gestalt Therapy,* which contains a series of exercises designed for self-awareness and change. The homework included writing, in free-association style, ideas about play, anxiety, and anger. It also included finger-painting, poetry-reading and so forth. Other Gestalt homework can be found in John Steven's *Awareness.* This book has a goal that matches the title and is a series of Gestalt assignments designed to move the student toward that goal.

Fritz Perls gave homework that was a review of the therapy session. He wrote:

> What we ask the patient to do, in line with our entire approach, is to imagine himself back in the consulting room. What does he experience? Can he go over the entire session without difficulty? Can he find blanks? If so, is he aware of these blanks—that is, does he feel there was something vaguely disturbing that he cannot put his finger on? Did he express everything there was to be expressed towards the therapist? Can he do it now and can he do it with his whole self? Can he become aware of avoiding and interrupting any of the aspects of the total expression—in other words, is he preponderantly involved with his emotions or his movements or his sensations or his visualizations or his verbalizations? Does he say what he feels and does he feel what he says?[40]

In TA literature, the books which include considerable homework as well as theory are those Dorothy Jongeward and I either coauthored or authored individually. I strongly believe that many people are capable of working out many of their problems with some guidance, and I enjoy designing exercises to accelerate this process.

In *The People Book,* a TA text for high school students, we use the words "suggested research." Students who were field testing the book before publication were strongly against the word "homework." Yet the same assignments labeled "suggested research" were acceptable to the Child in them and hooked their Adult with problem-solving techniques.[41]

If Gestalt therapy is explained from a TA perspective, is can be said that the major focus of Gestalt is to open up the blocks that may exist between ego states or within an ego state. For example, a common problem many people have is that they are out of touch with the Natural Child and Little Professor.

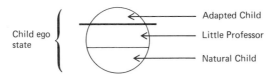

In such people, these important parts of the personality are walled off. They function primarily from their Parent and Adapted Child, and their Adult is often contaminated by both.

Gestalt techniques are very effective, sometimes faster than TA, in releasing the energy of the Natural Child and the creativity of the Little Professor. The release may break up the continuing top dog/under-dog dialogue. TA therapists also have this goal. In addition, they strengthen the Adult with information, reparent the Parent when appropriate, and encourage the clients to give up destructive transactions, games, and scripts in favor of authenticity and autonomy. Describing it in this way may imply that TA has more to offer than Gestalt. That is not so. The focus and techniques are different, but the goal is the same—mentally healthy clients.

Robert Goulding, who has designed unique methods for combining TA and Gestalt therapy, refers to three kinds of impasses that need to be broken up if the client is to be mentally healthy.[42] The first-degree impasse is experienced as dialogue between the Parent and Child ego states. Such is the case when a person's Parent says, "Work hard." The Child retorts, "I don't wanna." The impasse is broken when the Adult intervenes and decides to limit the number of working hours.

The second-degree impasse is between the Adapted Child and the Little Professor. It occurs when the Adapted Child receives negative scripting through comments such as, "I almost died before you were born." And the Little Professor concludes that he or she should not exist but does so in spite of the injunction. Using fantasy and other regressive techniques, the client can make a *redecision* from the Child, such as "I will exist," with accompanying affective relief.

The third-degree impasse is between the Adapted Child and the Natural Child. This is similar to a second-degree impasse but occurs in infancy or prenatally. In this impasse, as in the second-degree, the person also feels as if he or she should not exist and is worthless and without value. However, the client is often unable to put words to this third degree impasse, because it occurred before he or she could understand words.

Goulding has helped clients break through this kind of impasse in dream work. I have done the same with hydrotherapy in the South Pacific and Hawaii, where the water is saline and almost at body temperature. The client must be able to float in about waist-high water for about 15 minutes with eyes closed. I am also in the water, close to the client, giving brief, simple instructions. The gentle movement of the water often takes the clients back to the womb. This "preprimal" treatment can effectively break a third-degree impasse.

Another technique I use when the impasse has been experienced at an early age is to sit closer to the client than I normally would, use fewer words, and deliberately use nonverbal eye messages designed by my Adult for the infant in the person. The nonverbal message conveys, "I'm glad you're you," and "You can make it." This often induces some transference, which can be dealt with at a later time by double-chairing—specifically by putting me in the projection chair and discovering that bonds of affection are not the same as bonds of neurotic need.

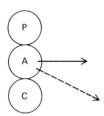

In conclusion, neither TA nor Gestalt therapy techniques can provide instant cures. Persons who are willing to get into the hot seat cannot be sure they will break through their impasses to autonomy and awareness. Nor can clients who make valid contracts in a TA group expect instant success.

Therapists who are thinking about using Gestalt techniques are strongly urged to do some personal work in a Gestalt group as well as read the literature. Gestalt therapy is for therapists who wish to use powerful tools in an ethical manner. It takes time for people to become aware of the many fragmented parts of their personalities. It takes time for opposing forces in therapists, as well as in clients, to become reconciled and integrated. In fact, all of life is a growth process.[43]

REFERENCES

1. The first and most complete text is: Perls, Frederick, Ralph Hefferline, and Paul Goodman, *Gestalt Therapy* (New York: Delta, 1951). It is also the most difficult to follow and requires commitment and discipline from the therapist who wishes to integrate academic information with experiential techniques.

2. Perls, Frederick, *Gestalt Therapy Verbatim* (Lafayette, Calif.: Real People Press, 1969).

3. ———, *In and Out the Garbage Pail* (Lafayette, Calif.: Real People Press, 1969).

4. Ibid.

5. ———, *GT Verbatim,* p. 53.

6. ———, *Ego, Hunger and Aggression* (New York: Random House, 1969), p. 15.

7. Ibid., p. 17.

8. ———, *Garbage Pail.*

9. ———, GT *Verbatim,* pp. 36, 37.

10. ———, *Garbage Pail.*

11. Wallen, Richard, "Gestalt Therapy and Gestalt Psychology," in *Gestalt Therapy Now,* edited by Joen Fagan and Irma Lee Shepherd (Palo Alto, Calif.: Science and Behavior Books, 1970), p. 9.

12. Ibid., p. 11.

13. Shepherd, Irma Lee, "Limitations and Cautions in the Gestalt Approach," *GT Now,* pp. 234–235.

14. Fagan, Joen, and Irma Lee Shepherd, *What is Gestalt Therapy?* (New York: Harper & Row, 1973), p. xii.

15. Perls, *Garbage Pail.*

16. Narango, Claudio, "Present-Centeredness: Technique, Prescription, and Ideal," *GT Now,* pp. 49–50.

17. James, Muriel, and Dorothy Jongeward, *Born to Win: Transactional Analysis with Gestalt Experiments* (Reading, Mass.: Addison-Wesley, 1971), p. 7.

18. Enright, John B., "An Introduction to Gestalt Techniques," *GT Now,* p. 108.

19. Levitsky, Abraham, and Frederick Perls, "The Rules and Games of Gestalt Therapy," *GT Now,* pp. 140–144.

20. Polster, Erving, and Miriam Polster, *Gestalt Therapy Integrated* (New York: Brunner/Mazel, 1973), pp. 18–23.

21. James and Jongeward, *Born to Win,* p. 8.

22. Levitsky and Perls, "Rules and Games of GT."

23. James and Jongeward, *Born to Win,* pp. 218–219.

24. Stevens, John O., *Awareness* (Lafayette, Calif.: Real People Press, 1971), pp. 240–242. This is a very useful book, filled with exercises to expand awareness.

25. James and Jongeward, *Born to Win.*

26. Levitsky and Perls, "Rules and Games of GT," p. 147: Cf Stevens, *Awareness,* pp. 15–17: Cf James and Jongeward, *Born to Win,* pp. 216–217.

27. Perls, Hefferline, and Goodman, *Gestalt Therapy,* pp. 127–135.

28. Stuntz, Edgar C., "Multiple Chairs Technique," *TA Journal,* April 1973, pp. 29–32.

29. McNeel, John R., "The Parent Interview," *TA Journal,* Jan. 1976.

30. Ibid., p. 68.

31. Perls, *GT Verbatim,* p. 2.

32. Berne, Eric, *Games People Play* (New York: Grove, 1964), p. 182.

33. Ibid.

34. Perls, Frederick, *The Gestalt Approach and Eye Witness to Therapy* (Palo Alto, Calif.: Science and Behavior Books, 1973), pp. 73–74.

35. ———, *Garbage Pail.*

36. Fagan, Joen, "The Tasks of the Therapist," *GT Now,* p. 96.

37. James, Muriel, "Self-Reparenting: Theory and Techniques," *TA Journal,* July 1974, pp. 32–39 (included in this volume).

38. Haimowitz, Morris L., "3,000 Hello's: What Happens When You Say Hello," *TA Journal,* April 1973, p. 37.

39. Fagan, Joen, "Anne: Gestalt Techniques with a Woman with Expressive Difficulties," *GT Now,* p. 170.

40. Perls, *The Gestalt Approach,* p. 83.

41. James, Muriel, and Dorothy Jongeward, *The People Book: Transactional Analysis For Students* (Menlo Park, Calif.: Addison-Wesley, 1975).

42. Goulding, Robert L., "Thinking and Telling in Transactional Analysis: Three Impasses," *Voices,* Spring 1974, pp. 11–13.

43. For extensive exercises that incorporate both Gestalt and TA, see James, Muriel, and Louis Savary, *A New Self: Self-Therapy with Transactional Analysis* (Reading, Mass.: Addison-Wesley, 1977).

CHAPTER 16

bioenergetics and TA

JOSEPH CASSIUS

REICH AND BIOENERGETICS

Wilhelm Reich discovered that character is based on movement and blocking of energy in the body. He called this energy bioenergy, or orgone (organism) energy, since it existed everywhere and radiated from living organisms. Emotions mean the manifestation of a tangible bioenergy, and "character" means specific blocking of energy flow. In treatment, Reich found that character could be changed directly by freeing biological energy or pulsations. He found that by working on muscular armor directly, as well as on the character, he could help patients achieve resolutions more rapidly. When the armor was dissolved in therapy it released the orgasm reflex.[1]

TA AND BODY ARMOR

From a Transactional Analysis viewpoint, if a child receives an injunction from his parents about sex, such as "don't feel" sexy or "don't think" about sex, that child may decide to block off sexual excitation as his natural energy builds up; he may choose to hold back to avoid parental disapproval, pulling his pelvis back, tightening the muscles of his thighs and buttocks, holding his breath or clenching his teeth, avoiding thoughts and feelings that alter his self-control. Eventually he cuts off the sensation of sexual desire and his or her body becomes contracted or armored.[2] All the muscles of his body become involved and the energy becomes blocked—counterpulsating and forming neurotic symptoms which affect communication.

REICH'S RINGS OF MUSCULAR ARMORING

According to Reich, seven rings of muscular armoring cut transversely across the body from front to back, obviously affecting one's functioning and way of being in the world. The primary purpose of the seven armor rings is to block the spontaneous flow of metabolic life energy longitudinally up and down the body as a whole.[3] This curtailment of longitudinal life energy is reflected in one's life script as the somatic component of the Script.[4] This decision made by the Child is sustained within the body tissues and is maintained by games and rackets (the defense mechanisms of the Child). Reich discovered that direct, systematic pressure on a "script-ridden" body—beginning with the ocular (eye) block, which is the upper ring, and moving down to the oral (mouth), cervical (neck), thoracic (chest), diaphragmatic, abdominal, and pelvic blocks— would lead to a disintegration of a client's defenses (games, rackets, and psychological positions). As the layers of character (or somatic component of the script) are peeled away with breathing, movements, and direct pressure, intense emotional release (authentic feeling) is experienced and the rubberbands to the past may become conscious. This gradual process is required to attain self-regulation or genitality, which is the orgonomic equivalent of the I'm OK, you're OK position. As a result of becoming a genital character (the position of the prince or princess), orgasm reflex would be achieved with spontaneous movement (pulsations) of the pelvis during breathing.

LOWEN'S ADAPTATIONS OF REICH

Alexander Lowen, who was a student of Wilhelm Reich, developed bioenergetics by expanding upon Reich's previous work on character structure. He combined the theories of Freud and Reich into his own bioenergetic formulations, rejecting some of Reich's clinical techniques and principles while accepting Reich's pioneering efforts which stemmed from vegetotherapeutic techniques. Lowen does not accept the principle that armoring must be dissolved from the top down. Lowen believes that it is equally feasible to start with the legs—emphasizing "grounding" and getting in touch with the reality of how one stands or moves in the world, feeling contact with the ground as a reality (Adult) of life. Bioenergetics makes less use of direct body contact than do the Reichians. The emphasis is on do-it-yourself exercises involving immobile stress positions, activity exercises, and emotional release, verbal techniques (e.g., psychoanalytic, gestalt or TA techniques can be effective here) as well as group work.[5]

Lowen's basic concern is to mobilize the metabolic energy flow throughout the body quickly and dynamically during each session. Bioenergetic stress positions and movements are very potent release techniques useful in making one aware of one's real feelings and in avoiding games or discounts. Chronic breathing restrictions, muscle contractions, and energy blockages dissolve and awareness of one's life patterns emerges rapidly. The patient becomes aware of having cut himself or herself off from longitudinal energy flow or "streamings." The Lowenian exercises rapidly precipitate pulsations, vibrations, tremors, and other energy currents with their required movements. The exercises get more feelings into the legs.[5] Bionergetics stresses recapturing the natural Child's capacity for pleasure, joy, and creativity.

EXAMPLES OF BIOENERGETIC TECHNIQUE

One of the voluntary exercises which is stressed to get in touch with grounding is a passive stress movement in which one stands with feet six inches apart with toes turned in and knees bent, while the head is held straight and fists are placed in the small of the back to get in touch with muscular tension. This position, if the body is unified, should form a perfect arch from the center of the foot to the center of the shoulders.[6] Tension is reflected in the pelvis if it is pulled back, or if the head is off to one side, or if the client is unable to bend his knees. When this exercise is done while breathing deeply, the client begins to feel contact with the ground as he pushes down with his heels and senses the energy flow through his body.[7]

Another passive stress position requires that the patient sit on a stool, with his or her feet on the ground, and arch backward while breathing deeply. By observing the client's breathing, the trained therapist can note where muscle tensions or blocks are located, and can ask the client to cathect his or her Child and investigate the significance of those tensions using TA and Gestalt methods. Active body movements and direct body intervention with bioenergetic positions are also useful in regressive analysis.

SWEATSHIRTS AND HOLDING PATTERNS

The character structure ("sweatshirt") of the patient is continually emphasized in treatment, since this structure is synonymous with the concept of the Child's resistance to change.[2] For adequate treatment to occur, the symptoms or games utilized to maintain homeostasis of the character structure (script) need to be understood. There are no pure character types, although one pattern may dominate the personality. The combination of several character types in each person makes for script uniqueness.

Chronic muscle tensions or blocks impede free longitudinal energy flow (Natural Child) and excitation in the body, and are observable in distortion of body form and movement. In bioenergetics they are identified as holding patterns and are related to script directives.[8]

There are five basic holding patterns which give use to five character types. Although pure types are very rare, one may have a dominant holding pattern which is reflected in one's stance, expression, and body structure.[7]

1. Schizoid The first holding pattern is the *schizoid* body, in which the body line appears broken. The legs, head, and trunk are at angles to one another. Marked tension in the waist appears to be dividing the body in two. The eyes appear out of focus, there is tension in the neck, which is rigid, and sensitivity and vulnerability to environmental stress is notable along with a feeling of peripheral disconnectedness. The Child in the schizoid is terrified of self-expression (injunction is "don't be"), believing this will lead to his destruction. Usually, a cold, mechanical, ambivalent response from a rejecting mother has led the Child to experience unsatisfied longing which is contrasted by rage. The individual escalates anger or paranoid ideation to ward off his or her intense fear of being annihilated.

Bioenergetic treatment emphasizes respiration and contact to make the Child's interruption of energy flow and the blocks observable. (When a small child, he internalizes the mother as a critical Parent to continue his fear of being destroyed.) The murderous rage can be released by twisting a towel or screaming as well as in other ways. Direct pressure on both sides of the jaws with fists gives the Child permission to physically relax some of the intense holding together and allows for expression of unsatisfied longing. The hands can be directly placed on the anterior scalene muscles (neck) to (permit the Child) open the throat and release the suppressed scream. Pressure applied to the pelvis releases and relaxes deep tensions there. The patient may be asked to reach with his hands to express the Child's longing and to ask for what he needs (which can optionally be gratified by the therapist's nurturing Parent), to counter the Child's fear of being destroyed by his self-created influencing Parent.[7]

2. Psychopathic The second holding pattern, bioenergetically, is that of the *psychopathic* personality, who holds up or pulls up (stays in his head) to avoid falling down into a state of helplessness, failure, and defeat. The center of gravity in this body type is displaced to the upper half which is generally larger and more charged than the lower half. The psychopath, according to bio-energetic concepts, experiences severe pelvic tensions when under stress. His legs and arms may be observed and experienced as rigid. There are also severe shoulder tensions. A need to be in control is experienced because to give in or surrender may imply a loss of self. Negative (Vengeful Child) feelings are expressed in superiority and contempt for others—using others to prevent them from using him. Hyperactivity or "acting out" is a typical reaction of the psychopath (Rebel Child). A deep underlying (Adapted Child) panic has led the psychopath to choose to run away (Get away from), discount, or deny reality when cornered. The bioenergetic dynamic core of psychopathy results from an internalized (Mother's Child) sexually seductive mother, so consequently the Child decides to inhibit his sexual feelings and counters the threat of seduction by internalizing the mother and being seductive (Adapted Child) as a way of gaining power over his own and external Parents. The Child's fear of being helpless and vulnerable and his lack of grounding (Adult contamination) are observable in his fear of falling.

Bioenergetic treatment physically emphasizes overcoming the client's lack of security and the subjective weakness in his legs. The holding patterns in the upper half of the body are stressed by using a stool to arch over to help the patient work through the exaggerated holding felt in the chest (to free the Natural Child). When a client is lying over the stool, pressure is applied on the chest to help the client to breathe out so he can "let down" and "give in." The overinflated chest (reinforced by games) is a physical defense against archaic panic. Direct pressure under the eyelids is utilized to get the patient to open his eyes and see what he avoids and discounts (injunctions in this area are uncovered). The therapist requests that the client reach with his arms to express longing for a father. This usually precipitates regression and awareness of the internal rejecting father in the psychopath. The mother may have stroked the Adapted Child for rebelling against and defying the father. By observing mother's fear of his father, the child models this same fear. Regressive work may bring out how the Child defends against his dependency and need, which involves the fear of being used and the Vengeful Child's impulse to destroy the user by using him first. The plea to the world is "Love me or I'll kill you."

If I described this holding pattern from a transactional model, I would say that the Child's decision is reflected in not giving in to avoid helplessness. The Vengeful Child manipulates and discounts others as an expression of his anger racket. The parents often played *Corner, Uproar,* and *NIGYYSOB* and a host of other games with him when he was little and may have further perpetuated his not-OKness with physical abuse. The Child utilizes the same games as the parent, as well as *Kick Me, Cops and Robbers,* etc. The Child experiences a lack of grounding related to a Child-contaminated Adult, or in some the Parent may be excluded. The fear of falling is part of the physical manifestation of his script. The exaggerated holding up of the chest reflects the vengeful Child's defiance and chip-on-the-shoulder attitude, whereas the weakness in the legs reflects his basic not-OK position and lack of responsibility in standing up to the world. As the holding up is gradually released, authentic feelings are expressed and excitement (I'm OK and You're OK) is experienced as the natural Child emerges.[7]

3. Oral The third bioenergetic body holding pattern is the *oral* type. The oral person holds on against the fear of being alone. The body structure is developed as a defense against the threat of abandonment and to curtail the overwhelming rage the Child experiences. The oral body usually appears thin and underveloped and there may be a pronounced indentation or protrusion in the sternum. The oral body appears elongated with small hands and feet, a narrow mouth, and knees locked tight. Deprivation (injunctions of "You don't count," "Don't Be," "Don't think," etc.) in childhood is the central issue in orality. Rather than thinking about the problem, the individual discounts his loss or his needs and displaces his need for parenting onto others. He tries to recreate the symbiosis by doing nothing and manipulating others to do for him.[9] Structurally the body is flaccid and the arms hang limp, and during body work he will not easily reach with his eyes or lips. Passive resentment is expressed by a reluctance to ask for what he needs or by doing nothing. This body structure usually tends toward experiencing deep depressions (I'm not-OK, you are OK), the anger of needs not being met and the reluctance to accept responsibility for this is turned against the self. The Child's impulses appear weak with little sustained attention or interest.

Regression usually reveals the need for a warm, loving mother (Nurturing Parent). Assertive movements are stressed in therapy, along with verbal demands to reach out and ask for strokes. Needs are also fulfilled by allowing sucking with the fingers and increasing energy flow with an arched body-bridge position with the arms holding the heels. When Parenting needs are satisfied and a nurturing Parent is internalized, a resolution with redecision is simplified.[9,7]

4. Masochism The fourth holding pattern reflected in the Child's holding-in against the fear of self-assertion is *masochism*. "Letting go" may lead to explosive, angry, behavior or the bottom may literally fall out. Therapy requires the expression of the anger. Structurally the body is heavy and holds in but also seems to collapse easily with stress positions. The collapse is notable in the waist region with a pulling in of the head, arms, legs, and buttocks. Tension is observable in the jaw, throat, and pelvis and a trapped feeling is sometimes verbalized. The injunctions may be "Life has to be difficult," "Don't be a child," "Don't enjoy," "Don't be you." A problem of toilet-training may be associated with the decision to be nonassertive and to please others ("Try hard," "Be strong") and not allowing the Child's needs to be important.[10] Exaggerated attention to oral and anal functions by a smothering mother leads to the Child experiencing pressure from above and below. Negative feelings are expressed in passive-aggressive whining and complaining. This hidden spite is often seen in *Kick Me* players, and it is reflected in the cardiac and anal sphincter. Their resistance to Parental authority was crushed. Temper tantrums were crushed and Free Child expression would lead to shame and humiliation.

In treatment, screaming is encouraged, as well as permission to let go and assert the right "to be." Kicking and shouting is used to express the Child's anger openly while the movement precipitates regression. Pressure is put on the pelvis to open up feelings and sensations. The body is characterized by a short, thick structure and overdeveloped musculature that serves the holding patterns. Hitting a pillow or bed and yelling "No" may bring out some emotional response which is difficult to elicit because of injunctions to "Be strong" and "Don't feel what you feel." Pressure on the cheeks is also useful to bring out the fear in the Child. When the fear is evoked and dealt with, Free Child excitement, tenderness, and pleasure may be observed. Conditional strokes were given to the Child by the parents who implied or stated, "I will give you love if you do what I want you to." (Counterscript of "Please me," "Try hard," "Be perfect")[10] The need for strokes or intimacy may be perceived as threatening to freedom and hence may be denied by the Child.[11,7]

5. Rigidity   The fifth body holding pattern is rigidity. Negativity in this pattern is expressed by indirect communication (lying and discounting) and holding back. In the male this is called phallic and in the female the label is hysteric. In this condition, the Child decides to hold back real feelings, fearing that showing them will exhibit his frailty or weakness and surrender. The body appears balanced or integrated with the main tension in the long outer layers of muscle. The eyes, hands, and genitals are highly charged and rigidity is evident in the back of the neck. The chest is inflated and tight. When regressive movements are encouraged, real feelings are expressed and the Child can face his fear of betrayal and openness. This character type reflects aggressive and competitive behavior as well as much control. There is a tendency to intellectualize or head-trip and avoid real feelings. If the rigidity dissolves, masochism may become apparent. The dynamic core is related to unfulfilled oedipal striving. The Child says "I want you," and is rejected by the parent of the opposite sex on the sexual level. Usually, the female child is not supported by either parent and deals with her angry feelings by being seductive. The male may be supported by one of the parents. Since the cause dynamically results from frustration of the Child's needs for erotic satisfaction at the genital level—i.e., infantile masturbation may be prohibited (e.g., "Don't be sexy") or contact with mother or father prohibited—the Child fears being betrayed if he expresses his forbidden desire. Therefore, he uses lying and all types of discounts to get what he wants.[7,12]

Therapy is directed toward opening up the Child and allowing feelings to flow freely into head and genitals. The partial bridge position, in which the patient arches over a bed, may be used or direct release of anger may be encouraged with screaming or twisting a towel or kicking. Feelings of sadness and authentic fear are beneath the frustration. Eventually, longing, intimacy, and tenderness are experienced naturally.[7]

BEFORE USING BIOENERGETICS

Prior to utilizing bioenergetic methods individually or in group, a script assessment should be completed on each patient. The script analysts using these techniques and dynamic formulations can recognize the value of holding patterns as the somatic component of the script. The injunctions, personal myths, and early decisions become apparent rapidly as the treatment progresses.[13]

PURPOSE OF BIOENERGETICS

The purpose of using Bioenergetics in a transactional framework is to remove the blocks to all the split-off parts and, through direct body work, become more aware of the Child's potential for pleasure and aliveness. The holding patterns decrease available energy and help to maintain the script. There are three basic body levels (script layers) to consider in terms of armoring:

1. The first is the peripheral or outer layer. This is equivalent to the game layer and reflects social roles and attitudes. The Child adapts, with the de-intensified movement, feelings and ideas that go with this layer. This layer conflicts with the body and the real feelings and is a layer of pseudo contact that prevents intimacy with the inner and outer world. It involves the muscular system (the organ system and brain), and as a block may hinder breathing each time game payoffs occur.[8]

2. The second layer contains racket feelings as well as some authentic feelings of blocked anger, fear, sadness, tears, looking, defiance, and stubborness—the reflection of Vengeful-Child reactions. The Adapted-Child layer involves deep muscle patterns, vegetative organs, and nerves. Vengeful-Child techniques of holding back and contracting impulses are repressed in this layer, which requires expression so that the third layer can emerge.

3. The third layer is the equivalent of the Natural Child, and yields the dynamic pattern of creativity, pleasure, aliveness, and love. This is the layer of intimacy, which gives us a sense of connectedness to the cosmos and allows for free energy flow.[14]

SCRIPTS AND CHARACTER TYPES

All character types are regarded as representing relatively fixed patterns of behavior determined by script directives. The labels of schizoid, oral, masochistic, psychopathic, and rigid prsonalities reflect the life script decision and are present to some degree in almost all of us. They become pronounced when we are invited into not-OKness by seductive counterscript directives such as

"Be perfect," "Be strong," "Try hard," "Please me," and "Hurry up." In TA the concept of think sphincter relates to the holding patterns of bioenergetics. To know which sphincter the patient is holding is to know the somatic component of the script. The ego states are the muscles of the personality and the personality functions of the ego states in terms of "holding patterns" can be a reflection of what you can do with your muscles—extend, contract, adapt, or use them in a natural (Child) way. The dynamics can be compared to Ernst's concept of personality operations (e.g., as noted in the *OK Corral*), that is, how you can use your muscles with other people—long for them, push them away, embrace them or use them.[15,16] This concept would apply to the holding patterns of holding together (Schizoid), where the conflict is existence versus need; holding on (Oral), where the conflict is need versus independence ("I need you"); pulling or holding up (Psychopathy), where the conflict is independence versus intimacy; and holding in (Masochistic), where the conflict is closeness versus freedom ("I don't need you"). The final holding pattern, Rigidity, is related to rejection by the parent of the opposite sex ("Don't be a man"). I am still exploring relationships of bioenergetic holding patterns to script directives and there is much to be done in this area.

The body is a reservoir of rubberbands to the past, and when the Child is discounted, spanked, or traumatized, the natural reaction is to tighten or hold. This is how holding patterns develop. The posture and how one stands (holding patterns) characterize the life scripts. In *Transactional Analysis in Psychotherapy,* Eric Berne has a diagram of groups of pennies as affected by various trauma. This concept also reflects how the memories are built into the muscle structure and posture and their related impasses.[17,18]

The script can be better understood and resolution can be more decisive if respiration and energy flow are increased and posture improved. Body changes can increase one's capacity for pleasure by resolving characterological attitudes which interfere with unitary movement of the Free Child. Every physical expression has a meaning in terms of which ego-state muscle is more highly charged. Handshake, posture, eye contact, voice tone, and movement reflect the script directives and rubberbands to the past. Releasing chronic muscle tension in the Adapted Child adds a new dimension to TA in terms of regressive analysis.[19] All scripts reflect fixations or decisive commitments to behavior evidenced in special body holding patterns.[15] A Frightened-Child ego state can be covered by an exaggerated expression of courage (Be strong) by squaring one's shoulders, inflating the chest, and sucking the stomach in. The Child may not be aware of this until he discovers he cannot drop his shoulders, relax his chest, or let his stomach out. When direct pressure is applied to contracted areas, or muscle tensions are released, the rubberbands to the fear and the commitment to the body holding patterns can be worked through.

SUMMATION

There are two factors obvious in this paper; the first is that any limitation of movement in the natural Child results from early script directives. These directives lead to the Child's decision to hold up, hold in, hold together, hold on, or hold back—Adapted-Child behaviors utilized for internal or external stroke value. (It would be interesting to explore stroke-pattern changes with this approach.) Persistent reinforcement through games serves to maintain the symbiosis and the holding pattern—sabotaging Adult functioning and blocking unitary, straight response to the environment.

The second factor is that restriction of breathing is the Natural Child's way of coping with fear of his Critical Parent. If prolonged breathing is impaired and armoring or holding is reinforced, the disturbance may be structured in the thoracic area with abdominal tension or it may be reflected in the body posture and shape. The Adapted Child's inability to breathe freely under stress is the somatic basis for reacting to fear physiologically. All armoring, holding patterns or blocks are rooted in the Adapted Child. One fear may be the blocked impulse (counterpulsation), another fear may be the source of the block. Release of blocked fear or terror with bioenergetics can be a very dramatic factor in leading to redecision. I have observed many patients in group regressing and releasing the physically ingrained counterscript and injunctive messages and the blocked anger and frustration (Vengeful Child) associated with injunctive messages. The release of the anger softens the body and permits a new capacity for trust and intimacy to emerge. Respiration and movement may be freed when the negative aspects of a script are given up cognitively as well as physically.[20] Deconfusion of the Child and decontamination of the Adult proceed together with cognitive, affective, and behavioral techniques being combined.

In my opinion, real change occurs when physical, behavioral and affective methods are used concomitantly.[20] The intensive movement encourages regression to the Child and deconfusion can begin.[17] The last value I can think of is as a form of desensitization, or the client becoming less upset about what was formerly traumatic by exaggerating repetitive movements and sounds. Stressing the muscles is one way to get to real feelings which the "professor" (Adult in Child) decided to "hold back" to survive and cope with situations usually fueled by fear.[21] Much remains to be investigated in the areas of body movement and physical contact approaches and it is the author's hope that this preliminary paper will start legitimate research projects.

REFERENCES

1. Reich, Wilhelm, *Character Analysis* (New York: Farrar, Strauss & Cudahy, 1961).
2. Berne, Eric, *What Do You Say After You Say Hello?* (New York: Grove, 1972).

3. Reich, Wilhelm, *The Function of the Orgasm,* Vol. 1. (New York: Farrar, Strauss & Cudahy, 1961.

4. Steiner, Claude, *Scripts People Live: Transactional Analysis of Life Scripts* (New York: Grove, 1974).

5. Brown, Malcolm, *Direct Body Contact Psychotherapy.* Unpublished ms. 1970.

6. Lowen, Alexander, *The Betrayal of the Body* (New York: Macmillan, 1967).

7. ———, *Bioenergetics.* A slide presentation. (New York: Institute for Bioenergetic Analysis, 1973).

8. ———, *The Language of the Body* (New York: Macmillan, 1971).

9. Schiff, Aaron, and Jacqui Schiff, "Passivity," *TA Journal,* 1, 1 (1971), pp. 71–78.

10. Capers, Hedges, and Taibi Kahler, *Miniscript Workshop,* ITAA Conference, 1974.

11. Samuels, Solon D., "Stroke Strategy: I. The Basis of Theraphy," *TA Journal,* 1, 3 (1971), pp. 23–24.

12. Schiff, Eric, personal communication, 1974.

13. Karpman, Stephen B., "Script Drama Analysis," *TA Bulletin,* 7, 26 (1968), pp. 39–43.

14. Harris, Thomas, *I'm OK, You're OK* (New York: Harper & Row, 1969).

15. Ernst, Franklin H., Jr., personal communication, 1974.

16. ———, *Who's Listening?* (Vallejo, Calif.: Addresso Set, PO Box 1530).

17. Berne, Eric, *Transactional Analysis in Psychotherapy* (New York: Grove, 1961).

18. Dusay, John M., "Eric Berne's Studies in Intuition," *TA Journal,* 1, 1 (1971), pp. 34–45.

19. Gebhart, Shepherd, personal communication, 1974.

20. Ellis, Albert, personal communication, 1974.

21. Kupfer, David, personal communication, 1967–1970.

client-centered therapy and TA

THOMAS J. LONG
LYNETTE A. LONG

INTRODUCTION

Transactional Analysis has not acknowledged much common heritage with the client-centered therapy best represented by Carl Rogers, its first expositor, and his followers, perhaps because of the perceived conflict between contractual treatment and process treatment and the oversimple dichotomy drawn between "feeling treatment" and "thought treatment."[1] There are, however, very real similarities in the development of both of these psychotherapeutic approaches. Eric Berne has been quoted as saying that transactional analysis was born as a result of his starting to listen to his patients rather than to his teachers. Rogers has drawn the hypotheses of client-centered therapy from the raw data of his therapeutic experiences. Both approaches are widely practiced in group treatment, though neither exclusively. Both put the client at the helm in determining treatment goals: In TA this is carried out in a contractual form in which the patient specifies what he wishes changed and the therapist indicates his intention to facilitate change under certain conditions, while in client-centered therapy client goals and ensuing change strategies emerge during the process of treatment—often without being explicitly outlined.

There are differences as well. Both approaches view therapy as a sharing of a common frame of reference, but in client-centered therapy the common frame of reference is communicated by the client during the process of counseling, while in TA this sharing involves a great deal of therapist-generated information transfer, including the principles of TA. Finally, client-centered therapy focuses on less-specified or less-defined change in the client, fostered by less directive action on the part of the therapist, while TA therapists work in a more direct and directive method on specific tasks, often prescribing "assignments" for clients.

The direct-active-contractual nature of TA stands in contrast to the accepted procedures of the client-centered therapist, who avoids manipulating events to produce specific changes in client behavior. The client is seen as the real change agent. The therapist is simply providing the proper atmosphere in which the client can slough off learnings which limit his behavior and acquire new unencumbered learnings and behaviors which constitute his growth.[2]

CARL ROGERS AS A PERSON

Carl Rogers was born in 1902, the fourth of six children, in a closely knit, hardworking and rather strict Protestant family. Rogers lived on a farm from age 12 until his college years. He received his B.A. from the University of Wisconsin in 1924, then attended Union Theological Seminary for two years. Finding himself increasingly attracted to courses with a psychological bent, he transferred as a graduate student to Teachers College, Columbia University, from which he received his M.A. in 1928 and his Ph.D. in 1931. He was for twelve years a psychologist in the Child Study Department of the Society for the Prevention of Cruelty to Children in Rochester, New York. There he spent his time diagnosing and interviewing delinquent and underprivileged children. During this same period Rogers taught courses at the University of Rochester on understanding and dealing with problem children. His first book, published in 1939, was entitled *The Clinical Treatment of the Problem Child*.[3] The Department became the Rochester Guidance Center in 1939. Rogers, who had been director of the Department since 1931, remained as Center Director for one more year before accepting a professorship at Ohio State University in 1940.

It was while teaching at Ohio State that Rogers realized that during his time at Rochester he had developed a unique therapeutic approach of his own. He set forth this theory in *Counseling and Psychotherapy*, a book published in 1942.[4] In this book Rogers outlined a therapeutic approach which was nondirective in form, warm and responsive in therapeutic style, and permissive in climate. This treatment approach ran counter to the two prevailing styles of treatment current at the time, psychoanalysis and directive counseling, both of which depended heavily on diagnosis, categorization, and explanation of problem causality by the therapist. *Counseling and Psychotherapy* is largely a technique-oriented book which sets forth procedures for helping the client gain insight into himself and his situation by creating a permissive atmosphere in which defenses would be reduced and the client could take positive steps for himself in light of his new understandings.

In 1945 Rogers accepted an appointment as Professor of Psychology at the University of Chicago. During his 12 years there, he wrote *Client-Centered Therapy: Its Current Practice, Implications and Theory* (1951)[5] and over 60 other papers. The most noteworthy paper was "The Necessary and Sufficient Conditions of Therapeutic Personality Change" published in the *Journal of Consulting Psychology* in 1957.[6] Here Rogers set forth the central hypothesis of client-centered therapy, namely that if certain conditions are present in the attitude of the therapist, then positive personality change will occur in the client. In 1958 Rogers published an orderly sequence of the positive changes an individual goes through in a therapeutic relationship.[7]

Rogers left the University of Chicago in 1957 to become Professor of Psychology and Psychiatry at the University of Wisconsin. While there he wrote *On Becoming a Person: A Therapist's View of Psychotherapy* (1961).[8] During the 1962–63 academic year he was a fellow at the Center for Advanced Study in the Behavioral Sciences at Stanford University, and in 1964 he joined the staff of the Western Behavioral Science Institute in La Jolla, California. In 1968 Rogers and a group of fellow researchers spun off from that Institute to form the Center for Studies of the Person, located in La Jolla. He is currently a resident fellow there.

Rogers' books written since 1961 have concentrated on the application of client-centered theory and methods to facilitate growth in normal individuals. *Person to Person: The Problem of Being Human* was written (with Barry Stevens) in 1967;[9] *Freedom to Learn: A View of What Education Might Become* in 1969;[10] *Carl Rogers on Encounter Groups* in 1970;[11] and *On Becoming Partners: Marriage and Its Alternatives* in 1972.[12]

While Rogers certainly was influenced in his early days by writers such as John Dewey and Otto Rank, the development and refinement of client-centered therapy has rested squarely on Rogers' shoulders. He has worked not only to define the therapy he drew together but, especially in his later years, served to extend its applicability into classrooms, bedrooms, and boardrooms.

PRINCIPLES OF CLIENT-CENTERED THERAPY

Central to this theory is the hypothesis that the potential possessed by any individual, but as yet unreleased, will tend to be put into action in a relationship in which a helper is both experiencing and communicating his own present and genuine reality, warm caring for the other, and nonjudgmental understanding—if the needing other perceives these qualities to be present in the relationship at least to a minimally facilitative degree.

This hypothesis rests on a view of the nature of Man which posits one motivational force, the tendency to full actualization of the self. It indicates that this motivational force will be most fully released in a relationship in which certain interdependent and related conditions exist. Of these conditions Rogers classes as most basic *genuineness,* or the ability not only to be aware of one's internal experiences but to be transparent in the communication of these experiences to another. The next quality demanded is a *positive regard* for the client. It is this quality of acceptance which elicits deeply meaningly material from the client and establishes the base for the *empathic understanding* of material communicated by the client.[13]

The correlations between these conditions are high.[14] Genuineness in the therapist indicates that what he says is in tune with what he experiences; that he is able to keep track of his own feelings and express them understandably to the client. I have found in my own practice that genuineness does not mean a continuous replay of all my moment-to-moment experiences, but a personal sensitivity to my internal experiences with a narration to the client of those that have a recurring pattern. It is not that I mistrust my experiences but I increase the probability of my accurate understanding by listening for recurring experiences or themes. Genuineness and accurate understanding are thus closely related.

Because I cannot directly experience what another experiences, I must rely on my own experiences to come to an understanding of the experiences of another. This coming to understand another through being attuned to oneself is not always a poor second choice, for in reflecting the experiences of another, we often help to clarify them in his own conscious awareness.

The truth that the individual is the only one who has the ability to know his inner world in any genuine or complete sense is expressed by Rogers in two propositions: (1) "Every individual exists in a continually changing world of experience of which he is the center,"[15] and (2) "The organism reacts to the field as it is experienced and perceived. This perceptual field is, for the individual, 'reality.' "[16] Rogers does not attempt to explain any concept of true reality. Reality for any individual is simply his perceptions of his world.

Healthy behavior depends on adequate awareness, and those things that interfere with one's awareness of significant life events or serve to distort clear perception interfere with healthy development. One does not learn to be aware. However, what one focuses one's attention on is a product of learning.

Characteristics of Normal Development

Together with the actualizing tendency or the basic "tendency of the organism to develop all its capacities in ways which serve to maintain or enhance the organism,"[17] Rogers projects that people, even as infants, have an inborn ability to positively value experiences which as individuals they perceive as benefiting them and to negatively value those experiences which they perceive as contrary to their ability to fulfill themselves.[18] The human organism's inherent valuing process serves to direct behavior toward self-actualization while the actualizing tendency serves to both maintain the person, as in protecting one's physical integrity, and enhance him, as in seeking events that result in new and pleasant experiences.

Rogers assumes that people are inherently capable of differentiating between desirable or undesirable responses because of this valuing process. Moreover he has an abiding faith that people will make personally and socially satisfactory responses unless their behavior is distorted by inappropriate learnings.

Learned Characteristics

As the child develops he also begins to discriminate among experiences differentiating the me and not me. This awareness of one's own being and function arising from one's interaction with the environment leads to a sense of self which is labeled self-concept. This construct is important in the client-centered system. It is an organized, dynamic, but consistent conceptual pattern of the individual's perception of himself, of himself in relation to others experienced in his environment, and of the values attached to these perceptions. In other words, self-concept entertains not only such thoughts as "I am a man," but "Other people like me," or "I am an accomplished racquetball player." These self-referent thoughts are organized into a consistent conceptual gestalt so that the whole pattern is altered when one aspect is altered.[19]

Rogers has not conceptualized the development of a self-concept as a static process. Self-concept is something like the picture a person has of himself together with his evaluation of that picture, but the picture and the evaluation of it are continually in flux, being heavily influenced by (1) a universal need in human beings for positive regard,[20] and (2) the fact that this need can only be satisfied by others.

Positive regard includes responses from others which produce a positive affect in the individual. This positive affect is satisfying. When one's responses are evaluated negatively, discomforting affect is produced in the individual. The human gradually comes to seek positive evaluation by others and to avoid negative or unsatisfying evaluation. Rogers believes that human beings acquire a need for positive regard. That is, we learn to need and seek affection from others because these responses are inherently satisfying.

Following in series individuals come to develop a second basis for evaluating their behavior and choosing their courses of action. They develop a need for self-regard. Individuals judge their own behavior according to their perception of the regard they receive from others. They can come to judge their behavior as good because others approve it, even though the behavior itself may be quite displeasing to them; conversely they can come to judge their behavior as bad because others disapprove.

According to Rogers' scheme, in the fully functioning, congruent individual, self-regard and the individual's direct evaluation of his own subjective responses are in tune. Innate and learned responses operate together and lead to the same behavior choices.

Development of Maladjustment

Rogers operates on a conflict model of disorder. According to Rogers "one of the first and most important aspects of the self-experience of the ordinary child is that he is loved by his parents."[21] The child sees himself as lovable and deserving of love and is satisfied in the interaction. Inevitably, the child's internal or organismic needs run into conflict with his need to retain the love of his parents. The behavior which springs from his internal values and needs runs counter to the behavior his parents value as acceptable. In an effort to deal with these perceived conflicts, that is, keep his perception of his behavior consistent with his self picture, the child begins to employ certain internal distortions in order to maintain his internal equilibrium. These distorting strategies serve for Rogers as the basis of maladjustment. "Psychological maladjustment exists when the organism denies to awareness significant sensory and visceral experiences, which consequently are not symbolized and organized into the gestalt of the self structure."[22]

This fundamental conflict, many of the seeds of which were learned in childhood even though it is continued as a life process, might be characterized as "It feels good, but other people disapprove of it. Since I want them to like me, I'll disapprove of it, too."[23] Rogers refers to this incongruence between self and experience as basic estrangement. He sees it as learned, not a necessary part of man's nature, but characteristic of most humans in an imperfect society and the basis of all psychological pathology in man.[24]

Several consequences follow from this learned conflict:

1. Inconsistent or contradictory behavior, as the individual's behavior is regulated either by the actualizing tendency or controlled by the self-actualizing tendency. These behaviors are not only discordant but often incomprehensible even to the individual himself.

2. Anxiety, or a state of uneasiness or tension; this is the response of the organism to the physiological organismic preawareness that a discrepancy

between the concept of self and experience is approaching awareness, which if symbolized in awareness would force a change in self-concept.

3. Vulnerability, or a state of incongruence between self and experience. Incongruence must exist as well as a lack of awareness of this incongruence. Then if any new experience irrefutably demonstrates the incongruence between self and experience the concept of self might be disorganized by a demand, which the subject is unable to refuse, to assimilate contradictory and unassimilable experience. As long as this state exists the individual is vulnerable to anxiety, threat, and disorganization, at least each time he is in conflict-arousing circumstances.

The greater the extent of threat to the self-structure, the more likely it will be that the defenses usually employed will not be equal to the task of maintaining perception of the self structure consistent with experience and those conditions of worth subsumed from others under extreme conditions. The controls demanded by defensive behavior give way and behavior becomes disorganized.

Psychosis can be equated with the disorganization of behavior; neurosis with the behavior arising from the struggle to maintain equilibrium between organismic experiences, the self-structure, and a greater or lesser number of conditions of worth that have been introjected. A truly healthy or fully functioning person would be one who accurately symbolizes and includes in his self-concept all self-experiences.

The Process of Therapy

For Rogers, psychotherapy "is a process whereby man becomes his organism—without self-deception, without distortion."[25] It is a return to basic sensory and visceral experience. The conditions for worth are eliminated and the client begins to ask "What do *I* want?" "What am *I* experiencing?" "In therapy the person adds to ordinary experience the full and undistorted awareness of his experiencing . . . ,"[26] and through this process, the client comes to be in awareness what he is in experience.

During the therapeutic process several experiences and discoveries emerge as the client moves toward a reowning of the self. Early in the relationship the client comes to discover that he is responsible for himself in the relationship. This discovery might be accompanied by a sense of aloneness or annoyance in the client while he comes to recognize the value of being responsible for himself.

Since the client has placed himself in a changeable posture, he in some sense desires change—and yet there is a kind of fear as to what change, only dimly seen, will entail. During this experiencing of exploration the client begins to discover inconsistencies in himself and, as his story unfolds, may even find contradictions. But as the inconsistencies are recognized, examined, and dealt with, the self is altered in ways which bring about consistency.

The result of the client's exploration is the discovery of attitudes previously experienced but denied to awareness. Rogers cites as one of the most profound phenomena of therapy the experience of discovering attitudes and emotions previously experienced organismically but never consciously recognized.

As the denied elements of experience are reowned in awareness the self begins to reorganize. This reorganization is necessary because the self-concept previously developed must change in order to contain these new perceptions. Depending upon the extent of change called for, the client may experience a great deal of pain and confusion or only a mild discomfort during therapy. It can happen, during this process of reorganization, that the personality goes through rapidly changing configurations until finally a new organization gains ascendancy over the old. Rogers indicates that "On the whole there are more experiences of unhappiness, fearfulness, and depression during the second half of therapy than during the first half; and rather violent fluctuations from elated to unhappy, or from confident to depressed, are the rule rather than the exception."[27]

The client finally determines when to end treatment. This termination is not infrequently accompanied by some fear, a sense of loss or perhaps even an unwillingness to face life without the support of the therapeutic contact. But there is also an accompanying sense of excitement.

What Rogers projects as happening in therapy is that in exploring behind the mask of what one thought was his real self, one arrives at a new exercise of his ability to be the person he truly is. He exercises this ability to experience all the emotions which organismically arise in him. "Thus to an increasing degree he becomes himself—not a facade of conformity to others, not a cynical denial of all feeling, nor a front of intellectual rationality, but a living, breathing, feeling, fluctuating process—in short, he becomes a person."[28] This person is more open to his experience, more aware of the reality existing outside himself, more tolerant of ambiguity and more expressive of his reality. He also comes to learn that his organism is a suitable instrument for discovering the most satisfying behavior in each immediate situation. Not that he will not make mistakes, but there will be a greater and more immediate awareness of the consequences of his behavior and a quicker correction of the choices which are in error.

Finally, the individual grows in his understanding that his locus of evaluation is within himself. He feels less afraid of his emotional responses and more responsible for himself. He emerges from therapy more content to be a process than a product, and herein lies his increased excitement for living.

TECHNIQUES OF CLIENT-CENTERED THERAPY

In keeping with the general format of this book we are listing this section as dealing with techniques of therapy, although the theory of client-centered therapy might better be headed "Attitudes of client-centered therapy practitioners." Techniques used in a textbook fashion would run counter to the formulation of client-centered theory since the therapist would not be acting genuinely. It is of course possible for attitudes, postures, even patterns of verbaliza... to be so incorporated into the habitual behavior patterns of a therapist that they can no longer be considered the employment of a technique, as though lifted from a text and inserted in a specific situation, but simply the human act of a therapeutic person.

Basic to the client-centered therapist's way of working is the providing of a certain type of relationship. This relationship, as previously noted, includes the following elements: the therapist is *genuine,* aware of his own feelings and willing to *be* and to express in his words and deeds the various feelings and attitudes existing in him; the therapist entertains *warm regard* for his client as a person—that is, accepts the client as he presents himself; and the therapist experiences a continuing desire to *understand,* coupled with an ability to sensitively *empathize* with each of his client's feelings and communications as they seem to him at the moment without the therapist owning these feelings and communications as genuinely emanating from the therapist rather than the client. Such a relationship establishes the environment for client self-exploration as well as the freedom and support to conduct it. Rogers believes that, given such a relationship, "change and constructive personal development will *invariably* occur. . . ."[29]

While Rogers believes that these three attitudinal conditions—congruence, positive regard, and accurate empathic understanding—come close to representing the core of the client-centered approach, he and his followers have spent considerable time and research energy exploring the implications of these core conditions and associated therapeutic techniques. Early work dealt with the differences between "reflection of feeling" and "restatement of content" and the technical problem of understanding the client's frame of reference. During the 1960's, however, a great deal of research data began to accumulate. It demonstrated that not only the core conditions put forward by Rogers lead to growth on the part of the client, but solid certain other conditions when offered by the therapist at measurably high levels. An equally important finding was that when these conditions were absent or only minimally present the client seemed to get worse.

Finally, Carkhuff, a colleague of Rogers at Wisconsin, refined, renamed, and standardized the core dimensions, adding operational rationales in order to round out a model for a helping relationship. Added to the original core conditions were the dimensions of concreteness, or ability to be specific; confrontation, or the pointing out of discrepancies; and immediacy, or communicating what one wants to communicate directly rather than through distorted, indirect comparisons.

Carkhuff outlined the phases of helping in somewhat more active, problem-solving terms than did Rogers. During the facilitative phase the therapist concentrates on establishing an atmosphere and a relationship utilizing the facilitative dimensions of understanding, warmth, respect, and concreteness. The goal expected in this phase is that the client explore for himself his relevant areas of concern while the therapist gradually establishes for himself a basis for experiencing and understanding the client's world.[30] The technique employed is a gradual crescendo in the therapist's delivery of the levels of the facilitative conditions, bringing about increasingly higher levels of self-exploration in the client as his experiences are sharpened and clarified. As the client comes to trust his own experience in the relationship and to be more disclosing, then the need for higher levels of genuineness in the therapist are called for. The therapist is seen as both model and agent, and the counseling process as an interacting, alternating, stepwise progress. As the therapist begins to offer higher levels of the facilitative conditions he gradually introduces the more highly action-oriented dimensions at minimally facilitative levels.

During this stage when the therapist presses for greater specificity on the part of the client or becomes increasingly more disclosing, the client frequently becomes more threatened. These dimensions press for greater transparency and intimacy in the relationship which produce a hopefully temporary elevated threat response in the client but also provide a bridge into the second phase of helping.

During phase two the client learns not only to reown his experiences but to act in terms of his experiential dimensions. Carkhuff sees this as a problem-solving stage which includes identifying the alternatives for action, evaluating each of them, and operationalizing the one perceived as best.[31] During this action phase dimensions of confrontation and immediacy may be employed if indeed the therapist has built an appropriate base.

Carkhuff describes the helping process as follows: "The more helpee self-exploration, the more helpee self-understanding; the more helpee self-understanding, the more clear the directionality; the more clear the directionality, the more focused the goals; the more focused the goals, the more clear the steps leading to the attainment of these goals."[32]

COMPARISONS WITH TA

Some general comparisons may be drawn between client-centered therapy and TA. Client-centered therapy has always been considered a "third force" psychology. Transactional analysis, despite the parallel frequently drawn between it and psychoanalysis, probably also has more rapport with those approaches which stress humanistic and phenomenological views of people. Both methods are applied in a wide range of settings and across the age spectrum, including dealing with a wide range of individuals and individual problems. Both Rogers and Berne were interested in research and researching their models. However, Rogers and his followers have been quite successful in carrying out research on client-centered therapy, while TA is frequently criticized for its lack of a research base. Both theories see the effect significant others have on the development of the child. Both hold that, if a person is dissatisfied with the impact of earlier life experiences on his present behavior, it is within the power of the individual to do something about these old decisions. Both theories work largely with present behavior in effecting a change to more appropriate behavior. However, while the TA therapist works to expose the client to his past misconceptions in order to institute present change, client-centered therapy avoids therapist-generated explanations of past behavior. This largely client-directed approach attempts to facilitate client self-exploration and thus effect adoption of present alternative behaviors. At its base, TA is an explanatory-action oriented therapy; client-centered therapy largely a permissive-facilitative therapy.

The two therapies share a similarity in defining some of the basic problems people encounter. Rogers has indicated that people experience problems when they deny their experiences to awareness; the transactional therapist is concerned when it appears impossible for his client to cathect an ego state when such apparently should be activated. Client-centered therapists attempt to establish a permissive atmosphere and relationship in which the client might dare to express personal experiences he otherwise could not admit to awareness. The transactional analyst attempts to establish a safe setting. He also attempts to give permission to have an otherwise dormant ego state cathected by giving an assignment to the client, for example. Recathexis and reowning the self appear very similar concepts.

The structural analytic and contractual nature of TA is considerably different from the process orientation of client-centered therapy. Even a specific termination point is established in TA, while in client-centered therapy the client-determined terminus evolves out of the treatment process.

While Carkhuff has added the dimension of confrontation to the list of facilitative qualities, this was not one of Rogers' dimensions. The permissive quality of client-centered therapy appears more overwhelming as compared with TA, yet the TA relationship is permissive in that it gives persons permission to activate their stages of being. The notion of the "cop-out" is a singularly less permissive aspect but might compare somewhat with the notion of confrontation in Carkhuff's scheme.

Both TA and client-centered therapy appear to be concerned with relationships and social interactions. Transactional analysis espouses control over relationships and social interactions through understanding (games, rituals, strokes, etc.) even though the goal might be the experiencing of intimacy as Berne defines it: "The direct expression of meaningful emotions between individuals without ulterior motives or reservations."[33] Client-centered therapy advocates development and control of positive interpersonal relationships through modeling and self-realization. The contrast between the two therapies might well be that the basic emphasis for TA is on the interpersonal while that of client-centered therapy is intrapersonal, yet neither is exclusive in its emphasis. Client-centered therapy makes use of interpersonal relationships in order to facilitate intrapersonal reorganization while TA continually uses the interplay of intrapersonal states in working with person transactions.

Comparisons Among the Mechanisms of Psychotherapy

It might be helpful to briefly compare TA with Carkhuff's stages of implementing a course of therapeutic action. Even though Carkhuff does not consider the tripartite division of personality into Parent, Adult, and Child ego states, his therapeutic procedures serve as a backdrop against which the mechanisms of TA and client-centered therapy might be compared.

Carkhuff outlines three stages of therapy: (1) client self-exploration, (2) client understanding, and (3) client action. All three stages are also present in TA. The differences lie not in the stages themselves but in the techniques used within each stage and the relative emphasis placed on each.

The first goals of helping in both therapeutic approaches are to establish a relationship and to come to understand the nature of the problem. These goals must be established before treatment can proceed. For the client-centered therapist, this is a most important stage of therapy. He or she spends a great amount of energy on the relationship utilizing the conditions of genuineness, accurate empathy, and respect to establish a nonthreatening environment. A key response style is the reflective response. Through it the therapist communicates to the client that he is listening without judging and that the client has the freedom to direct the flow of the interaction.

By contrast, the first stage of the TA relationship may be that of a meeting of a confused client with a benevolent parent. The therapist is direct in seeking the information he needs in order to establish a contractual relationship. The therapist asks questions and gives information to minimize as much as possible the differences in understanding between therapist and client. The therapist is not indiscriminately permissive. He does not excuse irresponsible behavior on the part of the client. The therapist does, however, express certain specific expectations of the client. During the first stage the therapist attempts to create a safe environment in which the client may begin to reown his Adult. This stage is one of experimentation in the safe environment created by the client's therapeutic alley, the therapist.

Because TA is usually carried out in a group, the initial stage also serves to develop the group into a community of meaningful others. Improved communication between group participants is hoped for and the therapist works to ensure the free flow of effective communication. For transactional analysts the major developments experienced during this first stage depend upon the skill and assurance of the therapist. Of the core conditions outlined by Rogers, the one most prominent in the TA therapist at this stage is genuineness, a quality which, while present for the client-centered therapist, is less asserted here than at later stages.

During Carkhuff's second stage the client-centered therapist attempts to foster client understanding of the problem expressed in stage one. Explanations of the problem by the therapist are avoided, for it is the client-centered therapist's belief that not only is it within the power of the client to come to understand his own difficulties but it is therapeutic for the client to arrive at such an understanding at his own pace under his own power. The function of the therapist is again to provide the conditions of respect, empathy, and warmth along with increasingly deeper levels of genuineness and concreteness. During this stage the therapist serves as model and friend, both allowing and guiding the client to explore himself, discover denied experiences, and begin the process of self-reowning. The levels of empathic understanding are deepened and the dimensions of specificity (concreteness) and self-disclosure are reinforced. The therapist does not, however, suggest specific expectations of the client.

By contrast, the TA therapist is responsible for explaining the client's behavior to him, using the information which was obtained during the first stage of therapy and integrating it with the model provided by TA. The TA therapist's tools here are structural analysis, transactional analysis, script analysis, and game analysis. The client leaves this stage of therapy with an understanding of the transactional analysis model of human behavior by which the client can interpret his behavior and reorganize old information using new TA vocabulary. It is indeed a goal of this stage of therapy that the client gain an understanding of the basic vocabulary and principles of TA. Moreover, the TA therapist is not hesitant to employ a variety of techniques by which the client might become more aware of his internal areas of conflict and explore his understanding of them. The task of directing this exploration appears to be largely that of the therapist.

Carkhuff's stage three of the therapeutic process is the action phase. During this stage a workable solution to the accepted problem is identified, outlined, implemented, and evaluated. The therapist must be able to help the client develop a plan of action that will lead to a successful resolution of the client's present problem as well as establish a method for approaching future problems. But the therapist does not determine the available alternatives or make choices for the client; he instead provides a resource and support for the client. The dimensions of confrontation and immediacy are added at this stage—that is, the therapist will point out inconsistencies in client behavior as well as focus on immediate behaviors and interactions. The therapist does not confront or emphasize the action dimensions until he has earned the right by establishing a firm relationship with the client and thoroughly understands the problem. Nothing can be more harmful for the client-centered therapist than to brutally confront his client without a firmly established relationship. The therapist thus has an effect on the client's problem solution without directly developing it.

In TA, once the problem is understood by the therapist and accurately defined for the client, the third stage of therapy is entered. This stage is often marked by confrontation. The therapist tries to keep the client in the present time frame while eliciting a commitment to some action. It is during this period that clients begin to appreciate their own value in the therapeutic process, an appreciation client-centered clients hopefully developed in stage one. Thus TA clients come to accept their own Adult as the true base of support for life activity and gradually can come to release the Adult of the therapist without experiencing a significant loss of security. The clients' self-confidence is further enhanced by the fulfillment of the therapeutic contract, and they depart from the course of therapy with the personal acknowledgement that "I'm OK."

REFERENCES

1. Colton, Helen, "Guts Don't Solve Problems, Contexes Do," *TA Journal* 4 (1974), pp. 13–14.

2. Rogers, C. R., *On Becoming A Person* (Boston: Houghton Mifflin, 1961), pp. 204–205.

3. ———, *The Clinical Treatment of the Problem Child* (Boston: Houghton Mifflin, 1939).

4. ———, *Counseling and Psychotherapy* (Boston: Houghton Mifflin, 1942).

5. ———, *Client-Centered Therapy* (Boston: Houghton Mifflin, 1951).

6. ———, "The Necessary and Sufficient Conditions of Therapeutic Personality Change," *Journal of Consulting Psychology* 21 (1957), pp. 95–103.

7. ———, "A Process Conception of Psychotherapy," *American Psychologist* 13 (1958), pp. 142–149.

8. ———, *On Becoming A Person* (Boston: Houghton Mifflin, 1961).

9. ———, and Barry Stevens, *Person to Person: The Problem of Being Human* (Lafayette, Calif.: Real People Press, 1967).

10. Rogers, Carl R., *Freedom to Learn: A View of What Education Might Become* (Columbus, Ohio: Charles E. Merrill, 1969).

11. ———, *Carl Rogers on Encounter Groups* (New York: Harper & Row, 1970).

12. ———, *On Becoming Partners: Marriage and Its Alternatives* (New York: Delacourte, 1972).

13. ———, "Client-Centered Therapy," in *American Handbook of Psychiatry* (3 Vols.), edited by Silvano Arieti (New York: Basic Books, 1959). See Vol. 3, *A Supplement to the Handbook* (New York: Basic Books, 1966), p. 184.

14. Delaney, D. J., T. J. Long, M. J. Masucci, and H. A. Moses, "Skill Acquisition and Perception Change of Counselor Candidates During Practicum," *Counselor Education and Supervision* 8, 4 (1969), pp. 273–282.

15. Rogers, *Client-Centered Therapy*, p. 453.

16. Ibid., p. 484.

17. Rogers, Carl R. "A Theory of Therapy, Personality, and Interpersonal Relationships, as Developed in the Client-Centered Framework," in S. Koch (Ed.) *Psychology: A Study of a Science*, edited by S. Koch. See Vol. III, *Formulations of the Person and the Social Context* (New York: McGraw-Hill, 1959), p. 196.

18. ———, *Client-Centered Therapy*, pp. 498–499.

19. ———, in S. Koch (ed.), p. 201.

20. Ibid., p. 223.

21. Rogers, *Client-Centered Therapy*, p. 499.

22. Ibid., p. 510.

23. Rogers, in S. Koch (ed.), p. 226.

24. ———, "The Actualizing Tendency in Relation to 'Motives' and to Consciousness," in *Nebraska Symposium on Motivation*, 1963, edited by Marshall Jones (Lincoln, Neb.: University of Nebraska Press, 1963), p. 24.

25. ———, *On Becoming A Person*, p. 103.

26. Ibid., p. 104.

27. Rogers, *Client-Centered Therapy*, pp. 81–83.

28. ———, *On Becoming A Person*, p. 114.

29. Ibid. p. 35.

30. Carkhuff, R. R., *Helping and Human Relàtions*, Vol. II (New York: Holt, Rinehart & Winston, 1969), pp. 28–29.

31. Ibid., p. 31.

32. Carkhuff, *Helping and Human Relations*, Vol. I, p. 240.

33. Berne, Eric, *The Structure and Dynamics of Organizations and Groups* (Philadelphia: J. B. Lippincott, 1963), p. 245.

CHAPTER 18

other
treatment modalities
and TA

DORIS WILD HELMERING

This chapter, utilizing edited transcripts from actual therapy groups, demonstrates ways to integrate other therapies and their techniques with Transactional Analysis. Freedom to utilize the knowledge and techniques of various therapies as they apply to each situation allows for optimal results. The format used in this chapter consists of three columns. The first column is a transcript of part of a therapy session. The second column describes techniques developed by other therapeutic models that were used in this group. The third column translates the technique into TA terminology and also defines TA theory. The pronouns his and her have been alternated throughout the chapter instead of writing as though the world is universally male.

The first edited transcript is that of a young woman, Suzanne, who, although 25 and presently working on her Master's Degree, has been unable to find a job. She has always lived with her parents who have continued to support her. In other group sessions Suzanne had stated that she wanted to find a job in order to achieve her independence. She had interviewed for numerous jobs but had never been hired.

When Suzanne first came into treatment her main symptom was depression. She was apathetic, rarely smiled, and would not volunteer any information about herself and/or her life style unless she was pressed to do so. Two months prior to her coming into therapy, she had attempted suicide with an overdose of sleeping pills. Suzanne was seen individually for four sessions at which time her script was done and her treatment goals were determined. Some of her script injunctions and attributions were: Don't grow up . . . Don't trust people . . . Be passive . . . Life is a struggle . . . Don't ask for what you want . . . Don't show feelings . . . Don't be angry . . . You're crazy . . . Be depressed.

The goals Suzanne had established for herself in therapy were: Grow up . . . Be independent . . . Get a job . . . Stop being depressed . . . Give and get strokes . . . Stop being passive . . . Express feelings.

In previous sessions, Suzanne had made contracts about getting strokes for herself in the group and giving strokes to other group members. This had helped her to give up her depression. She had begun to express her feelings and had become an active group member. She had consistently asked for time each week to work; however, it seemed that Suzanne's unwillingness to find a job was a way for her to hold on to her script. She could live with her parents, continue to struggle because she had no money, and continue following the injunction, "Don't grow up," as well as have her parents reinforce other script messages.

On the following pages, the first column is the transcript of Suzanne's working on the problem of finding a job. In the second column other modalities of treatment are discussed, and in the third column the material is translated into TA theory and terminology. To make it easier to follow, each concept that will be discussed will be given the same title in all three columns.

Group Process

Taking Responsibility

Suzanne: I'd like to work.
Therapist: Okay.

Other Modalities Used

Taking Responsibility

The idea of having the client verbalize his desire to work on a problem has its roots in Gestalt Therapy. Fritz Perls, one of the major developers of Gestalt, placed much emphasis on having the client take responsibility for himself. He firmly stated that he was responsible only for himself, and for no one else. He explained to the client that he was not responsible for him. He further made it clear that if the client wanted to go crazy, commit suicide, improve, get "turned on," or get an experience that would change his life, it was up to the client.[1]

Contract

Behavior Modification Theory makes use of the concept of contracts. Behavioral contracts are agreements between two or more persons specifying what each person will do for a stated period of time.[2] An effective behavioral contract:[3]

1. Contains clear expectations.
2. Specifies performance.
3. Sets reachable goals.

Contract

Suzanne: I had a contract with Doris to get a job by January 15th, but didn't keep the contract because I wasn't hired for a job. So, I need to work on how I keep myself from being hired.

TA Translation

Taking Responsibility

A norm usually established in a TA group is that a group member takes responsibility for working on a problem. Suzanne's intervention, "I'd like to work," is one way the client can do this. TA therapists generally agree that if a therapist calls on a group member to work, both the therapist and client are discounting the client's ability to ask for what he wants.

Contract

One kind of contract in TA is an explicit agreement to replace a specific old behavior with a new, more effective behavior. A contract is made between the therapist's Adult ego state and the client's Adult ego state. Many TA therapists believe, however, that it is important that the client's Child ego state needs to be in on the contract, because usually it is the Child ego state which has the most to give up.

4. Contains provision for renegotiation.
5. Establishes rewards.
6. Accents positive behavior.
7. Assesses outcome.

The theory behind the behavior contract is that it is helpful to the client to specify the kind of change that is desired. Through negotiation of the contract, the client and therapist determine what each wants from the other. Sometimes contracts specify what kinds of counseling goals are to be achieved. A contract is also useful in finding out the expectations of both the client and the therapist.

The behavior contract is also a method of specifying rewards in advance. It allows the client to participate in two ways. First, the client specifies the desired behavior. Second, she determines the specific reinforcements that will be used to reward this behavior.

Rogerian therapists use the concept of contracts in classroom teaching. They contend that "One open-ended device which helps to give both security and responsibility within an atmosphere of freedom is

For example, a client who makes a contract to give up smoking is giving up lots of strokes for her Child. If she has nothing to replace these strokes, she is not likely to keep the contract. However, if her Child is turned on by the contract and will get something out of the new behavior, i.e., strokes from a different source, the contract is likely to be kept. It is also helpful that the client's Parent agrees to the contract, but it is not as essential because the Adult and Child working together are more powerful than the Parent. Using the same example, a great many more people would give up smoking because their Parent agrees that smoking is a "bad habit" and "expensive," while their Adult knows that studies have shown smoking to be medically harmful. In this frame of reference, it is important that the therapist also makes the contract utilizing his own Parent and Child ego states. From his Parent comes the protection, permission, and potency to help the client change. From his Child ego state comes the enthusiasm which supports the contract. If the therapist is not aware of what his Child feels about the contract, he may inadvertently sabotage it even though

Group Process

Role-Playing

Therapist: Well, I know that you have qualifications for a job. And I know that you have interviewed for 25 or 30 jobs. So, how about role-playing a job interview?

Suzanne: Okay.

Therapist: You sit where you are and put Mr. Jones, your potential employer, in the other chair. How about being Mr. Jones first and start out the interview?

Other Modalities Used

Taking Responsibility

the use of student contracts." A contract made by the student is one whereby she determines her own goals for learning in agreement with the professor.[4]

Role-Playing

Role-playing as a technique goes back as far as drama itself. Moreno used it as a therapeutic tool, calling it "psychodrama." He contended that "therapeutic acting-out" in a controlled environment is both a preventive and curative measure against "irrational acting-out" in life itself.[5]

In a psychodrama group, when a member of the group experiences an emotional problem, she is urged to act out the situation, and a "stage" is provided for her to do so. Other group members may or may not join in.

Fritz Perls also saw a great value in role-playing. Perl's role-playing technique is

TA Translation

Taking Responsibility

his Parent and Adult ego states agree that it is a good contract. For example, a therapist who smokes and gets much gratification in his Child ego state may sabotage the contract with a smile when the client talks about giving up smoking. His Child is saying to the client's Child, "You'll (we'll) never give it up! Ha-Ha!"

Role-Playing

In TA a number of people have developed further techniques making use of role playing. Jack Dusay's Script Rehearsal,[6] and Pete Stuntz's Multiple Chair Technique,[7] are examples of these.

With the technique of Script Rehearsal, the therapist acts as "director." The "star" is the client who wants to work on a problem while the "co-star" is another member of the group who volunteers to role play a scene with the "star." Other group members take the role of the star's Parent ego state, Adult ego state, and Child ego state.

The session begins with the director

Suzanne: (As Mr. Jones) Hello. I'm Mr. Jones. I hear you're interested in applying for our secretarial position.

Suzanne: (Switches chairs) Yes, I saw your ad in the paper and I called for an interview.

called the "empty-chair" or "double-chair" technique. Unlike Moreno, he rarely used the other people to role-play with his client. He claimed that these other people would "bring in their own fantasies; their own interpretations." "Perls, therefore, required the patient to imagine and act out all the parts. He focused on *how* the patient was acting now, not on the *why* of his behavior."8

The double-chair technique entails placing an empty chair directly in front of the client. The client sits in what is called the "hot seat," which is a chair for the client who chooses to "work." The client imagines that another person is sitting in the empty chair. She begins the dialogue, and switches to the empty chair when she is playing the role of the person whom she imagines to be sitting there. She then responds to herself as she perceives the imagined person would respond to her. She continues the dialogue, switching chairs when she changes roles until she reaches some sort of resolution.

Virginia Satir uses a similar technique called "simulated-family technique."9
There are two ways this technique can be

telling the star and co-star to play their scene. As the star and co-star are involved in a dialogue, the star is bombarded by outside influences from group members playing the roles of Parent, Adult, and Child.

A discussion, or "rehash," follows the enactment of the scene which allows the star to determine which ego state is interfering with her being able to solve the problem.

In Pete Stuntz's Multiple-Chair Technique, three chairs are set up to represent the client's Parent, Adult, and Child ego state. The person moves from one chair to another as he changes ego states. His awareness of his different ego states is facilitated by his shifting from chair to chair. The person can then use this awareness for decontamination of his Adult ego state from Parent attitudes and Child feelings.

Other Modalities Used

Role-Playing

used. In one, the therapist can have family members simulate each others' behavior. For example, each member of a family plays the role of another family member, and behaves and thinks the way he believes that particular family member behaves and thinks.

A second way to use the simulated-family technique is to have the family members play themselves. The therapist constructs a situation to be role-played from her understanding of the family's system. An audiovisual tape is made of the family acting out the situation. The tape is then played back to acquaint the family with their behavior. The playback is then followed by a discussion with the therapist.

Behavior-modification theorists use a technique that is similar to both Perls' double-chair technique and Satir's simulated-family technique. This technique is referred to as "behavioral rehearsal."[10] The therapist himself takes the role of the person with whom the client is having difficulty relating. The therapist then in-

TA Translation

structs the client to express his ordinarily inhibited feelings toward that person. The aim of the rehearsal is to make it possible for the client to express himself with his real "adversary."

Data Processing

Suzanne: (As Mr. Jones) Can you tell me about your qualifications?

Suzanne: (Switches chairs) I type 50 words per minute and I've done typing at school. I've typed term papers and I've worked temporarily for a photo supply store.

Suzanne: (As Mr. Jones) I see by your application that you have a B.S. in Education. Why are you not using it?

Suzanne: (Switches chairs) After I graduated, I decided I didn't want to teach. I decided I'd rather work for a large company than work in a school with children. I'd like to be involved in some aspect of personnel.

Data Processing

This question, "Can you tell me about your qualifications?" is from Suzanne's Adult ego state. "The Adult ego state can be used to reason, to evaluate stimuli, and to store information for future reference." This procedure in TA is called data processing.

Group Process

Data Processing

Therapist: Now be Mr. Jones and offer her some wage.

Suzanne: (As Mr. Jones) The job I have open starts at $2.25 an hour. How does that sound? Would that be acceptable?

Suzanne: (Switches chairs) Yes.

Therapist: Do you need to ask Mr. Jones any questions about the job?

Suzanne: Hmm, yes—I'd like to know something about the hours of the job.

Suzanne: (As Mr. Jones) The hours of the job are 8:00-5:00 p.m. with an hour for lunch.

Suzanne: (Switches chairs) What exactly would my duties be?

Suzanne: (As Mr. Jones) You would be answering the phone, typing my reports and filling orders.

Suzanne: (Switches chairs) Can you tell me about the employee benefits?

Other Modalities Used

TA Translation

Suzanne: (As Mr. Jones) I don't know. (Group laughter)

Therapist: Switch chairs, Suzanne. I like the way you conduct and handle interviews. Do you really ask questions when you go on an interview?

Suzanne: I didn't use to, but now I do.

Therapist: In a real interview, would you ask something like, "What are the employee benefits?"

Suzanne: Yes.

Strokes

The concept of the need for stroking was recognized, defined, and researched by Harry Harlow and Rene Spitz. Harlow conducted an experiment using infant rhesus monkeys. He believed that the "contact comfort" the infant gets from clinging to his mother is not dependent on feeding.

From his studies, Harlow concluded that the infant monkey, and perhaps the infant human, is innately satisfied by tactile

Strokes

According to TA theory, a stroke is defined as "any act implying recognition of another's presence." Strokes can be either in the form of an actual touch or in the form of a symbolic recognition such as a word, a smile, or a frown. Berne summed up the importance of strokes by saying, "If the infant is not stroked, his spinal cord shrivels up."

With this intervention, "I like the way you conduct and handle interviews," Suzanne's

Group Process

Other Modalities Used

Strokes

stimulation, which is the basis of the at-tachment that baby monkeys showed to artificial terrycloth mothers. Consequently, this tactile quality, and not feeding itself, was the main source of gratification and security for the infant monkeys.

Spitz did research with infants raised from birth in institutions who had sufficient food and health care, but did not receive the affection that most children get from their parents. Spitz observed that infants that are deprived of physical contact in the first six months of life frequently be-come apathetic, dejected, and detached. In later life they continue to manifest lack of appetite, retarded physical de-velopment and stupor. As a result of these studies, many therapies make use of the knowledge of the basic need for stroking.

In learning theory, the concept of stroking is termed reinforcement.[11] Reinforcement is defined as any circumstance or event that increases the probability of a response. Many learning theorists, such as B. F. Skinner and C. L. Hull, believe that every

TA Translation

Strokes

Adult was stroked for thinking clearly and her Child was recognized by the therapist indicating additional interest.

response is a learned response; therefore, any desirable behavior can be learned by reinforcing the desired behavior with a pleasurable experience or reward, preferably during or immediately after the desired action.

Behavior modification therapists use the principle of reinforcement to strengthen positive habits in order to replace maladaptive habits. Reinforcement may consist of social rewards such as praise, attention, and special privileges. However, in some cases, more primary forms of reinforcement, such as food or cigarettes, may be used.

Feedback

Therapist: I think that's smart because it gives the employer information that you're concerned about the job and you don't want it just for two weeks, but that you really want to get involved in it. Any other feedback people have?

Kevin: I thought she conducted herself very well.

Feedback

The term "feedback," originally used in cybernetics, was adapted by Kurt Lewin to describe the process whereby one person feeds back or mirrors to another person what she has observed and often how she feels about her observations. Feedback has become an essential part of group dynamics and has been found to be most effective when it stems from here-and-now observations and when it closely follows

Feedback

The therapist's question, "Any other feedback people have?" encourages other group members to share their own feelings and/or thoughts with Suzanne.

Some TA therapists utilize the knowledge of group process and communication skills while other more traditional TA therapists do not. It is the opinion of this author that if a therapist does not encourage feedback, she is setting it up so that the group

Group Process

Other Modalities Used

Feedback

the generating event. To establish the validity of the feedback and to reduce perceptual distortion, feedback should be checked out with other group members.

In group psychotherapy, it is believed that each group member needs to find acceptance from other group members. This acceptance is accomplished through the group's giving and receiving of feedback with each other.[12]

Carl Rogers contends that feedback is a necessary part of group therapy in that each person learns how he appears to others and what impact he has in interpersonal relationships.[13]

Much research has been done in the area of communication. If a therapist is familiar with a concept such as the Johari Window,[14] she will establish a group norm of people responding to each other in the here-and-now.

The Johari Window is a graphic model of awareness in interpersonal relationships. It is based on four quadrants. Quadrant I,

TA Translation

Feedback

will only talk with her, thus reinforcing the magical belief that the therapist has all the answers.

When a therapist does give feedback, it can be from any ego state; however, the Adult is the executor for modeling how to give and receive effective feedback. The therapist also gives permission for the group members to learn and practice more effective communicative behaviors.

which is known as the Area of Free Activity, refers to behavior and motivation known to self and to others.

Quadrant II, which is known as the Blind Area, refers to where others can see things in ourselves of which we are unaware.

Quadrant III, which is known as the Avoided or Hidden Area, represents things we know, but do not reveal to others.

Quadrant IV, which is known as the Area of Unknown Activity, refers to certain behaviors or motives of which neither the individual nor others are aware.

According to the Johari Window, feedback is a way for the group members to aid each other in reducing the blind area and increasing the knowledge in the area of free activity. An enlarged area of free activity among the group members would immediately imply less threat or fear and greater probability that the skills and resources of group members can be brought to bear on the work of the group. It suggests greater openness to information, opinions, and new ideas about one's self as well as specific group process.

311

Other Modalities Used

Group Process

Direct Feedback

Therapist: Tell Suzanne directly.

Kevin: I thought you conducted yourself very well, except for a little lack of enthusiasm. I think I'm going to rescue her now. I was going to say that this was maybe due to the role-playing.

Rescuing

Therapist: That was a rescue, Kevin. How can you give Suzanne information about how she came on with Mr. Jones without giving her an excuse for her lack of enthusiasm?

Kevin: I like the way you conducted yourself with the interview, but I was aware of a lack of enthusiasm; and, this lack of enthusiasm might be a factor in your not getting a job.

Therapist: Good feedback, Kevin.

TA Translation

Direct Feedback

This intervention, "Tell Suzanne directly," was made in order that Suzanne would receive the stroke instead of the therapist.

Rescuing

The intervention, "That was a rescue," was made to confirm Kevin's statement that he was rescuing. In TA, a statement that that is a rescue is one which comes from the speaker's Parent which says to the client's Child, "I might take care of you. You need me to protect you and to do your thinking for you." In this intervention, Kevin's Parent was saying to Suzanne's Child, "I'll protect you. Here is an excuse for your lack of enthusiasm."

The therapist also gave Kevin permission to use his Adult to figure out how to give the feedback without rescuing Suzanne.

Discounting and Hidden Agenda

Diane: I thought one good question you asked was, "What does the job involve?"

Trudy: Suzanne, do you keep eye contact with your employer when you're talking with him?

Suzanne: I don't know.

Trudy: I think you probably don't keep eye contact. You came across as shy to me, and I think one of the things was the eye contact. You sort of looked down and it was a little girl looking down and not making any eye contact. That's what it seemed like.

Terry: At the very beginning you had a tendency to sit far back in your chair like you were trying to get as far away from the situation as you could. It looks to me like you are scared.

Therapist: Good feedback, Terry.

Discounting and Hidden Agenda

Groups work simultaneously and continuously on two levels. The surface, or the public level, is the formally stated topic or task on which the group has agreed to work. The second level is the hidden-agenda level. The hidden agendas represent all of the individuals and/or group problems that differ from the surface group job and therefore may get in the way of the work to be done on the surface agenda. Hidden agendas may or may not be within the awareness of the group member(s).

For example, in a group the public agenda is Joyce's working on her anger at her husband. Another group member, Joe, has a hidden agenda of which he is not aware. Hs is angry at Joyce for taking so much group time and consequently he has not been able to work in the group. On a conscious level, he attempts to praise her for her working through of the problem. However, as he goes to make his statement he sound angry to the other group members and the therapist. When it is pointed out that he sounds angry, he gets in touch with his hidden agenda.

Discounting and Hidden Agenda

Diane gave Suzanne a positive stroke which was discounted when Suzanne did not respond to the stroke. The therapist and the group also discounted Diane by not responding and by allowing Trudy to discount Diane by jumping in with another question. Diane also discounted herself as she did not confront Suzanne's acknowledgment of her stroke or Trudy's interruption.

It is important for a therapist to be aware of the dynamics of discounting in a group. If the discounting of positive strokes is not confronted, members of the group will soon find it more rewarding to say nothing or to give negative strokes. For example, a group member who was usually continually late was given negative strokes when he marched in the group late. He made a contract to be on time which he kept for three weeks. The fourth week he again came late. When analyzing what happened it soon became clear that because he had received no positive strokes for being on time, he resorted to his old behavior, which at least assured him of some recognition.

Other Modalities Used

Discounting and Hidden Agenda

Gestalt therapists clearly recognize the importance of a hidden agenda. In *Gestalt Therapy Verbatim*, Perls talks about The Bear-Trapper.[15] The bear-trapper is a person who encourages people to get close to him, but who, when someone takes the bait and moves in, then pulls a switch and brushes her off. The switch allows the bear-trapper to obtain control over others and in addition serves to build his own self-esteem by making him the victor in the game.

In addition, Perls claimed that questions are inventions we use to torture ourselves and others. He believed that the way to develop our intelligence is by changing every question into a statement. By doing this, "the background out of which the question arose opens up, and the possibilities are found by the questioner himself."[16]

TA Translation

Discounting and Hidden Agenda

The question Trudy asked had a hidden agenda (Trudy already knew the answer). This should have been confronted. By not confronting Trudy's discount of her own Adult, the game *NIGYSOB*, was played. Using Berne's game formula, the game was played as follows (Con plus Gimmick equals Response, and so on):

Con: Do you keep eye contact with your employer? *Plus*

Gimmick: (Suzanne's weakness to want to be rescued.) *Equals*

Response: I don't know. *Plus*

Switch: I think you probably don't keep eye contact. *Plus*

Cross-up: Suzanne is confused. Her Rescuer turns into a Persecutor.

Payoff: Trudy's payoff: She's one-up on Suzanne.

Her position: I'm OK, You're not-OK.

Feeling: Triumphant—looks bright at Suzanne's expense.

Suzanne's payoff: She is one down.

Her position: I'm not-OK, you're not-OK.

Feeling: Scared and angry.

Reinforces script: People can't be trusted.

Another way to look at this game is by use of the Drama Triangle.

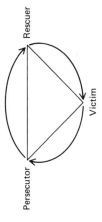

Trudy starts out obstensibly in the Rescue position: "Do you keep eye contact"? Suzanne appears as a Victim, but moves to the Persecutor position: "I don't know." The ulterior message is, "You must tell me." Trudy is now the Victim, she must respond but then quickly moves to the Persecutor position: "I think you probably don't." (The ulterior message is, "You don't because I just watched you, ha! ha!") Suzanne switches back to the Victim position.

To have prevented this game from being played out, a good confrontation would have been to ask Trudy to turn on her Adult and give feedback as to what she saw.

Group Process

Script Rehearsal

Therapist: We know what happens when you go on an interview, Suzanne, so let's see what goes on in your head when you are interviewing. This time other members of the group will need to participate in a different way. We will need a mom, dad, brother, and employer. Who wants to hire Suzanne?

Diane: I will.

Therapist: Now, who do you want to role-play your mom, Suzanne?

Suzanne: Trudy.

Therapist: Fine. Trudy, would you be willing to play Suzanne's mom and stand behind her?

Trudy: Um hmm.

Therapist: Who do you want to be your dad?

Suzanne: Michael.

Therapist: Okay. Would you also stand behind Suzanne, Michael?

Michael: Yes.

Other Modalities Used

TA Translation

Script Rehearsal

This technique, Script Rehearsal, helped Suzanne become aware of the Parent messages in her head. Each time Suzanne had gone on an interview, she had spent much of her time in her Child ego state, listening to her mother say, "You're wasting your time." Listening to the Parent messages was a way for Suzanne to turn off her Adult and mess up the interview. This reinforced the Parent message, "You're wasting your time," and resulted in Suzanne's remaining dependent upon her family. As Suzanne became aware of what she was doing, she then could decide with her Adult if she really wanted to get a job.

Therapist: Who do you want to be your brother?

Suzanne: Kevin.

Therapist: Kevin, sit down there next to Suzanne. Suzanne, what would your mother say as you were going out on an interview?

Suzanne: She would say I was wasting my time and I'm not going to get this job.

Suzanne: "You're wasting your time. You are not going to get the job."

Therapist: Got the idea, Trudy?

Trudy: Yes, I say the things that Suzanne's mother says to her in her head.

Therapist: Okay, Suzanne, what would your father be saying?

Suzanne: "Good luck. I hope you get the job."

Therapist: Would he say it as strong as mom?

Suzanne: No.

Therapist: What would your brother be saying to you?

Group Process

Other Modalities Used

TA Translation

Script Rehearsal

Suzanne: "Where are you going?"

Therapist: So, he would be asking questions. Okay. So your job is to look at your interviewer and answer her questions. Mom and dad and brother know what lines to feed you.

Diane: (As interviewer) How did you first hear about this job?

Suzanne: I saw your ad in the paper and called for an interview.

Diane: (As interviewer) Do you know what it involves?

Suzanne: No. In the paper it just said light typing. I'd like to know more about that.

Diane: (As interviewer) It will involve typing, being a receptionist, filing, and meeting people. I'm looking for someone who will be able to handle this. (Simultaneously Michael and Trudy talk)

Trudy: (As mother) You're wasting

your time. You're not going to get this job.

Michael: (As father) Good luck. You can do it.

Therapist: Suzanne, who are you listening to right now?

Suzanne: (Laughing) Trudy. (Group laughter)

Therapist: I think you all did beautifully. Got an idea why you are not getting a job?

Suzanne: Yes. (With much laughter)

Life Plan

Addendum: In the next group meeting Suzanne had this to say, "I want to make an announcement. I have a job and I start tomorrow. It looks like I've changed my script message, 'Don't grow up.'" (Group laughter, cheering, and clapping)

Life Plan

Albert Ellis, whose system of therapy is known as "rational emotive therapy," believes that most of man's illogical ideas are derived from his upbringing. He says that people get most of their irrational self-sentences, which are similar to the TA concept of "script messages," from their parents, teachers, peer groups, the general culture, and mass media. Ellis further points out that these illogical ideas lead to a certain amount of self-defeating patterns or neurosis. Much as the TA thera-

Life Plan

One of the most important concepts developed by Eric Berne is script theory. Berne defined a script as "an ongoing program developed in early childhood under parental influence which directs the individual's behavior in the most important aspects of his life."

One message in Suzanne's script was, "Don't grow up." According to Berne, this particular message would have been decided by Suzanne's Child ego state between

Other Modalities Used

Life Plan

pist helps the client to change his script messages, the rational therapist teaches his clients to change their internalized sentences, or self-talk.[17]

Alfred Adler's theory of "life plan" or "life style" is also similar to the TA concept of scripts.[18] Adler believed that a person's development was conditioned by his social environment. He stated that the therapist's job is to reeducate the client to healthier patterns and goals. This can only be undertaken once the client's life style is understood. He also added that if he knows the goals of a person, he knows in a general way what will happen in the future to that person.

TA Translation

Life Plan

the ages of five and thirteen, and was probably written through a series of transactions she had had with her parents. She had carried this message around in her head at all times. Consequently, she would not grow up and get a job. The games a person plays also are a part of the script. The game Suzanne had played in this group session was a result of her staying in her Child ego state and not thinking, while expecting someone else to think for her. Once Suzanne realized how she was living by her script message, " Don't grow up," she was in a position to change it.

Since the next transcript involves two therapists working with a client, the issue of co-therapy will be discussed. Clinicians differ in their opinion about using a co-therapist. Some of the dissenters are Berne, Slavson, Gans, MacLennan, and Yalom. Some proponents are Block, Demerest and Teicher, Heilfron, Moreno, and this author.

Some of the arguments given against co-therapy are:[19,20]

The use of co-therapists can add complications and pitfalls to an already complex arena. "In a group, transferences seem to be multiple, variable, and fragmentary and mobile, and they are made even more so by the addition of a second therapist."

A main difficulty encountered in a multiple leadership group arises from competition between therapists.

There can be a common source of antagonism if the two therapists have different therapeutic orientations.

Group members often attempt to separate the therapists, setting up one therapist against the other, which can cause problems in the group.

Two therapists who feel uncomfortable with each other and are not open with each other will add a strain which will result in a tense, inhibited group.

Eric Berne believed that a co-therapist is present because the primary therapist is reluctant to take full responsibility. He further argues that "what the presence of a co-therapist contributes in dynamic confusion usually outweighs what he offers intellectually or therapeutically."[21]

Some of the values of co-therapy that have been cited in the literature by Block and by Demerest and Teicher are:

- Co-therapy enhances limit-setting capacity, i.e., if a therapist confronts a game, the client may deny her responsibility in the game if only one therapist is present. Whereas, if both therapists confront the same game, the client may be more likely to hear, particularly if she has observed the therapists disagreeing openly in the group and not always seeing issues in the same way.
- Co-therapists who disagree openly and resolve their differences in a constructive rather than a destructive fashion are able to provide a good role model. Clients can experience that people can have differences and problems and that these problems can be solved.
- When one therapist is involved with a complex interaction with a client, the other therapist is oftentimes more objective in describing what is transpiring.

- In the training of a therapist, the multileadership approach decreases anxiety in the trainee and, in addition, promotes insight into problems within himself and with his interacting with others.

It is the opinion of this author that the benefits of having another therapist far outweigh the difficulties that may arise. In addition to the values of cotherapy that have already been stated:

- For one therapist to recognize, in front of the group members, the other therapist's perceptiveness, therapeutic ability, explanation, wittiness, new shirt, or new piece of office equipment can be very effective in teaching people how to stroke each other.
- A group has a better chance to continue uninterrupted from week to week as one therapist can cover for his vacationing or ill colleague. At times, difficulties do arise when one therapist is absent. However, if people are encouraged to say what they think and how they feel about the absence of a therapist, many valuable insights can and do occur.
- After the actual therapy session the co-therapists can do a rehash of the group. This is often valuable in determining what techniques or strategies may be useful in helping a person solve his problems.
- Lastly, this sharing with another therapist the experience of seeing a person change and grow can be extremely rewarding.

This next transcript shows how co-therapists worked together with Irv in a playful manner to help him recognize how he manipulates people into attacking him or leaving him. Irv, a young college student, was referred by a minister two months prior to this group session. His main complaint during the initial interview was that he felt very much alone. He did not relate well to his peers, considered himself friendless, and over the past two years was experiencing more and more problems relating to his parents. Also, his grades, "the only thing I have been proud of," were starting to slip. His script was done during the next two sessions and then Irv went into an ongoing therapy group.

His script messages were: Be a loser . . . Grow up fast . . . Do procrastinate . . . Don't show your feelings . . . If you can't do it right, don't do it . . . Be depressed.

The goals that Irv decided to work on in therapy were: Become aware of how I put people off . . . Stop setting it up so people kick me . . . Get a part-time job . . . Learn to recognize and express feelings . . . Stop being depressed . . . Make two friends in the next four months.

Group Process

Terminology

Irv: I spent the week in my Child thinking about my scared feelings and the other night I had a dream. I'm sorry now that I didn't write it down. What I got out of it was that I had an injunction from my father, that if I say something or do something I might get hit for it. It's like every time I open my mouth I'm taking a chance of getting hit and I would like information to break the injunction.

Therapist: I think you have the information.

A Con

Irv: What?

Therapist A: I think you have the information.

Irv: Well, what I was thinking about was that if I stay in my

Other Modalities Used

TA Translation

Terminology

A criticism often leveled against TA is that the language is very jargonistic and many people begin to use the language as a cop-out. Irv demonstrates this by beating around the bush with TA terminology instead of getting to the point. "I spent the week in my Child thinking about my scared feelings."

A Con

As was shown earlier, a con is the first step in a game. Irv's "what" is interpreted as a con in order to get more information from the therapist. The therapist did not respond to the con, but again gave Irv permission to think for himself. Irv responded

Group Process

A Con

Adult, I can tell myself not to get scared but I'm scared about not being able to tell myself that. When I do get scared, I have to shut it off. I guess I feel that I don't have any protection for myself.

Therapist A: What are you talking about?

Irv: I don't know how to break the injunction outside of just telling myself that you're an adult now, you handle it as an adult. But just telling myself, that doesn't seem to work for me.

Something from the Past

Therapist A: Is it really going to happen, that you're going to get hit?

Irv: Well, I'm really not sure. I don't know how I did it, but I know when I was younger, in school I attracted the bullies who were always picking on me.

Other Modalities Used

Something from the Past

The concept of transference[22] in Freudian terms is similar to the TA concept of rubberband. Freud believed that transference occurred when the client displaced to the analyst, in the present, such feelings as love or hate which were unconsciously attached to a significant person in his past. Freud found that when the trans-

TA Translation

A Con

to the permission of the therapist to turn his Adult on. His Adult knew what he needed to do, but his Child felt scared.

Something from the Past

Irv's "I'm really not sure," was his Child responding to the therapist. This was not confronted because Irv got in touch with a rubberband. "When something in the present situation triggers a response in the patient which appears out of place or stronger than the situation deserves this is a clue to the therapist that the feeling may

It was quite real. If I wasn't careful what I said, I would get hit.

ference became intense, the patient would reproduce and reenact important childhood conflicts and fears.

Getting in the Now

Doris: Irv, teach me how to get hit right now.

Therapist A: If Doris (Therapist B) wanted to get hit when she opened her mouth, what would she have to do?

Irv: Well, you have to antagonize the other person.

Doris: What would I have to say?

Irv: It's different for different people.

Therapist A: What would Doris

be archaic; a snap back, or rubberband to an old, familiar childhood feeling, which is being expressed *here* and *now*."[23]

An example of a rubberband is a person being extremely scared while observing two of her friends having a slight disagreement. Chances are, she is experiencing some old feelings which she had felt when she was a child and her parents would argue. She is, in effect, overreacting to the present situation since her feelings are out of proportion to what is happening in the now.

Getting in the Now

This intervention, "Irv, teach me how to get hit right now," made use of Frankl's technique called the Paradoxical Intention.[24,25] This technique requires the person to have his symptom right there. "It is carried out in as humorous a setting as possible." In this kind of setting, the person is usually able to place herself at a distance from the symptom. If the therapist succeeds in bringing the person to the point where she exaggerates her symptom rather than denying it or fighting it, the symptom may diminish.

Getting in the Now

The intervention, "Teach me how to get hit right now," was made in order to help Irv move out of his Child ego state where he felt scared and into his Adult ego state where he could figure out how he gets people to kick him and ultimately leave him.

Getting in the Now

have to do to get people to come down on her?

Irv: One good sure-fire way is to always be critical of them.

Doris: I would always be critical of other people and they would always come down on me?

Irv: Yeah.

Doris: What else would I do?

Irv: Um, never come through for people.

Doris: How would I not come through?

Irv: Say you're gonna do something and then don't do it and tell them you forgot.

Laughter

Doris: Oh, I forgot (Laughter) Okay, how else?

Therapist A: (Laughter) I don't know about that one.

Irv: Act like you don't care about them.

Laughter

In other modalities, laughter as a therapeutic tool has been mainly neglected. Freud gave some recognition to the concept of laughter in his article, "Jokes and Their Relationship to the Unconscious." He believed that laughter is essentially

Laughter

Most TA therapists put a good deal of emphasis on the "why" and "how" of a person's laughter in a group. While much laughter is healthy, productive, and helps people to move to intimacy, some laughter is very scripty and destructive. Eric Berne,

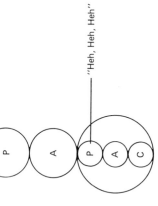

"Heh, Heh, Heh"

Doris: How would I do that?

Irv: If you see they're getting interested in something, wander the conversation off someplace else. (Laughter)

Doris: Okay.

Betty: What about if you talk real slow?

Irv: Oh yeah. Talk real slow. Bore them to death that way. Be hifalutin'.

Doris: How could I be hikaflutin', oops, hifalutin'?

Irv: Use big words.

Ellen: Like hifalutin'.

Irv: Talk about things you know the other person doesn't know anything about.

Doris: What would I talk about?

Irv: Talk about the fine art of torture. (Laughter) How to tell the difference between the vertebrae and the back, the finer points of classification, general knowledge on dinosaurs, obscure writers. (Laughter)

based on some release of repressed hostility.[26]

Luft, in *Group Processes*, states, "Because humor touches on vital matters...it facilitates communication and decision-making. Humor may, of course, serve as a means of expressing hostility in the group and may be exercised at the expense of some person or subgroups. Or humor may be a means of temporary flight from the situation at hand. There is probably no limit of the kinds of processes to which humor may be related."[28]

in his book *What Do You Say After You Say Hello?* distinguished a number of different kinds of laughter, both healthy and scripty.[27]

The first main category is the *scripty* laugh. This includes the "Heh, Heh, Heh" laugh, the Parental chuckle of the witch-mother or ogre-father who is leading his child to failure and defeat. In second-order structural analysis, this is the Parent in the Child.

Another type of scripty laughter is the "Ha, Ha, Ha" laugh. This is the Adult's chuckle of humor. It is also called the "gallows laugh." The "gallows laugh" (which results from a gallows transaction) means that if the client laughs while recounting a misfortune, and particularly if the other group

Group Process

Laughter

Doris: Any more ways I can get people to come down on me?

Irv: Be miserable about yourself.

Doris: How would I do that?

Irv: Well, that's a position. You simply take it, and then just communicate it to people.

Doris: How could I communicate my miserable position?

Irv: Sit slumped over. Have a long face.

Doris: Like this?

Irv: Yeah. Worse!! (Laughter)

Doris: Worse?? How's this?

Irv: Squinch in your toes a little. That's always a good thing.

Doris: I bet I look pretty miserable. (Laughter)

Therapist A: You gave Doris a lot of information about how to get yourself set up to get hit. Is this what you do?

Irv: Yeah, these are things I have been doing. (Laughter)

Other Modalities Used

TA Translation

Laughter

members join in the laughter, that misfortune is part of the castatrophe of the client's script. When the people around him laugh, they reinforce the payoff, hasten his doom, and prevent him from getting well. In second-order structural analysis, this is the Adult in the child.

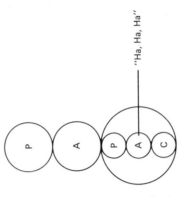

A third type of scripty laughter is the "He, He, He" laugh. This is the laugh of the Child when she is preparing to "pull a fast one." The Child thinks she is going to fool somebody, but usually ends up being the Victim instead. In second-order structural analysis, this is the Child in the Child.

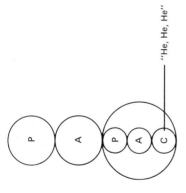

"He, He, He"

A second category of laughs is the healthy laugh. The first of this type is the "Ho, Ho, Ho" laugh. It is the Parent laughing at the Child's struggle to succeed. It lets the Child know there are rewards for non-scripty behavior.

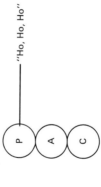

"Ho, Ho, Ho"

There is also a "Ha, Ha,Ha" laugh, which is a sign of the Adult's insight into how she has been conned by her own Parent.

Other Modalities Used

TA Translation

Laughter

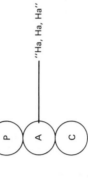

The last type of healthy laugh is known as "Wow, Wow." This is the Child's laugh of fun. "It only comes to people who are script-free or can put their scripts aside for the occasion. It is a spontaneous laugh of healthy people."

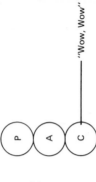

In the group, Irv's laughter was a healthy "Ha, Ha, Ha," coming from his Adult ego state. He was able to see how he set it up to have people kick him or leave him.

It is my thinking that all theories contribute to our understanding of people. Because people have different problems and encounter various difficulties in solving these problems, the more tools and knowledge a therapist has available, the better she is equipped to help her client get through the blocks which are keeping him from solving his problems. To ignore, or write off, other therapeutic models and their various techniques would be to deny that other models are effective in treating people.

REFERENCES

1. Perls, Frederick, *Gestalt Therapy Verbatim* (Lafayette, Calif.: Real People Press, 1969) p. 78.

2. Krumboltz, John D., and Carl E. Thoresen, *Behavioral Counseling: Cases and Techniques* (New York: Holt, Rinehart, & Winston, 1969), pp. 87–88.

3. Dustin, Richard, and Rickey George, *Action Counseling for Behavior Change* (New York: Intext Educational Publishers, 1973), p. 93.

4. Rogers, Carl, *Freedom to Learn* (Ohio: Charles E. Merrill, 1969), p. 133.

5. Moreno, J. L., *Psychodrama,* Vol. 1, 3rd ed. (New York: Beacon House, 1964).

6. Dusay, John M., "Script Rehearsal," *TA Bulletin* **9,** 36 (1970), p. 117.

7. Stuntz, Peter, "Multiple Chairs Technique," *TA Journal,* **3,** 2 (1973), pp. 29–32.

8. James, Muriel, and Dorothy Jongeward, *Born to Win: Transactional Analysis with Gestalt Experiments* (Reading, Mass.: Addison-Wesley, 1971) p. 8.

9. Satir, Virginia, *Conjoint Family Therapy.* (Palo Alto, Calif.: Science and Behavior Books, 1967).

10. Wolpe, Joseph, "The Practice of Behavior Therapy," in *Human Development: Selected Readings,* edited by Morris Haimowitz and Natalie Haimowitz (New York: Thomas Y. Crowell, 1973), p. 478.

11. Skinner, B. F., "Operant Behavior," *American Psychologist* (1963), pp. 503–515.

12. Yalom, Irving D., *The Theory and Practice of Group Psychotherapy* (New York: Basic Books, 1970), p. 348.

13. Rogers, Carl, *On Encounter Groups.* (New York: Harper & Row, 1970), p. 7.

14. Luft, Joseph, *Group Processes: An Introduction to Group Dynamics.* (Palo Alto, Calif.: National Press Books, 1963), p. 10.

15. Perls, *Verbatim,* p. 53.

16. Ibid., p. 38.

17. Harper, Robert A., *Psychoanalysis and Psychotherapy: 36 Systems* (Englewood Cliffs, N.J.: Prentice-Hall, 1959), pp. 122–123.

18. Berne, Eric, *What Do You Say After You Say Hello?* (New York: Grove, 1972), p. 58.

19. Davies, Frederick B., and Naomi E. Lohr, "Special Problems With the Use of Co-Therapists in Group Psychotherapy," pp. 143–157.

20. Heilfron, Marilyn, "Co-Therapy: The Relationship Between Therapists," *International Journal of Group Psychotherapy,* July 1969, pp. 366–379.

21. Berne, Eric, *Principles of Group Treatment* (New York: Oxford University Press, 1966), pp. 23–24.

22. Freud, Sigmund, "The Dynamics of the Transference," in *Freud: Therapy and Technique,* edited by Philip Rieff (New York: Collier Books, 1963), pp. 105–115.

23. Kupfer, David, and Morris Haimowitz, "Therapeutic Interventions—Part I, Rubberbands Now," *TA Journal* 1, 1 (1971), pp 10–16.

24. Frankl, V. E., "Paradoxical Intention: A Logotherapeutic Technique," *American Journal of Psychotherapy* 14 (1960), pp. 520–535.

25. Gerz, H. O., "The Treatment of the Phobic and the Obsessive-Compulsive Patient Using Paradoxical Intention," *Journal of Neuropsychiatry,* 3 (1962), pp. 375–387.

26. Freud, Sigmund, *Jokes and Their Relationship to the Unconscious* (1905) Standard Edition, Vol. 8 (New York: Norton, 1961).

27. Berne, *Hello,* pp. 337–339.

28. Luft, *Group Processes,* p. 28.

CHAPTER 19

Eric Berne
as group therapist:
a verbatim

ERIC BERNE

One of the last examples of TA as practiced by Eric Berne was released by him in the form of a tape made during group therapy at a closed ward of the McAuley Neuropsychiatric Institute at St. Mary's Hospital in San Francisco. This tape was transcribed and prepared for publication by the staff of *Roche Report: Frontiers of Hospital Psychiatry* and published in the May 15, 1970 issue, Vol. 7, No. 10, after several telephone consultations for clarification with Dr. Berne. A happy, smiling picture of Eric, one of the best we've seen, illuminates the piece.

The method he used here employs two groups of inpatients: a younger group and an older group. Following the observer method used by Berne in staff-patient conferences,* one group sits in the inner circle as "patients," while the other group sits behind as "observers," with the two groups alternating as "patients" and "observers." The session runs as a regular therapy group for an hour, then the groups change places and

From *Roche Report: Frontiers of Hospital Psychiatry* (Roche Laboratories, Nutley, N.J.) 7, 10 (1970). Reprinted by permission.

* Eric Berne, "Staff-Patient Staff Conference," *American Journal of Psychiatry* 125, 3 (1968), pp. 286–293 (included in this volume).

during the last half-hour the "observers" give their comments and reactions to what took place.

The therapy session transcription (names are fictitious):

Pearl: Dr. Berne, shouldn't we all be introduced before we start?

Dr. Berne: Not particularly.

Pearl: This is our dayroom. When strangers come—

Sam: We haven't time to waste.

Tom: Dumb ass! Every time Pearl says something, I know we're going off on a tangent.

Sam: Dr. Berne, why does a man have to stay in a hospital for eight weeks when he wants out?

Dr. Berne: What does he have to do to get in?

Sam: I just worked a little harder than the average.

Dr. Berne: What did you do that caused people to say you had to go to the hospital?

Sam: They got uncomfortable with the way I was acting. I thought I was acting pretty good.

Dr. Berne: How were you acting?

Sam: Working fast all day long. That's all.

Dr. Berne: Sounds all right to me. Why should someone put you in the hospital for that?

Sam: I've asked that question for three weeks.

Dr. Berne: What did you do to get in the hospital?

Sam: I asked for help. I said I needed a vacation in some far-off place. The doctor immediately said I had to go to the hospital.

Dr. Berne: What did you do to get in the hospital?

Sam: I was working 18 hours a day, sleeping four—having a grand time.

Dr. Berne: The reason you're here is because you don't answer questions. I still don't know why you're in the hospital.

Sam: I was losing control.

Dr. Berne: What did you do when you lost control?

Sam: Worked like two men.

Dr. Berne: Okay, that's why you're in the hospital.

Sam: How can they expect you to gain control when 18 people are telling you what to do?

Dr. Berne: I don't know.

Sam: I feel worse in the hospital than I did on the outside.

Emilio: Brother, find a way of talking to the doctor who signs the paper saying you're cured.

Ruth: You don't want to change, Sam.

Sam: Course not!

David: Dr. Berne, I've just been here a few days. I need a little help. I can't get along with people. I always have to have one guy I don't like, and when I quit not liking him, there's someone else I don't like. In the short time I've been here, I'm already mad at half the guys. I've been working on myself for 10 years and not getting anywhere.

Dr. Berne: What do you ask of life?

David: I'd like to be comfortable working with people—have a steady job so I could accomplish things, like buying a house. I can't look forward to anything now because I don't know from one day to the next if I'm going to blow up.

Pearl: You told me you get along with your mother and you work well with your mother and you work well with women.

Dr. Berne: How come you only want a little help?

David: I don't want a little help; I want help.

Dr. Berne: You said "a little help."

David: I've gone to a psychiatrist, and I've been in a state hospital twice. I found out that nobody can help you a whole lot. They give you a little bit, and you've got to do the rest yourself.

Dr. Berne: You're not really thinking. All you're doing is saying, "Oh, the tragedy of it." How come you only want a little help? You're really saying you don't want to get better.

Pearl: You told me last week the Child part of you didn't want to get better and the Adult part of you did. Don't forget a part of your personality is the free Child. You need to learn to let the free Child express himself.

Maria: What do you mean by free Child?

Pearl: Dr. Berne explained it in his book. In every adult there's a free Child who wants to run on the beach, make love, enjoy things, be happy.

Dr. Berne: Okay, Pearl. I'd like to talk about a few things with David. What did your parents tell you about life?

David: I don't know.

Dr. Berne: Where's your father?

David: I don't know. My mother and father were divorced when I was 6, and she married again. I never talked to my stepfather. He's so stern.

Dr. Berne: What did your mother tell you about life when you were young?

David: I don't know. She wanted me to be a lawyer or something. I stayed with her parents for a while after the divorce. My grandfather was a very grouchy man.

Dr. Berne: What did he say to you when he was grouchy?

David: "Goddamn you, kid, I'll take a razor strap to you if you don't do those dishes." He scared me. My stepfather scared me too.

Dr. Berne: What did your stepfather say to you?

David: Him! All he tried to do was make money.

Dr. Berne: What did he say to you?

David: "If you don't shut up, I'll knock your head off." He gave me an inferiority complex. I can't walk down the street without fear. I haven't confidence.

Dr. Berne: Okay. What did your grandfather say?

David: He said he'd beat hell out of me, that I'd never amount to anything.

Dr. Berne: How did he say it?

David: I think he said "that kid." I don't like him.

Dr. Berne: How about answering my questions? What did your grandfather say to you?

David: He said he'd knock the hell out of me if I didn't straighten up and do the dishes.

Dr. Berne: And what did your stepfather say?

David: "I'll knock your head off."

Dr. Berne: What did your mother say?

David: She never said anything. She went along with my stepfather. But when it came to doing anything, I had to ask her.

Dr. Berne: What did she say when you asked her?

David: She wouldn't let me go. Like going in a boat. She was afraid I'd drown. She was a worrier. I sometimes think I picked up worrying from her.

Ruth: Do you lack confidence in yourself?

Dr. Berne: Why did you ask David if he lacked confidence in himself?

Ruth: Because I lack it myself.

Dr. Berne: He already said he lacked confidence; so why did you ask him, and why do you want to know whether he lacks it or not?

Ruth: Because I like support from other people.

Dr. Berne: Why is it supportive when he says he lacks confidence?

Ruth: It's good to know someone else lacks confidence. It makes me feel better.

Pearl: David, does it make you feel more comfortable?

Dr. Berne: Hold it, Pearl. I want to get back to David. What you've really been saying, David, is that you don't want to get better. If you can find a few people who feel like you do, you won't have to get better.

Ruth: That doesn't make sense to me.

Dr. Berne: Why? You said it makes you feel better; if someone else lacks confidence, it makes you more comfortable.

Ruth: I follow you.

Dr. Berne (to Tom): Which of your parents doesn't like you?

Tom: My father. He thinks I'm stupid. He calls me a dumb ass kid.

Dr. Berne: Okay. So why are you like your father?

Tom: I'm not like him!

Dr. Berne: When we first started this session, you called Pearl a dumb ass, and you've muttered it each time she said something.

Tom: She is a dumb ass!

Dr. Berne: I don't know about that. *(Laughter)* The point is you say the same thing to her that your father says to you.

Tom: It's grown into me, I guess.

Dr. Berne: Is that the way you want it?

Tom: No.

Dr. Berne: What are you going to do about it?

Tom: Have patience with people.

Dr. Berne: Is that what your mother says? Have patience with people?

Tom: Yeah.

Dr. Berne: Have you any thoughts of your own—thoughts that aren't your mother's or father's?

Tom: Sure I do!

Dr. Berne: Let's hear one. When you talk to Pearl, it's your father. When you say, "Have patience," it's your mother. Now what do you say?

Tom: Whew! It's not one way or another. You got to find a happy medium.

Dr. Berne: That's your mother too. Can you say something of your own?

Tom: I'm not going to say Pearl is stupid anymore. I'll just keep it all inside of me.

Ruth: You use the same technique with us. When you don't want to be bothered, you clam up. That's because you're trying to fight society and its institutions.

Dr. Berne: I don't blame you for fighting institutions, because you have two institutions in your head telling you what to do all the time. I still haven't heard you say something that you think independently of your father or mother.

Tom: I want to get out of this place.

Dr. Berne: Okay. That's a beginning. Can you think of something else?

Tom: I want to be liked by everyone.

Maria: I can understand that you want to be liked by people. I do too. But sometimes we go at it the wrong way. To tell girls you'll get a knife and go after them, that's sadistic.

Tom: You think I'd chicken out? Do you know how many birds I've killed? I used to stick birds in the washing machine and then put it on spin.

Maria: I don't want to talk to you. You're a maniac. You're sick. It's good you're in the hospital. I want out, but I'm glad you're in. *(Laughter)*

Emilio: I have a gun, and sometimes I do things that are illegal. The other day I shot blackbirds. You know what I made? Spaghetti sauce.

Sam: What's your problem, Emilio?

Emilio: God knows.

Pearl: You're not coming on straight. They wouldn't let you go into the kitchen because you were on suicide precaution.

David: What put you in the hospital?

Emilio: I came to be circumcised. It's a nuisance to have to wash that thing every day. What if you don't have any water?

Sam: You told me you couldn't sleep.

Emilio: Because there's a Why? in my head. Why doesn't Pope Paul recognize us properly? I have kids. And maybe, when they grow up, they'll get married and divorced. They say in heaven you sit in a circle, and I want my kids to sit in the circle with me.

Dr. Berne: What crazy thing did you do to get in the hospital?

Emilio: I went to the emergency room.

Dr. Berne: To get a circumcision?

Emilio: Yes. And the doctor asked me why I wanted to do it and I told him—

Dr. Berne: Okay. It would take a lot of time to give all the details. Let's hear from people who haven't said anything (*turning to Mary*).

Mary: I didn't do anything. I just don't think right.

Dr. Berne: What were you thinking?

Mary: I didn't want to go places.

Pearl: There is something wrong with you, Mary. You went to college and trained to be a teacher, and then you were afraid to go out in the world. You stayed at home to be protected by your mother and you worked in your father's office.

Dr. Berne: You don't go to the hospital because you work for your father.

Mary: I told him I couldn't take it anymore. I blew. I was afraid I'd kill myself.

Dr. Berne: Anyone else?

Mary: Only my parents. I took a room by myself, but it was too lonely; so I went back home, and I—I—I (*becomes incoherent*).

Dr. Berne: Okay. (*To Bob*) You haven't said anything.

Bob: I set my room on fire.

Dr. Berne: Why did you do that?

Bob: I thought the world was coming to an end, and I might as well as start it off.

Dr. Berne: Why were you in a hurry to end the world? Why can't you let it happen? Why do you have to help?

Bob: I don't know.

Dr. Berne: Is there someone you want to die?

Bob: I guess myself.

Dr. Berne: There must be somebody else you want to knock off if you're set on ending the whole world.

Pearl: He smokes marijuana.

Dr. Berne: Do you know why you wanted to end the world?

Bob: I just wanted everything to be over.

Dr. Berne: What did your parents say to you when you were young? Do you remember anything they said?

Bob: No.

Dr. Berne: Do you still want to get it over with?

Bob: No.

Dr. Berne: Okay. I guess that's all we have time for today. Will the groups change places now? (*The younger patients move to the outer circle. The older patients take the chairs in the inner circle for their discussion.*)

Dr. Berne: If you can only talk about your own troubles, you should do it here. You were supposed to be listening to what went on. You may have something to say about the younger patients.

Male Patient Observer: I was in a group with Pearl at one time. She just doesn't want to be an adult. Emilio is terribly hung up on religion.

Dr. Berne: We're here to help people get better. What do you think we ought to do to help Pearl?

Male Patient: Staff and patients should try to make Pearl realize that she's an adult. Otherwise she'll be in institutions the rest of her life.

Dr. Berne: What about Emilio? How would you help him?

Male Patient: I have no idea. (*Dr. Berne asks the older patients for ideas on helping the younger patients. Except for one woman, the others have no comments.*)

Female Patient: Pearl should stop having babies. Everytime she has one she lands in here. She's had her share, and so have I. We both need to get some joy out of life.

Dr. Berne: What do you think about Mary?

Female Patient: I'm fond of her. Maria has beautiful children, and they need a father. I told her so. I told her she should marry a man with money. And that boy Tom! Why, he ought to go to school and obey his parents. I obeyed mine. Till I was 18 I didn't open my mouth.

Dr. Berne: Okay. Any others? If not, let's hear what the staff has to say.

Nurse 1: Pearl is really better now. But she doesn't listen. She only picks up a word or two so she can interrupt. She tried to cut you off when you were talking to patients.

Dr Berne: That's one of the jobs of a group therapist—to keep patients from cutting others off.

Nurse 2: Most patients were angry, and they went at each other in an angry way, but they rarely said why they were angry. It would be better if they could come out straight and say what it is about a person that's making them angry. Take Emilio. He keeps interrupting but he doesn't say what is angering him or why.

Dr. Berne: If he did, who would it help? The patient or Emilio?

Nurse 2: Both. Emilio could hear how he was coming along in the group, and the patient would be helped too.

Nurse 3: I was disappointed that those in the outer circle who were really listening didn't feel comfortable enough to say how they felt about what happened.

Nurse 4: I got the feeling that Pearl wanted to become the leader of the group.

Nurse 5: This is the first time I heard David speak about his father or grandfather. It was as if he was making a bridge to his difficulties.

Nurse 6: I was interested in your observation that Ruth can't come out and say she feels this way until someone says they feel this way.

Charles Berger, M.D. (Second-year Resident): Some patients cannot stand to see others get well. Pearl tried to sabotage anything going on. Ruth was more subtle about it. Emilio would come out with a lot of trash anytime you were making progress with a patient.

Dr. Berne: Any other staff people? No?

Dr. Berne's summary follows:

Then let me summarize a few things in this very complicated deal. The first thing that interested me was that when everybody was sitting close to each other in a circle they talked more to each other than when they sat at a table at other sessions. I think the idea of having other patients listen is rather good. I can't say the listeners contributed very much, but I think if we did this regularly they would start thinking. (*Note: This is strongly borne out by later experiences.* E.B.)

As far as the inner group is concerned: Tom, who likes to cut and kill birds, only repeats what his mother and father say. There must be an Adult in Tom. Try to get to the Adult. You could wander off with him, trying to find out why he wants to shoot birds, but it would be a waste of time. It would take years. So instead of analyzing, try to get to the Adult in Tom. Then he might start to get better.

The same thing applies to Ruth. I was interested in the maneuver with David. When he said he felt inferior, she asked him if he ever felt inferior. One thing she was after was to be comfortable while feeling inferior. But there's something else there I don't understand. Whatever it is, it's very pervasive. She's playing some game, and she's doing it 90% of the time.

I think Pearl's Child is out so much that you have to make the Child feel better before she can be Adult. That's the way to approach her.

About Sam, who wants out. Don't bother him. Let him rest for one or two weeks. Some people come to the hospital for a vacation. They will do all kinds of things to get in a hospital. They probably want a vacation, and they are entitled to one.

As for David, he probably has said all the things he said here when he was in a state hospital. He probably was told he was a masochist, had homosexual tendencies and so forth, and it didn't do any good. All the psychodynamic formulations are irrelevant in his case. The key thing he said here was that he wanted a little help. When he say he wants a lot of help, you'll be in a much better position to help him. That would mean he really wants to get well.

That's about all we have time for. Next week we'll reverse the circles and see what happens.

PART 5

special applications
of TA

Contributors

**A TRANSACTIONAL APPROACH
TO SUICIDE PREVENTION**
James D. Orten, A.C.S.W.

FAMILY THERAPY WITH TA
John James, M.A.

**CURING SEXUAL DYSFUNCTIONS
IN WOMEN WITH TA**
Lillian O'Hearne, M.D.

THE NURSE AS THERAPIST
Ann Chandler, R.N.

CURING "MORAL MASOCHISM"
David E. Kemp, Ph.D.

**SUPPLEMENTAL PARENTING OF
THE *KICK ME* PLAYER**
Michael Breen, Ph.D.

**STROKING THE REBELLIOUS
CHILD: AN ASPECT OF
MANAGING RESISTANCE**
Robert C. Drye, M.D.

A TA APPROACH TO DREAMS
Arthur Samuels, M.D.

**INSIGHT FOR THE SIGHTLESS:
A TA GROUP FOR THE BLIND**
Solveig H. Thomson, Ph.D.

**THERAPEUTIC EDUCATION
WITH OLDER ADULTS**
Elizabeth Fielding, M.A.

**REDECISION HOUSE: A PROGRAM
FOR DRUG TREATMENT**
Keong Chye Cheah, M.D.
William R. Barling, M.S.S.W.

**SOCIAL *RAPO*:
DESCRIPTION AND CURE**
Robert Zechnich, M.D.

CONFUSION RACKETS
Harry S. Boyd, Ph.D.

**EGO STATES AND STROKING IN
THE CHILDBIRTH EXPERIENCE**
Margot Edwards, R.N.

**THE FEMALE
JUVENILE DELINQUENT**
Mary Bentley Abu-Saba, B.A.

**TA IN VOCATIONAL
REHABILITATION:
THE REHABILITATION CHECKLIST**
John Mackey, M.S.

TREATING MALE BANAL SCRIPTS
J. Herbert Hamsher, Ph.D.

CHAPTER 20

a transactional approach
to suicide prevention

JAMES D. ORTEN

Suicide has been a significant cause of death for many years, not only in the United States but in most industrialized nations. Only recently, however, have the mental health disciplines accepted reduction of suicides as a professional responsibility. The reason behind this reluctance was probably not indifference to the problem, but because there was and is no really viable technology for interrupting suicidal patterns.

Sociological theories of suicide usually focus on the degree of support which the individual receives from the large society. Alienation is a key concept in such theories (Durkheim, 1951). Most psychological theories seek to explain the meaning of the suicidal act for significant others in the individual's life. Suicide is thought to be an expression of anger and retribution against those who were expected to fulfill needs but did not do so (Noyes & Kolb, 1963).

While both of the above approaches seem valid, neither gets to the point of why any particular person decides to take his life. An even more serious defi-

From *Clinical Social Work Journal* **2**, 1 (1974), pp. 57–63. Reprinted by permission.

ciency for mental health practitioners is that they offer only vague suggestions for how to deal with a suicidal client. Why, for example, does one person who is angry over unfulfilled needs decide to kill himself, while another commits homicide, and a third sublimates his anger into making money? As sympathetic as the treatment practitioner may be toward reducing alienation in society, his immediate need is for knowledge and techniques which will help him keep the person on the other end of the telephone line from coming to a violent end.

The purpose of this paper is to explain the phenomenon of suicide through Transactional Analysis (Berne, 1961; Harris, 1967; James & Jongeward, 1971), to classify traditional methods of intervention according to the transactions involved, and to suggest a more effective method of interrupting suicidal patterns. The approach outlined below is especially designed for use in crisis intervention by phone where time and distance make unique requirements. It is useful, however, in office consultations and with clients who are not as intensely suicidal as crisis-center callers are assumed to be. The hypotheses presented here speak specifically to suicides which grow out of depressions and do not apply to those which are culturally inspired (e.g., the protest immolations in Vietnam) or those which arise from organic damage or toxic conditions which produce idiosyncratic behavior.

THE ORIGIN OF SUICIDE

Suicide is the act of a miserable and helpless Child. Transactional Analysis postulates a personality consisting of three parts: Parent, Adult, and Child. These "ego states" are organized sets of feelings, perspectives for viewing the world, and congruent behavior patterns into which one shifts under certain stimuli. Since each is the whole person at the time one is in it, they are not comparable to the Freudian id, ego, and superego. In the Child, for example, one not only assesses his strengths as he did when a child but his view of the world and his adaptive behaviors are those which he possessed when he was a two-foot person in a six-foot world.

Locating the origin of the phenomenon within the Child part of the personality is based on the fact that it is the Child which feels despair and hopelessness. Had the Adult been in control he would have dealt realistically with the situation and Parent control would have furnished a constricting but less deadly counterscript (Steiner, 1966). The prototype is the latency aged child who feigns death to test his parent's love or cause them to change a situation that is painful to him. One of the best known examples, and one every young person identifies with, is described in *The Adventures of Tom Sawyer*. Tom allowed his Aunt Polly to think he had drowned, surreptitiously attended his own funeral, and delighted in the expressions of love he observed.

While the purpose of the self-destructive act is not at issue here, I believe it to be relief of the Child's pain rather than punishment to those causing it. Grudges are not held in the Child (that is a Parent activity); he simply wants what is pleasant and good for himself. The Parent of the suicidal subject might wish to punish others but the Child, who is in control of the depression, kills himself because he is hurting and perceives no other means of relief. In this respect all suicides are similar to that of the terminal cancer patient who is in unbearable pain and realistically sees no other way out.

This postulation does not preclude the idea of scripting to a tragic end. Those who study troubled persons regularly see individuals whose lives are moving dramatically toward a violent conclusion. Transactional analysts refer to such persons as following a life script. A tragic script, however, is produced for and played out by a miserable Child. Prototypic experiences, such as the one described above, may be seen as spontaneous "script rehearsals" for the real drama which will come later. The frequency and intensity of these early experiences are reliable indicators of the degree to which one has accepted a tragic script and thus the seriousness of his candidacy for suicide. I remember a sad-eyed little boy of seven who had already progressed from what his parents took as an amusing attempt to hang himself from a doorknob, to setting his bed afire, to running in front of speeding automobiles.

Professional handling of suicidal clients as well as laymen's reactions to threats of suicide are classifiable according to the directions of the transactions involved. (Transactions are analyzed by observing which part of the initiator's personality generates the stimulus and which part of the recipient's personality sends the response.) The first group described under the colloquial headings (TA emphasizes the use of down-to-earth language, see Orten, 1972) below consists of the principal traditional approaches distilled from the professional literature on suicide and conversations with practitioners. These approaches may be used in combination but one is often emphasized depending on the particular inclination of the therapist. Those described in the second group are common reactions of naive or hostile laymen.

PROFESSIONAL INTERVENTION

"Somebody loves you" is the message underlying most professional attempts at suicide intervention. This message may be stated openly, couched in phrases such as "human worth," or conveyed in behavior such as a willingness to talk with the client at any hour, but the implication is the same. It is most frequently described in the literature under the heading of "Reassurance and Support" (Bellak & Small, 1965, p. 62). Whatever the particular means of communication the design is to convince the client's wretched Child that "somebody cares whether he lives or dies" (Stengel, 1962, p. 726).

"Oh promise me" is a common approach in crisis call centers where the person answering the telephone serves principally as a bridge to get the caller in to talk (Feiden, 1970). The goal is to build enough of a relationship by phone to extract a promise that the client will not harm himself until he has talked with the therapist in person, usually the following day.

"I won't let you do it" is implied when the therapist tells the client he will hospitalize him, break confidentiality to alert others, or take various protective measures if he thinks the client intends to kill himself. To a lesser degree the same message is conveyed in a prescription of drugs for the suicidal patient.

All of the above approaches are based on transactions which originate from the therapist's Nurturing Parent and are directed to the client's Adapted Child. They are largely ineffective and one should logically expect them to be. One whose Child has accepted a script which calls for killing himself can hardly be expected to respond to contradictory Parent messages from the therapist, at least on such brief exposure. Promises extracted from one who is living in his Child will frequently go unkept for the Child is skilled at manipulation, and a therapist who takes the responsibility for not letting such a person commit suicide is setting himself up to be outwitted. More empirical evidence (and more poignant) of the ineffectiveness of conventional approaches is contained in a follow-up study of crisis callers in the city of Chicago (Wilkins, 1970). The suicide rate in that study population was approximately 75 times the national average. The picture is even more bleak if one considers that the above figures do not include several "unexplained deaths," "equivocal" cases, and "suicides by alcohol." The practice of staffing crisis call centers with volunteers is a tacit acknowledgment that ordinary professional approaches have little more to offer than kindness and common sense.

LAY RESPONSES

"I dare you to do it." The literature reflects a historic recognition of the fact that some people react with hostility when confronted with the prospect of another's suicide. This response is a part of the not uncommon attitude that those who try to kill themselves don't deserve to live anyway. If one accepts the premise it becomes logical to challenge the would-be suicide to either "put up or shut up." Those trained in human behavior should be expected not to respond in this manner. Unfortunately not all those who serve suicidal patients are so trained. Hospital emergency rooms and the medical and paramedical professions in general seem to acquire a number who think anger is an appropriate reaction to suicidal gestures. A similar attitude is observed in the treatment of drunks, drug users, unwed mothers (Levin, 1969), charity patients and other "undeserving" persons. The dynamics behind *I Dare You* transactions are closely related to those in the game *Now I've Got You, You S.O.B.* (Berne, 1964). In the latter game the supposedly misbehaving Child is caught and the aim is to punish him. In the former the Child is suspected and the goal is to tease out and expose him.

I Dare You transactions emanate from the initiator's Angry Parent and are directed to the receiver's Adapted Child. They are especially dangerous because they allow the respondent's Angry Parent to combine with and strengthen the subject's own, which may be sufficient to push him over the brink. The CBS movie "Hot Line" gave an excellent portrayal of the moves in such an encounter. The caller (to a crisis center) insisted he had a gun to his head and was prepared to use it. During a long, tense conversation the volunteer became angry and his shouts of "Go ahead, I dare you," were followed by a pistol shot on the other end of the line. This set of transactions occurs in a variety of less tragic settings and with a degree of frequency which probably entitles it to the status of a game.

The psychoanalytic explanation of such hostile reactions is that the sight of another's attempt is threatening because it encourages one's own repressed suicidal impulses to become conscious. While such a postulation is not amenable to an empirical test, the writer sees no evidence that *I Dare You* players are threatened by suicidal impulses. They seem rather threatened by any frank expression of Child, or put in common terms, emotion. Their judgmental attitude clearly indicates they live in their Parent and thus would likely be as displeased at an overt expression of the happy Natural Child. Such responses come from a cynical person who has subdued his own Child at great cost and is resentful of others who have not paid a similar price.

Rotav (1970) studied the "characterological types" of the physicians who had responsibility for 20 persons who committed in-hospital suicides. The behavior of those physicians described respectively as "benevolent" and "aggressive" appears to conform to what we have labeled here the Nurturing Parent and the Angry Parent approaches. The physicians in these categories were responsible for more than a random share of the suicides studied. Rotav's study supports the thesis of this paper that neither of the above approaches are effective, though the latter is more destructive than the former. Speaking specifically of the "aggressive" ones he said, "This type of physician can be quite destructive if allowed to manage his ward without supervision" (p. 226).

"The good-humor man" is a kind-hearted but naive attempt to cheer up the suicidal person. Some laymen respond to the depression in the suicidal subject by trying to make him laugh. If the effort is an honest attempt to convince him his troubles are not as bad as they seem (as opposed to teasing), it may be described as a healthy Natural Child reaching out to a weak and troubled one. It is seldom effective and even somewhat dangerous for the suicidal person's Natural Child is too weak to respond and the humor can easily be mistaken for disparagement.

TA AND SUICIDE

Transactional theory provides techniques for handling suicide calls which have not been fully exploited, specifically in the area of shifting clients from the Child state to Adult. Engaging the Adult is imperative since only the client's Adult, not the therapist's Parent, can protect his hurting Child. The Parent-Child exchanges in conventional practice tend to reinforce the process which has brought the client to where he is. Even reassurance should be a supplementary feature of the intervention and not the main thrust.

Two specifically Adult activities are seeking information and giving it. Since the caller will not likely be seeking information the counselor's surest means of engaging his client's Adult is by eliciting it, which can be done by asking questions which require specific, straight, and nonthreatening answers. What is being proposed is that the therapist assume he is speaking with the caller's Child and begin with a series of questions designed solely to shift the client to the Adult state. "Nonthreatening" means unrelated to the problems causing the depression.

A premature rush into consideration of a client's problems strengthens his Child position and makes moving him from it later more difficult. It also starts the counselor off on an insecure footing for he does not know the caller as a person. A counselor must prepare himself and his client for problem discussion with care equal to that with which the surgeon prepares himself and his patient for an incision. In the writer's experience most clients take this approach as evincing personal interest in them, as opposed to commitment to an ideology that life is good and therefore suicide is bad.

Attention must be given to see that the caller does not take the initial conversation as an indication the counselor is not concerned about his problems. This can be accomplished by a lead-in statement such as, "I'd like to get to know you as a person. Can we do that before we go on to talk about why you want to kill yourself?" This should be followed by specific questions, e.g., "How old are you?" which will not be directly related to his problems and will facilitate straight answers from the Adult. One who uses this technique should have a list of such questions to use as a reference. Questions regarding the client's physical person, occupation, and the like, are appropriate. When the counselor knows the client, questions such as, "Where are you now?" "What are you wearing?" etc. can be substituted. General leads such as "Tell me about . . ." should be avoided in this initial phase. The questioning process should be deliberate and unhurried. The client should be allowed to elaborate his answers but only to the extent that the conversation does not drift into a premature and depressive discussion of problems. Whenever the dialogue gets weary it should be immediately interrupted with a specific question on a nonproblem subject. The counselor's own ego state is quite important. An overly solicitious tone, fear, criticism or other indications of Parent or Child on the part of the therapist will be detrimental.

During this initial process the counselor should be alert to the client's tone, phrasing, and the other characteristics which reveal particular ego states. When these indicators signify the client is established in the Adult a decision can be made whether to proceed into a direct discussion of his problems. Many clients experience a significant degree of relief from this process alone and it is not always wise to carry the conversation immediately to a deeper level. Their relief is valid and understandable for in the Adult (where they probably haven't been lately) they not only feel better, they see the world differently and are more capable of dealing with it. They have gotten locked in the Child by their own feelings and others' reaction to them. A naive dismissal of the caller the moment he is ensconced in the Adult ego state is not what is suggested. If, however, he can make a commitment to see you the following day, make with you plans to constructively spend the intervening time, and demonstrate a knowledge of how to get to your office, all from the Adult, then he will survive and probably be at your office at the appointed time.

If a decision is made to do problem discussion immediately the counselor should be alert to signals the caller is slipping back into Child. When this happens, as it probably will, the process above should be repeated to recontact the client's Adult. One can do this without offending the caller by suggesting, "Our discussion of this subject seems to be depressing you. Let's go on to other things for the moment and come back to this point later." This procedure works equally well in office consultations.

Transactional Analysis has a unique contribution to make in suicide prevention. More than other personality theories TA provides the concepts for explaining "who" is hurting in a depressed person and "who" in him can protect him from that hurt. (There is, for example, no comparable concept in psychoanalytic theory which provides for shifting one from id to ego.) Traditional methods of intervention have utilized chiefly the Good Parent approach which provides either nurturance or protection. The argument here is not that such ingredients are never needed but rather that they should not be the principal feature of the intervention. The real thrust should be to move the client to an ego state which will not only make him feel better but will also provide a mental perspective which will enable him to work realistically on his problems. Transactional Analysis provides the basis for an approach which is considerably more deliberate and, in the writer's experience, more effective.

REFERENCES

Bellak, L., and L. Small, *Emergency Psychotherapy and Brief Psychotherapy* (New York: Grune & Stratton, 1965), p. 62.

Berne, E., *Transactional Analysis in Psychotherapy* (New York: Grove, 1961).

Berne, E., *Games People Play* (New York: Grove, 1964).

Durkheim, E., *Suicide: A Study in Sociology,* trans. by J. Spaulding and G. Simpson (New York: Free Press, 1951).

Feiden, E., "One Year's Experience With A Suicide Prevention Service," *Social Work* 15, 3 (1970), pp. 26–32.

Harris, T., *I'm OK—You're OK* (New York: Harper & Row, 1967).

James, M., and D. Jongeward, *Born to Win* (Reading, Mass.: Addison-Wesley, 1971).

Levin, P., "Games Nurses Play," *TA Bulletin* 8, 32 (1969), pp. 99–100.

Noyes, A., and L. Kolb, *Modern Clinical Psychiatry,* 6th ed. (Philadelphia: W. B. Saunders, 1963).

Orten, J., "Contributions To Stroke Vocabulary," *TA Journal* 2, 3 (1972), pp. 104–106.

Rotav, M., "Death By Suicide In The Hospital," *American Journal of Psychotherapy* 24, 2 (1970), pp. 216–227.

Steiner, C., "Script and Counter-script," *TA Bulletin* 5, 18 (1966), pp. 133–136.

Stengel, E., "Recent Research Into Suicide and Attempted Suicide," *American Journal of Psychiatry,* 118, 8 (1962), pp. 725–729.

Wilkins, J., "A Follow-Up Study of Those Who Called A Suicide Prevention Center," *American Journal of Psychiatry* 127, 2 (1970), pp. 155–161.

CHAPTER 21

family therapy
with TA

JOHN JAMES

A RATIONALE FOR FAMILY THERAPY

I believe it's a miracle that we continue to wake up each morning and can say hello to the green grass, the world, and other human beings. Many families get into a rut where they become overly focused on their inadequacies or inconsistencies and ignore the miracle of the moment which is possible and available. Possibly the real task of the family therapist is to assist persons in regaining their vision so they can see through the fog of everyday life, so they can "see the coffee-pot as it really is," and so they can gain a sense of awe when they see a tree, the stars, or another person struggling to find meaning, friends, and joy.

The decision to seek out family therapy is often made because one or more members of the family still have a vision of what a happy family can be. This vision is often distorted by specific problems.

Common problems that affect families include childrens' misbehaving, being friendless, getting low grades, using drugs, fighting with siblings or parents, not doing the chores, etc. When a school, clergyman, or court recommend family counseling, many parents who want their children to change are willing to at least initiate the process. Sometimes parents do this on their own, feeling unable to continue living with the battles, arguing, door-slamming, tears, sulking, snide remarks, complaining, boredom, overdependence, or rebelliousness. They seek family therapy for self-preservation, often hoping a miracle will occur.

Who Comes

The decision to start family therapy is seldom unanimous. Often one or more family members feel as if they're being dragged in, forced to come, or conned into participating. They may resent "being made" to join in, or they may not see themselves as a part of "the problem," or they may be scared of what might happen, or they may feel they don't have time, or they may think psychology is "a lot of baloney," or their work schedule may interfere with attending, or they may be separated or divorced.

After strongly encouraging the entire family to attend, if someone is not going to participate, I meet with those who *are* willing to come. I don't want others to suffer because of one person. If all goes well, family growth often acts as a magnet to uninvolved family members and attracts them to therapy.

If a parent calls and asks me to meet with a *child*, I do so only if at least one parent attends. It would be counter-therapeutic to accept parents' inclinations to see a particular child as the "identified patient."[1] However, if *teenagers* ask for the initial appointment, I will meet with them. I do this because such requests are unusual and I respect people who are trying to make sense of their lives regardless of their parents' commitments.

Hot Potatoes And Protection

The trouble or predicaments children get into are often similar to the trouble and predicaments their parents got into when they were young. Berne notes that "every parent is openly or secretly delighted when his children respond the way he does, even when they follow his worst characteristics."[2] These "worst characteristics" are often played out, when things go wrong, in Rescuer, Victim, or Persecutor roles. Thus parents may, without awareness, encourage their children to play the interlocking roles. Thus they toss their children the "hot-potatoes" they don't want,[3] which are the problems they haven't solved for themselves.

A therapist needs to be alert for hot potatoes, to discourage vicarious living on the parents' part, and to encourage more self-chosen behavior on the kids' part. Therefore, one of the first issues confronting a therapist is who's coming and for what reasons; who is blaming whom?[4]

It is important to provide protection for any person not participating, and this can be done by encouraging members to accept responsibility for their part in the family turmoils rather than avoid their needs and energies by scapegoating. This protection is a way to maintain the therapeutic environment so the nonparticipating family member(s) may sometime feel interested and safe enough to attend future sessions. It's also necessary to provide this sort of protection because underneath all the "garbage," family members usually love each other and feel some resentment when others are not protected.

The Drive For Health

Protection is possible if five principles are considered when thinking about individual family members, family systems, family stroking patterns, and therapists' interventions in the family processes. These principles are:

1. *Families are groups of related individuals.* As Darwin noticed, individuals strive for both their own survival *and* for the survival of the species. This is similar to the way individuals in families operate. Each person is trying to make sense of his or her own life while living with and caring for the others (even if the caring is not obvious).

2. *The individual is striving for health.* This is a belief which many psychotherapists support and Berne held it to be one of his three basic "therapeutic slogans," stating *"Vis medicatrix naturae*—the patient has a built-in drive for health, mental as well as physical."[5,6]

3. *Each person is operating with all the knowledge* (visceral, intellectual, and emotional) *that he or she has.* We are all trying to make the most sense of life that we can. We're acting on the basis of all the information we have at each moment. We're doing the best we know how on the data we've got, and if we had proof that we could live more successfully and knew how to safely do it, we would make the changes required.

We are all acting on what we figure is true. Sometimes our information and perceptions are inaccurate. Sometimes our Adult ego states are contaminated by Parent opinions or Child feelings and/or decisions. Even so, we are all acting on the basis of what we believe to be true, and we are acting as best we can at each moment.

4. *Each family also strives for health,* operating on the best knowledge it has. The question is: What is a healthy family? How do you recognize a healthy family? For example, is it advantageous or not for parents to insist a child go on a family outing, to worry about what time their kids get home, or to be more involved in their own lives than the lives of their children? What are the fine lines of health vs. nonhealth?

Albert Einstein invested his energy in discovering new scientific theories which affected all mankind's perceptions of the universe and its workings.

But his children and first wife left him because of his apparent lack of interest in them.[7] Would he be called healthy or not?

Beniamino Bufano, the famous Italian-San Franciscan sculptor, also ignored his family for his craft.[8] Does this mean that Bufano was a failure? What kind of therapy would seem indicated for such a recluse? Who knows which value has the most merit for his life? Who is to judge—Bufano, his art critics, his daughter, his therapist (if he had one), his confidant (if there was one), his ancestors or benefactors or . . .[9]

5. *Any family is a system.* One way to think about a family system is to recognize the various relationships. Like a pebble thrown into a pond, whatever influences the individual will affect each of the other relationships.

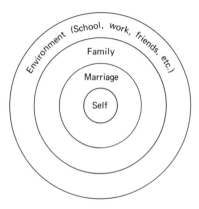

If a person does something unexpected, others in the family react in response to the change. Families tend to seek a homeostatic balance,[10] whether its healthy or not. To experience your own family system, recall a time when you came home, and someone in your family was upset. Remember how that upsetness filtered through to the other family members. Berne noted that the family system could be analyzed as a simple group (A) or as a complex group (B).[11]

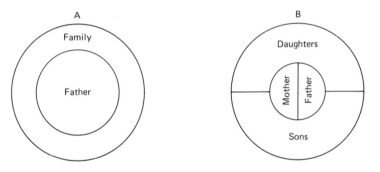

Berne remarks:

> In everyday life, a family may act at times as a simple group in which the father represents the leadership and the others the indifferentiated membership, and on other occasions as a compound or complex group in which the group leadership is split between the father and the mother, and the sons and daughters or older and younger children must be differentiated in the membership. . . A family that acts like a true complex group with organized splits in the membership is probably in trouble.[12]

Families can be helped to look at the splits and pressures by using the following diagram to represent each individual:

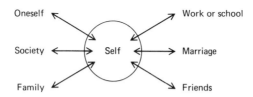

Each person experiences needs and demands in each of the "spheres" of his or her life. For example, a woman may experience expectations (both internally and externally programmed) to be a leader at the office, a nurturing mother at home, a sexy spouse in bed, an enjoyable and energetic person with friends, an involved church leader or political driver in the community, and a growing and learning and relaxing person in her own right.

People experience different degrees of success and satisfaction in the various spheres. For example, a man may experience a sense of accomplishment and pride at work but feel inadequate as a father and unloved as a husband. A teenage girl might feel popular with friends, yet unable to please her parents. Naturally, people want to invest their energy in those spheres of their lives in which they experience the greatest success.

The Therapist's Response to the Drive for Health

Therapists, being people, use all three ego states. From the Parent ego state they may give the kind of advice that they once received from their parents. A therapist who was told in childhood, "You should have done it the way I told you the first time," may feel defensive and get into an authoritarian blaming game. A therapist told, "If you don't succeed at first, try, try again," may feel ready to explore new options in treatment. The therapist who was told, "When the going gets tough, the tough get going," is likely to expect families to see crises as challenges and to discount their feelings of sadness, confusion, panic, or despair. The therapist who often heard, "Why can't you do it like your brother," may use the same words with siblings. A therapist who was told, "Don't worry about it, things will turn out all right in the long run," is likely to wait till the impasse is resolved with the expectation that any crisis can be weathered. And the therapist who was told in childhood, "You can figure it out, but if you need any help I'll be available," would probably spend time thinking the issue through, considering what the facts and options are, do any research which might be useful, and if still unsure or unsuccessful, meet with his or her clinical consultant.

The therapist's Adult has the obvious task of being the executive of the therapist's personality during the treatment session. The therapist's Adult operates with the theoretical data it knows, the internal reactions the therapist experiences in himself or herself, and the external information and behavior the therapist observes in the family. The therapist needs to be able to use his or her Adult in a clear, informed, and potent manner to illuminate both the contaminations the family has previously maintained and the new possibilities for success which are now available to them.

The Child of the therapist is useful in treatment for its skills in intuition and creativity, also for some of its childhood experiences and adaptations to life. Therapists who have not had enough exposure to personal and social variations, who haven't spent some time "on the street" and in some unusual environments, may be less likely to recognize subtle treatment clues, and, if they don't think quickly, may at times appear (and be) naïve. On the other hand, therapists who "have been around," who have associated with many different kinds of people in various environments, often see through the fog quickly. They recognize subcultural subtleties, understand the binds of various social niches, and consequently are better able to see the world from the family's shoes. Berne says: "The diagnosis of ego states is a matter of acuteness of observation plus intuitive sensitivity. The former can be learned, while the latter can only be cultivated."[13] Intuition is an important ability of the Child. So is the joy of laughter. The healthy TA therapist enjoys both.

The ways therapists meet and treat clients are statements of the therapists' philosophies and goals. Therapists' behaviors are far more poignant than their words. Their "hot potatoes" encourage negative feelings and behavior; their authenticity encourages the drive toward health.

Personal modeling becomes part of the professional therapeutic response. The expectation is not that therapists "be perfect," but rather that therapists direct their lives so as to be able to enjoy success, learn from failure, and make changes in their lives which are consisent and ethical and made with awareness and concern for others and for themselves. Such a person is what Berne referred to as a "cowboy therapist who has permission to be happy himself and can transmit this license to his patients."[14] I would add that cowboy therapists also treat their clients with a respect and caring. As M. James notes, "Although it may not be possible to love everyone, it *is* possible to show loving kindness to all people."[15]

THE INITIAL SESSION

The first session with a family is critical for long-range success in counseling. TA therapists present themselves as positive, potent, and protective. This means they (a) form an initial relationship based on Adult-Adult transactions, (b) enable the Child of each family member to experience a sense of trust and security, and (c) challenge the family members to begin to think in new ways about one another.

If these goals are achieved, the Adult ego state of each family member begins to join forces with the therapist for the task ahead. They become co-therapists, in effect, and the family leaves the first session with a sense of excitement and hope.

Getting clear is the "inner preparedness" of therapists. It puts them in the here-and-now which is part of the ethical and financial contract assumed and deserved by the families. In fact, therapists are paid to turn off much of their own lives and be here-and-now. One technique for achieving this attitude is to use some sort of preparation ritual. I have discovered that washing my face and hands with soap and cold water refreshes me physically, gives me a clean smell, and is my signal to shift gears. In this way, when I meet the family and say "hello," I'm prepared to mean it, am ready to move on, and to get on with our goals/contracts. Another technique I use is to ask myself, "I wonder what I will learn new today." With that, I'm also ready to work in the here-and-now.

Setting the climate of trust in the first minutes offers safety and security to the Child of each family member. One way to do this is to briefly state basic expectations. For example, a therapist might say, "I'd like to tell you how I work with families. I don't work miracles on anyone's head, nor do I make people change according to what I think they should be. Instead, I show you how to use TA as a tool. Then you can perhaps get what you want out of life. I also referee, coach, interrupt, or do whatever seems useful to encourage you and your family to get what you want."

A therapist can extend this potent protection to adolescents by adding, "I like to find out just what each person would like to change about his or her life. I will work with you individually and as a family toward achieving the goals you set for yourselves. I won't work with you for something illegal. I will work with you on how you *may* be able to negotiate for use of the car, or how to get more friends, or how to get your parents to let you make more of your own decisions."

Then to the parents, in much the same way: "I want to work with you to get what you want for you. You may want your kids to get along better, so there's less hassling around the house and so they're not always putting each other down. That's OK. You also may decide you want to start having more fun for yourself, or that you may want to get nurturing from each other, or whatever. The point of family therapy, as I see it, is that it's an opportunity for you folks to get things going better at home so you can make each of your own lives more enjoyable."

This sort of introductory statement of the therapist's goals gives the family members Adult information and the Child some immediate comfort and structure.

Getting family facts next gives this expectation a chance to "soak in." This is done by asking questions. Basic fact-questions include: "Is this your first marriage? Are there any other siblings? Where are they? How old are they and what are their sexes? Is there anyone else living at home with you? Who is your doctor? Do you have any medical needs? Are you using any drugs—prescribed or otherwise? When was your last checkup and what were the results? Who referred you?" etc. This gives family members a sense of confidence that the therapist is setting the pace and direction of the treatment sessions.

Openers. Next I lead with an "opener" to encourage each person and the family to get on stage. Common openers are: "What's going on for you folks?" "Why have you come?" "What's the pain-point in your family?" "What's going wrong at home for you?" "You look mad ... You folks seem like you're already into a battle." "Who decided you would come? How did you feel about that? Why? etc." All are designed to allow each person to begin to present his or her picture of the family world as he or she experiences it. If one person interrupts another or talks on and on, I intervene and say, "I'd like to hear briefly from each person."

Openers let the family open the steam valve. Now the therapist listens, allowing the members and the family to let off some of the pressure, to ventilate, to get some things "off their chests." This is the beginning of the treatment.

Script information. Another goal for the first session is to gather script data. As the clients talk, bits and pieces about their early childhood experiences, decisions, script positions, etc. will surface. This is especially true in the first session and is facilitated by questions such as: "If your family continues to act as it now does, what will happen next?" or "Give me three words to describe your mother . . . your father . . . yourself." Or, "How do you get mad? Sick? Show sadness?"

Initial contracting is another goal of the first session. I want to know what it is the family members want for themselves so I can evaluate whether I can be of assistance to them.

The most successful way I have to get contracts that are alive and useful is to ask the family how they'd like their family life to be different. When I know the overall goal, I ask more specific contract questions as we go along, such as: "What's your hunch about what needs to happen to make your family operate in a more healthy fashion?"

One new idea is given toward the last ten minutes of the therapy session so that the family has something to think about and work with until the next session. Depending upon the course the session had taken, I might present the Drama Triangle, or the Ego States, or the Game Plan, or whatever. I present one idea simply—to avoid confusion or scare—and with illustrations from the session to make it alive and useful for the clients.

A caution regarding the presentation of TA theory. Jargon can turn clients off. Even more of a turn-off to clients is when a therapist plays *Look How Smart I Am*. Once a mother and daughter came to me and in the first session I was able to discover much about their scripting. I told them what their scripts seemed to be and how they interlocked. They never returned. Effective therapy requires that the clients be allowed to discover for themselves, not that they get analyzed by a "smart-kid" therapist.

Closing the session, I tell the family, "Now that you've met me and have a feel for my style, I'd like you to think it over and then call me back for an appointment if you think we could work together to your best advantage." This provides a nonauthoritarian structure and reaffirms their ability to think and decide for themselves. It also affirms my willingness or acceptance to work with them. As Berne notes:

> Acceptance is not used here in its ill-defined, sentimental sense; it means specifically, that I am willing to spend more time with him (them). This involves a serious commitment which may in some cases, mean one or more years of patience, effort, ups and downs, and getting up in the morning.[16]

Thus, as the family leaves, they have been stroked for their Adult skills, their Child needs, energy and intuitiveness, and their Parent caring and concern. The therapist has made a therapeutic "bullseye" in the first session.[17]

MIDDLE STAGES OF TREATMENT

The first sessions in family therapy are a bit like a courtship and honeymoon. If the family is compatible, the members will commit themselves to joining efforts and dreams. They will experience excitement and hope for the future.

The middle stage of therapy is a "working-through" period, sessions in which the therapist's major goal is to encourage healthy change in the family relationships. Change and growth are natural, yet difficult. Change in a family needs to be a real growth, not a temporary readjustment; a growth toward script freedom, not a shift into counterscript or antiscript behavior; a growth toward more independence and interdependence, not a reversal to a renewed dependence. The family members need to experience new strength and success. They need to learn to stand on their own two feet while standing near each other.

Openers are also used during the middle stages. Some are: "Where are you at today?" "You look as if . . . " "How did you do on your contracts this week?" "What do you want to deal with today?" Another way to open a session is to say nothing and wait for family members to initiate the transactions.

However the session opens, the basic treatment strategy is to encourage the family members to deal directly with each other, to take the lead, and to develop their own agenda. As they deal with concerns, i.e., why the son couldn't use the car, how the mother was still mad at the father for withdrawing rather than helping with the children, how the daughter worries that Dad is feeling ignored and mother feeling lonely and bored—the therapist has the opportunity to observe their family interaction patterns and use appropriate techniques.

Hooking the Healthy Child with a Nurturing Adult is a technique for a potent therapist who has the inner freedom and agility to pack each transaction with information and affirmation. Each person's Natural Child is tender, loving, and healthy. The therapist can capitalize on this health by *responding to the client's Adult while sending subtle messages of affirmation to the client's Child.* The messages to the client's Child are often nonverbal. There is no "con" intended, rather it is a procedure based on a genuine belief that the client needs to be affirmed as OK while tackling the task of trying out new, script-free thinking and behavior.

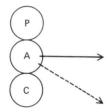

For example, in one session a mother started to cry as she realized she had some "unfinished business" about her father's death. I moved to a chair next to hers and spoke in a soft voice. My intention was to be closer to give her Natural Child a sense of support while I continued to talk to her Adult. Later she commented that she experienced my action as a subtle means of support that strengthened her.

Other "Nurturing Adult" transactions with families include applauding success, teaching new skills, being patient, and caring as much about the person as the therapy task. In this sense the therapist is much like a gardener who is patiently caring for a tomato plant, providing it with necessary protection, water, and soil, while all along knowing that it is the natural action of growth of the plant which is the miracle and which will bring it to the stage where it bears healthy fruit.[18]

Target stroking provides strokes that are healing and the ability to give and get strokes works like the rise and fall of a "stroke reservoir." As more needs are met, the stroke reservoir fills. In fact, our reservoir may be so filled it overflows with healthy nonexpectant joy, concern, loving fun, etc. However, like a reservoir that is low because of a dry spell, if people are stroke hungry, they give very little. They tend to become stingy.

In a family, parents operate on the stroke reservoir principle. Many parents try to give, give, give without paying attention to how they will keep their own reservoirs replenished. If this goes on for too many years, a parent might realize his or her drought and go on a separate journey, withdrawing from the family psychologically if not physically, in an attempt to find other ways of getting the stroke reservoir filled.

People give strokes based on their success at getting strokes. D. Baruch notes that "A reservoir without water cannot take water to those who are thirsty. Neither can a starved person feed another out of bounty."[19] The family stroke reservoir is essential for a therapist to recognize.

People often stroke others in the way that they stroke themselves. They do unto others as they do to themselves because they use the same Parent ego state in both situations. I recall once hearing a man berate his wife with the same critical statements he used on himself in his internal dialogue and which kept him feeling inadequate. A shortage of healthy, tender, and fun strokes brings families in for treatment.

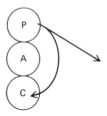

All people need strokes for each ego state. Everyone needs strokes for caring, for thinking, and for being creative and fun to be with. The therapist needs to give and encourage stroking for all ego states. Skilled family therapists continually give subtle positive strokes to all family members—by listening to them, asking each how he or she feels, asking their ideas and opinions, speaking straight to them, showing loving kindness, etc. The therapist's stroking serves two purposes—it aids in the healing of wounds and the filling of low stroke reservoirs, and it serves as a new model or option.

Therapists also need to *stroke strengths* which are counter to the person's scripty magical beliefs. If a Sleeping Beauty believes that Prince Charming will rescue her, then she needs to be stroked for her ability to stand on her own two feet and think for herself. If a Dumbo seeks advice and parenting, the therapist needs to stroke him or her for rebellious strength and thinking. If a Lone Ranger expects to save others, he needs to be stroked for his little boy excitement and his openness. We all need to have our hidden talents recognized and encouraged.

Being consistent and unpredictable provides safety and excitement for the Natural Child. Therapists should be predictable, keep appointments, etc. This can assure families that the therapist's good will, Adult skills and Child tenderness and intuition will be used to their advantage, that their therapist will deal gently with their dreams, considerately with their feelings, and respectfully with their thinking and opinions.

Therapists also need to be unpredictable, always moving and keeping their clients "on their toes." Asking the unexpected questions, or making the uncomfortable observation, or not intervening at every game, all add to the excitement and thinking of families.

One mother and daughter I was counseling had an agreement that the girl would come home on time rather than stay out most of the night. The mother had been wishy-washy about time in the past, so they decided that if the daughter was late, she would go to juvenile detention facilities rather than get into an uproarious battle. The daughter, naturally, had to test the new limitations. I got a call from the mother one evening while I was out. I guessed what was happening and decided the mother needed to take responsibility for her own decisions. The next session we had, the mother said, "I knew you wouldn't call me back. At the time I was worried but now I'm glad you didn't respond." She could predict my behavior and felt safe with it. The mother had her daughter put in detention for the weekend. Following that episode, both mother and daughter found new consistency around their time expectations and were able to keep contracts while working through script issues.

Being flexible can make family therapy alive. With one 10-year-old client, for three sessions he role-played being a rock and I role-played being the boy. With a family of five, I saw each person alone for ten minutes each session. With another family, I met with the parents regarding their marriage rather than focus on the family interactions. With another family, I met individually with the mother, then with the family, then individually with the father. With another family, I let them decide and would ask, "Who wants to come next session?" Each would decide for themselves on the basis of their own interests and needs. With another family I worked with a co-therapist; we would meet at times as a total group and sometimes my co-therapist would meet with some family members while I would meet with others on a flexible schedule.

Giving new information often repairs family dysfunction. People do what they do because they don't know what to do that would work better. Families grow by getting new bits of information about how people are, or what the common social mores are, or what kids are like, and so on.

I give families the common information that all people need time to play and time to be alone, that each person likes to think, that sarcasm never works as a positive educational tool, and that a parent also has an inner Child with needs.

I also give information regarding the hours most young people are permitted to keep on weekends, what juvenile hall is like, how to find out the marriage and divorce laws in the state, ways of determining whether a child is using drugs, etc. I also talk about other families' experiences and what has sometimes proven useful to them as they solve similar problems.

Explaining TA is another technique. The more cognitive understanding families have of what's going on in a treatment session, the more they will be able to use TA effectively outside treatment on their own time. To stimulate this,

I often explain in TA terms what is happening as it happens. This means giving feedback on what I observe without interpretation. This way, family members can see if they are aware of their behavior and/or if they agree with the observations made. There need be no secret operations or maneuvers. When a family member asks, "Why did you ask that question?" I give a direct answer to explain the logic behind my actions.

Using the process is listening for the patterns of interactions.[20] Therapists can use this procedure when they feel they've been part of a game or when the session seems to be going nowhere. For example, I felt like giving advice to one teenager who complained that he "couldn't get his life together." I wondered if this fit a family pattern, so I asked him what would happen if he said the same thing to his parents. He said his mother would be encouraging and would give him suggestions about what he might do. I then asked him how her response would miss the target. He said that he liked her encouragement but that he needed to think for himself and get support for his own ideas. He also recognized that support and encouragement for his own ideas was what he wanted from his father. As we clarified this pattern, I told him that in the future I would be encouraging and ask him what he thought rather than give him my "good ideas."

Separating issues. It is amazing how fast people act and react, think and respond. We are continually taking in myriads of stimuli and selectively deciding how to code and respond to them. Sometimes our speed, however, makes communications unclear and unsatisfying. Children have a vast amount of physical energy, but they tend to think slowly. This is true of the Child in many persons. The Adapted Child may be conditioned to respond quickly, but the wonderings of the Natural Child and the Little Professor often require time. Separating issues is a way to sort out ulterior transactions when two messages are sent at the same time and are received as an ambiguous or "loaded" statement.[21]

Separating the issues makes it possible for the two messages to be dealt with. This can be done simply by saying, "I hear you saying one thing and I notice your forehead is wrinkled and your voice is quiet. What are you also meaning to say?" This implies that both messages are OK, just that they have been combined and need to be separated.

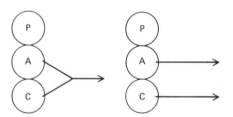

Therapists can use their Little Professors as their "third ear" to see below the surface to additional needs and concerns being expressed in transactions. By slowing down or pacing the family's interaction, feelings or ideas which are often discounted or combined can be recognized, sorted, and responded to.

Experimenting. One way to elicit creative contracts during the middle phases is with a fantasy. I suggest that therapy is like going to a clothing store; people can come to try on new clothes (behavior) to see how they might fit, feel, and look. If they like the new clothes, they can take them home. If not, they can try on something else, all in a safe environment.

For example, a boy who often acted out in "obnoxious" ways was encouraged to ask for a positive stroke from his older sister. He hesitated, then asked her in an awkward manner. She said she liked the way his new haircut looked and that she appreciated that he cleared the dinner table the night before. He had a smile of obvious new-found pleasure and success. Subsequently, he became more comfortable in asking for "warm fuzzies." This behavior was some new clothing he tried on and decided to keep.

Contracting for success. As therapy progresses, total family contracts may become appropriate. Contracts have the greatest likelihood of success if they are made around specific issues. Sometimes a mother says something like, "I want to stop being depressed and be able to help the kids like each other and respect their father's need for quiet."

This is too large a goal to begin with. Immediate, smaller goals that are readily achieved make larger ones possible. So I may respond, "Those goals are all worthwhile. To achieve them, however, you'll probably experience more success by working on one at a time. Which has the higher priority or immediacy for you now?" Some simpler goals might be: "I'll take one hour each day for myself," "If no one nags me I will stop yelling," "We won't fight if you (parents) won't get drunk," etc. As we set easier and quickly achievable goals, we (therapist and family) still keep long-range goals in mind.

Offering hope is necessary when persons come for treatment. They come out of frustration and disgust, not success and strength. Therapists can reverse the family's negative cycle of thinking with a simple operation. An example was a teenager who came for counseling because he had no friends:

C: I want to have some friends.

Th: OK. How many would you like?

C: Four or five.

Th: Four *or* five? Which would you prefer? They're to be your friends.

C: Five.

Th: OK, that's easy. And what kind of friends would you like?"

The words "OK, that's easy. And ... " offers hope. Hope can often be offered if therapists experience hope in their own lives. Hope is catching because it's normal and congruent with our inherent instincts.[22]

Laughing. While therapy is "serious business," no one has yet proved that sourness or seriousness gets clients well any more quickly or effectively than laughter and fun. "Anger and weeping," according to Berne, "are highly regarded by the majority of group therapists as 'expressing real feelings,' while laughter is for some reason not so highly thought of, and is sometimes lightly dismissed as not expressing a 'real feeling'."[23]

Viktor Frankl, father of logotherapy, included laughter as one of his procedures. Paradoxical intention or laughing at the absurdity and nonessential nature of most woes enables clients to break out of programed adaptations to a natural sense of OK-ness.[24]

Many people direct their behavior according to the expectations of "significant others." If therapists expect therapy to be a hard struggle, families will intuit this and probably follow suit and struggle. On the other hand, if therapists see life as a challenge with laughs and moments of tenderness and meaning along the way, families will begin to incorporate and demonstrate this behavior, too. Therapists can exude hope by the well-timed use of humor and laughter. It's hard for families to stay sour and unsuccessful when they're having fun and laughing.

Applauding. Changes in families can be "adjustments," or shifts within a script, or shifts to a counterscript, or they can be new decisions, free of script limitations and programing.[25] It is important that therapists reinforce positive behavior, not script shifts. Therefore, the applause for change needs to be carefully timed. When a family announces that they have made some changes and are excited, I tell them I support their success, I like their enthusiasm, and I'll applaud later after we're both sure the change has "taken hold" and the script has been changed.

Withholding applause for awhile allows clients not to feel guilty if things don't go as perfectly as they hoped. There's no need for them to "save face" if they backslide briefly.

Bridging time takes finesse. Since people change at different rates, bridging time consists of keeping one family member ready for change while another is still getting ready. Family members need to be willing to wait for others to catch up. To encourage this patience, I explain the concept to the family, then ask how each person can give the others the elbow room and time that is needed to effect the change. This is especially necessary in the development of new, Nurturing Parent and in the freeing up of a Fun-loving Child.

TRANSITION TO LAST STAGES

As families gain new skills and awareness and experience new success, their joy of life increases and their confidence in their own strengths flowers. The role of the therapist changes from that of catalyst to "concerned neighbor."

Sometimes termination of therapy is by default, because of summer vacation, moving, or lack of finances. Ideally, termination occurs when the family finds success in establishing and achieving mutually constructive goals. Termination can occur fairly abruptly, or it can be a tapering off process, i.e., a family who has come weekly may come only once per month. Either the therapist or the family may suggest the termination.

Reviewing past contracts is an important reinforcing technique to family growth. Such a review leads to surprise and a sense of satisfaction as the family members realize how far they've come. The therapist can also talk with the family about issues that still need to be explored and problems to be resolved. This allows the family to leave with a clear picture or statement of their situation and possible future goals.

To offer protection, a therapist can tell the family what they might expect to encounter after termination, that set-backs, misunderstanding, and old habitual behaviors may occasionally reappear; that low periods do not necessarily mean all is lost or that they have backslided. Rather, such momentary set-backs can be weathered with confidence until new successes resume.

DISCOVERING POSITIVE PAYOFFS

One of the most important ideas I present to families in the final stages of treatment is that their negative transactions are acually designed to get positive payoffs.[26]

Games are played for the positive payoffs that follow the negative payoff. Darwinian logic posits that animals would use only those behaviors which enhance (not retard) their growth and drive for survival. Currently, many psychotherapists believe that people, like animals, have a natural drive for health.[27] Virginia Satir, for example, considers this premise to be one of her "three primary beliefs about human nature." She states that, ". . . every individual is geared to survival, growth, and getting close to others, and that all behavior expresses these aims, no matter how distorted it may look."[28]

Berne considered this natural drive for health to be one of three basic "thera-peutic slogans." Thus, although the idea of a positive payoff may at first seem contradictory to some traditional TA theory, it is, in fact, consistent with one of Berne's basic beliefs. The positive payoff can be diagrammed by adding it to the end of Berne's Games Formula.[29]

$$\text{Con} + \text{Gimmick} = \text{Response} \to \text{Switch} \to \text{Cross-up} \to \frac{\text{Negative}}{\text{Payoff}} \to \frac{\text{Positive}}{\text{Payoff}}$$

Games begin with a con or ulterior transaction which leads eventually to a negative-feeling payoff. *It is after the negative payoff that some sort of positive payoff follows.*

For example, a couple in a bitter fight might withdraw, feeling mad (negative payoff). After a period of time they approach one another, possibly with an apology, then talk and listen to each other, and end up feeling close and cared-for (positive payoff). The underlying reason for this game is the positive attention (given by apologies, listening, time together) each receives and the excitement created in the process.

Another example is a woman who at work often tries hard to help others. She gets home feeling depressed because no one seems to care enough to want to nurture her. After feeling depressed long enough she has a long cry (time alone) and goes out and buys herself some new clothes (positive attention). Therefore, her real need underlying this game is to nurture herself with some time off and some new clothes.

It's a "positive payoff" again if Dad comes home from work and plays with his son, meeting his son's need for Dad's time and attention. But if Dad is "too tired to play," his son may go into his bedroom and "accidentally" stub his toe, at which time Dad comes in and takes care of his son. Thus, the son, by being clumsy, gets his positive payoff—time with his father.

The "positive payoff" that follows the "negative payoff" in a game is the *basically healthy need that underlies a game.* The pattern of behavior can take many different forms:

• After acting confused, a teenage girl may get an hour of nurturing explana-tion (attention) from her grandfather.

• After a harried week at the office, an executive may get sick and consequently stay home in bed to relax (time alone).

• After storming out of the house from a morning battle with his parents, a teenage boy may go to school and complain to his friends, who provide a listening ear and sympathy (attention and T.L.C.).

- After a long sulk while working overtime on house chores, a housewife may tell herself that she's special even though her family doesn't recognize that fact (positive self-stroking).

Everyone has needs for attention and excitement. Using Berne's terms, each of us has stimulation and recognition hungers.[30] If these needs are not met directly, people play games (use indirect routes) to get what they want. They have been conditioned in childhood to believe that the negative payoff is "the price they have to pay" to get their needs met.

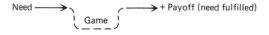

Need ────→　Game　────→ + Payoff (need fulfilled)

The positive payoff may come from an *external* source: from Dad, who at last gives some time and attention, or from a spouse who apologizes tenderly. It can also be internal: when people reassure themselves after feeling unloved, or when people give themselves days off for relaxing or playing.

By use of the Game Plan[31] or Game Formula, a game is easily recognized. Then these questions are asked to discover the positive payoffs that follow:

- At the end of a game, what bad feeling (negative payoff) do you experience?
- When you're feeling that negative feeling, what do you say to yourself about you and about other people? Or, how would you complete this sentence: "That just goes to prove that ..."
- After you feel bad, how do you nurture, rescue, or do something for yourself or how does someone else give you a positive payoff?

For some people, this is enough. For others the answers may not come easily. If this is the case, additional questions for historical diagnosis and script material lead to rediscovery of positive payoffs:

- Which one of your parent figures might have said or felt what you do when you're experiencing your negative payoff?
- Who came to his or her rescue and how (positive payoff)? Or how did each parent take care of themselves when feeling those negative feelings?
- Are you currently experiencing something similar to his or her positive payoff, getting it from others or via your internal dialogue?
- When was a time in your childhood when you felt the same negative feeling as you do currently?
- Who nurtured or rescued you then? In what way? Or how did you nurture yourself?

- Might you currently experience something similar to your childhood positive payoff, either internally or externally?

When the underlying needs and related positive payoffs have been discovered, a person has new awareness. This awareness speeds up decontamination and often leads to a new contract because new options are now available: (1) the person can choose to go for a healthy payoff more directly, for example, by asking for it or giving it to oneself rather than playing games to get it, or (2) he or she can evaluate the healthy payoff and develop other positive payoffs that might fulfill the need for positive attention and excitement in an even more complete and fulfilling way.

In recognizing the positive payoff for games, families become aware that their needs and struggles have an OK aspect to them, and that they can discard their game with negative payoffs in favor of Adult-chosen means to take care of their own Child needs. They also begin to understand other people's needs and responses in more direct, compassionate, intelligent, playful, and other mutually satisfying ways. Then there is no further need for therapy.

REFERENCES

1. Satir, Virginia, *Conjoint Family Therapy* (Palo Alto, Calif.: Science and Behavior Books, 1964), p. 1.

2. Berne, Eric, *What Do You Say After You Say Hello?* (New York: Grove, 1972), p. 297.

3. See English, Fanita, "The Episcript and the Hot Potato Game," *TA Bulletin* **8** (Oct. 1969).

4. Cf. Berne, *Hello,* pp. 304 ff. "Given a free choice, the patient will choose a therapist according to the needs of the script."

5. ———, *Principles of Group Treatment* (New York: Grove, 1968), p. 63.

6. ———, cf. *Transactional Analysis in Psychotherapy* (New York: Grove, 1961), p. 110.

7. Clark, Ronald, *Einstein: The Life and Times* (New York: World, 1971).

8. Falk, Randolf, *Bufano* (Millbrae, Calif.: Celestial Arts, 1975).

9. James, Muriel, and Dorothy Jongeward, *The People Book: Transactional Analysis for Students* (Menlo Park, Calif.: Addison-Wesley, 1975), Ch. 1.

10. Satir, *Conjoint Family Therapy,* p. 1.

11. Berne, Eric, *The Structure and Dynamics of Organizations and Groups* (New York: Grove, 1966), p. 59.

12. Ibid., p. 60. Cf. Berne on "family sphincters" in *Hello,* pp. 160 ff.

13. Berne, *TA in Psychotherapy,* p. 69.

14. ———, *Principles,* p. x.

15. James, Muriel, *Born to Love: Transactional Analysis in the Church* (Reading, Mass.: Addison-Wesley, 1973), p. 198.

16. Berne, *Hello,* p. 9.

17. ———, *TA in Psychotherapy,* p. 236.

18. For more on the Nurturing Adult and effective coaching, see: James, Muriel, *The OK Boss* (Reading, Mass.: Addison-Wesley, 1975), and Gallaway, W., *The Inner Game of Tennis* (New York: Random House, 1975). For information on the Integrated Adult, see: James, Muriel, and Dorothy Jongeward, *Born to Win: Transactional Analysis with Gestalt Experiments* (Reading, Mass.: Addison-Wesley, 1971), Ch. 10, and James, *Born to Love* pp. 197 ff.

19. Baruch, Dorothy, *One Little Boy* (New York: Dell, 1964), p. 24. See also: Steiner, C., "The Stroke Economy," *TA Journal* **1,** 3 (1971).

20. Cf. Luthman, Shirley, and Martin Kirschenbaum, *The Dynamic Family* (Palo Alto, Calif.: Science and Behavior Books, 1974), p. 27, regarding process analysis.

21. Cf. Jackson, D., "The Study of the Family," *Family Process* **4,** 1 (1965), p. 10, regarding "the report-command duality of communication."

22. For a comprehensive study on friendship see Muriel James and Louis Savary, *The Heart of Friendship* (New York: Harper and Row, 1976).

23. Berne, *Hello,* p. 340.

24. Frankl, Victor, *The Doctor and the Soul* (New York: Bantam, 1965), pp. 178 ff.

25. Holloway, W., "Beyond Permission," *TA Journal* **4,** 2 (1974).

26. James, John, "Positive Payoffs After Games," *TA Journal,* July 1976.

27. Cf. Perls, Frederick, Ralph Hefferline, and Paul Goodman, *Gestalt Therapy* (New York: Dell, 1965), p. 112; Jourard, Sidney, *The Transparent Self* (New York: Macmillan, 1958), p. 81; and Lowen, Alexander, *Bioenergetics* (New York: Coward, McCann and Geoghegan, 1975), pp. 33 ff.

28. Satir, *Conjoint Family Therapy,* p. 96.

29. Berne, *Hello,* p. 23.

30. ———, *Games People Play* (New York: Grove, 1964), pp. 13 ff.

31. James, John, "The Game Plan," *TA Journal,* Oct. 1973.

CHAPTER 22

curing sexual dysfunctions in women with TA

LILLIAN O'HEARNE

OVERVIEW OF THE PROBLEM

One big concern many American women have, as well as their partners, is the failure to achieve the stereotype of the "proper" orgasm. Many women are hesitant to admit that they do not have an orgasm each time they have coitus, and many men think that there is something wrong with themselves or their mate when she does not have a "proper" orgasm. A "proper" orgasm may mean a slight pleasure to some and great pleasure to others. Some people would describe a proper orgasm as one of simultaneous orgasm with their partner.

Kinsey records that 30 percent of the women in his sample did not have orgasms when they were first married, but that only 10 percent were still inorgastic after they had been married for ten years.[1]

Helen Kaplan writes that in her clinical experience, 8 to 10 percent of the female population never experience an orgasm. Kaplan believes that one-half or even fewer of these orgastic women regularly reach a climax during coitus without additional clitoral stimulation.

Her method during the initial phase of treatment is "to get the dysfunctional patient to function adequately just one time. It restores her confidence, imbues her with optimism, and demonstrates dramatically that her problem is solvable."[2]

This paper is based on the successful treatment of five women I have cured of sexual dysfunction ranging from vaginismus to disinterest in having sex to not quite having an orgasm. Transactional Analysis, the theory developed by Dr. Eric Berne, was the method used to effect these cures.

Dr. Edward M. Clark developed the five-spot diagrams shown here and their application to sex therapy.[3] In Diagram A the Nurturing Parent and the sexy and fun-loving part of the Natural Child are not cathected. The Critical Parent and Adapted Child are in operation. The Adult ego state is frequently contaminated by both Critical Parent and Adapted Child. In Diagram B all ego states are cathected and there is no contamination.

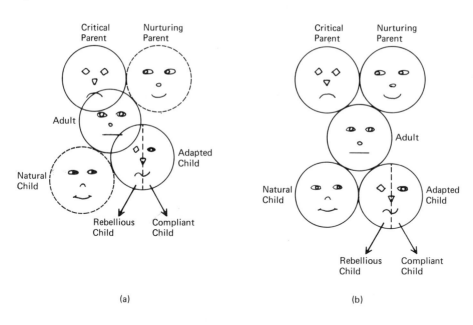

(a)   (b)

TREATMENT PROCESS

The treatment I use consists of the following steps:

1. Take a history.

   a) How does this problem affect your life and your mate's life?

   b) In what way is your sexual life unsatisfactory?

   c) When did you start masturbating?

d) Any sexual relations with people of own sex?

e) Any experience with family members or older people when you were a child?

f) What were your parents' attitudes to sex and sexual parts of the body?

g) Why change?

(Questions (b), (c), and (d) are recommended by Masters and Johnson for general practitioners to ask patients.[4])

2. Make a contract.

3. Give information and new data for the Adult ego state, including a book list.

4. Teach verbal exercises by asking what kind of encouragements appeal to the individual. For example, one person may like to hear, "This is good stuff," and another may like to hear, "It's okay to begin to enjoy sex." I encourage the individual to write down his or her favorite phrase on a recipe card and have it easily accessible to read and say out loud. This is a method of developing a new Nurturing Parent.

5. Help them become aware of the internal Critical Parent by asking what fault-finding thoughts they think in reference to themselves. By becoming aware of when they are listening to the internal voice, they can say, "Stop it," and then say the Nurturing Parent phrase that appeals to them.

6. Show what games are being played by teaching each person to detect whether they are Persecutor, Rescuer, or Victim. Next, options of ego states are taught in responding to an invitation to a game. I do this by role-playing.

7. Teach each individual what favorite or "target strokes" they have by asking them what they like to hear from whom. Saying it is okay to let the other person know and to ask is a way to get the target strokes.[5]

8. Restructure time by asking the patient to write down what she or he likes to do for her partner or have the partner do for her. This helps in clarifying what one wants.

Case Illustration:

Sally was a 73-year-old woman who was referred by her internist because of her threat of suicide. Her initial complaints were: "No one cares for me or wants me. I feel neglected. My husband leaves me alone and doesn't console me. He never touches me." She also had poor appetite and "crying spells," was withdrawing from people, thought of suicide, and had not had intercourse for four years.

When I asked about her early life, she said her mother had died when she was two years of age and she had been reared by several different relatives. She remembered feeling rejected and that "I shouldn't be around." Her first attempt at suicide was when she was in high school. At that time she took an overdose of sleeping pills.

Her early childhood decision[6] was "Don't be," which she experienced many times when moved from relative to relative. Her Adapted Child then followed this injunction by attempting suicide as a teenager and again by being hopeless, depressed, and suicidal when I first saw her.

Treatment consisted of:

1. A no-suicide contract[7] for the Adult ego state. I do that by asking the patient to make a commitment and say, "I will not accidentally or on purpose kill myself." Then I ask the patient to write that statement down and sign it.

2. Giving her some new information of how she was functioning in an ego state. For example, feeling neglected as she did as a Child, being uninformed in her Adult, and copping out as her mother had done, or being unkind as her parent surrogates had been.

3. Decontamination of her Adapted Child which regarded her worthlessness as a fact.

4. New Nurturing-Parent permission[8] to live and to enjoy by saying "You can live and enjoy."

5. Protection by giving her permission to call on the phone and talk a few minutes when she became frightened in the process of change.

Even though her 77-year-old husband refused to come with her, he gained from Sally's treatments. Sally decided what she wanted to do for fun by herself and with her husband. She invited him to join her every night in bed for "touching time." This led to sexual intercourse approximately one to two times a week, which they both enjoyed. At last report they were not only both alive but enjoying life, enjoying touching and having sex.

Case Illustration:

Minnie was a 24-year-old housewife with two small children. She was referred by her gynecologist because of painful intercourse after the birth of her second child. Her initial complaint was painful intercourse and anger at her husband for spending too much time at his work.

Her early script decisions were: (1) I should be perfect, and (2) I must suffer. They were discovered by asking her to recall early outstanding experiences, such as: what her parents told her over and over, how they showed her to live, accidents, illnesses, moves, a birth in the family, and how she got along in school. Once we had determined what the script was, I proceeded by:

1. Directing the patient to verbalize past experiences with her mother, such as pretending that her mother is in the room.

2. Encouraging her to make new decisions, such as: "I don't have to keep a perfect house or have a perfect baby." I helped her to become aware of her "Be Perfect" driver[9] and "Please Me," and then change to a new Nurturing Parent and choose what to do well without demanding perfection in herself or others. With the "Please Me" driver I asked her what she wanted to do for fun, like sex, and then told her that it was okay to enjoy activities that were safe and legal and still choose when to please others.

3. Giving her new Nurturing-Parent permissions to enjoy by inserting her finger into her vagina while doing relaxing exercises such as deep breathing.

4. Strengthening the Adult ego state by stating the fact that her husband was required to be away from home some evenings. During that time, with the new Nurturing-Parent permissions, she could think what she wanted to do by herself for fun, including masturbation, and follow with it.

She then structured her time in another way. Instead of saying "Ain't it awful," and playing the game *If It Weren't For Him* ("If it weren't for my husband, I'd be happy."), she got positive strokes from herself and her husband. She also recognized that it was impossible to do everything perfectly. She stopped her misery racket and was intimate with her husband, and her husband was not resentful that she stopped her pattern of being in a long-suffering Child ego state while he was a Critical Parent.

Case Illustration:

Shirley was a 23-year-old married woman who was in college. When first married she enjoyed sex only for a few months. She came to me wanting to stop losing control of her anger and start enjoying sex again. She did not like living in Kansas City and resented her husband's long hours away from home.

Early in life, she learned to be very critical of herself and others and to yell when angry. She said, "I take little incidents and blow them up." (A typical angry racket.) Her early script decisions were: (1) I won't make it, (2) I won't be happy, and (3) I can't control my anger. These script decisions became part of her awareness after I asked her to recall early life experiences and what she decided at that time.

My treatment consisted of:

1. Giving her permission to say what she didn't like without exploding by telling her "It's okay to say what you don't like without yelling." Her husband responded by listening, and in the joint session he agreed to arrange some special time with her each day.

2. I gave her permission to play and enjoy by telling her "It's okay to play and enjoy and be sexy with her husband." By restructuring her time on her drive home she started thinking erotic thoughts rather than resentments toward her husband.

Case Illustration:

Beverly was a 28-year-old housewife married for two years. She complained that for the past six months intercourse had been painful. She was referred by a gynecologist who had told her there was no physical disease or abnormality in the pelvic area.

This woman was tense and hostile. When I questioned her about her relationship with her husband, she said she was angry with him a great deal of the time. She also thought that men in general were "odd." She told of many arguments. "When my husband yells at me and is shitty, I think of a hard penis." She liked to feel a soft penis, which she associated with pleasant feelings.

She remembered early life experiences in which her mother taught her how to dislike men, including her father. Her father was a "man" alcoholic, and she feared and hated him. Her early life decisions were: (1) "I hate men," and (2) "I will not trust men."

My treatment consisted of:

1. Working through the unfinished business of her hatred of her father with a Gestalt exercise.[10]
2. Role-playing an angry scene between Beverly and her husband. (I role-played Beverly and she her husband, replaying actual incidents in which he was persecutor. In my role of Beverly I refused to be the victim. I remained in the Adult or Nurturing Parent, shifting at times into the Fun-loving Child. In this way I taught her options[11] which she never knew existed when she was in the Adapted Child ego state. Furthermore, such role-playing provided her a role model.)
3. New Nurturing Parent permissions included looking at reality to see that her husband was not "mean" like her father, even though he did get angry with her occasionally. From my Nurturing Parent I gave her—and she took —permission to play and enjoy and be sexy with her husband.
4. Another change was helping her decontaminate so she could associate a hard penis with strength, rather than with "yelling and shitty" behavior.

By refusing to be the victim she no longer needed to play *If It Weren't For Him*. She then refused to collect resentful feelings. Since her resentments were contributing to her tenseness she began to relax and enjoy both her husband and herself and to experience pleasurable intercourse.

Case Illustration:

Susan was a 31-year-old housewife who had been married one year. Her complaint was she did not like sex with her husband. She liked him as a person, but sex was distasteful.

Among the questions I asked her were: "Did you ever like special sexual parts such as breasts and genital area?" and "When did you start masturbating?" Her answers revealed that she never did like the sexual parts of her body and never had the experience of masturbating.[12,13] When she had sex she would think of how her mother would disapprove.

When Susan thought back to early life experiences, she remembered her mother's scornful attitude toward any woman who dressed or acted sexy. Any jokes with a sexual flavor were strongly disapproved by mother and father. Her early decisions were: (1) Don't enjoy your body, and (2) Don't be sexy. She was still pleasing her parents in her Adapted Child ego state by not enjoying sex with her husband.

Treatment consisted of:

1. New Nurturing Parent permissions to like herself and her sexuality. Permission to disobey her parents' early injunctions of "Don't be sexy" and "Don't masturbate." Daily practice at looking and touching self in front of the mirror and talking aloud to self with her new encouragements of "You're OK," "This is natural and fun," were recommended for homework. While in my office she wrote down the phrases she liked to hear so she could easily follow through with her homework. This approach worked for her, and she later related that she and her husband were happy that both could finally enjoy sex together and that she had experienced her first orgasm.

Of all these women, Susan exemplified most clearly the woman who has been actively taught to dislike her physical sexual characteristics. With her and with women like her, I use a system devised by my husband, John J. O'Hearne. We have patients draw—or we draw—sketches of a nude man and nude woman. We tell patients that everyone is interested in his own body and the bodies of others unless they are taught that they should not be. We then tell them that we shall use + symbols to represent the interest that the opposite sex invests in different parts of their bodies. A woman who has learned to dislike her own sex has often also been taught to hate or fear the opposite sex. On the sketch of the male such women tend to put only a few + symbols on hair, eyes, nose, shoulders, etc., and to concentrate most + signs on the penis.

When we have them assign + symbols to the sketch of their own body, they usually place them heavily on hair, face, neck, and shoulders. They frequently make derogatory comments about their own breasts, hardly notice the female curve at the waist, assign very few, if any, + signs to female genitals.

This method helps patients to see that they have literally learned to overlook their own sex. When we ask how they learned to inhibit their curiosity and their healthy narcissism, answers are quick to follow. They see that they are disowning a valuable part of their own existence as though their survival still depended on getting parental approval. Though some might anticipate that such women would have an injunction of "Don't be the sex you are," our finding is that they usually have been taught "Don't enjoy." They need decontamination, permission to enjoy their own Natural Child impulses safely. By getting this Child "on our side," there is much less Parent resistance than if the focus is specifically on sexual enjoyment.

In each of the above cases, the woman rather than the man sought treatment even though both were experiencing sexual dissatisfaction. I invited the husbands to join in the treatment sessions, for in each case there were unresolved resentments which interfered in a close relationship and contributed to the sexual dysfunction. In two cases the husbands refused to come in, yet they, too, profited when their wives became sexy and enjoyed it.

REFERENCES

1. Kinsey, A. C., W. Pomeroy, C. Martin, P. Gebhard, *Sexual Behavior in the Human Female* (Philadelphia: Saunders, 1953).

2. Kaplan, Helen, *The New Sex Therapy: Brief Treatment of Sexual Dysfunctions* (New York: Brunner/Mazel, 1974).

3. Clark, Edward M., "TA and Sexual Dysfunctions," *TA Journal,* April 1976.

4. Masters, William, and Virginia Johnson, *Human Sexual Inadequacy* (Boston: Little, Brown, 1970).

5. James, Muriel, *The OK Boss* (Reading, Mass.: Addison-Wesley, 1975).

6. Goulding, Robert L., "Decisions in Script Formation," *TA Journal,* April 1972.

7. Goulding, Robert L., and Robert Drye, "No-Suicide Contract," *American Journal of Psychiatry,* Jan. 1973, p. 4.

8. Crossman, Pat, "Permission and Protection," *TA Journal,* July 1966.

9. Kahler, Taibi, and Hedges Capers, "The Miniscript," *TA Journal,* Jan. 1974, p. 6.

10. James, Muriel, and Dorothy Jongeward, *Born to Win: Transactional Analysis with Gestalt Experiments* (Reading, Mass.: Addison-Wesley, 1971).

11. Karpman, Stephen, "Option," *TA Journal,* Jan. 1971.

12. Colton, Helen, *Sex After the Sexual Revolution* (New York: Association Press, 1973).

13. Berne, Eric, *Sex in Human Loving* (New York: Simon & Schuster, 1970).

CHAPTER 23

the nurse
as therapist

ANN CHANDLER

Bill Smith, age 52, is the president of his company, husband, father of four, and deacon in his church. He is considered, by those who know him, to be logical, intelligent, strong, and emotionally well-balanced.

Bill Smith, age 52, enters the hospital and, as the identification bracelet is snapped on his arm, he becomes little Billy Smith, age 5. This ego shift is dramatic and visible to those people who understand Transactional Analysis. Nursing personnel become therapists willingly or unwillingly, skilled or unskilled. Bill Smith's problems would be eased if the hospital personnel were aware of his ego shifts, and therefore could respond to his needs more appropriately.

The hospital routine keeps Bill in his Child ego state in many ways. He is asked to undress and be in his bed clothes even during the day. He is told when to eat, sleep, and bathe. He is invited to feel helpless because all those "Parents" (nurses, doctors, and allied personnel) know more than he does about what's going on. Often there is an element of secrecy concerning his tests and their results. It's OK for the "Big Folks" to know but Billy wouldn't understand. Even the physical position of being in bed looking up is one of Child to Parent.

Bill's existential position, while in the hospital, is likely to be "I'm not OK because I'm sick and helpless—You're OK because you're well and in control." His not-OKness may be intensified if he has a "Be strong and don't need'" script message from a parent figure. There is considerable discomfort in going against this injunction or message.

It is important for the hospital staff to know how the patient feels about the hospitalization. Is he worried about his job or family? Is she worried about her children and who will cook and clean? Does the patient feel guilty about not being at home taking care of all the "You Shoulds"?

The patient comes into the hospital as a member of a family and a community, and these relationships come with him in varying degrees. If the patient is in the middle of a divorce, or a law suit against his neighbor's dog, or running for election to the school board, his emotional reactions will have a direct influence on his physical well-being.

RACKETS AND STAMPS

According to Berne, Rackets are "self-indulgence in feelings of guilt, inadequacy, hurt, fear, and resentment."[1] English says rackets are played to "collect transactional currency, namely strokes."[2] She further states that "it is the 'Racket' feelings that represent what the young child was most stroked for in early childhood, whether the strokes were positive, negative, or crooked." James and Jongeward point out that "Not all feelings are rackets. Some are genuine."[3] It is my experience and observation that a person's rackets will accelerate after a few days in the hospital. A patient spends most of his time in the Child ego state and is egocentric as children normally are. His "feelings" are likely to be exaggerated and real or imagined slights grow out of proportion. If a patient has an Anger Racket he will find many opportunities to collect Stamps and will even take some that he would let pass under normal conditions. Other Stamps are offered as well, such as scared, hurt, feelings, lonely, apprehensive, inadequate, and "suffer."

Since the Child ego state is hypercathected, the Little Professor, or Adult in the Child, is very active. The patient "tunes in" on the health care people and often makes incorrect assumptions. For example: Mrs. Jones turns on her light and the Nursing Assistant answers, looking sullen and angry. Mrs. Jones' Little Professor intuits that the Nursing Assistant doesn't like her and feels hurt. She will hesitate to turn on her light next time and reports to the doctor and family that she "hates to bother the staff because they get angry." She doesn't

have the Adult information that the Nursing Assistant had just been repri-
manded by the Head Nurse and was in fact, in her own Child ego State.

A patient's Little Professor watches the facial expressions and body language
of the personnel in an attempt to discover his or her position in this strange
new hierarchy. The patient used this ability as a child to "psych-out" his or
her position in the family, and may have formed wrong conclusions then—
and therefore is often mistaken now. If the nurse frowns when taking the
patient's blood pressure, the latter may collect a "worry" Stamp and decide
that the pressure is either too high or too low—without even considering that
the nurse may have a headache. The patient, being egocentric, will feel that
all frowns and sighs must be related to his or her self and welfare. Adult information from the nurse would be useful to the patient at this time; a simple
statement concerning what is going on with the nurse would be sufficient.
The nurse would have to be aware of where the patient is, ego-wise, in order
to respond appropriately.

STROKES

"People" are often stroked in one way and "patients" in another. Patients receive strange strokes from strange folks. It is important to remember that the
patient has given up the familiar sources of strokes as well as the familiar
strokes themselves. Example: a 70-year-old woman who lives alone may have
gotten her strokes from the milkman, the mailman, and a daily call from a
friend. When she enters the hospital she loses these dependable sources of
strokes. She now gets strokes from the Laboratory, X-Ray, and EKG folks.
Since these are strange strokes it will take more of them and she may become
demanding and fearful.

One often neglected point can be illustrated by the following case: Mrs.
Henry, age 74, lives alone and cares for her own needs. She does fairly well
and gets by on very few strokes. One day, however, she has a heart attack and
discovers herself in the Medical Intensive Care Unit of a hospital. There, she
is monitored. medicated, bathed, fed, and massively stroked by many people.
After several weeks she is discharged, as well as before, and no one thinks
about the acute stroke deficit she will face when she goes home. She may well
be calling her doctor to complain that she can't sleep, has no appetite, and
feels depressed. She is most likely to be suffering from "stroke withdrawal."
This could be minimized by some planning before she is discharged. A staff
person could talk with her about ways to decrease her aloneness when she is
at home. Perhaps a call to her minister, priest, or rabbi could enlist some
definite sources of strokes. Hospital volunteers might be useful in making a
daily phone call for a week to newly released patients who live alone. Shut-ins

could also fill this need and get their own strokes as well. The nurse as therapist can use her Adult to help the patient do effective problem-solving.

Conscious patients who are admitted as emergencies have a special stroking need. Here the first consideration is to save the patient's life by whatever procedure is necessary and to do so as quickly as possible. The staff members transmit their anxiety to the already anxious patient by their facial expressions, movements, words, and the equipment they use. In order to cathect the Adult of the patient and obtain his or her cooperation, it is of vital importance to *first stroke the Child.* This can be done by the nearest Nurturing Parent and must be by physical touching as well as by verbal reassurances. Procedures can also be explained in simple terms as they are being performed. This gives the patient some information that the Adult ego state can use to help protect the Child. All conversation during an emergency should either be about the patient or should include him or her. It's a painful and frightening experience for the patient to have the staff talk over him or her about other matters. If a tedious tendon repair is being done under a local analgesic, it's helpful to talk and take the patient's mind off the sounds of cutting and suturing so long as the patient is included. The patient can be invited to stay in his or her Adult in this manner, but will go to the Child or Critical-Parent ego state if the doctor and nurse start a private conversation. Patients have a right to feel that they are "number one" in these circumstances.

Especially when a patient is admitted on an emergency basis, the friend or relative standing by in the waiting room should not be ignored. Depending on the closeness of their relationship to the patient, their need for positive strokes may be as great as the patient's own. While it is up to the nurse or the doctor to assess the degree of that need, it almost always exists, and the newly admitted patient's friend or relative should not be allowed to leave unstroked.

DISCOUNTS

Patients can really be hurt by discounts from the staff. A discount occurs when a light isn't answered and no explanation is given; when a request is forgotten; when flowers die due to lack of water; when food is cold; when no one comes in to say goodnight and lower the head of the bed; when doctors stand impatiently in the door instead of coming into the room; when they don't listen; when the Nursing Assistant sighs deeply over a simple request as if he or she is exhausted. Patients feel discounted if no one takes a few minutes to acquaint them with simple things like using the phone, the TV, and electric bed controls.

The nurse is acting as therapist when she truly listens without discounting.

Hospital discharge is often a sadly neglected time for patients. They can feel discounted when the only farewell statement is, "Stop by the Business Office on your way out and here are your prescriptions." Even the busiest staff can smile, wave, and wish good-luck. If the hospital stay has been a long one, the patient may well be apprehensive about going home and back into the family and social community. His or her Child needs a stroke!

Staff often discount a patient's feelings. Example: "You're not afraid of a simple D & C, are you? That's nothing to cry about." The patient won't stop feeling scared but will, however, stop expressing feelings that are discounted.

GAMES

Games played by patients are often the same ones they play outside the hospital.[4] Frequent examples are *Ain't It Awful?, Poor Me, Why Does This Always Happen? Let's You And Him Fight.* This last game can involve the nursing staff, the doctor and the staff, or the members of the doctor's group. Example:

Mrs. Faultless: (to the Evening Shift Charge Nurse) I want to go down to the Coffee Shop and visit my little granddaughter.
Ms. Strict, R.N.: Sorry, you can't leave the floor without a written order from your doctor.
Mrs. Faultless: Well, Miss Smith on the day shift always lets me because she understands how lonely I get. I wish she worked evenings!"
Ms. Strict: Well, Miss Smith isn't in charge on evenings, I am, and rules are rules!

Ms. Strict may let it "accidently" drop to the Supervisor that Miss Smith isn't following the rules and the game can accelerate in a number of ways.

Another example: "Doctor, I'm so glad you're the one visiting me today, Dr. Curt just rushes me through and never tells me anything and he's so rough when he changes my bandages!" Patients usually feel that they are Victim in the game drama but often end up as Persecutor. The health care personnel need to understand games so that they won't play them. Games take up time that could be used for the benefit of the patient. The nurse, as therapist, can spot and stop games or reduce their intensity. He or she will need to understand why the game is being played. If strokes are needed, the nurse can see that they are given; if the game is from boredom he or she may check on occupational therapy or the library cart.

TIME STRUCTURE

There are only six ways in which time can be structured: Withdrawal, Ritual, Pastime, Activity, Games, Intimacy. The person who enters the hospital must learn a completely new way of structuring his or her time: An earlier with-drawal pattern is disturbed by hospital routine; rituals and pastimes are now with different people; activity time is over-turned with little to replace it; time will now be structured by other people, whether it is time for sleeping, eating, treatments and tests, or even visiting. No wonder Games flourish and Stamps are collected!

Patients could spend more of their time in Intimacy if the staff knew how to allow and invite the intimate sharing of real feelings between themselves and their patients. When people become patients, they need Intimacy more than ever. They need strokes that are authentic and rich with warmth. They need to have their Child recognized and valued. They have a right to have their emotional as well as their physical needs met.

Example: Father William R., a Jesuit priest, was recovering from a coronary which left major heart damage. After several visits from the TA-trained nurse, he told her, "When I was so sick and felt that I was dying, I wanted some one to hold my hand and say, 'Hang on Willie, hang on!' That's what my mother called me." This information was given to the Medical Intensive Care nurse. When Father R. came into the hospital again, the nurse held his hand and called him "Willie" as he died. She discussed her feeling of discomfort at call-ing this most distinguished man "Willie" and her great feeling of intimacy at the same time. She valued his Child and met his emotional needs.

Here again is the nurse as therapist in another example of intimacy: Mr. K., age 60, black, with strong religious faith, was told that the spot on his leg was malignant and the leg itself must be amputated. When the TA-trained nurse talked with him she became aware that his belief that "It is the will of God" was keeping him from grieving over the impending loss. She sat on the bed and put her arm around his shoulder saying, "I know you believe in God and it's also very sad to lose a part of your body. I think I'd feel scared and cry." With that remark and "permission," the patient did cry and later talked about his anxieties. The nurse then helped him move beyond the loss into the future with talk of prosthesis, physical therapy, and a job transfer.

Webster defines a nurse as "a person trained for the care of the sick or in-jured; a woman tending another's child." Only a slight change is necessary for the nurse as therapist: "a woman/man tending another's Child."

Where health care personnel understand and utilize the concepts of Transac-tional Analysis, the journeys back through the time tunnel of all the Bill Smiths can be less frightening.

REFERENCES

1. Berne, Eric, *Principle Of Group Treatment* (New York: Random House, 1966), p. 308.

2. English, Fanita, "The Substitution Factor—Rackets and Real Feelings," *TA Journal,* Oct. 1971 and Jan. 1972.

3. James, Muriel, and Dorothy Jongeward, *Born To Win: Transactional Analysis with Gestalt Experiments* (Reading, Mass.: Addison-Wesley, 1971), p. 189.

4. Berne, Eric, *Games People Play* (New York: Grove, 1964).

CHAPTER 24

curing
"moral masochism"[1]

DAVID E. KEMP

This is a "how-to-cure" paper, based on my experiences with ten women[2] who could be "diagnosed" as "having" "masochism," "moral masochism" or "passive aggressive personality disorder."

These are all lousy words, but the problems to which they refer are so frequently encountered that they persist in the clinical folklore. What we have in mind here are "injustice collectors"; people who recurrently "find themselves" in painful, destructive interpersonal relationships. More specifically, the patients I saw shared these attributes:

1. Their "ticket of admission" is "depression," seemingly engendered by a situational problem. However, the onset of the "depression" is in fact undateable, since the patient has rarely been free of feelings of worthlessness. Further, the patient herself has, more often than not, initiated the "precipitating incident."

2. These women live very chaotic lives, which revolve around intense, locked-on relationships with men. Even though they are miserable, and

From *TA Journal* **2,** 4 (1972). Reprinted by permission.

attribute this misery to the male with whom they are involved, they cannot leave these relationships, and will actively resist any suggestion that they should. They are convinced that a "white-knight Santa Claus" exists and will be shortly along; in the meantime, they are equally convinced that they are hapless, and blameless, victims of "typical" men.

3. They can be very trying patients. Not that they are hard to keep in treatment. In fighting an army dedicated to defeat, it's hard to make mistakes; the more you make the harder you hook the patient. And what you have hooked is a person who has attended the post-post graduate school for developing a repertoire of provocations to exasperation and anger: The therapist into stamp-collecting will find a home here, because vigorous *ITHY* with the patient, and prolonged *AIA* with colleagues are lead-pipe cinches.

4. They have lived in perfectly horrid families. The nasty details vary, but one feature is invariant: disturbed, very cruel fathers. Their behavior toward their daughters comprises consistent, unremitting cruelty; insistence on absolute obedience; and a promise that all sorts of good outcomes will follow, if . . . only . . .

TA is specifically indicated for such patients because, simply, it can cure them. The actionistic nature of TA tends to "head off at the pass" the proclivity of these patients to get into "real-time" messes that render more contemplative therapies as irrelevant as angel-on-pinhead counting. TA provides a simple, clear description of these patients, and an equally-clear set of therapeutic strategies, as will now be demonstrated:

STRUCTURAL ANALYSIS

A structural analysis of these patients is given in the accompanying figure, in which appear the persistent refrains of each ego state.

The internal dialogue of a moral masochist

Mother   Father

Don't ask me, I just work here.

I am an angry, dirty Santa Claus.
You must be a frog, the wartier the better

All men are god-damn dirty Santa Clauses.
I am a frog.

About "dirty Santa Claus": These patients perceive their fathers as having all the goodies and gifts there are, but as dispensing these gifts in a capricious and thoroughly evil fashion. In short, they experience their fathers as a combination of Santa Claus and obscene phone caller. A good example is found in these recollections of a patient whose father beat her regularly, often sufficiently to prevent her from attending school the next day: ". . . When he was beating me, he had a peculiar look in his eyes. Sorta glazed, or glassy. You know, the way men look when they're looking at dirty pictures or . . ." Right from Kraft-Ebbing, sure; but not at all atypical.

Mother ("Don't ask me . . .") stands idly by, which, given the provocation, is clear-cut, covert encouragement.

The internal dialogue of these patients consists of severe, vicious, Parent-to-Child put-downs; and Child-to-Parent *covert* anger. Both the real child and the Child know that openly handling this anger is likely to worsen the situation.

The Adult is weakly cathected, and outvoted 2 to 1. Sometimes these patients' interpersonal hassles are maintained at a level of distortion that may lead a clinician to suspect "psychosis," or some other dread "disease," but however ominous or crazy the patient's thoughts seem to be, the "thinking disorder" stops at whatever level is required by the game, and *never* includes other mainifestations such as hallucination.[3]

It is worth a digression to point out that this structural analysis sheds some light on the clinical folklore that reads, "all masochists are really *sado*-masochists." These patients are, indeed, sullenly angry much of the time. Psychoanalytic thought ascribes this to an "identification with the aggressor." Insofar as "Parent" is a close familial relative of that idea, the TA approach is not particularly innovative. However, the structural analysis does clearly identify an additional source of aggression: the covertly-angry Child, brimming over with "sadism," which is *historically* justified. This way of looking at things has considerable implications for treatment; for example, see the "Control of the *NIGYSOB* component" and "Permission to be OK" sections below.

GAME ANALYSIS

The moves in these patients' game are:

1. Pt.: "Be my Santa Claus."[4]

2. Male: "OK"

3. Pt.: Why don't you love me more?"
   Male: "Take this"

   Or

4. a. (payoff) Pt: "Oh, this is terrible; nothing can be done."
   and/or

   b. "You've let me down."

Move No. 3 is optional, because sometimes the patient arrives at a contract with a genuine S.O.B.; and other times finds that it is necessary to provoke kicks.[5]

The thing to take note of is that in close conjunction to easily-recognized *Kick Me*, these patients also play a reasonably subtle version of *NIGYSOB*.[4] Through their sulking and pouting, they are able to make it perfectly clear to their protagonists—which sometimes includes the therapist—that he has "let them down," and "who wouldn't be angry."

For these patients, *Kick Me* and *NIGYSOB* are family names; related variants, like *Ain't It Awful. Blemish, Harried Housewife, inter alia.*, abound. But the threat of escalation is chronic. If, for example, *AIA* founders, tears (*Kick Me*) or accusations of "You don't really care" (*NIGYSOB*) will quickly ensue (See therapeutic procedures Nos. 4 and 5).

TREATMENT PROCEDURES

From this framework, treatment procedures are quite precise and specifiable:

1. De-commission the Parent.
2. De-fuse *NIGYSOB*.
3. Give the patient permission, protection, and encouragement to be OK, especially with regard to wanting good things.

These procedures are listed in *exactly* the serial order in which they should be undertaken. Wherever you are in this series, these two steps *must be followed:*

4. Do not give blue stamps.
5. Do not give red stamps.

Steps 4 and 5 *must be scrupulously adhered to,* because they mean the difference between a successful outcome and prolonged treatment which is mutually noxious to therapist and patient. They work like this: When the patient enters treatment, the games of *Kick Me* and *NIGYSOB* gain a potential third player —the therapist. The patient comes to the therapist and relates the latest dreadful episode, ending with *two* tearstained "hooks": "Ain't it awful; what did I do wrong." The therapist could agree with *Ain't It Awful*; it usually *really* is awful. This is of course, giving blue stamps. Nothing will go dreadfully wrong with this intervention, except that you will soon discover that *Ain't It Awful* can go on for a *very* long time. The therapist could take the other hook, and state: "You brought this on yourself as follows . . . " Zingo! Faster than a speeding bullet, you've made it, because the patient now either kicks herself ("you're absolutely right, Doctor.") or points out how mean you really are ("How can you kick me when I'm down!"), or both of these simultaneously.

This is *the* pitfall with masochistic patients. Imagine the advantage to the patient of having a *scheduled* time for being kicked, and perhaps being drained financially, to boot! It is easy enough for the therapist to become a firm favorite under these conditions, all the time congratulating himself for "freeing" ("freeing" = "replacing") the patient from her persecutor.

As to the other strategies:

De-commissioning the Parent.   Berne's recommendation of structural analysis first, transactional analysis second, must be adhered to rigorously in the treatment of moral masochism. The Child's lock-on to the Parent is so tenacious that until the Parent is de-commissioned there is only a very slim chance that the patient will ever hear you "straight," and most interventions—no matter what you intend—will break Rules 4 and 5.

The strategies involved here are straight forward.

1. The patient must *experience fully* the *internal* dialogue of not-OK Parental messages. It is difficult for the patient to hear the Parent *within,* because of the patient's lock-on to *If It Weren't For Him,* and because *Him* is often a real-time S.O.B. Some techniques for doing this will be spelled out in a moment.
2. The patient must perceive the real parent as the *historical* source of the "not-OK" message.
3. This message must be moved back to its proper time; a friendly divorce from the Parent must be arranged.

Control of the NIGYSOB component.   When the Parent is becoming de-commissioned, the anger which the patient saved-up from her childhood will be increasingly obvious. When the historical source of the anger becomes clear to the patient's Adult, *she* will be able to control it by moving it back to the past where it belongs, rather than its being addressed, willy-nilly, to any man who steps into range. Two cautionary notes here: Keep in mind that you're dealing with the *historical* parents, Otherwise, the patient will go home, try to get even with her real parents, and create one hell of a mess. Furthermore, the anger must not be a mild *Ain't It Awful,* with the chronic, low-grade bitching to which the patient is well-accustomed; insist on the genuine article. Some of the anger will be "irrational," but that is OK: feeling indignant over real slights has been out-of-bounds for so long that a little overshoot should be tolerated; and the therapist should avoid "That's not right either." It is helpful here to remember that the Child has a perfect right to be angry, given the kind of cruelty to which she was exposed.

One of the persistent therapeutic contretemps in this area is moving past the tenacious *Ain't It Awful* monologue, dripping with "justified" hurt-anger. The problem is, of course, that you know the patient's Child is mad, but the patient's Adult doesn't. Now hopefully, the readers of this *Journal* will recognize that the classically-recommended response to "repressed anger"—"you must have been angry"—is a dead-end street. What *does* work is to say something like: "I understand that this guy has hurt you and you feel very sad about this. But, it's curious isn't it, that this S.O.B. never makes you *mad*." This usually, eventually, hooks the scientific curiosity of the Adult, and you're off and running.

The other way to work with *NIGYSOB*: While listening to the gruesome details of a completed *Kick Me* game, the therapist may well be startled to notice a smile on the patient's face. This, of course, is the Child chortling with glee at her success in the game. At this point the therapist can, if his timing is perfect, remark: "You got the son-of-a-bitch, didn't you!", or some such. If this works, both of you—that is, both of your Children—will have a good laugh on the Parent, which is often followed by a direct engagement of the Adult, grappling with her revenge motives. Of course, this is a Child-to-Child intervention, which means that while it can be spontaneous; zingy; and intuitively accurate, it is risky, because it cannot be computed in advance, and the therapist must know his own Child well.

Permission to be O.K. One of the remarkable things about the *Kick Me/ NIGYSOB* cycle is that it is often used to get rid of a man that the Adult (and therapist) clearly recognizes as outright bad luck. The patient cannot act more directly (as in *Get Lost*), for reasons which the structural analysis diagram will make clear. The Adult has spent a lifetime watching passively while its two neighbors do their dirty work. This creates a situation in which first, ordinary "wants" are confused with anger; secondly, there is no Parent permission for taking initiative; and finally, the Adult's "muscle" is flabby. Thus, these patients have a great deal of difficulty in stating unequivocally "I want, I should have, I'm entitled, etc." They usually judge these thoughts as being "pushy," "mean," or "asking for too much." The solution to this has, at this state of treatment, been partly achieved through the neutralization of the angry Parent, and extending Adult control over the rebellious Child. However, in addition to this, one needs to encourage, ratify, permit, and protect the patient's "getting on with it," that is, in actively prosecuting an OK life. This is probably the time for the therapist's strokes, because once you reached this stage, the Buddha-like patience required to avoid the patient's gimmicks is no longer so uniformly required.

How to make hay when the sun isn't shining. The perpetual roadblock to this sequence of interventions is the tenacious *If It Weren't For Him.* However, the therapist can count on a situation recurring which, though painful to the patient, can break this roadblock.

These patients cannot tolerate being alone.[6] Their reaction is inevitable: They will contact their most reliable S.O.B. and invite him over. The resulting events, predictably disasterous, are related to the therapist the following hour, usually with the patient's feeling quite angry about herself, being aware that she has committed another mistake.

As painful, frustrating, and repetitive as these episodes are, they are paydirt because: (1) The patient can realize that something about being alone leads them to repeat their errors. (2) That "something" is the not-OK internal dialogue. (3) It is one of the few times that the patient can experience the not-OK message as coming from *within,* rather than from *without,* because unlike 95% of the rest of their experiences, there are no persecutors in the room.

The episode can be successfully dealt with by intervening in *exactly* this order: First, one of you should specify, *out loud,* that whatever is happening in the patient's head while she is alone is what triggers the pattern of *Kick Me.* Then, the obvious question: "What *is* going on in your head while you are alone?" The response is almost certain to be a not-OK quote from the Parent. It's downhill the rest of the way.

THE END

Cure, means that *Kick Me/NIGYSOB* is dropped, and the patient leaves in the midst of busily getting a new, and shinier, show on the road, and knowing there are *now* better things to be doing than talking to psychotherapists.

And this should occur far faster than with more traditional treatment modes. However, what I have so far treated somewhat light-heartedly now needs to be considered seriously: the considerable and real abuse inflicted upon these patients as children. One of the implications of this is that a little patience is definitely good form, for we do *know* that the greater the abuse, the longer the "unabusing" takes. To be sure, we are constrained to examine with a Martian eye prolonged treatment; yet, we must be wary of being inhuman by virtue of "ideals," which can, of course, be Parental *and* destructive.

Specifically, the therapist can expect one year of work; and not necessarily be dismayed by two. Longer than that, though, requires a search for Parental injunctions not to cure.

REFERENCES

1. It is ultimately "masochistic" that whereas any school child knows about De Sade, very few people remember L. Von Sacher-Masoch. Concerning the diagnostic term, "moral masochism," the less said the better, for not only is it rather bad English (how does a moral masochist differ from an immoral one?) but it also represents an attempt to make-believe that the psychoanalytic understanding of the *sexual perversion* of masochism could explain a dedicated *Kick Me* player. This was about as successful as other games of make-believe, and make it necessary for Berliner, in a series of very good articles, to go to great lengths to establish that psychoanalytic methodology could *not* be be used in these cases. See: Berliner, B. "On Some Psychodynamics of Masochism." *Psychoanalytic Quart.*, 1947), 16, 459–471; and, "The Role of Object Relations in Moral Masochism." *Psychoanalytic Quart.*, 1958, 27, 38–56.

2. Why only women? Well, that's who came to my door—but that, of course, explains nothing. Steiner says that psychiatric problems can be understood by this formula: oppression + self-deception = alienation. (Steiner, C. Radical Psychiatry: Principles. *The Radical Therapist,* 1971 2 (No. 3, October), 2.) For the problem at hand, I would alter the formula: masochism in women = deception + oppression × male chauvinism. But, let's stay clear on one thing: Masochism is not a disease of the womb! There *are* cases of male masochism. It would hardly do to repeat that bit of history.

3. Thus, psychoactive medications are very rarely necessary; even more to the point, they should be vigorously avoided or ignored because they so often are props in games.

4. Groder (*TA Bulletin,* 1969, 8, 35–36) discusses both the "Santa Claus" gimmick and identifies *Kick Me/NIGYSOB* as an interlocking family of games. The situation in which *one* person plays *both* games of an interlocking family is explained by Berne's observation that although people typically have preferred games, they know the game that "fits" theirs, and, in a pinch, can play it. "Pinches seem to happen a lot for these patients.

5. Of course, the men are "in" on the contract, knowing perfectly well how the action is to unfold. The male players—and, as you might expect, the father of masochists —*seem* to be men whose Parent is dead-set against anger of any sort, but whose Child is very angry. Periodically, their Child overcomes the Parental surveillance, and they have temper tantrums. Immediately following, they are overcome with remorse (that is, the Parent regains the upper hand), which makes the patient's *NIGYSOB* extremely effective.

6. Easy enough to understand this: staying at home with a sadistic Parent and a hostile, rebellious Child would rarely be chosen by anyone.

CHAPTER 25

supplemental parenting of the *kick me* player

MICHAEL BREEN

A *Kick Me* player is an individual who obtains his strokes by evoking criticism and bullying from others.

He enters therapy complaining of a combination of bad feelings—depression, anger, guilt, anxiety—but the bad feeling commonest to Kick Me players is anxiety or tension. He announces that no matter how hard he tries, he doesn't seem to get anywhere in life and he doesn't know how to deal with people. He is pessimistic and down-trodden and complains a lot.

PRECISE RECOGNITION OF THE *KICK ME* PLAYER

There are ten indications to the therapist that he has a *Kick Me* player in treatment.

1. The favorite game of the *Kick Me* player is *Yes, But* . . . He will appear eager for advice but discard each offered solution by finding a fatal imperfection.

From *TA Journal* **3**, 3 (1973). Reprinted by permission.

2. In terms of differential diagnosis, a *Kick Me* player can be distinguished from a paranoid or depressed patient by the ego state immediately "induced" in the therapist. An induced ego state is defined as an ego state which is drawn out or "hooked" in the therapist and which is very similar in functioning to the patient's actual parents when the patient was younger. A depressed patient will make the therapist feel Parental apprehension. A paranoid patient will make the therapist feel Parental frustration and irritation.

3. There is no way to proceed with orderly problem solving in the initial stages of therapy. Before the therapist's "authority" the patient is in an Adapted Child ego state which is both compliant in regard to "advice" but rebellious in regard to carrying it out. The very procedure of defining problems in the beginning stages is affected. The subject is changed every few moments and there are "too many problems" to get a contract. Little asides bait the Critical Parent of the therapist, such as, "I don't really know what I'm doing here," or "Maybe I should go see my palm reader," or "I just don't know, I'm beginning to feel more confused now than when I came in." An almost classic, one-line clincher is the pause at the door—after forcing the therapist to run overtime with scattered questions about emotional emergencies—and the statement, "Well, Doc, how did I do?" Also, he may fall silent during inquiries and play *Stupid* with an "I dunno" answer to simple Adult questions, which he is hearing as Critical Parent grilling.

4. The *Kick Me* player cannot accept positive strokes and he clearly dislikes compliments. He believes that anyone who is coming on positively toward him is either being manipulative or is a fool. He readily will accept many types of negative strokes as "realistic."

5. The *Kick Me* player attends therapy late or irregularly and sometimes fails to pay his bills.

6. He may make suicidal gestures from the position "I'm fed up with myself" more than from the position of depression. He will usually say, in a self-kicking way, "But I'm really too much of a coward to do it."

7. He cannot tolerate success and tends to be a loser in the script sense. Often he cannot settle down to any plan or job for long because this would bring him the positive recognition of being at least a stable and reliable person. He commonly draws up new and daring plans that are poorly conceived and end in minor catastrophe.

8. He is malaprop. He does not operate in his Adult for sufficiently enduring periods of time in transacting with others so that he would win their respect. He is easy to criticize, ridicule, put down, push around. He attracts critical or

mean people. He readily criticizes himself but he does not effectively criticize others in Critical Parent versus Critical Parent showdowns.

9. His predominant childlike emotion is crying. There is a plaintive tone in his voice. He is usually whining, whimpering or being demanding from a "hurt" position.

10. He generally has a mild paranoid feeling that others are looking at him critically. He tends to avert his eyes and fiddles with something in an annoying way when talking to others, for example continuously picking lint off his trouser legs. He is fearful of this imagined criticism but tends to agree with it rather than feel the need to counter-attack.

First Stage of Treatment: Counter-Gaming and Child-Child Pastimes

There are two procedures to be *avoided* in the first stage of treatment. (1) The patient should not be analyzed transactionally, that is, "introduced to TA" and presented with his games and script matrix. (2) The patient should not be confronted or criticized. All Adult and well-meant Critical Parent transactions will be perceived as cruel and bullying.

The first stage of therapy is devoted to establishing a good relationship. In reference to a *Kick Me* player, this means the therapist must (1) control the interview and (2) have fun with the patient. In all other transactions the patient accomplishes the reverse—he controls the transactions by playing *Kick Me* and guarantees bad feeling, irritation in the other and anxiety and feelings of rejection in himself.

The interview is controlled by countering the game of *Kick Me* with a game of *Kiss 'Em* (referred to as an "antithesis" by Zechnich). It is a game because the therapist must come on Benevolent Parent despite the fact he may be in another ego state, usually swinging between Critical Parent, which the patient is inducing, and Adult, which is making strategy. The patient will continue to escalate, but the therapist continues Benevolent Parental stroking. A typical example:

Patient: I don't know whether I'm an idiot to be coming to see you or whether you're an even bigger idiot for trying to help me.
Therapist: One of the things I've always liked about you is the honest and open way you express your feelings.

The *Kick Me* player is not fooled by this maneuver. There is a quality of artificiality about counter-gaming in psychotherapy. But he does not notice that unless he takes extreme measures, you cannot be forced to kick him. An example of an extreme measure:

Therapist: Well, I'll see you next week. I'm sorry we have to stop because what
  you were saying was so interesting but I have another patient waiting.
Patient: Just one more question. How am I going to get better?
Therapist: "We'll talk about that next week.
Patient: But . . .
Therapist: So long.

This is a mild kick forced out of the therapist and one which he could not
really control. This should not unduly distress the therapist because some playing of the game will raise the question in the patient's mind whether or not
he will be able to play out his game fully and intensively, and this suspense
holds the patient to therapy in the initial states (Berne).

When the patient cannot play *Kick Me,* there will be a transactional vacuum
which should be conscientiously filled by the therapist with Child-Child
pastiming. The therapist finds a topic which he and the patient deeply enjoy
discussing. For example, it is appropriate for the patient and therapist to discuss sports cars for several months. If the patient complains that "I'm not
getting anywhere," then the therapist allows the first moves of *Why Don't
You . . . , Yes, But* and other *Kick Me* games but disallows payoffs by countering
with Benevolent Parent transactions.

Second Stage of Treatment: Analysis of Script Matrix

When the *Kick Me* player is partially convinced that the therapist will not
kick him from the therapist's Competitive Child position, and will not be
overly critical from a Critical Parent position, his anxiety and tension will
lower and he will be able to cathect Adult upon request. The therapist proceeds with P—A—C formulations and analyzes the nature of the Critical
Parent and Adapted Child ego states of the patient and the patient's parents.

The historic roots and dynamics of *Kick Me* follow:

1. The Critical Parent of the most influential parent, usually the patient's
mother, is dominated by her own Adapted Child. When the patient did something inappropriate at an early age, the Critical Parent message was supplemented by an Adapted Child message from the mother that fouled up the
initial Critical Parent message. An example follows of mother-child transactions when the patient did something that required Critical Parent correction
from his mother.

Mother (from Critical Parent): Why didn't you make your bed this morning?!
Child (from Adapted Child): I forgot, Naturally, ha, ha.
Parent (from *Adapted Child*): Do you know what you are? A slob! A hopeless
  slob! And you'll always be a slob!

The mother switched from the Critical Parent position to an Adapted Child position of the competitive, bullying Child. This is not appropriate for accomplishing the job, which is to get the child to make his bed. The appropriate response would be for the mother to remain in her Critical Parent and get her way. For example:

Mother (continuing in Critical Parent): Well, you are not going to "forget" anymore! No allowance this week! And you know what's going to happen when your father gets home! I expect everyone in this house to make their bed in the morning! In fact, get in that room right now and clean up the clothes from the floor!!!

It should be made clear to the patient that the patient's Child and the mother's Child are in a collusion where (1) the mother's Child can competitively lord it over the patient's Child by obtaining a monopoly on competence and have the enjoyment of *Ain't It Awful,* complaining to everyone about how put upon she is, and (2) the patient's Child has covert permission to be lazy and cowardly because he does not have to be competent, he is not expected to succeed, he may be a "slob" or "loser."

2. There is little authentic effort made by the patient to solve problems effectively and succeed because he does not believe that it is actually possible for him to have a success. (Even obvious successes are detracted from by the patient, who will launch into *Blemish*.) The essential message from the Child in the mother to Child in the patient is some version of *"You're a hopeless case."* If it is hopeless, why try? This explains the "lack of motivation" or "wrong attitude" noted in *Kick Me* players. Why should the *Kick Me* players tolerate the initial anxiety that commonly accompanies an effort to learn a new approach if he expects failure? If there is always failure, then the anxiety will never subside. And so the *Kick Me* player will take the position, "I'll do it when I feel like it, and it's your job (the therapist's) to make me feel less anxious, and *then* maybe I'll do it." If the therapist agrees to this, he is playing into the pathology and will get nowhere.

3. The Child in the mother has an aggressive and competitive attitude toward others, and imparts a distorted picture of human nature to the patient. The *Kick Me* player often feels that people get their major gratification out of bullying or bettering others, rather than out of affection, love, care, friendliness, and so forth. Positive stroking is always suspect to them, and their feelings about life tend to be ones of distrust and pessimism. Many aspects of human existence may be seen as futile and hopeless. "It's a dog-eat-dog world," "Life is a rat race," and similar sentiments are common. The therapist must flatly disagree with such gross stereotyping of reality in the second phase of treatment.

4. The patient believes that the only authentic transaction is a negative one and that in truth he deserves to be put down and bullied. Therefore he cannot even say "Thank you" to a compliment. It is important to teach the patient to accept positive strokes with at least simple rituals of recognition.

In making these analytic observations clear to the patient, the following script matrix is used:

Third Stage of Treatment: Supplemental Parenting

Supplemental parenting in the case of the *Kick Me* player means that the Critical Parent of the therapist is added to the other ego states of the patient. It is important that the therapist tells the patient about the procedure before he commences so that the patient can learn to distinguish on an Adult level the difference between the therapist's adequate Critical Parent, which gets in its way, and the patient's own Critical Parent, which is inadequate because it settles for failure.

Warning! Under no circumstances is this procedure to be used before the patient is prepared by successfully proceeding through the first two stages of treatment. Remarks from the therapist's Critical Parent prematurely delivered may minimally lead to firing of the therapist and at worst may increase the patient's potential for violence or suicide. The only exception to this rule occurs when the patient threatens this type of behavior at an early stage in treatment, in which case the therapist must authoritatively order the patient not to carry out the activity.

The Critical Parent of the therapist can only be transmitted to the patient effectively if the Natural Child of the patient is finally cathected in the process, as indicated in the following example. Also note that the Critical Parent of the therapist is not to be confused with the Competitive Child of the therapist, which *must not be hooked*. The patient is not to get a general pounding by the therapist's Child. The patient is to be placed in discomfort by the Critical Parent of the Therapist until the Critical Parent gets its way.

Patient (Adapted Child): I'm lonely. Where can I meet people? (The first move in *Yes, But . . .*)
Therapist (Critical Parent): If you're lonely, do something about it!
Patient (Adapted Child): Like what?
Therapist (Critical Parent): I expect you to solve that problem yourself!
Patient (Adapted Child): Yes, but I've never had a friend!
Therapist (Critical Parent): Baloney! You're lying! You had a friend a year ago.
Patient (Adapted Child, moving into *Blemish*): That wasn't a *real* friend.
Therapist (Critical Parent): Don't try to screw me up with a lot of that "Well, it wasn't perfect" jazz! Go find a friend!

Patient (Adapted Child): I'm too anxious to meet people.

Therapist (Critical Parent): That's a poor excuse. If you force yourself to meet them and treat them right, you won't be anxious forever, so put a move on, please!

Patient (Adapted Child): You don't know me, ha, ha.

Therapist (Critical Parent): I don't think it's funny, I think it's tragic! You know I've told you not to knock yourself! What are you doing!

Patient (Adapted Child): I dunno.

Therapist (Critical Parent): What are you going to do about meeting a friend?

Patient (Adapted Child): I dunno.

Therapist (Critical Parent): I don't accept "I dunno" as an answer! What are you going to do about finding a friend? And look up at me when you are talking and stop picking the lint off your pants, please!

Patient (*now* under the pressure cathects Natural Child): Aw, get lost!

Therapist (Critical Parent): I'll get lost when you start doing something about finding a friend!

Patient (Natural Child shifting to a *new* Adapted Child position, which is simple Compliant Child): All right, all right, so I'll join the Sierra Club!

Therapist (Critical Parent): And don't give me any more of that jazz about your anxiety, please. If you make an honest effort to do something and do it right, your anxiety will go away. I'm not here to make everything perfect for you, you know!

Patient (new Adapted Child): O.k., o.k.!

Therapist (Adult): What else do you want to talk about?

Successes on the part of the patient are to be responded to enthusiastically, either from a Benevolent Parent position—"Good work!"—or from a "buddy" or "hurrah for our team" Child-Child basis—"Great!"

Supplemental parenting with Critical Parent is deemed functional if the patient reports he is getting new messages when faced with problems. Example:

"I was given a promotion in assignment, and boy I was really sweating bullets and I almost turned it down. But then I said to myself, 'Do it! Are you going to be a chicken for the rest of your life! Do it and do a good job!' So I did it, I did a good job, and I wasn't nervous after a while. Boy, did I feel great!"

GENERAL CONSIDERATIONS

Stages One and Two generally take from six months to a year in individual psychotherapy. Stage Three takes about a year. Group therapy, unsupplanted by individual sessions, is ineffective with *Kick Me* players in the author's experience.

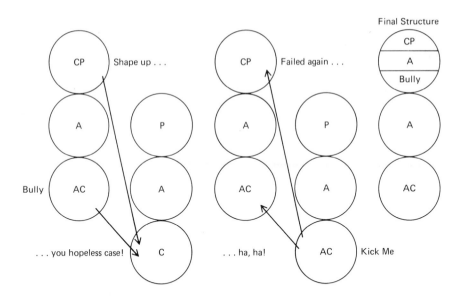

Note that the patient is not reparented (Schiff) since this requires the adoption, regression and re-raising of the patient, procedures which the author has been unable to carry out in a clinic or private practice setting.

The result of supplemental parenting is that the patient will have two Critical Parents, and although this will place him under conflict at choice points, he will have a clear option.

CHAPTER 26

stroking
the rebellious child:
an aspect
of managing resistance

ROBERT C. DRYE

In this paper I will define the Rebellious Child ego state, describe some of the powers in it and note ways of recognizing when the patient is in this spot in therapy. The thesis of this paper is that once the therapist recognizes the Rebellious Child position in his or her patient, it is useful to bring it to the awareness of the patient and even to stroke *positively* for the creativity, strength and excitement the patient has, and may be able to be in touch with, in the position. Failure to bring it to the patient's attention often leads to persistent impasses and premature interruption of treatment. The way I define Rebellious Child is: behavior organized around the position "whatever it is someone else wants me to do (or not do), I will do my utmost to not do (or do) it, or at least not their way." Externally directed this becomes "Try and make me, ha-ha!"

All of us experience rebelliousness as we grow. I must, from the very start, experience "I want to but I can't; I don't want to but I must." As I begin to perceive my parents as separate people, much of this becomes "I want to but you won't let me [touch, eat, play or whatever];" or, "I don't want to but

From *TA Journal* **4**, 3 (1974). Reprinted by permission.

you're making me [sleep, eat, shit, stop playing, etc.]." For example, "I may have to take it in my mouth but you can't make me swallow it or like it" or "I may have to sit on the toilet but you can't make me go." I can counter Parental injunctions such as "Don't feel!" (what you feel) by external compliance and internal rebellion.

The Natural Child wants to do something and doesn't like—in fact, positively hates—interference. "Leave me alone, I want to do it my way." The Adapted Child disguises the intensity of what he wants to get strokes from his parents and he may eventually disguise it even from himself. Adaptation includes rebellion as well as compliance. So the Rebellious Child I locate as part of the Adapted Child, the other part being the Compliant Child.

Depending on the kind of strokes around rebellious behavior, I develop various adaptive techniques in work and play which allow me to maintain my feeling of doing it my own way without necessarily letting it be known to those around me. I may make Decisions, such as "I'll never," which may be expressed as "whatever you want . . . I won't." Note that this is not freedom or autonomy since I depend on someone else with whom I can fight, and deny myself the option of doing what I want, if you also want it. I may feel it as autonomy, however. The script is written from "I'm OK—You're not, and I'm not so sure about me if I do anything your way."

The Rebellious Child position may be expressed in a number of ways: as a major life style, such as procrastination; in a tragic game, such as the alcoholic games described by Steiner;[1] or a major symptom of illness, such as some patients described by Schiff[2] as passive. If a therapist is aware of the Rebellious Child in himself and each of his patients, he and the patient can decide what to do therapeutically with each patient's unique way of expressing his or her rebelliousness. While some clinical conditions, such as alcoholism, drug abuse, perversions or delinquency, are likely to have rebellion as an important theme, the Rebellious Child may occur with any diagnosis. The best place to observe and point out the existence of this phenomenon is as it occurs in transactions between the patient and the therapist.

DETECTION

Occasionally a patient simply tells me, "I wish I could succeed even though I know you want me to." A fuzzy contract is a clue, in which what the patient's Child wants is unclear. "I'd like to, I ought to, I need to, for my wife's sake." If the therapist asks "why?" clear Parent messages may emerge and the patient can then be asked directly, "How do *you* [your child] feel about that?"[3] The patient may then recognize the difference between what he feels he should do and modify his contract to be more straight—or he may simply smile, wink or laugh. The slightly inappropriate smile or laugh is the most important single tipoff. If the patient is unaware of this behavior, ask him to stay alert to it, until he can pick it up and report his feeling. Rebellious laughs feel good and strong to both the patient and the observer, not spooky. At this point I might observe in an interested way, "You seem to be enjoying telling me this." I give the patient Permission to enjoy his strength and excitement and to explore what is happening and I find that the patient is more willing to link his rebelliousness to his laugh and to identify his own good, strong feelings as Rebellious Child.

For instance, one patient entered therapy with the contract "I want to get close to women, so I can get married." He seemed genuinely lonely and quick to reach out to women within the group. He began to smile as he described a lengthy mental checklist he had for a girl to seem marriageable; for some reason as soon as he gets to know a girl she doesn't meet the list. As the list got longer, he and the group broke into laughter, and he recognized how much fun he was having in not getting married. The part of his contract about getting married was from his father, who had suggested most of the items on the list. As he decided he really wasn't interested in marriage at the moment, he recognized that he had actually let himself get close to two women recently, that he was enjoying them and was quite satisfied with himself. He decided he would rather have fun that way than through his rebellion and felt comfortable discontinuing therapy.

Another way of spotting the Rebellious Child is to be aware of whether or not the patient is doing what the therapist or others in the group are asking him to do.

Therapist: "How are you feeling right now?"
Patient: "Before I answer a question I like to think about it for a while."
Therapist: "Will you say: 'I don't want to answer your question' and see how that feels?"
Patient: "I don't see how that would be useful."

I tell the patient that instead of saying "no" or "I won't" he gives me explanations for *not doing* what I'm asking. I bring his rebelliousness to his attention. His message seems to be "I won't do what you want me to do when you want me to do it: maybe I will in my own good time when I'm ready." The patient smilingly comments that he intellectualizes. I am aware of irritated frustrations in myself (another clue) and I might say something like "it really is important to you to act slowly on what I say." Instead of kicking his behavior, I am stroking it positively (and I may be the first person in his life who has ever reacted in this way). A Child stroke here would be "You sure are good at keeping me waiting for a straight answer."

To continue with the list: A depressed housewife was hospitalized when she was no longer eating or sleeping. She hinted at marital troubles and feeling like a failure at her part-time job, but mainly responded "It's just too much— no use talking about it." Her face was sad and immobile. Her husband confirmed that he had been dissatisfied with her for the past year. In the hospital she was asked to fill out a check-sheet psychological test and I asked her to write down, at her own speed, what (if anything) she'd like to see change in her marriage. After three days she had done little with either project. As I walked from the ward to her room, behind her, I was struck by a sort of kicking motion to her walk, like a sulky little girl kicking rocks. I told her my impression and then asked, "When you were a little girl, what was it your mother wanted you to do that she couldn't get you do to?" With a big smile she sat up and said cheerfully, "Eat my oatmeal." She vividly and proudly described how she flushed it, hid it under her saucer, and so on, as I admiringly encouraged her report. She then returned to her depressive posture but was more willing to discuss her marriage and work on her testing.

Note the strength of these positions. The man can dodge my questions indefinitely while ostensibly cooperating (after all, he is coming to group to get help). The woman can sit and do nothing and keep both her husband and myself waiting helplessly. Note also the pleasurable excitement at defeating the powerful parent-therapist who thinks he knows everything. To emphasize the patient's power ask him to substitute "I won't" for "I can't," "I'd like to," or "I will if." These are, of course, the "buts" from the *Yes, But* game.

Another example: a housewife complained of mild chronic depression, specifically an inability to play. She pictured herself as a young adolescent sitting sadly with her sad mother. She knows her mother is sad because she (the patient) isn't slender and popular. Until her mother feels better she has no right to feel good. She must scold herself for not being slender and making mother feel better. She quickly decided to feel good whether her mother did or not, experiencing this as rebellion, for which she was extensively stroked by the group (at a weekend marathon). She began to play. She then recognized how deep her rebellion against mother's ostensible instructions on how to make her happy were. Writing to me recently, she said, "All my life I remember being called 'difficult.' From my present understanding, I see that my being difficult was very important to my being me. If I had not fought with my mother, I would be even more depressed, laden with guilt she wanted to share with me. It seems my father wanted an attractive daughter he could show off, a possession perhaps. My need to be the exact opposite of what he wanted was my only way of feeling a separate person, different, superior. Now that I am experiencing intensive feelings of closeness and security with my therapist, I think my Rebellious Child refused to take what it could get on someone else's terms. It's my own terms or nothing. I will resist being cooperative and easy. If I become so, I will disappear as me. My 'difficulties' is not one of the things I want to change for anyone. I like it." Note that this patient can only be more flexible in using her Rebellious Child, as she finds additional ways to feel "me."

The Rebellious Child is useful in several ways to this patient. It appears not only when she experiences demands (to be and feel what someone else wants— the injunctions from her parents) but when she is afraid of a submissive merger because she feels the therapist understands her. She relies on her Rebellious Child to carry her through these crises. My most useful role in this spot is to recognize how difficult she is (not negatively by sadness, like her mother, or by withdrawal, like her father, but by excitement). But what if the patient's Rebellious Child is threatening dangerous behavior?

MANAGEMENT

At this point I want to return to an earlier point. *Rebellious laughs feel strong, not spooky.* The question is, by stroking the patient for rebellious behavior am I risking that he will experience me as he did a parent's crazy Child, approving his hurting himself? I haven't seen this happen in the complete sequence I'm advocating. First, I demonstrate my Potency by demonstrating I know where he is, and that I know he is very strong in that position. This is a stroke for the position, not for the behavior. Secondly, I stroke him for his strength (which undercuts any failure scripts based on weakness). From this position of mutual respect I can invite him to share the importance of this position in his current life (particularly for excitement) and how he'd miss it if he dropped it, which he (I predict) won't until he finds something at least as exciting. Note that I am using my Child and my Adult openly, encouraging straight transactions from his Child and Adult. The parent's crazy Child is much more likely to have operated nonverbally and in crossed communications. If, after this approach, the patient appears immediately headed to some disaster I can continue interpreting "When you were a kid who told you really straight stuff that you agreed with but still wouldn't use?" or switch to a strong Nurturing Parent position.

The patient who wrote me may move slowly, but we both know where she is, and each outbreak of Rebellious Child will correspond to a Child feeling of fear or excitement that can be identified with and decontaminated. In addition, I check the script importance and the outcome of the rebellion behavior. This may be inferred from the transactions with the therapist, but it may be more adaptive outside therapy than in it.[4] Rebellious behavior may be to collect stamps, or a stamp payoff, or part of script or anti-script.[5]

Getting in touch with my own Rebellious Child has helped. For insance, I'd like to write a longer paper than the Editorial Board likes to accept. Reluctantly, I will leave discussion of related ideas (such as how the patient chooses Rebellious Child instead of some other ego state that might get the same result[6]) to another paper.

SUMMARY

An aspect of the Child ego state sufficiently distinctive to be recognized separately is proposed. Ways of recognizing this state are described, and some beginning ideas about its development and clinical importance are suggested. Positive stroking is recommended to bring the power of the Rebellious Child into cooperation with the therapist.

REFERENCES

1. Steiner, Claude, *Games Alcoholics Play* (Grove: New York, 1971), pp. 72–73.

2. Schiff, A., and J. Schiff, "Passivity," *TA Journal* **1**, pp. 71–78.

3. Goulding, Robert L. Personal communication.

4. English, Fanita. "I'll Show You Yet (ISYY)," *TA Bulletin* **9**, 33, pp. 13–15.

5. Berne, Eric, *What Do You Say After You Say Hello?* (Grove: New York, 1972), pp. 132–133.

6. Cohan, Carolyn. Unpublished manuscript.

CHAPTER 27

a TA approach
to dreams

ARTHUR SAMUELS

In TA terms, a dream may be thought of as a dynamic symbolic representation of one's existential position within a life script. If viewed closely it is like an exquisitely detailed painting of where one is in life at the moment of dreaming. Moving back from the detail, one can see the larger flow—where one has come from and where one goes in or out of the script. This paper illustrates a method by which the symbolism can be translated into clinically useful TA terms.

We start our dream work with a classical Gestalt Approach.[1] The dreamer first re-experiences the dream by relating it in the present tense. He is then asked to identify (again in the first person) with various people, objects, or feeling tones in the dream. In a short dream, every part is experienced; in a long dream with many components, those parts are chosen which are of most interest to the dreamer, or which appear to be most significantly useful to the therapist at that particular phase of therapy.

From *TA Journal* **4,** 3 (1974). Reprinted by permission.

Each of these parts, after it has been authentically experienced, can then be assigned to an ego state role: Nurturing Parent, Prejudiced Parent, Adult, Adaptive Child, or Free Child. The assignment of ego roles is made by the dreamer who has been trained in previous sessions using Stuntz' Technique.[2] The therapist's guidance may be necessary here, to recognize ego states where a lot of contamination exists. It is important that the therapist not intrude his own internal imagery. This part of the dream work in itself can provide important insights. For example: Arn has a dream about a group of people who have survived a perilous canoe trip. He has been asked to "Be the canoe."

"I'm solid, aluminum, straight, sturdy, agile, dependable. I maneuver accurately, darting my way through many dangerous situations. The people in me trust me and depend upon me. I'm their only support."

Arn feels competent and Adult as the canoe and moves into the Adult chair. He then realizes that the canoe has no ability to direct itself and is being battered unmercifully by the torrential river which is identified immediately as the Prejudiced Parent. He then feels like moving into the Adapted Child Chair.

The therapist helps Arn to see how his Adult is contaminated by his continually battering Parent. Though he usually makes Adult decisions that are successful, he ends up criticizing himself until he feels like a sad inadequate child.

More than one dream component may be assigned to the same ego state, each one providing a different perspective. The dream work can be facilitated by using a modification of Stuntz' five chair technique[2] in which the dream components are assigned to the appropriate chair and the dreamer moves from chair to chair as dialogue is pursued between the dream components. As significant insights are attained it is easy to translate them into TA terms. The dialogue can be moved out of the dream symbolism into present conflictual areas or into past conflicts with mother and father.

An alternate approach in groups is to use group members to role play the various parts, emphasizing the particular characteristic of the ego state assigned. Parts may be cast to facilitate the on-going therapy contracts of the other group members, e.g., the overly controlled member might be given a Free Child role to practice, while the overly impulsive member might benefit from practicing an Adult role.

Categorizing the dream content into ego states adds fascinating possibilities to the use of dream material. Some of the more important uses are:

To add subtle qualitative description to the ego states, defining them more accurately and showing their influence on each other.

By making an egogram[3] of the dream, the parts of the personality that need diminishing and those needing bolstering may be shown.

By placing the existential message of the dream in the context of script controls, games and rackets, and contracts leading to script antithesis, may be presented.

Transference can be clarified in TA terms.

Present conflicts can be clarified and resolved.

The following dream demonstrates many of these features. The dreamer is Betty, an attractive, compulsively hard-working professional woman in her early fifties. Betty left her punitive, rigidly moralistic, parents when she was eighteen. In the course of therapy, she has successfully given up a severe depression racket. Looking more attractive, she finds men to be very responsive to her. As these relationships grow she finds herself to be in constant conflict as to whether or not to please them by doing what they want to do or to stay free of them. She is slowly giving up tremendous guilt feelings about her own sexuality.

Dream

"I am swimming hard over a swampy area littered with grass, weeds, and dirt. I feel wary of snakes and bugs in the area."

As the Swamp: "I filter out all dirt and debris . . . Oh—I'm Prejudiced Parent. I inspect you constantly to see that you are doing the chores around the house and if I see you even looking at boys I'll attack you like a snake and call you a whore." (She continues to speak as her mother in the swamp, evoking the atmosphere of her poverty-stricken childhood home.) "I want you to be free but I'll feel frightened and angry if you actually are free—so I'll hold on to you forever."

As the Snake and Bugs: "I hide in here. I'm dangerous, you can't really see me but if you come too close I'll attack. I'm dark and ominous." (Betty went into the Adapted Child chair for this. She identified it as her own depression with snake-like projection of rage extending out towards mother and her demands.)

As the Water: "I flow freely in and out wherever I want to go. I'm the Free Child—Whee! I flow everywhere." (She gets up and flows around the room, gives me a hug.)

As the Swimmer: "I'm the Adult. I can observe potential danger and decide to swim away from it. I can keep myself in the clear water."

The existential message came out strongly here. "I'm the one who hides out in the swamp. I've never really let mother go, I hold on to her by expecting things of myself. Then I hate myself if I don't do it. I also stick my mother inside of men. I'm constantly running away from what they want and am furious at their demanding, selfish ways and I never stop to see what I want to do. I just stay in the swamp with mother and feel dirty and intruded upon."

In the working through process Betty saw the need to develop her Nurturing Parent which was buried in the swamp. She had experienced a bit of the nurturing part of her mother via parental concern that had been covered over by fear. She understood how she symbolically had kept herself from leaving her parents' home by making herself feel guilty and depressed whenever her Free Child emerged. She saw how she was currently doing that with men by playing, *If It Weren't For You* I'd be free to do what I want to do.

She made a contract to develop her own Free Child by identifying and expressing her feelings. When she feels guilt she will replace the Critical Parent with Nurturing Parent who loves her for having the free feeling. This contract was specifically spelled out and carried out on her next date.

REFERENCES

1. Pearls, F., *Gestalt Therapy Verbatim* (Lafayette Calif.: Real People Press, 1969).
2. Stuntz, E. C., "Multiple Chairs Technique," *TA Journal* **3,** 2, pp. 105–108.
3. Dusay J. M., "Egograms and the Constancy Hypothesis," *TA Journal* **2,** 3, pp. 37–41.

CHAPTER 28

insight
for the sightless:
a TA group
for the blind

SOLVEIG H. THOMSON

For blind people, the problem is not only "what do you say after you say hello?" but even more crucially, "how do you say hello in the first place?" If you cannot see, your howdy-do travels to others and back again through a blind alley echoing with tension, uncertainty, and misunderstanding. This paper reports on an educational-therapy group aimed at helping blind people explore that alley from a TA point of view. To date, there are no publications on the use of TA theory and techniques with blind people, and very little literature on group treatment with the blind.[3,11]

The original group members were nine legally blind residents of a dormitory where students live while taking individualized classes on such topics as mobility, vending, and home management at the nearby Services for the Blind agency in Seattle, Washington. Five group members were men and four were women; of the nine, five were totally blind and the others had very minimal vision. Ages of the original group varied from 17 to 35, but as the membership changed the overall average age was about 21. No selection procedures were used and members volunteered to participate in the group which met for an hour and a half

From *TA Journal* 4, 1 (1974). Reprinted by permission.

weekly for six months. Group members shared in common the fact that they were legally blind, were members of a stigmatized minority, lived in the same dormitory, were receiving government supported services, and most had similar institutional school backgrounds. They were very diverse, however, in regard to the degree and kinds of blindness, intelligence, personality, family and socioeconomic background, and life goals.

The focus of the original group, viewed as an experimental program by the agency, was educational in that it explored basic TA ideas in discussions of ego states, transactions, life positions, scripts, games, rackets, time structuring, and others. Special materials such as tape recordings of *I'm OK, You're OK* and *Born to Win* were made available at the agency. Members did not listen to them, however, partially because of passivity and the inconvenience of reel tapes, but mainly because the group's primary payoff was interpersonal stroking. An ingenious technique developed by Roger Craven,[4] using plastic sheets melted over an aluminum mold in a Thermoform machine, created an efficient braille version of basic TA diagrams such as ego states, transactions, contaminations, and exclusions. (A printed version is shown in the accompanying figure.)

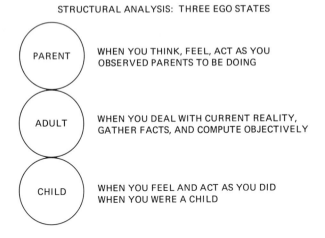

STRUCTURAL ANALYSIS: THREE EGO STATES

PARENT — WHEN YOU THINK, FEEL, ACT AS YOU OBSERVED PARENTS TO BE DOING

ADULT — WHEN YOU DEAL WITH CURRENT REALITY, GATHER FACTS, AND COMPUTE OBJECTIVELY

CHILD — WHEN YOU FEEL AND ACT AS YOU DID WHEN YOU WERE A CHILD

Visual aids for sighted persons differ from tactile tools for the blind in their audience impact. A sighted group can simultaneously see the same diagram, get an overview, and watch additional lines being added or features being pointed out. A blind group must go through a sequential touching process which makes tactile aids less spontaneous, flexible, and potent in a group teaching situation. Learning through the fingertips is a more individualized process in that it takes time to pass out materials, arrange for support, distinguish top from bottom, and find the beginning of the text. Individuals then read these materials at varying rates, depending upon their skill and motivation.

In the educational discussions, members turned their happy little kids loose with much enthusiasm, laughter, curiosity, and "Wow! I play that game," or "Let me tell you about," responses. On other occasions, they got in touch with their hurting kids who wanted to blow off steam about blind alley transactions relating to families, peers, jobs, agencies, living situations, school and other social situations. Many were in the "I'm not very OK" position, feeling themselves "made into blind men"[15] by the expectations of a rejecting society. Some people do not accept physical disability and substitute an "eye" for an "I" by discounting the uniqueness of the blind individual's identity.

Many examples were shared of discounting transactions and negative stroking through: overprotection (not being allowed to eat with a fork until age 14 was one example); rejection (being a drag on siblings or friends who resent guiding the blind); miscommunication (a congenitally blind teenager wanting to give books on blindness to his father); unrealistic expectations (constantly being reminded of famous blind people or not being allowed to help in the home); and games played by blind and sighted alike (a mother who moves the furniture often without warning or the blind person who seeks special privilege).

After 11 weeks, and following a favorable written evaluation by group members, the group chose to move into a therapy model involving individual contracts about personal problems. Examples of contracts included: "I want to understand and stop a hostile game-playing relationship with my mother;" "I want to quit taking on responsibility and then resenting it;" "I want to be able to express a broad range of emotion authentically instead of clowning all the time!" "I want to develop more self-confidence, assertive behavior, and get rid of my 'I'm sorry' syndrome."

To break through the verbalizing and to add a little therapeutic zip, the following experiential techniques were adopted: double-chair dialogues; performing a psychodrama with each member playing the role of a family figure at a crucial decision point in one member's life; modeling and practice of new behaviors during group (saying "No!" for example, when the group tried to get one member to take on unwanted responsibilities or helping another to assertively tell his roommate to wash the ring out of the tub); a "growing up" experience acted out by a youth who grew from a position on his knees to his adult stature while experiencing the changing relationship with encircling group members, and so on.

The group, which in general had many depression rackets and seemed stimulus deprived, really enjoyed getting in touch with a sense of play. Some members made considerable progress on their contracts, others less so, and some members, especially the less intelligent ones, failed to develop and work on clearly defined contracts. One girl's Little Professor came up with a nifty plan to have her mother read *Born to Win* to her, thus opening up mutual opportunities to intimately explore the sticky games they were playing.

There are some unique characteristics of group work with the blind.

First, non-verbal communication between the therapist and the group and between group members is totally or substantially lost. Obviously, much information about emotional expression and the ability to monitor changing emotions is lost in transactions where much of one's sweatshirt (i.e., dress, posture, body tension, facial movement, and bodily gestures) is not seen by others. Lacking visual information, the blind person focuses on verbalizing his feelings, listening to verbal feedback, and checking out what is perceived from others by further conversation. This makes for a more intellectual, verbal atmosphere where transactions are often less potent and clearly understood in that only verbal portions can be shared. Consequently, group members made fewer comments such as "you look sad" which recognize emotion in others and trigger further reactions. Also, a blind person cannot use the subtle, shifting, non-verbal cues given by a listener to adapt his ongoing conversation. Instead, he must await verbal feedback, which makes his transactions slower, less precise and less intense.

The body language of the blind, directed at an unseen goal, may be experienced by the sighted as somehow strange and less spontaneous. There can be considerable differences in the body language of the congenitally blind and those who have had sight at one time or who have minimal sight. The congenitally blind may not have learned much of the culturally shared non-verbal language as a result of never having had the opportunity to observe and imitate others. Consequently, a blind person may have such mannerisms as a grimace, an adapted smile, a rigid handshake, a rocking motion, a passive expression, a turned-down face with closed eyes, or a quiet posture associated with listening. The sighted person may respond to such unfamiliar messages with discomfort and a flustered realization that much of his own body language is not being perceived, a recognition which can lead to a cycle of still more stilted communication.

In addition to the loss of non-verbal communication, there is a second, less obvious, characteristic of group work with the blind.

The therapist suddenly becomes a sighted minority of one, with all the accompanying feelings of uncertainty in a world of new experiences. For example, wearing a blindfold for part of one session quickly put me, a sighted therapist with a lifelong dependency upon visual cues, in touch with a loss of orientation and clout. I felt a loss of sensory information, the frustration of not being able to give and get non-verbal strokes like smiles and hand gestures, and a self-conscious awareness of lazy, undeveloped listening skills. At another session, the lights were turned out with resulting associations of restful intimacy for me but with no change in the experiential world of the blind. On one occasion, a blind youth placed his chair so close to mine that I felt he unknowingly violated my territory; his boundaries, perhaps as a function of his blindness, were simply different from my own. Several times I used a stroking touch but it was a funny "feeling" in that I had to give warning of my approach and this powerful interaction could not be observed by others in the group. I also found a little hesitation in using techniques which I had only experienced with the sighted and had to adapt to blind use by describing each step of what I was doing with one individual so that others could share (e.g., moving people into positions in a group sculpt). I became aware of talking more, filling ambigious silence, and increasing my rate of stroking "yeah's" and "Um-hmms" to acknowledge that messages were being heard.

A sighted therapist may have to deal with delicate areas of personal uneasiness about physical disability and blindness which may show in censored language such as avoiding the words "blind" or "I see," in nervous mannerisms, in discounting with oversympathetic attitudes, or in behaviors maintaining physical distance and avoiding touch. Subtle conditioned values and attitudes regarding physical beauty, effectiveness, and interpersonal attractions are challenged in that blind people may move in a tentative, awkward way, may bump into things, may have eyes that are clouded or move in an unusual manner, and may need realistic help on occasion. Deep-rooted cultural biases which associate looking someone in the eyes with honesty, directness, or emotional arousal are also questioned.

A third feature of group work with the blind is that housekeeping duties are slower and more complicated. For example, a blind person entering the room does not know who is there or where to sit, and those in the room may not be aware someone has entered. Small talk and directions, then, are necessary at the beginning of each meeting for everyone to identify the presence and position of others. Furniture and ashtrays have to be identified and arranged carefully. People who want to leave the room, get a match, or adjust a window usually have to make a verbal request or take interrupting action, whereas in a sighted group people can meet their needs more quickly and independently.

Working with a blind group suggests many stimulating research ideas. For example, it would be fun and beneficial to develop a training program in such "give to get" transactions as practicing body language (which maximizes the possibility of good strokes from the sighted) or learning other techniques (like leaving your seeing-eye dog home when apartment hunting). The differences in transactions and ego states between congenitally blind, adventitiously blind, and partially sighted; the nature of fantasy in the blind person; and the process of forming group images for the blind, are all interesting areas of study. A theoretical paper speculating on the development and manifestation of ego states of the blind is being considered.

In summary, TA groups have much to offer the blind and other disability groups in many settings. TA offers a fun, informal, hopeful, comprehensive set of tools as a framework for living. It has a vital language, simple concepts, a frisky literature, and combines well with experiential techniques. For this group, the high attendance rate, the favorable written evaluations, the positive subjective comments, the friendly atmosphere, and the progress on meeting contacts indicate that the group felt it was a worthwhile experience. For the therapist, it was "out of sight."

(Note: The braille teaching materials mentioned in this article are available at minimal cost. Also, *I'm OK, You're OK* has been published in braille and is available, together with *What Do You Say After You Say Hello?* on tape cassettes. Contact your local agency for the blind.)

REFERENCES

1. Bauman, Mary K., and Norman M. Yoder, *Adjustment to Blindness-Reviewed* (Springfield, Ill.: Charles C. Thomas, 1966).

2. Berne, Eric, *What Do You Say After You Say Hello?* (New York: Grove, 1972).

3. Cholden, Louis S., *A Psychiatrist Works With Blindness* (New York: American Foundation for the Blind, 1958).

4. Craven, Roger W., "The Use of Aluminum Sheets in Producing Tactual Maps for Blind Persons," *The New Outlook for the Blind,* November 1972, pp. 323–330.

5. Goldman, Herbert, "The Use of Encounter Microlabs With a Group of Visually Handicapped Rehabilitation Clients," *The New Outlook for the Blind,* September 1970, pp. 219–226.

6. Manaster, Al, and Sue Kucharis, "Experimental Methods in a Group Counseling Program with Blind Children," *The New Outlook for the Blind* **66,** 1 (1972).

7. Miller, William H., "Group Counseling with the Blind," *Education of the Visually Handicapped* **3,** 2 (1971), p. 46–51.

8. Routh, Thomas A., *Rehabilitation Counseling of the Blind* (Springfield, Ill.: Charles C. Thomas, 1970).

9. Rusalem, Herbert, *Coping with the Unseen Environment* (New York: Teachers College Press, 1972).

10. Saul, Sidney R., "Group Work with Blind People: Helping Them to Develop Emotionally and Socially," *The New Outlook for the Blind* **52** (1958), pp. 166–72.

11. ———, "Group Work and Integration," *The New Outlook for the Blind* **53** (1959), pp. 58–60.

12. ———, "The Evaluation of Social Group Work," *The New Outlook for the Blind* **57** (1963), pp. 44–51.

13. ———, "New Uses of Social Group Work." *The New Outlook for the Blind* **59** (1965), pp. 66–68.

14. ———, Nadine Eisman, and Shura Saul, "The Use of the Small Group in the Helping Process," *The New Outlook for the Blind,* April 1964, pp. 122–125.

15. Scott, Robert, *The Making of Blind Men* (New York: Russell Sage Foundation, 1969).

16. Wilson, Edouard L., "Group Therapy in a Rehabilitation Program," *The New Outlook for the Blind* **64,** 7 (1970), pp. 237–239.

17. Wilson, Edouard L., "Programmed Individual and Adjunctive Therapeutic Services for Visually Impaired Clients in a Rehabilitation Center," *The New Outlook for the Blind* **66,** 7 (1971).

CHAPTER 29

therapeutic education with older adults

ELIZABETH FIELDING

THE PROBLEM: THE NEED FOR THERAPY AND THE AVOIDANCE OF IT

Old age often brings new problems and magnifies old ones. Yet, in spite of the physical and emotional suffering that often accompany problems, older people seldom seek psychotherapy. It is not in their frame of reference. They have not been educated to recognize its value. Even the words "mental health" and "mental illness" are new and strange and frightening. Because the concepts are not familiar they are threatening. The popularity in recent years of encounter groups and various types of therapy directed toward developing human potential does not seem to have spread significantly among older adults.

Late maturity for many people is a period characterized by increased stress resulting from a variety of problems. Physiological changes with aging include: loss of speed and strength, changing physical appearance, sensory decrements in all modalities, and increased susceptibility to chronic disease. Short- and long-term memory may also be affected by aging. In our youth-oriented society such changes are experienced as contributing to personal devaluation.

For some women the first of the later life adjustments occurs when the last child leaves home. If a woman's role as a mother has been her major—or only —role, and she has not prepared for new personal involvements, the period of adjustment may be traumatic. In addition, this may come when her husband is at the height of his work involvement, when he has little excess energy for increased activities with her. Growing demands from his job may coincide with his first feelings of waning physical strength. Overtaxed by work responsibilities, he may also be experiencing concern about sexual performance, which can generate anxiety and perhaps experimentation with extra-marital involvement as a way to reestablish his self-confidence. He may therefore be unsupportive of his wife, or even leave home in search of new and more rewarding relationships.

Retirement brings major role changes for employed men and women. This milestone *may* involve enthusiastic anticipation, especially with advance planning accompanied by good health, adequate income, and emotional investment in personally rewarding activities to replace work and work-related roles. *Forced retirement* for those not so foresighted or fortunate will be more traumatic.

Loss of spouse, a major crisis of aging, leaves the survivor not only alone but deprived in areas of life once shared with the person now dead. For instance, poor nutrition and increasing susceptibility to disease may result from reluctance to cook for one or to eat alone. Widowhood may mean financial problems which are particularly overwhelming for women with no work experience or skills.

Decisions about living arrangements are a major problem for some older people; for example, moving from the family home to a different type of housing —an apartment, retirement community, or lifetime care facility. Others may move to reduce expenses or to be near adult children. Forming new friendships and making adjustments to new communities may be difficult. Living with adult children for reasons of economic or physical dependency may reduce feelings of self-worth and leave older people isolated and lonely.

Family problems may revolve around late-life marriages, relationships with adult children, or changing dependency needs of senile parents.

In addition to characteristic age-related stresses, the life review process, identified by Robert Butler,[1] revives for some people unresolved conflicts from earlier years. Problems and conflicts may benefit from the integrative healing process occurring in warm and supportive groups with skilled leadership, where similar concerns are shared.

THE SOLUTION: THERAPEUTIC EDUCATION

A Community Case Study

In California's Contra Costa County (across the bay from San Francisco), people over 65 comprise over 10% of the population. Yet most mental health care for this age group is for those in crisis who require emergency care and/or institutionalization as the result of severe impairment or incapacitating emotional disorder.[2] There have been no mental health resources for older people who are able to function in the community and are *not* on welfare. The cost of private counseling or therapy is prohibitive for many aging persons because of limited financial resources and escalating living costs.

To solve this problem a therapeutic education course was developed. It was called "Fun after 50 with TA," and it was designed for the purpose of applying Transactional Analysis to the problems of late middle age and aging. It was viewed as therapeutic by the instructor; as educational by the participants.

The goals were: increased understanding of self and others; realization of the existence of multiple options for problem-solving and decision-making; and growth in capacity to cope and take responsibility for feelings, attitudes, and behavior, thereby increasing self-esteem and life satisfaction.

In TA the simple nontechnical language and easily understood concepts were particularly valuable for meeting the needs of older people with varying education, experience, and social skills. TA concepts were made clear by means of illustrations from everyday experience and exercises[3] in applying them to personal situations. As a result, TA theory became immediately relevant and usable.

Introductory Courses. There were two introductory courses in "Fun after 50 with TA." The first was offered through the Oasis TA Training Center, in Lafayette, California. The regular course fee was reduced by half in order to attract older people, and, of the twelve women enrolled, about half did office work at the center in exchange for the fee. Nine completed the program: four in their 50's, four in their 60's, and one in her 70's.

The course consisted of eight sessions of one and a half hours and covered: relevance of TA to the adjustments of the last third of life, autonomy and the contract process, ego states, ego boundary problems, transactions, strokes and discounts, rackets and trading stamps, time-structuring, psychological positions, games, and scripts. Each topic was accompanied by exercises to increase familiarity with the concepts. Reading assignments from *Born to Win*[4] were optional. Friendships developed, and participants felt comfortable in bringing in personal problems for gaining insights and exploring varied solutions. Personal philosophies were shared, and group members appreciated the supportive environment.

All of those who completed the course felt that they understood TA concepts fairly well and were beginning to use some of them, but some wanted the experience of another class in order to do so more effectively.

As a result of this experiment the community college offered the course tuition-free through a community center. Thirty-two women and six men signed up; and thirty-four completed the eight two-hour sessions. Three were in their 70's, and of the remainder about half were in their 60's and half in their 50's. Because of its size the group met in two sections.

The course plan was basically the same as in the Oasis Center course, although illustrations in lectures and exercises were changed because a few from the former course attended. The innovative technique in this program was the addition of fantasies for enhancing sensory awareness and growth of personal insight through identification and value clarification. Fantasies were also used as a way of getting in touch with happy events in the past and potentialities for the future in order to enrich experience. After each fantasy, without exception, a few people commented on the beauty or wonder of the experience or the fact that they were learning new things about themselves.

Following the introductory courses, there were two additional types of courses. The first was a series of five three-hour workshops on: strokes and discounts, the Child, games, scripts, and problem-solving. The second was an advanced course in which participants formulated contracts.

TA Workshops. Twenty-one women and five men participated in the workshops. Two of the men were in their 70's, and the remainder of the group were evenly divided betwen the 50's and 60's. All had read *Born to Win,* at least in part. At the beginning of the course they were asked to share their personal goals. These included: being able to apply TA better; understanding games and scripts better; making better decisions; feeling more OK in specific areas; improving relationships with spouse and children; learning to age gracefully; planning time better; being able to speak up in groups; and deciding about marrying again.

The general objectives in the workshops were to increase familiarity with the principles of TA and to develop the ability to apply it in everyday living. The program, therefore, consisted of brief reviews of theory (providing clarification as needed) and in-depth work projects and experiential exercises. Small-group projects and role-play were particularly useful in providing opportunities for insight and redecision in regard to personal concerns.

Exercises on strokes and enjoyment gave participants understanding and insights into ways of spending time alone and with people in meaningful ways, increasing good feelings, and experience of OKness. In an exercise on intuition involving two strangers imagining things about each other aloud, participants generally made remarkably accurate discoveries about each other, and this exercise and others in awareness provided major insights into several areas, in addition to enjoyment of the experience and at least two new friendships.

A workshop for the Child focused on the paramount value of some of the Child activities of the individual such as: fun, creativity, imagination, discovery, and new experience.

A workshop on games provided insights and options as groups worked out games based on their own experiences and then devised ways of breaking them up. Games were selected to portray Victim, Persecutor, and Rescuer roles, and after each game was role-played by the work group, the members demonstrated a way to break it up. This session was considered particularly valuable to the whole group.

During the workshop on scripts, participants worked individually on their own scripts by first writing fairy tales[5] and then analyzing them to see how they were like their own lives. Using the script matrix,[6] they then worked to identify the verbal and nonverbal messages received from their parents or parent figures. Script formula[7] analysis of positive and negative experiences resulting in script decisions was considered valuable by the group. Emphasis in this workshop was on the fact that the individual made his or her own decisions as a small child on the basis of often inadequate information, and that there existed here-and-now possibilities for redecision.

One woman in her late 60's commented: "All my life I've lived to please other people, not that I've been unhappy; but now I have a lot of living to do in a short time. Now I enjoy every new day because I'm always finding some new experience."

Using the technique in *Winning with People*[8] problem-solving exercises (with problems presented by participants) were effective in demonstrating the process to participants and giving them practice in it. Circumstances surrounding the sale of a house and placing an elderly parent in a nursing home were explored.

Advanced Course. At the end of the workshops, twenty women asked for some additional work with TA. Twelve were in their 50's, seven in their 60's, and three in their 70's. They said they would like particularly to have more practice in breaking up games, another workshop for the Child, further ex-

ploration of their own scripts, and some work with contracts in the group setting. This third type of course has been labeled the "advanced course."

The first distinctive aspect of the advanced course was the work with contracts,
which reflected decisions for change in feelings or behavior. Although contracts had been discussed in all the other courses, participants lacked enthusiasm
about using them in the group. Some, however, had made individual contracts
which they shared from time to time. All the advanced class worked on contracts, although three chose not to describe them in the group. Among the
contracts made by the participants were contracts to:

- Lose weight (4).
- Ask my daughter for feedback instead of feeling she is constantly criticizing
  me.
- Speak up once a week in bible class.
- Improve my image in appearance and dress as a result of changing my bal-
  ance of money and effort expenditure.
- Stop nagging my husband; give him positive strokes (2).
- Use "I" when talking to people to increase my feeling of potency.
- Treat men like friendly people instead of keeping them at a distance.
- Find things for my husband and me to do together.
- Find other options instead of feeling and acting shocked at things my daugh-
  ter does.
- Release my children to make their own decisions, dealing with my internal
  anxiety about them through accepting their need to be independent.
- When I feel blue, stop calling negative people who reinforce my depression;
  develop other things to do.
- Be decisive and honest when my children ask my preferences, rather than ask-
  ing them to decide for me.
- Manage my time to have one hour of pure enjoyment just for me. (Woman
  with a full-time job and an invalid husband.)

About half of each session was devoted to work on contracts: reports of progress, changes and new decisions, difficulties and problem-solving. Descriptions
of successes were reinforced and problems were explored to identify options.
Role-play of crossed and ulterior transactions was often helpful and acted as
reinforcement of new patterns.

This is different from contract work in the therapy group setting in that there
was no confrontation or probing. The instructor used active listening and
Adult questions or information-giving, providing permission to think through
problems. Interaction from group members was often supportive and never

more than gently critical. They shared insights, without becoming deeply involved in rescue games, and demonstrated patience and concern.

The second major emphasis in this course was on adaptations of therapeutic techniques to the educational setting. A "bragging" session was a meaningful exercise in self-affirmation. Work with strokes led to discussion of personal philosophy with regard to aging. Several women described older people who had provided inspiration and insight to them about successful aging. They identified four patterns for aging: doing things for people, as in volunteer work or focusing on grandchildren; recreation, such as bridge, golf, travel; personal growth through going back to school, starting a second career, or philosophizing; and being wholly involved with oneself and withdrawing to television and loneliness. There was general agreement that some balance of the first three would be most personally rewarding for them.

A session on self-reparenting[9] gave permission to all participants to foster the welfare of the Child within them. As a group they identified a list of twenty-seven qualities of an ideal parent—in general, to provide nurture, encourage, broaden opportunities, and set reasonable limits. They then worked on selecting qualities to adopt for parenting themselves and others.

Freeing the Natural Child for greater awareness and joy has been a major goal for many of the participants, and the group workshop for the Child seemed effective in involving them in shared experiences of fun, sensory awareness, and new discovery. For three people who saw their lives as mostly work and little, if any, play, it seemed particularly valuable.

At the end of this workshop was presented some material on sexuality in the last third of life, summarizing the findings of Masters and Johnson[10] and Mc-Kain's[11] research on retirement marriages. Sexual problems were not discussed in the group situation, but two of the women later expressed relief at getting information on the causes of impotence in middle-aged men. Each could see a direct relation to other aspects of the marital situation, job situation, and/or alcohol. They explored tactful ways of passing the information along to their husbands, as they believed this would be a difficult thing to discuss.

Centering exercises—relaxation and breathing exercises to facilitate an experience of inner balance and strength—were introduced in the advanced course and were much enjoyed and appreciated. Several students reported using them in moments of stress or fatigue, and some stayed after classes for additional exercises in the group situation.

Some members of this class plan to continue study of TA in new courses currently being planned.

THE THERAPEUTIC EDUCATOR

A teaching style characterized by simplicity, warmth, enthusiasm, and appreciation for contributions of the participants contributes to a comfortable learning climate, particularly with older people who are not academically oriented.

In addition, there is a constellation of attitudes and behavior in the instructor which contributes to healing and growth in the participants—belief in the essential OKness of people and acceptance of them as individuals with unique qualities and resources which can be mobilized to solve problems and enrich personal experience, and the capacity to convey such acceptance and beliefs and to refrain from solving people's problems or conveying criticism. Creating an atmosphere of acceptance and goodwill gives participants permission to take responsibilities for their own unique decisions for growth and change.

This program also requires an understanding of the problems of aging and a degree of comfort with personal aging; ability to use and adapt TA concepts to meet the needs of older people; skills to provide any indicated counseling after class and to make appropriate referrals to community services; and the ability to use group process effectively, limiting individual discussion to meet needs of the total group.

Three tools of the psychotherapists are valuable in this therapeutic education program: permission, protection, and potency.

Participants should have permission to set aside overly rigid or nonconstructive Parent direction (verbal or nonverbal) without antagonism, and to distinguish Child feelings and wishful thinking from here-and-now reality. For the instructor to give that permission contributes to his or her effectiveness in this process of learning and change.

The solutions for the problems presented by Mary and Martha illustrate these two types of permission. Mary, who had been overweight all her life and had lost fifty pounds, discovered that she was uncomfortable with compliments related to her being slender and subsequently gained back thirty pounds. Some work with Parent messages in the class disclosed that she had double-binds from both of her parents about her weight. In addition, she had been adopted at age two and a half and remembers being told frequently that her parents decided to take her because she was "such a pretty chubby little girl." She was given permission by the instructor and the group to feel lovable regardless of her weight and is again on a low-calorie diet.

Martha's husband seemed completely engrossed in his business, and she described herself to the group as "nagging him constantly to retire so he would be free to travel." In a counseling session after class she saw her nagging as a childlike technique which was reinforcing her husband's procrastination about retirement. She was given permission to explore other options and decided to take a trip by herself while he was attending a business conference. On her return he set the date for his retirement.

Protection of participants who are experiencing excitement or stress against revealing things about themselves they might later regret is a valuable tool which depends to a large extent on intuition and skill in focusing on areas which are less emotionally charged. Adult questions or, more radically, direction from the Nurturing Parent, may be used effectively in this connection. It has been useful to close off a topic directly by suggesting postponement to a later time because of the amount of material to be covered. Giving the individual concerned a particular question to consider for later discussion on a one-to-one basis encourages cathecting of the Adult. For example, "When your son is critical of you, you say you usually cry. What other things could you do or say?"

Responsible professionalism involves respect for people's defenses and avoiding occurrences which may be demeaning to participants. Labeling and diagnosing should be considered counterproductive. The instructor has a responsibility for awareness of personal games and for continuing attention to avoid involvement in drama roles.

The potency of the leader in a program such as this exists in some degree through modeling another person on a pilgrimage of growth and change, together with skills and techniques for enabling the class to experience stages in their pilgrimage as pleasurable and meaningful. Checking out the realities of the human situation to recognize previously unidentified resources—internal and external—contributes potency for healing and growth. There is, in fact, potency in the process of people joining together to work toward these common goals. The relationships which develop in the process add meaning and act as facilitators for further growth and enrichment.

CONCLUSION

Motivation and readiness for change seemed important factors in this growth experience. Participants came with hopes and/or expectations, and in some cases they were aware of particular decisions or changes which they wanted to put into effect. Some, who had had much experience with Adult decision-making, moved ahead in an organized fashion to change their patterns of feelings and behavior. Others focused on freeing up Adult processes from Child feelings to move toward increasing autonomy. In some cases, Parent messages which constituted double-binds were identified, and some major decisions and permissions were possible.

Work with, and evaluations of, the courses discussed here indicate that most of the participants have to some degree experienced: growth in self-aware-ness and sensitivity to others, increasing control of feelings and behavior, dis-covery of interpersonal behavior patterns which seem increasingly effective in promoting meaningful relationships, some success in making contracts, increas-ing feelings of self-confidence and self-worth, and a growing enjoyment of living.

Comments made by participants included:

• This course has helped me work through some problems about my life that I just couldn't face.

• I enjoy my children and grandchildren more now I've stopped so much of this Critical Parent stuff. They act as though they like me better too.

• This course has really helped me understand I don't have to feel helpless. Sometimes, with my husband gone, I just have felt I can't go on living with all the problems I have. I'm learning to take one thing at a time and not get panicky.

REFERENCES

1. Butler, Robert N., "The Life Review: An Interpretation of Reminiscence in the Aged," in *Middle Age and Aging*, edited by B. L. Neugarten (Chicago: University of Chicago Press, 1968), pp. 486–496.

2. Contra Costa County, Mental Health Services, "Annual Plan, 1975–1976, Mental Health Plan on Aging."

3. See the Resources for Exercises which follow these References.

4. James, Muriel, and Dorothy Jongeward, *Born to Win: Transactional Analysis with Gestalt Experiments* (Reading, Mass.: Addison-Wesley, 1971).

5. Jongeward, Dorothy, and Muriel James, *Winning with People* (Reading, Mass.: Addison-Wesley, 1973), p. 25.

6. Steiner, Claude M., *Scripts People Live* (New York: Grove, 1974), p. 88.

7. James, Muriel, and Dorothy Jongeward, *The People Book: Transactional Analy-sis for Students* (Menlo Park, Calif.: Addison-Wesley, 1975), p. 160.

8. Jongeward and James, *Winning with People*, pp. 95–96.

9. James, Muriel, "Self-Reparenting: Theory and Process," *TA Journal* 4, 3 (1974), pp. 34–39.

10. Masters, William H., and Virginia E. Johnson, *Human Sexual Response* (Boston: Little, Brown, 1966).

11. McKain, Walter C., "A New Look at Older Marriages," *The Family Coordinator*, January 1972, pp. 61–69.

RESOURCES FOR EXERCISES

Anderson, Marianne S., and Louis M. Savary, *Passages: A Guide for Pilgrims of the Mind* (New York: Harper & Row, 1973).

Hesterly, S. Otho, *Leaders Guide to the Parent Package: To Raise a Winner* (Little Rock, Ark.: 1974).

James, Muriel, *Born to Love: Transactional Analysis in the Church* (Reading, Mass.: Addison-Wesley, 1974).

——, and Dorothy Jongeward, *Born to Win: Transactional Analysis with Gestalt Experiments* (Reading, Mass.: Addison-Wesley, 1971).

Jongeward, Dorothy, and Muriel James, *Winning with People* (Reading, Mass.: Addison-Wesley, 1973).

Kirst, Werner, and Ulrich Diekmeyer, *Creativity Training* (New York: Peter H. Wyden, 1971).

Stevens, John O., *Awareness* (Moab, Utah: Real People Press, 1971).

redecision house: a program for drug treatment

KEONG CHYE CHEAH
WILLIAM R. BARLING

We all started in life as winners. We are all the result of
the winner in the swim of life, a spermatozoon, meeting
the egg of the month (the egg of the year).

Having insight or awareness or knowledge of psychodynamics alone is like being given a million
dollars in small denominations in a suitcase. If
we carry the suitcase around and do not use the
money, this will become a burden. Inflation will decrease
the value, exposure to the weather will cause the
money to rot, and after a period it becomes useless.
Keong Chye Cheah*

INTRODUCTION

The main tenet behind the operation of the program herein described is that
basically we all have the ability to be and remain winners. Some through their
behavior have stuck themselves in positions to lose. Decisions made early in
life based on incomplete information have contributed to feelings of not-
OKness of self or others or turning this into a position of feeling OK only at
the expense of others.

---

* These are two thoughts that have been proposed to residents of Redecision House.

There are manifold possibilities of OKness as translated into specifically defined behavior patterns. Steiner[1] has offered several examples for consideration. His reference to harmartic scripts[2] provides an understanding of how well drug addicts and drug abusers put their not-OKness into rigid behavior patterns. These individuals have placed themselves in positions of self destruction—social, financial, physical, and emotional. Much work is required in changing these destructive patterns.

Many approaches have been made in treating drug addiction and abuse. Various claims have been made regarding success by exponents of these various and diverse treatment efforts. The authors are making no attempt here to unveil a "magic" solution or to discredit the success that others claim. The product that has evolved—Redecision House—as a specific treatment program grew out of wanting a therapeutic stance or frame of reference which could be utilized with a somewhat diverse population. The information offered in the paper is based upon the authors' experience in designing and operating a comprehensive treatment program within a large Veterans Administration Hospital.

We believe that the most critical aspect of our treatment program is the modified therapeutic community referred to hereafter by name—Redecision House. This is described in detail. We briefly discuss detoxification and follow-up care to point out their relatedness to the operation of Redecision House.

The authors were members of a rather small staff which decided that Transactional Analysis (TA) as a frame of therapy offers a structure which could serve as a foundation for developing a multimodality treatment program. Two TA tenets were most appealing.

TA emphazies the basic OKness (worth) of the individual and offers the very real probability of change potential which is inherent in every individual. TA offers an easily understandable theoretical base with language which can be communicated in clear, specific terms. Professional staff as well as patients who might reflect very diverse backgrounds in intellect, education, culture, and experience can come together in this common frame of refernce.

PHYSICAL STRUCTURE

The Treatment Center consists of three semi-autonomous operations, namely: (1) the Detoxification Unit ("Detox"), (2) the Residential Treatment Program (Redecision House), and (3) the Outpatient Treatment Program. All of these operations are housed in the same building in rather close proximity. This allows for continuity of treatment and better staff utilization.

The Detoxificaion Unit ("Detox") is the primary intake unit where prospective recipients of the treatment program enter the system. As the name implies this unit provides: (a) medical care for those individuals who require medically managed withdrawal from the chemicals abused and (b) diagnostic evaluation to rule out any significant medical conditions. Physical rehabilitation is emphasized. Nutritious diet, regular sleeping and eating habits, and physical exercises are important during this phase of treatment. In those situations in which medical illness requires intensive or specialized care, use is made of the larger hospital system where appropriate consultation is available. Throughout the process of the patient's medical treatment in "Detox" he is being evaluated for the Redecision House.

Redecision House is a 15-bed unit which operates essentially as a modified therapeutic community staffed by a multidisciplinary treatment team. As a member of the program the resident is expected to be totally involved in a therapeutic milieu of which intensive group psychotherapy is the major thrust. A residential government made up of the residents themselves has the responsibility for the day-to-day operation of the program as well as other duties.

The Outpatient Treatment Program is operated in an adjoining area within the same building as "Detox" and Redecision House. It is primarily for those residents who have graduated from Redecision House. In some rare exceptions services have been offered through this program to individuals who have not gone through Redecision House. Here as well, group psychotherapy is the main thrust, and regularly scheduled individual, family, and couples groups are available. Over the past few months we have been able to expand our Outpatient Treatment Program by starting two additional individual therapy groups in cities some 50 miles away from our hospital setting.

FUNCTIONAL DESIGN AND RATIONALE

Physical structure, building locations, program components, and administrative structure certainly have profound influence upon the design, function, and treatment outcome of any program. In any program there are the elements of program design and rationale that go beyond the physical structure. Within each of the separate but interdependent units of the Treatment Center ("Detox", Redecision House, and Outpatient Treatment Program), the essence of the program lies in the functional aspects and the rationale behind these functions.

Individuals admitted to "Detox" do not automatically qualify to enter the community. The detoxification period lasts for one or more days, depending upon the physical and emotional condition of the patient. As soon as he is admitted to the detoxification unit he is referred to Redecision House for evaluation by a screening team made up of staff and residents* for acceptance into the Redecision House. The evaluation teams review with the individual his social and interpersonal history, any significant adjustment problems, desired changes he sees for himself and provides him with information about Redecision House.† The individual's level of motivation‡ for change in the area(s) he identifies is assessed. A positive level of motivation is deemed necessary for the individual's treatment and for the maintenance of a high level of therapeutic change within the group. This is also necessary to maintain morale of the whole group.

If the screening team and the individual reach a concensus that Redecision House will best meet his needs and if he is willing to endorse the formal therapeutic agreement, he is then accepted. The formal treatment agreement follows with comment related to the specific rationale.

Treatment Agreement

Redecision House

Before admission to Redecision House, it is necessary that the applicant agree to the following terms:

1. I agree that the main reason I have enrolled in the program is to get off drugs, including alcohol. [Many drug abusers have been known to switch to heavy alcohol intake, thus continuing self-destructive behavior.]

2. I also fully realize that this is a Self-Help Program, and I will actively participate in all activities in order to better achieve the above goal (No. 1). [Adult commitment—No magic.]

3. I understand that: The taking of any drugs not prescribed by the physicians on this unit, the drinking of alcohol, or the smoking of Marijuana is contrary to my above purpose and can be considered sufficient reason for an immediate discharge from this program. [Information and protection for all participants on the program.]

4. I will do nothing harmful to the image of the Redecision House or my fellow residents. [Cathect Adult and Nurturing Parent.]

---

* An individual in Redecision House is referred to as a resident rather than patient in order to deemphasize the connotation of "sickness" and pharmacological treatment.

† Exercise of Adult ego state is fostered by offering a copy of the Resident's Manual to the potential candidate. As a further measure he is given the opportunity to observe a psychotherapeutic group session (with group consent) prior to signing the formal treatment agreement.

‡ Elimination of "shoulds," "oughts," and focus on "wishes," "wants," and "needs" is made.

5. I will be aware that it is my responsibility to know the time and place of all personal assignments and group activities, and I agree to attend these and participate to my fullest. [Adult.]

6. If my behavior and group participation merit a pass, I agree to conduct myself responsibly and project the same image as I do while on the ward. [Positive "strokes" for appropriate behavior.]

7. I agree to remain in the Redecision House Program for a minimum of 30 days with the option of continued individualized treatment as needed at the end of that period. [Adult commitment elicited.]

8. I am aware that the information shared by all group members during the process of therapy is confidential and is not to be discussed outside the therapy situation. [Permission and Protection.] [3]

9. I will abide by the no hand-holding rule, which is as follows: If I have any knowledge or suspect any person connected with this program of doing anything destructive to himself, someone else, or to the program, I will confront him with this and then bring it up in the next group therapy session, if that person fails to do so. [No contamination of Adult function by using excuses.]

It is noted that the detoxication process is important prior to starting intensive psychotherapy in the residential program. It would be futile to require an agreement from a "fogged out" individual. For this reason every effort is made to elicit the Adult ego state functions of the individual while he is in the "Detox" Unit. Here he is offered protection from making agreements in a state of unawareness.

Each resident in Redecision House is required to write a contractual agreement within the first seven days of admission outlining his own therapeutic goals while in the program. This contract is a written statement of observable behavioral changes (problems→solutions) the resident would like to make and is willing to work to achieve. The contract is explored in detail in group therapy as this (the contract) is the essence of what the resident will do while in treatment. He is required to attend and participate in all group therapy sessions and personal assignments which may include education therapy, occupational therapy, manual arts therapy, vocational planning and special interest groups. The new resident is assigned a resident sponsor by the Resident Governor for the initial seven days. (Sponsor is an "older" resident who is responsible to the new resident to help orient him to the program and assist him in his initial adjustment to the program.)* He is considered and treated as responsible for his behavior, feelings, and thoughts. It is his responsibility to ask questions and obtain information when he needs it. There is no room for assump-

---

* Provides for being taken care of. Exercises Child ego state trust and shows Parent ego state protection and permission.

tions, excuses, or secrets. It is every resident's responsibility to know what is going on about him and to find ways of changing anything that does not suit him. He is encouraged to make known when and how he wants to work on his therapy contract. He is encouraged and provided the means to become more aware of his behavior which has caused him problems, to discover alternatives, and to put them into action.

Monitored urine samples are taken two or more times per week to determine if the resident is maintaining his abstinence from drugs.* Anyone in the program (resident or staff alike) has the right to request this urine test of anyone else in the program. After the resident's second weekend, if he has a "good image" (working on his therapy contract, remaining drug free, and following program guidelines) he is eligible for a weekend pass, and he can make a formal request to the resident motivation board which approves all passes.

Functions of Resident Government

Ward management problems are referred to the Resident Government for appropriate corrective action. The offices of the Resident Government consisting of the President, Vice President, Secretary, and Sergeant-at-Arms are elected by the residents in the program. Each officer has well defined responsibilities which are spelled out in the Constitution and By-laws. The Constitution serves as an official mandate outlining the structure of the Resident Government, job descriptions of the officers, guidelines for rewards and penalties, and unit policies and procedures.† The Constitution also provides for four categories of offenses; category One being minimal and category Four being the most severe. The disciplinary actions (penalties) range from a verbal reprimand to a recommendation of dismissal from the program.

Operationally the Resident Government provides the overall therapeutic milieu with the necessary ingredients of a functional structure and a reference point to evaluate individual performance. A miniature of the "real world" is actualized with opportunities to win, fail, and test out new experiences. Laws and regulations, each very specifically spelled out, as well as rights and privileges, are a part of each day's living. The Resident Government also provides a means for participation in group task achievement and commitment to the group. The resident learns to accept recognition for "being" and for performance in this structure. He is also given an avenue for learning social inter-

---

* This will reflect a clear record (if this the case) which the resident has made for himself, and it reveals his "image."

† The Constitution was originally written and developed by a group of residents themselves. The Redecision House motto is "People Activating Change." Over a period of some three years of use, it has undergone some revision without any significant changes.

action. Rewards (positive strokes) and penalties (negative strokes) are provided (for Adult ego state to evaluate) in appropriate circumstances. We use penalties rather than punishment because we have observed that residents actually work toward receiving (earning) the penalty just as they do in earning rewards.

Although it may appear that we only stroke for doing (conditionally) because of the written structure, the provision for stroking for "being" is very much emphasized in the daily functioning of the program. This is not formally structured because stroking for being requires spontaneity. When this is done as a response to formal guidelines, it comes across as "phoney" and is really the Adapted Child performing.

Upon completion of the initial 30 days in the program the resident may desire to extend his in-residence contract.* If he so desires he reviews his contract in therapy and formally petitions the motivation board for as much additional time in the in-residence program as he thinks he needs. A night-hospital status is also available to those who have completed 30 days in residence, have a good image, and who need this type of structure prior to community re-entry. These and all special adjustments in a resident's activity schedule are initially evaluated by the resident motivation board and, if approved, referred to the staff treatment team.

Group Therapy and Other Related Activities

A major portion of the resident's daily routine is devoted to intensive group psychotherapy. This occurs every weekday with two sessions comprising four hours each day. Additional sessions are held if staff or resident decide there is a need. In the morning the group meets with trained staff therapists.† All sessions are either audio- or videotaped in order to maximize the opportunity for the resident to review his work and spot and eliminate his not-OKness. In the afternoon session the group meets without staff and reviews the morning tapes or reviews contracts. These sessions are also taped and may be used as a springboard for further work the next morning.‡

---

* Others have reported of hard core drug abusers needing as much as 90 days to clean out their physical systems from the influence of drugs.

† Presently primary staff therapists include social workers, drug counselors, psychologists, and registered nurses each with considerable training in group psychotherapy utilizing TA. Since high level of confrontation requires much energy and involvement, we routinely use multi-therapists.

‡ The technique using resident group (without staff) tapes as a springboard for further therapy is, with modifications, based on work done by George Wiggins, M.D., of Houston V.A. Hospital. Our staff have further employed the use of video tapes by making them available for residents' use during free time at night. This employs an exercise in taking charge of one's own function and treatment and is enthusiastically received by our residents.

In our psychotherapy sessions our staff utilize a wide variety of techniques drawn from various methods of psychotherapy. We use techniques drawn from TA, Gestalt, Reality Therapy, and Behavior Modification. Several of our staff, for example, use the Gestalt chair work effectively. Frequently, specific "self-discovery exercises" * are assigned, and occasional use is made of role-playing for the rehearsal effect. Although much of our work in the session is directed to one individual at a time, group process as a dynamic is neither ignored nor restrained. Our staff have been exposed to varied training experiences, nevertheless; they have been able to achieve, utilizing TA as a basic framework, a viable blend of therapy which is creative, spontaneous, and exciting for both staff and residents.

Some of the other activities that are offered throughout the week include relaxation sessions, vocational counseling, educational therapy (which may include study for G.E.D. or college level courses), manual arts therapy and resocialization activities such as cooking labs, and Veterans Benefits counseling.

In addition to the daily program, the resident is required to attend the Out-patient/Family Therapy Group his first two weeks in the program. This gives him an opportunity to explore his family constellation and to meet former residents who are "winning," making it in the community. He is encouraged to invite any "significant other" (e.g. family, friend, spouse) to these therapy sessions. A couples therapy group is currently active, and others are planned.

Out-patient Treatment Program

Following completion of the in-patient phase of treatment, the resident can be given an out-patient discharge, if he so desires and is willing to continue his updated therapy contract on an out-patient basis. This therapy group meets regularly once a week. The former resident is encouraged to report on his successes and work on further problems. He is eligible to return as often and for as long as he feels is beneficial, provided he maintains a good "image." He is permitted to visit the residential program and participate in that therapy group as an observer. This contact between residents and out-patients (former residents) is encouraged to take advantage of the effects of modeling. Several of our former residents have gained considerable awareness and skill in TA techniques. They volunteer their time and energies in a number of ways in our program. Two of these official volunteers are serving as co-therapists to a staff therapist in our satellite out-patient groups.

The main objective of the out-patient program is to keep in contact with the "graduate" and offer constant review of his needs. Urine checks (to determine

---

* Some call this "homework," but "homework" brings memory of doing a chore. Muriel James was the first to note this.

the maintenance of a drug-free life) are a necessary part of the out-patient therapy contract. As with residents, the out-patient is expected to be responsible for his continued therapy and returning to out-patient meetings. Telephone calls are made, periodically, to maintain personal contact and show a continuing concern for the individual in his efforts in maintaining his constructive lifestyle.

CONCLUDING COMMENTS: THE THERAPEUTIC THRUST

For a therapist, especially working with drug abusers—or for that matter, any self-destructive individual(s)—the following are the ingredients of a basic stance in therapy which we refer to as the therapeutic thrust.

1. Ability to see potential winners in all of us (I+, U+)* and to encourage through permission and protection further OK growth.

2. Avoidance of blaming maneuvers: blaming patients, parents, society, "the Establishment," ourselves, or others. In other words, refusing to be Rescuer, Persecutor, Victim (Karpman),[3] or Patsy (Steiner).[1] (Therapist: "I am not the cause of your self-destructive behavior and will not feel responsible for being the cause. I will not feel guilty nor be responsible for being the cause. I will be responsible for my relationship with you . . . etc.") [I+, U+; we are responsible for our own actions and decisions.]

3. Refusal to believe that as therapists we have any "magic cure" and rejection of any assignment of magical powers by individuals desiring such "witchcraft." [Decontamination of Adult—Berne[5]: "No Discount"—Satir[6,7] and Schiff.[8]]

4. Rejection of moralistic stance as Persecutor or as inappropriate Parent. The therapists can provide information on drug abuse as self-destructive/"suicidal" activity. "Suicidal" activity includes social suicide (decrease/negate social options), financial suicide (negate options of employment), and physical suicide (getting unknown, impure, or too pure drugs; chemical effects of drugs, etc). [Utilize Adult and decontaminate.]

5. Recognize and build on positives and provide guide to alternate options regarding self-image and getting positive strokes. [U+ and can exercise your Adult to see your OKness.]

6. Show that in the pursuit of illicit drug use the individual has shown strength and creativity in his Rebellious Child (Drye)[9] not only to obtain the drugs

---

* I + = I'm OK; U + = You're OK.

but in surviving in the street and keeping from being arrested. Encourage efforts in the use of this strength and creativity in a positive direction.

7. Not be caught in the middle of having to provide a detrimental report to court or police (Federal Confidentiality Law actually prohibits this) and that if any report is to be made it will be with consent of the individual and his selected attorney. If a positive report is made, let it be based on factual behavioral changes, etc. A good plan is not to get into any prior commitment to provide such a report, so that one does not feel victimized if a positive report is not justified.

8. Not be placed in a position of having to "hold patient/client in treatment" because of a third-party agreement when the individual is unwilling to do anything besides be bodily present.

9. Stay aware that the individual drug abuser has an image, which, if unattractive, has been the result of his own efforts. To change this image he will have to work in treatment to explore and develop new behavior patterns in his daily living. The therapist is not able to change fairness or unfairness of the other people in the world but can provide the know-how so that an individual can determine how he wants to be treated by others and behave in such ways that these outcomes are maximized.

10. The most productive treatment is accomplished when an individual voluntarily participates and seeks out specific positive changes.

11. The structure of the program or the modality of treatment per se does not guarantee successful treatment outcomes. Most successful therapists are competent, well trained, concerned and believe in their work. Therapeutic tools either provided by TA, Gestalt, Behavior Modification, Reality Therapy, etc. applied alone or in combination(s) do not guarantee good treatment. An inexperienced and untrained therapist using TA is no better than any other untrained therapist. There is no magic in TA or in any other form of therapy. TA can be utilized to increase effectiveness in doing therapy. TA provides a greater advantage as a theoretical framework of development, as a means of communication, and as a methodology to evaluate therapy. This means that an individual is not "therapeudized upon" but is actively involved in the whole process.

12. Effective therapy utilizes the education or re-education of individuals, but education or re-education is not equivalent to therapy. Through therapy the individual applies his "redecision(s)" (Goulding)[10] and thus is equipped to

deal with other situations he encounters in the future. He also learns when and how to seek future help.

ACKNOWLEDGMENTS

1. The Veterans Administration for providing the support to make Redecision House possible.

2. Muriel James for providing encouragement to continue the program and for making it possible to get the ideas and workings of the program into print.

3. The staff and residents past and present who have contributed and involved themselves in the workings of the program. The teachers past and present of Psychiatry and especially in Transactional Analysis, among these being Harry Boyd, Robert and Mary Goulding, Muriel James, and Jonathan Weiss.

4. Sandra M. Cheah and Ann Barling for initial reviewing.

5. Caroline Pasierb for a neat job of getting the manuscript ready.

6. Joe Golenor for proof reading.

7. Joe E. O. Newton and Otho Hesterly for Adult evaluation of the manuscript.

REFERENCES

1. Steiner, C., "The Alcoholic Game," *TA Bulletin* **7**, (1968), p. 6.

2. ———, *Games Alcoholics Play: The Analysis of Life Script* (New York: Grove, 1971), p. 23–26.

3. Crossman, P., "Permission and Protection," *TA Bulletin* **5**, 19 (1966), p. 152.

4. Karpman, S., "Fairy Tales and Script Drama Analysis," *TA Bulletin* **7, 26** (1968), p. 39.

5. Berne, E., *Transactional Analysis in Psychotherapy* (New York: Grove, 1961), pp. 144–145.

6. Satir, V., *Conjoint Family Therapy* (Palo Alto, Calif.: Science and Behavior Books, 1967, pp. 63–90, 178–180.

7. ———, *People Making* (Palo Alto, Calif.: Science and Behavior Books, 1972), pp. 30–79.

8. Schiff, A. W., and J. L. Schiff, *TA Journal* **1**, 1 (1971), p. 71.

9. Drye, R. C., "Stroking the Rebellious Child: An Aspect of Managing Resistance," *TA Journal* **4**, 3 (1974), p. 23.

10. Goulding, R.: "New Directions in Transactional Analysis: Creating an Environment for Decision and Change," in *Progress in Group and Family Therapy*, edited by C. J. Sager and H. S. Kaplan (New York: Brunner/Mazell, 1972), pp. 105–134.

GENERAL READING

1. Berne, E., *Transactional Analysis in Psychotherapy* (New York: Grove, 1961).

2. ———, *Principles of Group Treatment* (New York: Grove, 1966).

3. ———, *What Do You Say After You Say Hello?* (New York: Grove, 1972).

4. James, M., and D. Jongeward, *Born to Win: Transactional Analysis with Gestalt Experiments* (Reading, Mass.: Addison-Wesley, 1971).

CHAPTER 31

social *Rapo:* description and cure

ROBERT ZECHNICH

According to the original description of *Rapo*,[1] it is a sexual game, in which the male pursues and the female is pursued. It has since become clear that *Rapo* has much deeper and broader applications thatn the original description encompassed.

The first recognition of the broader possibilities was Karpman's description[2] of a variant which he called *Reverse Rapo,* in which the female pursues and the male is pursued. Next, it was noticed that *Rapo* is not strictly a heterosexual phenomenon that it is extremely common among (male, at least) homosexuals, too. It may even be that homosexuals who do *not* play *Rapo* constitute a rather negligible minority, numerically, in the homosexual community. *Rapo* is still *Rapo,* regardless of which partner does the pursuing, and even if both partners are of the same sex.

These two expansions are still sexual ones. There is, in addition, a social (non-sexual) form, which is at least as common as the sexual game. The clinician who notices *Rapo* in the sexual context only is missing between 50 and 75

From *TA Journal* **3,** 4 (1973). Reprinted by permission.

percent of all the *Rapo* his patients are playing. He certainly is overlooking a great deal of *Rapo* that patients play through completely under his very eyes, right in the therapy group.

DESCRIPTION

There are two basic patterns, two basic sequences of transactions, which characterize *Rapo* in both its social and sexual forms. The patterns are identical in the two areas. The first sequence of transactions is:

1. Offer made.
2. Offer accepted.
3. Offer withdrawn.

In the nonsexual context it looks like this:

Example 1.

Red: Would you like to go to the movies with me Thursday evening?
Blue: Let's see . . . I have no commitments that night, yes, I'd like that.
Red: (typically this move comes on Thursday afternoon): Oh, I just remembered I have to go to a board meeting, and won't be able to go to that movie with you after all.

Example 2.

Red: Would you like a piece of chewing gum?
Blue: Oh, It's Spearmint, my favorite kind. Thank you very much.
Red: On second thought, it's my last piece, I think I'd better save it for after lunch.

In each case, Red offers something, Blue accepts the offer, and then Red withdraws the offer.

The second basic sequence for *Rapo* is:

1. Request made.
2. Request granted.
3. Request withdrawn.

In the nonsexual context it goes like this:

Example 3.

Red: I noticed you have a copy of *The Red and the Blue* on your bookself. I've been dying to read it for some time and haven't been able to find a copy. Do you think I could borrow it?

Blue: Sure. I've already finished it. I think you'll enjoy it. It's a pleasure to lend it to you.

Red: Well, come to think of it, I have an awful lot of things to read. I don't think I'll be able to get to it. Anyway the review in the *New York Times* was not very favorable.

Example 4.

Red: I'm terribly thirsty. Would you get me a drink of water please?

Blue: Certainly. Here it is. I put ice cubes in it, too.

Red: On second thought, I'll be having lunch soon. I'll just wait 'til then. (Or, alternatively, Red simply, without comment, fails to drink the water.)

In each case, Red makes a request, Blue grants the request in good faith, and then Red, by withdrawing the request, rejects it.

Example 5. (A Consulting Room Variant)

Patient: Would you please explain to me why . . . ?"

Therapist: OK. The reason is that . . . and furthermore . . . and therefore it follows that . . . Understand?

Patient: I knew that already.

What therapist has not been "had" by *Consulting Room Rapo* of this kind, saying or thinking, "If you already knew the answer, what the hell did you ask the question for?"

Example 6. (Third Degree Social Rapo)

Red: Let me pick up your symphony tickets for you. The box office is right near my work, and I can do it easily on my lunch hour.

Blue: That would be great.

Red: Here are your goddamn tickets. God, what a hassle. I had to stand in line for three hours and of course I missed my lunch and was late for work and the boss is mad at me. I wish I'd never let you talk me into getting your tickets for you.

Here Red—just as in sexual *Rapo*—actually fulfills the offer, and then, by professing that the whole thing had been Blue's idea forced upon an unwilling Red, makes Blue feel guilty.

These two basic patterns can be played out in an almost infinite variety of specific content, and in an almost infinite variety of situations. But the framework itself, the essential transaction-sequence, is constant, whether the arena is sexual or nonsexual. The *feelings* of the players when the payoff comes, are also the same for both types. Emotionally, as well as objectively, social *Rapo* and sexual *Rapo* are the same game. This does not seem surprising when one recalls how often a problem which a patient might present and regard as "sexual" turns out on analysis to be only the sexual aspect of a problem in getting-along-with.

In my experience to date, people who play *Sexual Rapo,* do not necessarily play *Sexual Rapo,* although many do. On the other hand, I have not yet seen a *Sexual Rapo* player who did not also play *Social Rapo.*

TREATMENT AND CURE

The steps and procedures for curing *Rapo* will be given for Red players first, and then for those who preferentially play the Blue hand. The same procedures equally well describe the steps in curing *any* game, except that 2, 4, and 5 are specific and different for each game.

1. Point out the game to the patient.

2. Be sure he understands exactly how the game goes, and at least generally what gains are involved. For the Red end of *Rapo,* the main advantage is the opportunity (with an alleged "justification") to slap Blue psychologically, to *hurt* the partner by disappointment (by generating guilt, in third degree *Rapo*).

3. Ask him if he wants to stop, i.e., give up the game; this of course means giving up the advantages of the game, too.

If—and only if—he agrees to stop playing *Rapo,* proceed to:

4. Establish the rule that he *must* go through with all offers he makes, once they are accepted, without pretending he was forced into it; and,

5. Establish the rule that he *must* go through with all actions of others generated by his own requests.

6. As he carries out steps 4 and 5, deal with the dynamics, and the pressures to play *Rapo,* and the inevitable "static" from Parent and Witch, as they come up.

7. Give strong, effective Permission,[3] and then Protection,[4] in specific instances of 4 and 5 as they occur, in the group and outside.

Do not allow any cop-outs, however well the patient rationalizes them. He must deliver on *every* offer he makes, and he must accept delivery on *every* one of his requests.

8. Stay with the patient during the period of despair and existential vacuum, after *Rapo* is clearly obliterated from his repertoire for getting-along-in-the-world.

9. Work with the patient to generate strokes to replace the ones lost as a result of his resigning from *Rapo.* (Note: sometimes this can be done or partly done between steps 3 and 4.) This means to find nonhurtful ways of dealing with

others, ways of exchanging positive strokes, and/or delivering hurtful strokes, when appropriate, in a straight way rather than through a game.

10. Watch out for the patient's proclivity to play *Rapo* with the therapist over the offer-made-and-accepted cure for *Rapo!* It would be easy for a *Rapo* player to announce at any stage in the cure process that, on second thought, maybe he'd just as soon go on playing *Rapo* like he used to. "I've changed my mind," he's tempted to say at some point, "I don't want to get cured of *Rapo* after all." The therapist needs to counter this move: "It's too late for that; you decided to get cured and made a contract, and now you're committed to follow through."

For patients who prefer the blue side of *Rapo,* the same program works, except that steps 2, 4, 5, and 9 need to be modified. It is essential to keep in mind that no matter how much Blue *feels* like an innocent victim being "taken" by Red, no matter how much Blue *appears* to be an innocent victim, it takes two to play the game, and Blue is in fact an active, willing player. The necessary modifications in Blue's treatment program are:

2. The payoff for Blue is *getting hurt,* getting disappointed (or being made to feel guilty).

4. Establish the rule that before acceding to any request, he must think first, and say "yes" only if he is genuinely willing. These patients are inclined to say "yes" indiscriminately, without making a real choice, simply because they cannot say "no." They do not realize that it is *possible* to say "no," that they have that right; so they need permission to say no. Also, they assume that saying no would necessarily hurt the other's feelings (while overlooking the fact that to say "yes" and then fail to follow through hurts more). So they need permission to say "no," even if it does hurt someone's feelings.

Establish the rule that once Blue has said yes, Red is obliged to accept delivery, and Blue is to act on that expectation. That means confronting Red with his cop-out and pressing for follow-through, much as the therapist does in step 10, above.

5. Establish the rule that he is to think before accepting an offer: "Is the offer real, does Red intend to keep his commitment?" These patients tend to discount clues available at the outset, that Red has no intention of following through on the contract. They need permission to be suspicious, to recognize that there are people, namely Red *Rapo* players, who make agreements only to break them and thereby hurt the other.

Establish the rule that once an agreement has been made between Blue and Red, Blue is not solely responsible for it, as Red may claim—it is bilateral, and Blue need not feel guilty.

9. The strokes lost by giving up *Rapo,* for Blue, are hurts. Ways will need to be developed for the ex-Blue *Rapo* player to replace these with loving strokes.

SUMMARY

Rapo needs to be understood as a much broader phenomenon than "he pursues —she protests." Clinically the social form accounts for at least half of all instances of *Rapo*. The basic sequences are:

1. Offer made—offer accepted—offer withdrawn.

2. Request made—request granted—request withdrawn.

The steps for effective cure of *Rapo*—sexual or nonsexual—are spelled out in chronological order.

REFERENCES

1. Berne, Eric, *Games People Play* (New York: Grove, 1964), pp. 126–129.
2. Karpman, Stephen, Oral report at SFTA Seminar, 1969 (unpublished).
3. Crossman, Patricia, *TA Journal* **5**, 19.
4. Ibid.

CHAPTER 32

confusion rackets

HARRY S. BOYD

In most therapy groups there are several patients who seem to spend a lot of time being confused. They may look puzzled and shake their heads negatively while the therapist is working with another patient; when asked, they report "I'm confused," "I don't get it," "I read the booklet and I didn't understand a thing it said," "Would you explain that last part one more time?" and so on. The element that distinguishes this set of moves from *Stupid* is that the patient ends up feeling "blocked" or "unable to think," while the *Stupid* player usually ends up feeling kicked and mistreated.

Frequently the questions they ask are so vague and unclear that if the therapist attempts to answer, he leads himself into a morass of nonsensical questions and replies. If the therapist does not make the attempt, it is a pretty sure bet that in all but the most sophisticated groups someone will, leading to the same results. If the therapist is keeping close track of his own reactions, he will frequently observe increasing frustration, irritation, impatience or the like, which he tends to deny because of the obvious helplessness/innocence of the patient.

From *TA Journal* **3,** 3 (1973). Reprinted by permission.

At this point, the patient is in the Adapted Child, and attempts by the therapist to explore, expose or ignore the game are futile, more often than not.

The following is a suggested approach that I have found quite useful. Further, while curing one patient of this racket, usually several others will work the process out for themselves. Explanation of the tactic to be suggested should be saved until later when the patient's Adult is freed up enough to integrate the data. The therapist intervention is best timed at the point where the patient clutches his head or drops his head into a Thinker (Constipated Type) position. The signal may range in obviousness from the above to knitted brows and a pained expression. Frequently the patient will say something on the order of "I just can't think," or "My mind is a total blank." At this point the therapist suggests an experiment to the patient, if the patient is willing to do it. The patient is instructed: "Whenever you ask me a question and you get confused, I want you to say to me: I just can't understand a thing you say, Ha, Ha!, and simultaneously give me the finger." These instructions are sufficiently shocking to hook the attention of the patient's Child. Typically, the patient gets in touch with the triumphant aspect of his pay-off almost immediately, and can then be encouraged to spend some time enjoying the operation in the open. One especially adroit patient managed to hook me into giving unnecessary explanations six more times during the same group session, with increasingly delighted laughter, until I belatedly got wise.

At this point the patient is usually able to understand the scripted element in his confusion. He typically reports hearing a Parental admonition "Now, *think!*" He experiences an Adapted Child response of "I'm trying, but I just can't!" A little exploration soon demonstrates that the hidden injunction from the parent's Child was Don't Think (so I can worry/exhort/think for you, stupid). The decision the patient makes is "I'll try to think and go blank, ha, ha." As a reward, he gets to frustrate his parent and salvage a mixed win from the battle, at the cost of feeling confused and blank.

Correct identification of the confusion feeling is important. On one occasion, the patient reported confusion which turned out to be a mislabeled fear response. Many of the patients with severe confusion rackets have been brought up in families in which *Corner* was a dominant game. For them, the danger is that if they get unconfused enough to make a straight statement, someone may kill them. On occasion I have seen a brief acute disorganization occur, in all cases followed by very rapid recovery.

REFERENCE

Groder, Martin, "Four Contributions," *TA Bulletin* 7, 26 (1968).

ego states
and stroking
in the
childbirth experience

MARGOT EDWARDS

In this paper, I explore childbirth as experienced by all ego states[1] in the pre-pared participating woman. Typically,[2] this woman is having her first or second baby, and has attended eight three-hour sessions of pre-natal classes with her husband. Classes offer information regarding pregnancy and labor, teach com-fort measures such as exercises, body mechanics, relaxation, and controlled breathing. They offer a setting where expectant couples can freely discuss their feelings about having a baby. Parents are present at many classes to share their own birth and parenting experiences, lead rap sessions, and pass their babies around. The expectant woman and her husband practice relaxation and breathing for two months. They are encouraged to communicate with touch, and learn simple massage techniques. With such involvement, they often de-velop an increased mutual awareness which prepares the husband to be a "sophisticated helpmate"[3] to his wife during the birth. To promote this col-laboration, preparatory education includes Parental permission to enjoy labor, Adult skills to cope with labor, and ample assurances for the Child. Assurance is offered by stroking in the class setting, both verbally and with touch. Par-ticipants enter class with assorted goals, and learn they have many options for

From *TA Journal* 1, 4 (1971). Reprinted by permission.

labor. Their good feelings about the birth, normal or complicated, depend on the strokes they give each other, and receive from attending persons. During labor, hospital personnel become particularly significant to the couple's birth experience. Stroking and You-are-OK messages can eliminate the performance aspect of prepared childbirth.

Labor, a major event in the sexual life of a woman, is largely experienced by the Child ego state. The prepared woman responds to mechanical forces which she perceives as hardening and tightening, pressure and stretching, with Adult skills if her Child is guided and stroked throughout labor. When isolated or scolded, the Child part of her clutches and cries out (flight). If discounted ("How dilated am I?" "The doctor will be along soon."), confused Child will sabotage Adult functioning ("It didn't work from then on."). The hurting Child likes to be touched, not told, or commanded. She quickly spots the rescue operation, and exploits it to remain helpless ("They wouldn't let me move."). The Child who has permission to be stroked during labor (prepared mother), can moan, squat,[4] grunt, and still feel OK. She'll be less balky when her Adult needs to cathect. Biological stroking such as massage, effleurage, and touching cues (nonverbal hints to release voluntary muscles), are more reassuring than verbal stroking. The guide (husband) is Child's best friend.

Although the Adult is less active in true labor, she needs to plug in at strategic times to direct appropriate physiological activity. The Adult has pertinent information regarding her body and what's happening to it. She recognizes the suggestions in her guide's touching cues, and responds with muscular release and respiratory patterns. The Adult selected a sympathetic medical manager (obstetrician who isn't threatened by patients who think), and was straight with him on her goals for labor. Knowing the reality of labor, she does not use it as a test for OK-ness. She has more options than success or failure. The Adult is tuned in by the guide's cues, nurse's information, and physician's direction. Adult knows her Child needs care, and she's important enough to ask for it. Familiar with old Parent tapes, Adult intervenes to inform the Child, "the facts are . . ."

Parent programming rarely involves a stroking contract. A-woman-should, the-best-way, if-I-can-make-it, are good set-ups for disappointment. The cultural Parent says, "Labor is scary." Exceptional biological mothers may say, "I enjoyed having you." Nurturing Parent models need to be mustered when lacking in the pregnant woman's own head. The medical manager, teacher and comfortable mother peers often provide such a model. During labor, straight transactions with medical attendants encourage good messages—"You're doing fine. Labor is like this sometimes," (You are OK.) "Call me and I'll be here. Your husband will be a lot of help," (We'll take care of you.) provide assurance that good Parents are around. Bad Parent messages ("If you can stand it. You might not make it. It gets a lot worse.") are particularly undermining when they re-inforce the mother's own witch messages (Things never work out for you, Mothers have it hard.). The Parent needs to protect the Child, permit her to be touched, and feel OK while experiencing pressure and pain. The kindly Parent forgives Child when she takes more medication than she planned, or defecates in the delivery room. Parental expectations need to make sense, or be turned off by the discerning Adult. The Adult has many choices, but can function in la-bor only when the Child is liberally stroked.

Labor Chart

Labor means hard work. It consists of three stages. During the long variable first stage, the uterus contracts and retracts to thin and open its bottle-neck cervix (opening of uterus). The cervix dilates from zero to ten centimeters, per-mitting the baby to exit to the birth canal (vagina). The prepared woman re-laxes and breathes in first stage labor. **Duration: 12 to 16 hours**

Second stage begins with full dilation and ends with the birth of the baby. This stage is fast and can be painless. The mother breathes and pushes for second stage. She relaxes the muscles of her pelvic floor. **Duration: 1/2 to 2 hours**

During the third stage, the membranes and placenta are delivered. The mother relaxes and nurses her baby to contract her uterus after birth. **Duration: 1/2 to 2 hours**

Summary of Progress of Labor	*Associated Feelings*
0-4 centimeters	Excitement, elation
4-6 centimeters	"True labor," concen-tration, helplessness
7-10 centimeters	Anxiety, apprehension
Crowning of the head	Burning of the vulva, fear of splitting
Birth	Relief, exhilaration

There are, in labor, characteristic feelings making up a pattern of predictable shifts in ego state. Termed emotional menaces by Grantly Dick-Read,[5] these shifts indicate Child is in charge at an inappropriate time. The Adult needs to be alerted by the intervening guide. Reassurance to the fearful Child is pro-vided by touching techniques (cues, effleurage, massage, and position changes).

The first emotional menace occurs about four centimeters dilation (see labor chart). The Child part of the laboring woman feels trapped and helpless (I can't get out of this). In new territory (hospital), wearing odd clothes, the Child may feel bewildered and embarrassed before an assortment of strangers. She may respond to exams as to sexual attack, and to moderate contractions, with tensing. Her pain threshold drops if Adult is not cathected, and she can experience her entire labor with flight. If Adult makes the decision to cope, and the Child is stroked, Child will settle down, let go, and breathe with the brisk contractions. She has hurdled the first emotional menace.

From seven to ten centimeters, the transitional phase of labor makes up the most difficult portion of childbirth. The Child fears her trembling legs, powerful contractions, and pressure from the descending baby's head. She is discouraged, irritable, and angry with her guide's ministrations. She cannot predict the future, and sees no end to the contractions. The guide can recognize this phase, verify it with the nurse, and identify it to the laboring woman's almost absent Adult. With a change of position, and shift in breathing levels, the Adult can get her bearings. The Child can be led through the emotional menaces of transition with short directive phrases—"Blow away the pain. Breathe your baby down. Let go and lean forward." When heard by the Child, and accompanied by massage and positioning, the mother can handle transition.

Second stage can be the truly joyful part of labor. Permission to push after complete dilation affords relief, as Adult choices are at a minimum with the work of pushing. The Child says, "It feels so good to push." If she is afraid to soil or split, however, she will hold back and hurt. Colorful, explicit directions from the medical manager ("Let your bottom go. Open the gate."[6]) need to be repeated by the guide. The woman often cannot hear clearly from the foot of the table, and she exhibits an unawareness of her surroundings with her absorption in giving birth. The husband can chant directions from the obstetrician and reassure while the mother pushes with abandon. During second stage, the Child forgets.

Crowning is the final emotional menace. The stretching of the cervical fibers leads to a characteristic burning sensation.[7] Frightened (I will rip), the Child panics and squeezes down on the baby's head. Stroking by the guide, and explicit instruction by the medical manager ("Pant. Let your perineum go. Now you can push.") brings in the Adult who directs the release of the soft tissues. The Child feels relieved and excited after the birth of the head. When the hospital setting offers permission, she may cry with joy, or shout out her accomplishment. Viewing her baby, she switches to Parent ego state, arranges her hair, and demands her baby.

REFERENCES

1. Berne, *The Structure and Dynamics of Organizations and Groups* (New York: Grove, 1966), pp. 130–138.

2. "Typically refers to the average woman who attends my class as taken from 300 follow-ups after delivery. Unmarried women attend, as well as women expecting their fourth or fifth child. They are a minority. (Unpublished follow-up studies.)

3. Chabon, *Awake and Aware* (New York: Dell, 1969), p. 97.

4. Dick-Read, *Childbirth Without Fear* (New York: Harper & Row, 1949), p. 156.

5. Dick-Read, *The Childbirth Primer* (New York: Harper & Row, 1955), p. 5.

6. These two phrases are suggested by Sheila Kitzinger and are unpublished. She conducted a workshop at UC Medical Center, San Francisco, 1969.

7. Dick-Read, *Childbirth Without Fear,* p. 157.

CHAPTER 34

the female
juvenile delinquent

MARY BENTLEY ABU-SABA

People who work with society's "deviants" become painfully aware of the inter-action between internal crazy behavior and crazy social structures and laws. A great dilemma arises in deciding whose change to work for first: the individ-ual's or the society's. Eventually, an uneasy decision is made to throw one's efforts toward one end of the spectrum, rather than another. But an astute change agent always has her eye over her shoulder to see how the variables which she chose *not* to deal with directly will affect, negatively or positively, the variable she decided to change. Though this holds true for the whole arena of mental health,[1] it is poignantly true in working with the female juvenile delinquent. To be unaware of the weaknesses of the law, court, and social structure which have assigned this questionable title to a young woman is humanly and professionally irresponsible.

The irony of the situation is, however, that many young women in legal trouble are in great need of acquiring the internal attitude which says: "I am respon-sible for my life. I will not let others be in charge." This essential attitude is the key reason for the success of TA with delinquents.[2] Before discussing thera-

---

From *TA Journal* **5,** 1 (1975). Reprinted by permission.

peutic problems, however, let us take that necessary hard look at the legal framework which has called her to our attention.

Females have had a strange history with the American correctional system. They have been treated under a double standard on several counts: the nature of their offense, a longer period of confinement for similar offenses, and a differential age limit under which they can be considered wards of the court. In most states, girls can be so categorized up to 18 years of age; for boys the limit is commonly 16. Any official record will readily point to the higher delinquency rate of boys as compared to girls, usually about 15 to one. Yet the boy-girl ratio of those institutionalized in the whole nation is about three to one.[3] There seem to be more girls in institutions than their number of offenses would warrant.

In a nation-wide survey conducted with a view toward discovering the nature of female offenses, two authors[4] categorized these offenses into a "big five" listed here in order of frequency: running away; incorrigibility; sexual offenses; probation violation; and truancy. However, these authors go on to show that in many instances "incorrigibility" and "ungovernability" are used as official euphemisms for sexual misconduct; otherwise, sexual misconduct would have taken first place.

The same study showed only four percent of the offenses committed by boys as being of a sexual nature. Certainly one would not assume that girls are sexually more promiscuous than boys, rather one would immediately perceive the double ethical standard operating in the expectations placed on female versus male sexual behavior. The general platitude "boys will be boys" is commonly accepted when it involves their sexual experimentation. When girls are apprehended because of this kind of action, however, they are labeled as incorrigible, or ungovernable, or more blatantly, sexually deviant.

The President's Commission on Law Enforcement and Administration of Justice in 1967 stated that:

> Children's Bureau statistics based on large city court reports reveal that more than half of the girls referred to juvenile court in 1965 were referred for conduct that would not be criminal if committed by adults; only one-fifth of the boys were referred for such conduct. Boys were primarily referred for larceny, burglary, and motor-vehicle theft, in order of frequency. Girls for running away, ungovernable behavior, larceny, and sex offenses.[5]

It is immediately apparent, then, that in dealing with apprehended female offenders, we are not confronting "hardened criminals." In many cases the girl has been reacting to a difficult home situation. She repeatedly runs away, a foster family is not available to her, so the court has little recourse except to institutionalize her. The reason for institutionalization is, therefore, a particular social condition, and not the commission of a crime.

"Persons in Need of Supervision" is the euphemism used in New York State for juveniles who have had trouble with the law, but who have not committed any criminal act. The statute applies to boys under 16 years of age, and girls under 18 years of age. It is not a protective law for juveniles who have committed a criminal act. They still may be subject to criminal prosecution. But it entitles the court to adjudicate minors for noncriminal acts. And in this case, girls can be subject to court supervision two years longer than boys.

The juvenile court system is a product of social reforms of the late 1800's. At this time there was considerable agitation from humanitarians over the treatment of wayward youth. The general policy was to lock them up along with adult criminals. This was perceived as the worst thing to do for a child. Illinois served as a model for other states by passing the Illinois Act of 1899 in which juveniles were to be treated under a whole different system of philosophy and law. This Act was a just and sincere reflection of the best notions of the time on how to treat youth. It asserted that punishment and cruelty were no way to insure that a child would grow up to be an acceptable citizen.

Our laws have become complex and the juvenile population needing attention has become considerably larger. While at one time it may have seemed a good idea for the judge to act as substitute parents, today no judge has the time to give juveniles this kind of attention. Too often the informality of the juvenile judge's court proceedings has denied a juvenile the sort of due process she could expect as a legal adult. And by the time a youth has come before the judge she has too often already felt the brunt of police procedures: apprehension, searching, questioning, detention, and all of the resultant psychological upheaval.

Females brought into Family Court in New York are given as a matter of course vaginal tests for venereal disease, even if their offense had nothing to do with sexual activity. There is a questionable violation of the female's body here, not to speak of the consequent terror on the part of a juvenile who is sexually naive.

It is not unusual in many states to find that females are given longer sentences than would be given males for the same offense. The rationale for the longer sentence can best be described by quoting Judge Hall of the New Jersey Supreme Court in a 1971 statement:

There are decisions in other jurisdictions concluding that disparate legislative sentencing schemes based upon sex are not constitutionally invalid. These cases, generally speaking, reasoned that the legislature could legitimately conclude that female criminals were basically different from male criminals, that they were more amenable and responsive to rehabilitation and reform—which might, however, require a longer period of confinement in a different type of institution—and that therefore the legislature could validly differentiate between sexes with respect to the length of incarceration and the method of the determination thereof.

The laws to deprive females of their liberty are plentiful, but there are no laws that give women the right to suitable treatment. Girls who are brought before the attention of the courts are not automatically given information on the physiology of their bodies, on contraceptives, or the therapeutic reaffirmation that women have the right to control their own bodies, as well as their lives. They are not given guidance of a vocational nature to assist them in choosing means of taking care of themselves in some adequate way other than depending on males.

Girls who engage in sexual activities, are truant from school, or run away from their homes, do not need county jails, court procedures or police questioning. They are in search of identity, love, security—and sometimes intense adventure to express the anger which is not traditionally allowed to the female. They have often come from extraordinarily inadequate homes. They need our best counsel, our firm guidance, alternatives for identification other than a submissive dependent role, opportunities for vocational competence, love, and acceptance from a compassionate adult community. They have been neglected by a social order providing unequal opportunities for them. They need institutions with people dedicated to the healing of human hurt, and to the nurturance of the will so that they may live with hope.

So, then, therapists have this as a first imperative in treating the female delinquent: to recognize the inconsistent body of laws which declare her a delinquent, and to work for their rectification. This would be also a first step in delinquency prevention. Those laws regulating clearly noncriminal behavior which is of potential harm only to the youth herself should be examined carefully and struck from the criminal code. Such laws include smoking, truancy, running away from home, violation of curfews, and sexual activity. It has become obvious that we cannot continue to expend our resources in the area of policing and enforcing private morality.

When females are involved in potentially self-detrimental activities (prostitution, drug abuse) they can be required to attend therapy sessions which emphasize the rights of women, to acquire accurate sexual and drug information, and to assess their own needs and how they can be fulfilled. This does not mean that the female must accept this point of view, but she could at least be channeled to those forces within the society which are of a consciousness-raising nature.

Recognizing the illogical social and legal structure, the therapist still finds him or herself in the ironical situation of confronting the female client with the question: "How have you been responsible for getting yourself in this situation, and what are you planning to do about it?" There is an analogy here to the person who has been physically handicapped by sudden illness and confined to a wheelchair. Fate was in no way fair to visit this unhappy state of affairs on this particular person, yet there it is, and the person must learn skills he or she did not know before.

TA is an effective therapy because it insists that each person has an Adult to figure out how to take care of him or herself and stay out of trouble. The major emphasis is on people being responsible for what happens to them. With this as an underlying tenet, the client can then move to analyze all those people and events which influenced his or her choice of a not-OK position. Script analysis then becomes a powerful tool in this analysis.

A young "delinquent" can see how many of her activities are designed to get negative strokes, and she can learn to get her Child needs met in more positive ways.

She will also understand that many of her behaviors which are aimed at declaring her independence ("You can't tell me what to do—I'm my own boss,") do not achieve this at all, but rather reinforce her dependence. By not choosing alternatives from her Adult, but reacting from her Rebellious Child, she further embroils herself in situations where someone else (an institution, or a man) will have to take care of her. Though they often declare themselves more independent than their "straight" peers, female delinquents are equally caught up in the notion that marriage and/or pregnancy will "solve" their problems. This is reinforced by the lack of vocational preparation designed for girls in our society.

The TA therapist who is knowledgeable about the pitfalls of the social-legal framework which categorizes a female "delinquent," and one who is also sensitive to those ways in which the female declares herself to be "delinquent" will be able to effectively confront the client with a full battery of tools for "Getting On With It."

REFERENCES

1. R. D. Laing's work refers to the craziness of society.

2. Jesness, Carl, *The Youth Center Research Project* (Sacramento: California Youth Authority, 1972).

3. Eldefonso, Edward, *Law Enforcement and the Youthful Offender* (New York: John Wiley & Sons, 1973).

4. Vedder, Clyde B. and Dora B. Somerville, *The Delinquent Girl* (Springfield, Ill.: Charles Thomas, 1970).

5. *The Challenge of Crime in a Free Society*. Report by the President's Commission on Law Enforcement and Administration of Justice, 1967.

CHAPTER 35

TA in vocational rehabilitation: the rehabilitation checklist

JOHN MACKEY

The application of Transactional Analysis in therapeutic, teaching, and industrial settings has been discussed in the literature.[1,2,3] The following is an outline of a specific clinical application of TA in a comprehensive program of vocational rehabilitation.

During the last 20 to 30 years the federal government, state governments and the public at large have become more aware and more responsive to the rehabilitative needs of thousands of disabled and handicapped persons. This concern with the real problems of the disabled is reflected, in part, by the allocation of millions of dollars for case service fees, expansion of rehabilitation facilities, and training of specialists to assist the handicapped in dealing with their difficulties. Because of his special interest and training in the psychology of disability, the rehabilitation counselor is especially equipped to work with the handicapped. At this time, the rehabilitation counselor is particularly concerned with the effectiveness of his services. I propose that the systematic application of the theory and principles of TA in vocational rehabilitation is of significant value in the rehabilitation counselor's technical and treatment services, which include work evaluation, personal adjustment training, individual counseling, remedial education, and group treatment.

I suggest that a disability, whether as a result of trauma, disease process, or congenital factors, represents an insult to the total personality of the person but most especially to the Child. The process of rehabilitation cannot proceed to a satisfactory conclusion without an eventual structural analysis of the ego states and the related attitudes, data, and feelings concerning the disability.

I have become aware that when a client has initiated a discussion of her or his disability or symptoms in a treatment group, this has not always been a pastime, a racket, or the opening move in a game. Rather, it has been a reflection of the Child's (A_1) need for stroking for OK-ness in spite of the disability. The therapist can exercise the option of staying with a structural analysis of the ego states in relation to the disability rather than moving, perhaps prematurely, to the transactional, game, and script analyses which would be indicated if the client's discussion of his symptoms included ulterior motivations (leading to *Wooden Leg, NIGYSOB, Do Me Something.*)

A useful instrument for the therapist who elects this option is the *Rehabilitation Checklist.** Questions useful in determining the Adult's (A_2) awareness of the disability are:

1. What is your disability? (The client is asked to name it in medical terms, if possible.)
2. Is it progressive? (A knowledge of the prognosis as well as diagnosis reduces discounting of the client.)
3. Can treatment help you? (What can realistically be changed by medical and surgical techniques?)
4. What kind of work can you do now?

Questions for the Parent (P_2) are:

1. What did your parents say about handicapped people? About the blind? About the deaf? About skid-row alcoholics?
2. What do you guess they said when you weren't around?
3. How would your father or mother have acted if they had a disability?
4. How do they feel about you now?
5. Did your problem make any difference in the way they raised you?
6. How would you raise a handicapped child?

Questions for the Child (P_1 and A_2) are:

1. What happened to you?
2. Did anyone do this to you?

---

* Credit is given to Liz Allen for naming the Rehabilitation Checklist.

3. What might happen now?
4. Were you being punished?
5. Did you decide to suffer? For how long?
6. Are there any advantages to your disability?
7. Do you use your handicap in any way?

The questions designed for the Child may tap archaic fears or rage, those for the Adult elicit the extent of reality-based data, and those questions for the Parent discover the client's traditional counterscript instructions in regard to the handicap. The questions tend to "hook" the Adult (A_2) of the client and intrigue the Little Professor (A_1) without Parental (P_2) objection.

This early structural approach to capture the interest of the client and enlist the support of his Adult for later operations is essential before the therapist attempts more advanced levels of analysis for two reasons. First, the client views his disability almost exclusively as the main reason for his dependence, vocational failures, interpersonal problems, etc. The Child invariably and magically concludes that he has to be cured and made "whole" again. Secondly, the process by which the client is referred to state and federal agencies is essentially Parental because of its bureaucracy and authoritarianism which offers strokes primarily for compliance rather than assertiveness and individuality. Consequently the client approaches the rehabilitation facility with an Adult contaminated by both his Parent and Child. Functionally, his early responses and overtures to the facility are either rebellious or compliant as he has adapted to the "processing" in order to maximize his supply of strokes (A_1).

The process involving the referring agency, rehabilitation facility, and client is further explained in terms of the dynamics of the Karpman Drama Triangle. For example, a social service agency may threaten a disabled client with termination of his welfare (or social security or compensation) allowance because he has been on the "dole" too long (Persecutor). The rehabilitation facility may be cast in the role of the Rescuer who will get the client back to work. The client is the Victim and may play *(Just Try and) Do Me Something* or *Poor Me.*

Role switches occur at two points. First, the rehabilitation facility becomes Persecutor when discussing the results of the work evaluation process and begins placement efforts with the client (still Victim) who asks *Who Me?* or says *I'll Bet You Can't!* The social service agency may then rescue with, "If you can't find a job right away, we'll continue your allowance a while longer." The payoff point occurs when the client (now Persecutor) asks, *What Do You Expect of a Man with An Ill-Fitting Prosthetic Device?* or who *NIGYSOB*'s the whole facility (e.g., "They were really inadequate to meet my needs"). The social service agency may again rescue by saying, "Let's try this other program down the road." The Victim is the agency who, having discharged the client, gains the internal and external social advantages from the game of *We Were Only Trying to Help Him*.

The rehabilitation counselor skilled in TA is wise to consider the meaning of the disability to the client in terms of structural analysis before attempting the transactional and game analysis necessary to confront the ulterior transactions inherent in the Drama Triangle. It may then be possible to do the more involved script analysis resulting in the client's increased ability to change his life position and direction.

REFERENCES

1. Berne, E., *Transactional Analysis in Psychotherapy* (New York: Grove, 1961).

2. Ghan, L., "Transactional Analysis in University Teaching," *TA Bulletin* 5, 20 (1966), p. 183.

3. Berne, E., *The Structure and Dynamics of Organizations and Groups* (New York: Grove, 1963).

CHAPTER 36

treating male banal scripts

J. HERBERT HAMSHER

MALE-FEMALE LIBERATION MOVEMENTS

Increasing numbers of men are experiencing intense discomfort around issues of their sexuality and role definitions. To a considerable degree the surge of anxiety and unhappiness in males has been fostered by and represents a reaction to the Women's Liberation Movement. Women have done men the service of "upsetting the apple cart"—initiating a dialectic process in which the traditional banally scripted ways of behaving and relating no longer work. The previously "required" ways of "being a man" do not now so predictably produce either stability in relationships or strokes to the Adapted Child. For a long time the definition of socio-personal maleness has been overtly clear and definitive. Men were given powerful messages about how to act in order to be able to feel good about themselves. The price that has been paid for fitting into this pattern—in terms of the reduced freedom, spontaneity, emotionality, and the genuine loving of the Natural Child—has been discussed for several years in the TA literature (for example, Allen[1] and Hamsher[2]). It is this awareness of constriction and inhibition that has been facilitated by women's enhanced ability to depart from the constraints of their own traditional role definitions.

BANAL SCRIPT: DEFINITION

The concept of "banal scripts" was first focused on in TA literature by Steiner[3] and Wyckhoff[4] who emphasized women's issues. The banal script is one which, although not overtly tragic, produces a constricted, stereotyped way of being which severely limits the capacity for joy, spontaneity, and autonomy. Berne[5] refers to the banal script as a non-winner one, while James and Jongeward[6] discuss these issues within the context of a "going-nowhere" pattern. The dictionary defines banal as "trite, hackneyed, commonplace, trivial." The banal script restricts people to centering their lives around their social roles and converts into major issues the variety of concerns that are quite irrelevant to the Free Child. What is produced by the banal script is indeed a life that is "commonplace, trivial," a person who is, in James' and Jongeward's terms "treading water"[6] and not experiencing the joy of authenticity and the exhilaration of growth.

FREEDOM VS. NEW ADAPTATIONS

Humans are social organisms and exist, grow, and experience themselves in the context of relationships. It is important to remain aware that the treatment of male banal scripts involves in some direct or indirect way what is occurring in the scripts of women and other men with whom a particular man is relating. The first question of diagnostic importance is, "What is the source of the current discomfort and unhappiness?" As much as the social pressure of feminism assists men in realizing their own scripted limitations there is also associated with it a potential trap of extraordinary therapeutic significance. If a man changes to please a woman he is *continuing*, not escaping, the confines of adaptation. I have seen many men who have sought treatment because of the pain they were experiencing in a relationship with a woman who was becoming herself, more free and less stereotypically female. While the pain of these men was real, it covered a basic fear about losing the relationship, a thundering proof to them of their own OKness. It is essential to work first on providing permission to "feel what you feel" and "be what and who you are" before moving to changes which are desired by another. No matter how ostensibly positive the change, any change that is promoted unwittingly in the service of adaptation rather than freedom reinforces basic not-OK messages.

Very often men are dealing not only with banal script messages but with the interlocking script messages as well. The counterscript message, "Be strong and potent," is accompanied by an even more limiting and destructive injunctions, "Don't feel," "Don't be you," or "Don't leave me (mother)." To rebel against the banal counterscript, then, may in fact be to drive oneself further into the script.

JERRY: A CASE STUDY

Jerry entered treatment because he was having difficulty adjusting to the new liberated lifestyle of his wife, Linda. After seven years of relatively stable married life they were having many arguments and problems centered around her working and requiring that he give her more assistance with the house and children, and with her becoming more free to be sexual and to ask for sex for herself. Jerry was an intelligent and aware man who knew that his problems were stemming from his inability to free himself from programing that defined the man as the bread winner and the woman as the homemaker. He came in announcing that he wanted to "raise his consciousness." My first question was "Why?" which astonished him and led him to question whether I was in fact the one that he had heard was invested in the development of men's liberation. It seemed apparent to him that the reason the relationship was not going well was his being "out of step with the times." While I assured him that what he had heard about me was true, it was also true that my primary investment was in the liberation of the Natural Child, and not the strengthening of the Adapted Child for whatever benign and desirable purposes.

What emerged in our work was that Jerry had parents with the stereotypic relationship in which father was a successful professional and mother was in charge of the home and children. We established that the basic message from mother was "Don't disappoint me," which covertly gave Jerry responsibility for mother feeling OK about herself as a mother. Jerry remembered two occasions on which he started doing something his mother disapproved of: one when he was dating a girl in high school who came from a lower-class family and another when he was going to change his major in college from premedicine to art, which he loved with enthusiasm. His mother developed an ill-defined illness and was bedridden at the height of the tension surrounding both situations. When Jerry went to his father to discuss the college decision his father's response was "For Christ's sake, Jerry, can't you see that you've gotten your mother so upset that I can't think of anything now but getting her well."

Our work together moved from Jerry's taking care of himself, even if Linda was disappointed, and only subsequently into expanding his own options to include those which would please the "new Linda." The two of them worked on how to deal with the problem of Linda wanting freedom when Jerry didn't want to take care of the kids, and how they could relate to Linda's being sexually aroused when Jerry was not and didn't want to "perform." Compromise in the Adult was supported; adaptation was not.

TECHNIQUES AND CRUCIAL ISSUES

What this case highlights is the crucial issue, that liberation from a banal script can only work in the context of dealing with Natural Child feeling and can only proceed from the foundation of "permission to be you." All banal scripting stems from parental programing and parental control. It is this locus of control that must be dislodged to assure that development of options will proceed in the service of the Natural Child and not in the direction of supporting alternative parental programing.

It is because of the tie to parental directives and parental reactions that much of the therapeutic work in relation to banal scripting profitably takes the form of confronting "projections" and of providing permissions. One of the major areas of focus with men is highlighted by the question, "What would people think if you . . . ?" This is a useful question both in working with the attributes and the behaviors on which men falsely base their OKness and in working on those feelings and behaviors which men suppress out of fear of consequences. I often ask men to relate to this area by identifying first the things about themselves about which people would react negatively if they were no longer true. What emerges is how men are invested in feeling OK because, for example, they: are successful, take care of others, are responsible, are good fathers, are good bosses, etc. We then proceed to identify those things which are positive by virtue of their absence; for example, men often have much invested in *not* breaking down in a crisis and *not* being undone by feelings and *not* running away from risks and challenges.

Two things are of considerable importance in working in this area. The first is to continue pushing to develop a list. There is a tendency for work to proceed from the superficial and relatively emotionally uncharged to the deeper and more significant. The second related issue is the value of constantly searching for things that have symbolic significance. A man may, for example, work for a long time thinking that he is getting beyond the issue of having to be a success and be brought up abruptly if it is suggested that he get rid of his Mercedes or his Jaguar. The symbol is very often the point of intersection between parental programing and child connectedness. It must be remembered that the resolution or outcome to all script-related programing is ultimately determined by the Little Professor and represents what I call a "mini-max solution."

A mini-max solution is a statistical computer concept in which the constraints are programmed into a problem solution and the computer searches for the most desirable solution possible within the limitation defined. If the requirement is to be a success, then the Child will find a symbol of success that contains its own element of pleasure, such as a fancy automobile. The associated value of working with representative things (representative behaviors in the form of symbols) is that the Child functions in relation to simplicity—and while very complicated, fancy, analytical work can be done, it is only when there is dramatic simplicity that the Child will be cathected. Just as I have men add to a list of the positive things about them that they would have to maintain to continue to feel OK, so also I use my own Child to associate with the specific symbolic situations, behaviors, and things which capture the essence. As a man, for example, talked about his feeling good that he is a good husband and father, I responded by asking how it would be for him if he lost his job—or, better yet, if he chose to quit his job and not work for awhile.

There is a rule of thumb which I find very useful in assisting men in extending their own sense of themselves, and that is that everything is imaginable to the Natural Child even though it may not be desired; it is only to the Adapted Child and the Parent that something is unimaginable, inconceivable, and upsetting. I therefore will often exaggerate issues by using an example which a person considers bizarre. I will ask, for example, "What if you no longer wanted to have sex with your wife: how would you feel, and how would she feel?" To the degree that a person is free and unprogramed the response is likely to be to the effect that, "That would be ok, only having sex is a lot of fun so I can't imagine wanting that to be true." The more typical response is, "That is ridiculous and that would mean that something is wrong with me, and of course a wife would not want to be with a husband who was not interested in her sexually." One of the most difficult things to remember in working with banal scripts is that banal script input builds from and overlaps with Natural Child feeling, and that operating from programing is still not the same as operating from spontaneous freedom. It is true, for example, that it is "not natural" not to have sex. It is also true that the Natural Child experiences total comfort in not having sex as well as in having sex. What most men require most in achieving liberation is decontamination, which separates their doing what is natural because it is natural and because it would not be OK not to do so.

One of the exercises that I use with men to clarify importance and unconscious areas of contamination is to have them describe a person who is completely opposite to themselves. The aspects of themselves which are omitted in describing their opposite are often those aspects which are so solidly programed that a man does not even experience an option about being different. For example, a man may identify his opposite as not being responsible, as being inadequate, incompetent, etc., but not identify that it would also be the opposite of him not to value having women look at him in a way that indicates that he is attractive to them. Identifying this and focusing then on his opposite, being unattractive or ugly, clarifies the programmatic importance of his feeling validated by women's response to him.

INTERLOCKING BANAL SCRIPTS

In working in groups that contain both men and women there are repeated instances which provide an opportunity for dealing with banal scripting for both sexes in terms of their relating to each other. It is, for example, very difficult for men *not* to rescue women when they are in trouble and for women *not* to provide assistance to men when they are struggling. In working with men it is important to interfere with their obtaining assistance from women and to invite them to obtain nurturance, support, and assistance from other men in the group. Working with this transactional situation frequently elicits issues related to what men got from their mothers that kept them feeling inadequate and "needing" their mothers, and what they did not get from father. It also frequently highlights how mother is unwittingly invested in there being some separation between father and son. What frequently is not recognized is that if father were providing for all of the needs of the son, mother would experience herself as "useless," therefore intimacy between father and son is interfered with by mother and feared by both father and son. It is because of this primitive triadic situation that so many issues occur in relation to men relating to men. At the first level men avoid intimacy with each other and run away from nurturing and loving each other. At the deeper level men acquire the capacity to relate warmly to each other first only in the absence of women. It is as if there may be permission to seek from father what is naturally obtained from mother only if mother isn't around. To ask father in mother's presence for that which mother is offering elicits the greatest anxiety for all members of the triad.

It is because of the dynamics involved in the mother-father-son relationship that men's liberation first involves permissions which are socially a replay of the adolescent "homosexual" experience, that is to say permission for men to love men and to achieve intimacy with other men. If men, however, remain stuck at the level of achieving intimacy with men only by virtue of the absence or exclusion of women, the dynamics of the parental triad continue to have power. It is only when love, nurturing, intimacy can be experienced in the presence of women and without its being defensively sexualized, that a man is truly liberated. I believe homosexual sex that is *chosen* rather than compulsive is not based on dislike of or exclusion of the opposite sex.

The following are some issues that are important to deal with and some questions which are useful in exercises in working to free men from their banal scripting: It is important to work with men around all of the issues of sexuality and sensuality. Men need to experience permission to be sensual without having to be potent and to be able to enjoy their bodies—to enjoy sensuality with women without the necessity of that producing a coital demonstration of their adequacy. It is important also to identify what men think both other men and other women feel about them in relation to sexuality. What do they expect would be someone's reaction to, for example, discovery that they are impotent or have experienced, impotence. In this regard it is often valuable for men to be able to discuss in the presence of women their feelings about their body and their perceptions of others' reactions to their body. Despite all of the reassuring input from experts in the field of sexuality, American men remain concerned about penis size, and it is of great value to be able to discuss with a man his fear that his penis is too small or his conviction that he is powerful and male because it is large.

It is also useful to identify what father stroked a son for and what mother stroked him for. One of the questions that I ask is, "What could your father not tolerate being true about you?" "What could your mother not tolerate being true about you?" Another useful question is, "If your mother had only two 'dos' and two 'don'ts' that she could communicate to you to govern your life as a man, what would they be?" The same question, of course, is repeated for father. It is also instructive to ask what aspects of father's personality and behavior were upsetting to mother.

OTHER FORMS OF BANALITY

It is often difficult for a man to perceive with accuracy the pervasive influence of the script inputs that have been discussed to this point. Many men have started to develop themselves in vocations and avocations and have suddenly "copped out" on themselves because of the pull of messages which keep them stuck in relatively humdrum existences. They often lack permission to ask a partner to leave the family-of-origin to move to a new place, or to take an exciting risk and initiate a new venture. They may drop out of college after two years to "assume responsibility" for bringing home a better paycheck for a wife and baby. They may, in fact, find it difficult to admit not wanting a child at a time when it puts strain on them and limits their development in a free and autonomous fashion. This is rendered even more powerful when a wife is scripted to stay home and "care for the family"; not to have children is then to deprive the woman of her sole means of feeling OK about herself.

While men are sometimes admonished to "sow their wild oats" as adolescents and young adults, it is seldom recognized how little real freedom is involved. This message typically means "impress others and show what a man you are"; it doesn't mean "have fun and discover what it is like to experience joy." I frequently work with men around issues of joy and excitement since these emotions are often the first to be sacrificed to the banal script inputs. Answers to the question, "What would fill your life with joy and excitement?" often provide insight into what has been given up in order to "be strong," and other banal script directives. The answers to this question can provide direction for career changes, reorient primary relationships, and get a man in touch with his Natural Child feelings about his life. One man who pursued the answer to this question went back to school at age 38 to become a successful trial lawyer, another gave up a very successful career in sales to open up his own small business. In both cases, the men discovered how constricted their lives and their relationships had been and experienced much excitement and joy, as well as travail and struggle, in becoming less "solid" and programed and more spontaneous and authentic.

LIBERATION

Freeing up the Child from the confines of banality is at the same time exciting and scary. Life and relationships become more authentic while they also become less safely predictable. It is important for therapists to have a sense of both the feeling of excitement and the sense of danger that requires Adult safeguards and potent protection.

REFERENCES

1. Allen, Brian, Liberating the Man Child, *TA Journal* **2**, 2 (1972), pp. 68–71.

2. Hamsher, J. Herbert, "Male Sex Roles: Banal Scripts," *TA Journal* **3**, 2 (1973), pp. 23–28.

3. Steiner, Claude, *Scripts People Live* (New York: Grove, 1974).

4. Wyckhoff, Hogie, "The Stroke Economy in Women's Scripts," *TA Journal* **1**, 3 (1971), pp. 16–20.

5. Berne, Eric, *What Do You Say After You Say Hello?* (New York: Grove, 1972).

6. James, Muriel and Dorothy Jongeward, *Born to Win: Transactional Analysis with Gestalt Experiments* (Reading, Mass.: Addison-Wesley, 1971), pp. 37–39, 68–100.

PART 6

selected
papers

Muriel James, Ed.D.

CURING IMPOTENCY WITH TA

SELF-REPARENTING: THEORY AND PROCESS

**THE DOWN-SCRIPTING OF WOMEN FOR 115 GENERATIONS:
A HISTORICAL KALEIDOSCOPE**

THE USE OF STRUCTURAL ANALYSIS IN PASTORAL COUNSELING

**EGO STATES AND SOCIAL ISSUES:
TWO CASE HISTORIES FROM THE 1960'S**

TA THERAPY WITH CHILDREN

ONE-SESSION CURE FOR FRIGHTENED EXAM-TAKERS

curing impotency with TA

One American stereotype, held by many people, is that a man should be sexually virile, able to make love spontaneously and to respond to his sexual partner erotically—at the drop of her handkerchief or the drop of his neckline. When a man is unable to do this, when he is impotent for one reason or another, it is a painful, humiliating experience.

This paper is based on the successful treatment of nineteen men cured of impotency with the use of Transactional Analysis. One involved an organic factor. The others were due to malconditioning, childhood trauma, or situational anxiety of a nonsexual nature.

"Impotency is usually rooted in both minor and major psychopathology. In some cases it is a consequence of temporary fatigue; in others it is the first sign of a developing depression. In most instances it is a symptom related to a developed self-image and to a diminished conception of one's adequacy as a male. It may be highly selective (as toward one's wife and not to mistresses) or it may relate to all women."[1]

From *TA Journal* **1**, 1 (1971). Reprinted by permission.

Symptoms included in the description of impotency, or sexual inadequacy in the male, often overlap. They are, according to Wolpe and Lazarus:

1. complete or almost complete absence of sexual arousal.
2. complete or partial inability to obtain an erection despite considerable, and even strong sexual stimuli.
3. complete or partial inability to maintain an erection.
4. premature ejaculation.
5. retarded ejaculation.
6. absence of pleasure in sex, especially ejaculation without sensation.[2]

Transactional Analysis, the theory developed by Dr. Eric Berne (*Games People Play, Principles of Group Treatment,* et al.), was the method used to cure these nineteen men of impotency.* This method includes four phases of treatment which are:

1. *Structural Analysis*—a theory for analyzing the structure of personality based on the concept of ego states. An ego state is defined as a system of feelings accompanied by a related set of behavior patterns.[3] Each person has three ego states—Parent, Adult, and Child—which are three separate sources of attitudes and behavior.
2. *Script Analysis*—the theory that people have an unconscious, or preconscious, life drama that they act out compulsively and that this drama contains replays of early childhood scenes.
3. *Analysis of transactions* between people—the theory that any interaction between people involves the interaction of the ego states in one person, with the ego states in another, and that these transactions can be analyzed.
4. *Analysis of the psychological games* people play—the theory that in many transactions between people there is a series of ulterior transactions which lead to a "pay-off."

One of the basic principles of Transactional Analysis is that the therapist uses simple language and colloquialisms that most people understand. I will try to apply that principle to this paper.

No doubt some of you are interested in techniques other than TA and have had success in using them. I would rather not enter into a comparison game of "My brand of therapy is better than yours." Instead I wish to present some cases that will illustrate Transactional Analysis theory and the treatment process I have found useful in my private practice.

---

* This paper was first presented as a lecture at the Golden Gate Group Psychotherapy Society, San Francisco, June 1970, and later became the author's first publication in TA.

Historically, men have always had sexual freedom. They have usually determined the when, where, and how of sexual intercourse. Many men have expected women to concede to their terms without question and without threatening their masculinity. Many women have, and enjoyed it—especially if the man is potent.

The basic tools a Transactional Analyst works with are: his intuition, his brains, his scientific training (including a knowledge of his own ego states, his own script, and the various ways he himself transacts with others) and last, but not least, his blackboard.

When using TA to cure impotency there are several basic questions to keep in mind. (1) Is the impotency situational, maybe temporary and due to illness, job anxiety, etc.? (2) Is it due to long-term negative conditioning or due to childhood trauma? (3) Is it reflecting the prejudicial attitudes and behavior of the client's parents? (4) Is the impotency somehow related to inadequate or incorrect data in the Adult ego state? (5) Is it a problem related to the man's current sex partners? (6) Is it a dramatic replay of a childhood script being compulsively played out now? If so, who is the director of the drama? What roles are being played? (7) In summary, which ego states are involved and in what ways?

Following are very condensed summaries of two men whose childhood dramas were re-activated in later years when the working requirements of their jobs were changed.

CASE ILLUSTRATIONS

Childhood Trauma: 1

Al was a banker, age 33, and in the early years of marriage, was highly potent. However, when his job was changed and extensive travel was required, it became impossible for him to gain an erection. Both Al and his wife, Jean, were distraught; both were confused because of the abrupt change in his sexual performance.

When they came for treatment, Jean hesitantly said to Al, "Maybe you've got someone else and don't want me any more. Maybe you *like* to travel to be with her." He denied this; his denial seemed genuine.

A TA question was asked Al, "What do you think about on your way home from a business trip?" He replied, "It's kind of odd, 'cause I know Jean's faithful but I keep wondering what she does when I'm out of town." Later another question was asked, "Can you recall any early childhood dramatic scenes played by either of your parents that might be related to this?"

Al was asked to use the creativeness in his Little Professor and project what he knew of his parent's sexual life onto an imaginary movie screen. In time, the original scene emerged. As a young boy, Al had walked in on his mother at the climactic moment. She was having intercourse with his uncle while his father was away. His mother threatened him, "Al, if you ever tell anyone, I'll kill you. What I do when your father's away is my own business."

The recovery of this traumatic scene gave Al additional options. He chose to resign from his traveling job. As he said, "It isn't worth it to fight that kind of anxiety. There's no point setting up the stage for a poor drama like my father did."

Childhood Trauma: 2

Another case of sudden impotency which occurred with a change in jobs and was related to childhood trauma was that of Joe, a trucker, age forty-eight. Joe, with his eighth grade education, felt embarrassed but desperate when he came for counseling. His sudden impotency, like that of Al the banker, began when his working situation changed. Joe's job change was a shift from day work to night work.

For many years his Tuesday and Friday habit of sexual activity had been to go home after work, have a big dinner, read the paper, and have intercourse.

But Joe had not objected to his changed work shift since both he and his wife expected to continue a comparable sex life—with intercourse after breakfast rather than dinner. However, Joe found himself totally unable to achieve an erection in spite of his wife's efforts to arouse him. With a deep blush he explained, "She's a nice looking woman but when I see her naked I feel sort of sick and just can't do it. I'm all bound up."

Joe was asked, "Did you ever feel that way when you were a kid?" After thinking it over briefly, Joe started pounding his leg and shouted, "Yes, damn it. I *was* bound up. Once my ma caught me peeking at her through a keyhole when she was undressing. She was so mad she tied me to the bed post and left me there all day. Just for looking at her! Well I made up my mind then, I'd never look at another woman." And Joe hadn't. For 20 years of marriage he and his wife had had intercourse only at night and only in total darkness.

The suggestion, made to Joe's Adult ego state, was that he try having intercourse according to their previous pattern—in the evening when it was dark—rather than in the daylight when he came home after work.

His potency immediately returned. Jubilantly he phoned with, "Hey, I don't need any more counseling. That contract I made—to get potent again—well,

I made it. I found out we can do it at night before I go to work. . . . Hey, I'm thinking of getting some of those blackout shades. Then it will be OK anytime, day or night, when we're in the mood."

In my practice, recovery of the traumatic childhood scene and a new decision, made by the Adult ego state, to "take that show off the road and get a better one going" led to a cure of situational impotency in a very few sessions. Joe the trucker had only two sessions; Al, the banker had four.

However, when the sexual pathology in the Adapted Child is primarily due to long term negative conditioning in childhood, rather than to a single traumatic event, the cure is not as rapid. The person has taken a basic position about himself which is "I'm not-OK as a man."

In such cases of impotency it may take several months for the personality structure to be analyzed and the games and script to be revealed; it also takes that long for the "permission to be potent," which is given by the therapist, to be permanently accepted by the client. Part of a cure may require the therapist to give subtle, positive messages of "Yes you are OK." "Yes you really can be a strong, potent man." This nonverbal message helps break the "curse" of the negative conditioning.

Eric Berne, who was one of my clinical training supervisors, once suggested that I try giving this message indirectly, by commenting to the client's wife, in the presence of her husband something like, "Did you notice that strong, masculine statement your husband just made?" This procedure has never failed. The wife always gets the message that her husband may really be a man. He invariably begins to feel potent once more.

In TA terms, when a therapist gives "potency permissions"—either verbally or nonverbally—the permissions are often in opposition to the original *impotency* scripting which was given to the client in childhood by his actual parent figures. TA permissions can be used to countermand original negative messages.

Along with permission, the client may need "protection" from a replay of what are called in TA "witch" and "ogre" Parent tapes. Any ego state may be activated, as though with an electrode, and become the executive of the personality when a stimulus enters a person's awareness and triggers off original messages—verbal or nonverbal—which are then often experienced once more. If negative and reactivated in a person's head they can create severe anxiety in his Child ego state. His internal Parent "beats up" his internal Child and reinforces the old negative feelings.

The therapist may offer "protection" to the client—sometimes in the form of allowing the client to make a brief phone call to him—out of his own sense of potency. This potency of the therapist is important because if the client's Little Professor is active he will know, *intuitively,* if the therapist is real or just trying to "put something over on him" as his parents once did.

Prejudicial Parent

In the following case, the original message Tom received was, "women are a useful commodity but secondary to everything else." This had come from both his parents. Tom's father, who always retreated from people into work, showed him how to play the male role in this script; his mother played the expected female part.

Tom was a nationally known physicist. His Adult ego state was strong in his professional field. He could gather data well and was competent at probability estimating based on the data. However, at home Tom was a flop according to Suzy, his wife.

The company Tom worked for, being involved in national security, had a policy that a single man was a poor security risk. They entered therapy because Suzy was threatening divorce.

Tom was on the spot. He liked his job but would lose it if Suzy left him. Her complaint was, "He goes to bed with his company, never with me. He uses all his energy to keep the company happy. He doesn't even pick up his socks. I'm supposed to say 'Poor You; You work so hard.' Well let me tell you I'm mad. If he wants to make love to his company in the name of science, let him! I got married for a lot more than his *professional potency.* I got married for some *sexual potency* as well. I thought his big shoulders were a sign he'd have it. Well, he doesn't have it and he never did and I'm fed up."

In TA terms Suzy's last remark was an "exit" line. In script analysis language, an exit line is either the end of the act or the end of the entire marriage drama. Suzy had saved a big collection of resentment—psychological "trading stamps." Her book was full and she was about to cash them in for a big "prize" which was to be a divorce. The final curtain on their marriage drama was about to fall. Tom would not only lose Suzy, he would also lose his job.

The TA treatment in this case was for Tom and Suzy to gain awareness of their psychological scripts, the prototypes of which are often found in children's stories and ancient myths.

Tom, like Atlas of Greek mythology, was under the delusion that the world was held up by his efforts—his research. One of his favorite games was, *Look How Hard I'm Trying.*

Suzy was unwilling to play the Herculean role that Tom expected—that of applauding his performance while cleaning up his mess. She was bored with her Pollyanna role and her game of *Sunny Side Up*. Suzy also wanted to be "on stage." She wanted to play a role like that of Europa, who in Greek mythology was "carried away" by Zeus, king of the Gods, disguised as a "lot of sweet-smelling bull." But Tom was not the type of man to carry women away.

In a sense, they were reading from different scripts. Although they were performing on the same marriage stage, they played roles that were at odds. Their scripts, which were in their Adapted Child and received from their parents in childhood, were not compatible.

Although it may not be necessary to live on the basis of a childhood script, most people do. In this case, Tom and Suzy's marriage script needed to be changed. Atlas was an OK role for a single man with aspirations for holding the whole world on his shoulders but it was too limiting for a woman who wanted a strong erection instead of strong shoulders.

One phase of Tom and Suzy's treatment involved the use of "homework." They liked Greek myths and reread them in an attempt to find different dramatic themes and roles that might be mutually satisfying in their marriage. At the time of this writing they are experimenting with the parts of Ulysses and Penelope. Tom recently said, "Wow, I feel like I just came home from the wars and here she is, Wow!"

The use of recommended reading—selected erotic literature and scientific information on sexual behavior—often is a major factor in curing impotency with TA. The data strengthens the Adult ego state so that the prejudices in the Parent that often control a person's behavior, can be reevaluated and, when appropriate, can be rejected. Another value of erotic literature is that it may "turn on" the Natural Child.

Inadequate Data in the Adult

Neither Ron nor his wife Betty had had any sexual experience before marriage. They had had similar backgrounds including parents who, in answer to their questions on sex, often said, "You'll learn enough about sex after you're married."

Ron's potency problem was premature ejaculation. This was the behavior of the Natural Child who always wants what he wants when he wants it. His Adapted Child hadn't learned to delay gratification. According to Betty, all he did was, "Roll on, do his thing, roll off, and go to sleep."

Ron's pattern of ejaculation left Betty sexually frustrated. Her resentment sharply increased after she attended a young women's class organized by Women's Liberation Movement and read some books on sexuality and woman's rights.

Ron was confused at her changed attitude. He claimed, "Since she's been reading those books she's always criticizing me. She never used to complain about our sex life. Now, *nothing* I do is right. Anyhow I don't know what in the hell she wants."

Both had neglected the obvious—Betty hadn't told him what she wanted sexually; Ron hadn't become informed. His Adult ego state needed information on women's sexuality and the varieties of sexual stimulation. He needed adaptation to delay the gratification of his Natural Child until she could become aroused.

Ron's TA treatment included specific reading to strengthen his Adult ego state, to retrain his Adaptive Child to the needs of his wife, and to liberate his Little Professor to be more creative during intercourse. His Parent, who had given him the "ogre" message that women were objects to be used, was decommissioned.

In cases where strengthening the Adult through education is useful treatment, the Transactional Analyst may convey, verbally and/or nonverbally, the idea that it is neither his, nor his wife's fault that they were not well informed sexually, also that the new information they can get as grown-ups will make their sexual life more exciting and satisfying. Accurate data often is a major factor in curing impotency. It straightens things out.

Even Briefer Case Summaries

One man in his late sixties was cured when he discovered in three counseling sessions that the smell of his brandy nightcap so offended his wife that she nonverbally gave him a "don't be potent" message. This man's cure was simple. He switched to bourbon as the odor was not as offensive to his wife as brandy was.

Another was cured when the anxiety of his wife, who feared being overheard by neighbors through the paper-thin walls of their retirement apartment, was easily alleviated. They simply moved their bed to the other side of the room and away from the neighbor's wall.

Still another case was of a man with one of his testicles undescended. He discovered he was not "half a man," but was instead fully potent. The discovery came with two important permissions. His wife, a nurse, got permission that it was OK to stop acting like a nurse in bed. He got permission to invite her to be nurse only on her job and to be a sexy Child and informed Adult in bed.

In curing impotency it is often useful to let a man's wife "in on the act." She may play the part that spoils the show. If so, she can learn that it is possible for the curtain to fall on a scene of the prematurely ejaculating, or retarded ejaculating uneducated spouse who, to her, has been like a frog. She can also discover that the curtain can go up on a new act, with her as a princess and the frog transformed into a "prince" of a man.

QUESTIONS USEFUL IN CURING IMPOTENCY

Following are samples of useful questions that can be used in marriage counseling when working with an impotent male and his wife.

- What about this woman (this man) turns you on?
- What about this woman (this man) turns you off?
- What do you want more of?
- What do you want less of?
- Are there external problems that worry you and interfere with your masculine (feminine) feelings of sensuousness?
- Can they be solved, or can they be temporarily set aside?
- Is there a physical problem that needs consideration?
- Do you need to be better informed?
- Are you playing some old negative memory tapes that interfere with a good sex life?
- What is your pay-off in replaying them?
- Are there words, gestures, actions that you could use to turn on your spouse?
- Would this behavior hurt or discount either of you?

REFERENCES

1. Wolberg, Lewis R., *The Technique of Psychotherapy,* 2d ed. (New York: Grune & Stratton, 1967), Part Two, p. 984.

2. Wolpe, Joseph, and Arnold A. Lazarus, *Behavior Therapy Techniques* (Oxford: Pergamon Press, 1966), pp. 102–103.

3. Berne, Eric, *Games People Play* (New York: Grove, 1964), p. 23.

4. ———, *Transactional Analysis in Psychotherapy* (New York: Grove, 1961), p. 32. Cf. Berne, Eric, *Principles of Group Treatment* (New York: Oxford University Press, 1966).

5. James, Muriel, and Dorothy Jongeward, *Born to Win: Transactional Analysis with Gestalt Experiments* (Reading, Mass.: Addison-Wesley, 1971).

CHAPTER 38

self reparenting:
theory and process

Self-reparenting is a procedure for updating and restructuring the Parent ego state. It includes both *a theory and a process and is related to Berne's differentiation between parental behavior and behavior that comes from a Parent ego state.* In my private practice I have found this differentiation is often important, both in diagnosis and treatment.

PARENTING AND THE PARENT EGO STATE

Parent ego states are "borrowed from parental figures and reproduce the feelings, behavior, and responses of these figures."[1] They are experiential, behavioral, and civil realities: you can find the telephone number of a Parent.[2]

Parental behavior is not always from the Parent ego state. Parental behavior may come from any ego state, and be uniquely different for different people. Berne clarified this: "The pointed index finger may be a Parental admonition, an Adult indicator, or a Child's accusation."[3] This may be one reason that "parenting styles vary with different cultures."[4] The most intelligent parenting

From *TA Journal* **4**, 3 (1974). Reprinted by permission.

often comes from using the Adult as a substitute parent or as an executive determining when and how behavior from the Parent ego state is appropriate.

The accusation "You're in your Parent" that some people make toward others who shake their fingers is simply not universally true. Berne again writes that a therapist, *playing a supportive Parent role,* may really be in the Child ego state, "very much like a little boy playing doctor."[5]

Consequently I believe it is useful for both therapists and patients to know the difference between using some kind of parental behavior (which can come from any of their ego states) and functioning from their unique Parent ego state *as their parents once functioned.* "The Parent ego state is (1) a biological reality and (2) a transmitter of rules and traditions that mainly favor the survival and betterment of the human species,"[6] not a little boy or girl playing at being a parent. This fact was recognized by one client, who when speaking of her brutal parents, said, "They were so incredibly horrible, but some parent figure up there in my top circle must have sometime done *something* that was OK. Otherwise, I'd be dead now."

RATIONALE FOR SELF-REPARENTING

I firmly believe that whatever is OK in that "top circle" needs to be affirmed as such and used appropriately. The OKness in the Parent gives the Child some comfort and encouragement. It may not be much, but even if it's something like, "Mom was an OK cook even though she was kind of crazy," or "Dad was good at reading stories to me when I was little even if he was mean when he was drunk."

Babies do not need to be thrown out with the bathwater. Parents don't need to be discarded for a patient to get well. "Patients get well when they learn how to parent well."[7] The old parents in the Parent ego state, being historical figures, cannot be updated, but through the self-reparenting process the ego state can be restructured. When people learn to parent well they have developed a New Parent ego state which, in this process, includes the old parents. Knowing there was something OK about their natural parents accelerates the self reparenting and the reeducation of the Child.

The process is called self-reparenting because each client independently decides what the New Parent ego state will be. When beginning treatment it is not unusual for clients to talk about their parents as though looking at them through rose-colored glasses. This is natural. They were once children; and children, looking for Santa Claus, expect "perfect" parents. When the Adult is plugged in they recognize the humanness of all people and give up that delusion.

"Children begin by loving their parents, later they judge them, sometimes they forgive them."[8] During the process of self reparenting, clients often start to judge their parents (if they have not already done so). They do this *phenomenologically* from their Child, sometimes aided by gestalt techniques, and *analytically* from their Adult, using specific data-processing techniques. Eventually clients forgive and once more love their parents because they understand how it happened; have kept what is OK in their Parent; and defused what is not-OK by developing a New Parent.

SELF-REPARENTING AND REGRESSIVE REPARENTING

Throughout the process of self-reparenting, a person's Adult is the executive, even if techniques to regress the Child are used. This is very different from the Schiff process of reparenting.[9] In the Schiff modality, the historical parents are *excluded* from the Parent ego state and the therapist becomes the new Parent, sending better messages to the Child than the original parents once did. This can be very useful. A difficulty may arise, however, if unsolved problems in the therapist's ego states are also incorporated.

In self-reparenting, the natural parents are recognized and accepted for what they were. They, like all parents, exhibited some critical and nurturing behavior; some rational Adult behavior, and some free and some adapted-Child behavior. As the frequency, intensity, and appropriateness of this behavior varies from individual to individual, a New Parent is created by the Adult to balance off the negative characteristics—but not to get rid of the old parents who were less than perfect. Using the Adult as executive allows a person to get a *friendly* divorce from their parents, as recommended in *Games People Play*,[10] instead of a hostile one.

DIAGNOSIS OF THE PARENT EGO STATE

Ego states can be diagnosed four ways: behaviorally, socially, historically, and phenomenologically. The use of Dusay's egogram[11] is effective for behavioral and social diagnosis and for changing *parental behavior*, if that is contracted for. Berne says historical diagnosis is also needed. Without this, the new behavior can be a new mask, an adaptation that the Child puts on to please others rather than a restructuring of the Parent ego state.

Historical diagnosis can start in many ways, including Berne's question,[12] "Which of your parents...," followed by a specific, such as, "hit you with uncontrolled anger as you say you did to your son last week?" Or it can start with a question, such as, "Did any of your parents frown, as you are now frowning, to get you to obey?"

If the patient says, "None of my parent figures did that, but *I* do," the behavior is *not* from the Parent ego state; it is probably from the Child. In the
first example above, it could be the Child playing a brutal parental role. In
the second example, although the frown may look parental, it could also be
the Child who wants to be seen as "trying hard."

If people become aware that when they are in their *Parent ego state,* they use
behavior incorporated from their significant parent figures in childhood, they
can, by using their Adult, freely choose when, how, and with whom to use
such behavior. When they become aware that their *parental behavior* may be
coming from their Child or Adult they can also choose whether or not to use
it. "Child and Parent are distinct personalities, each with its own separate and
complete organization; they are not necessarily opposed to each other, they are
simply in many respects inconsistent with each other."[13]

When developing a New Parent a person will, in essence, imagine reducing
the parents in their ego state so that there is room for a New Parent who will
replace part of the old one. The New Parent will have positive qualities,
planned by the *Adult* to balance the negative qualities incorporated from
the historical parents. This process can be conceptualized as shown here.

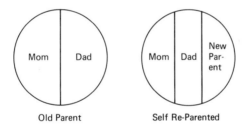

All ego states are subject to change and many people unknowingly incorporate
significant parent figures throughout their lives. These can be part of a New
Parent.

THE NEED FOR A NEW PARENT

Everybody may need milk, but not everyone needs a New Parent. A rapid
technique to discover whether or not a New Parent is appropriate is to ask the
following questions:

- What are five words to describe your mother, the way you perceived her
  when you were little?

- What are five words to describe your father, the way you perceived him when
  you were little?

• Did you have other significant parent figures or people who took care of you when you were little? If so, who were they? What words would describe them?

(The third set of questions above is necessary to determine how many people are in a person's Parent ego state and how they were perceived by the person.)

If the adjectives selected are positive, the client will exhibit these same positive characteristics *when in the Parent ego state* and may not need a New Parent. If negative, these characteristics will also be exhibited and may be an indication that a New Parent is needed. Most people seem to have a mix of positives and negatives in their Parent ego state. These can be separated so that the positives can be consciously used and the negatives balanced off by the potent New Parent. The adjectives originally used may later be seen as distortions, but this can be verified during the decontamination process.

Prejudice, for example, is most often associated with the Parent ego state. On the social level it may appear that way when actually it can be coming from the Child. With historical diagnosis, the ego state where it originates and the *reason* for the particular prejudice becomes clear.

Case illustration   Bill, an engineer working with an interracial group of scientists, often displayed strong prejudice against people of other races. He was belligerent, demanding, and used many distancing techniques with others. Bill was "sent" to treatment to discover why this was so. As he wanted to keep his job, Bill was willing to make a decontamination contract to discover which ego state in him used this behavior, how, and why.

In two sessions of historical diagnosis, Bill decided that it was his Child acting "as though it were a parent." According to Bill, his parents had been easy going, had not been demanding, and seemingly had little prejudice. (This was verified through Bill's brother who worked well with people of other races.)

Bill had made a childhood decision to act like a "bossy" parent because as a little boy he had been the oldest child in an interracial neighborhood and was able to get away with it.

When Bill discovered his prejudicial behavior was a contamination due to his childhood experiences and decisions, he redecided:

• That he would use his Parent ego state and be easygoing as his real parents were instead of his bully Child.

• That his bully Child could be restrained by his Adult.

- That he did not need to have everything his way (as he had in his childhood neighborhood).
- That he would enjoy getting closer to people of different races.

The rationale for developing a New Parent as *part* of the old Parent ego state is based on the belief that a New Parent can defuse the negative parts of the old.[14] Those old parents that interfere with children's growth toward autonomy include: overly critical parent; overly protective parent; inconsistent parent; conflicting parent; uninvolved parent; super-organized parent; overly needy parent.

Overly critical parents say things such as, "You're stupid, you'll never amount to anything," or "Can't you ever do anything right?" or "Go get lost." When in the Parent ego state, a person who had overly critical parents will use these same words, or imply them with nonverbal ulterior transactions, toward others. When in their Child ego state, listening to their Parent tapes like a ventriloquist's dummy, they may say things such as, "I don't get it. I guess I'm getting stupid," or "I'm sorry, but I don't understand," or "I'm lost."

Overly protective parents say things such as, "I'll drive you whenever it rains," "Let me do it for you," "Don't worry, I'll take care of everything," "Now you just tell me if those kids are mean to you." When in their Parent ego state, a person who had overly protective parents will act "syrupy" towards other grown-ups as well as toward children. When in their Child ego state, they will act overly dependent, always looking for care and protection.

Inconsistent parents say one thing one day and something different the next. On a Tuesday such a parent may say, "I worry about you. You must come home on time," and on Wednesday say, "I don't care what you do, just leave me alone." Persons with inconsistent parents will, when in their Parent ego state, act similarly and vacillate in what they expect from others and may be seen by others as "unfair." When in their Child ego state they will feel unsure and frequently "check others out" looking for the nonverbal signs that indicate where the other person is at that particular minute.

Conflicting parents argue over many issues. The arguments may, for example, be loud, even vituperous, or quiet, even rational, or bitter, even cruel, or laughable, even fun. Conflict may arise over work, education, money, leisure time, sex and sex roles, how to rear children, and so forth. Each parent may take an opposing view such as, "Work until you drop dead" vs. "Don't work, let someone else support you." People with conflicting parents often have an inner battle within their Parent ego state. They are likely to act toward others, first as one parent, then as another. They may frequently "go looking for a fight" as their parents did. When in the Child ego state they may feel frightened by loud voices and tend to withdraw when faced with conflict.

Uninvolved parents are those who stay away from home a lot or when home don't listen, or don't share their feelings and ideas, or who isolate themselves in a particular room or workshop, or activity and say things such as, "Don't bother me, I'm busy," or who act like a proverbial absent-minded professor, forgetting birthdays and other special occasions. People who had uninvolved parents will act distant when in their Parent ego state. They will withdraw and be uninvolved as their parents once were. When in their Child ego state such people often act friendly but unsure. They may search diligently for someone who will act like an involved parent, but at the same time, doubt that it could ever happen.

Super-organized parents data-process continually, do not often show child-like warmth and impulsiveness, nor critical or nurturing parental behavior. People with super-organized parents are, when they are in their Parent ego state, well-organized themselves and expect others to be likewise. When in their Child ego state, they usually have a pattern of rebellion, indifference, or compliance toward organizations in general and toward organized people in particular.

Overly needy parents continually expect to be babied and taken care of, or expect to be cheered up and made happy, or expect to be criticized and forgiven. Such parents often manipulate their children into taking parental roles at home. People who have had emotionally overly needy parents will, when in their Parent ego state, express similar emotional needs. When in their Child ego state they are likely to act parental, as they were trained to do in childhood, and choose a spouse to take care of and a job in which they will take care of people.

Except in rare cases, people seem "stuck" with their parents and consequently with their Parent ego state, for better or worse. Therefore, creating an additional parent, a New Parent for the Parent ego state, seems reasonable. The New Parent does not replace the old parents, but it does change the Parent ego state. People have different combinations of parent figures. Therefore their Parent ego states, before and after reparenting, might be diagrammed as shown in the accompanying figure.

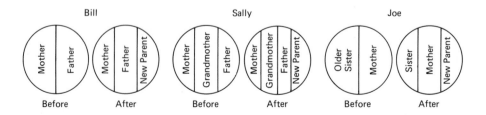

The development of a New Parent, carefully designed by the Adult, increases the options a person has when in her or his Parent ego state. The value of options is so well discussed by Karpman[15] that the usefulness of this does not need proving. The development of a New Parent is not necessarily the same as developing new parental behavior because parental behavior can come from any ego state.

Many TA techniques can be used to change parenting *behavior*. For example, egogram theory and methods combined with contracts for change are especially valuable for a person who wishes to increase Nurturing Parent *behavior*. This new parental behavior may unknowingly contribute to the formation of a New Parent, although in some cases the new behavior can be merely Child compliance to the therapist or to group pressure. In others it can be the newly informed Adult.

The natural parents in the Parent ego state are what they were and consist of historical figures with names, addresses and phone numbers. The New Parent which is carefully designed by the Adult and aided by the creative Child, need not be a historical figure. It can be an intelligent, loving, imaginary parent created as characters in novels and dramas are created.

Imaginary characters in novels and dramas often have real power in a person's life. When authors construct such characters they incorporate ideas and experiences from many sources to create effective characters. The process a person goes through when creating a New Parent is similar to that of a creative writer. Ideas for the New Parent can come from many sources.

SELF-REPARENTING PROCEDURE

The procedure for self-reparenting follows specific steps, with the therapist (if there is one) acting primarily as a facilitator. The steps are as follows:

Awareness of the need for a New Parent that will compensate, supplement, or defuse part of the old parent. Awareness comes when people get in touch with their negative childhood injunctions and their negative feelings about self/or about others, their games, script, or parenting behavior that isn't working.

Historical diagnosis of each childhood parent figure. This is facilitated by homework—detailed lists of strengths or weaknesses of each parent. Exercises from *Born to Win* at the end of the chapter on Parent ego states can be used to energize this process.

Education on the subject of parenting. Attending classes on parenting, reading books such as *Parent Effectiveness Training* or *What Do You Do With Them*

Now That You've Got Them? And, very important, observing real parents. Observation of real parents may be in playgrounds where young children may be protected, overprotected, ignored, encouraged, etc. It may also be in parent co-op nursery schools, in supermarkets, movies, or any place where children are likely to be accompanied by parents. Observation of grownups, who are parenting other grownups, is also important and may include deliberate observation of the group therapist and group members who may or may not parent appropriately.[16]

Inner dialogue between the Adult and the Second Order Child. The purpose of this step is to discover what each part of the Child ego state needs. These needs often differ. For example, the Natural Child (being body-centered) may need better nutrition; the Little Professor may need to play its hunches; the Adapted Child may need Permission to stop listening to puritanical Parent tapes and creatively explore sexuality and gourmet eating.

Because each person's ego states are unique, each is likely to have unique needs. For example, one person may need Permission to think, another to be less self-indulgent or more self-indulgent, and still another to be creative.

Regressive techniques with the Child, as described by Berne, Stuntz, Schiff, or James and Jongeward, or techniques adopted from the Gestalt movement, such as double-chairing, exaggeration of body movements and verbal statements, etc., can be very effective at this step.[17] Fantasy or memory trips, the perusal of a childhood photograph album, and "target stroking" can also be used to cathect the Child. Phenomenological ego state diagnosis can be accomplished at this time and the ego state boundaries realigned.

The Adult can then talk to the inner Child at various stages of development. It can ask the inner Child what would be helpful and what would be harmful, and can listen to the Child's answers. Some answers will be adapted responses learned in childhood, some will be hunches from the Little Professor, some may be uncensored feelings of the Natural Child. All have value in the therapeutic process. Clients, as well as therapists, can learn to potently intervene and referee between the Parent and Child to give permission to themselves and to protect themselves if necessary.

Evaluating the data. The Adult is now in the position to data-process the data it has collected from three sources: the Parent, the Child, and the external world. The old Parent is evaluated as inadequate in specific ways, and as needing to be supplemented or balanced with a New Parent in specific ways. Discussion clarifies the specifics.

Contracts and practice. On the basis of the data, the Adult then contracts to be a substitute parent to the inner Child and to practice the specific parenting behavior that has been decided upon. This pleases the Child whose needs are *at last* being met.

Recognizing the New Parent. Although the new parenting behavior may seem uncomfortable, superficial, even phony when first tried (like learning a foreign language or a new skill), with practice it becomes automatic.

Case illustration Although my mother and father were very caring, responsible parents in many ways, I cannot remember if they ever *asked* me how I felt (they probably told me how they thought I was *supposed* to feel). Nor did they ever touch me, so far as I can remember.

Some years ago I decided, from my Adult, that they were wrong in rearing children that way. My Child ego state probably pushed my Adult to make that decision. After all, children, including the Child in me, *do* want to be asked about their feelings and they *do* want to be touched and held. So I started asking people how they felt and started touching other people and my own children more. I also looked for friends who were warm and touching as well as friends who were interesting intellectually.

At first this new touching felt very uncomfortable, but in time it became automatic and formed part of my New Parent in my Parent ego state. Naturally it pleased my Child, and my Adult thought then—and still thinks—that it's a better way to be.[18]

This New Parent, however, still needs Adult supervision. Recently I led a workshop for upper management executives and was taken to the plane by one of the participants. Instead of a cordial Adult or a warm, grateful Child "thank you," I came on strongly with my New Parent. Some people wouldn't have liked it. Fortunately he did. But since then I've been more aware that what I experience as the good New Parent in me is not always appropriate to use with someone else.

SUMMARY

In brief, parental behavior can come from any ego state. Although any ego state can be used or abused by the client or the therapist,[19] *all ego states have merit,* even some parts of a person's old Parent. Those parts of the old Parent that are without merit can be defused and the personality can be restructured by the process of self reparenting.

REFERENCES

1. Berne, Eric, *Principles of Group Treatment* (New York: Oxford University Press, 1964), p. 220.

2. Ibid., p. 216.

3. Ibid., p. 312.

4. Samuels, Solon D., "Parent Ego State: Can a Therapist Take One to Lunch?" Unpublished paper. Cf. Kaufman, Dorothy N. and Jack Kaufman, "The Sources of Parenting Behavior: An Exploratory Study," *TA Journal* 2, 4 (1972), pp. 191–195.

5. Berne, p. 105. Cf. Berne, Eric, *Principles, Transactional Analysis in Psychotherapy* (New York: Grove, 1961), pp. 233–234.

6. Samuels, "Parent Ego State."

7. Ibid. Cf. Sudhalter, Trava, "Hello, My Nurturing Parent," *TA Journal* 1, 3 (1971), p. 43.

8. Oscar Wilde, quoted in James, Muriel and Dorothy Jongeward, *Born to Win: Transactional Analysis with Gestalt Experiments* (Reading Mass.: Addison-Wesley, 1971).

9. Schiff, Jacqui. *All My Children* (New York: M. Evans, 1970).

10. Berne, Eric. *Games People Play* (New York: Grove, 1964), p. 183.

11. Dusay, John M., "Egograms and the Constancy Hypothesis," *TA Journal* 2, 3 (1972), p. 37.

12. Berne, *Principles,* p. 296. Cf. James and Jongeward, *Born to Win,* pp. 101–126.

13. Berne, *Principles,* p. 298.

14. Cf. James, Muriel, *What Do You Do With Them Now That You've Got Them?* (Reading, Mass.: Addison-Wesley, 1974), pp. 96–104.

15. Karpman, Stephen B., "Options," *TA Journal* 1, 1 (1971), pp. 79–87.

16. Cf. James and Jongeward, *Born to Win,* pp. 241–242.

17. See Berne, *TA in Psychotherapy,* pp. 224–231. Cf. Schiff, Aaron, and Jacqui Schiff, "Passivity," *TA Journal* 1, 1 (1971), pp. 71–78. See also James and Jongeward, *Born to Win,* especially pp. 6–10 and 155–156, as well as Stuntz, Edgar C., "*Multiple Chairs Technique,*" *TA Journal* 3, 2 (1973), pp. 29–31.

18. James, *What Do You Do With Them?,* p. 100.

19. James, Muriel. *Born to Love* (Reading, Mass.: Addison-Wesley, 1973), pp. 48–49.

the down—scripting
of women
for 115 generations:
a historic kaleidoscope

A kaleidoscope, made of bits of glass and a cardboard tube, is a toy many children enjoy. With a slight turn of a wrist the color and design miraculously change. New patterns come into focus.

The purpose of this article is to offer a kaleidoscopic view of some historical patterns from Greco-Roman and Judeo-Christian cultures that have contributed to the down-scripting of women for 115 generations. These cultures are selected because of their pervasive influence on the western world.

History repeats itself, a fact that points to the repetition compulsion in individual and cultural scripting. Yet many people believe history is only for school children and do not consider it for insights to the present. Hopefully, this kaleidoscope will provide another option.

The brief scenes focused upon will illustrate how the down-scripting of women was the accepted cultural expectancy since the myths of Pandora and Eve were first transmitted in verbal form and later as written word.

From *TA Journal* **3,** 3 (1973). Reprinted by permission.

DOWN-SCRIPTING IN MYTHS

Pandora and Eve, two well known ancient myths, the first from Greece, the second from Palestine, are so similar that a reader might easily assume they are modifications of the same story passed from one culture to another via the busy trade routes used in that time. Both myths emerged between 850 and 750 B.C. Both are stories of how and why the first woman was created.

The Greek myth of Pandora, meaning "all-gifted," tells how Pandora as the first woman, was made in heaven with every god contributing something that would make her perfect; Venus gave her beauty, Mercury gave her persuasion, etc. In one version of the myth, Zeus, king of the Gods, sends Pandora to men as a curse; in another, Pandora is sent as a blessing. In both stories, however, she is depicted as insatiably curious.

In the version where she is seen as a curse, Pandora opens a jar out of curiosity and all the *evils* of the world escape to plague man; only hope remains. The less well-known version says that when Pandora, out of curiosity, opened a box, all the *blessings,* except hope, escaped. Hesiod, an important early Greek poet who lived about a century after Homer, a century after this story was recorded, used the myth of Pandora to prove woman is a necessary evil and is responsible for the ills of the world. Greek writers and those who followed them continued this down-scripting emphasis.

The Hebrew myth of Eve, the first woman, also supports sex prejudice. This myth, found in Genesis 2 of the Old Testament, tells of Eve, born from the rib of Adam tempted by a walking, talking snake to eat from a forbidden tree, blamed by Adam when, sharing the fruit with him, they are confronted by God. She is punished with promised pain in childbirth. The myth establishes Eve as physically, morally, and intellectually inferior to Adam (meaning Everyman). A second Old Testament story (Genesis 1) tells of woman created at the same time and equal to man. However, leaders in synagogues and churches have chosen throughout the centuries to ignore the positive myth and promote the anti-feminist view of Eve.

DOWN-SCRIPTING IN GRECO-ROMAN CULTURE

Greek civilization was male dominated. Homosexual love was regarded as of a higher order than heterosexual. Women had neither freedom, education, nor legal rights. From birth to death they were merely chattel to be bought, sold, or given away. Athenian houses had separate quarters for men and women. Bolts and bars imprisoned the women.[1] They were allowed out of the house only to attend an occasional women's festival. Men did the shopping and used slaves to carry their purchases.[2]

Greek literature, over and over again reflects this downscripting. For example, Pythagoras (540–510 B.C.) wrote: "There is a good principle, which has created order, light, and man; and a bad principle, which has created chaos, darkness, and woman."[3]

Plato (428–389 B.C.), in his famous dialogue, *The Symposium* claimed that the female mind thinks differently than the male mind. Since Plato, many have assumed that because women think differently, their thought is inferior. This kind of prejudice, culturally transmitted through both Parent and Child ego states, contributes to the psychological position, women are not-OK.

Aristotle (384–322 B.C.) claimed that women were an unsuccessful act of pro-creation, "female by virtue of a certain incapacity . . . weaker and cooler than males and we must regard the female character as a kind of natural defectiveness." Furthermore, Aristotle wrote, woman is only matter, whereas movement, the male principle, is "better and more divine."[4]

Rome took over Greece but the status of women in their enforced passive roles remained the same. In the Roman household fathers had unrestricted authority, including the right to inflect death penalties on any in the household, which was a large unit and included blood relatives, in-laws and slaves.

In the late Roman period women achieved minor rights. Now they were allowed to sit at the dinner table with their husbands! Now they were allowed some basic education from their fathers so that they could in turn educate their sons during pre-school years. A few became involved in politics. Yet Cato the Censor, an important Roman statesman active in both military and civic affairs, strongly upheld the rights of men over women with, "If you catch your wife in adultery, you would kill her with impunity without a trial; but if she were to catch you, she would not dare lay a finger on you, and indeed she has no right." Until very recently, in the state of Texas, a similar law was accepted.

JUDEO-CHRISTIAN DOWN-SCRIPTING

At the same time the Greeks and Romans were writing about the inferior nature of women, so were the Hebrews. Their views of down-scripting women are reflected in many of their ancient laws. For example, a wife was a possession along with slaves, house and land, ox and ass.[5] A man could divorce his wife on numerous grounds including a poorly cooked dinner. She could not divorce him. Neither wife nor daughters could inherit unless there were no male heirs.[6] When universal compulsory education began in Judah in 64 B.C. it was only for boys.

Anti-feminism has always been tied to anti-sexualism, especially in the Christian churches. This is not surprising. It is rooted in its early Hebrew traditions that claim women's sexuality is unclean. As early as 600–400 B.C., the writer of the biblical book of Job affirmed: "Man that is born of a woman is of few days, and full of trouble . . . Who can bring a clean thing out of an unclean?"[7]

And in another passage he reinforces it with: "How then can a man be righteous before God? How can he who is born of woman be clean?"[8]

These ancient Jewish traditions, strongly masculine and anti-feminist, are revealed in many ways today. For example, a daily prayer recited by the orthodox Jewish man is: "Barush Atah Adonai, Elohaynu Melek Ha-Olam, SHELOH ASSANI YISHAH." (Blessed art Thou, O Lord, Our God and King of the Universe, *that Thou didst not create me a woman.*)

An exception to the pervasive downscripting of women is found in the records about Jesus of Nazareth who by some of his followers was called the Messiah (Christo in Greek). Jesus was seemingly free of many cultural stereotypes related to women. He respected their opinions, and defended them against public censure.

Paul of Tarsus was not as gracious. Although in the book of Galatians he claimed all people were equal, Paul obviously preferred male company. He seemingly believed in the historicity of Adam and Eve, the doctrine of sin that blamed it all on women, and the need for them to be subordinate and obedient to men.

An ecclesiastical hierarchy, called the Early Church Fathers, continued the emphasis on evil being related to a woman's body. One of these men, Tertullian (*circa* 220 A.D.) defined woman as a "temple built over a sewer." "Women! You are the gateway of the devil. You persuaded him whom the devil dared not attack directly. Because of you the Son of God had to die. You should always go dressed in mourning and in rags."[9]

St. Ambrose said the same, "Adam was deceived by Eve, not Eve by Adam . . . it is right that he whom that woman induced to sin should assume the role of guide lest he fall again through feminine instability."

Monasticism, which arose about 370 A.D. out of this environment, continued to encourage the renouncement of sexual pleasures in favor of a life of celibacy and chastity. This continued throughout the middle ages.

DOWN-SCRIPTING FROM THE MIDDLE AGES TO MODERN TIMES

By the time of the Middle Ages, the Church, which was a patriarchal system, ruled the secular as well as the religious worlds. Women were still servants of men. De Beauvoir writes, "for the first time in history a mother kneels before her son; she freely accepts her inferiority."[10] This is the supreme masculine victory, consummated in the cult of the Virgin.

The cult of the Virgin became popular perhaps as a response to the over-emphasis on Eve. In contrast to Eve, the sinner, the Virgin was celebrated as totally sinless. Both concepts of woman were stressed simultaneously.

Women were elevated, worshipped, and treated as superhuman. They were also degraded, ridiculed and treated as subhuman. The distinction between "super" and "sub" is not as vital as the fact that both words and corresponding behavior place women in a nonhuman category.

The writing of Thomas Aquinas (1223–1274 A.D.) reflects Aristotle's influence 1500 years earlier. Aquinas wrote that women were misbegotton males, "defective and accidental . . . a male gone awry . . . the result of some weakness in the (father's) generative power . . . or of some external factor, like the south wind, which is damp."

Aquinas' ideas, originating in pagan Greece and perpetrated for generations, that women are "naturally" defective physically, are "naturally" defective intellectually, leads to the conclusion that they should "naturally" be subject to men.

Consequently, although a father had to get his daughter's consent when giving her in marriage, he was entitled to lock her in a tower, flog her daily and feed her on bread and water until she said "yes." Canon law allowed husbands to beat their wives whom they "bought" under the dowry system. Women had no say over their money, were considered legally incompetent and only four careers were open to them: housekeeper, prostitute, nun, or witch.

Those who followed Aquinas continued the down-scripting and people such as Ignatius, founder of the Jesuits (1491–1555) equated women with Satan with, "The enemy conducts himself as a woman. He is a weakling before a show of strength, and a tyrant if he has his will."[11]

The witch hunts which lasted from the 14th to the 17th century were based on these kinds of beliefs. Thousands upon thousands of women were executed throughout Germany, Italy, France, and England. For example, at Wertzberg, 900 were killed in one year; at Toulouse, 400 were killed in a day.

Written in 1484, *The Malleus Maleficarum* and its directory of tortures was used by courts for three centuries to force women to confess they were witches and had intercourse with the devil. Women were always associated with sex and enjoyment of sex was condemned.[12]

The Renaissance, following the Middle Ages, gave a few upper-class women new opportunities. For example, Italian women could at last get an education, could dress erotically and use cosmetics without fear or guilt. However, although knighthood was in flower and a few wealthy women gained some freedom, the denial of women's full humanness continued. In fact, a debate of the 16th century Reformation following the Renaissance was on the question, "Are women human?"

In the 17th, 18th and 19th centuries women, such as Mme. de Pompadour and Mme. du Barry, became influential in politics, but the opinion of women in general was, as usual, that they should be subordinate. Rousseau wrote, "Women's entire education should be relative to men . . . woman was made to yield to man and to put up with his injustices."[13] As late as 1797, men in England were selling their wives for 3½ guineas!

THE DOWN-SCRIPTING AND SCRIPT-BREAKING OF AMERICAN WOMEN

When America was first being settled, English common law, which was based on Roman law, predominated, both in the colonies and in the religious denominations. Consequently, women had "many duties but few rights."[14] She could not own property or sign a contract, a husband could restrain her, require her to submit sexually, and to live where and as he chose.

In frontier life women became indispensable. Consequently, they became more aware of their ability to think. They began to challenge both church and state. This was a breaking of a cultural down-script pattern. It led some women to death, led many to ridicule and imprisonment.

Abigail Adams believed women should have equal rights in the Constitution. She was angry at taxes without representation and wrote to John Adams, her husband, who was later to be the second president of the United States: "In the new code of laws which I suppose it will be necessary for you to make, I desire you would remember the ladies and be more generous and favorable to them than your ancestors. Do not put such unlimited power into the hands of the husbands. Remember, all men would be tyrants if they could. If particular care and attention is not paid to the ladies, we are determined to foment a rebellion, and will not hold ourselves bound by any laws in which we have no voice or representation."[15]

Abigail Adams was ahead of her times. Women's suffrage did not begin in America until 1838 in Kentucky when widows with children were allowed to vote in school elections. The suffragette movement expanded rapidly and, flamed by the same movement in Britain, provided a stimulus for women to re-decide for themselves against that which was decided for them by secular and religious authorities 115 generations earlier. Women are still redeciding. More and more are refusing to be exclusively identified with feminine roles as portrayed in *Good Housekeeping, Playboy,* or Henry Miller's *Sexus.*[16]

In 1964, in the House of Representatives, an amendment was proposed to the Civil Rights Bill which was against discrimination on the basis of "race, color, religion, or national origin." The amendment was that the word "sex" be added to the anti-discriminating clause. When the amendment was read, the House exploded into laughter. Public ridicule of women and their rights became common, so common that indignation also grew, a counter-movement developed, and the amendment passed. One hundred thirty-three representatives were opposed and 168 in favor of women having equal rights.[17]

WOMEN'S SCRIPT AWARENESS—SCRIPT REWRITING

Historically women have been culturally scripted to be supporting characters, stage hands, or applauding audiences for male achievements and men's dramas. Historically, women have tended to avoid the spotlight, avoid "promoting" their own skills, avoid authority unless delegated to them, and avoid jobs that are defined as masculine. They have not expected nor have they received adequate salaries or important positions and have often resisted open conflict and negotiating in their own behalf because of being taught to feel not-OK.

The down-scripting of women, generation after generation, with mottos such as, "Woman's place is in the home" implies that if a woman goes out into the male oriented world she is not-OK. A reinforcing message often given, "You're only a girl," also implies a secondary role.

This kind of anti-feminism is obvious in Freud's work. It reflects centuries of prejudice and no doubt affected his followers. It might have been better if Freud had said less about women whom admittedly he did not understand. Writing to Marie Bonaparte he confessed, "the great question that has never been answered and which I have not been able to answer, despite my thirty years of research into the feminine soul, is, "What does a woman want?"[18]

In one of his lectures Freud showed further uncertainty, "If you want to know more about femininity, you must interrogate your own experience, or turn to the poets, or else wait until science can give you more coherent information."[19]

Scripted to see women as inferior, Freud, like Aristotle, defined women in negative terms because of her "lack" of penis, and based his psychology of women on penis envy related to passivity, masochism, narcissism. His Parent prejudice, contaminating his Adult ego state, is obvious in the invidious terms he used: "the boy's far superior equipment," "her inferior clitoris," "genital deficiency," and "original sexual inferiority."[20]

His Child's delusion, also contaminating his Adult ego state, is reflected in his subjective reasoning that the size of a penis means it is superior to a clitoris and that the period of clitoral autoeroticism is the "phallus" in girls. (Actually a little girl could conclude that her body is the norm and that a penis is an excrescence.)

When people are unaware of their scripts and counter-scripts, their Adult ego states are contaminated. This includes Freud. Such people compulsively expect and repeat outdated behavior and live up to outdated expectancies.

"To become aware of some of the elements of one's script is the first step of changing it. If a person is unaware their Adult is unknowingly contaminated. Awareness gives power to the Adult. A person who is alert to being in his script can suddenly stop the 'play acting' of the inner Child who may expect something magical to happen,[21] or can stop inappropriate negative feelings, thoughts, and behavior that can lead to an unhappy ending. A person, aware of the script, can 'get a better show on the road' by deciding to do so. In the process of becoming aware and making new decisions, the ego state boundaries are realigned. The clear thinking Adult becomes the excutive of the personality and directs the new action."[22]

Ego boundaries and script awareness

Counterscript

Script

Without Adult awareness

With Adult awareness

Currently many women are beginning to rewrite their "stay-down" scripts. They are getting bored with the "same old acts" and refusing to play the expected roles. They are denying that woman's place is in the home, that woman's work is prescribed by her anatomy, that women are unable, mentally and physically, to do men's work.

The down-scripting is changing. A kaleidoscope view in the future may show the new woman as neither subhuman nor superhuman, simply fully human. It may show men as comparable human beings, no longer threatened by woman's sexuality and therefore no longer needing to see them in stereotyped roles.

Utopia? Maybe. After all, the mythical Pandora, in both versions, always had hope. As one of her "daughters," I am aware of this ancient script element within myself. The belief in full humanness for both sexes could be unrealistic, but I *hope* it is not.

REFERENCES

1. Xenophon, *Oeconom.*

2. Aristophanes, *Lysistrata.*

3. De Beauvoir, Simone, *The Second Sex,* translated by H. M. Parshley (New York: Alfred A. Knopf, 1953), p. 74.

4. Ibid, p. 73.

5. Exodus 20:17; Deut. 5:31.

6. Numbers 30:4–17.

7. Job 14:1–4.

8. Job 25:4.

9. PL 1, 1418b–19a. De cultu feminarum, libri duo I, 1.

10. De Beauvoir, p. 188.

11. *Spiritual Exercises,* "Rules for the Discernment of Spirits."

12. Kramer, Heinrich, and James Sprenger, *The Malleus Maleficarum,* translated by Montague Summers (London: Pushkin Press, 1928).

13. Rousseau, Jean-Jacques, *L'Emile or A Treatise on Education* (New York: W. H. Payne, 1906), p. 263.

14. Flexner, Eleanor, *Century of Struggle* (Cambridge: Harvard University Press, 1968), p. 7.

15. Ibid, p. 15.

16. See Millet, Kate, *Sexual Politics* (New York: Doubleday, 1970).

17. Bird, Caroline, *Born Female* (New York: Pocket Books, 1969), pp. 1–15.

18. Quoted in Jones, Ernest, *The Life and Work of Sigmund Freud,* Vol. II (New York: Basic Books, 1953), p. 421.

19. Freud, Sigmund, "Femininity", *New Introduction Lectures on Psychoanalysis*, translated by James Strachey (New York: Norton, 1964), p. 135.

20. Ibid, pp. 126, 127, 132.

21. James, Muriel, and Dorothy Jongeward, *Born To Win: Transactional Analysis with Gestalt Experiments* (Reading, Mass.: Addison-Wesley, 1972), pp. 35, 40, 73, 154–155, 157, 160–162.

22. James, Muriel, *Born To Love: Transactional Analysis in the Church* (Reading, Mass.: Addison-Wesley, 1973), p. 146.

the use
of structural analysis
in pastoral counseling

At least 40% of those who seek psychiatric help go to a pastor first. Though pastors often counsel in areas that are within the scope of secular therapists, they are more frequently called upon to respond to problems that fall uniquely within the religious sphere. The psychiatrist, Eric Berne, has developed a theory called Structural Analysis which is a valuable tool when used by the pastor who has neither the training nor the time to do long-term intensive therapy. It is designed for working with individuals and can be introduced during the last fifteen minutes of the initial counseling session. (The subsequent use of Transactional Analysis, a form of group treatment, focuses on the interactions or "transactions" between persons, including the "games" people play.)[1]

The use of Structural Analysis immediately gives the counselee some confidence that he is going to learn how to control his life in more satisfying ways and with less conflict because he has gained a measure of autonomy. This new sense of autonomy comes quickly. Frequently, with as few as three to eight interviews,

---

From *Pastoral Psychology*, October 1968, pp. 8–15. Reprinted by permission.

the counselee begins to recover the sense of awareness, spontaneity, and intimacy—those components out of which autonomy is made. This is not to imply that all problems can be solved rapidly, only to state that the initial counseling process can be *immediately* effective; the tools learned in a brief period can have value for the balance of one's life. When the counselee learns he is to be given a tool that is both interesting and fun to use—a tool that, potentially, is a magic key to self-understanding—he has already started to get well.

Structural Analysis is a way of analyzing the structure of a personality. It is the process of identifying and separating what Berne calls the Parent, Adult, and Child ego states which are phenomenological realities of every personality. *An ego state is a system of feelings, related to a given subject, which motivates behavior patterns.*

The purpose of Structural Analysis is to strengthen the Adult so that it can (1) be the executive of the personality, (2) regulate the activities of the Parent and Child, and (3) mediate between them. For example, if someone has the concept of a Santa Claus God, he will act accordingly. If someone has the concept of God as a wrathful, punishing father, his natural sense of guilt, which could lead him to make amends, may become so neurotic that the creative aspects of his personality are stifled. The case of Mrs. Martin, which will be reviewed later, will illustrate this.

The *Adult ego state* does what Berne calls "data processing" because it operates like a computer by gathering data, arranging and filing it mentally on the basis of past experience. The Adult is not so-called because it data-processes accurately (it may not have enough education or facts to decide correctly), but by its ability to deal with the facts it has. The Adult, though objective and oriented toward probability estimating, is also able to have fun, to experience gratifications, and accept disappointments.

The *Child ego state* does not refer to some concept of childish behavior, but to a specific child within each one of us. This Child is (1) *natural*—free, spontaneous, affectionate, self-centered, rebellious, and (2) *adapted*—adapted by parental influences to respond in certain ways to specific situations. In the more advanced theory of Structural Analysis, one learns that there is a part of the Child that may be called the "Little Professor." Professors are usually intelligent and know some of the answers. The Little Professor is no exception. He knows many things, often intuitively. A mother told her four-year-old son, "Don't go away from the house or you'll get lost." The boy replied, "I can't get lost 'cause I know where I am and where I'm going." This Little Professor had the potential wisdom of a philosopher.

The *Parent ego state* is the executor when a person talks or acts in the precise way that his *own* parents, or parent substitutes, acted. The functions of parents are to judge and nurture their children. Some do this well, some poorly. However, even if a person had admirable parents, Structural Analysis encourages differentiation from them. Martin Buber, the great Jewish philosopher-theologian, tells of a rabbi who, on his death bed, commented that in the world to come he would not be asked why he was not Moses but why he wasn't himself.[2] To help a person become *aware* of his unique individuality is more important than to encourage that person in the imitation of another. The release or recovery of awareness is crucial to becoming an autonomous Adult; it is "the capacity to see a coffee pot and hear the birds sing in one's own way, and not the way one was taught."[3]

A forty-five-year-old distinguished looking Air Force chaplain came to me for counseling because of a drinking problem. Although he drank infrequently, he was unable to stop once he got started. The Adult in him was fully aware of the effect his behavior could have on his work. His inner Child anticipated that I would say, "Stop drinking," and that I, being a minister, would reenforce this advice with theological reasons. In essence, he anticipated my playing a parent role, which in this case would not have been appropriate. It would have led to his continuing to play the "game" of alcoholic. "Alcoholic" is played out of a feeling in the Child that it is not acceptable, so the alcoholic creates situations in which he or she will be punished and subsequently forgiven.

The counseling procedure was to assign homework to his Adult, to gather data on: (1) why, when, and how often he drank, (2) how many ounces he was accustomed to pouring, as a measured drink is quite different from one poured by guess, and (3) what happened the next day with his spouse and superior officers.

These facts were gathered by the chaplain, and, because his motivation was high, his Adult was strengthened and enlarged by this homework and became able to referee between his Parent and Child. When his Child said, "To heck with things; I'm going to start drinking," and his inner Parent said, "God will punish you if you do," his Adult could ask the question, "Shall I or shall I not drink in this situation?"

The result of eight counseling sessions was *not* that this chaplain stopped drinking but that he learned to allow his Adult, rather than his Child, to drink in moderate ways that were acceptable to himself, his wife, and his associates. In the two years since counseling he has not returned to his former behavior patterns.

The procedure in pastoral counseling after the initial problem is presented is for the counselor to pick up a small blackboard, diagram the three circles representing the ego states and explain the basic principles of Structural Analysis. He should then state that this is the method he is going to employ and ask if it seems useful to the counselee. If the response is affirmative, the next question comes, "Why are we here?" This is a crucial step to establishing an initial "contract." A contract is a commitment by the pastor to use this method with integrity to help the counselee achieve a specific goal. The goal which is decided by the counselee can be amended or ratified if appropriate and should be referred to frequently.[4]

One woman who came for counseling said her goal was to find courage to stay with her husband; another's goal was that she find courage to leave her husband. These became the initial contracts, but "this does not mean that the ultimate goal is merely the alleviation of symptoms or the attainment of control over social responses . . . the therapist will always be on the lookout for the determinants underlying the symptoms or responses."[5]

Seemingly, Mrs. Martin was an intelligent, well functioning person, active in the church, happily married and with two normal children. She claimed to experience deep feelings of guilt without knowing the cause. The therapeutic goal (contract) she established was to understand why she felt this way. After some preliminary questioning to determine whether the guilt feelings were normal or neurotic, it became clear that Mrs. Martin's Child had the delusion of being evil and that this was a case of contamination. The most common examples of contamination in Structural Analysis are hallucinations, which generally stem from the Parent and contaminate the Adult; and delusions which generally stem from the Child and also contaminate the Adult. Intensive therapy did not seem to be indicated in the case of Mrs. Martin, who was basically healthy. She grasped the principles of the three ego states rapidly, so at the end of the second interview I gave her Adult an assignment. It was, "Since the Adult in you does not seem to have cause for guilt feelings, it is probably in your Child ego state. Therefore, when your Child is experiencing feelings of guilt, let your Adult data-process. Recall as many past experiences as you can and feed them into your Adult computer. If it gets jammed, remind your Child that she has permission to remember even very negative acts; that there is nothing for her to be afraid of; and that all children do 'naughty things' at times. It's normal."

Six weeks later Mrs. Martin was able to terminate, freed from her sense of guilt. She had recalled that, "At the age of four I stole five pennies from a friend living next door. After I took them home, it must have been my 'adapted Child' or my Parent who told my 'natural child' that this was wrong. On my way to return them, I dropped one in the grass and can still feel my panic. I was scared stiff. My friend might come home and find out. I looked and looked but couldn't find the penny so I only put back four, instead of five. I didn't dare tell anyone; I still feel perfectly horrible about it." (She started to cry.) As she relived this traumatic event, the counselor asked, "What ego state in you now feels so guilty?" Of course, it was her Child. At this moment, Mrs. Martin's Adult became her executor. Though annoyed at her parents for not having created a home where error could be talked about and forgiveness offered, she realized she had created the same kind of home for her own children. Mrs. Martin no longer needed to feel guilty. Instead she could say, "What a strange idea; the loss of one penny made me feel lost myself."

One of the values of Structural Analysis is that it becomes challenging and fun to find out about one's ego states. It seems to have a built-in protection against a sense of total despair because it allows the Adult an escape hatch—the Child or the Parent can be the scapegoats. The Adult can say, "Part of me feels very negative but not all of me." This escape hatch, when a person is overwhelmed by memories of childhood traumas, is useful in the healing process.

It is often useful to remind a person that each ego state may feel *differently* about a specific subject; or two, even three of the ego states may *agree*. This was illustrated at a social gathering where an obese college girl, trying to diet, was observed picking up a piece of rich cake, then putting it back. An astute friend commented, "Your Child wanted the cake, your Parent gave it permission, but your Adult moderated so you put it back."

Mrs. Smith came for pastoral counseling because, according to her, she wanted desperately to attend church but whenever she would get ready she would have a pseudo heart attack. She had had three years of individual therapy, knew her heart attacks were false, yet was unable to get to the source. Mrs. Smith's physician and psychoanalyst confirmed the facts. After introducing Mrs. Smith to Structural Analysis, including drawing the circle diagram, the basic question was asked, "What does each of your ego states feel about attending church?" The reason this was basic was that it was part of the initial contract and could be used to initiate the further identification and separation of the Parent, Adult and Child:

Pastor: Did you go to church when you were a little girl?
Mrs. S: No, my mother wouldn't let me. She didn't go herself. When I was older, in Junior High, she let me go with friends. (This answer begins to show the influence the mother had on adapting the Child in Mrs. Smith.)
Pastor: I hear you saying that as a child you wanted to go to church but your mother said 'no.' (Mrs. Smith nods.) The Child in you still wants to go but the Parent still says 'no.' (Mrs. Smith nods again.) Now, what about your Adult?

Mrs. S: My Adult wants to go but is afraid, I think. I don't know if it's my Child or my Adult that has the pseudo heart attacks but I'm afraid that if I go to church, I'll hear something I don't want to hear.

Pastor: Such as?

Mrs. S: Well, when I went to church as a Junior Higher, the minister talked a lot about our obligations to other people. I guess I don't want to hear about responsibilities, obligations, and so forth. I guess I'm a selfish, spoiled brat; at least my mother *says* I am. My husband says I'm not, but I know I sure act that way sometimes.

Pastor: Are you saying that part of you, the Child, doesn't want obligations— that because obligations are part of growing up you'd rather not grow up?

After a long pause, it came out. Mrs. Smith had an older sister who was severely retarded, unable to care for herself even in minimal ways. The sister had lived at home, in seclusion, cared for by Mrs. Smith's mother who had made her promise that, when she died, the sister could live with Mrs. Smith and her family.

Structural Analysis revealed the Child in Mrs. Smith who was afraid to grow up for two reasons: (1) that she might turn out like her sister, or (2) she would have to assume an obligation with which she felt unable to cope. The Adult in her agreed with this second point. The Parent in her was always criticizing the Child. Consequently, conflict and fear had prevented her Adult from being the executor of her life.

As Mrs. Smith gained an understanding of her ego states, she became able to attend church without pseudo heart attacks. At church she heard what her Child *feared* to hear, but yet her Adult *wanted* to hear. It was the same call to responsible behavior that St. Paul wrote to the Corinthians:

> When I was a little child I talked and felt and thought like a little child. Now that I am a man my childish speech and feeling and thought have no further signicance for me.[6]

Childishness and childlikeness are not the same but both do have significance. The natural child has a sense of wonder, spontaneity and trust, which Jesus of Nazareth said was a pre-requisite to enter the Kingdom of God. It needs to be emphasized—*childlikeness* is a good part of the personality; it adds something special, like having real children around at Christmas. *Childishness* is similar to what Mrs. Smith called her "spoiled brat" behavior, or the "pettiness" of some grownups.[7] Mrs. Smith decided that the "call to responsible behavior" included considering the effect on her husband and children if her sister were to live with them. Her Adult data-processed the effect of a broken promise on her Parent ego state and on her actual mother, yet remained aware of her Child's anxiety. In time, her Adult successfully mediated between the two.

The introductory principles of Structural Analysis had not been difficult for Mrs. Smith to grasp. But to grasp these principles is not the same as having Santa Claus come with exactly what one has asked for; it does not imply that all problems can be easily solved. Even with her Adult in control, Mrs. Smith had a difficult decision. Nevertheless, the support she found in the church helped her make it and keep to it.

We all know that people do not always agree. In Structural Analysis the Adult ego states of two individuals may be uncontaminated, have adequate facts to process, and still come to different conclusions. Following are two self-evaluating statements which illustrate this point. One gives reasons for remaining in the church, the other for leaving the church.

1. Mrs. Jones, in her statement, uses "Before Berne" and "After Berne" almost like B.C. and A.D., perhaps because her decision to stay in the church felt like the Christmas event:

> Before Berne—the church was where I went to gain some measure of hope and courage for life. But quite often I came away feeling dissatisfied with myself and sensing that maybe there really was no hope for me since I wasn't and couldn't be perfect.

> After Berne—what a difference! Now I realize that my Child ego went to church. The church, as a parent figure, was making me aware of how bad I was and reminded me of the wrongdoings rather than encouraging the potential for good.

> My Child was, and is, afraid to express views contrary to what it thinks are the church's views. But my Adult has a greater sense of responsibility. It should express its opinions on what it sees as right and wrong about the present church and help bring about beneficial changes.

> My relationship to the church is becoming more meaningful and rewarding. I am eager to find out how to think for myself theologically, not just accept what others tell me. This is involving study, but it's very exciting.

2. Mrs. Brown's Adult had different data to process. She decided to leave the institutional church and wrote:

> When I was four years old, my father was murdered. My mother was (is) a very devout follower of a religion which refused to admit the reality of negatives—such as death and loneliness.

> All through my childhood, adolescence and early adult life, the Child ego state in me felt desperately insecure and afraid. To my frightened Child, God became the unchangeable Father upon whom I could depend to intervene in

my life and make everything all right—but only to the extent that I got myself out of the way, and in direct proportion to my ability to pray. My Child was so insecure and fearful of change that it substituted 'prayer,' 'listening,' and 'receptivity' for decision and responsibility—with the result that I entered the middle years of my life with practically no self-knowledge, no self-confidence, and the conviction that planning and decision were sinful because they conflicted with divine guidance.

Until I gained some insight into structural analysis, I was completely blind to the fact that what I considered (with no small amount of pride) to be a strong, uncompromising religious faith was really the controlling influence of my frightened Child.

When my Adult began to data-process, I decided that neither my reason nor my experience supported this concept of a God who would manifest Himself in my life only 'if I negated myself, my personality, my own desire and ambitions. My Adult is beginning to admit—without guilt—that the instances when I have felt most free, satisfied, and fulfilled have been instances characterized by a sense of self-confidence and competency.

My Child still experiences fear and sometimes intense anxiety when I face up to the fact that my Adult cannot accept the concept of a Santa Claus type God who is going to direct my life by remote control if I just 'listen.' My inner Parent still experiences real guilt feelings that my Adult would even dare to disbelieve in this kind of a God. But more and more my Adult is getting the upper hand and is concluding that if there is a transcendent, personal God who is responsible for my creation, He certainly intends for me to affirm, not negate myself. Data-processing tells me that the way I am best able to feel self-affirmed is by making decisions and taking responsibility for them. In the light of this, my Adult is considering the possibility that the whole concept of God as a transcendent power, having a character in some way identifiable with human personality, may not be acceptable—at least not to my Adult. Maybe 'God' has something to do with decision, and with real relationship, and with responsibility? At least my Adult seems to be able to consider these possibilities for the first time—without being paralyzed by fear and guilt.

I am no longer going to church because the preaching, teaching and liturgical acts of worship have become somewhat offensive to my thinking Adult.

When someone writes this strongly, many pastors would feel threatened and defensive. Yet, as Mrs. Brown says, the way in which she is able to feel self-affirmed "is by making decisions and taking responsibility for them." Berne would say she had achieved the feeling of being "O.K."[8]

The "O.K. positions" are a useful tool for sorting out the games one plays. A knowledge of them is vital for the pastor who wishes to understand his relationship to the counselee. Games are played by the Child from the inner conviction of "I am O.K. or I'm not O.K." There are four basic convictions: (1) I am (we are) O.K.; (2) I am (we are) not O.K.; (3) You (they) are O.K.; (4) You (they) are not O.K. These convictions lead to the following possible combinations between persons:

1. I am (we are) O.K., you (they) are O.K. (intrinsically constructive)

2. I am (we are) O.K., you (they) are not O.K. (intrinsically paranoid)

3. I am (we are) not O.K., you (they) are O.K. (intrinsically depressive)

4. I am (we are) not O.K., you (they) are not O.K. (intrinsically schizophrenic)

The term O.K. is an Adult term, a sort of middle of the road term, which says the person is neither great nor "not great" but, nevertheless, is O.K. When the Adult is executor, the person who has become better, or even well, feels this way about other people and about his own Parent and Child ego states. It's a worthy goal for the counseling pastor to work toward, feeling that someone like Mrs. Brown, who rejects the church, is nevertheless O.K.

A young college student, trying to sort out his feelings on intercessory prayer, said that his Child thought it was an O.K. thing to do; his Parent also thought it an O.K. thing to do, and, furthermore, that it made a difference; his Adult thought it was an O.K. thing to do but seriously wondered, "Does it make any difference?" His Adult finally decided that even if God is not subject to scientific data-processing, it might still be O.K. to pray because: (1) if there wasn't a personal, intercessory God it wouldn't hurt, it might even be good because he at least would be more conscious of the other person and his needs, and (2) if there was a God who enters into man's destiny, he might "tune in" like a radio to Him as the religious dimension of all existence.

The Reverend Kelly, an energetic parish minister, came for counseling because, according to him, he wanted "to be more like Jesus," yet he was considering a divorce because his wife claimed she no longer believed in God. The Reverend Kelly could not tolerate this rejection. Six counseling sessions were required to give him the Structural Analysis tools so that he could recognize his personal feelings of rejection and associated problems. Inasmuch as he wanted to be more like Jesus, who allowed people to reject Him, he decided to do the same. He decided to stop acting as a Parent to his wife, to permit her the freedom to think as an intelligent Adult rather than a compliant Child.

Out of this decision, which involved his marital relationship, came a new contract which was to reevaluate his theological beliefs by asking himself, "What does each of my ego states think about specific doctrines?" As the sixth generation of ministers in his family, he had assumed everything he believed was true. His inner Parents and his adapted Child were in total agreement, though his

Adult had never analyzed his theological position. The answers were amazing! He gained a new autonomy by asking "Where did I get my theological concepts? Did either of my parents ever talk (or act) like that? At what age did I talk (or act) like that? On what points do my ego states agree or disagree? How can my Adult data-process the religion of my Parent and my Child who is still looking for a God who is like Santa Claus? How does this affect my philosophy of life? Do I, like the four-year-old Little Professor, know where I'm going?"

To be a counselor is to be a person to whom others go for help—help which inevitably involves the examination of previous decisions. "If the primacy of the Adult is established during therapy, not only can the Child's decision be reconsidered, but the Parent can usually be brought to terms as well."[9] Pastors who decide to help others in a counseling relationship by using Structural Analysis need to become very aware of their own ego states. They should be willing to recognize their own limitations and refer counselees to someone more skilled when appropriate. If possible, they should seek out adequate supervision so that in clear conscience they would know from which ego state they speak and be able to estimate the effect of this on others. This self-knowledge and training is not an impossible goal; it is necessary. As Berne writes:

> A dilettante knows what to do; a professional knows what not to do. A mediocre therapist is like a bull, who charges whenever he sees the cape; a good one is like a matador.[10]

REFERENCES

1. Pastors will find Dr. Berne's books, *Transactional Analysis in Psychotherapy* (New York: Grove, 1961), and *Games People Play* (New York: Grove, 1964), useful. His *Principles of Group Treatment* (New York: Grove, 1968), is a detailed academic textbook that can be studied and used with great profit.

2. Buber, Martin, *The Way of Man* (New York: Citadel Press, 1966), p. 17.

3. Berne, *Games People Play*, p. 178.

4. The one exception to establishing a specific contract is in the case of paranoid conditions. See Berne, *Principles*, p. 90.

5. Ibid., p. 91.

6. I *Corinthians* 13:11 (Phillips Translation).

7. See the exposition by John Short in *The Interpreter's Bible*, Vol. X (Nashville, Tenn.: Abingdon Press), p. 190.

8. Berne, *Principles*, pp. 269–280.

9. Ibid., p. 266.

10. Ibid., p. 358.

ego states and social issues: two case histories from the 1960's

PROBLEMS AND ISSUES

Social *problems* are those situations in which some segment of society is injured, physically or psychologically. The injury may be due to some natural catastrophe, such as a flood which leaves many people homeless. It may be due to some form of discrimination which restricts people from developing or using their full potential.

Social problems become social *issues* when someone (or a group of someones) becomes aware that there really is a problem and determines to "make an issue" out of it. However, making an issue out of something is not enough to solve problems effectively; a well-functioning Adult ego state is required.

Take a moment to think about some of the current world or national leaders who have made issues out of problems, have elicited support from others, have actually been change agents. Which of their ego states seems to have been the executive of their personality?

From *TA Journal* **5,** 1 (1975). Reprinted by permission.

Now think about some of the groups that have done the same thing. Did these groups seem to have a *collective* ego state that was the executive?

My observation is that all or at least two ego states are likely to be involved when specific problems become issues to individuals and groups.

INDIVIDUAL CASE STUDY

I remember the day in 1964 when I decided to go to Selma, Alabama, and march with Martin Luther King, Jr. I had not been active in the civil rights movement, yet all of my ego states were involved. My inner Child was both curious and empathetic. Could it really be as horrible as was reported in the mass media? My Adult had very few facts and no direct involvement with racially discriminatory situations. My Parent ego state, an incorporation of mother, father, and grandmother,[1] was also involved.

My father, a research scientist, had frequently told me to think about things and to get the facts before drawing conclusions. My grandmother was a pioneer, doing unexpected things like going to Alaska during the gold rush and, later in life, renting out rooms in her large home near the University of California campus to anyone who was an interesting person or conversationalist, regardless of sex, age, race, or religion. My mother, a concert pianist, acted as though the world would be saved if everyone just played the piano. Until I decided to go to Selma, I was unaware of her concern over voting rights—one of the social issues of 1964. Although she always went to vote, no matter what, we did not discuss politics. Nevertheless, I went to see her. I expected her to be critical because very few White women were involved in the march, and because I had never been in the south, was going alone, and the situation was potentially dangerous. We pastimed about the weather until, on my way out, I casually remarked, "Mom, I'll be gone a few days as I am going to Selma, Alabama, to see what it's all about." I expected she would parentally try to talk me out of it. Instead she started asking questions from her Adult, many of which I could only partially answer as I had only partial data.

Mom: Where will you stay?
Muriel: I don't know. The small area is tightly surrounded by police and has no hotels, so I'll probably sleep on a church pew or maybe within a black family as only Blacks live there.
Mom: What will you eat?
Muriel: I'm not sure, but I understand that the church there will provide something.
Mom: What will you take with you?
Muriel: Nothing. I called Brown's Chapel in Selma where the marchers are registering and told them I was white, close to middle age, uninformed,

and asked if it was OK for me to come. They told me it was OK, but not to bring a sleeping bag (as many of the men were doing) or a suitcase. Either might provoke an incident when switching planes in Montgomery and would be a nuisance in Selma.

And so, the conversation with my mother continued with the giving and getting of information on an Adult-to-Adult level. As I finally left, I asked, "Mom, how come we've talked like this today?" She responded, "Muriel, you probably don't know how important I think voting is. When I was a Gibson Girl, I used to pass out women's suffrage pamphlets at Sather Gate at the University of California!"

EGO STATE ANALYZING

So, each of my ego states was obviously involved in the above incident—my Child with its curiosity and empathy, my Parent father tapes on the importance of research, mother's tapes on voting, and grandmother's tapes on pioneering and interesting people, and my Adult in getting facts and taking action. They often are involved whenever I am faced with a social problem which has become a social issue to me.

Such was the case when, as a safety engineer in Kaiser Shipyards in Richmond, California, during World War II of the 1940's, I was paid less than men who had identical jobs. "After all, you're only a woman," I was told. I was told the same when I was part of a surveying team measuring reservoirs for a public utility company.

Such was also the case when, as a minister, I was paid less then men who had equal or even less theological education and experience. Such was the case as an elementary school teacher, an interior decorator, and on and on, with the implication that women have less value than men.

It is not surprising that I served with keen interest as an advisor to the State of California's first Commission on the Status of Women. My Child resented the continuing societal putdowns of women in general and intuited that the time was ripe for change. My Adult had information and knew how to get more facts by holding public hearings, etc. Each of my three Parents in my Parent ego state had a similar opinion—that it was OK to be a professional woman.

GROUP CASE STUDY

The *collective* ego state of a group of people came to my attention when working on an interracial crises intervention team. The job of this team was to go into situations where there was a potential for violence due to racial tensions.[2]

The day after Martin Luther King, Jr. was assassinated, we received a crisis call asking us to hurry to the only high school in a small, wealthy community in southern California. This school had about 1200 white students and 80 black students. Few Blacks had graduated, none had gone on to college, Discrimination was rampant.

Our usual procedure with angry groups such as this one included teaching TA as a way of understanding conflict. Rage was high, a town riot was being planned, so teaching TA and showing how it could be used had to be done in the first 15 minutes of training if we were to hook the students' *collective Adult ego state.*

First, the Parent ego state was explained. The students almost with one voice, claimed, "Our parents were losers, just 'stoop' labor, and we aren't going to be. We're going to take things into our hands. We sure don't have a chance the way things are!"

"How did you decide this?" we asked. "Where did you get the message it was OK not to be losers like you say your parents are?"

"We've been hearing it loud and clear lately, 'Black is Beautiful,' and 'I'm black and I'm proud,'" claimed their *collective Child,* now programmed by strong Black leaders.

Next came additional questions including were they angry at anything else in the school? One of their grievances was the fact that the pom-pom girls, who received a lot of attention at athletic events, had been chosen by the same faculty members for years. The girls were always blondes with long hair and were introduced to the student body as "typical American girls." "Who are we," asked the group, "are we nontypical?"

Clearly, some of the grievances could be corrected if they learned to use Adult strategies at a less contaminated level. To effect this, specific questions were posed: What would be the results if they went on a town rampage? What did they want that would make them feel better *and* improve their situation at the same time? What would they be willing to do to get what they wanted? How might they sabotage themselves either individually or as a group?

Using their *collective Adult,* this group of students set contracts. They planned strategy, decided what they wanted to say, to whom, and how they were going to say it. Then they acted. First, they got the principal's support then the superintendent's to confront the faculty members and change procedures for pom-pom girl selection. Next, they presented their ideas and feelings to the Board of Education at a widely publicized community meeting. Finally, significant changes began to happen in the school. Perhaps the crisis intervention team was a catalyst, yet the actual leadership came from the cathected collective Adult ego state in black students.

A DECONTAMINATION TECHNIQUE

The choice of any individual or of a group when faced with a social issue is whether to: first, respond from the Child with, for example, defensiveness and hostility or confusion and inadequacy or hopelessness and withdrawal; or second, respond from the Parent ego state as parent figures would have done in similar situations, for example, with prejudice and criticism, concern and nurturing, indifference and apathy; or third, respond with the Adult, gathering data, processing it, and making decisions and taking action based on rational probabilities. For me, the third choice is the most effective because the Adult not only processes the social issues involved, it also processes the

Child feelings and Parent opinions. By doing this, decontamination is possible. The inner motivators to action or inhibitors against action come into awareness. The accompanying figure presents a simple method that I use and teach others to use in similar situations.[3] It requires a pencil and paper as writing things down helps cathect the Adult.

Second-order structural analysis of the Adult

The problem to be solved is: _____ .

P — What would each of my Parent figures *say* about it? _____ _____ .
What would each of my Parent figures *do* about it? _____ .
How would each of my Parent figures *feel* about it? _____ .

A — What facts do I have about possible solutions? _____ .
What facts do I need to get? _____ .

C — What are my conditioned feelings about similar problems? _____ .
What are my hunches on the possible solutions now? _____ .
What are my uncensored feelings about the problems and solutions? _____ .

On the basis of the above, the contracts I need to make are: _____ .

First comes a clear statement of the problem or issue, such as voting rights or equal pay. This is followed by analyzing each ego state.

In summary, "making an issue" out of something is relatively easy to do. This is often an automatic or impulsive C or P response. Analyzing ego states in reference to social issues is harder; this is Adult thinking. It requires a willingness to look at one's own prejudiced Parental opinions, archaic Child feelings, and incomplete Adult information. "Self Analysis," wrote Berne, "is like giving oneself a haircut: with sufficient care and practice it can be done."

REFERENCES

1. Berne, Eric, *Principles of Group Treatment* (New York: Grove, 1966). Berne says that Parent ego state represents psychological, historical, and behavioral realities borrowed from parent figures. It may exert itself as an indirect influence or be directly exhibited in parental behavior (p. 366). For example, in the Parent ego state a woman is behaving as mother behaved; under the parental influence (meaning when in the Adapted Child) she is behaving as mother would have liked (p. 222).

2. This was a three-year program funded by the Ford Foundation through the Universities of Michigan and California.

3. James, Muriel, *What Do You Do With Them Now That You've Got Them?* (Reading, Mass.: Addison-Wesley, 1974), p. 70. If people are reparented—either by self or others—this new parent in the Parent ego state also needs analyzing as well as the historical parent figures. See Schiff, Jacqui Lee, with Beth Day, *All My Children* (New York: M. Evans, 1971), pp. 210–211. See also, James, Muriel, "Self-Reparenting: Theory and Process," *TA Journal* 4, 3 (1974), pp. 32–39, (included in this volume).

CHAPTER 42

TA therapy
with children

BACKGROUND

This paper is based upon my experience in doing therapy with children seven years old or older. Having taught school for several years, I felt comfortable working with children as well as with adults. The children were sent to me from a variety of referral sources. Some of them had been previously hospitalized; all had serious problems with themselves and/or peer or family relationships, or their school. Sometimes they came to therapy alone, often they came with other family members. The precipitating incident that led them to therapy was some kind of complaint being made against the child by a teacher or parent who—gradually or suddenly—felt unable to cope with the problem.

SYMPTOMS AND THE THERAPIST'S TRAINING

Symptoms of problems are often ignored for years by parents and teachers who hope the children will outgrow them. Sometimes the children do. Perhaps symptoms are ignored because they are so similar to those observed in grown-ups and therefore feel familiar, almost normal, to others. Among those symptoms often ignored are: obsessions, fears, sleeplessness, nightmares, excessive activity, or continuing withdrawal patterns.

Other symptoms, more likely to be noticed, and often punished, include: rocking, thumbsucking, fecal retention or soiling, aggression, stammering, problems about eating, poor adjustment in school or with peers, and learning disabilities. These symptoms often develop because temperament is not recognized and dealt with as part of genetic endowment.[1]

Whether a symptom develops gradually or suddenly (often as the result of crisis), children's emotional difficulties are to be viewed against developmental norms. Therapists working with the children need to be well-trained in understanding developmental stages, including developmental psychology, educational psychology, and learning theory, as well as pathology commonly related to specific ages. Therapists need the ability to evaluate the developmental norms to see if those norms make sense in assessing a particular child. Many people who have made major contributions to civilization have not fit into the expected norms in their childhood.[2]

A THERAPEUTIC STYLE

Usually when I am successful with children, it is partly because of the co-operation of parents who are willing to share *responsibility for the problem and for the cure*. The person the family identifies as the patient is not always the one with the major problem. Therefore I work on *relationships* between children, and between children and authority figures. I often focus on the *transactions* and what each person gets out of transacting in certain ways, and show, during one of the early therapy sessions, how transactions are involved in stamp collecting.

I prefer being friendly, active, and supportive, rather than objective and uninvolved. I often model new behavior for parents as well as children by role-playing various options. As I am concerned with positive values, I build the therapeutic relationships on the basis of the children's strengths, rather than on the basis of their weaknesses. Because of this, transference is seldom a major issue. The exception is in the case of children (or grownups) with schizophrenic symptoms who have not had competent parents. Such children I sometimes hold and rock during the middle phases of treatment and deliberately allow for a positive transference, which in some cases may become a friendship when the treatment is successfully finished.

SITUATION AND ORGANIZATION

My therapy room is in warm colors with large windows against which roses grow and through which the fluttering leaves of birch trees can be seen. On many occasions this setting has been an important factor in turning on the Child in children to the natural world.

I am always in the room before any child clients come on their first visit and appear unhurried as well as totally interested. After a casual, "Hi," I suggest they choose whatever chair they would like to sit in. They often try several. The chairs are of various heights, styles and colors. The low-to-the floor basket-style swivel chairs covered in soft leather are most often selected by the children. As they snuggle down and swivel slowly around in them, their anxiety decreases almost immediately. (The Child has been relaxed, been comforted in this brief process, and I am then more able to talk to the Adult ego state.)

On the wall of the counseling room is a large, lovely photograph of a free, natural child. The child stands at the edge of an ocean, low waves lap at her feet; her arms are flung wide open as if to accept all of creation. I do not comment on the picture. However, as the Adapted Child gets deconfused in the therapy process, children invariably talk about it and compare their emerging sense of freedom to the nonverbal invitation of the photograph. For example, phrases such as "I'm beginning to feel happy, just like that picture," are not uncommon.

The only other kinds of specialized equipment in the room are a small blackboard which has cartoon figures from children's stories around the edge; an ugly beanbag in the form of a frog; a plaster-of-paris princess who has "real" jewels in spite of being made of plaster, and several books of photographs of children and families which they sometimes peruse intently.

In situations where parents are unwilling or unable to participate in therapy —individually or with their children—I have found it useful to work with groups of not more than six children. The groups are established for a specific period of time, such as once a week for six weeks, or three times a week, or for three weeks during summer vacation, etc.

Individual treatment, either before, after, or between group sessions, is often useful. It gives children more time to work through painful feelings and experiences with a therapist who will focus exclusively—often as their parents never did—on the problem areas.

CASE STUDY

Following is (1) a brief description of a single-parent family and three children, (2) an overview of the first session, (3) a transcript of the second session to give the reader a feel for how therapy often goes with children, and (4) a summary.

The family consists of a divorced mother and three children: Sally, age eight; Jim, age ten; and Lucy, age thirteen. The mother, who had been in therapy for two months, was severely depressed and confused. She brought in the children because family tension was so high. Lucy frequently indulged in temper tantrums and more extreme forms of violence. Jim had been caught stealing from local stores on several occasions. Sally was having difficulty eating and sleeping and had become phobic about attending school.

Living with this family was Grandma, highly critical, sometimes even cruel. Much of the family's tension and unhappiness was directly related to her. At a previous session with the mother, a long-term plan had been established that would eventually result in a separate living situation for the grandmother. For the children, the first therapy goal was for them to learn how to cathect their Adult so that they could solve problems and begin to feel better about themselves.

The First Session

The first step of the first therapy session was *primarily* to get acquainted and to establish trust. The getting-acquainted stage developed through an exploration of names. The children discussed what to call me and why. They decided to use my first name. We also discussed their names, the expectancies they had for themselves, or that others had for them because of their names. Lucy had been named after Grandma, whom they called "the mean one"; Jim after Grandpa, who they said was "nice"; and Sally for Mother's older sister, who was beautiful and had died at age ten in an accident. Concepts from the name exercises in *Born to Win*[3] and *The People Book*[4] were used. Only the positive aspects of their names were discussed, as they needed to be protected, at this time, from the negative scripting that was implied.

During the second stage of the first session I led them gently and slowly into an exploration of the pain points in their family. Each was encouraged to express his or her own opinions (starting with the youngest), without interruptions from others. Toward the end of the first session I told them that learning Transactional Analysis would help them feel happier and show them how to solve problems.

Second-Session Transcript

Following is a transcript of part of the second session (slightly edited for space). The focus is on ego states, how different people express them differently, and how feelings are used as trading stamps.

Jim: Muriel, I don't understand about how TA can help me understand my feelings at home.
Lucy: How come you don't understand? What are you, dumb!
Muriel: Lucy, you said last week you don't like your grandma being critical and sarcastic, yet you seem to be copying her now. Will you explain what

you know about TA to Jim without using a critical tone of voice and give some family examples?

Lucy: Yeah. I know what you mean about my critical voice. It's like Grandma's. Grandma also gets hurt pretty easily. So do I, but not for the same reason. I get hurt if someone gets mad at me or does something that gets me upset. I've gotten this habit of getting hurt from Grandma, so it's part of me. You know how traits are handed down in families? It's kind of like that.

Muriel: Does your mother also get hurt easily, like you and Grandma?

Lucy: Mother gets hurt, too, but she doesn't show it the same way until it builds way up. Then she really gets mad. Usually she doesn't show when she's beginning to feel hurt, so we don't know that she is. Maybe if we did know, we wouldn't keep getting at her. We could maybe do better, like trying not to make her mad or upset or anything.

Jim: Yeah. You, Mom, and Grandma *are* kind of alike.

Muriel: (Draws three sets of circles on the board.) OK, this first set of circles represents Grandma and her personality. One circle is called the Child ego state because it's like she was when she was a little girl. Another part of her is the Adult ego state. She uses this when she thinks clearly and acts with good sense. The third circle is called the Parent ego state and is made up of the Parent figures she had when she was little. Whoever took care of her when she was a little girl, these people are in her Parent ego state.

Everyone has three ego states, and remember, each of you has an Adult ego state—that's this middle circle. Even if Sally is only eight, she has an Adult in her. For example, she knew that would happen last week when she threw jam on the ceiling.

Sally: Yeah, I knew I'd get in trouble or that people would laugh.

Muriel: See, that's what I mean. That shows you've got an Adult ego state in you. You can figure out what might happen if you do certain things. That thinking part of you is your Adult. Grandma also knows what's going to happen, too, if she does certain things. For example if she's too crabby, what will happen to her?

Jim: Well, if she crabs at me, I usually get mad at her and crab back. Then she yells just like a *little kid.*

Muriel: OK. Now how about Mom? (Points to second set of circles.) Your Mother has an Adult that can think and a Child ego state that gets hurt and explodes. She also has a Parent ego state. Who would be in her Parent ego state?

Sally: I think Grandma is there.

Jim: Is Grandpa there, too?

Muriel: Yes, you're both right.

Lucy: Grandpa died a long time ago.

Sally: Yeah, and when Grandma talked about Grandpa, she said he was real nice and everything. So's Mama, sometimes. So's Jim, but *not* Lucy!

Muriel: OK. So here's a diagram of part of your Mom's personality. In some ways she's *like* Grandma. She gets hurt feelings and feels like nobody loves her and then gets critical. Now how is your Mom different from Grandma?

Lucy: Well, I think she knows how to cope better when problems come. I don't know exactly how to say it, but I think she gets along better with problems.

She doesn't take things so hard like Grandma. She doesn't act up as Grandma does either. Grandma is always saying, "Poor me." Mom doesn't do that very often. Also she isn't *always* crabby and telling us we're doing things wrong like Grandma does *all the time*—"The room's not clean enough," or "You're always messy." Mama tells us, but not quite as much.

Jim: Mom's also different from Grandma because Grandma makes a big thing out of something when it's really no big thing. Like when there are no crackers, she tells Mom, "Those kids ate up *all* the crackers," but Grandma's always telling *us* to eat them. Then sometimes she squeezes my arm till it hurts, or pulls my ears.

Muriel: So Grandma complains a lot, "If it weren't for the kids ..." She acts "Poor me," and sometimes she's mean. Mom doesn't do that so much, right?

Lucy: Once we had salmon at night and there just wasn't any lemons in the house and Grandma said, "I just can't stand my salmon without lemon. Your Mother didn't even go to the store today," or "The soup won't be any good without crackers, so I'll have toast." And on and on.

Muriel: Alright, now let's go back to how your Mother is different from Grandma. I'll bet you're glad she's different.

Sally: Yes, I wouldn't want my Mom to be like Grandma because then she'd be crabby. She'd even be crabbier because she wouldn't get all her sleep.

Muriel: Right. OK, now one of the reasons your Mamma is different from Grandma is because your Grandpa, who you said was nice, is also in her Parent ego state even if you didn't know him well.

Lucy: I remember him. He was scared of Grandma, too, but he was nice.

Jim: Muriel, is it Grandma's Child that gets so crabby and hurt?

Muriel: Yes, the Child in her *collects* hurt feelings much like stamp collectors collect stamps.

Sally: I don't know anything about stamps. I don't understand.

Jim: I do. I think I collect jealousy feelings when Laura gets to go out on a date or gets an extra baby-sitting job. I kind of feel jealous when I go to bed and I still feel that way when I wake up.

Muriel: Sally, how do you feel most of the time when things go wrong?

Sally: I feel icky. I don't know why, so I just go and do something.

Muriel: Like what?

Sally: To make everybody mad and get even with them.

Muriel: You want to get even and hurt them back, hum?

Sally: Well, kinda. If they do something to me, then I want to get them back and how am I going to get back at them if I don't do something?

Muriel: How do you usually feel, Lucy?

Lucy: I always feel hurt, like Grandma, and then feel sorry for myself all the time. Sometimes I'll yell like Grandma if Jim and Sally don't do something right, or not right through my eyes anyway. I don't know—it kinda takes me awhile to get into a bad mood and awhile to get out of it if someone gets mad at me or I don't get all my chores done, and Mom says something about it. I blew up sort of like Mom does sometimes. I don't know why, but I don't like to be reminded about things.

Muriel: (to Mom) What's your most commonly felt feeling when things go wrong?

Mom: That I'm not doing a good job.

Muriel: That's what you *think* when something goes wrong. How do you *feel?*

Mom: Frustrated, then hurt.

Muriel: Frustrated, then hurt. OK. Now the feelings you experience and save up are sort of like trading stamps that you get when you buy groceries or gas.

Sally: We save Blue Chip Stamps and one day our dog tore up two books and we had to wait and wait to get more stamps to get a prize.

Jim: Yeah, and some stores give Green Stamps. That really messes things up 'cause then we have two different stamp collections that don't go together.

Muriel: And if you put the wrong kind of stamps in one of your books, what would they say when you went to collect a prize when the book was full?

Sally: That you couldn't have it.

Muriel: That you couldn't have it, right! It seems as if you've got a lot of stamp collectors in your family. Jim saves jealousy stamps. Sally saves icky, "I'm gonna get even" stamps. Grandma and Lucy both feel hurt, then critical, and Mom feels frustrated, then hurt. Then you cash them in for a prize of yelling or crying or something like that.

Jim: That's it! That's right on, Muriel!

Muriel: Did you ever go to school where they gave out gold stamps or gold stars?

Sally: Some kids in our class get a gold star for being door monitor or getting 100 percent in spelling or cleaning the blackboard.

Muriel: OK, if you want to stop collecting bad feelings you'll need to collect gold star feelings that feel good.

Sally: I don't know how.

Muriel: How about having a box of *gold stamps* around your house? Then you can give them to each other or give them to yourself, just for being you. Your Mom might come along and say, "Wow! You went to school on time or cleaned up your room and I didn't have to tell you, and here's a gold star for you." Now suppose your Mom doesn't notice that you cleaned up your room or went to school on time? Then you can say to yourself, "I deserve a gold star," and give it to yourself for being you and for doing OK things. When you've saved up a bunch of gold stars you'll feel WOW!!, because you've got a collection of good feelings.

Mom: I guess some people learn to collect gold stars when they're little and some people, like me, don't start collecting gold stars 'till they're forty. I've wasted a lot of years with the wrong collection. (Stamps her feet and weeps quietly)

Lucy: Now Mom, don't feel bad now. Feel good . . . I see what Grandma does. She saves little stamps of "Nobody loves me," "Poor me," and so on until she gets a book full of them and then she gets mad. Getting mad is like she's getting a prize. *She* feels sad first, then mad. Mom, you feel mad, then sad.

Jim: Yeah, that's right.

Muriel: Does this make sense to you, Sally?

Sally: Kind of. You mean, when Grandma gets a little book *full* of bad feelings she just kinda lets them all out.

Muriel: Yes, she's saving hurt stamps.

Lucy: Sally, she saves them in her mind. Grandma doesn't really and truly have a little book that she holds in her hand.

Sally: Grandma doesn't know that she saves stamps, does she?

Muriel: Probably not.

Jim: Mom doesn't seem to collect as many bad feelings as Grandma.

Sally: Well, maybe it's because we don't bug Mom as much as Grandma.

Lucy: Mom's *never* been as crabby as Grandma but Grandma's been more crabby just this year. She's been getting sick a lot and it's kind of hot, and she was an orphan when she was little, so I guess I understand. And *I'm going to stop being hurt and crabby like her.*

Jim: Thank goodness for that!

Lucy: I'm going to get you for that, Jim. You just wait.

Muriel: Hey Lucy, if you're not going to be hurt and crabby like Grandma, you may need to count to ten before exploding and you, Jim, need to do the same before you pick a fight.

Mom: (Suddenly smiling, speaking clearly, while looking directly at the children) I like what went on here today. I think you kids are pretty darn good.

Sally: Hey, that's a stamp! Thanks Mom!

SUMMARY

Obviously, many issues were yet to be solved when this second session ended. In fact, ten additional sessions were required. What was important about the second session was that the participants: (1) increased their understanding of ego states, (2) learned about psychological trading stamps and how negative feelings could be exploited and positive feelings pursued, (3) recognized similarities and differences in the feelings and behavior within family members, (4) became aware of the cause of Grandma's problems and began to forgive her, and (5) became ready for contracts to be crystallized, for this family, in the third session.

Common contracts with children include: "Get a friend," "Be nice, not mean," "Feel OK instead of scared," "Stop having temper tantrums," "Feel good in my stomach instead of bad," and "Learn something new, like how to ride a bike."

Each child that comes for therapy is unique. Each is vulnerable and trying to cope and make sense out of a world that is often insensible. For the therapist, parent, and teacher who works with children, Khalil Gibran has some good advice: He says, "Seek not to make them like you. . . . Their souls dwell in the house of tomorrow, which you cannot visit, not even in your dreams."

RESOURCES

1. Thomas, Alexander, Stella Chess, and Herbert G. Birch, *Temperament and Behavior Disorders in Children* (New York: New York University Press, 1969). See also Blacklidge, Virginia, "Nature and Nurture of the Natural Child, *TA Journal,* July 1976.

2. Goertzel, Victor, and Mildred Goertzel, *Cradles of Eminence* (Boston: Little, Brown, 1962).

3. James, Muriel, and Dorothy Jongeward, *Born to Win: Transactional Analysis with Gestalt Experiments* (Reading, Mass.: Addison-Wesley, 1971), pp. 160–164, 179–180.

4. James, Muriel, and Dorothy Jongeward, *The People Book: Transactional Analysis for Students* (Reading, Mass.: Addison-Wesley, 1975), pp. 8–11.

SUGGESTED READING

Axlin, Virginia M. *Dibs in Search of Self* (New York: Ballantine, 1964).

Erikson, Eric H., "Identity and the Life Cycle," *Psychological Issues* (Monograph) **1**, 1, (New York: International University Press).

Fraiberg, Selma, *The Magic Years* (New York: Charles Scribner's Sons, 1959).

James, Muriel, "Transactional Analysis with Children: The Initial Session," *TA Bulletin,* January 1969.

———, *TA for Moms and Dads: What Do You Do With Them Now That You've Got Them?* (Reading, Mass.: Addison-Wesley, 1974).

———, and Louis Savary, *The Heart of Friendship* (New York: Harper & Row, 1976).

———, *A New Self* (Reading, Mass.: Addison-Wesley, 1977).

Kaufman, Barry Neil, *Son-Rise* (New York: Harper & Row, 1976).

Maslow, Abraham, *Motivation and Personality* (New York: Harper & Row, 1954).

Moustakes, Clark, *Who Will Listen?* (New York: Ballantine, 1975).

Satir, Virginia, *Conjoint Family Therapy* (Palo Alto, Calif.: Science & Behavior Books, 1964).

Spitz, R., "Hospitalism: Genesis of Psychiatric Conditions in Early Childhood," *Psychoanalytic Study of the Child* 1 (1945), pp. 53–74.

Sprinthall, Richard, and Norman Sprinthall, *Educational Psychology: A Developmental Approach* (Reading, Mass.: Addison-Wesley, 1974).

one-session cure for frightened exam-takers

THE CURED EXAMINEES

This is a procedure for instant therapy, a one-session cure for graduate student exam-takers who have previously failed major exams one or more times. I have used this method with nine people: four of them Ph.D. candidates who wanted to pass their orals, three who wanted to pass the bar exam to become attorneys, one who had his goals set on the National Medical Boards, and another who wanted to become a Certified Public Accountant. In this paper, two case studies are included to illustrate the procedure.

What these nine persons had in common was that all were highly educated in their respective fields and all had previously failed a particular exam—the exam that for them was crucial. All were highly anxious as the time approached for retaking their exams. Their fear of failing again was almost incapacitating. Although people often do better when retaking an exam, and these students knew it, each expressed a *certainty* for failing again. After the one-session cure, all of them passed.

THE INITIAL CASES

Case 1: Roy

The discovery of this technique occurred some years ago when I was meeting with the son of a black professional woman. She and I knew each other as colleagues, having worked together on several racial crisis intervention projects. She asked me to see her son who attended an eastern university, was in town only for the day, and was very fearful of his upcoming Ph.D. comprehensives. I agreed.

Roy phoned for an appointment and we scheduled a single two-hour therapy session which was to include my arranging for lunch. This seemed practical as I had not had breakfast and had a full afternoon scheduled. It certainly was different from my usual procedure. Later I concluded that preparing and eating food together was an important part of the one-session cure as it symbolized a caring parent.

When working with clients of different racial, ethnic, educational, or geographical background I am interested in our cultural similarities and differences and how they might affect the therapeutic process, so I asked Roy, "Why did you come to see me?" The response was, "Well, Mom sent me." "Why would your mother send you to me in particular?" I inquired. "She said you're our kind of people and might have special understanding into the kind of hangup I've got," he said in a straightforward, trusting manner. I intuited we were off to a good start.

His "hangup," as he saw it, was that his mind felt fragmented and he was unable to concentrate on his studies. He thought it was related to his current situation, which was living with a white woman, also a graduate student, who had chosen this particular time to press him for marriage. He said he didn't want to marry her, rather wanted to continue studying so that he could pass his exams.

While he presented this problem for discussion, I started fixing lunch and he continued talking. Over the meal I started drawing the three circles, explained structural analysis, and asked, "How do you think each of your ego states is involved in passing or not passing the exams?" He was sure his Parent wanted him to pass and we agreed that anyone of Ph.D. caliber had enough intellectual capacity and probably enough academic information in the Adult to succeed with the exams. After mulling this over a bit, Roy claimed it was his inner overanxious Child that seemed to be interfering with his Adult planning and performance. Clearly it was a case of contamination. I drew a diagram to illustrate the point. He quickly comprehended. Thus the process of decontamination began.

The next step was for him to learn how to analyze transactions. Remembering my own anxious experience with my committee when I was defending my doctoral thesis, I drew transactional diagrams to illustrate the process while using a major question: "How might the members of your examining committee use their ego states to transact during the orals?"

Subordinate questions that flowed into the discussion of transactions were:

- Do you imagine they are going to want to support you and your anxious Child?
- Are they going to want to impress each other with their questions?
- Is there likely to be some competition between them?
- If there is competition, will they be trying to outdo each other to show how stupid you are or to show how supportive they can be of you?
- Or will they see you a a potential peer, perhaps still in the process of learning?

After discussing his potential committee at length, we turned to the application of ego states and transactions to his current life and to the woman he was living with. She was white and from a very conservative background. He guessed that the parents in her head would be strongly against their relationship if they knew about it. He said they would see him as not-OK because he was black and undermine him if they could. Her Adult ego state was competent and informed. They often studied together and exchanged academic information. Her Natural Child was warm and joyful; her Adapted Child tended to be rebellious and sometimes tricky.

When I drew the inner dialogue diagram, he surmised that old tapes in her Parent ego state probably relayed negative things about Blacks to her Child. He also surmised that although she would sometimes rebel against the tapes, she might also listen. This was clearly detrimental to him, as well as to their relationship.

Roy then concluded that he needed to protect himself from the Prejudiced Parent and Adapted Child parts of her personality during the next months, which were crucial study time. He decided to tell her, "Some things, like marriage, are going to be put on ice until after the exams are done."

I suggested he also do something for his own inner Child, like having some private time alone each day, not to study, just to be. I also refused to charge him for the session. A month later I received a thank-you note. He had passed his exams with a high rating.

Case 2: Sam

The second case is of Sam, age 32, who had twice failed his bar exam to become an attorney. The exam in California is a three day written event. During the two exams Sam said he felt frozen, that he could hardly push the pencil across the paper. He claimed his sentences were incomprehensible although he had been a good graduate student.

After going through the same steps I have listed in Case 1, we discussed his current close relationships. The "significant other" for this man was his wife. Her parents were not well educated, and were indifferent about an advanced degree or his proposed profession. "People don't need degrees to make money," they claimed. Sam said strongly that her parents were not against his performance, merely somewhat indifferent and uninformed. Her Child ego state fluctuated, sometimes agreeing with her Parent, other times sticking up for him, like a cheerleader does for a team. Her Adult was better informed than her Parent and would see the value of his passing the exams. Sam decided to ask her to transact with him like a strong, positive, nurturing Parent, instead of an indifferent one.

Ultimately each person needs to learn how to take care of his or her own Child. After all, nice, nurturing parents are not always available. I intuited that for Sam to take care of his own anxious Child he would need to give it a treat, not a treatment. So, I asked him what he wanted when he was little that he was not allowed to have or that he wanted more of. It was Hershey bars with nuts because they were bad for his teeth. I suggested that he take candy bars for a special treat when he went for the exam. The session, which was again over a home-cooked lunch, was concluded, again without payment.

Sam phoned in a report some weeks later. He said that on the first morning of the exam he felt unable to write as clearly as he needed to do, although it was better than on previous occasions. Then he went out to lunch, put his hand in his pocket, discovered his Hershey bar, ate it, and talked to his inner Child: "Now lookit, kid, all you have to do is to relax in the exam room for three days while I work, and then you can have a big treat." After this inner dialogue and self treat, Sam was able to write fluently. He easily passed his exams. Now when faced with an important case in his law practice he takes along a candy bar "just in case".[1]

DELINEATING THE PROCESS

I do not know if this method would be effective with poor students who have not studied. I have used it only with graduate students who have done reasonably well academically. Therefore I have assumed that they knew their specialty, were motivated to pass in spite of previous failures and fear of subsequent failures, and were seriously blocked by their own inner dialogue or by the transactions with their "significant other."

With all nine of the frightened exam takers I used essentially the same therapeutic procedure and in the following order:

1. Reviewed the problem and feelings related to the exam.
2. Explained ego states.
3. Explored how the examinee's ego states were involved in the exam process.
4. Fantasized about the ego states of the oral examiners or how ego states of those who prepared a written exam might show through the questions.
5. Analyzed the ego states of the person who was the "significant other" at that time.
6. Planned how to be helped, not hindered, by that person.
7. Decided how to care for the inner Child when anxious.

During the second step I took the lead; the sixth was determined by the client. We worked together on the other steps. No mention was made of games, scripts, time structuring, or other TA concepts. Only ego states and transactions were discussed. This was enough for a single one-session cure, considering the purpose of the session.

Along with these TA techniques, I continued to use a single, two-hour session with each person. During the session I prepared an informal meal and we talked while we ate. At the end of the session I gave at least one positive suggestion for caring for the inner Child. I did not accept any payment and we had a few laughs together by ending the session with the good game, *And Furthermore,* when each of us "bragged" about our competencies.[2]

"Yes, but . . . " some readers might say, "that's not *real* therapy, that's just chicken soup, apple pie, and Mom." Well, maybe so—but it *works. And Furthermore,* I sometimes enjoy playing the "good" games of *Happy to Help* and *They'll be Glad They Knew Me.*[3] They feel good and actually are effective.

Perhaps an OK parent or friend could have the same success. I think so. Therapists aren't the only people with power to cure others as well as themselves. In fact, perhaps therapists also need an occasional one-session cure!

REFERENCES

1. This case was briefly summarized in James, Muriel, and Dorothy Jongeward, *Born to Win: Transactional Analysis with Gestalt Experiments* (Reading, Mass.: Addison-Wesley, 1971), p. 239.
2. Zechnich, Robert, "Good Games," *TA Journal,* Jan. 1973, pp. 52–56.
3. Berne, Eric, *Games People Play* (New York: Grove, 1964), pp. 163–168.

index

index